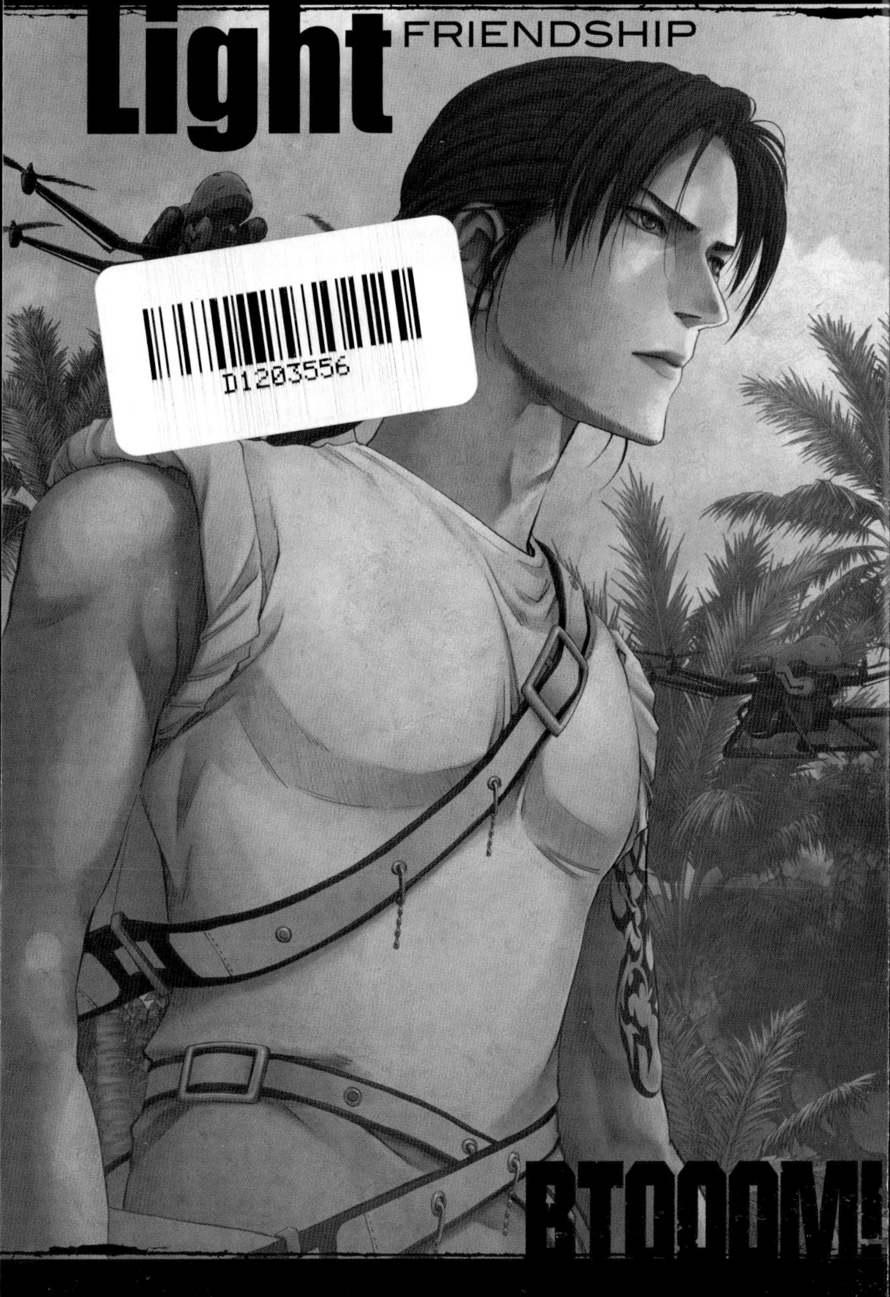
Light
FRIENDSHIP
BTOOOM!

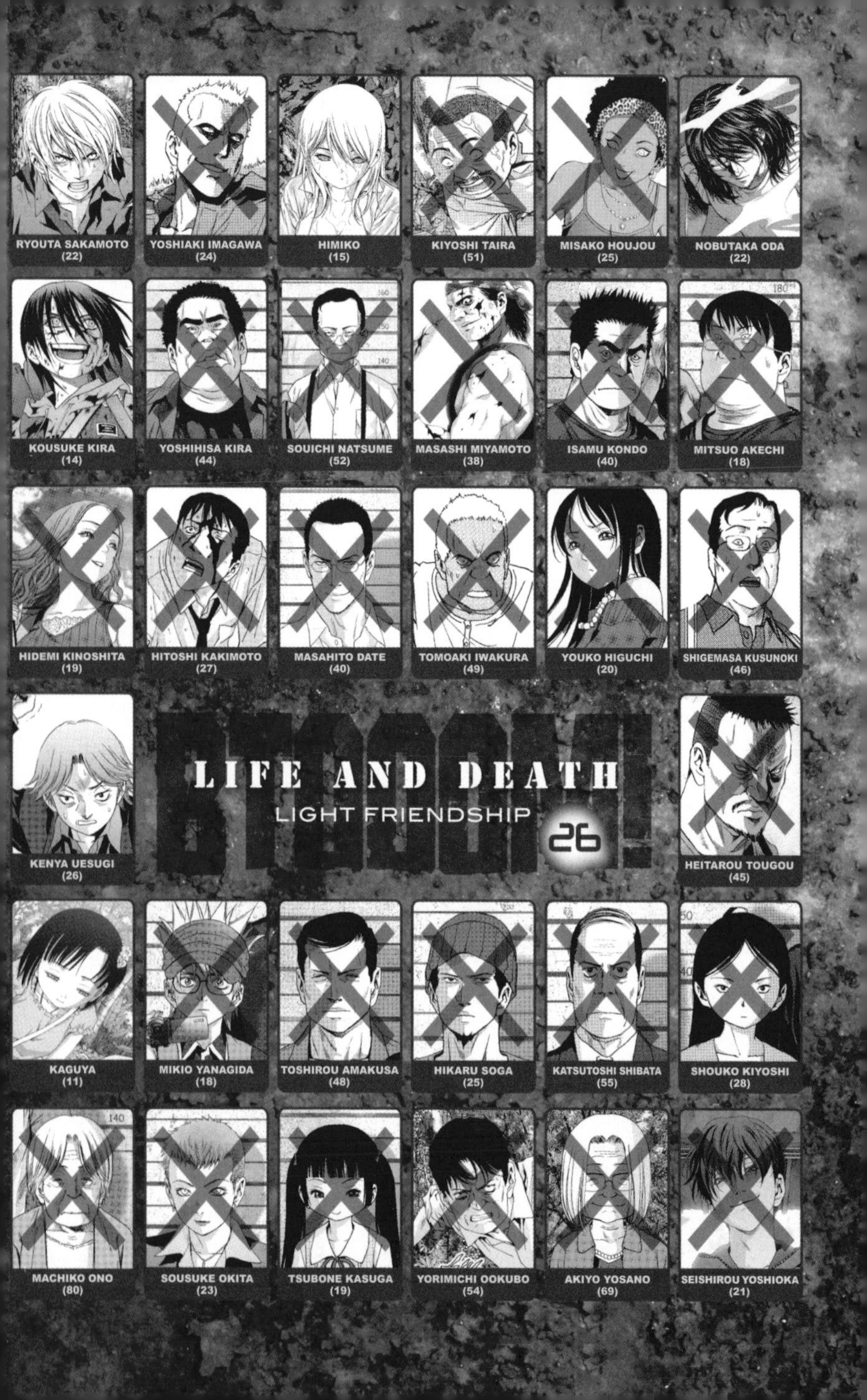
RYOUTA SAKAMOTO (22)
YOSHIAKI IMAGAWA (24)
HIMIKO (15)
KIYOSHI TAIRA (51)
MISAKO HOUJOU (25)
NOBUTAKA ODA (22)
KOUSUKE KIRA (14)
YOSHIHISA KIRA (44)
SOUICHI NATSUME (52)
MASASHI MIYAMOTO (38)
ISAMU KONDO (40)
MITSUO AKECHI (18)
HIDEMI KINOSHITA (19)
HITOSHI KAKIMOTO (27)
MASAHITO DATE (40)
TOMOAKI IWAKURA (49)
YOUKO HIGUCHI (20)
SHIGEMASA KUSUNOKI (46)
KENYA UESUGI (26)
LIFE AND DEATH
LIGHT FRIENDSHIP
26
HEITAROU TOUGOU (45)
KAGUYA (11)
MIKIO YANAGIDA (18)
TOSHIROU AMAKUSA (48)
HIKARU SOGA (25)
KATSUTOSHI SHIBATA (55)
SHOUKO KIYOSHI (28)
MACHIKO ONO (80)
SOUSUKE OKITA (23)
TSUBONE KASUGA (19)
YORIMICHI OOKUBO (54)
AKIYO YOSANO (69)
SEISHIROU YOSHIOKA (21)

BTOOOM!

Light

Friendship Version

JUNYA INOUE

26

CHARACTER

NOBUTAKA ODA

GENDER: Male
AGE: 22
BLOOD TYPE: AB
JOB: Restaurant manager
HOME: Tokyo

Sakamoto's biggest rival and an old classmate of his from high school. His elaborate plans and surprisingly daring athleticism have helped him procure chips at a rapid pace as he plans for his own departure from the island. Engaging in life-or-death battles with his former best friend Sakamoto, he has demonstrated himself to be an unequaled master at combat.

HIMIKO

GENDER: Female
AGE: 15
BLOOD TYPE: B
JOB: High school student
HOME: Tokyo

A foreign high school girl who has teamed up with Sakamoto. She harbors a deep resentment against men after a sordid experience in her past, but after surviving some battles thanks to Sakamoto, she begins to trust him. Her character in the online version of "BTOOOM!" is actually married to Sakamoto's character, and she has fallen in love with the real Sakamoto too.

RYOUTA SAKAMOTO

GENDER: Male
AGE: 22
BLOOD TYPE: B
JOB: Unemployed
HOME: Tokyo

After spending every day cooped up in his home gaming online, he suddenly finds himself forced to participate in "BTOOOM! GAMERS," a killing game taking place on a mysterious uninhabited island. As a world ranker in the online third-person shooter "BTOOOM!", he uses his experience and natural instincts to survive and concoct a plan to get off the island with his comrades, only for it to end in failure. At the Sanctuary, he teams up with Kaguya and Soga to beat Torio.

KAGUYA

GENDER: Female
AGE: 11
BLOOD TYPE: AB
JOB: Grade schooler
HOME: Tokyo

A mysterious little girl who came across Sakamoto when he washed ashore. She doesn't speak and uses a tablet to communicate. She's the figurehead of the Order of Moonlight, a religious cult, and can see dead people. In the Sanctuary, she worked with Sakamoto and Soga to defeat the real villain behind the tragedies, Torio.

KENYA UESUGI

GENDER: Male
AGE: 26
BLOOD TYPE: AB
JOB: Office worker
HOME: Tokyo

A cowardly and easily flattered young man who used to dream of becoming an actor. He was almost killed by Kira, but he escaped thanks to Higuchi's lie-detecting ability. He was previously a part of Tougou's team.

KOUSUKE KIRA

GENDER: Male
AGE: 14
BLOOD TYPE: AB
JOB: Junior high student
HOME: Tokyo

This junior high student harbors a dark, brutal, murderous past. On the island, he blew up his own father and is genuinely enjoying this murderous game of "BTOOOM!". He's always been a big fan of the online version of the game, and his dream is to defeat "SAKAMOTO", a top world ranker. Unfortunately, he keeps failing at it. Tougou's death makes him realize for the first time ever how precious life is.

BTOOOM! 26

LONGER SCHWARITZ

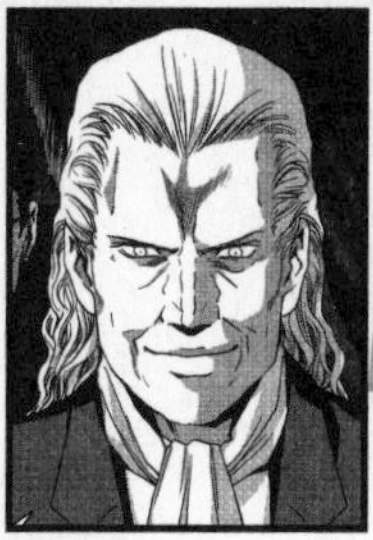

GENDER: Male
AGE: 77
BLOOD TYPE: O
JOB: Capitalist
HOME: New York

A descendant of European aristocracy, he is a man of power who controls the world behind the scenes with his considerable capital. In order to more thoroughly control the online realm, he founds the THEMIS project and has high hopes for "BTOOOM! GAMERS."

XAVIERA FRANCISCA

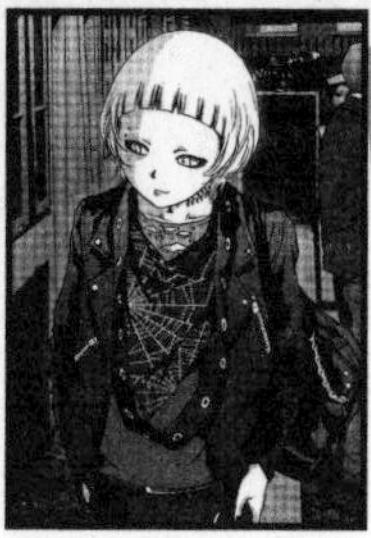

GENDER: Female
AGE: 22
BLOOD TYPE: O
JOB: Freelancer
HOME: Washington

The operator of the drone that dropped the medicine case on the island. Instead of BIMs, she attacks the players with a machine gun. Her skill is universally acknowledged, and in the online version of "BTOOOM!", she is the reigning world champion. However, she's never beaten Sakamoto, so she's obsessed with doing so.

TAKANOHASHI

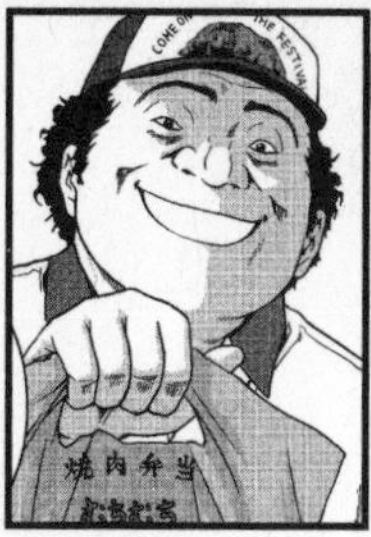

GENDER: Male
AGE: 45
BLOOD TYPE: AB
JOB: Game planner
HOME: Hokkaido

An executive staff member at Tyrannos Japan, he is the leader behind all the development of the online and real-life versions of "BTOOOM! GAMERS." He considers Sakamoto a valuable player and debugger. As a result of Sakamoto's plan to hijack the helicopter, Takanohashi's precious game was almost forced to come to a premature end.

HISANOBU

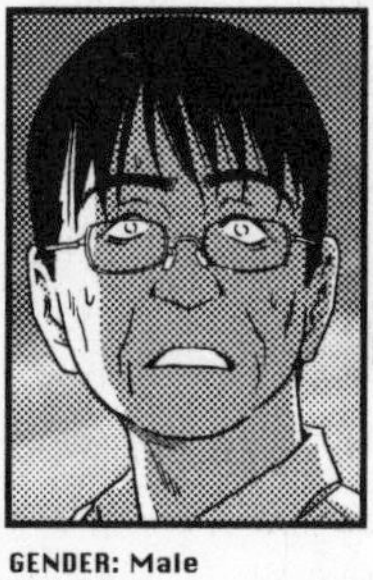

GENDER: Male
AGE: 55
BLOOD TYPE: A
JOB: Unemployed
HOME: Tokyo

Yukie's new husband and Sakamoto's stepfather. He's worried about how much time his stepson spends up in his room and scolds him, only to be attacked. Having just been laid off, he racks up debt because of his praiseworthy efforts to preserve his family's lifestyle. However, Yukie is frail in body and mind and attempts to kill herself. Fate has dealt him an unfair card in life.

TSUNEAKI IIDA

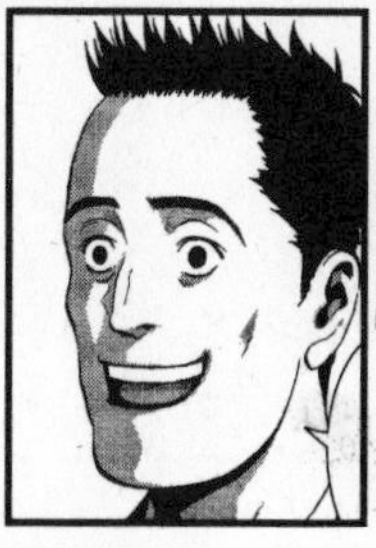

GENDER: Male
AGE: 24
BLOOD TYPE: A
JOB: Programmer
HOME: Tokyo

An employee at Tyrannos Japan and Sakamoto's senpai from college. He's an excellent programmer and works under Takanohashi on the development of "BTOOOM! GAMERS." But he doesn't agree with the inhumane nature of the game and approached Sakamoto with the proposal and strategy to put a stop to the game's development, only for the plan to fall apart.

MATTHEW PERRIER

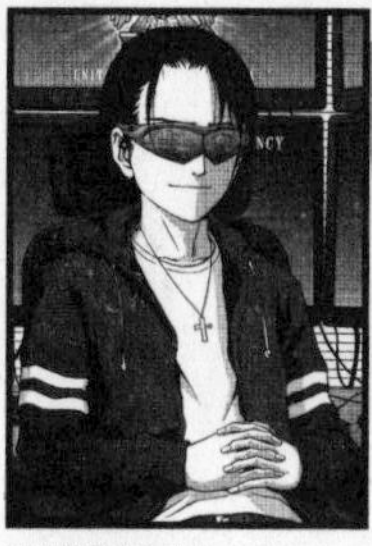

GENDER: Male
AGE: 27
BLOOD TYPE: O
JOB: Ex-NSA programmer, political refugee
HOME: Washington
(location unknown after exile)

A former programmer with the NSA (U.S. National Security Agency), he's a capable hacker and curbed a number of cyber-crimes while with the NSA. But after learning about the government's darker side, he made off with sensitive data about the THEMIS project—in a way, the evidence of their nefarious plans—and defected to another country.

INTRODUCTION

Light

FRIENDSHIP

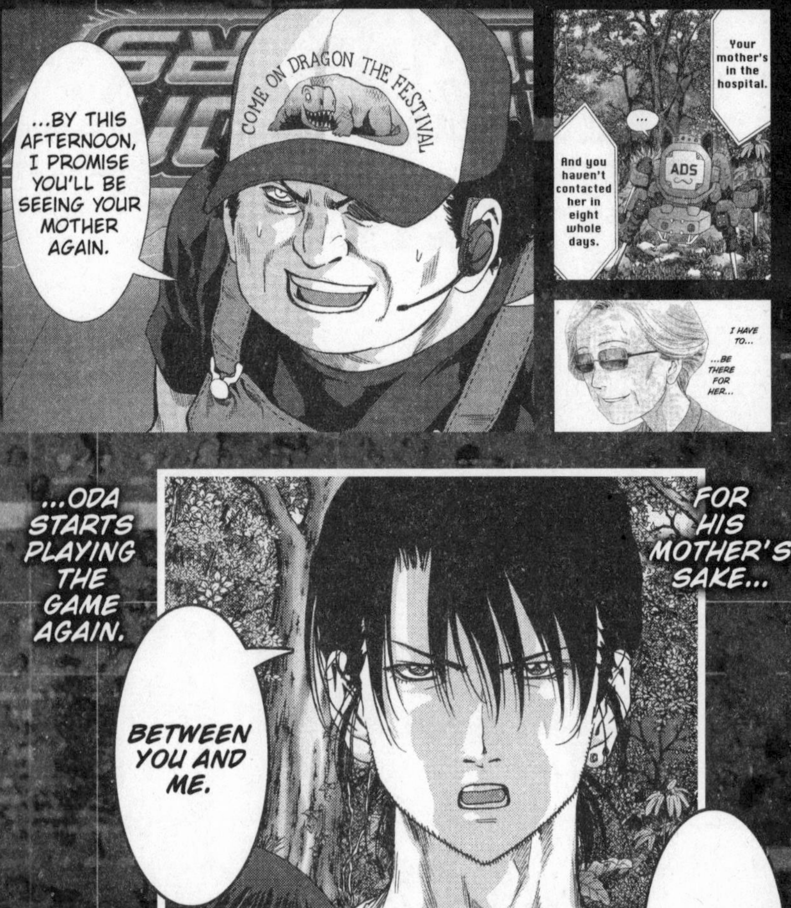
Your mother's in the hospital.
...
And you haven't contacted her in eight whole days.
ADS
I HAVE TO...
...BE THERE FOR HER...
COME ON DRAGON THE FESTIVAL
...BY THIS AFTERNOON, I PROMISE YOU'LL BE SEEING YOUR MOTHER AGAIN.
FOR HIS MOTHER'S SAKE...
...ODA STARTS PLAYING THE GAME AGAIN.
I PROPOSE A DUEL.
BETWEEN YOU AND ME.

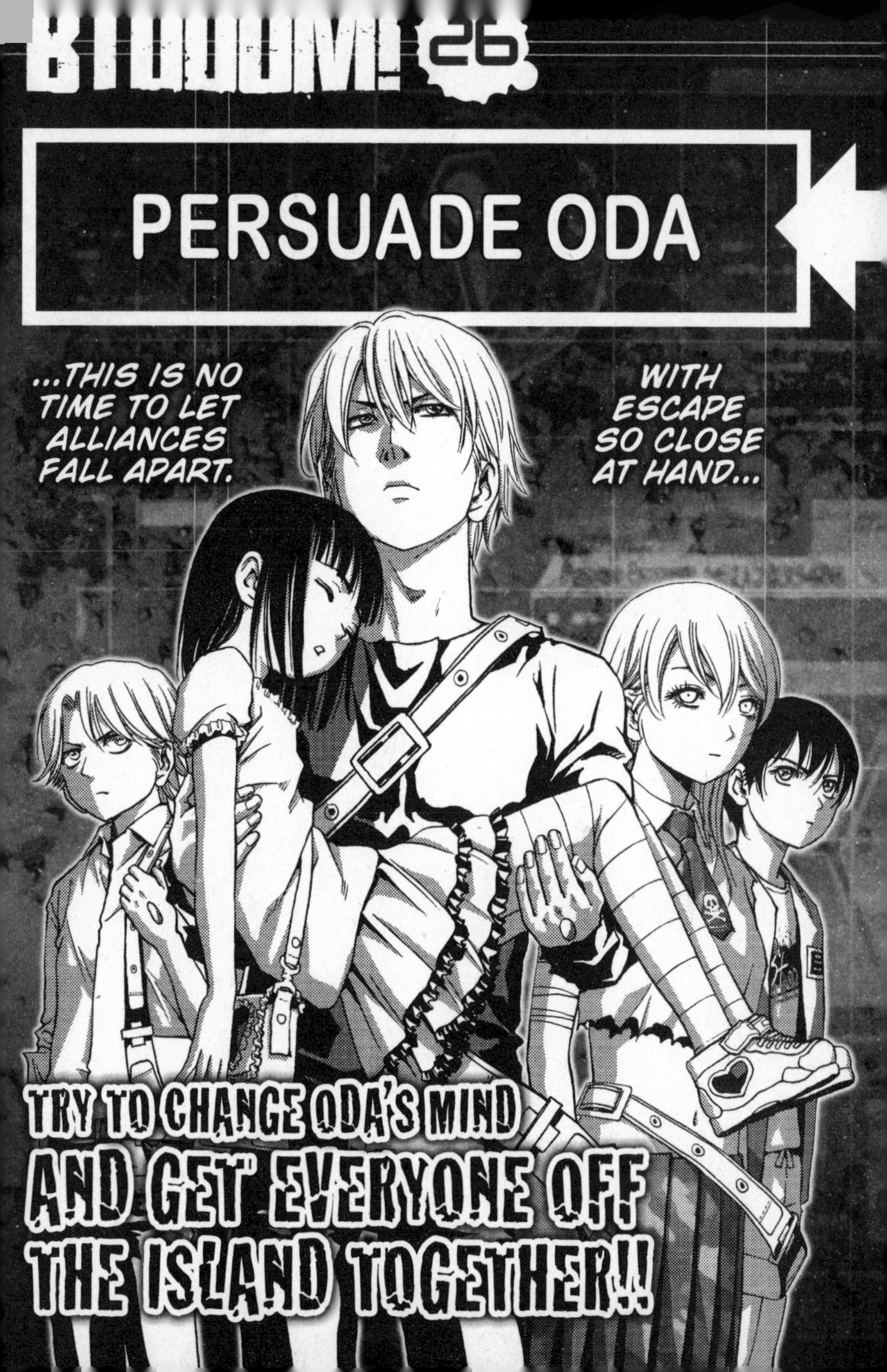
BTOOOM! 26
PERSUADE ODA
...THIS IS NO TIME TO LET ALLIANCES FALL APART.
WITH ESCAPE SO CLOSE AT HAND...
TRY TO CHANGE ODA'S MIND
AND GET EVERYONE OFF THE ISLAND TOGETHER!!

Light
FRIENDSHIP
CONTENTS

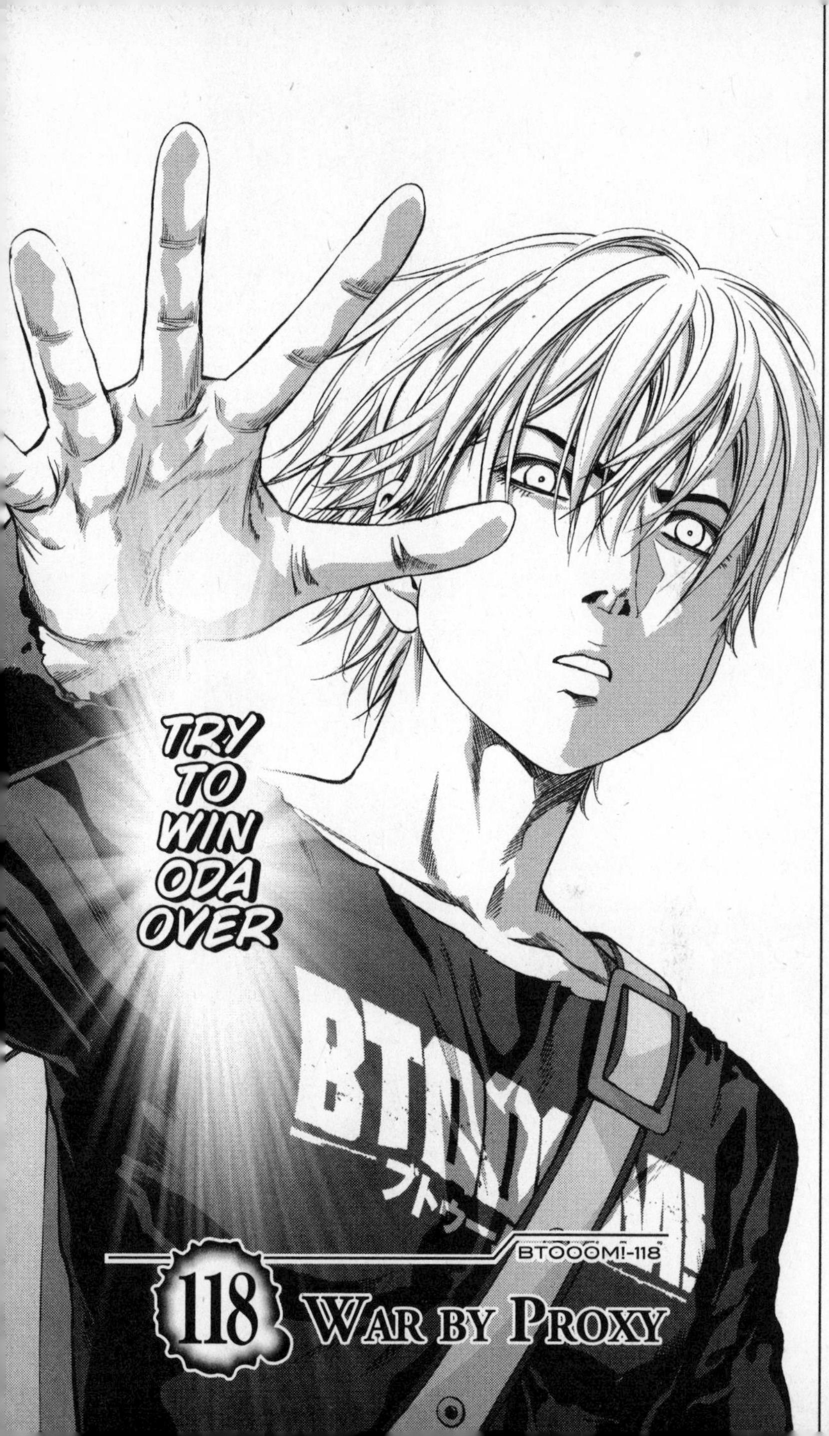
TRY TO WIN ODA OVER
BTOOOM!-118
118
WAR BY PROXY

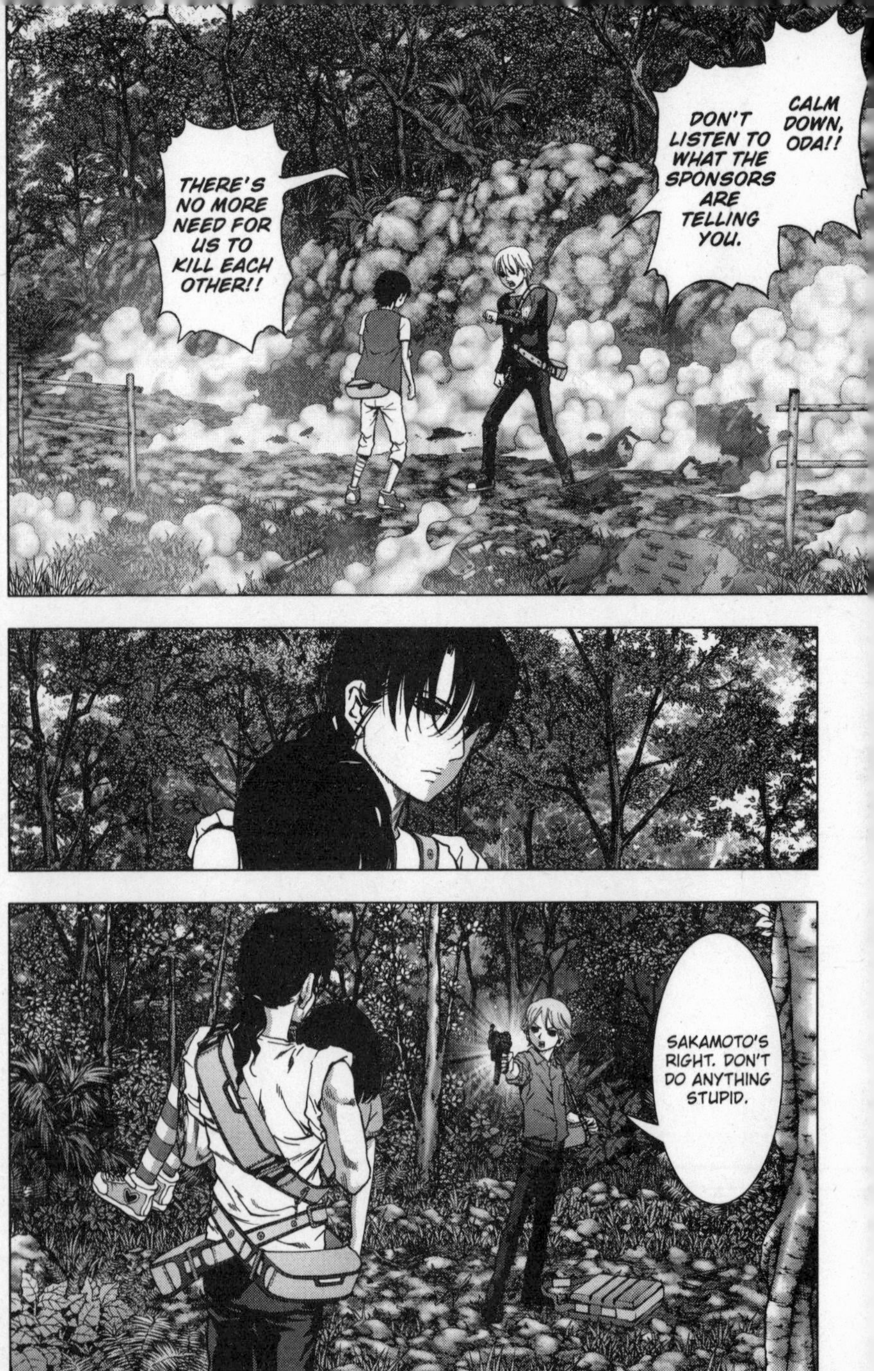
CALM DOWN, ODA!!
DON'T LISTEN TO WHAT THE SPONSORS ARE TELLING YOU.
THERE'S NO MORE NEED FOR US TO KILL EACH OTHER!!
SAKAMOTO'S RIGHT. DON'T DO ANYTHING STUPID.

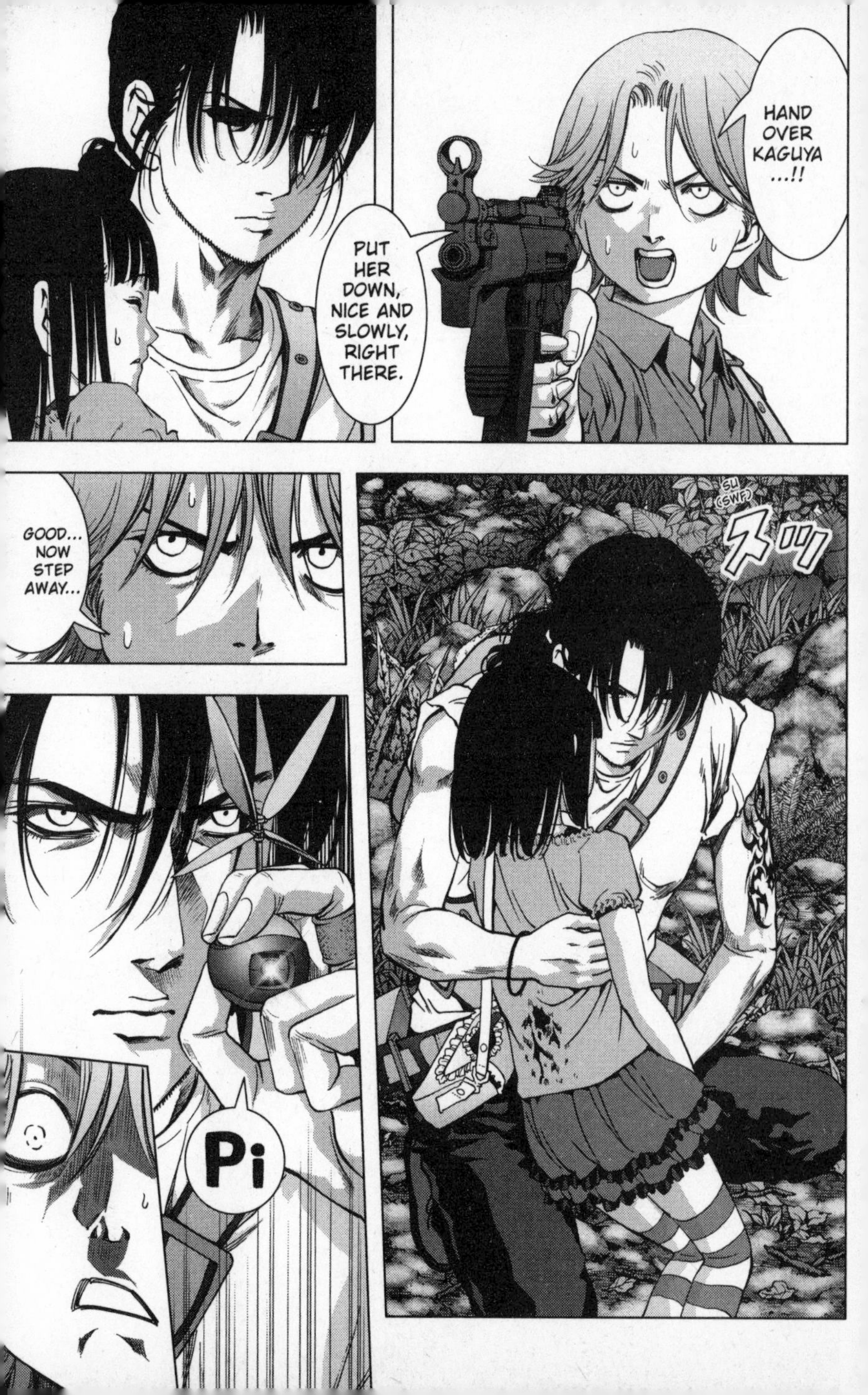
HAND OVER KAGUYA ...!!
PUT HER DOWN, NICE AND SLOWLY, RIGHT THERE.
SU (SWF)
GOOD... NOW STEP AWAY...
Pi

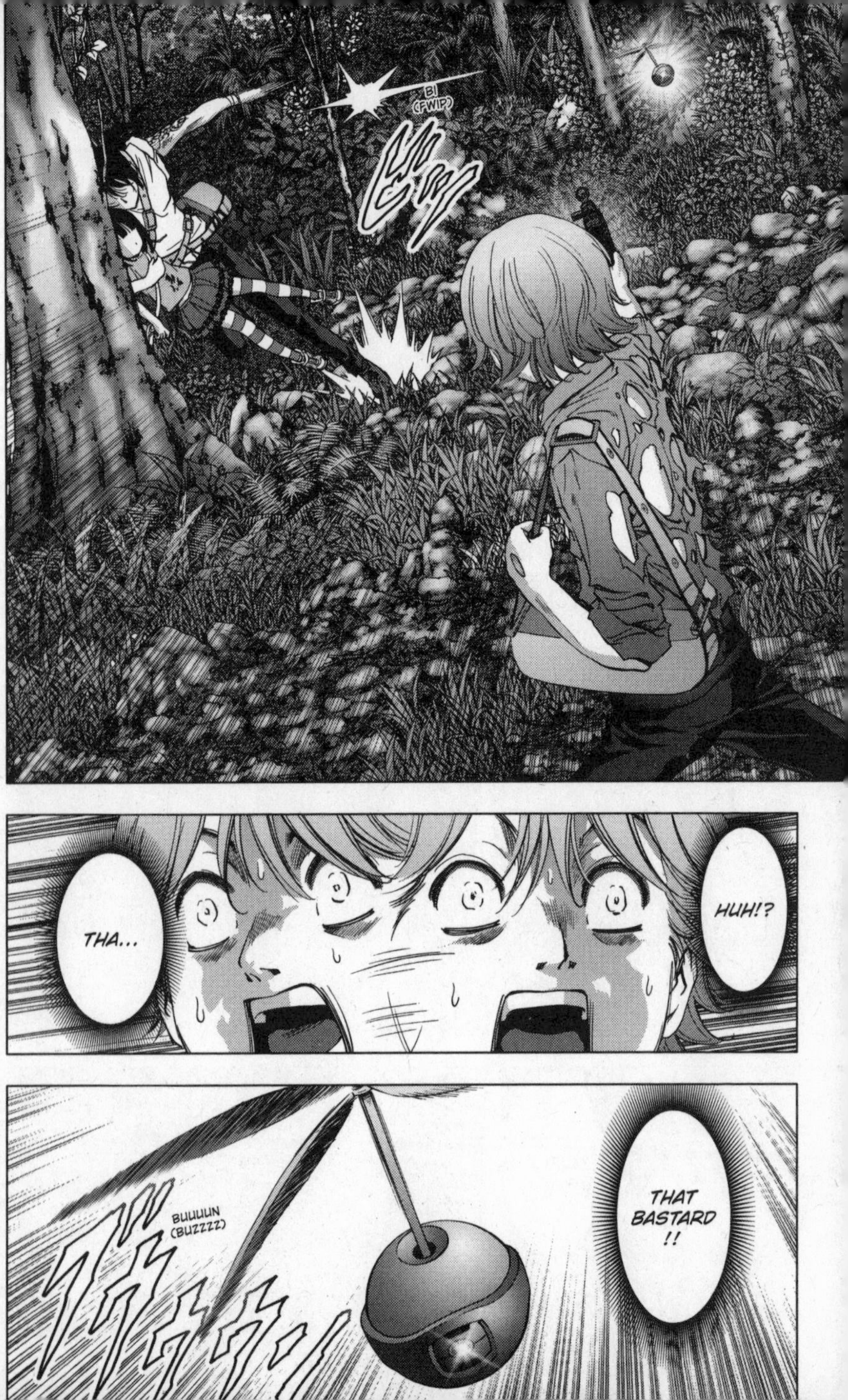
BI
(FWIP)
HUH!?
THA...
THAT BASTARD !!
BUUUUN
(BUZZZZ)

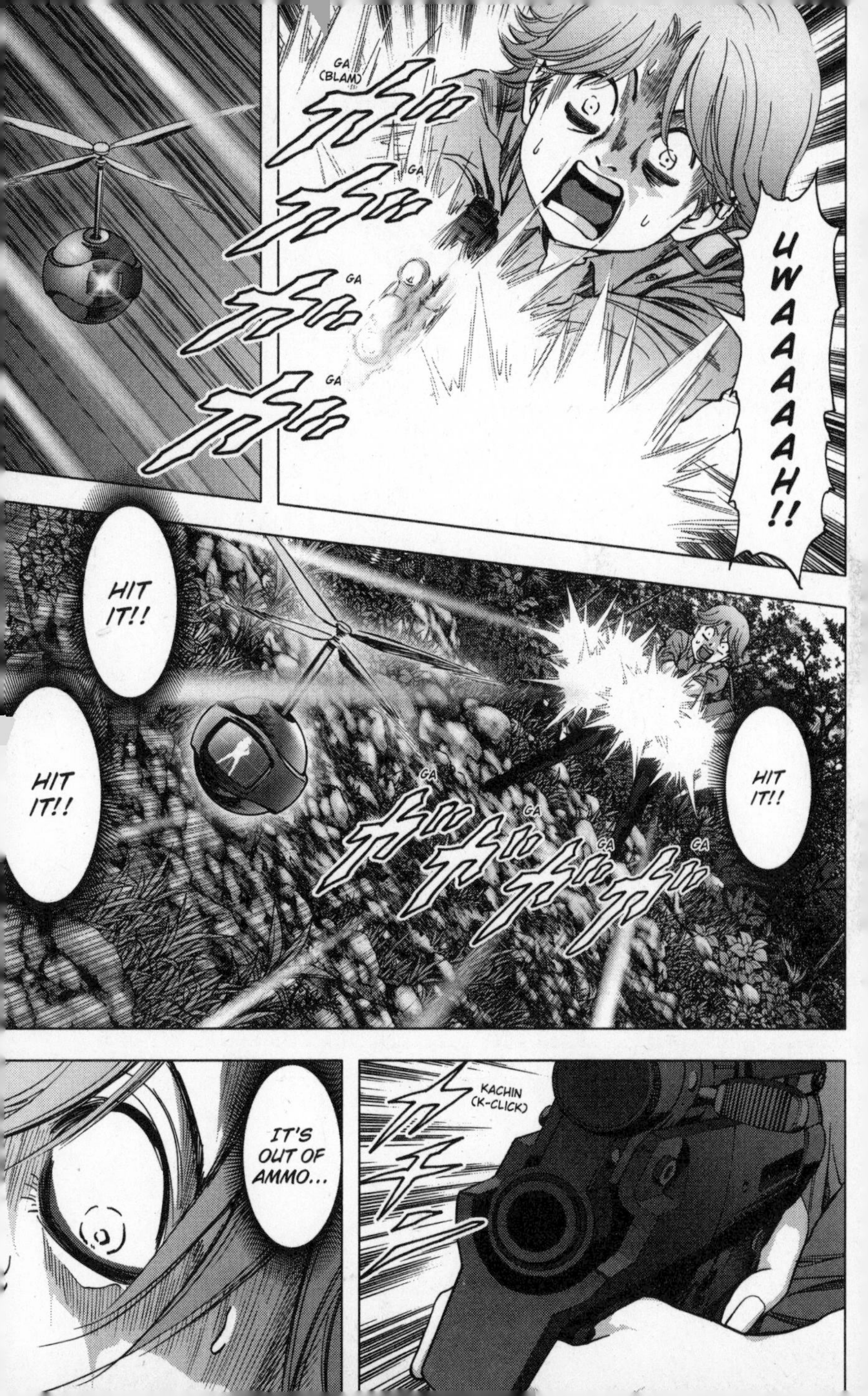
UWAAAAAAAH!!
GA (BLAM)
GA
GA
GA
HIT IT!!
HIT IT!!
HIT IT!!
GA
GA
GA
GA
KACHIN (K-CLICK)
IT'S OUT OF AMMO...

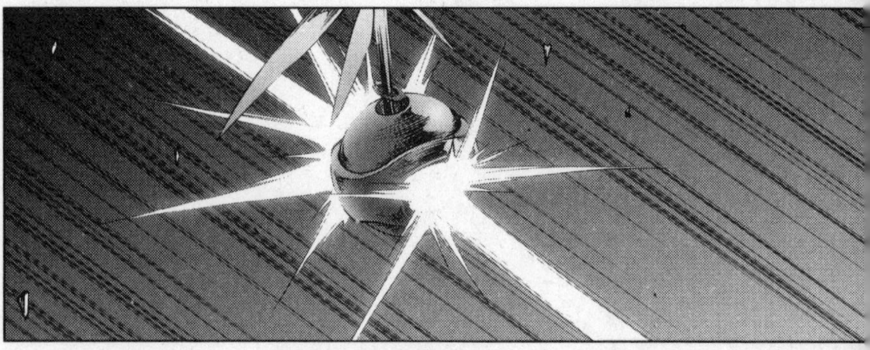

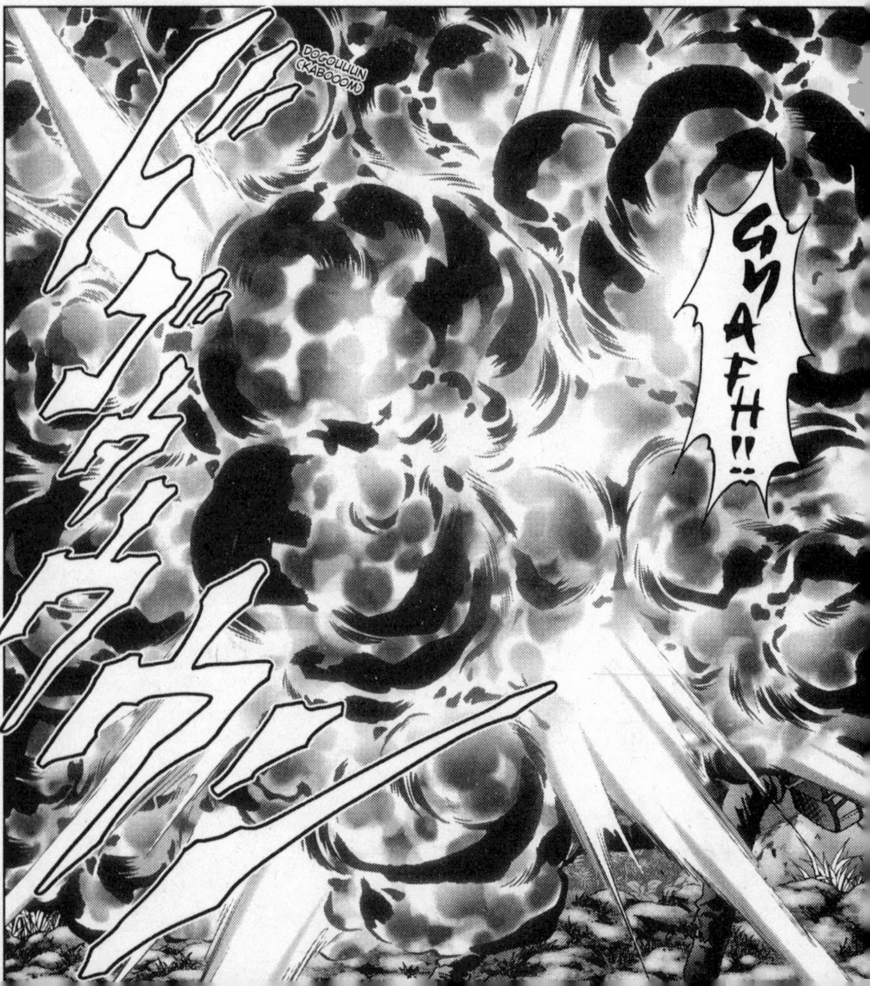
DOGOUUUN (KABOOOM)
GYAFH!!

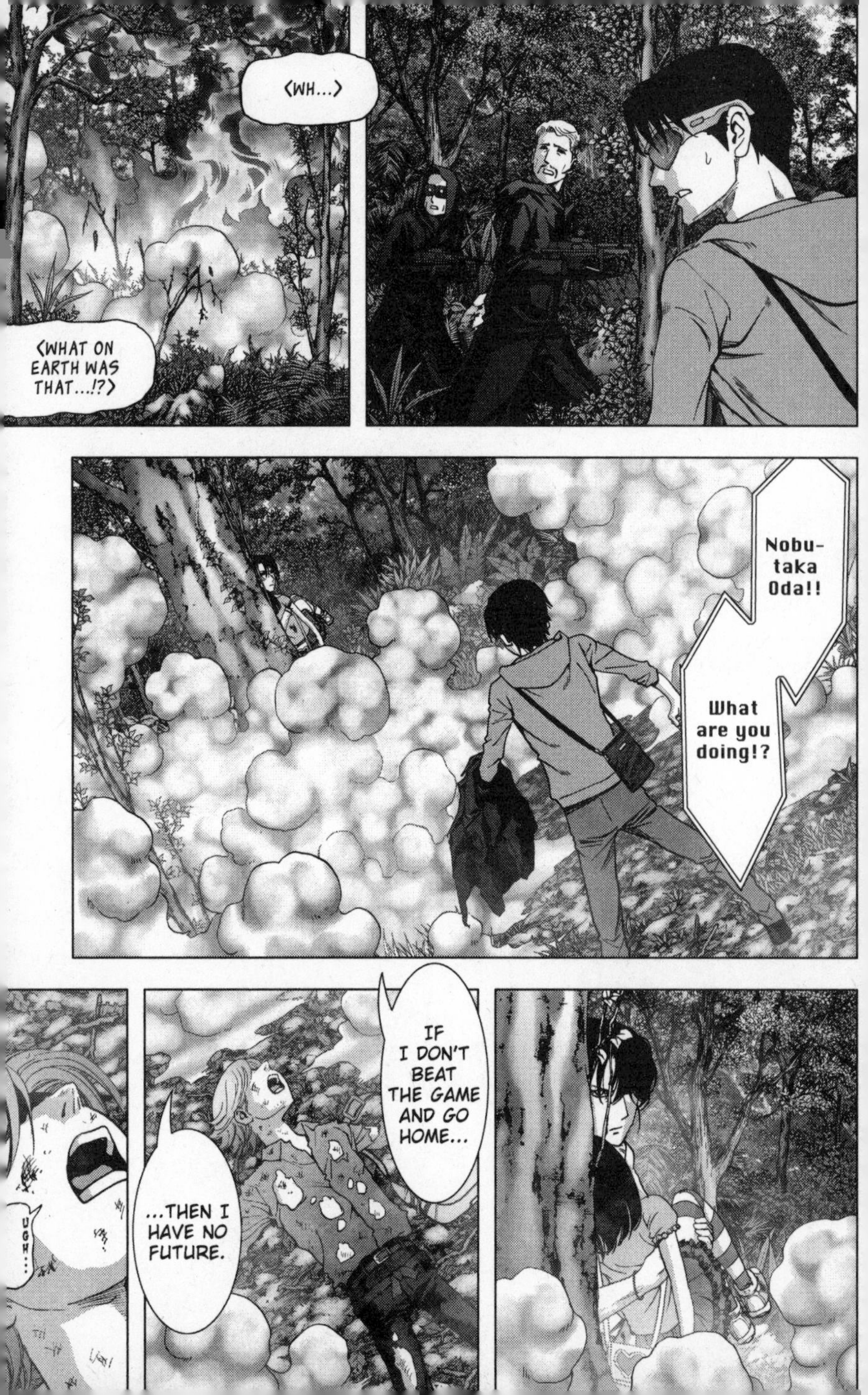
〈WH...〉
〈WHAT ON EARTH WAS THAT...!?〉
Nobu-taka Oda!!
What are you doing!?
IF I DON'T BEAT THE GAME AND GO HOME...
...THEN I HAVE NO FUTURE.
UGH...

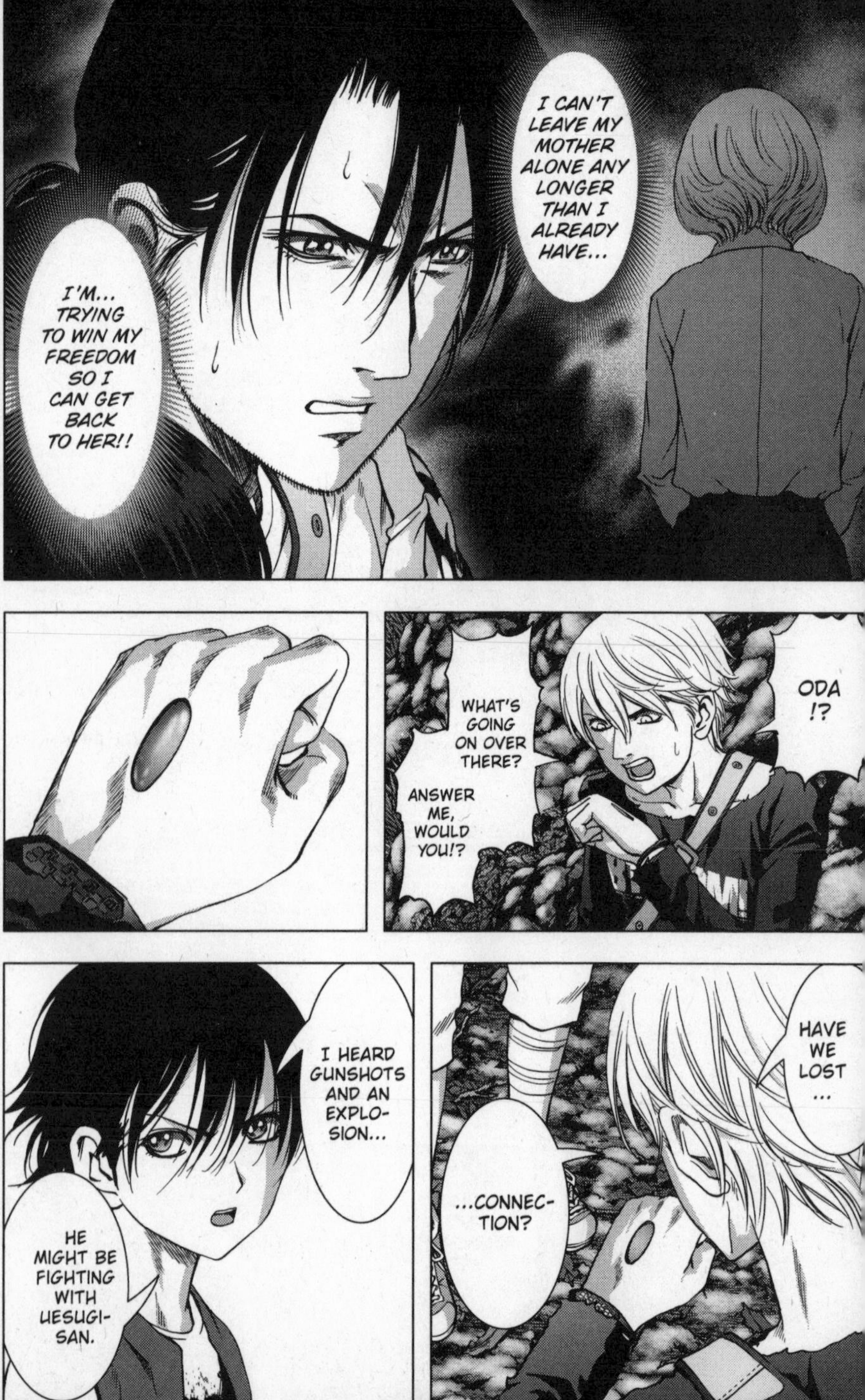
I CAN'T LEAVE MY MOTHER ALONE ANY LONGER THAN I ALREADY HAVE...
I'M... TRYING TO WIN MY FREEDOM SO I CAN GET BACK TO HER!!
ODA !?
WHAT'S GOING ON OVER THERE?
ANSWER ME, WOULD YOU!?
HAVE WE LOST ...
...CONNEC-TION?
I HEARD GUNSHOTS AND AN EXPLO-SION...
HE MIGHT BE FIGHTING WITH UESUGI-SAN.

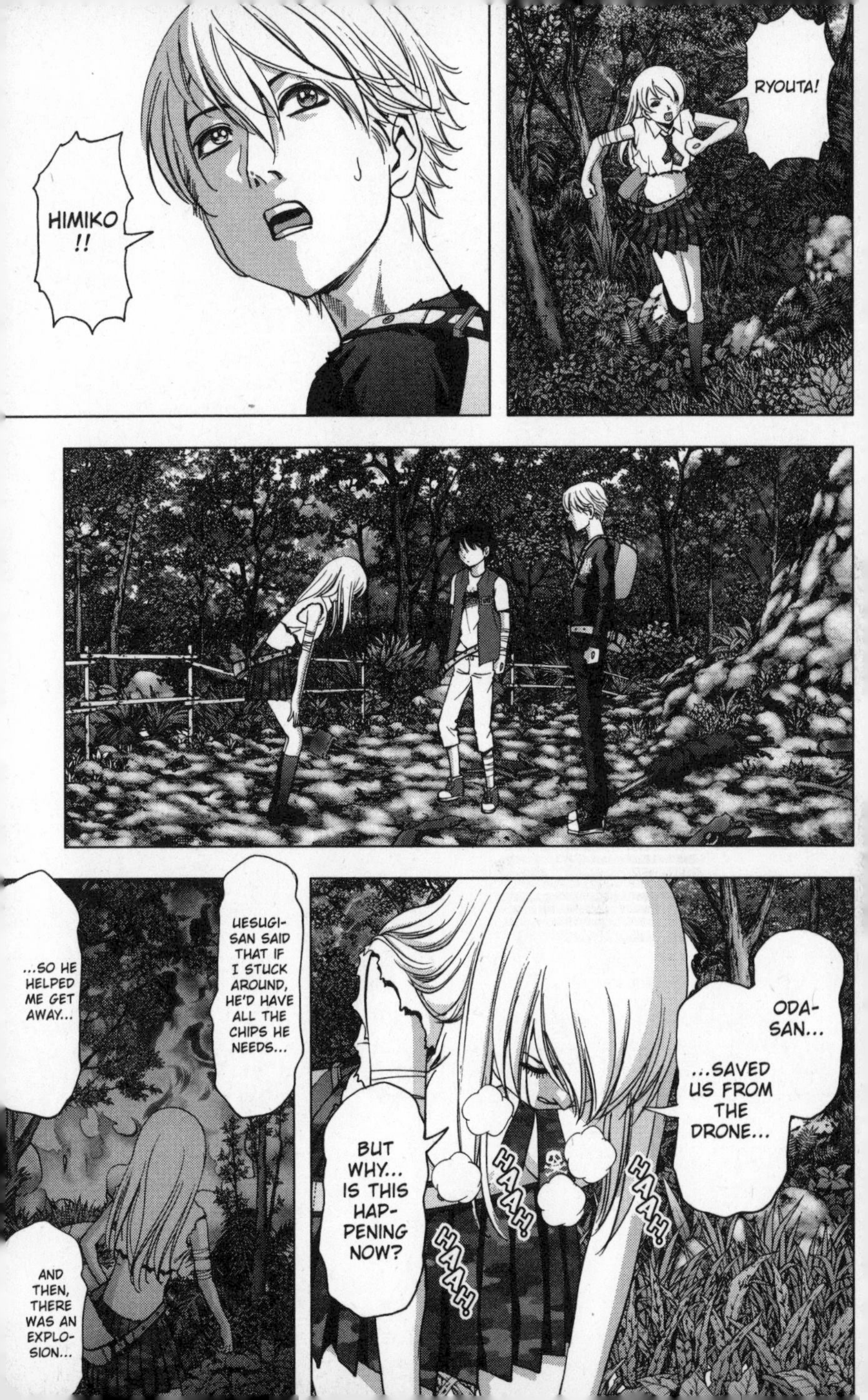
RYOUTA!
HIMIKO !!
ODA-SAN...
...SAVED US FROM THE DRONE...
HAAH.
HAAH.
HAAH.
BUT WHY... IS THIS HAPPENING NOW?
UESUGI-SAN SAID THAT IF I STUCK AROUND, HE'D HAVE ALL THE CHIPS HE NEEDS...
...SO HE HELPED ME GET AWAY...
AND THEN, THERE WAS AN EXPLOSION...

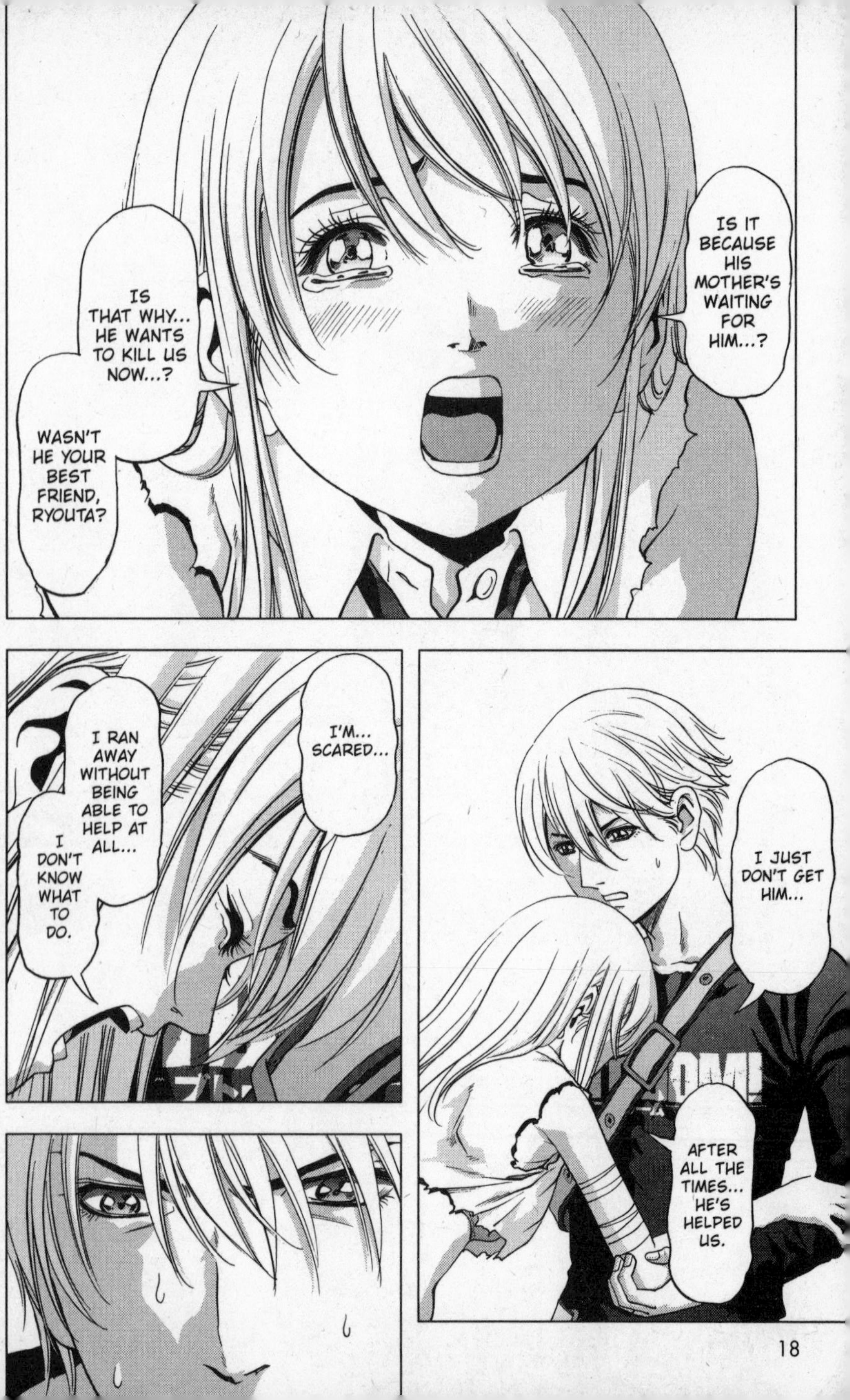
IS IT BECAUSE HIS MOTHER'S WAITING FOR HIM...?
IS THAT WHY... HE WANTS TO KILL US NOW...?
WASN'T HE YOUR BEST FRIEND, RYOUTA?
I JUST DON'T GET HIM...
AFTER ALL THE TIMES... HE'S HELPED US.
I'M... SCARED...
I RAN AWAY WITHOUT BEING ABLE TO HELP AT ALL...
I DON'T KNOW WHAT TO DO.

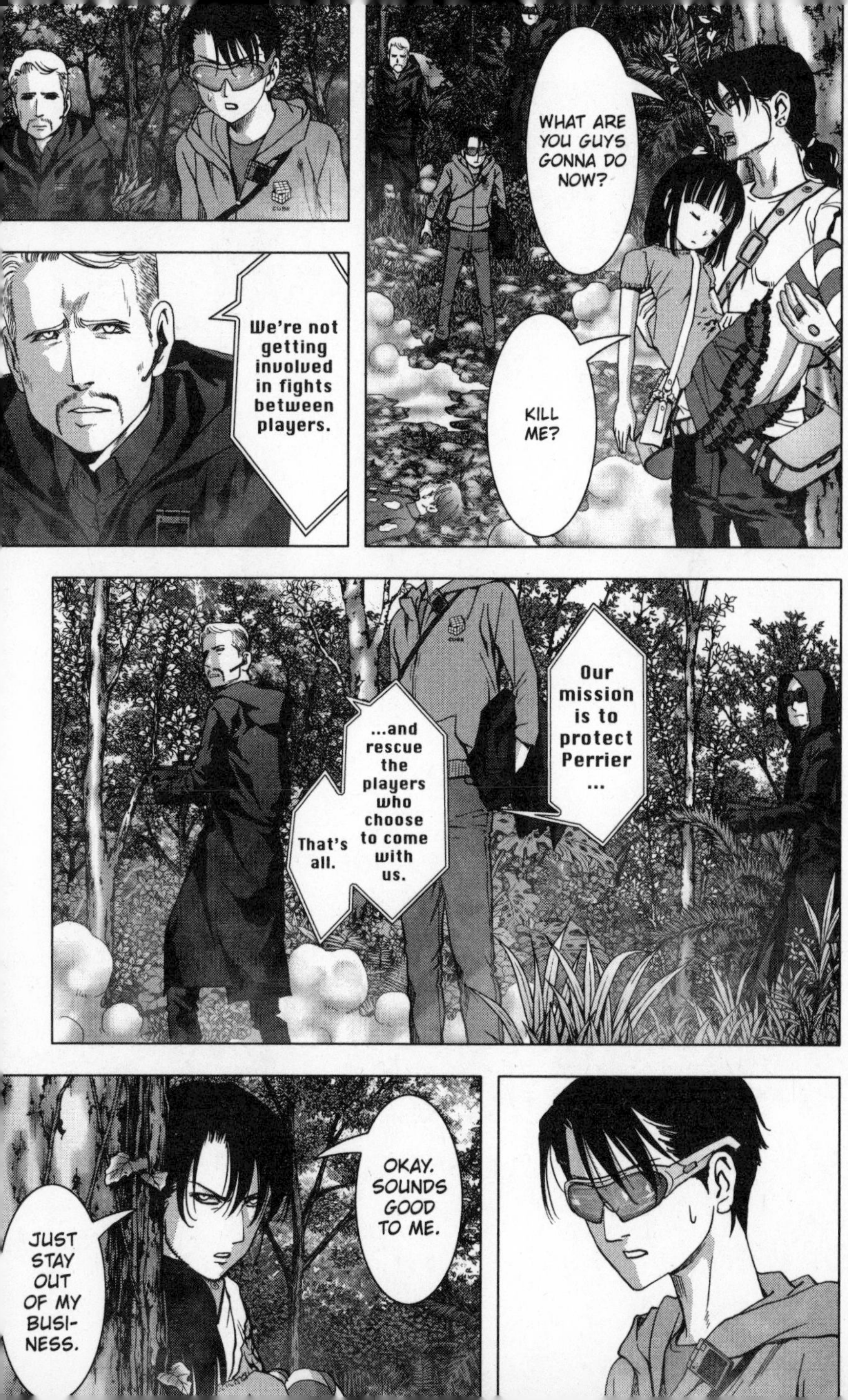
WHAT ARE YOU GUYS GONNA DO NOW?
KILL ME?
We're not getting involved in fights between players.
Our mission is to protect Perrier ...
...and rescue the players who choose to come with us.
That's all.
OKAY. SOUNDS GOOD TO ME.
JUST STAY OUT OF MY BUSI- NESS.

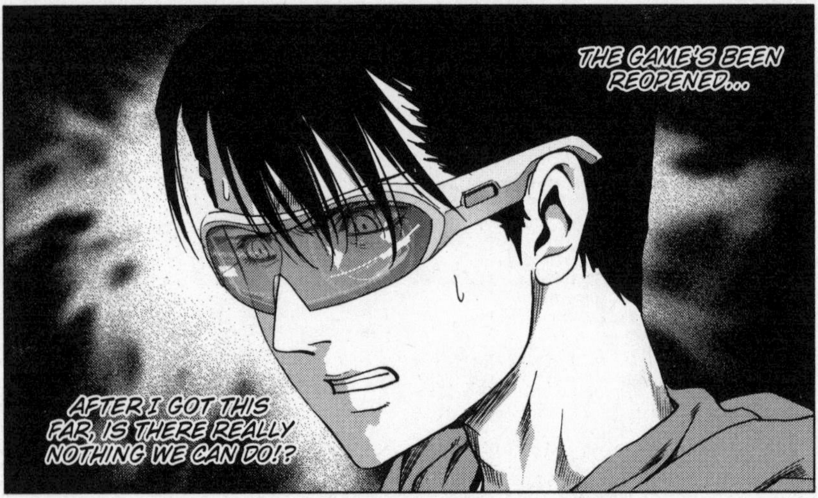
THE GAME'S BEEN REOPENED...
AFTER I GOT THIS FAR, IS THERE REALLY NOTHING WE CAN DO!?

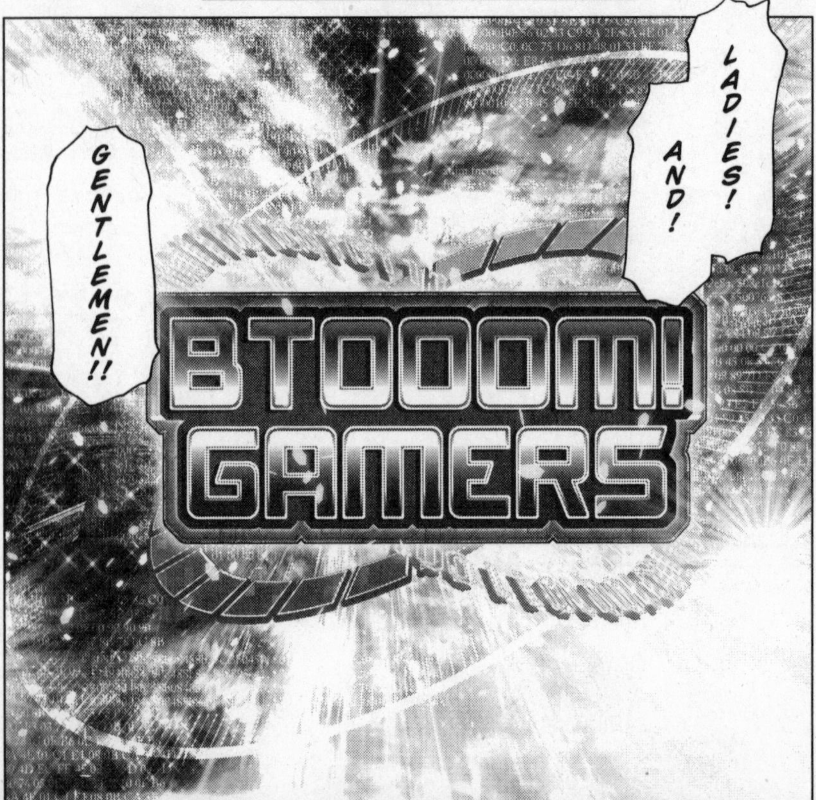
LADIES! AND!
GENTLEMEN!!
BTOOOM! GAMERS

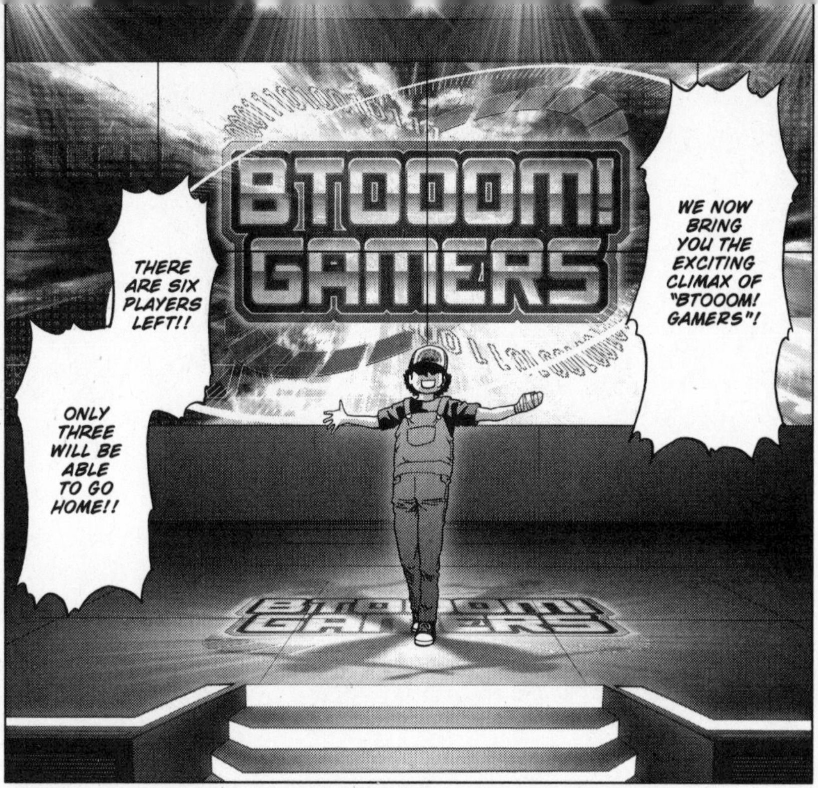
BTOOOM! GAMERS
WE NOW BRING YOU THE EXCITING CLIMAX OF "BTOOOM! GAMERS"!
THERE ARE SIX PLAYERS LEFT!!
ONLY THREE WILL BE ABLE TO GO HOME!!
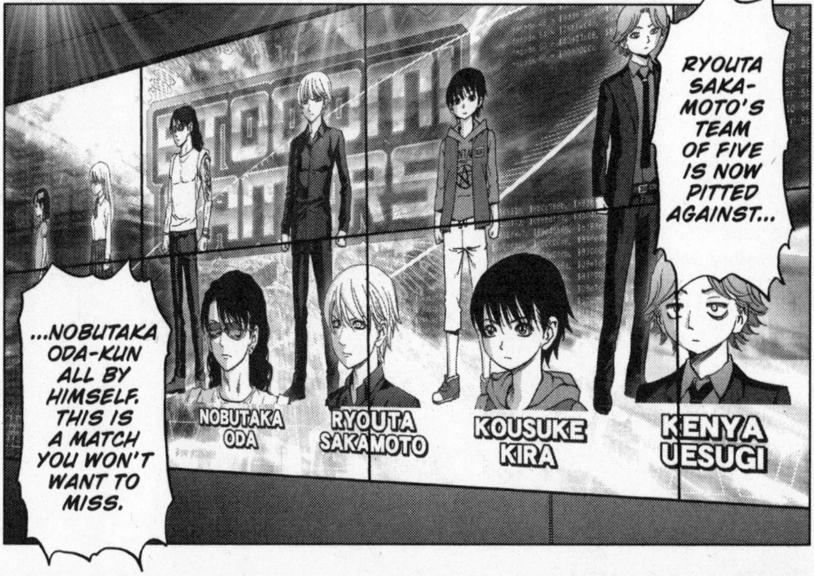
RYOUTA SAKAMOTO'S TEAM OF FIVE IS NOW PITTED AGAINST...
...NOBUTAKA ODA-KUN ALL BY HIMSELF. THIS IS A MATCH YOU WON'T WANT TO MISS.
KENYA UESUGI
KOUSUKE KIRA
RYOUTA SAKAMOTO
NOBUTAKA ODA

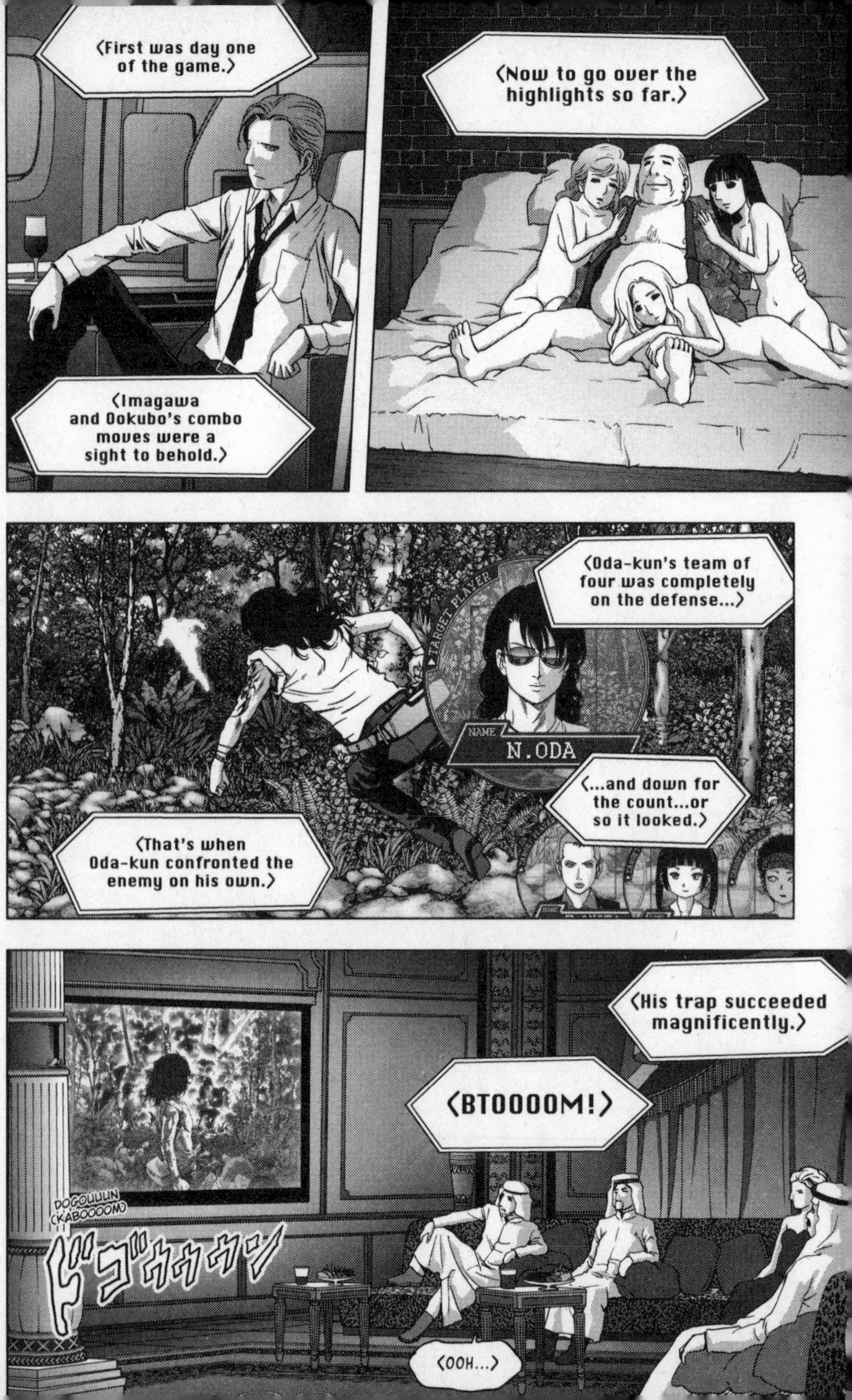
〈Now to go over the highlights so far.〉
〈First was day one of the game.〉
〈Imagawa and Ookubo's combo moves were a sight to behold.〉
〈Oda-kun's team of four was completely on the defense...〉
TARGET PLAYER
NAME
N.ODA
〈...and down for the count...or so it looked.〉
〈That's when Oda-kun confronted the enemy on his own.〉
〈His trap succeeded magnificently.〉
〈BTOOOOM!〉
DOGOUUUN (KABOOOOM)
ドゴゥゥゥン
〈OOH...〉

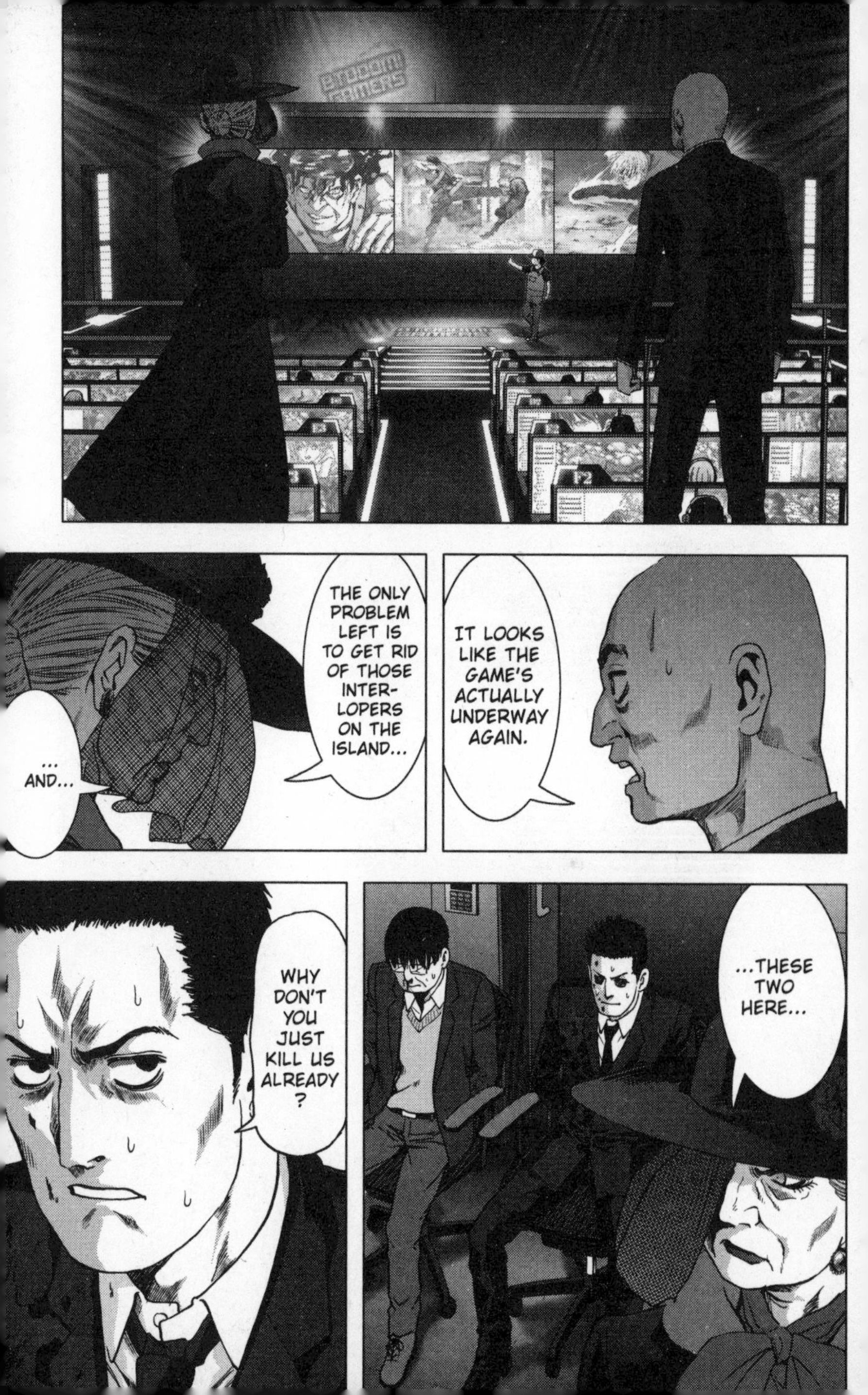
IT LOOKS LIKE THE GAME'S ACTUALLY UNDERWAY AGAIN.
THE ONLY PROBLEM LEFT IS TO GET RID OF THOSE INTER-LOPERS ON THE ISLAND...
... AND...
...THESE TWO HERE...
WHY DON'T YOU JUST KILL US ALREADY?

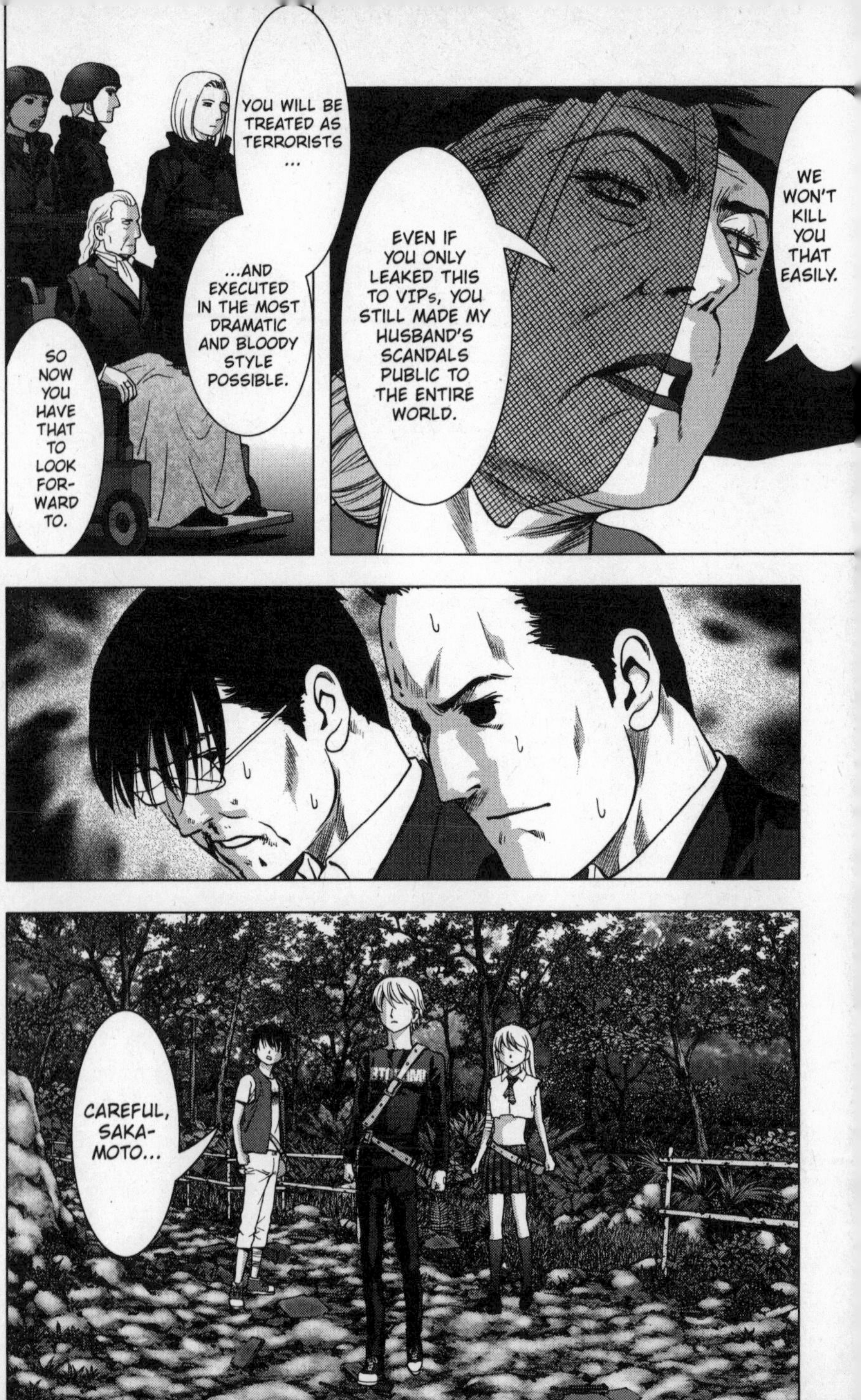
WE WON'T KILL YOU THAT EASILY.
EVEN IF YOU ONLY LEAKED THIS TO VIPs, YOU STILL MADE MY HUSBAND'S SCANDALS PUBLIC TO THE ENTIRE WORLD.
YOU WILL BE TREATED AS TERRORISTS...
...AND EXECUTED IN THE MOST DRAMATIC AND BLOODY STYLE POSSIBLE.
SO NOW YOU HAVE THAT TO LOOK FOR-WARD TO.
CAREFUL, SAKA-MOTO...

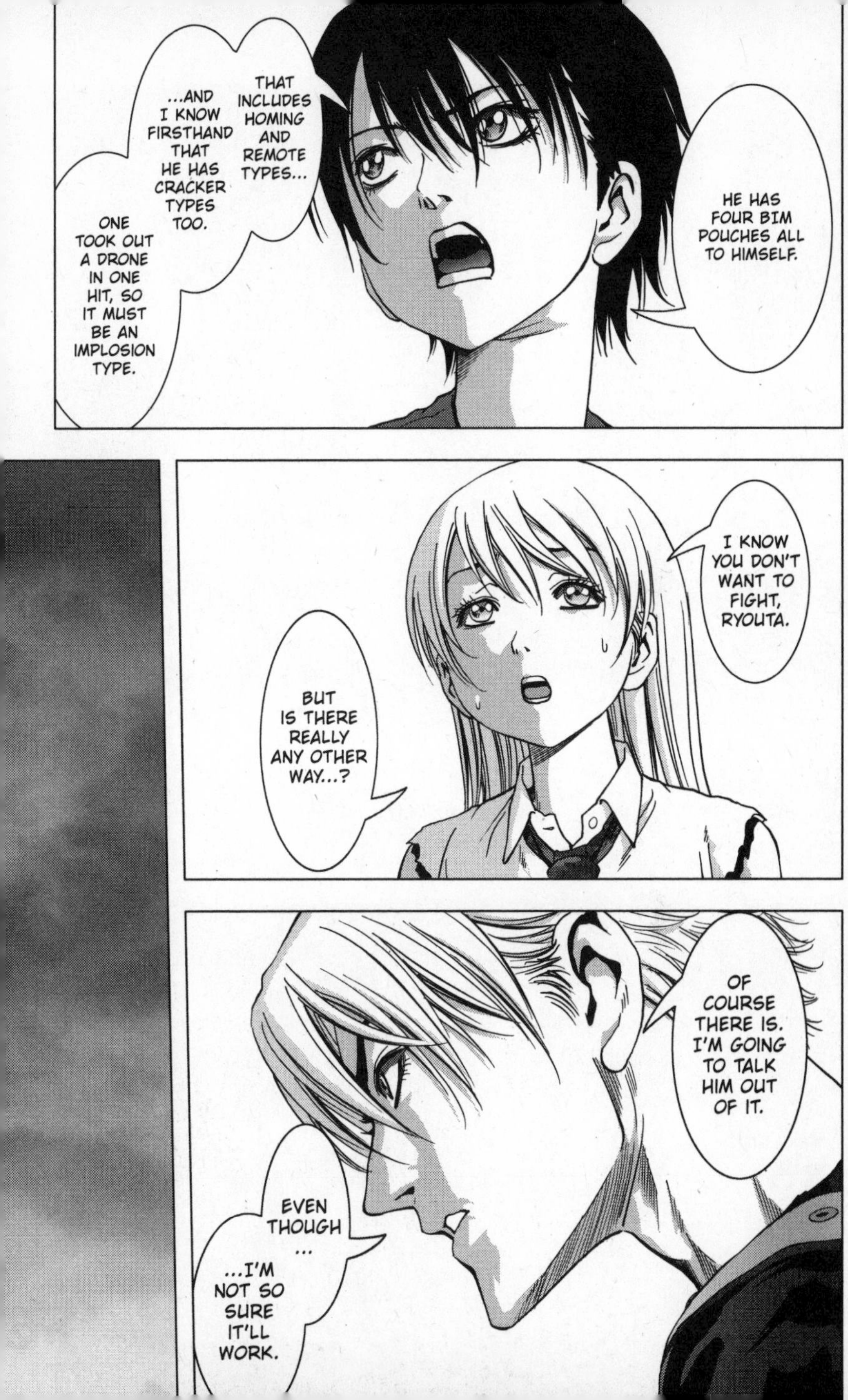
HE HAS FOUR BIM POUCHES ALL TO HIMSELF.
THAT INCLUDES HOMING AND REMOTE TYPES...
...AND I KNOW FIRSTHAND THAT HE HAS CRACKER TYPES TOO.
ONE TOOK OUT A DRONE IN ONE HIT, SO IT MUST BE AN IMPLOSION TYPE.
I KNOW YOU DON'T WANT TO FIGHT, RYOUTA.
BUT IS THERE REALLY ANY OTHER WAY...?
OF COURSE THERE IS. I'M GOING TO TALK HIM OUT OF IT.
EVEN THOUGH ...
...I'M NOT SO SURE IT'LL WORK.

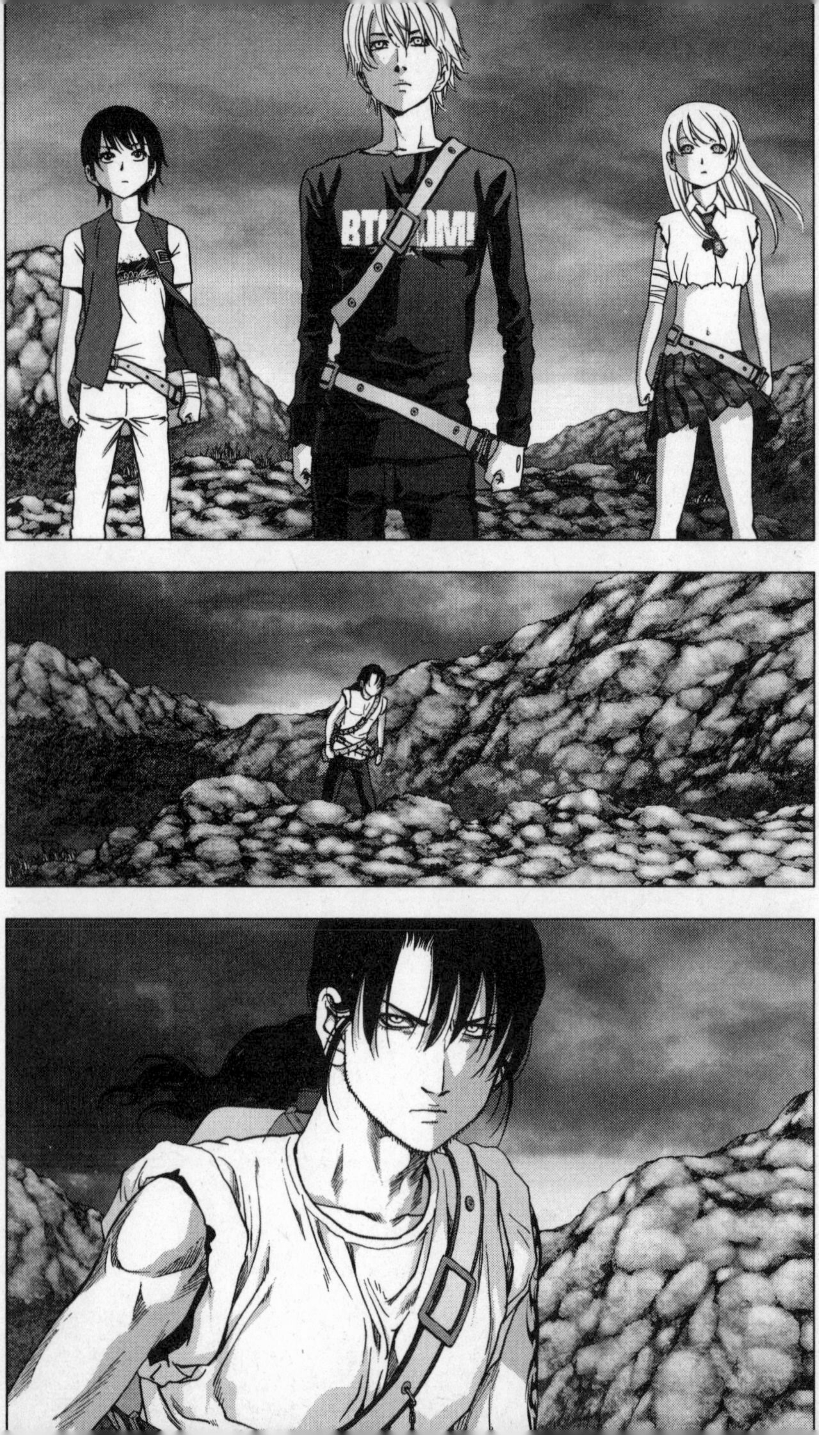

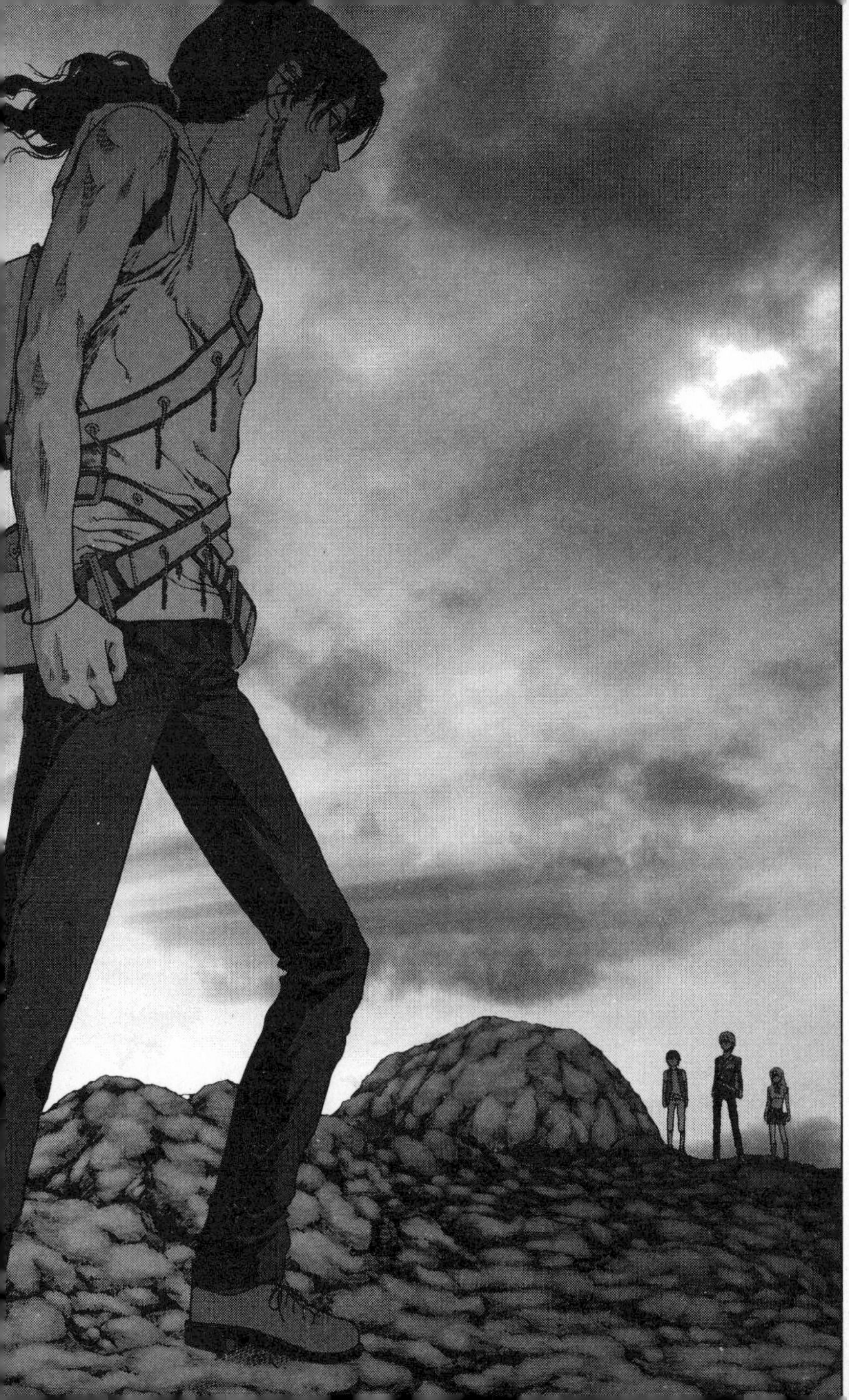

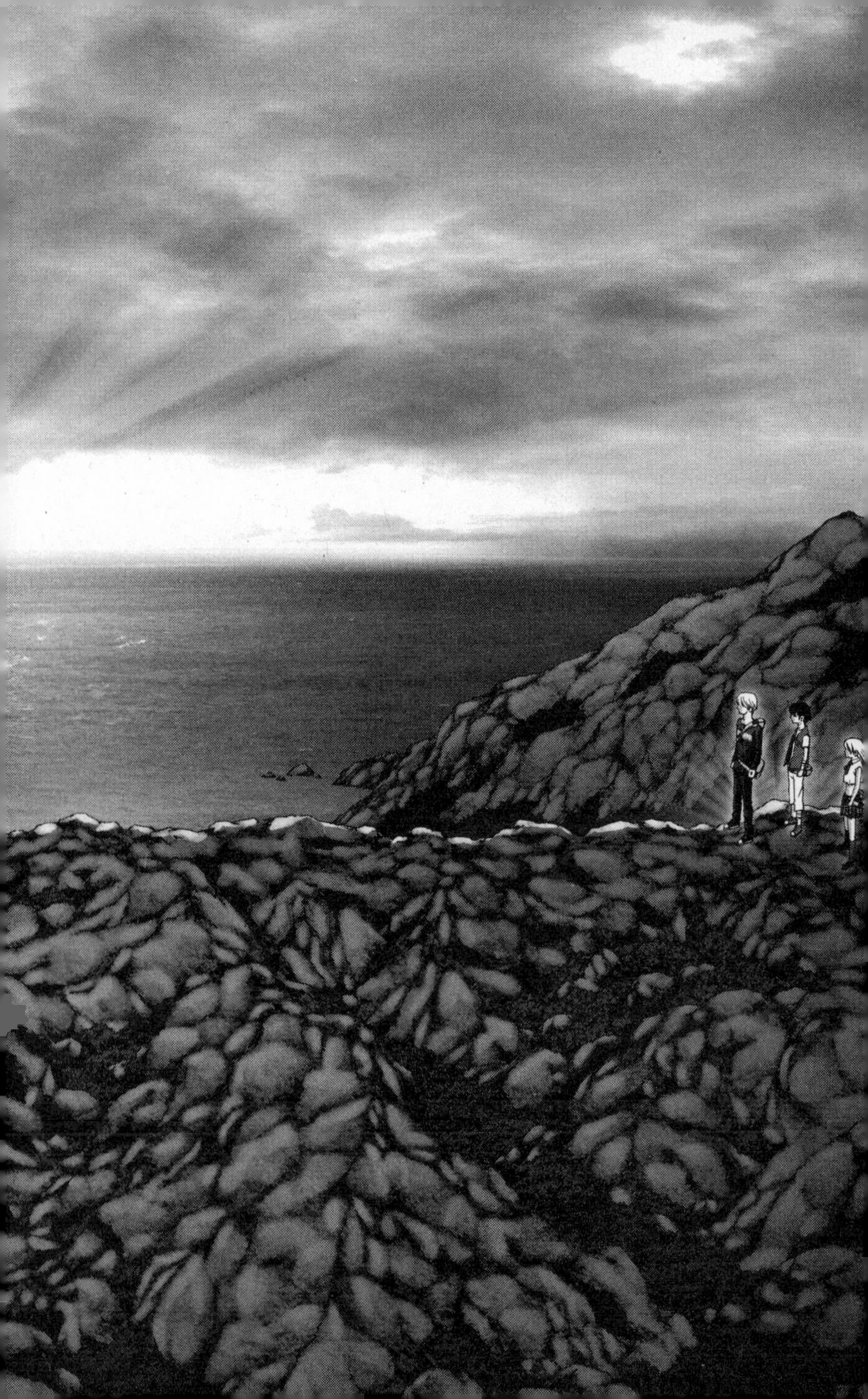

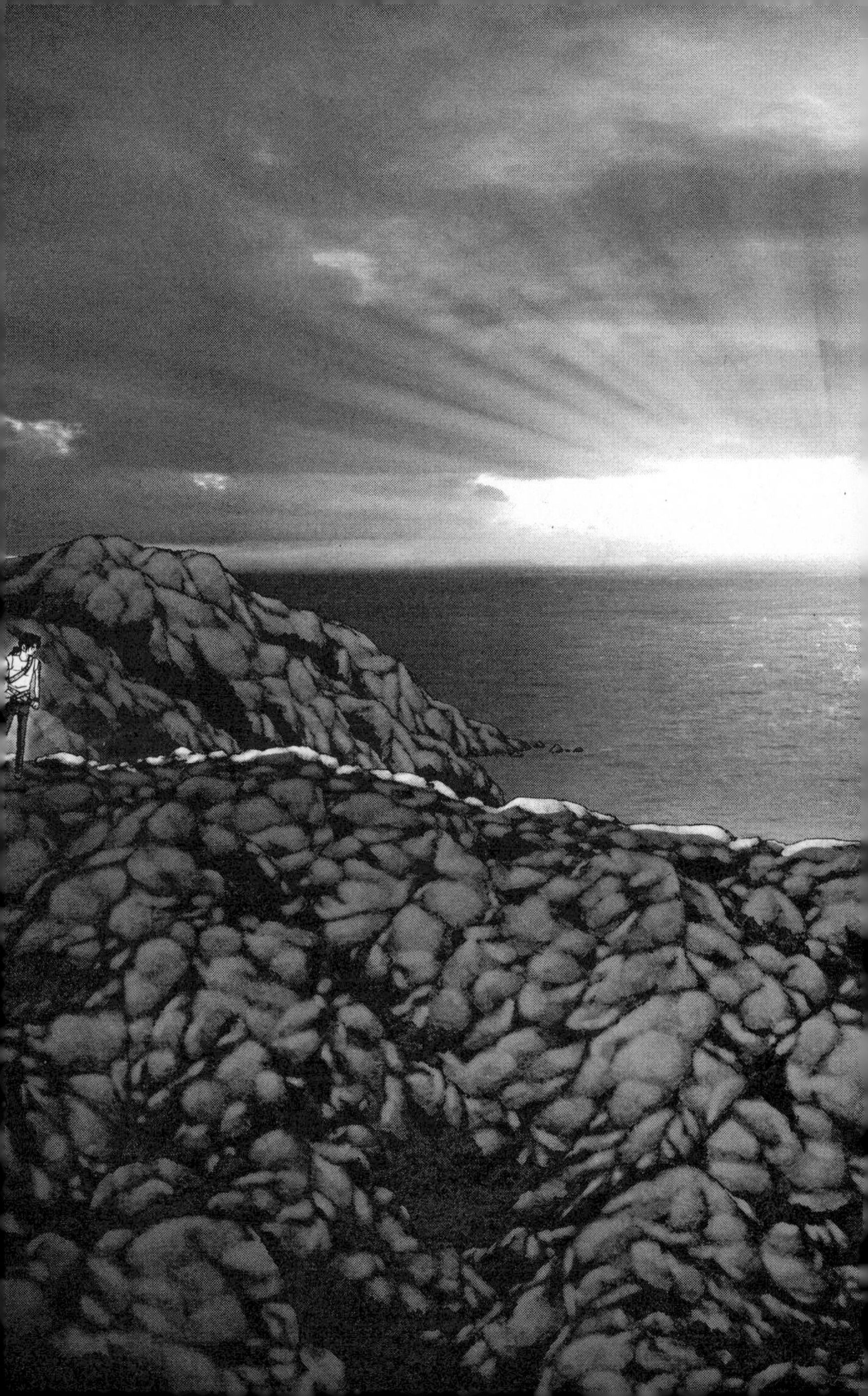

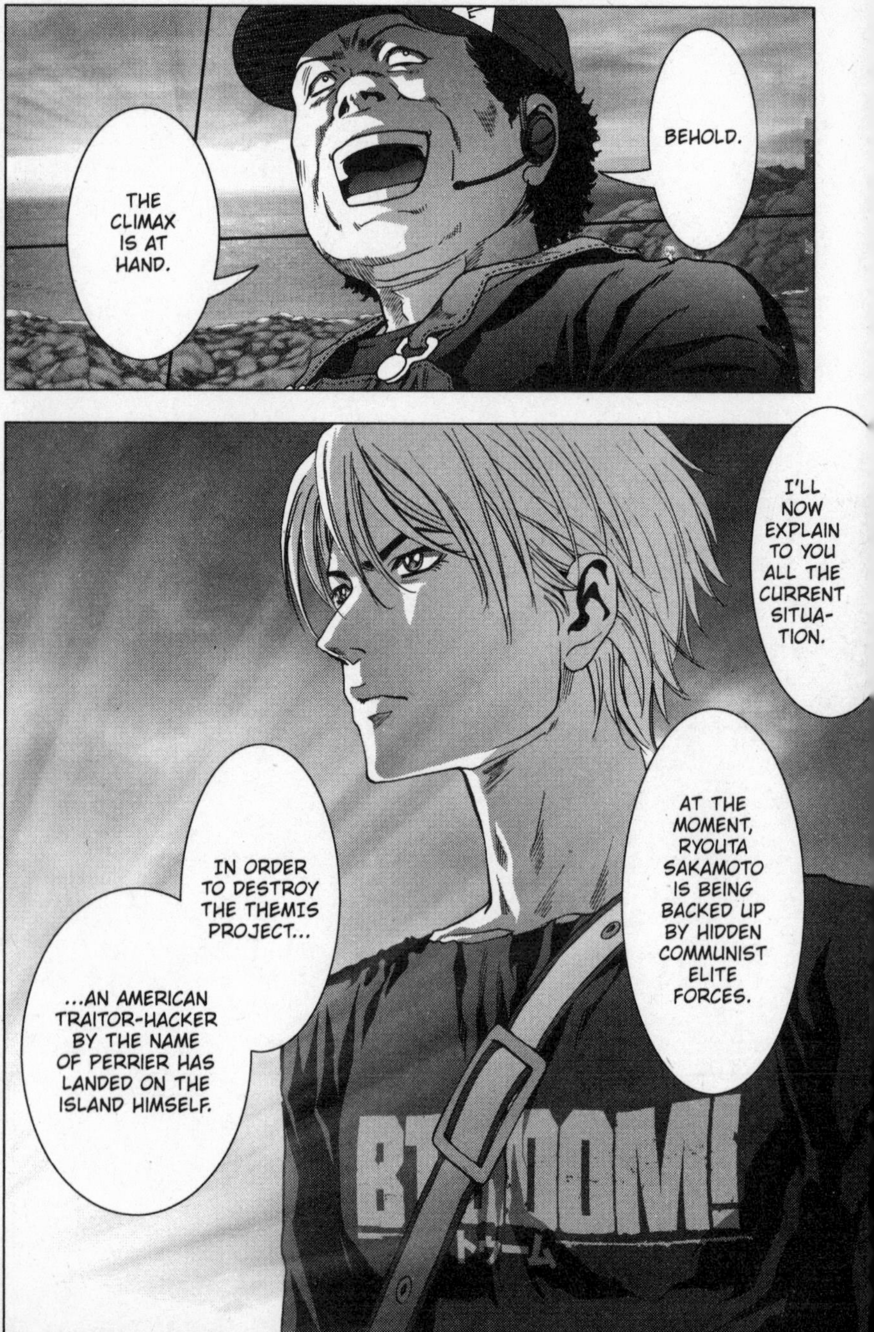
BEHOLD.
THE CLIMAX IS AT HAND.
I'LL NOW EXPLAIN TO YOU ALL THE CURRENT SITUATION.
AT THE MOMENT, RYOUTA SAKAMOTO IS BEING BACKED UP BY HIDDEN COMMUNIST ELITE FORCES.
IN ORDER TO DESTROY THE THEMIS PROJECT...
...AN AMERICAN TRAITOR-HACKER BY THE NAME OF PERRIER HAS LANDED ON THE ISLAND HIMSELF.

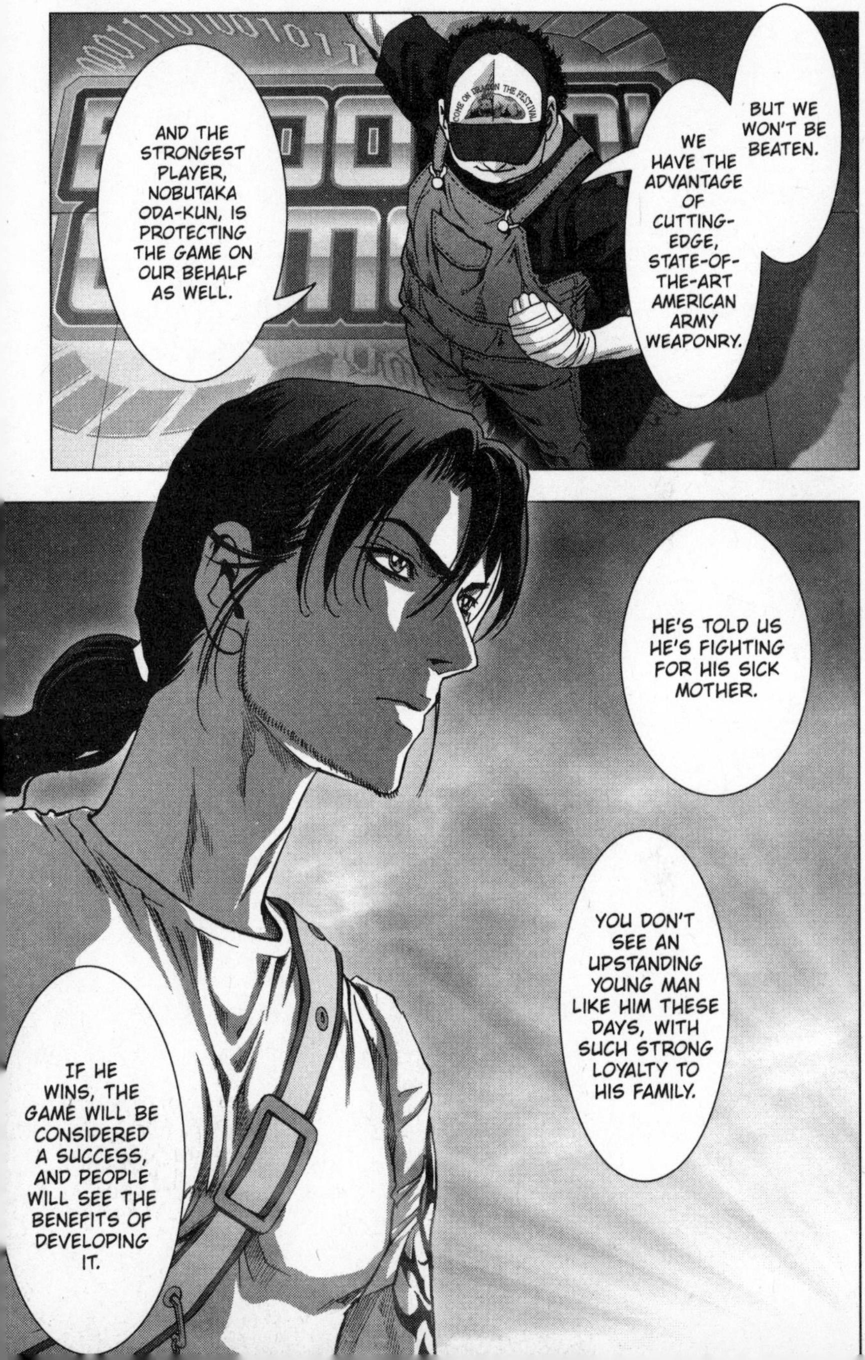
BUT WE WON'T BE BEATEN.
WE HAVE THE ADVANTAGE OF CUTTING-EDGE, STATE-OF-THE-ART AMERICAN ARMY WEAPONRY.
AND THE STRONGEST PLAYER, NOBUTAKA ODA-KUN, IS PROTECTING THE GAME ON OUR BEHALF AS WELL.
HE'S TOLD US HE'S FIGHTING FOR HIS SICK MOTHER.
YOU DON'T SEE AN UPSTANDING YOUNG MAN LIKE HIM THESE DAYS, WITH SUCH STRONG LOYALTY TO HIS FAMILY.
IF HE WINS, THE GAME WILL BE CONSIDERED A SUCCESS, AND PEOPLE WILL SEE THE BENEFITS OF DEVELOPING IT.

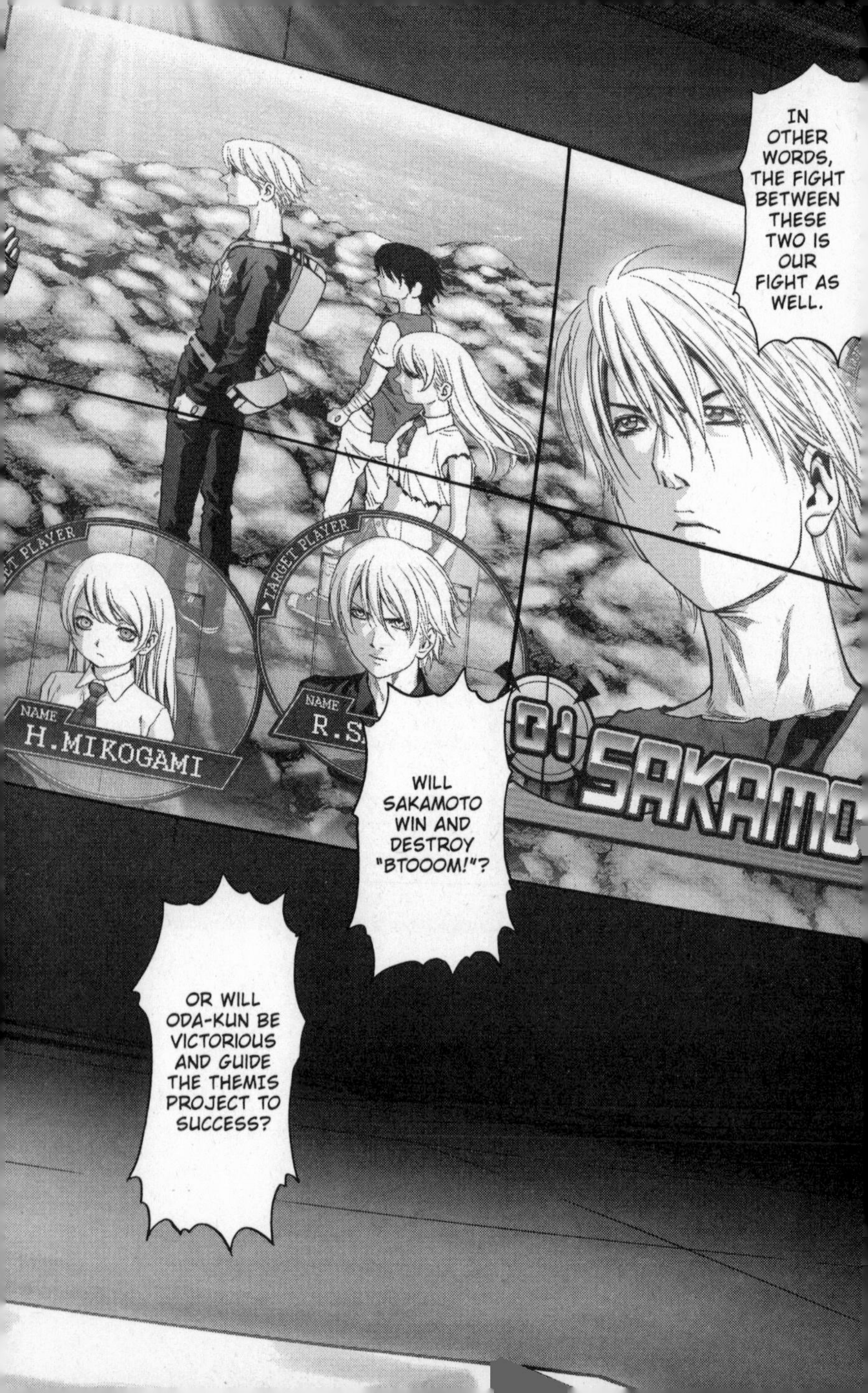
IN OTHER WORDS, THE FIGHT BETWEEN THESE TWO IS OUR FIGHT AS WELL.
TARGET PLAYER
NAME
R.S.
01 SAKAMO
TARGET PLAYER
NAME
H.MIKOGAMI
WILL SAKAMOTO WIN AND DESTROY "BTOOOM!"?
OR WILL ODA-KUN BE VICTORIOUS AND GUIDE THE THEMIS PROJECT TO SUCCESS?

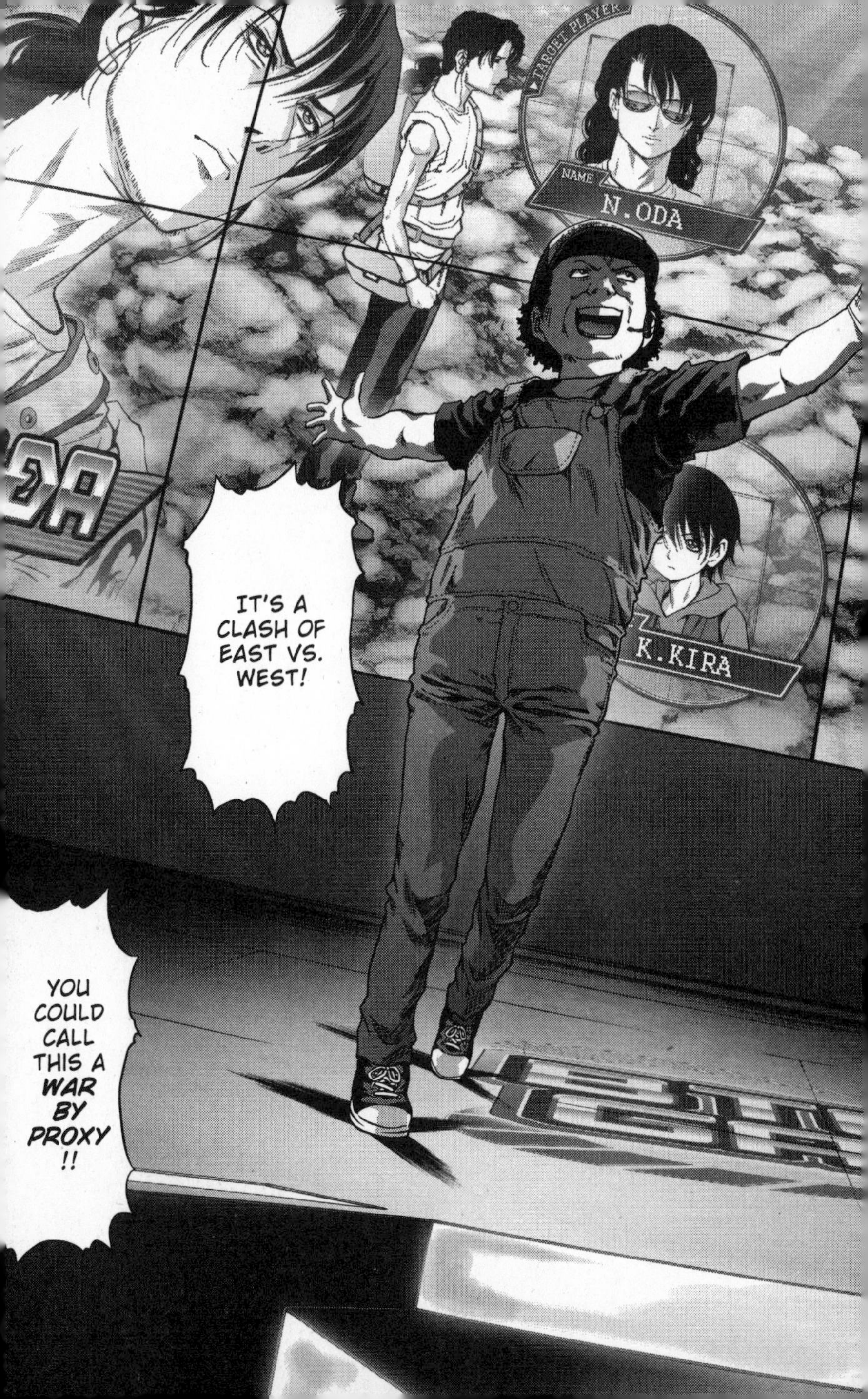
TARGET PLAYER
NAME
N. ODA
K. KIRA
IT'S A CLASH OF EAST VS. WEST!
YOU COULD CALL THIS A *WAR BY PROXY* !!

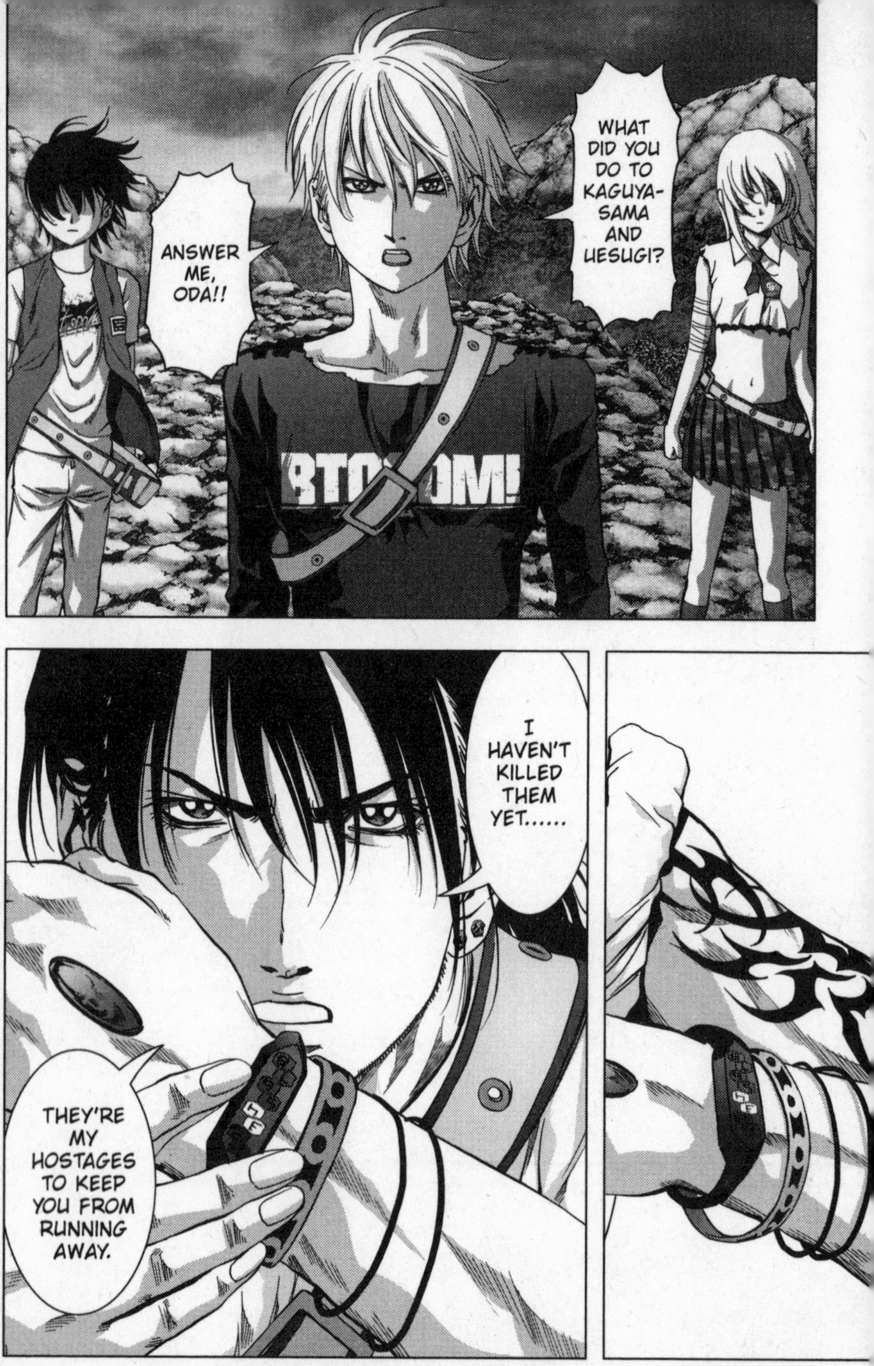
WHAT DID YOU DO TO KAGUYA-SAMA AND UESUGI?
ANSWER ME, ODA!!
I HAVEN'T KILLED THEM YET......
THEY'RE MY HOSTAGES TO KEEP YOU FROM RUNNING AWAY.

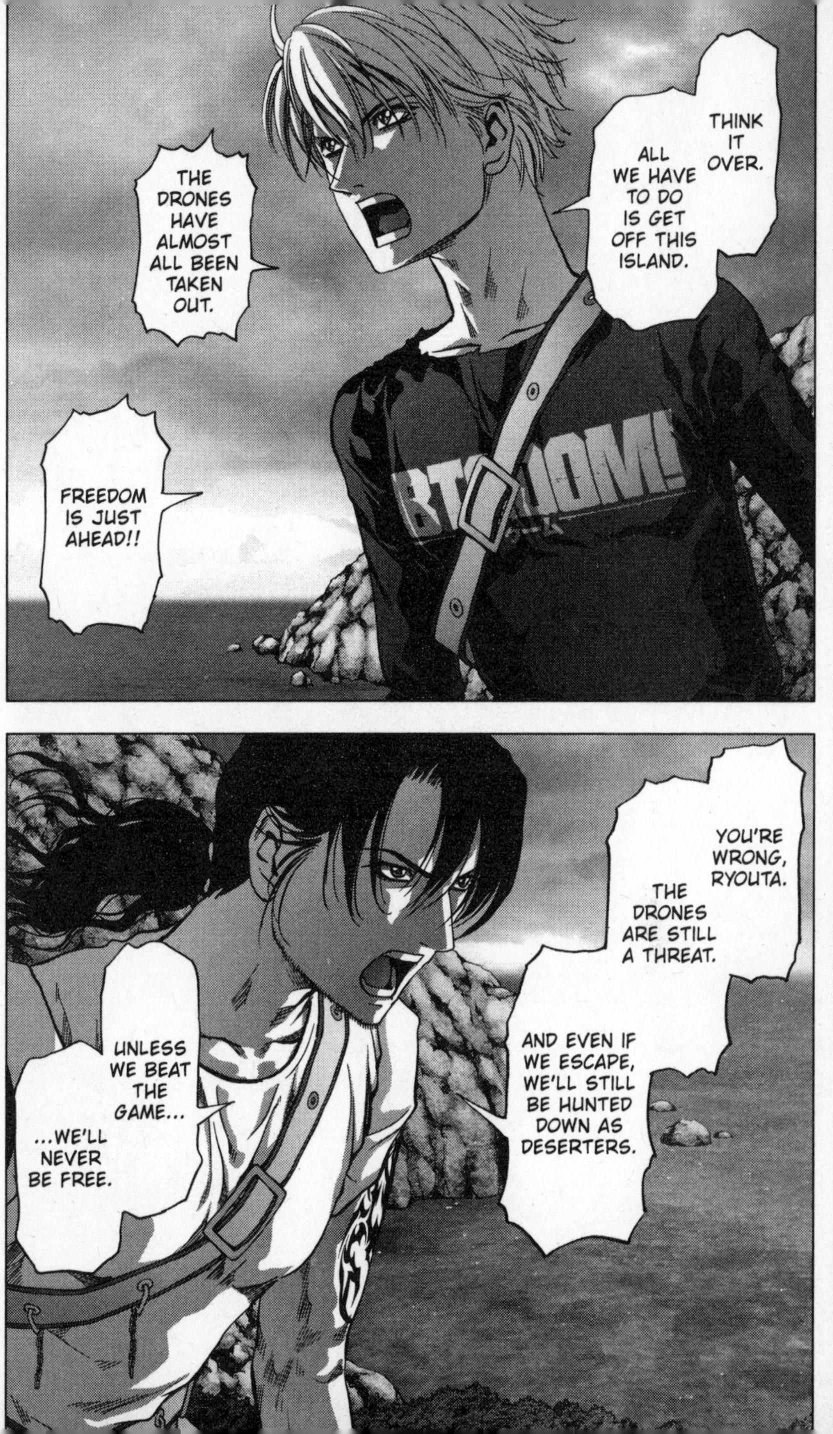
THINK IT OVER.
ALL WE HAVE TO DO IS GET OFF THIS ISLAND.
THE DRONES HAVE ALMOST ALL BEEN TAKEN OUT.
FREEDOM IS JUST AHEAD!!
YOU'RE WRONG, RYOUTA.
THE DRONES ARE STILL A THREAT.
AND EVEN IF WE ESCAPE, WE'LL STILL BE HUNTED DOWN AS DESERTERS.
UNLESS WE BEAT THE GAME...
...WE'LL NEVER BE FREE.

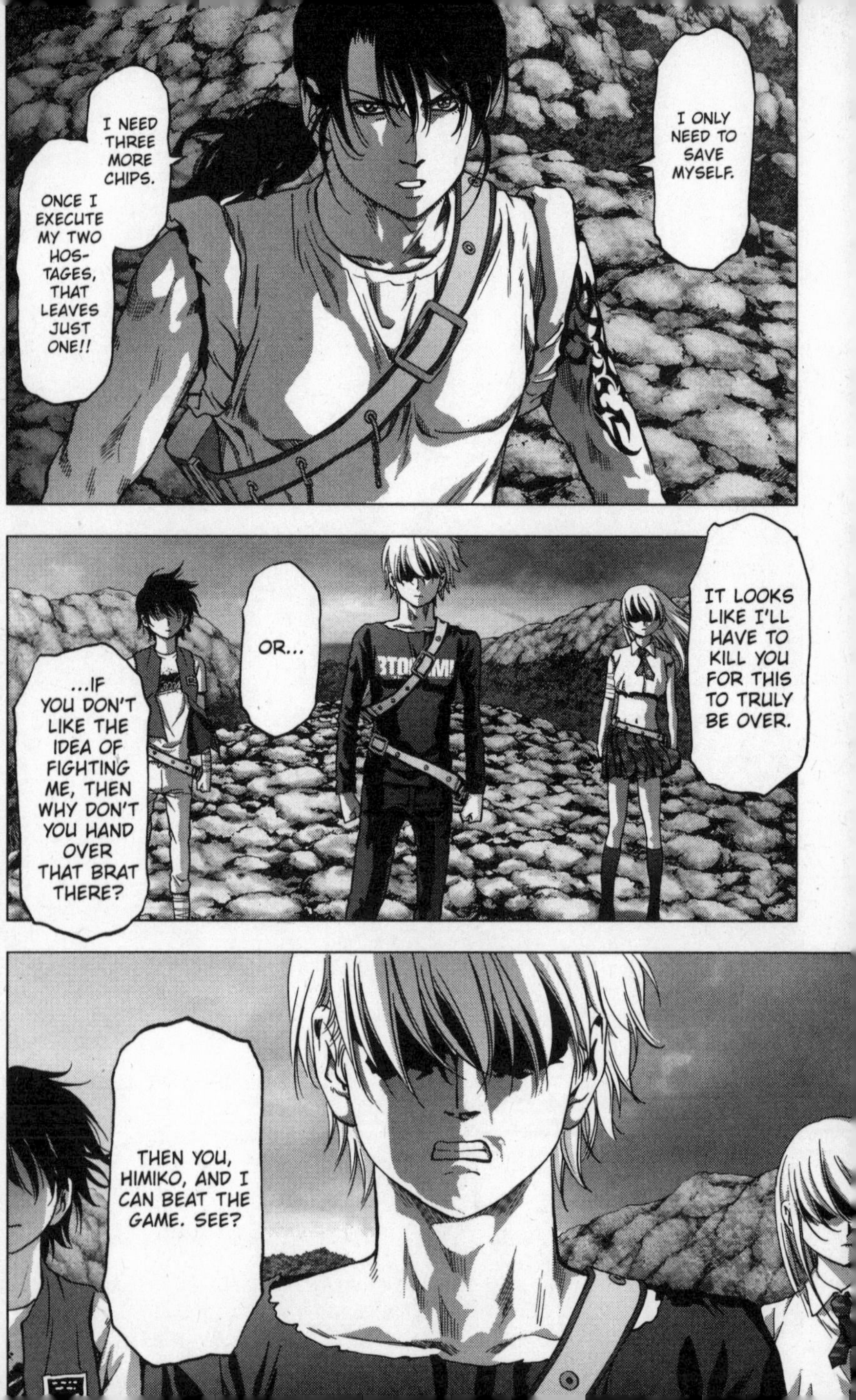
I ONLY NEED TO SAVE MYSELF.
I NEED THREE MORE CHIPS.
ONCE I EXECUTE MY TWO HOS-TAGES, THAT LEAVES JUST ONE!!
IT LOOKS LIKE I'LL HAVE TO KILL YOU FOR THIS TO TRULY BE OVER.
OR...
...IF YOU DON'T LIKE THE IDEA OF FIGHTING ME, THEN WHY DON'T YOU HAND OVER THAT BRAT THERE?
THEN YOU, HIMIKO, AND I CAN BEAT THE GAME. SEE?

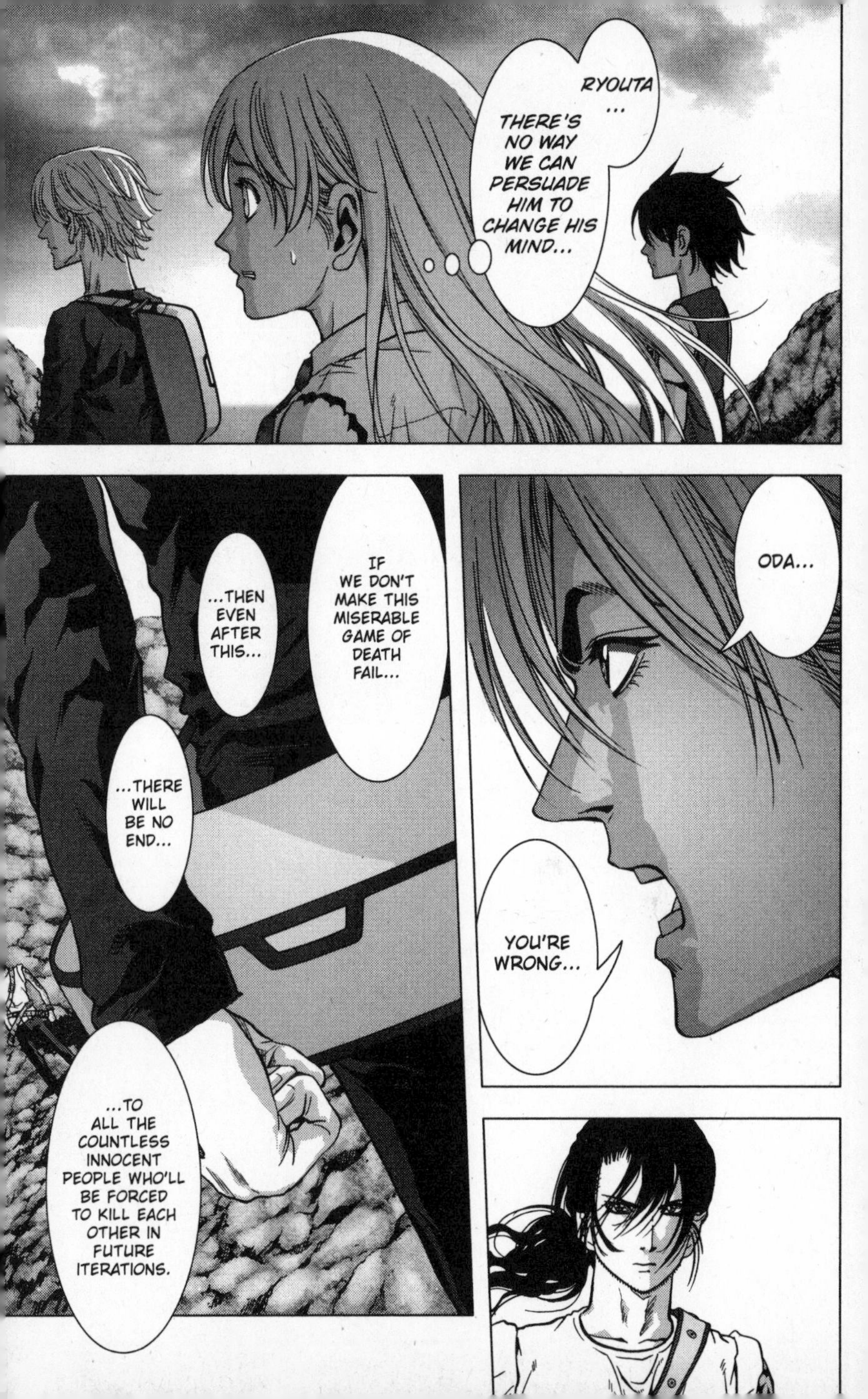
RYOUTA... THERE'S NO WAY WE CAN PERSUADE HIM TO CHANGE HIS MIND...
ODA...
YOU'RE WRONG...
IF WE DON'T MAKE THIS MISERABLE GAME OF DEATH FAIL...
...THEN EVEN AFTER THIS...
...THERE WILL BE NO END...
...TO ALL THE COUNTLESS INNOCENT PEOPLE WHO'LL BE FORCED TO KILL EACH OTHER IN FUTURE ITERATIONS.

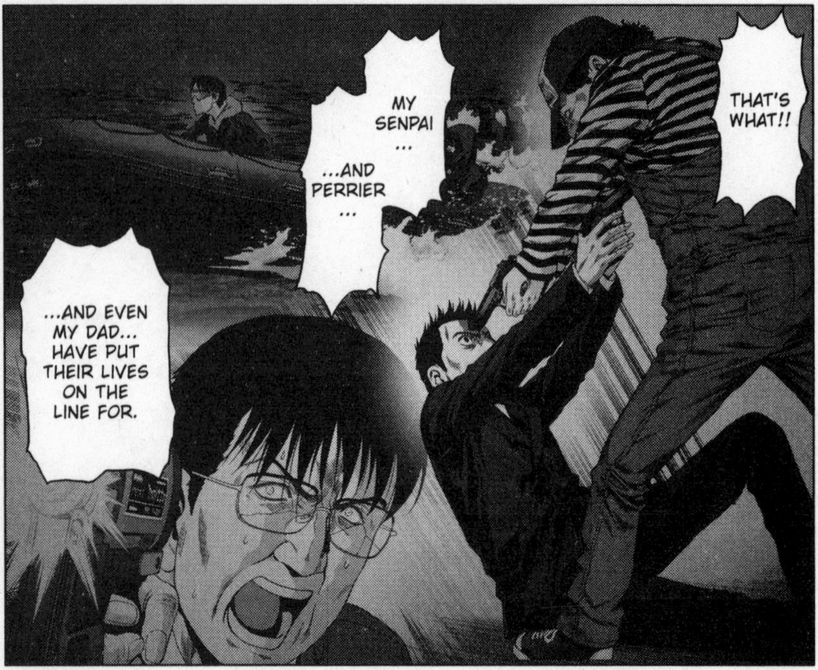
THAT'S WHAT!!
MY SENPAI...
...AND PERRIER...
...AND EVEN MY DAD... HAVE PUT THEIR LIVES ON THE LINE FOR.

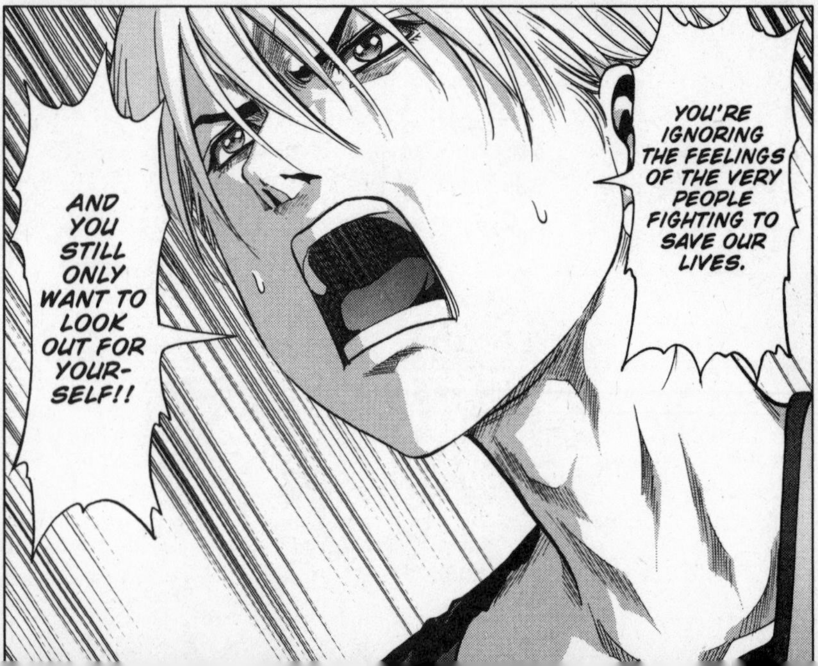
YOU'RE IGNORING THE FEELINGS OF THE VERY PEOPLE FIGHTING TO SAVE OUR LIVES.
AND YOU STILL ONLY WANT TO LOOK OUT FOR YOUR-SELF!!

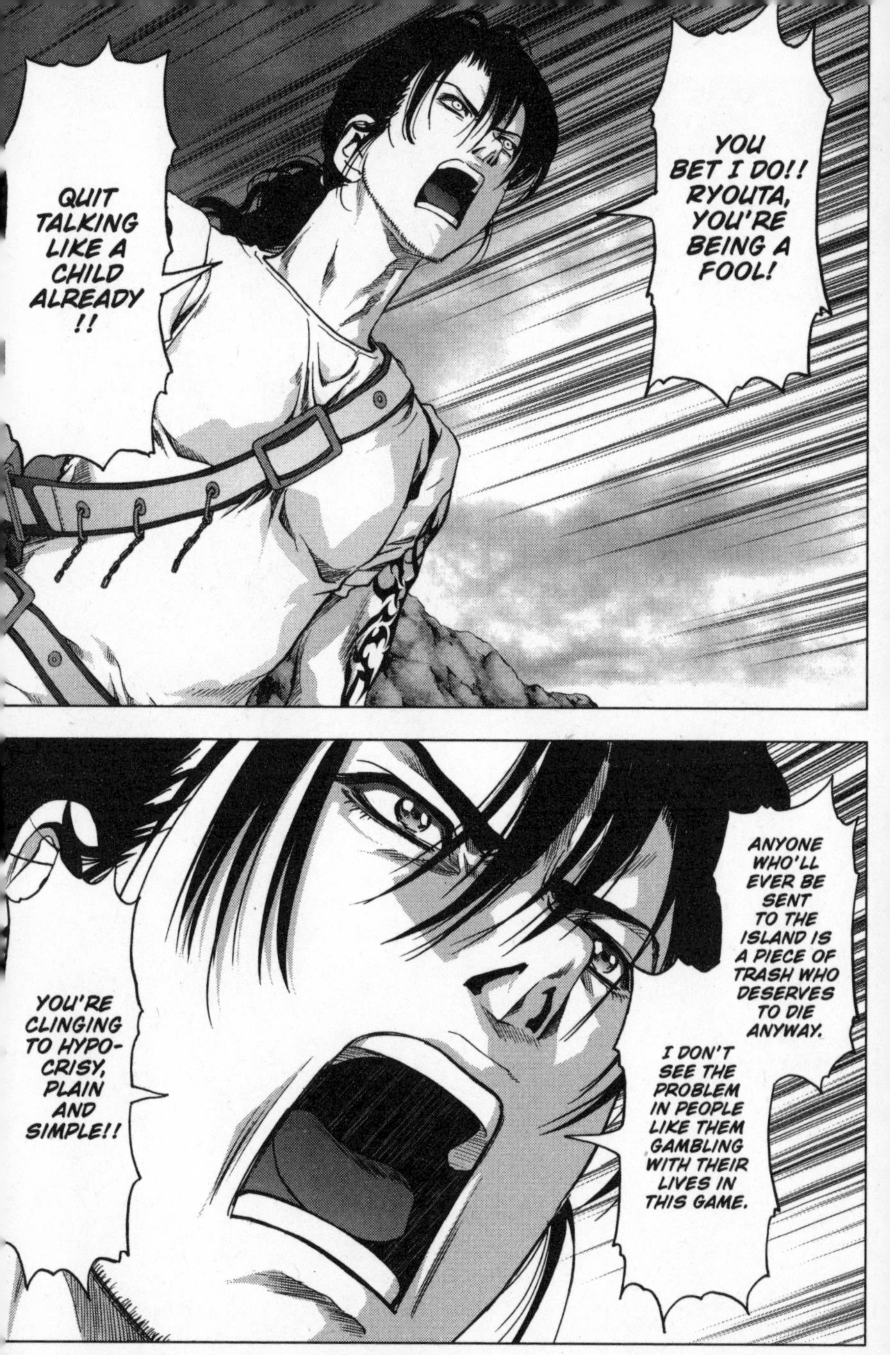
YOU BET I DO!! RYOUTA, YOU'RE BEING A FOOL!
QUIT TALKING LIKE A CHILD ALREADY !!
ANYONE WHO'LL EVER BE SENT TO THE ISLAND IS A PIECE OF TRASH WHO DESERVES TO DIE ANYWAY.
I DON'T SEE THE PROBLEM IN PEOPLE LIKE THEM GAMBLING WITH THEIR LIVES IN THIS GAME.
YOU'RE CLINGING TO HYPO-CRISY, PLAIN AND SIMPLE!!

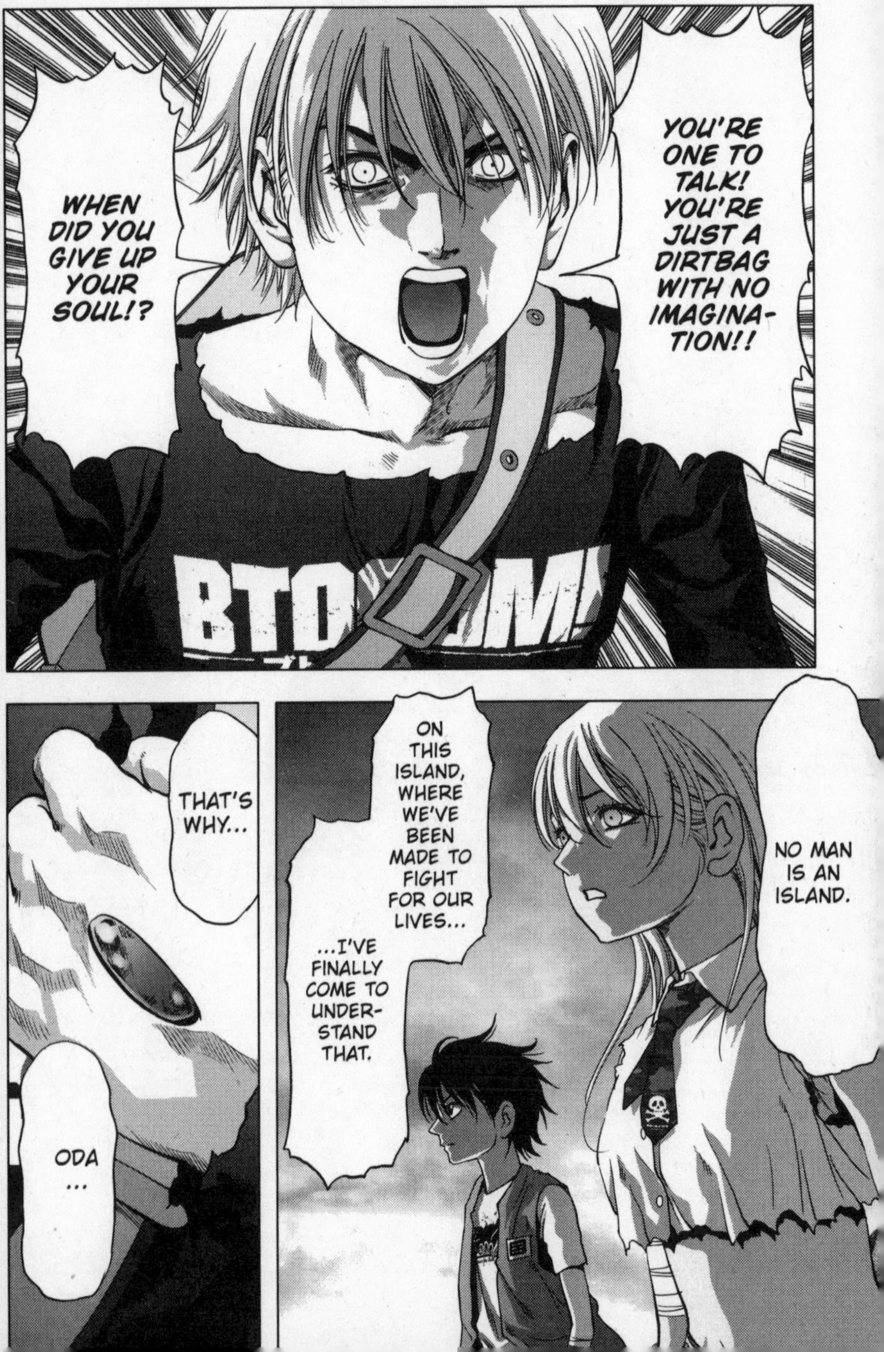
YOU'RE ONE TO TALK! YOU'RE JUST A DIRTBAG WITH NO IMAGINA-TION!!
WHEN DID YOU GIVE UP YOUR SOUL!?
NO MAN IS AN ISLAND.
ON THIS ISLAND, WHERE WE'VE BEEN MADE TO FIGHT FOR OUR LIVES...
...I'VE FINALLY COME TO UNDER-STAND THAT.
THAT'S WHY...
ODA
...

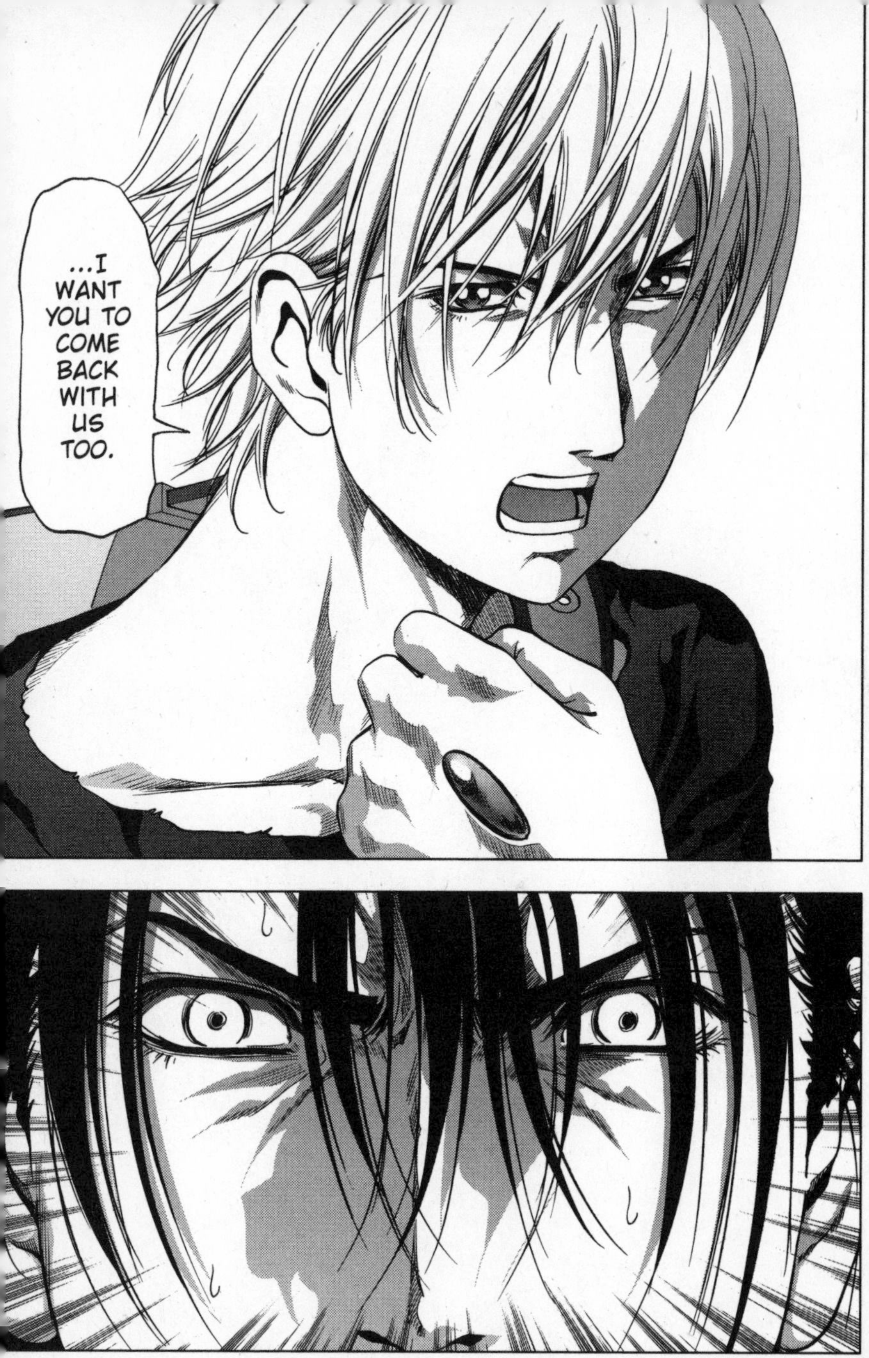
...I WANT YOU TO COME BACK WITH US TOO.

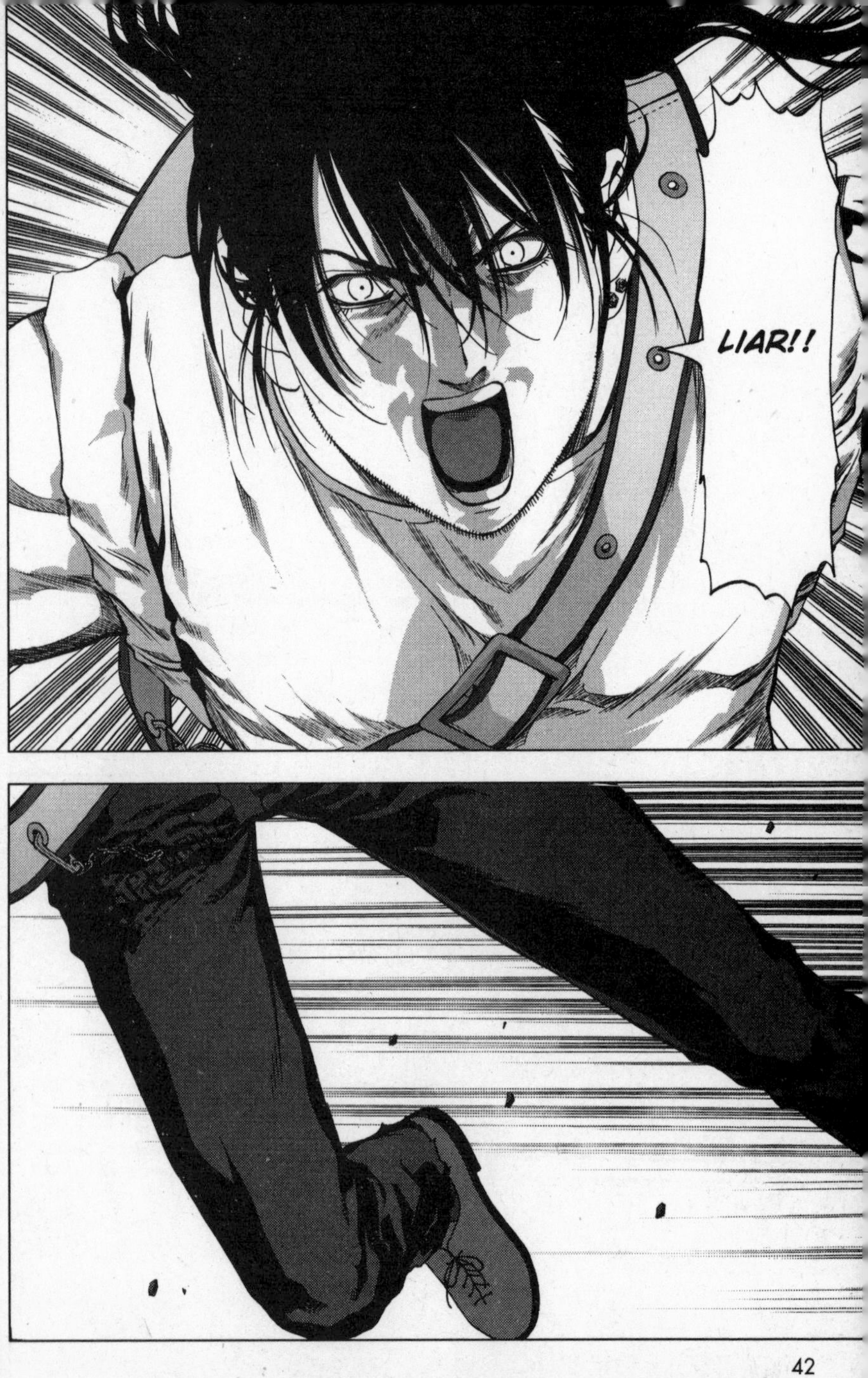
LIAR!!

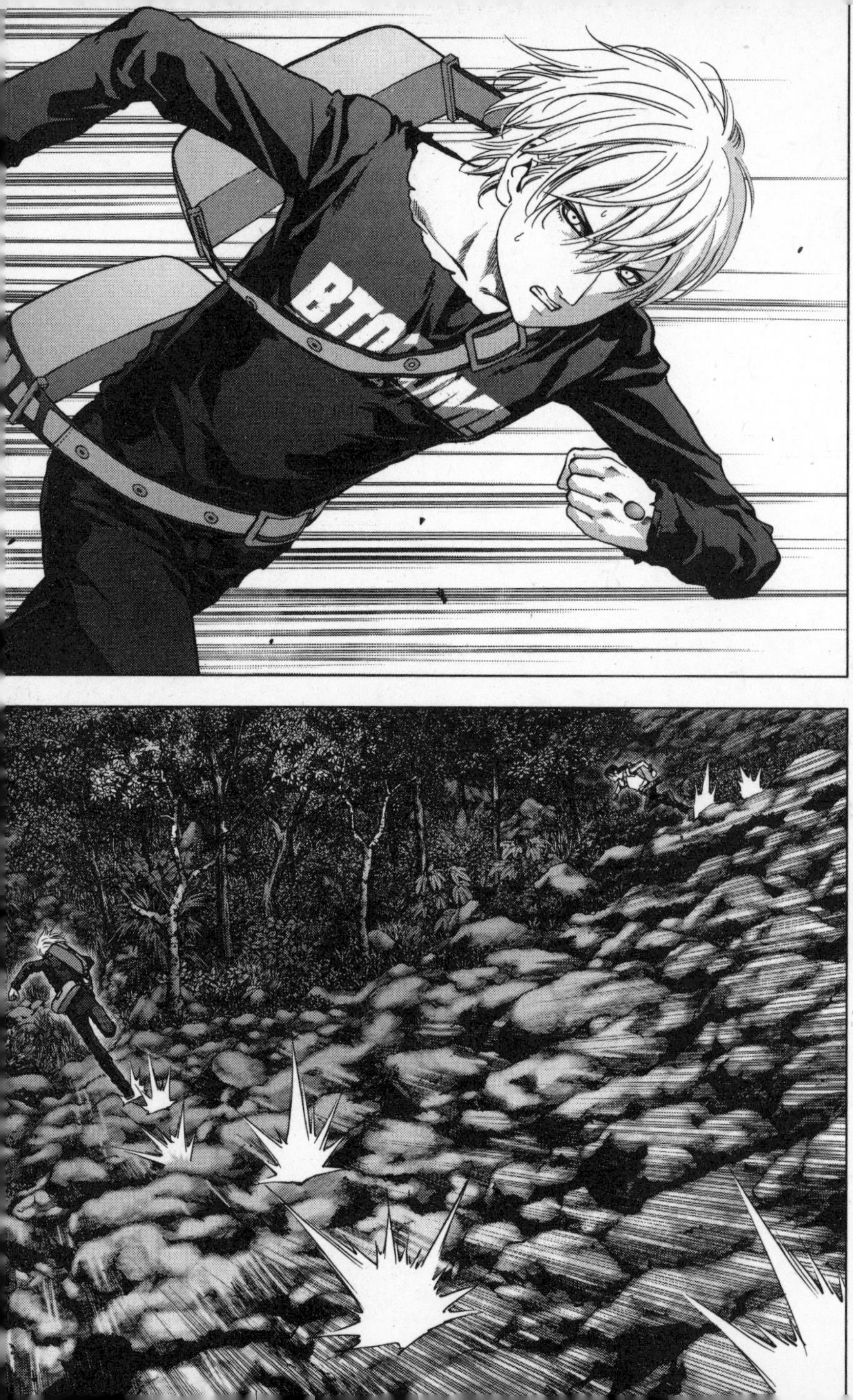

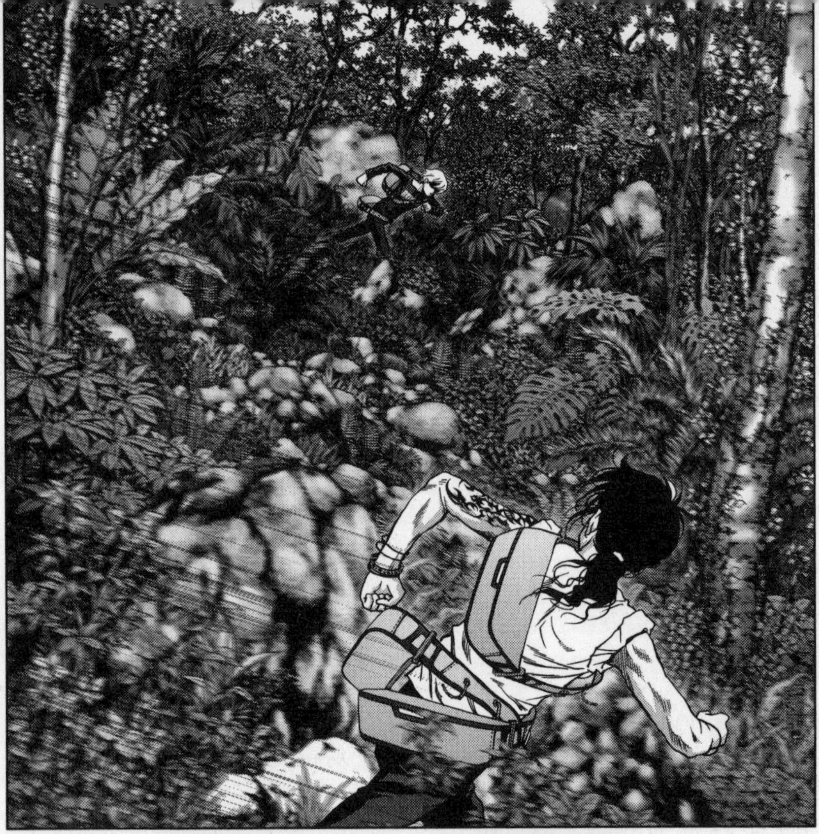

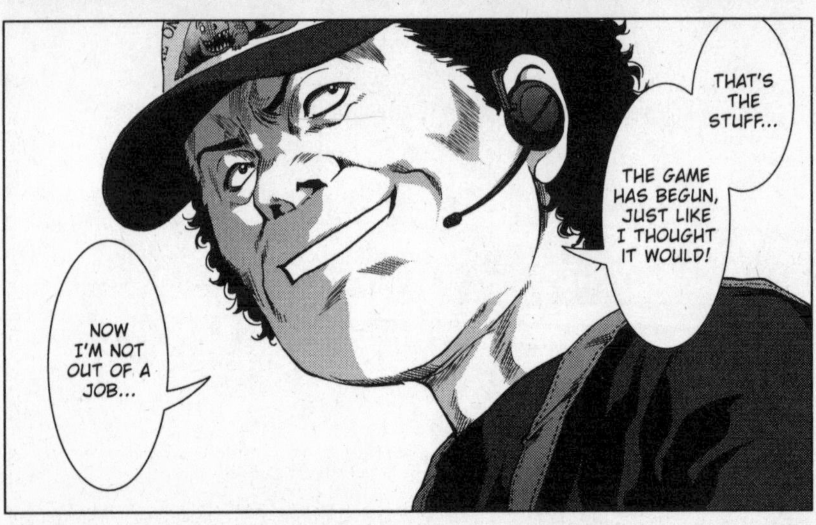
THAT'S THE STUFF...
THE GAME HAS BEGUN, JUST LIKE I THOUGHT IT WOULD!
NOW I'M NOT OUT OF A JOB...

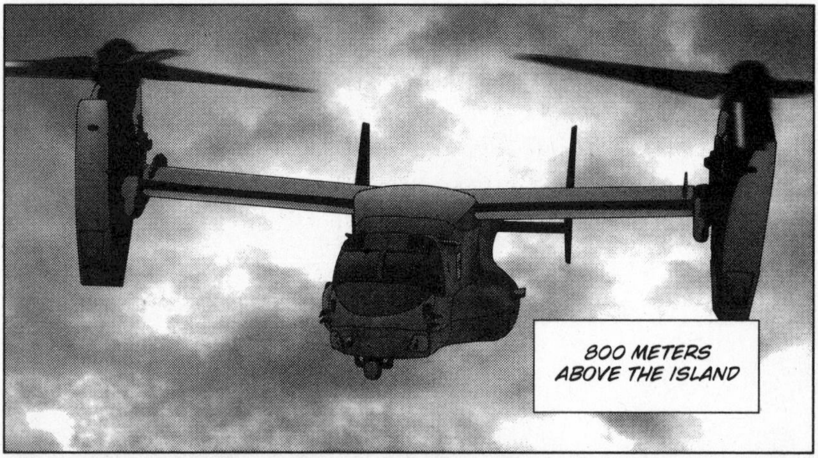
800 METERS ABOVE THE ISLAND

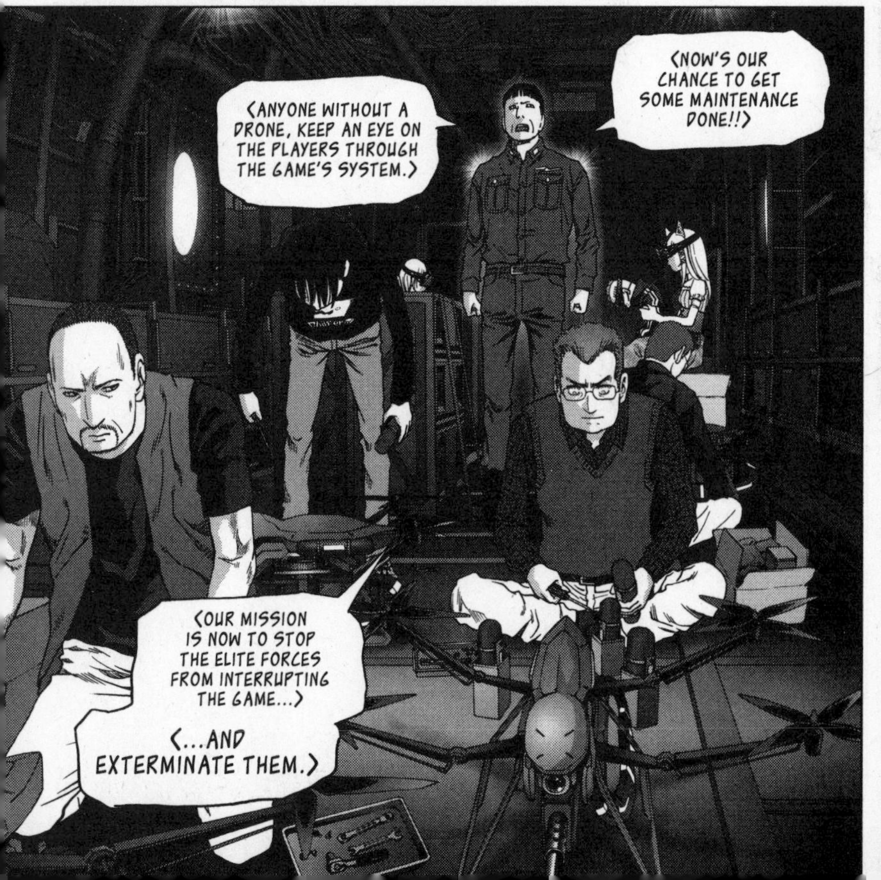
<NOW'S OUR CHANCE TO GET SOME MAINTENANCE DONE!!>
<ANYONE WITHOUT A DRONE, KEEP AN EYE ON THE PLAYERS THROUGH THE GAME'S SYSTEM.>
<OUR MISSION IS NOW TO STOP THE ELITE FORCES FROM INTERRUPTING THE GAME...>
<...AND EXTERMINATE THEM.>

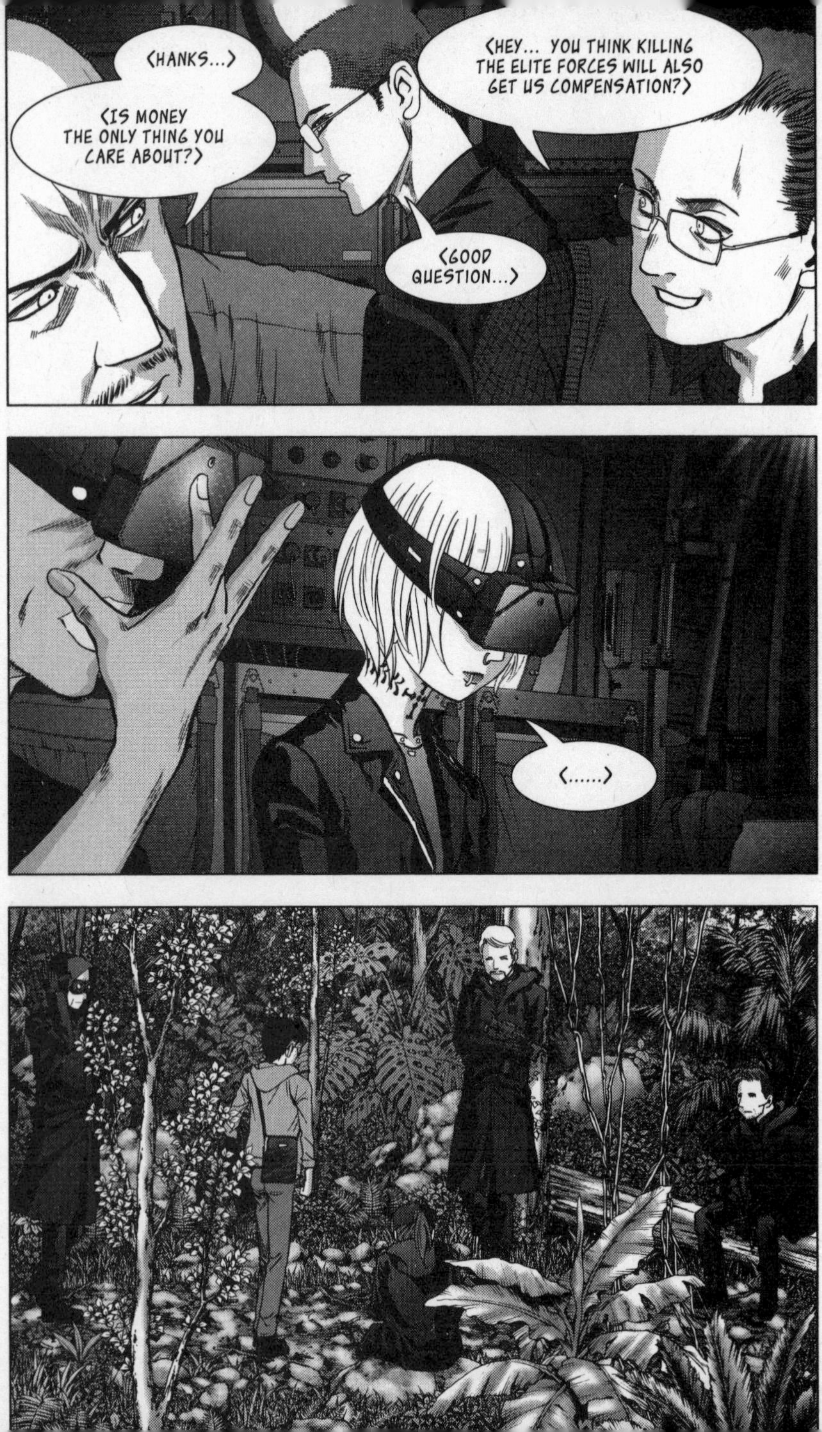
<HEY... YOU THINK KILLING THE ELITE FORCES WILL ALSO GET US COMPENSATION?>
<HANKS...>
<IS MONEY THE ONLY THING YOU CARE ABOUT?>
<GOOD QUESTION...>
<......>

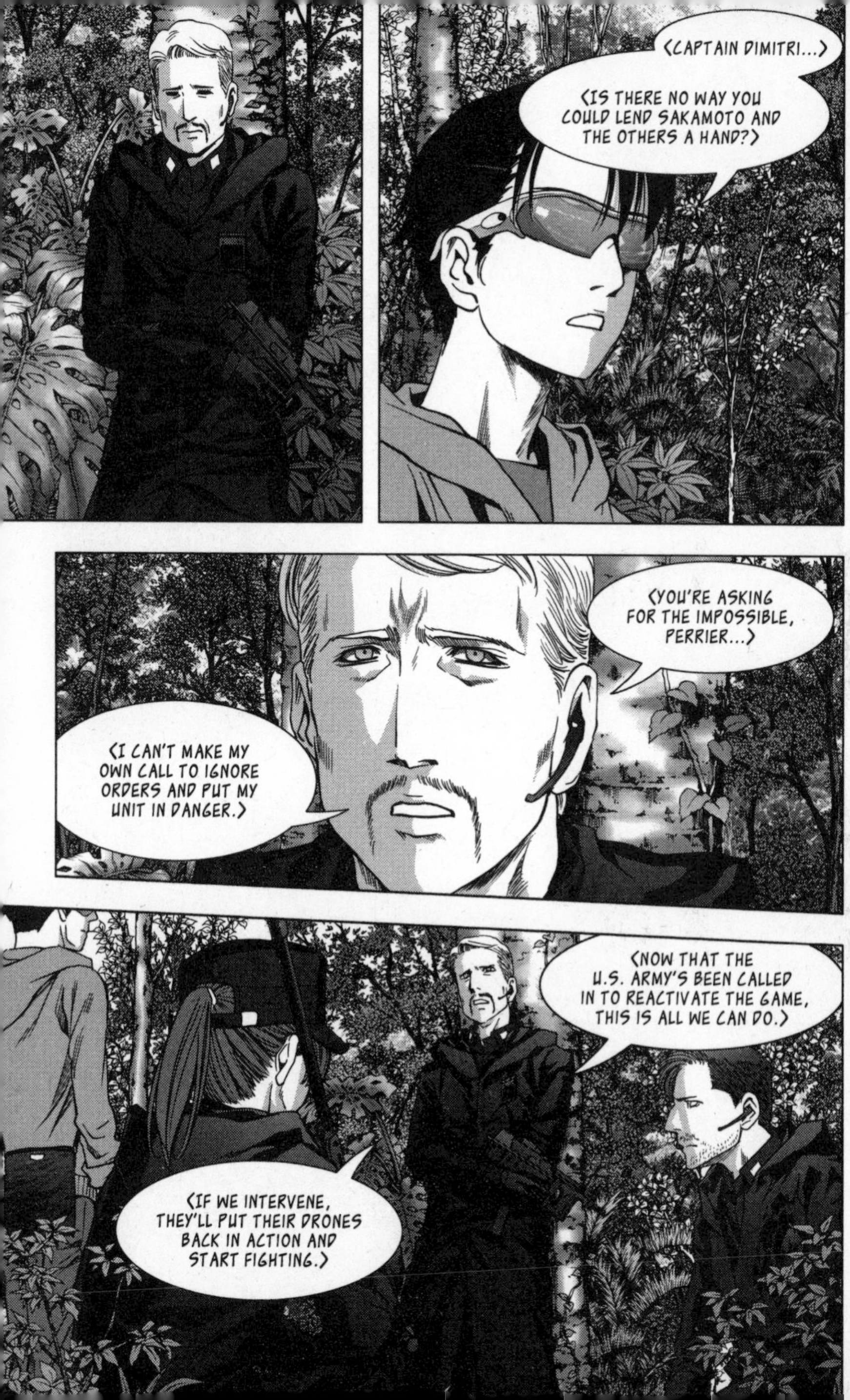
<CAPTAIN DIMITRI...>
<IS THERE NO WAY YOU COULD LEND SAKAMOTO AND THE OTHERS A HAND?>
<YOU'RE ASKING FOR THE IMPOSSIBLE, PERRIER...>
<I CAN'T MAKE MY OWN CALL TO IGNORE ORDERS AND PUT MY UNIT IN DANGER.>
<NOW THAT THE U.S. ARMY'S BEEN CALLED IN TO REACTIVATE THE GAME, THIS IS ALL WE CAN DO.>
<IF WE INTERVENE, THEY'LL PUT THEIR DRONES BACK IN ACTION AND START FIGHTING.>

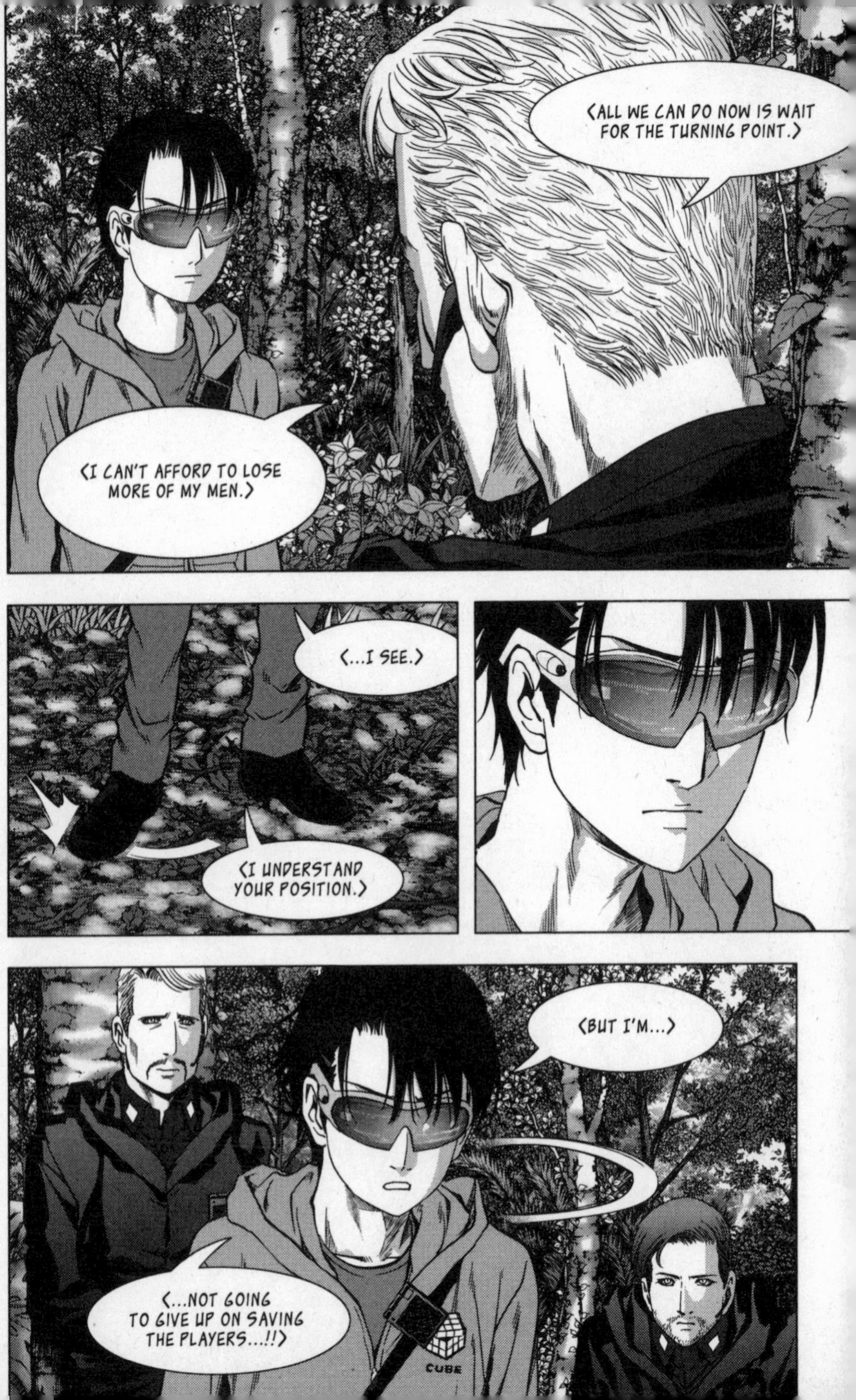
‹ALL WE CAN DO NOW IS WAIT FOR THE TURNING POINT.›
‹I CAN'T AFFORD TO LOSE MORE OF MY MEN.›
‹...I SEE.›
‹I UNDERSTAND YOUR POSITION.›
‹BUT I'M...›
‹...NOT GOING TO GIVE UP ON SAVING THE PLAYERS...!!›
CUBE

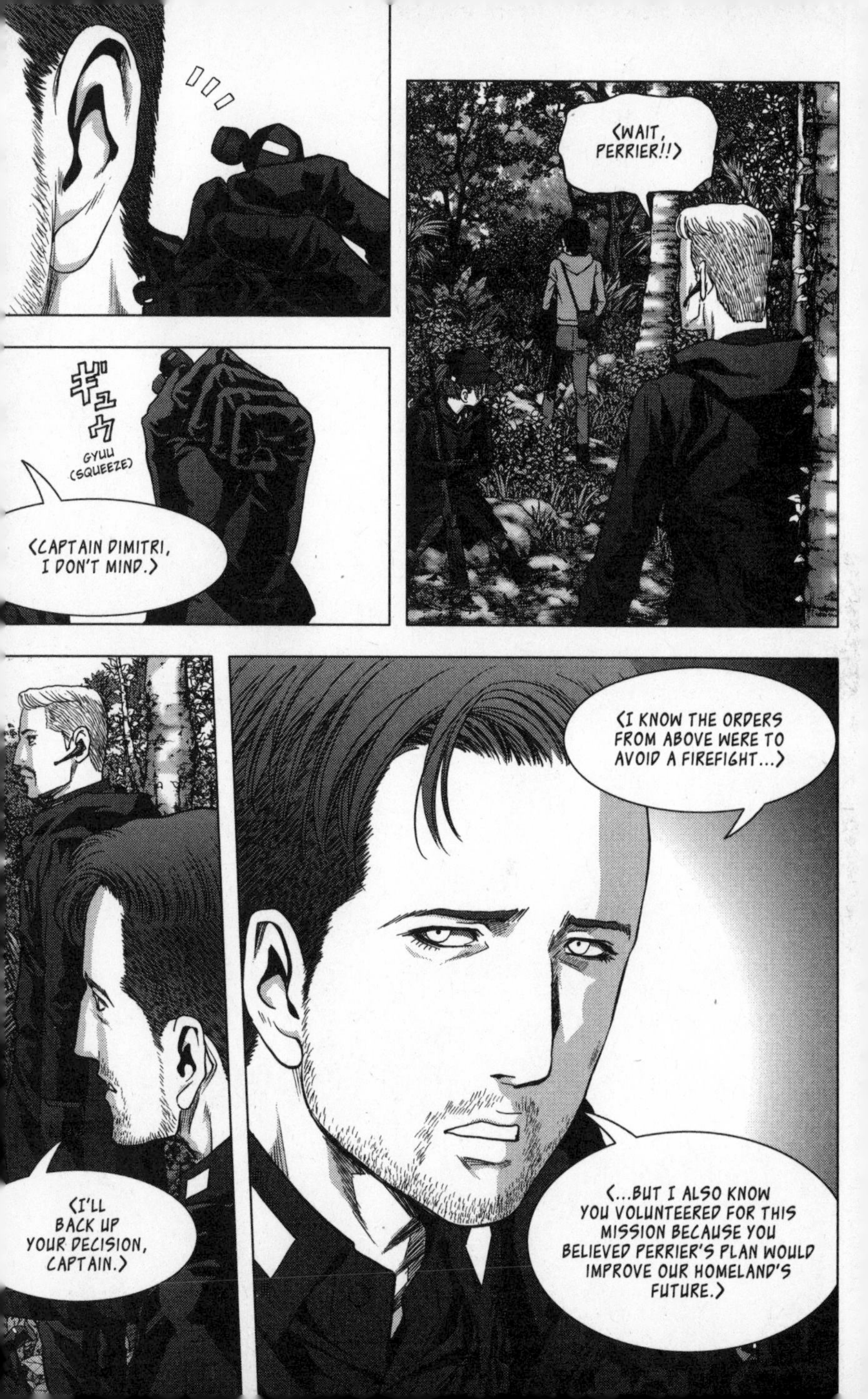
<WAIT, PERRIER!!>
ギュウ
GYUU (SQUEEZE)
<CAPTAIN DIMITRI, I DON'T MIND.>
<I KNOW THE ORDERS FROM ABOVE WERE TO AVOID A FIREFIGHT...>
<...BUT I ALSO KNOW YOU VOLUNTEERED FOR THIS MISSION BECAUSE YOU BELIEVED PERRIER'S PLAN WOULD IMPROVE OUR HOMELAND'S FUTURE.>
<I'LL BACK UP YOUR DECISION, CAPTAIN.>

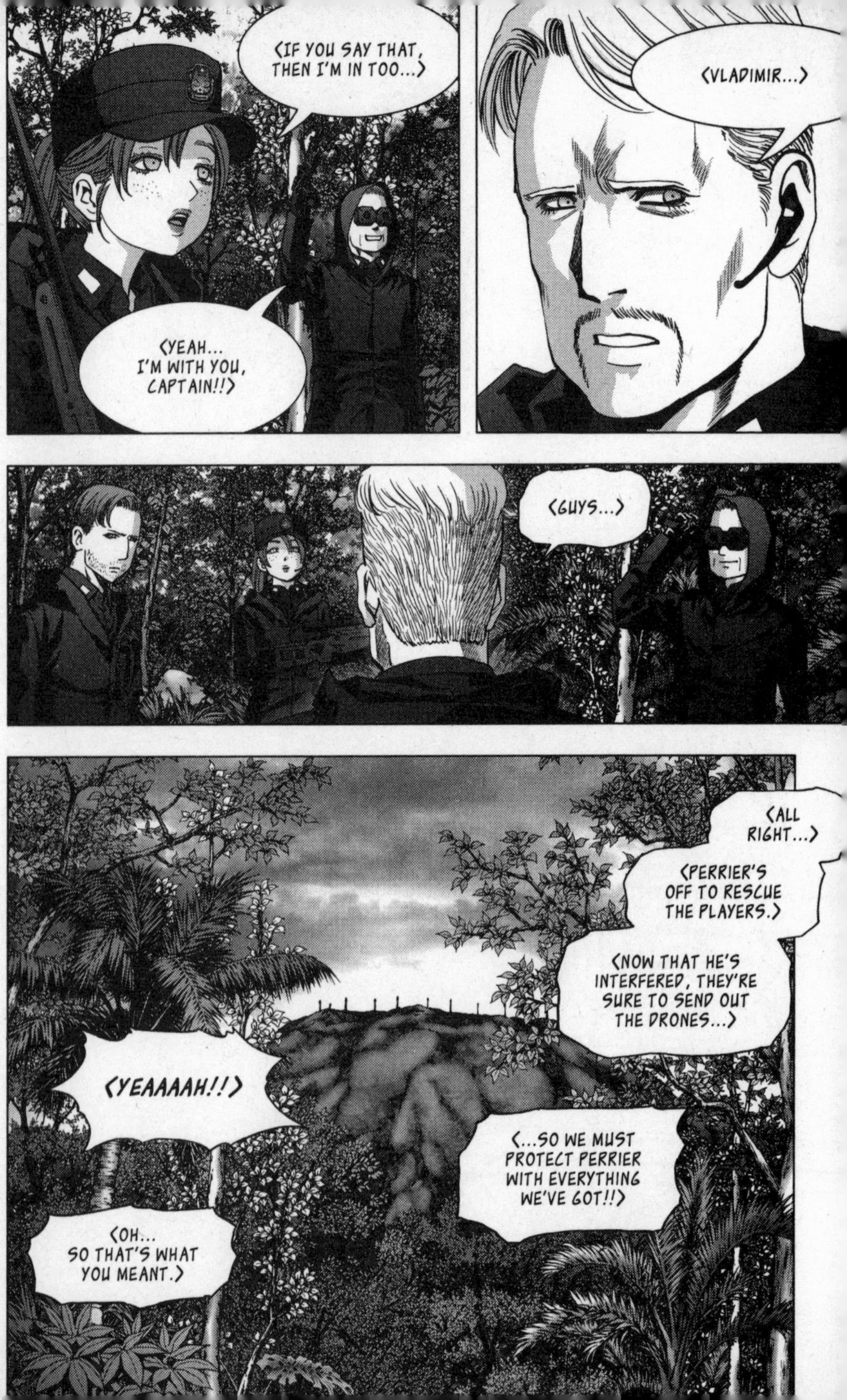
‹VLADIMIR...›
‹IF YOU SAY THAT, THEN I'M IN TOO...›
‹YEAH... I'M WITH YOU, CAPTAIN!!›
‹GUYS...›
‹ALL RIGHT...›
‹PERRIER'S OFF TO RESCUE THE PLAYERS.›
‹NOW THAT HE'S INTERFERED, THEY'RE SURE TO SEND OUT THE DRONES...›
‹...SO WE MUST PROTECT PERRIER WITH EVERYTHING WE'VE GOT!!›
‹YEAAAAH!!›
‹OH... SO THAT'S WHAT YOU MEANT.›

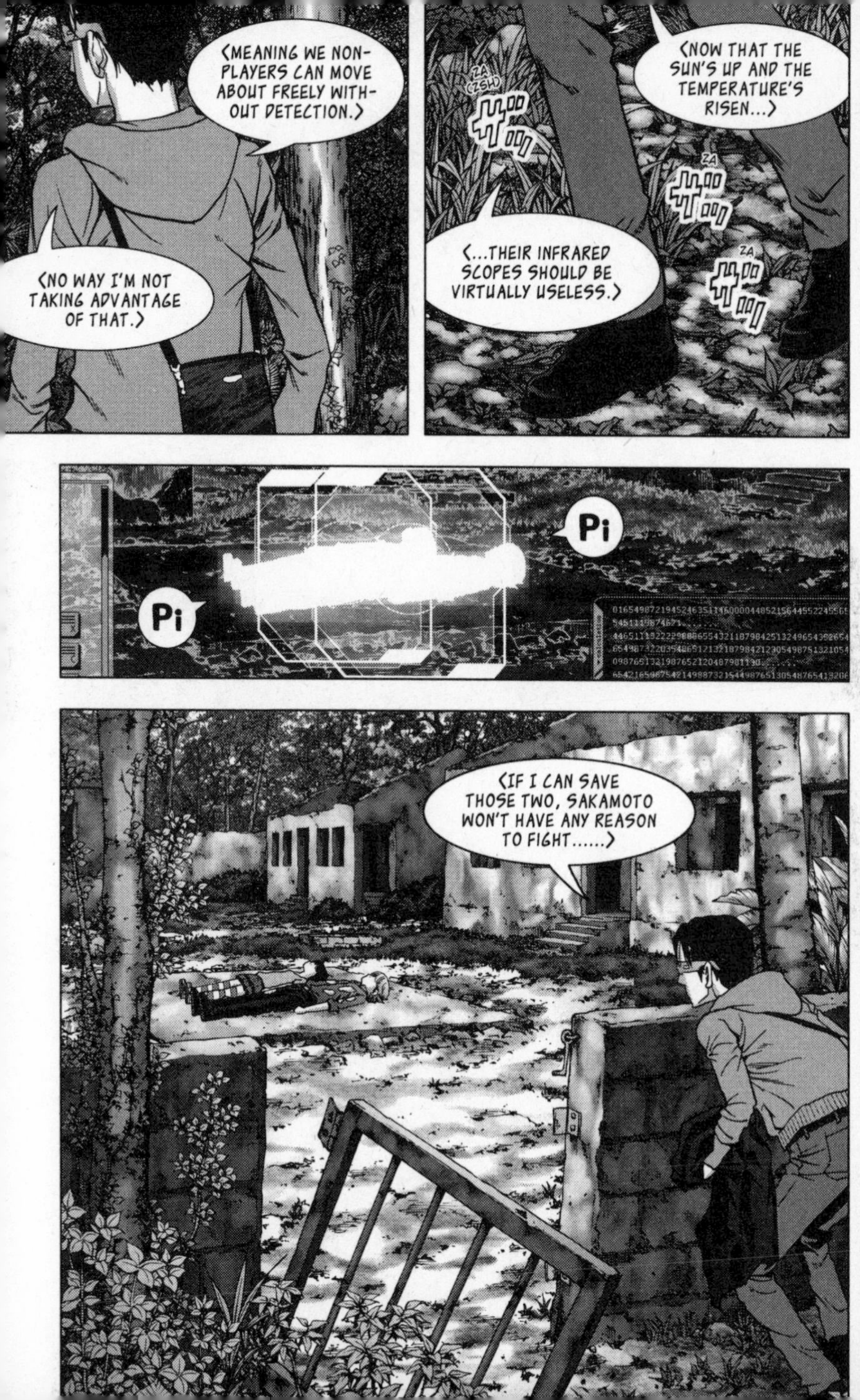
〈NOW THAT THE SUN'S UP AND THE TEMPERATURE'S RISEN...〉
ZA (ZSH)
ZA
ZA
〈...THEIR INFRARED SCOPES SHOULD BE VIRTUALLY USELESS.〉
〈MEANING WE NON-PLAYERS CAN MOVE ABOUT FREELY WITH-OUT DETECTION.〉
〈NO WAY I'M NOT TAKING ADVANTAGE OF THAT.〉
Pi
Pi
〈IF I CAN SAVE THOSE TWO, SAKAMOTO WON'T HAVE ANY REASON TO FIGHT......〉

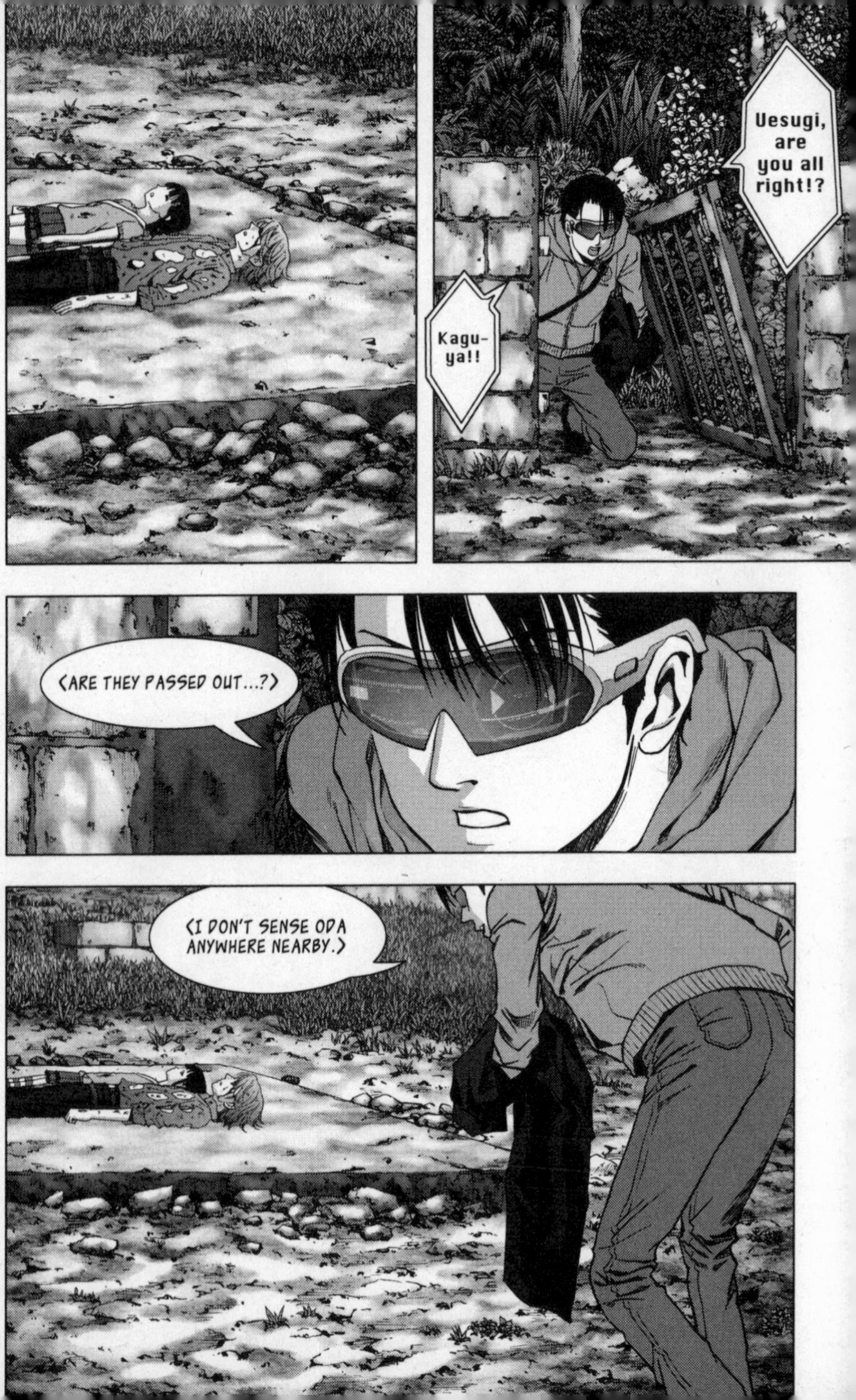
Uesugi, are you all right!?
Kagu-ya!!
⟨ARE THEY PASSED OUT...?⟩
⟨I DON'T SENSE ODA ANYWHERE NEARBY.⟩

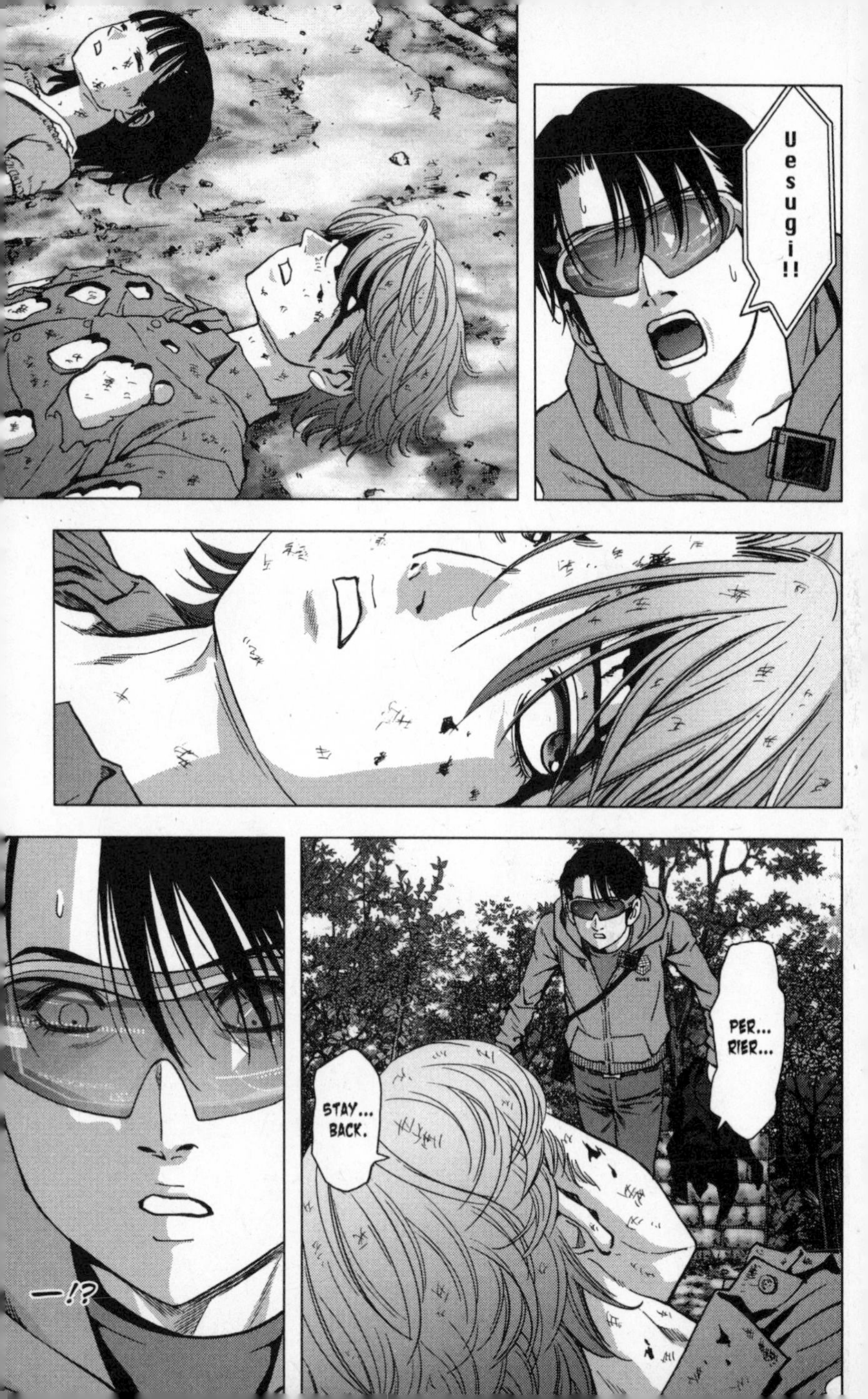
Uesugi!!
PER... RIER...
STAY... BACK.
—!?

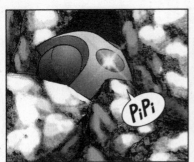

PiPi

DOGOUUUN
(KABOOOOM)

BTOOOM!

REFERENCE MATERIAL TRIP LOG

#6: OGAMI ISLAND, OFF MIYAKO ISLAND

OGAMI ISLAND IS A SMALL ISLAND FOUR KILOMETERS AWAY FROM MIYAKO ISLAND. IN A VERY LIMITED STRETCH OF LAND, THEY HAD ALL THESE RESIDENTIAL BUILDINGS ERECTED IN A MAZELIKE STYLE THAT GIVES OFF THE FEELING OF A STRANGE MINIATURE GARDEN OF SORTS. FOR SOME REASON, IT REALLY GAVE ME THIS EXCITED, GIDDY FEELING. DUE TO TIME CONTRAINTS, I COULD ONLY SPEND AN HOUR THERE, WHICH IS MY ONLY REGRET... THIS ISLAND WAS THE BASIS FOR THE SANCTUARY WHERE KAGUYA AND THE OTHERS RESIDED.

JUNYA INOUE

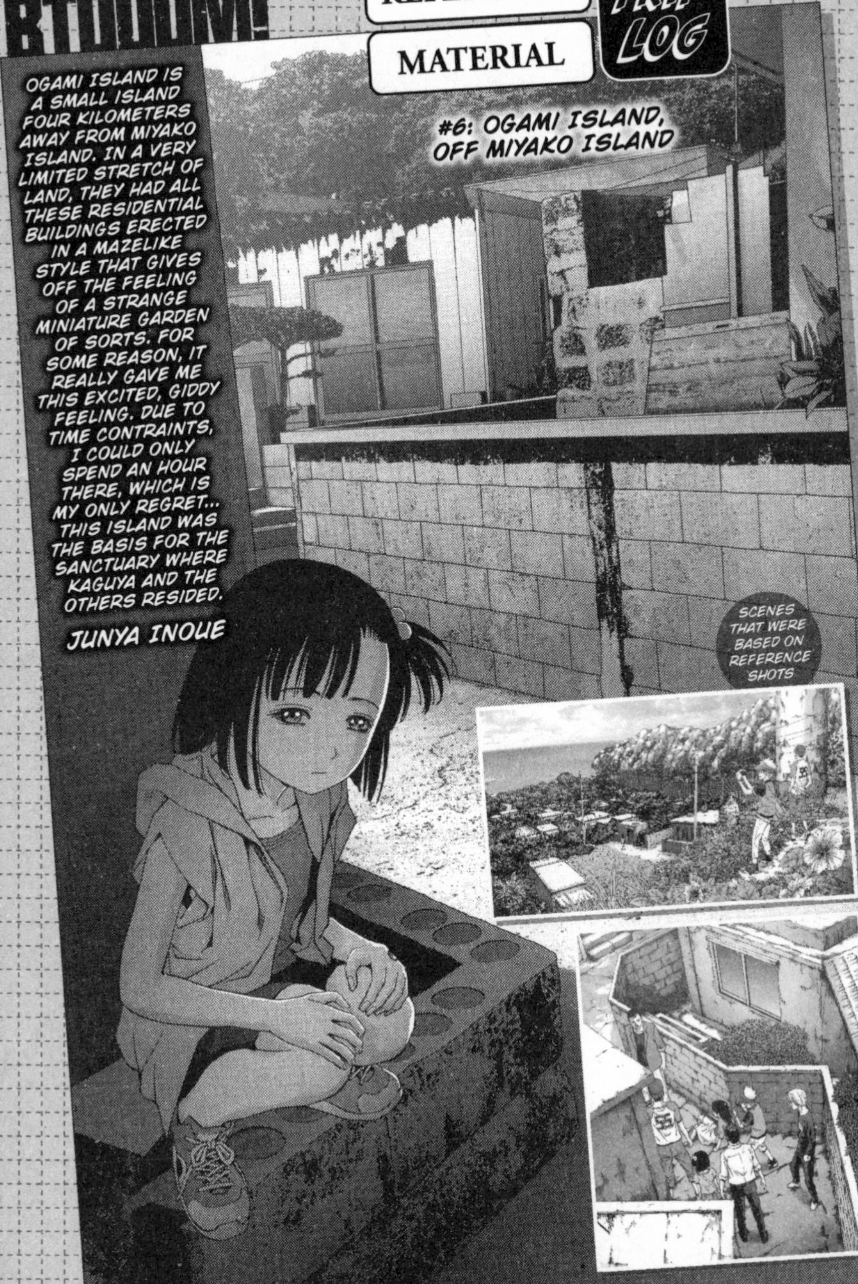
SCENES THAT WERE BASED ON REFERENCE SHOTS

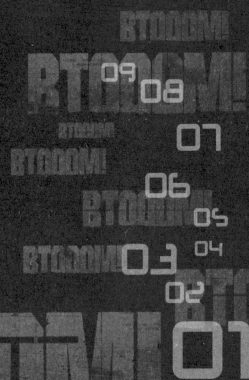

BTOOOM!

BTOOOM!

BTOOOM!

09 08

BTOOOM!

07

BTOOOM!

BTOOOM!

06

BTOOOM!

05

04

BTOOOM! 03

02 BTOOO

DOOM! 01

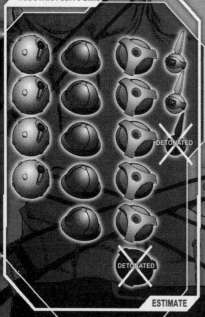

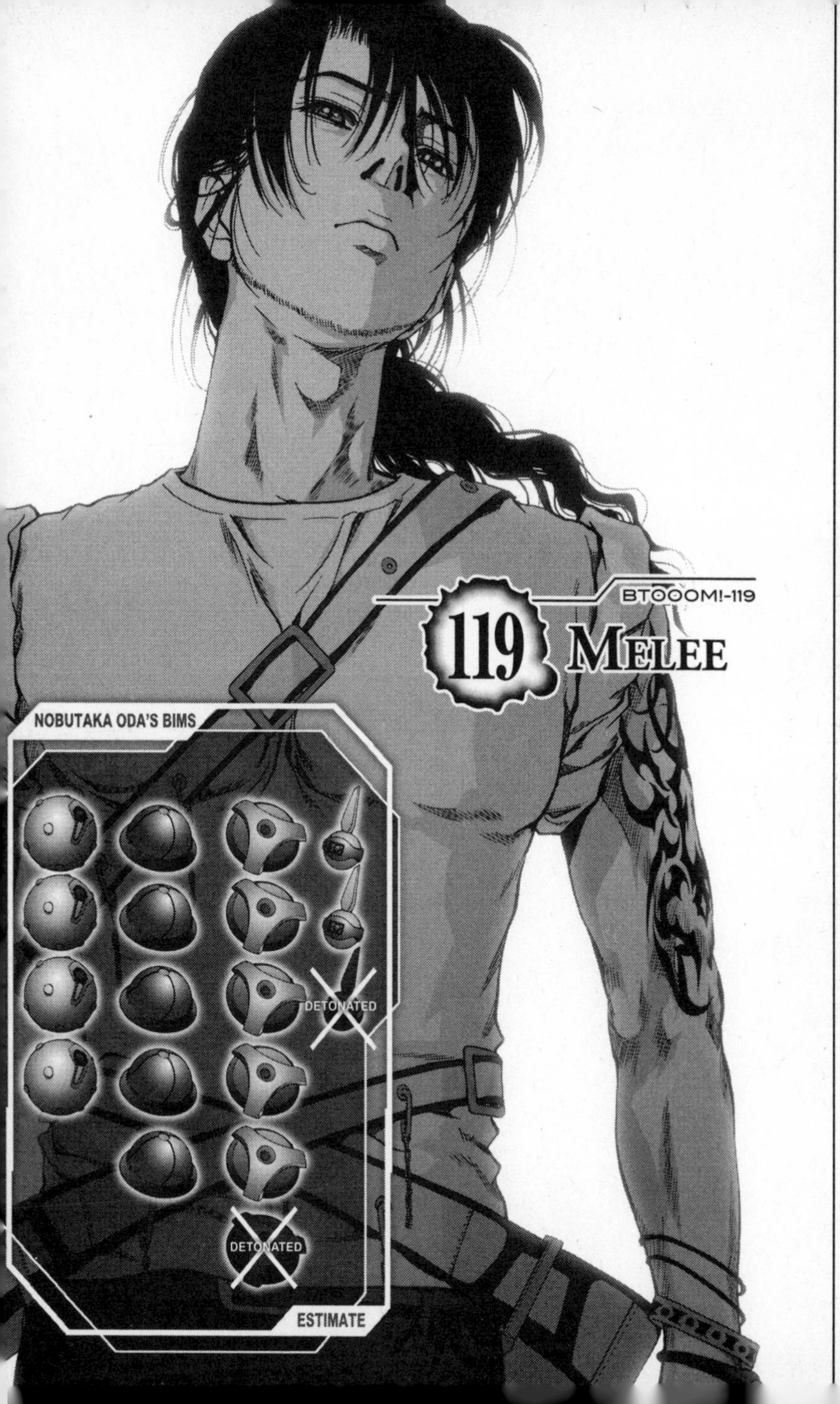

119 MELEE

NOBUTAKA ODA'S BIMS

DETONATED

DETONATED

ESTIMATE

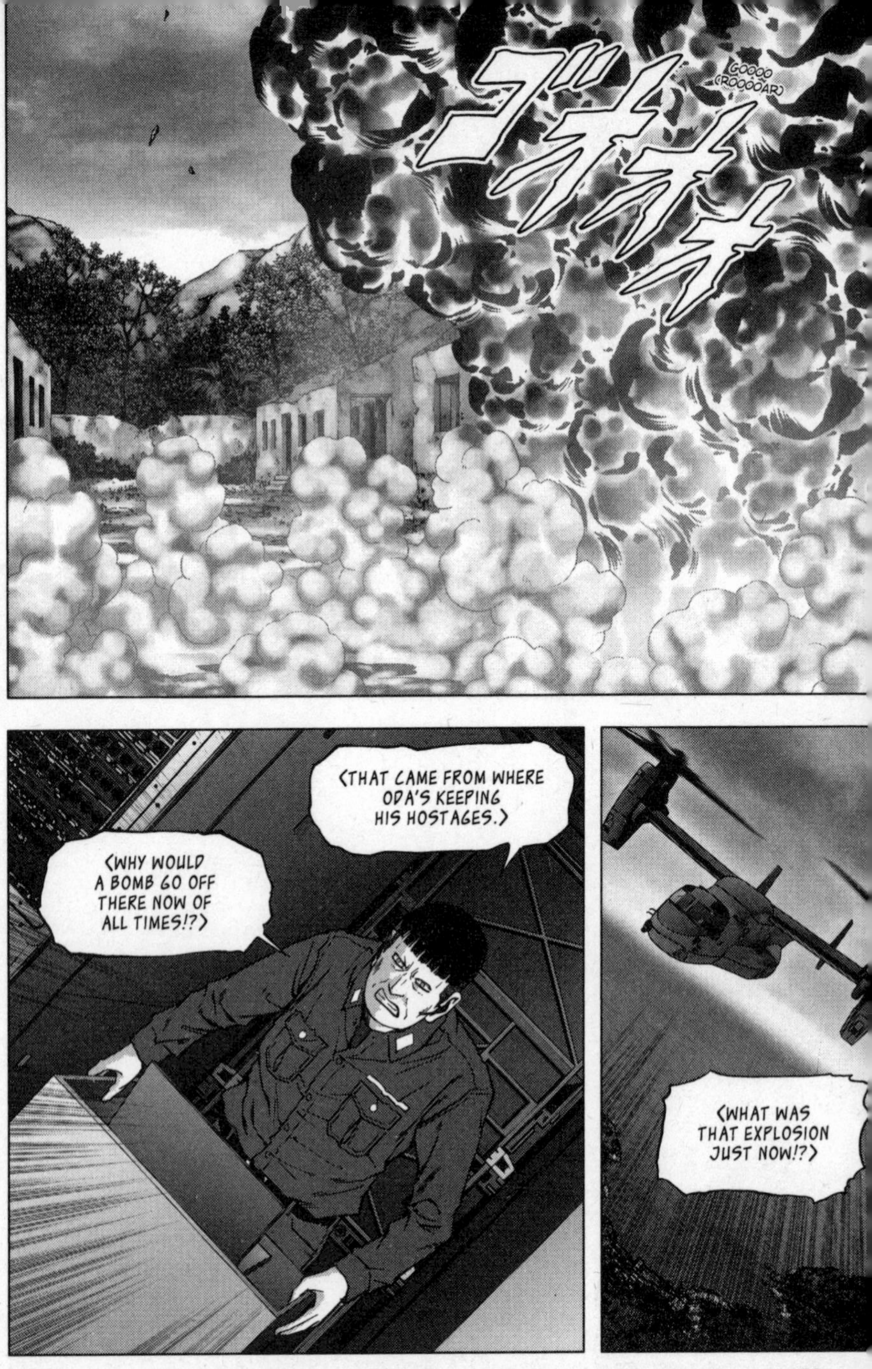
ゴオオオ
GOOOO
(ROOOOAR)
<WHAT WAS THAT EXPLOSION JUST NOW!?>
<THAT CAME FROM WHERE ODA'S KEEPING HIS HOSTAGES.>
<WHY WOULD A BOMB GO OFF THERE NOW OF ALL TIMES!?>

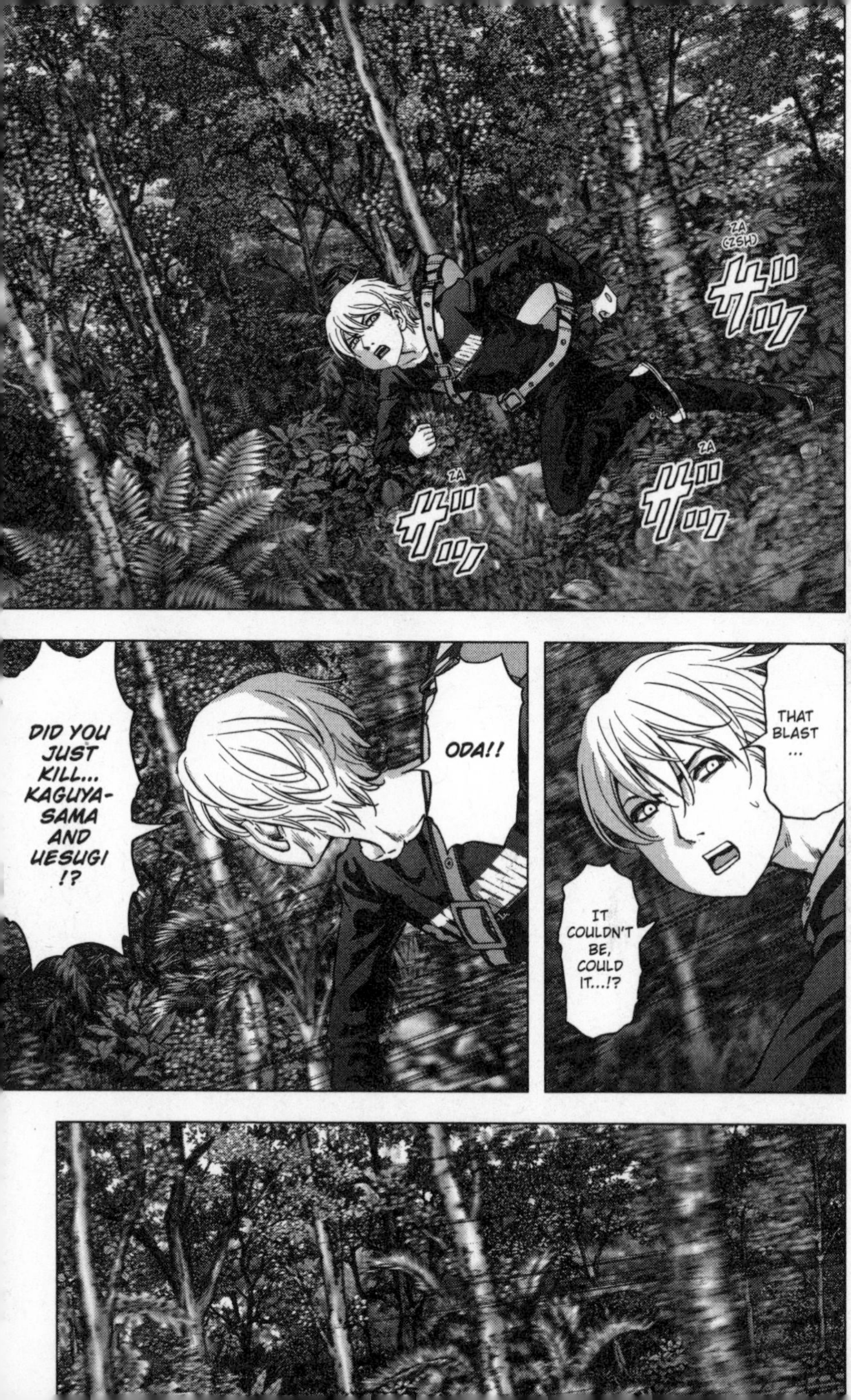
ZA (ZSH)
ZA
ZA
THAT BLAST ...
IT COULDN'T BE, COULD IT...!?
ODA!!
DID YOU JUST KILL... KAGUYA-SAMA AND UESUGI !?

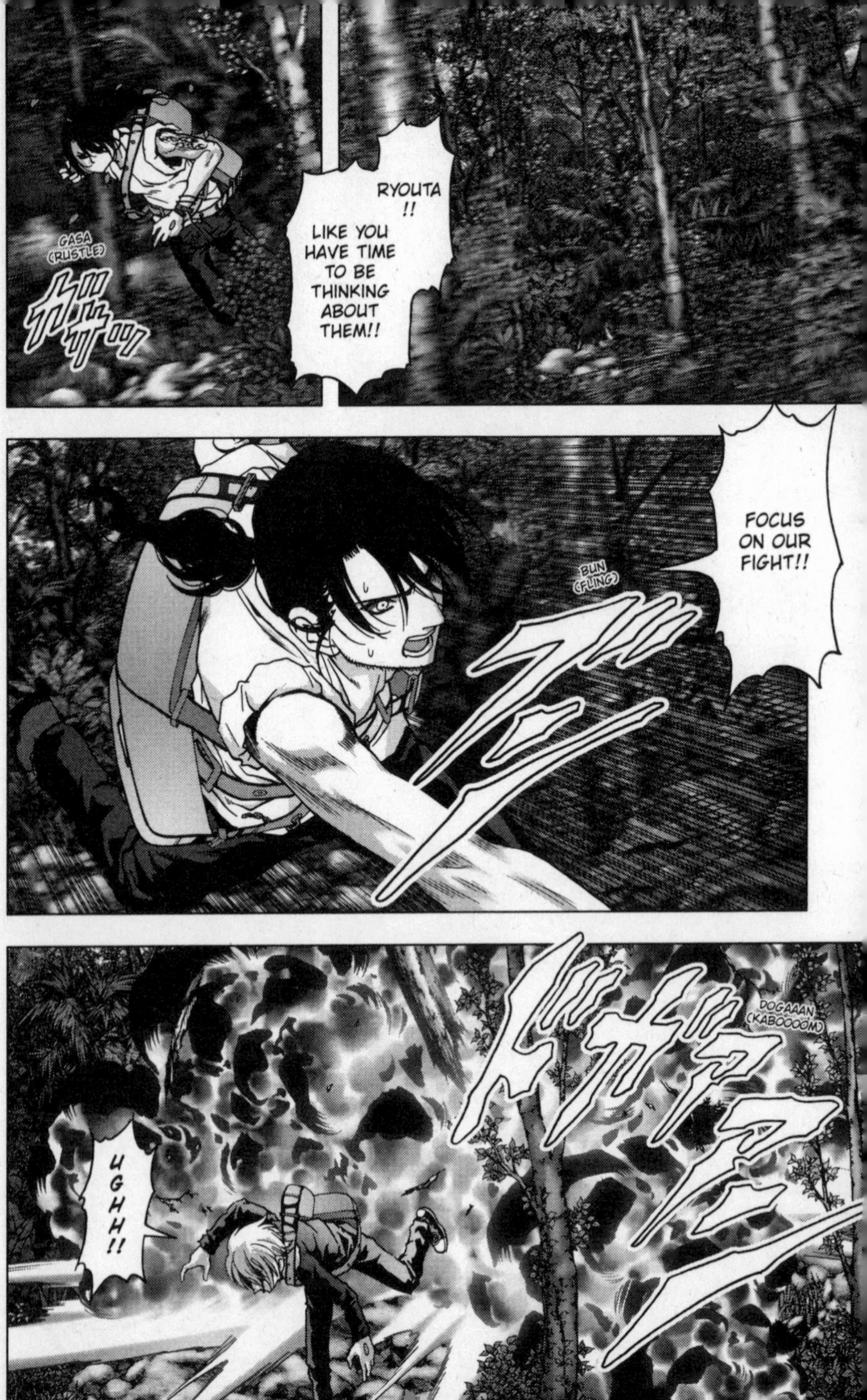
RYOUTA !!
LIKE YOU HAVE TIME TO BE THINKING ABOUT THEM!!
GASA (RUSTLE)
FOCUS ON OUR FIGHT!!
BUN (FLING)
DOGAAAN (KABOOOOM)
UGHH!!

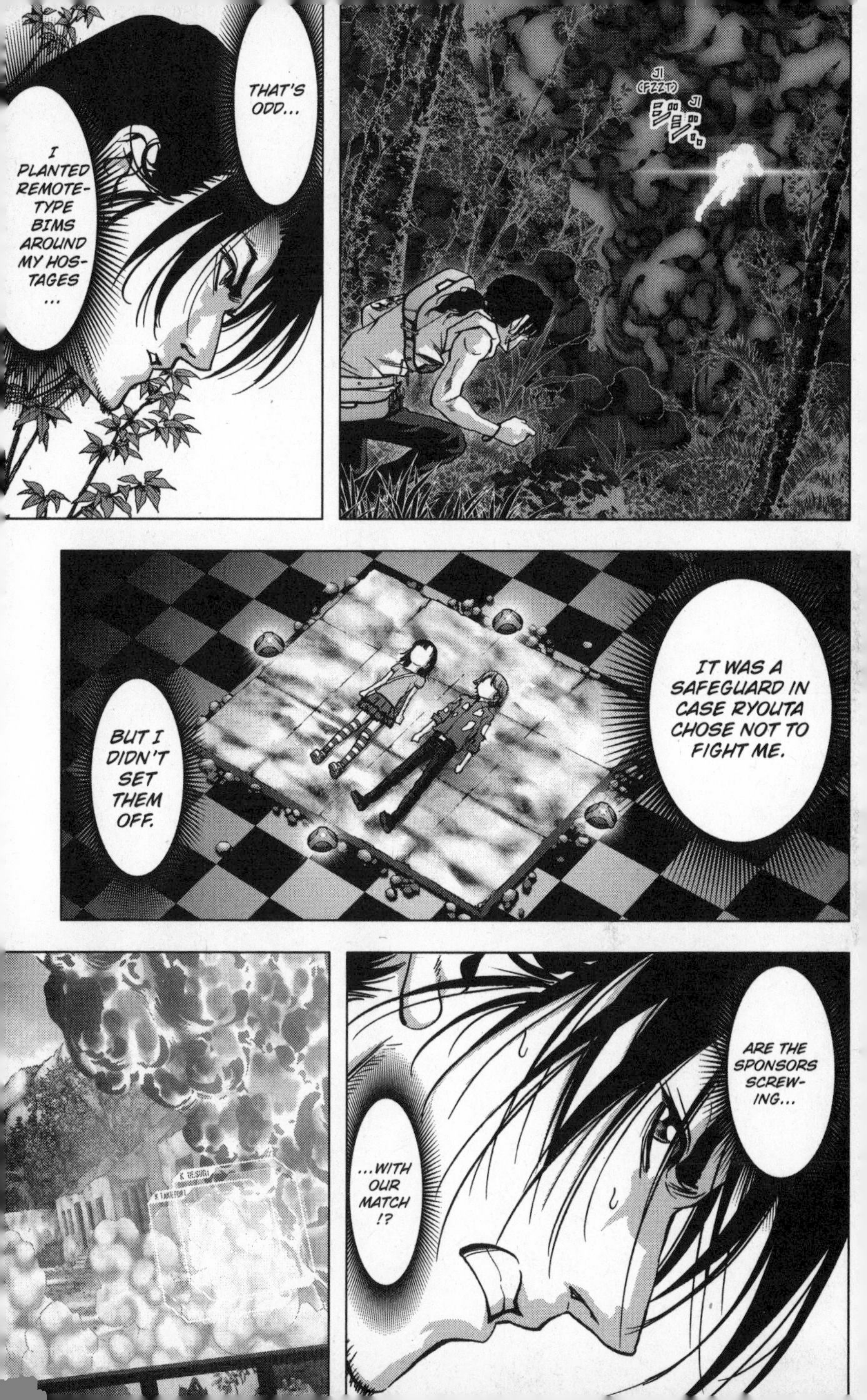
JI
(FZZT)
JI
THAT'S ODD...
I PLANTED REMOTE-TYPE BIMS AROUND MY HOSTAGES...
IT WAS A SAFEGUARD IN CASE RYOUTA CHOSE NOT TO FIGHT ME.
BUT I DIDN'T SET THEM OFF.
ARE THE SPONSORS SCREWING...
...WITH OUR MATCH!?

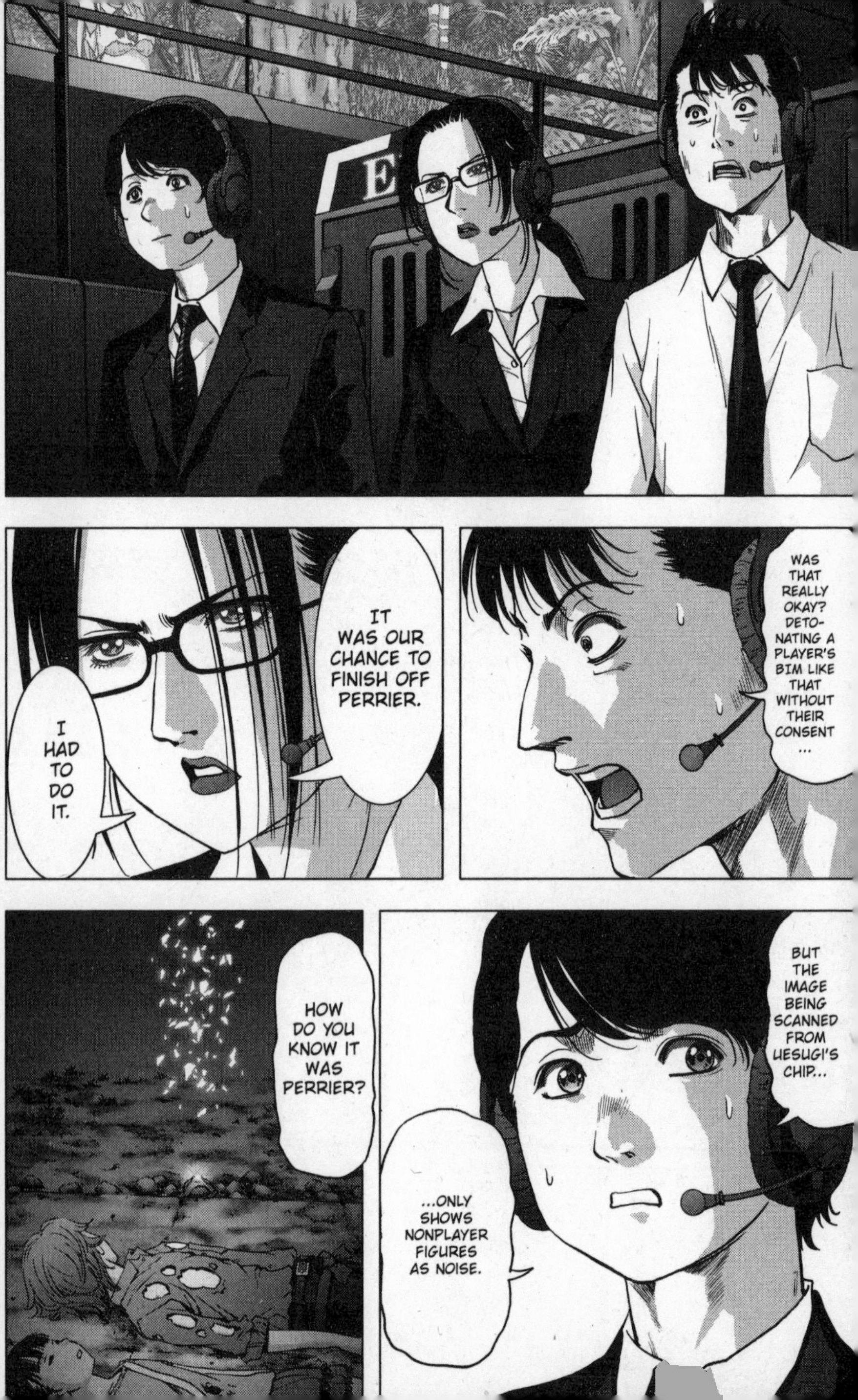
WAS THAT REALLY OKAY? DETONATING A PLAYER'S BIM LIKE THAT WITHOUT THEIR CONSENT ...
IT WAS OUR CHANCE TO FINISH OFF PERRIER.
I HAD TO DO IT.
BUT THE IMAGE BEING SCANNED FROM UESUGI'S CHIP...
...ONLY SHOWS NONPLAYER FIGURES AS NOISE.
HOW DO YOU KNOW IT WAS PERRIER?

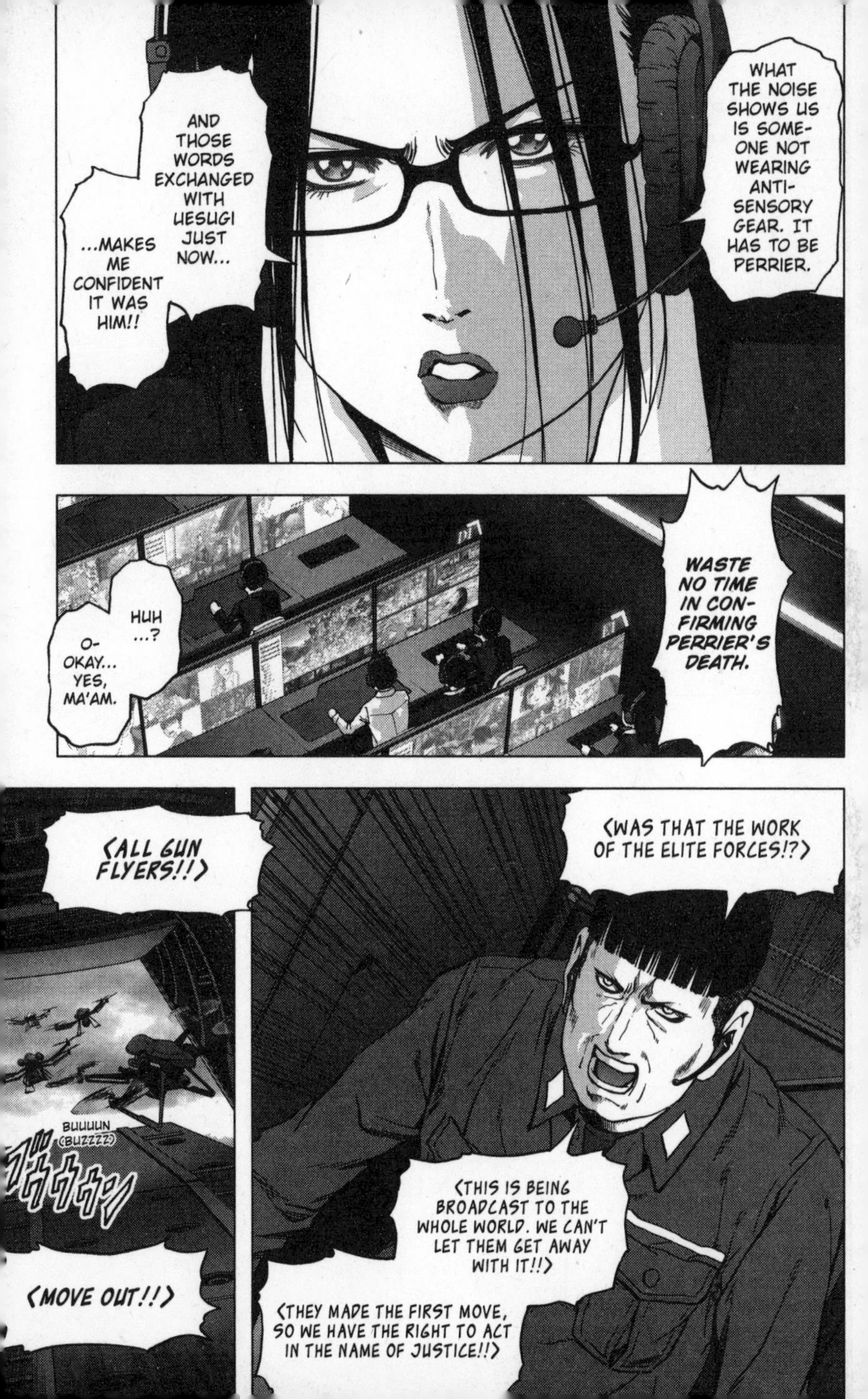
WHAT THE NOISE SHOWS US IS SOMEONE NOT WEARING ANTI-SENSORY GEAR. IT HAS TO BE PERRIER.
AND THOSE WORDS EXCHANGED WITH UESUGI JUST NOW...
...MAKES ME CONFIDENT IT WAS HIM!!
WASTE NO TIME IN CONFIRMING PERRIER'S DEATH.
HUH ...?
O-OKAY... YES, MA'AM.
<WAS THAT THE WORK OF THE ELITE FORCES!?>
<THIS IS BEING BROADCAST TO THE WHOLE WORLD. WE CAN'T LET THEM GET AWAY WITH IT!!>
<THEY MADE THE FIRST MOVE, SO WE HAVE THE RIGHT TO ACT IN THE NAME OF JUSTICE!!>
<ALL GUN FLYERS!!>
BUUUUN (BUZZZZ)
<MOVE OUT!!>

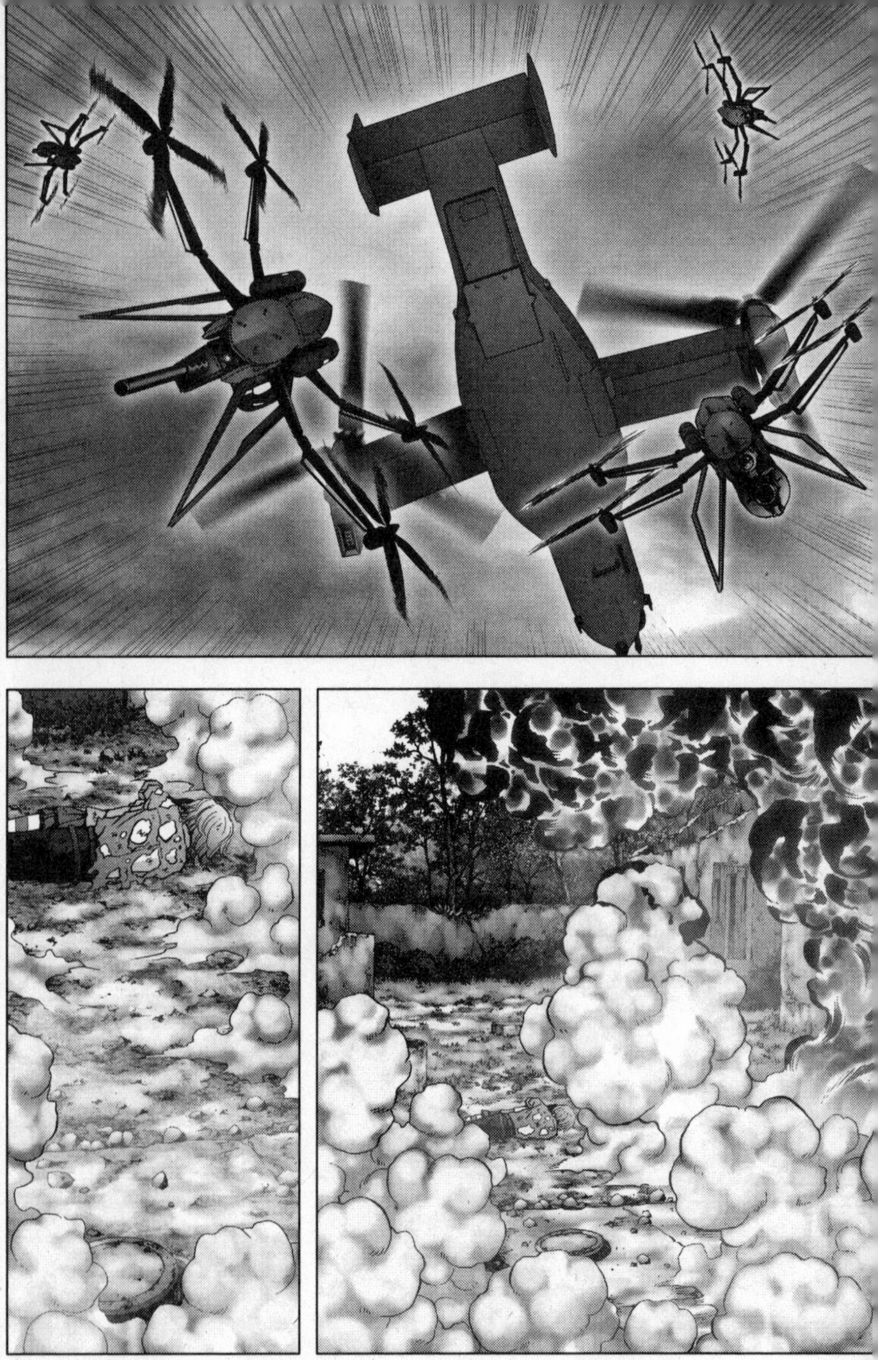

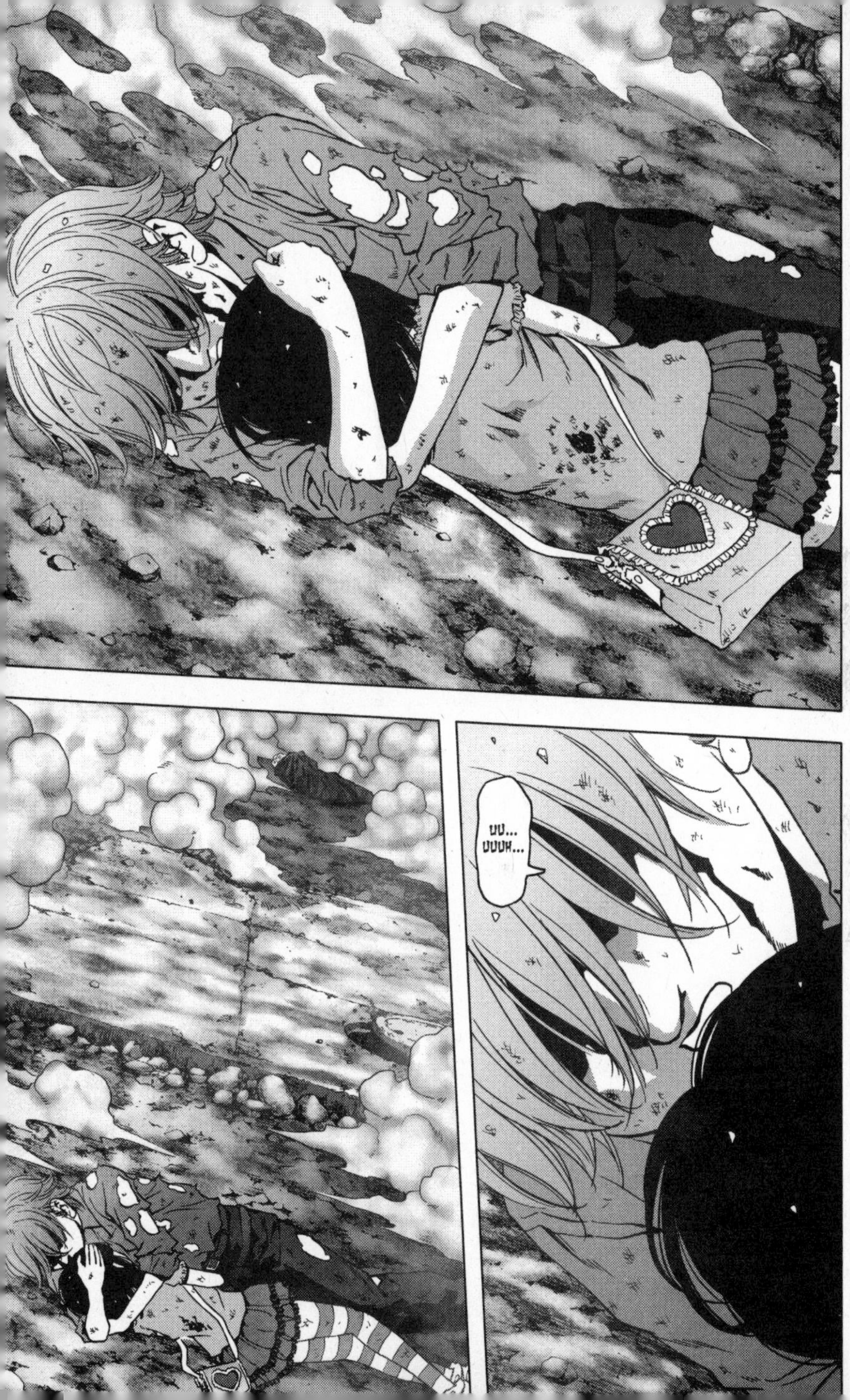
UU... UUUH...

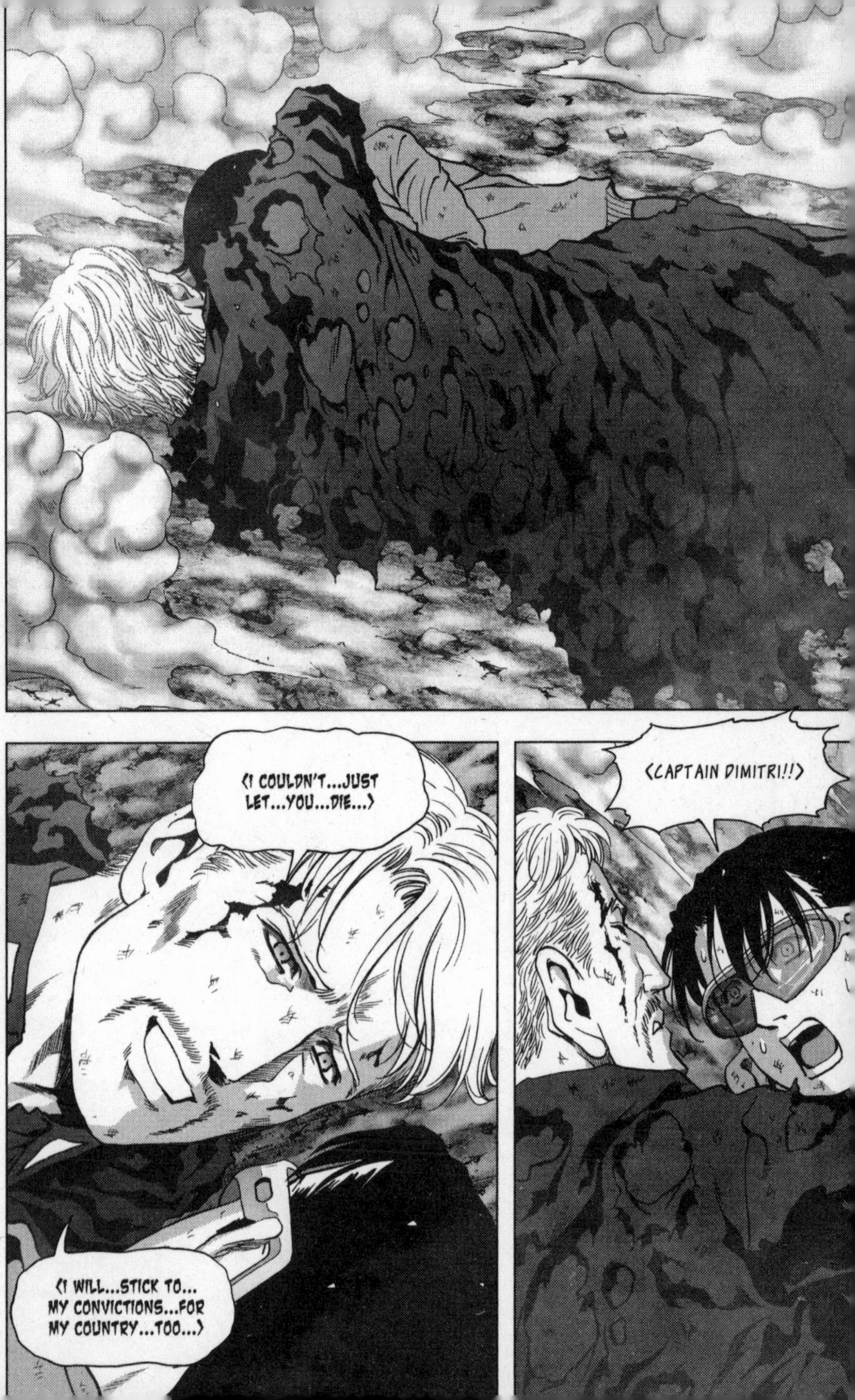
<CAPTAIN DIMITRI!!>
<I COULDN'T...JUST LET...YOU...DIE...>
<I WILL...STICK TO... MY CONVICTIONS...FOR MY COUNTRY...TOO...>

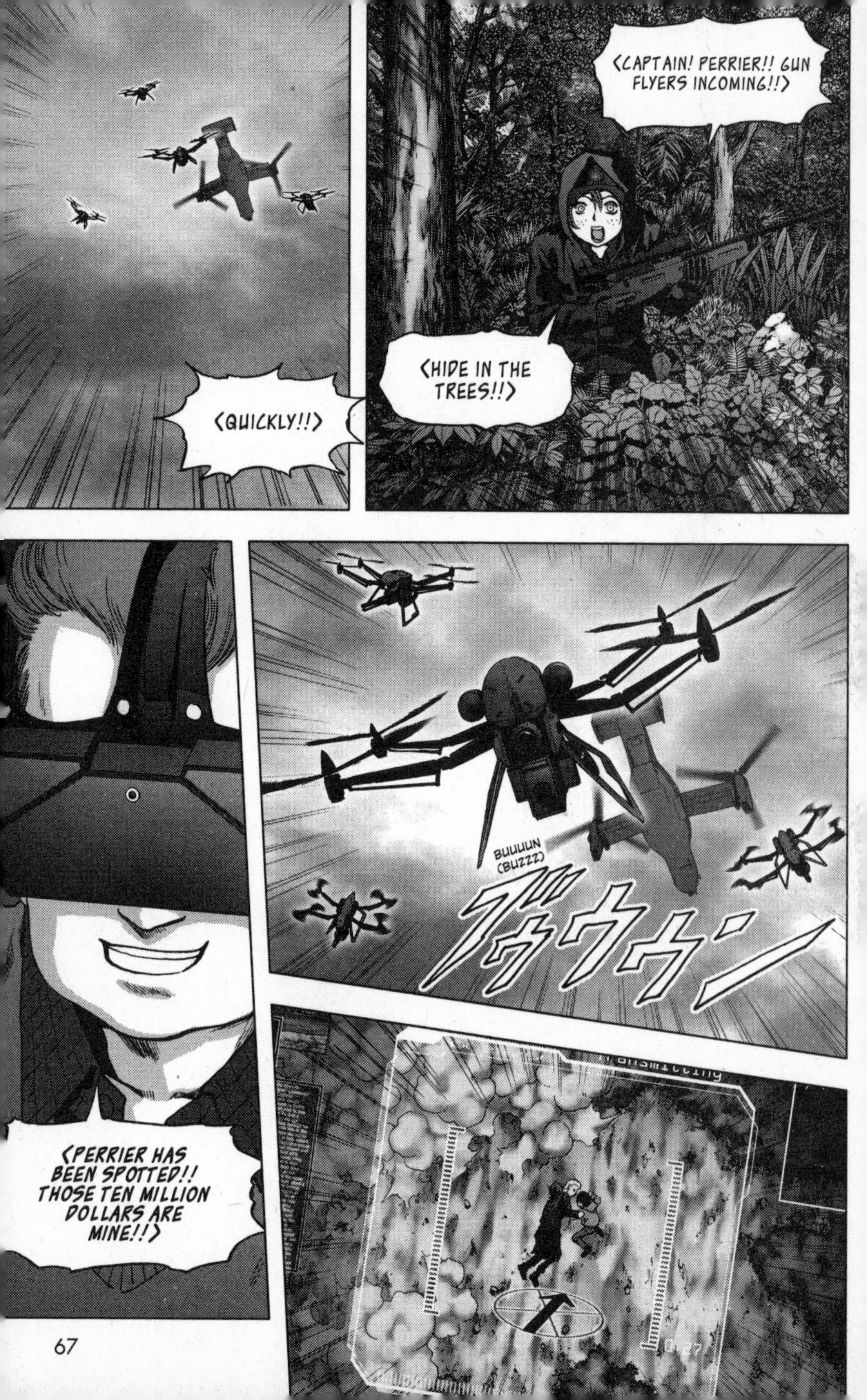
〈CAPTAIN! PERRIER!! GUN FLYERS INCOMING!!〉
〈HIDE IN THE TREES!!〉
〈QUICKLY!!〉
BUUUUN (BUZZZ)
ヴゥウゥン
〈PERRIER HAS BEEN SPOTTED!! THOSE TEN MILLION DOLLARS ARE MINE!!〉

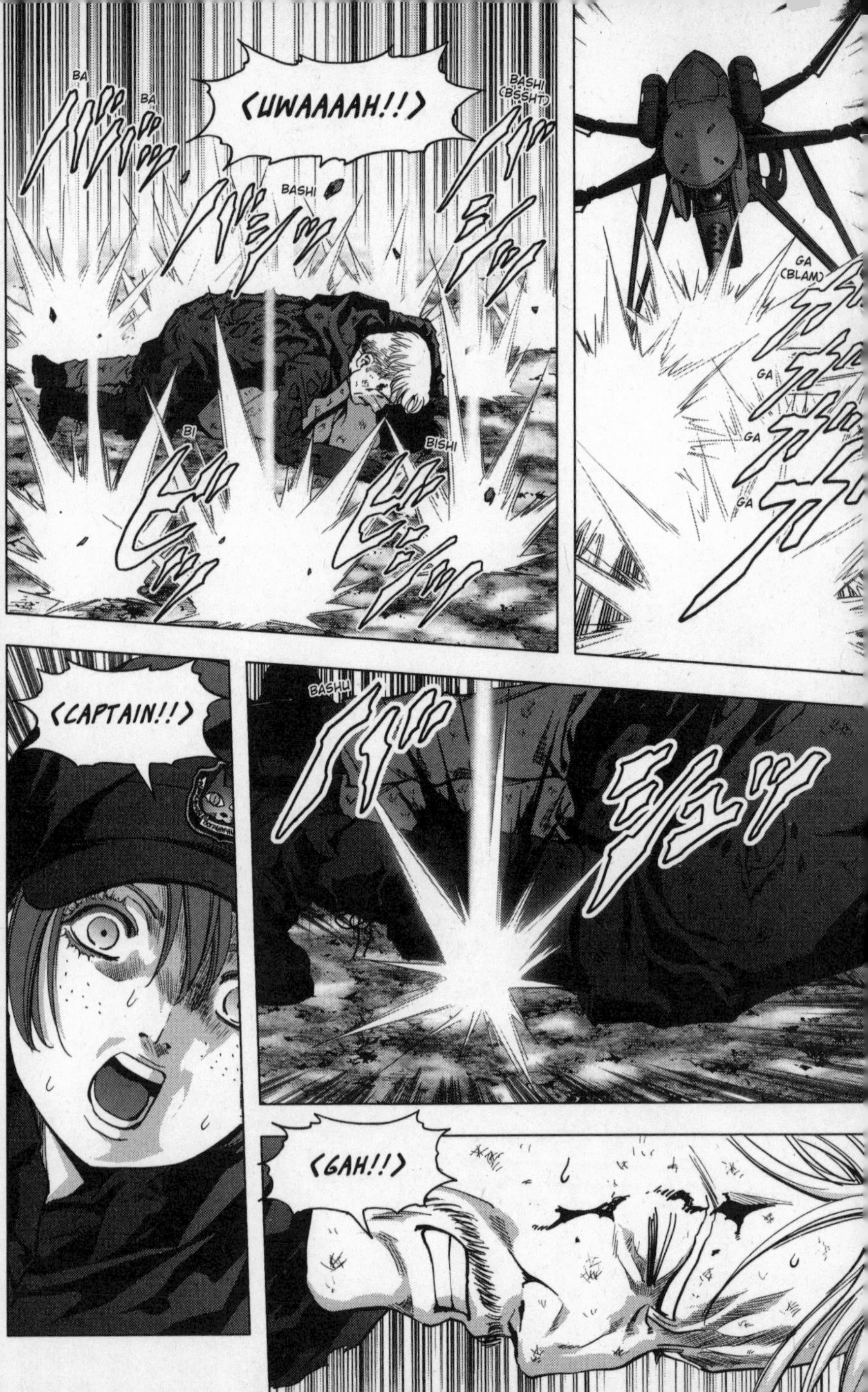
GA (BLAM)
GA
GA
GA
BASHI (BSSHT)
<UWAAAAH!!>
BA
BA
BASHI
BISHI
BI
BASHU
<GAH!!>
<CAPTAIN!!>

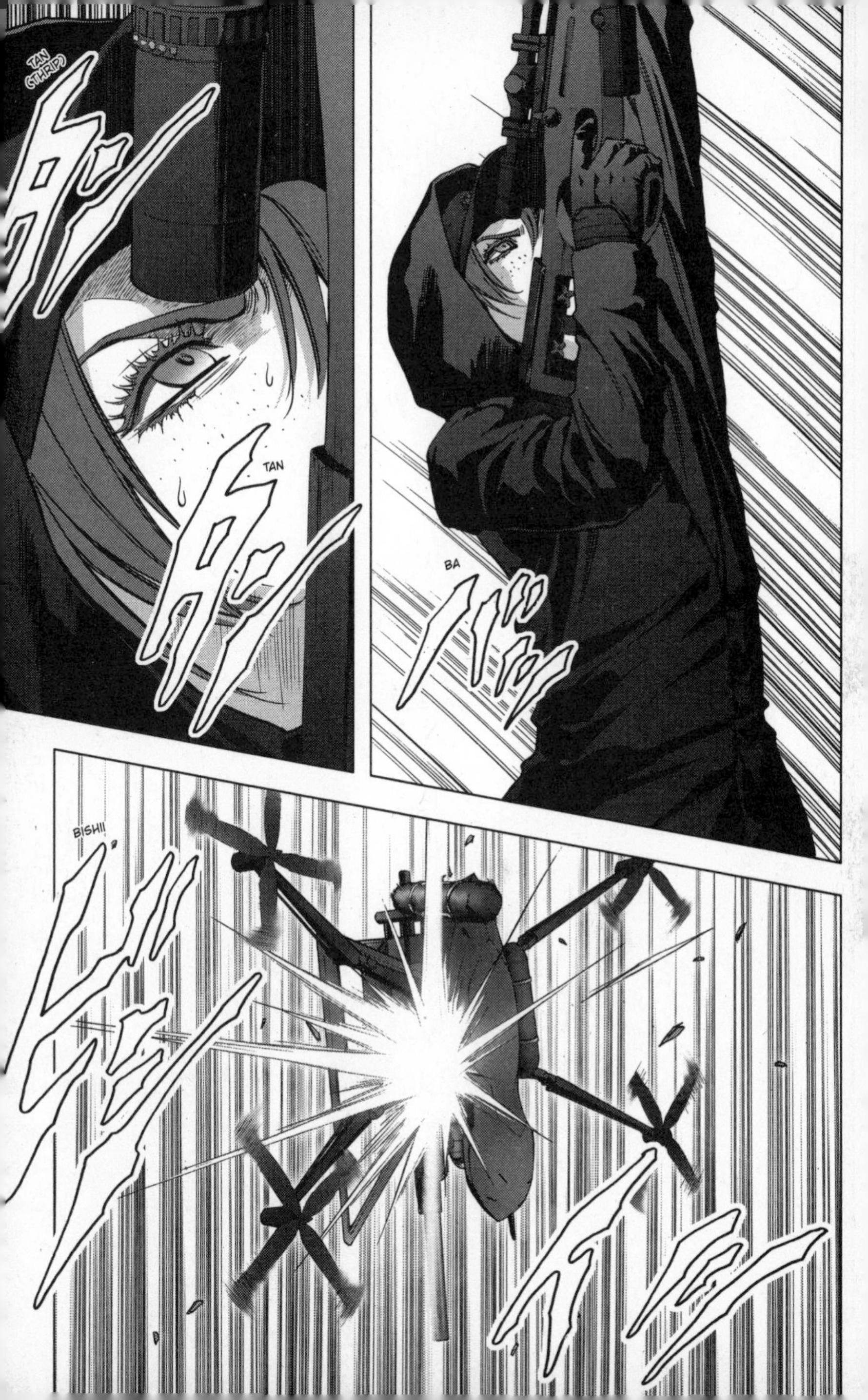
BA
TAN (THRIP)
TAN
BISHI!

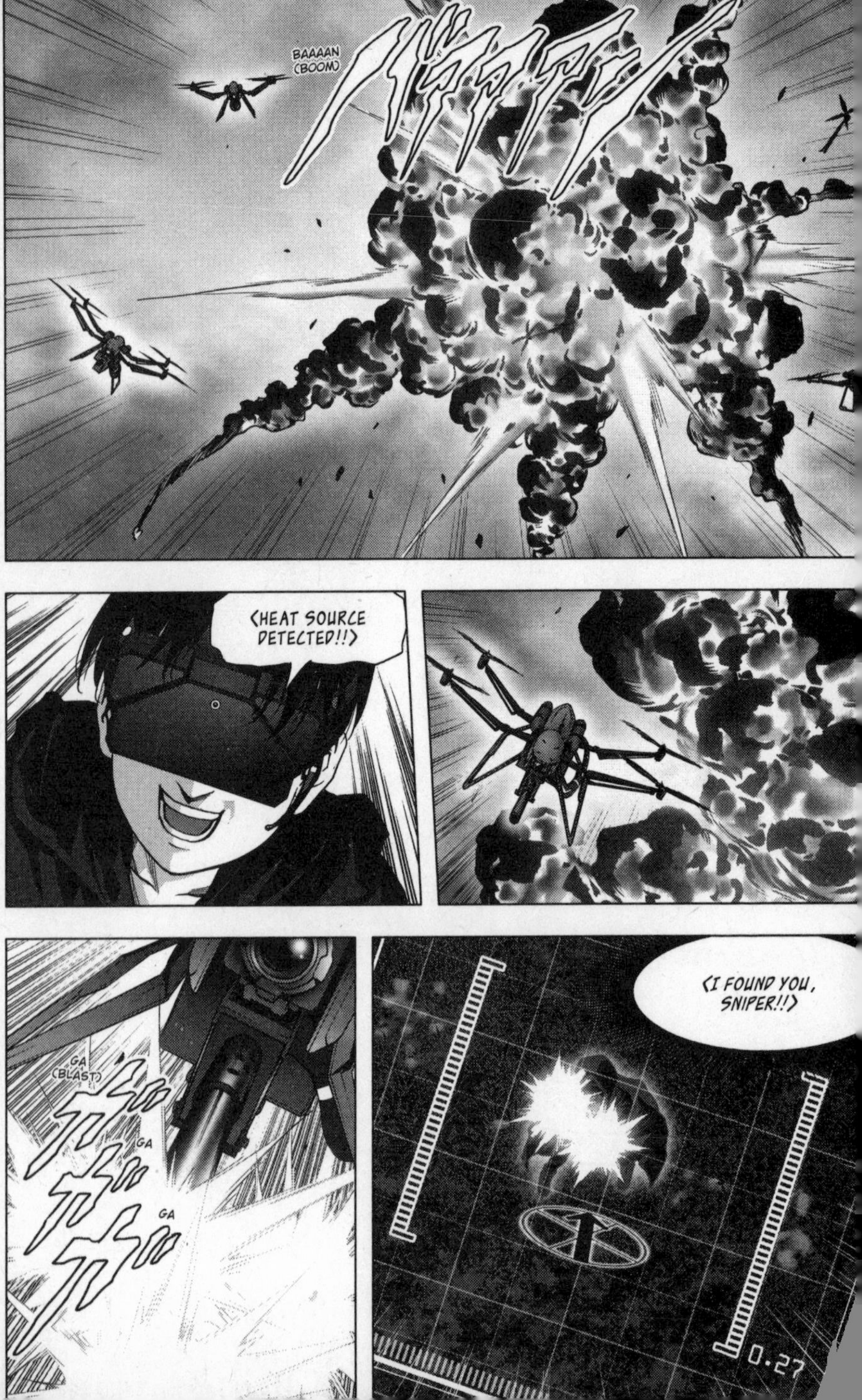
BAAAAN (BOOM)
バァァァン
〈HEAT SOURCE DETECTED!!〉
〈I FOUND YOU, SNIPER!!〉
0.27
GA (BLAST)
GA
GA

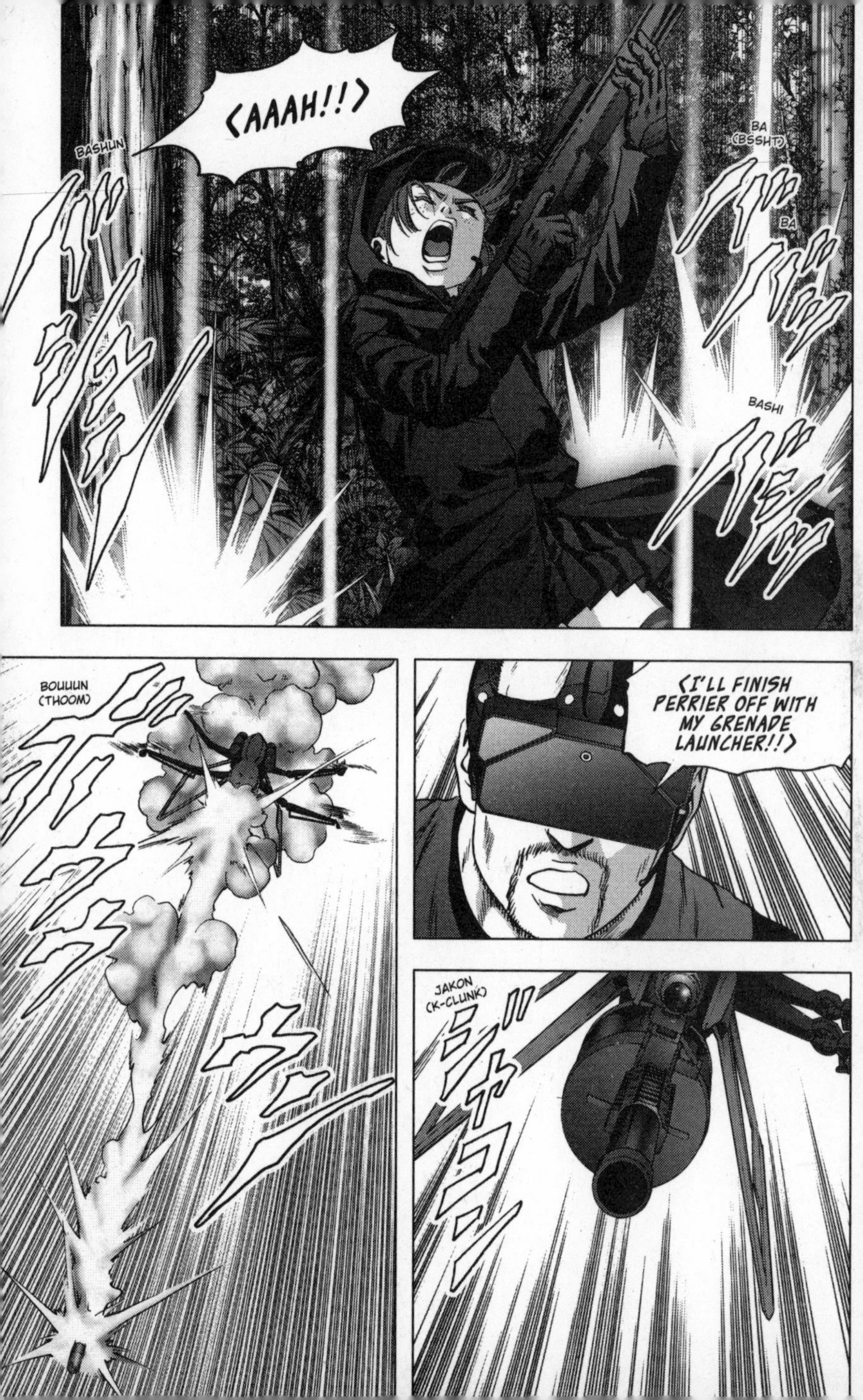
BA (BSSHT)
〈AAAH!!!〉
BASHUN
BA
BASHI
〈I'LL FINISH PERRIER OFF WITH MY GRENADE LAUNCHER!!〉
JAKON (K-CLUNK)
BOUUUN (THOOM)

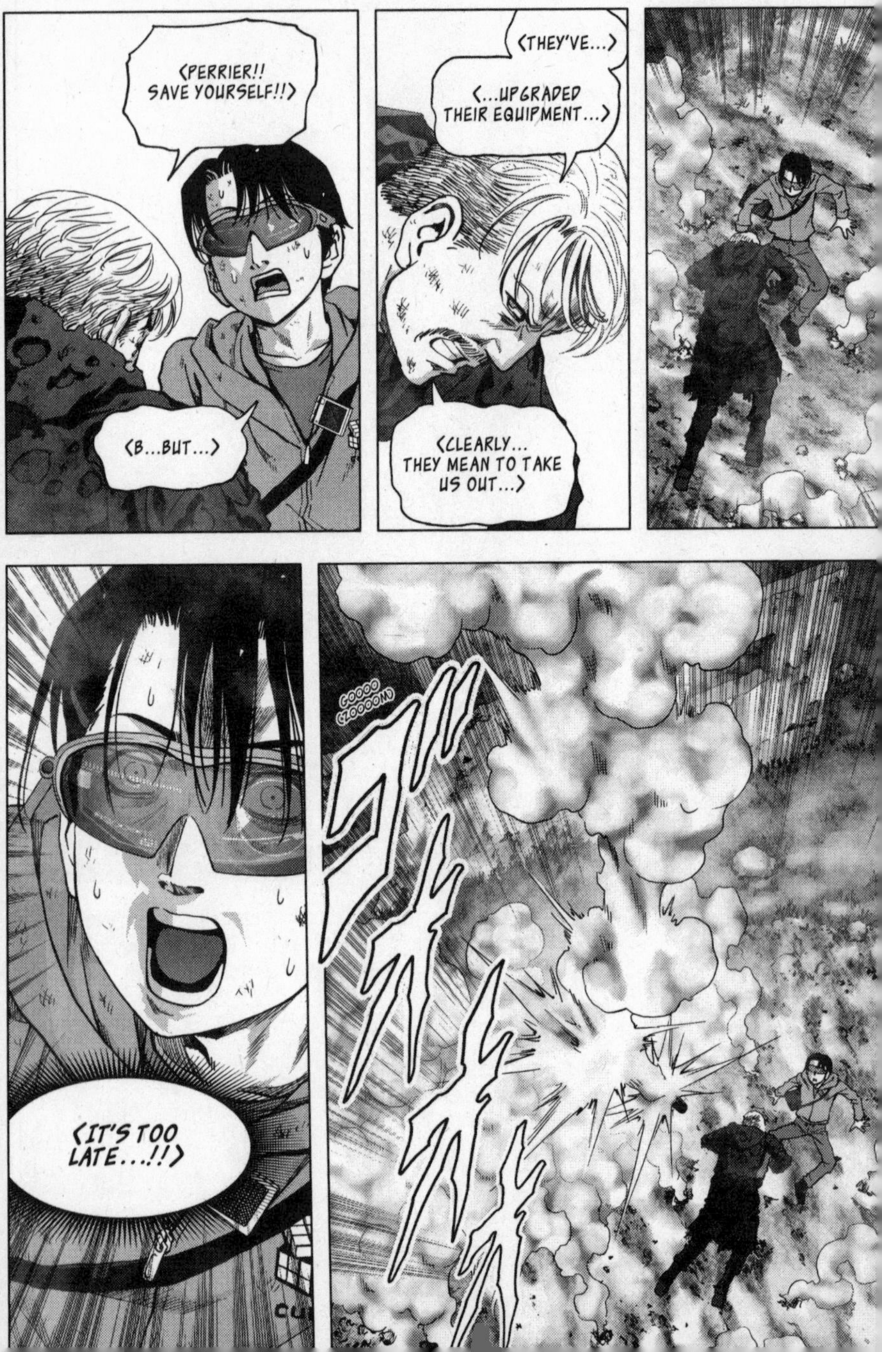
〈THEY'VE...〉
〈...UPGRADED THEIR EQUIPMENT...〉
〈CLEARLY... THEY MEAN TO TAKE US OUT...〉
〈PERRIER!! SAVE YOURSELF!!〉
〈B...BUT...〉
GOOOO (ZOOOOM)
〈IT'S TOO LATE...!!〉

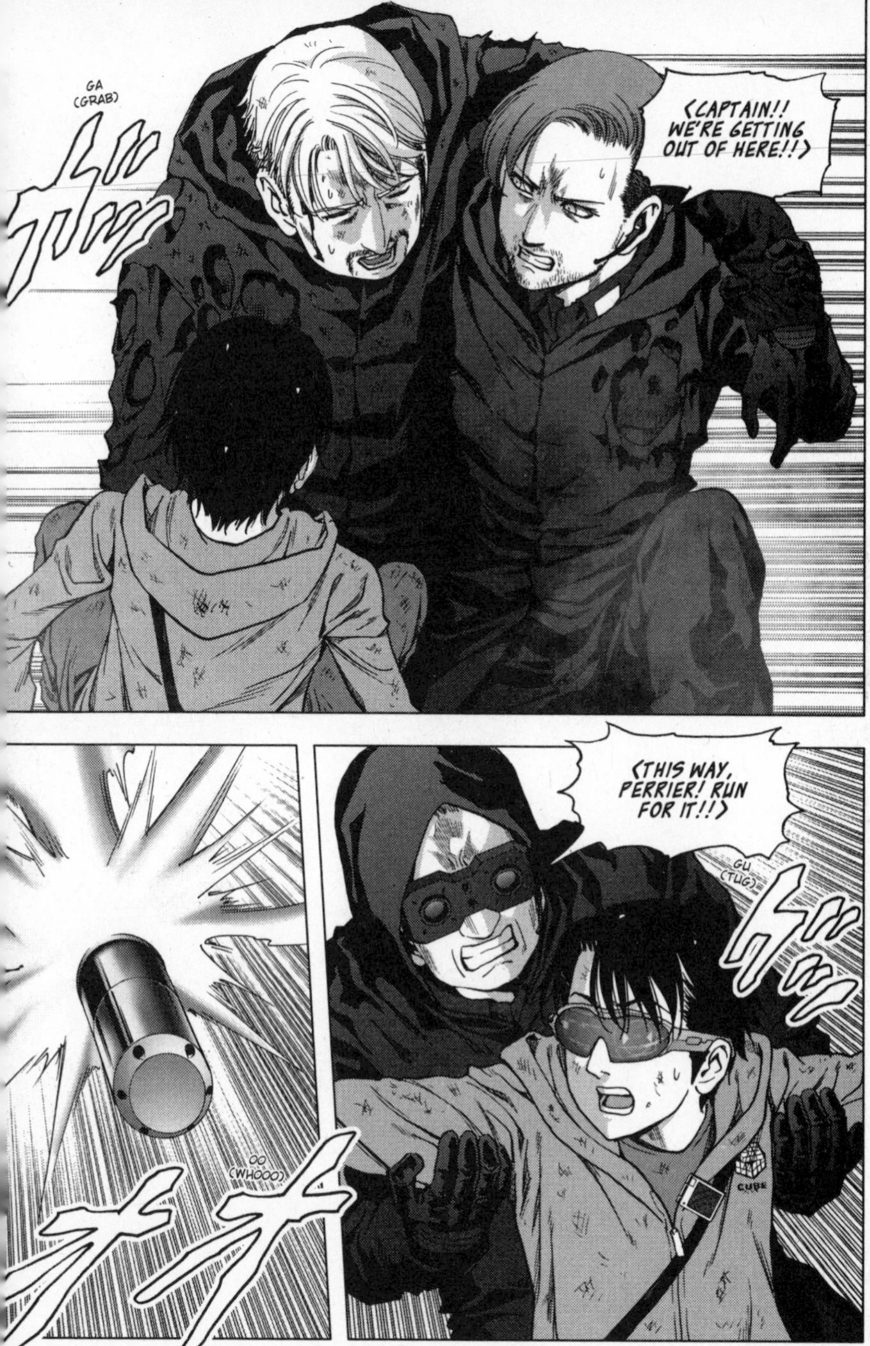
<CAPTAIN!! WE'RE GETTING OUT OF HERE!!>
GA (GRAB)
<THIS WAY, PERRIER! RUN FOR IT!!>
GU (TUG)
OO (WHOOO)

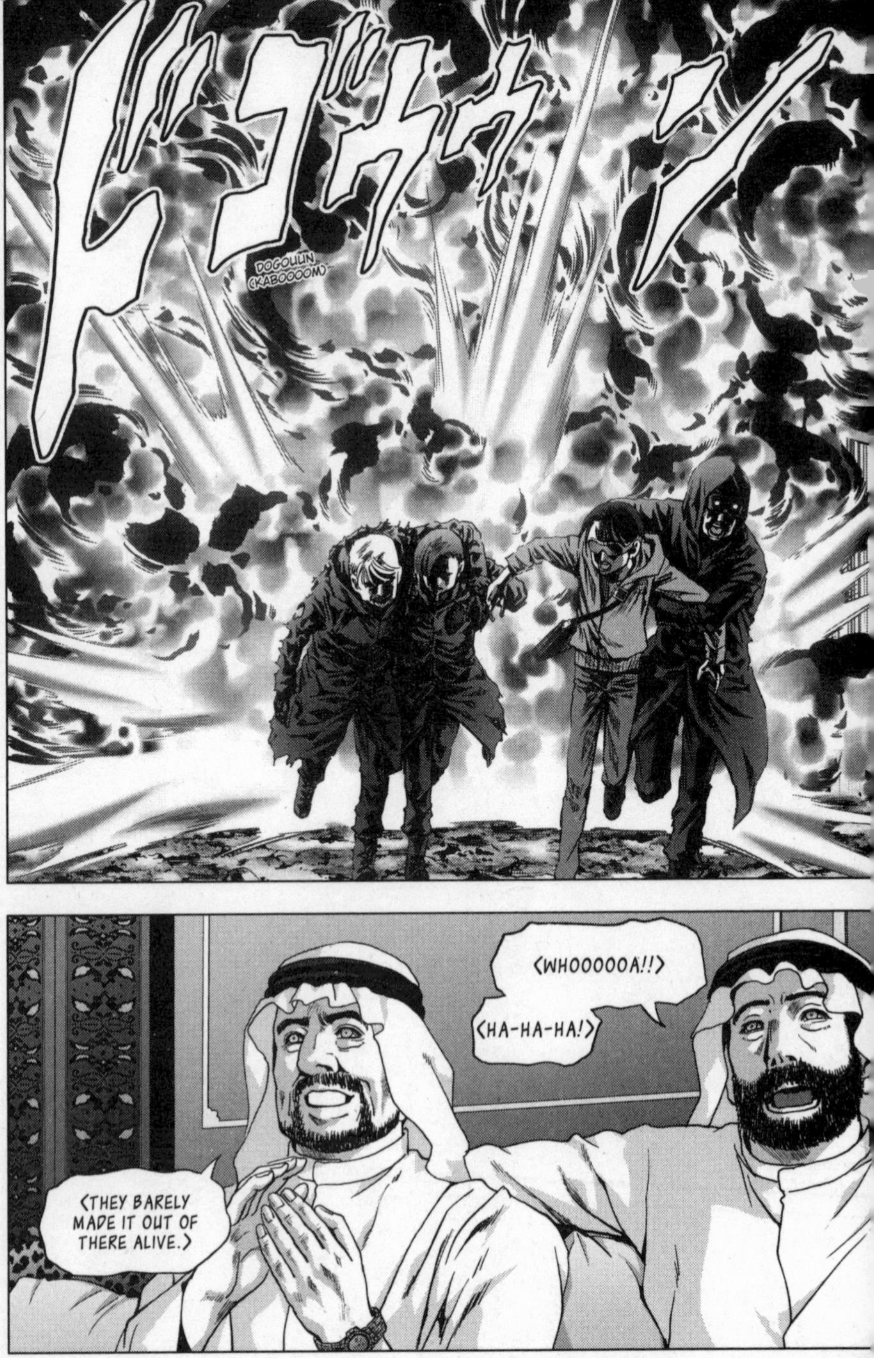
DOGOUUN
(KABOOOOM)
<WHOOOOOA!!>
<HA-HA-HA!>
<THEY BARELY MADE IT OUT OF THERE ALIVE.>

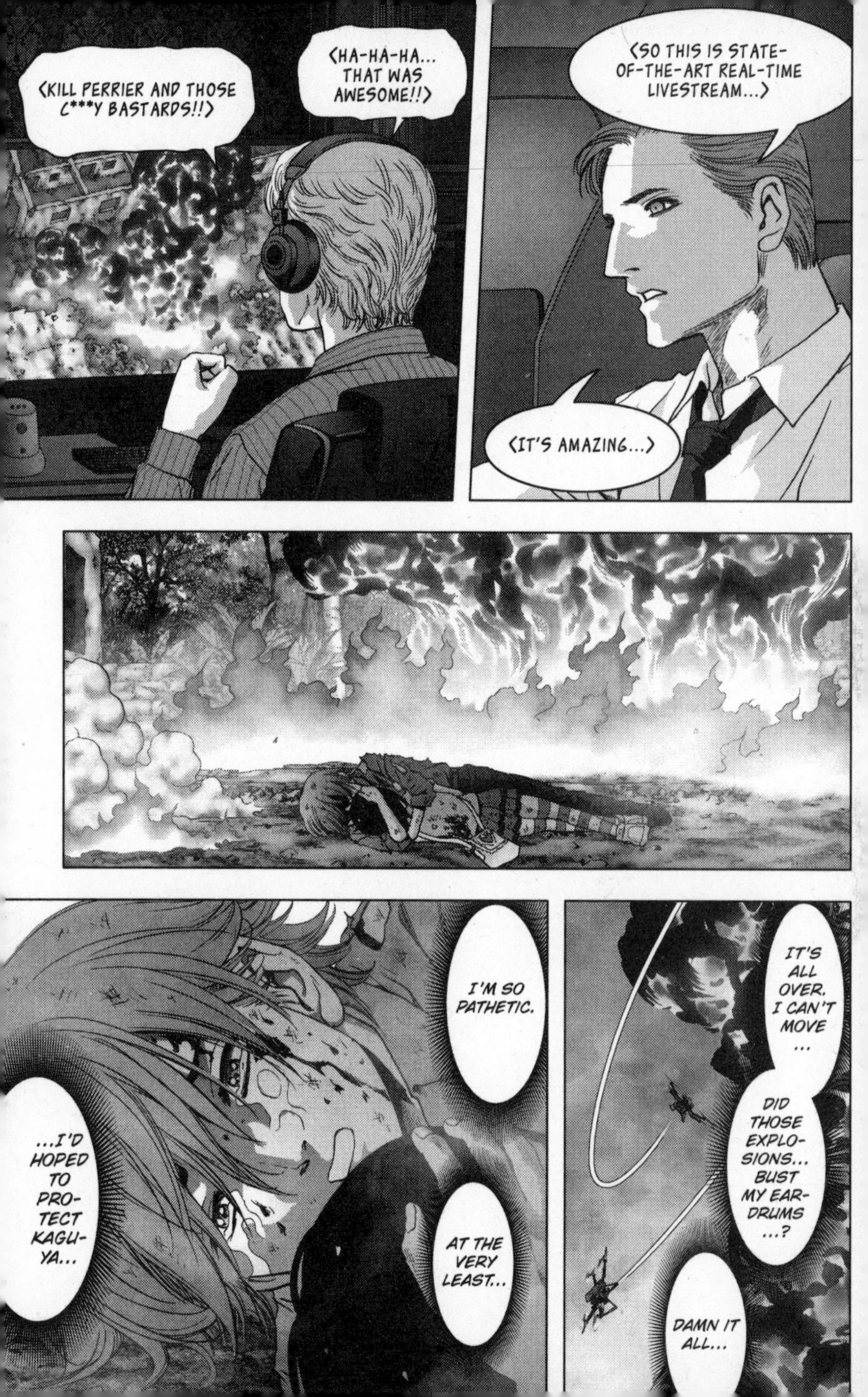
<SO THIS IS STATE-OF-THE-ART REAL-TIME LIVESTREAM...>
<IT'S AMAZING...>
<HA-HA-HA... THAT WAS AWESOME!!>
<KILL PERRIER AND THOSE C***Y BASTARDS!!>
IT'S ALL OVER. I CAN'T MOVE...
DID THOSE EXPLOSIONS... BUST MY EARDRUMS...?
DAMN IT ALL...
I'M SO PATHETIC.
AT THE VERY LEAST...
...I'D HOPED TO PROTECT KAGUYA...

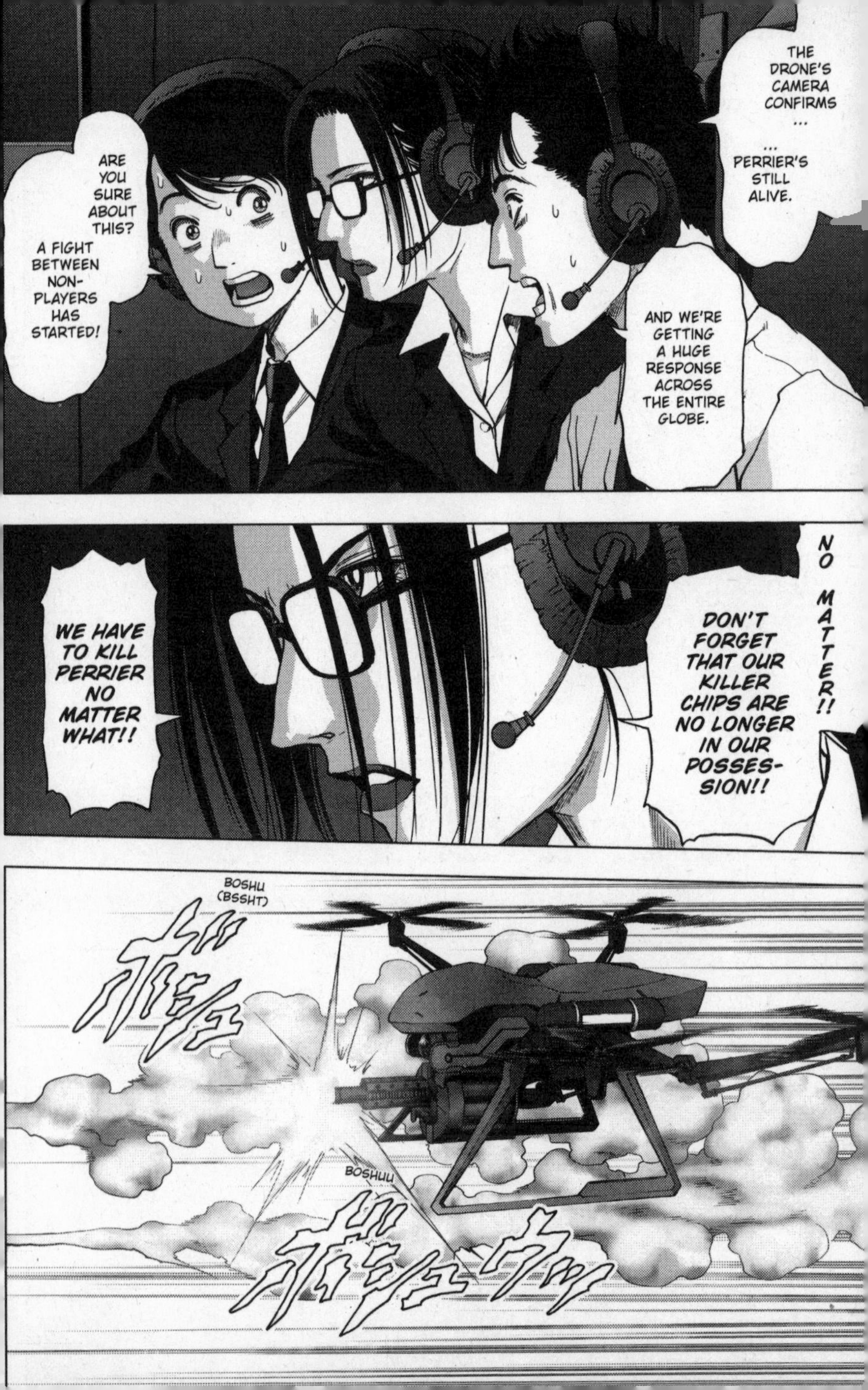
THE DRONE'S CAMERA CONFIRMS ...
... PERRIER'S STILL ALIVE.
AND WE'RE GETTING A HUGE RESPONSE ACROSS THE ENTIRE GLOBE.
ARE YOU SURE ABOUT THIS?
A FIGHT BETWEEN NON-PLAYERS HAS STARTED!
NO MATTER!!
DON'T FORGET THAT OUR KILLER CHIPS ARE NO LONGER IN OUR POSSES-SION!!
WE HAVE TO KILL PERRIER NO MATTER WHAT!!
BOSHU (BSSHT)
BOSHUU

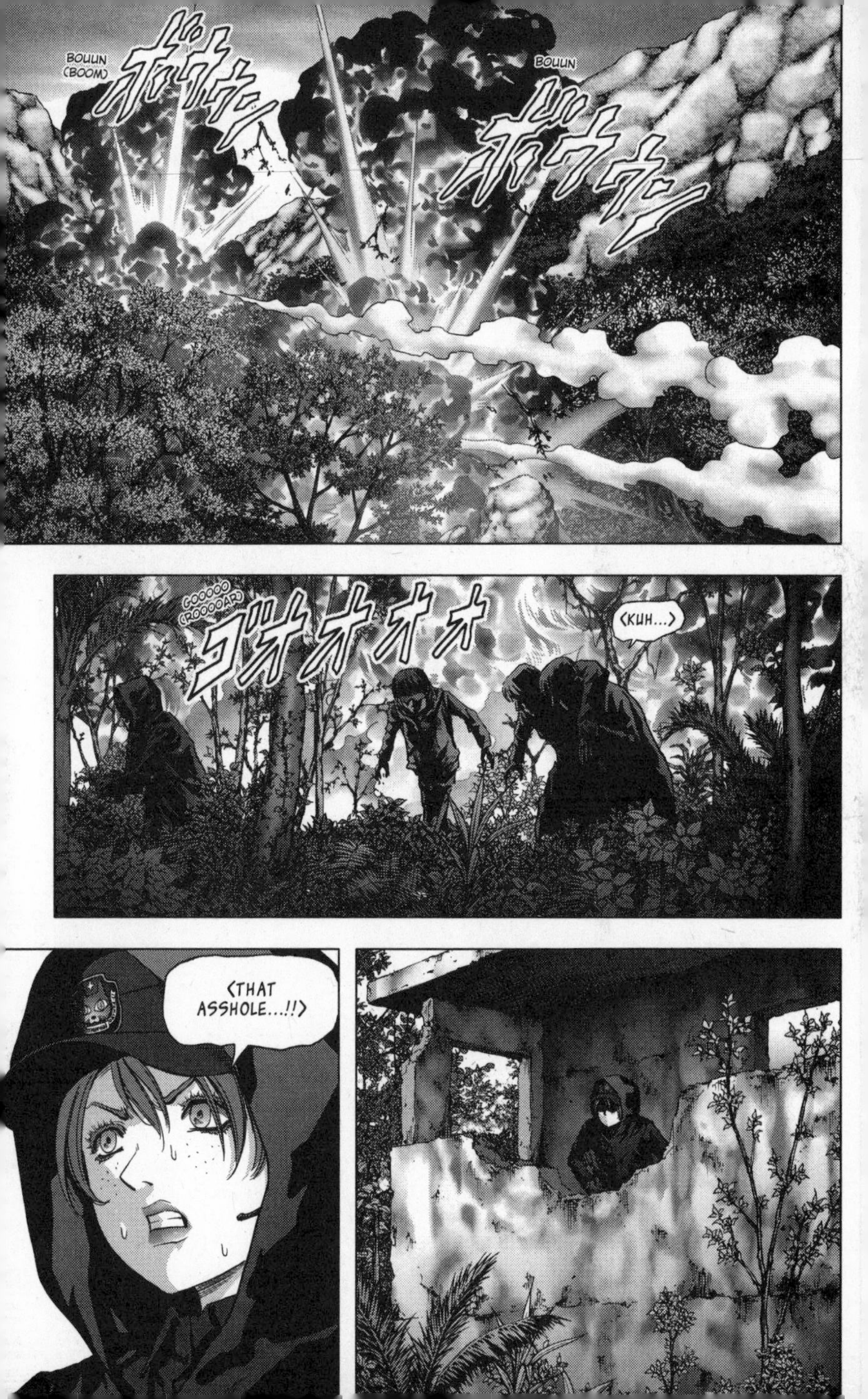
BOUUN
BOUUN (BOOM)
〈KUH...〉
GOOOOO (ROOOOAR)
〈THAT ASSHOLE...!!〉

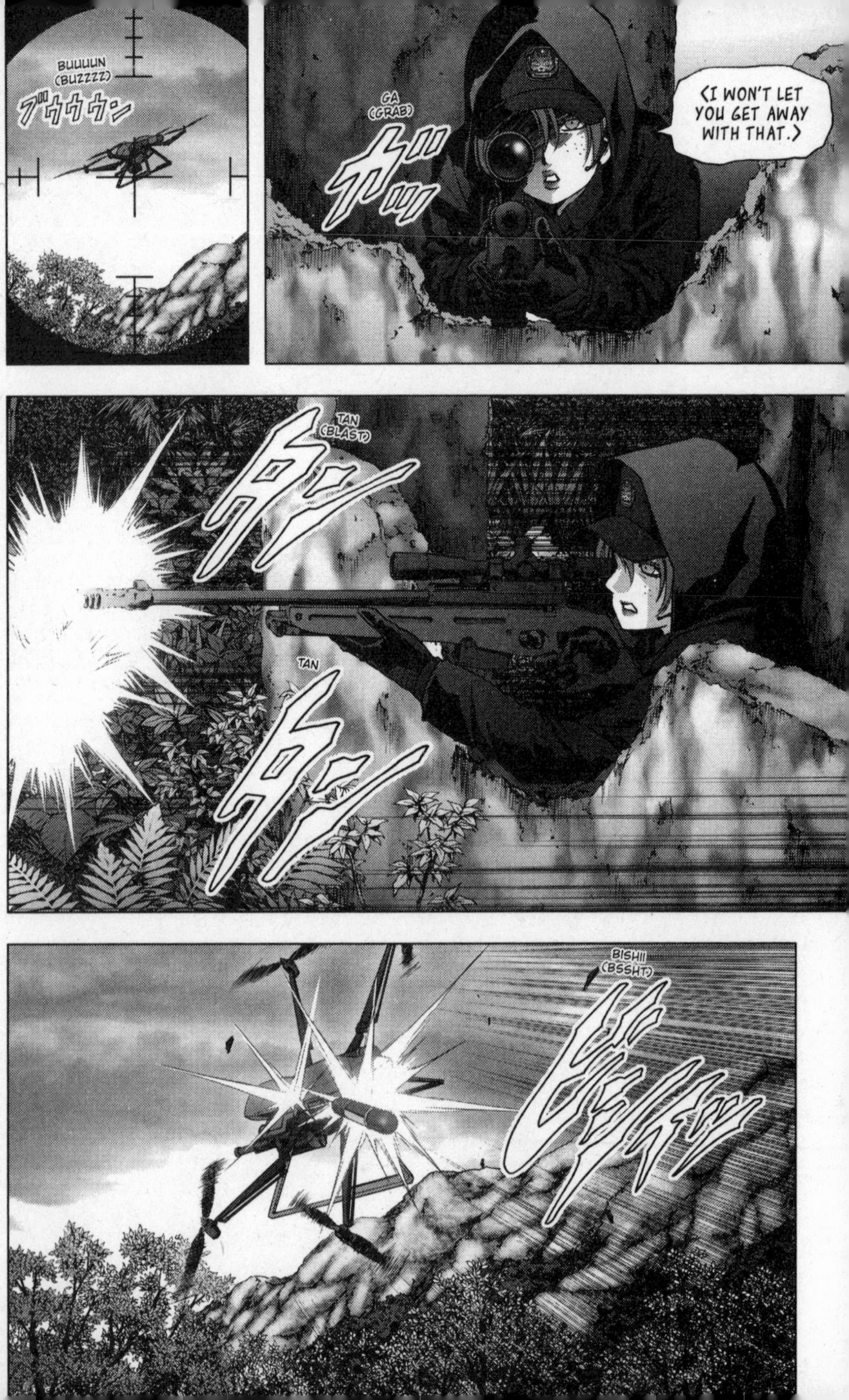
〈I WON'T LET YOU GET AWAY WITH THAT.〉
GA (GRAB)
BUUUUN (BUZZZZ)
ブウウウン
TAN (BLAST)
タン
TAN
タン
BISHII (BSSHT)

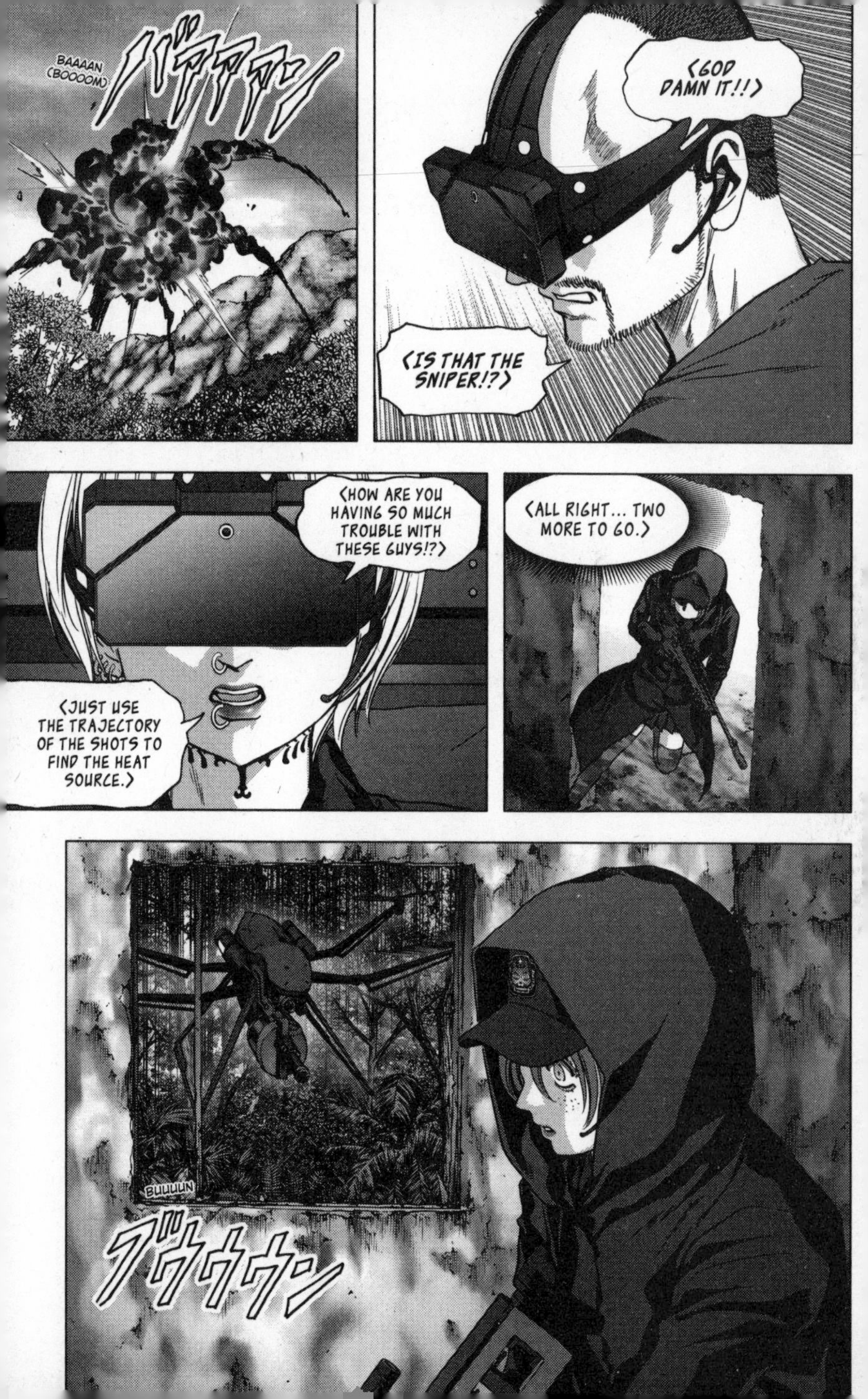

<GOD DAMN IT!!>
<IS THAT THE SNIPER!?>
BAAAAN (BOOOOM)
<ALL RIGHT... TWO MORE TO GO.>
<HOW ARE YOU HAVING SO MUCH TROUBLE WITH THESE GUYS!?>
<JUST USE THE TRAJECTORY OF THE SHOTS TO FIND THE HEAT SOURCE.>
BUUUUN

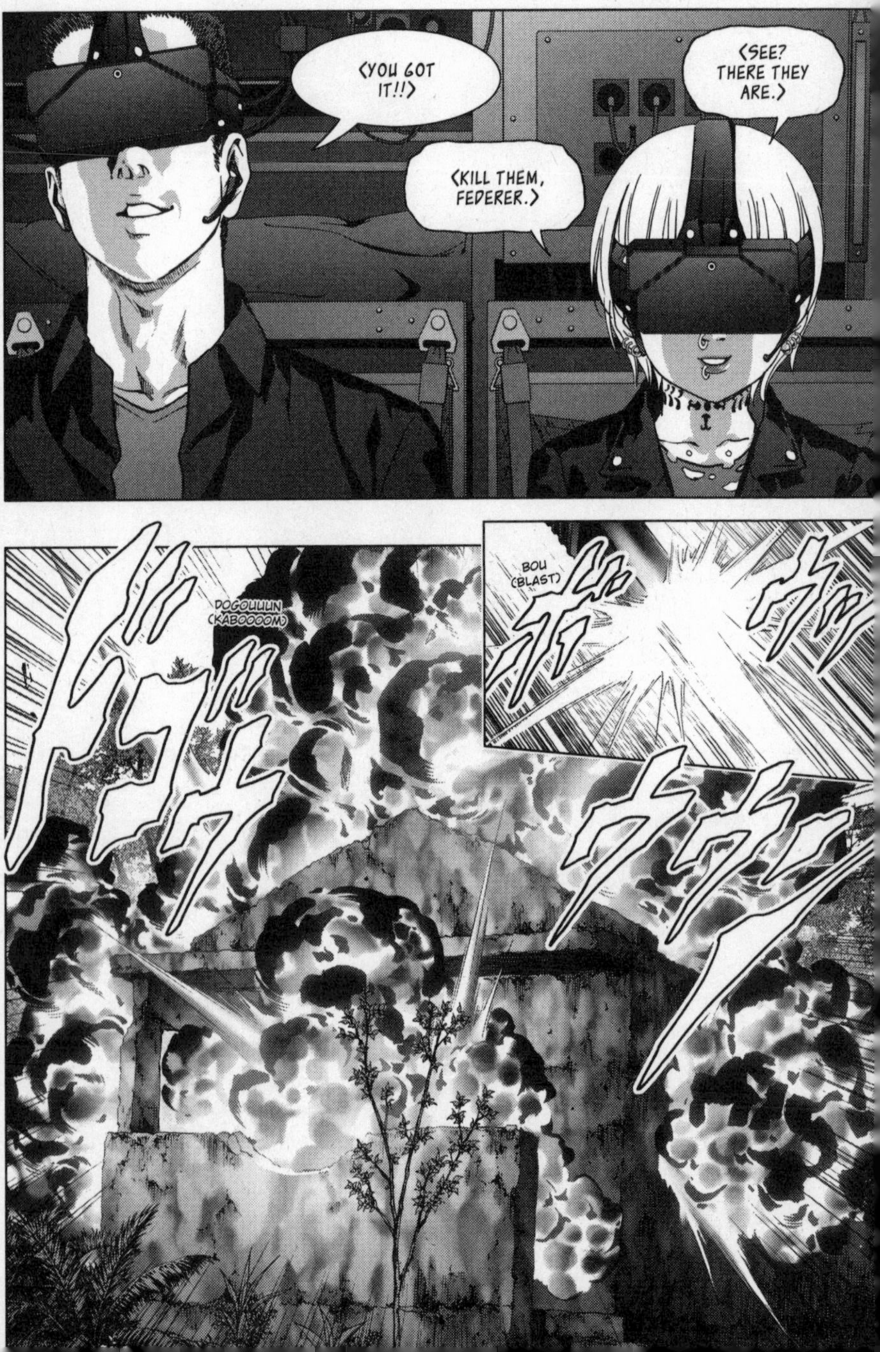

⟨SEE? THERE THEY ARE.⟩
⟨KILL THEM, FEDERER.⟩
⟨YOU GOT IT!!⟩
BOU (BLAST)
DOGOUUUN (KABOOOOM)

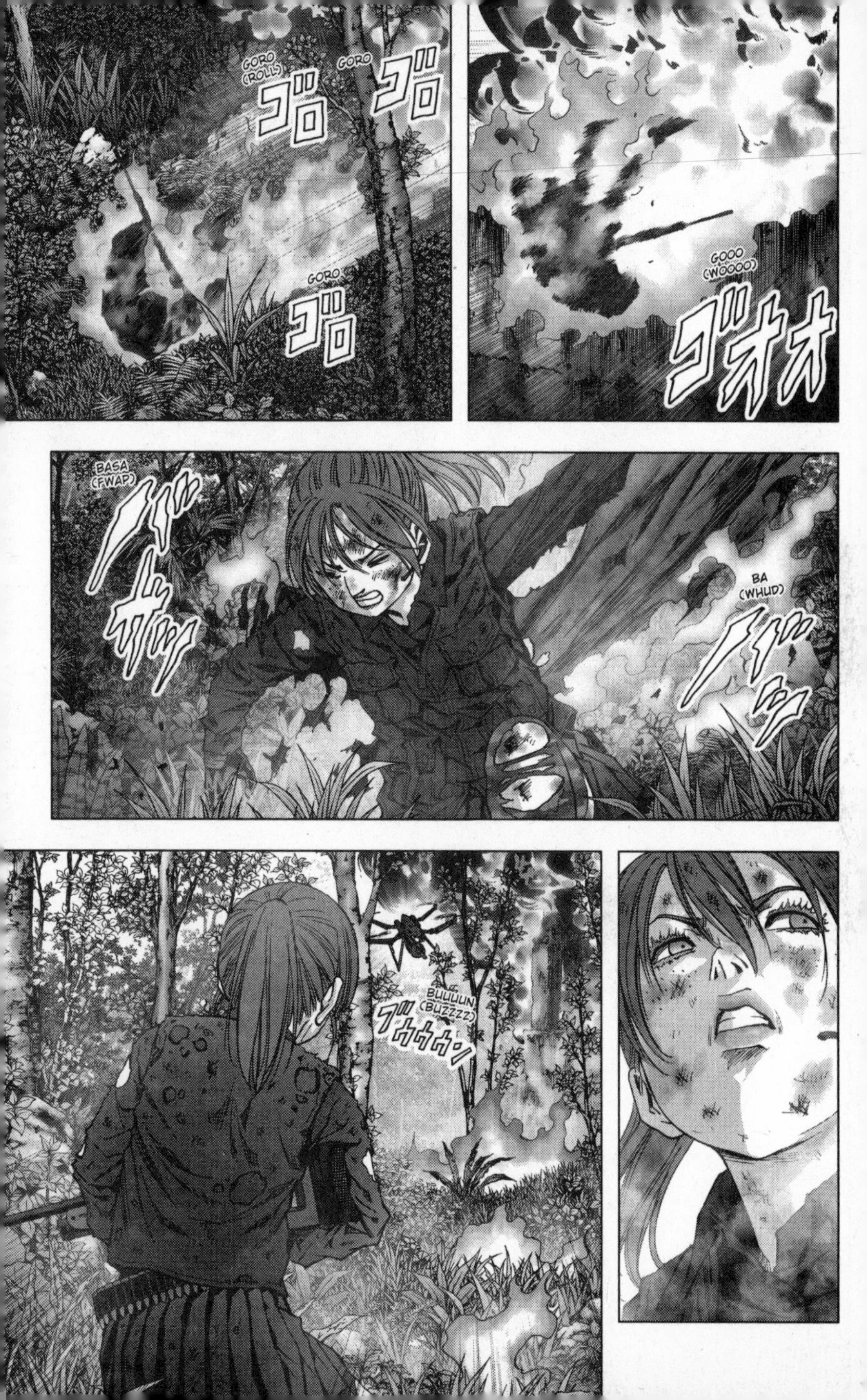
GOOO (WOOOO)
ゴオオ
GORO (ROLL)
ゴロ
GORO
ゴロ
GORO
ゴロ
BA (WHUD)
バッ
BASA (FWAP)
バサッ
BUUUUN (BUZZZZ)
ブゥゥゥン

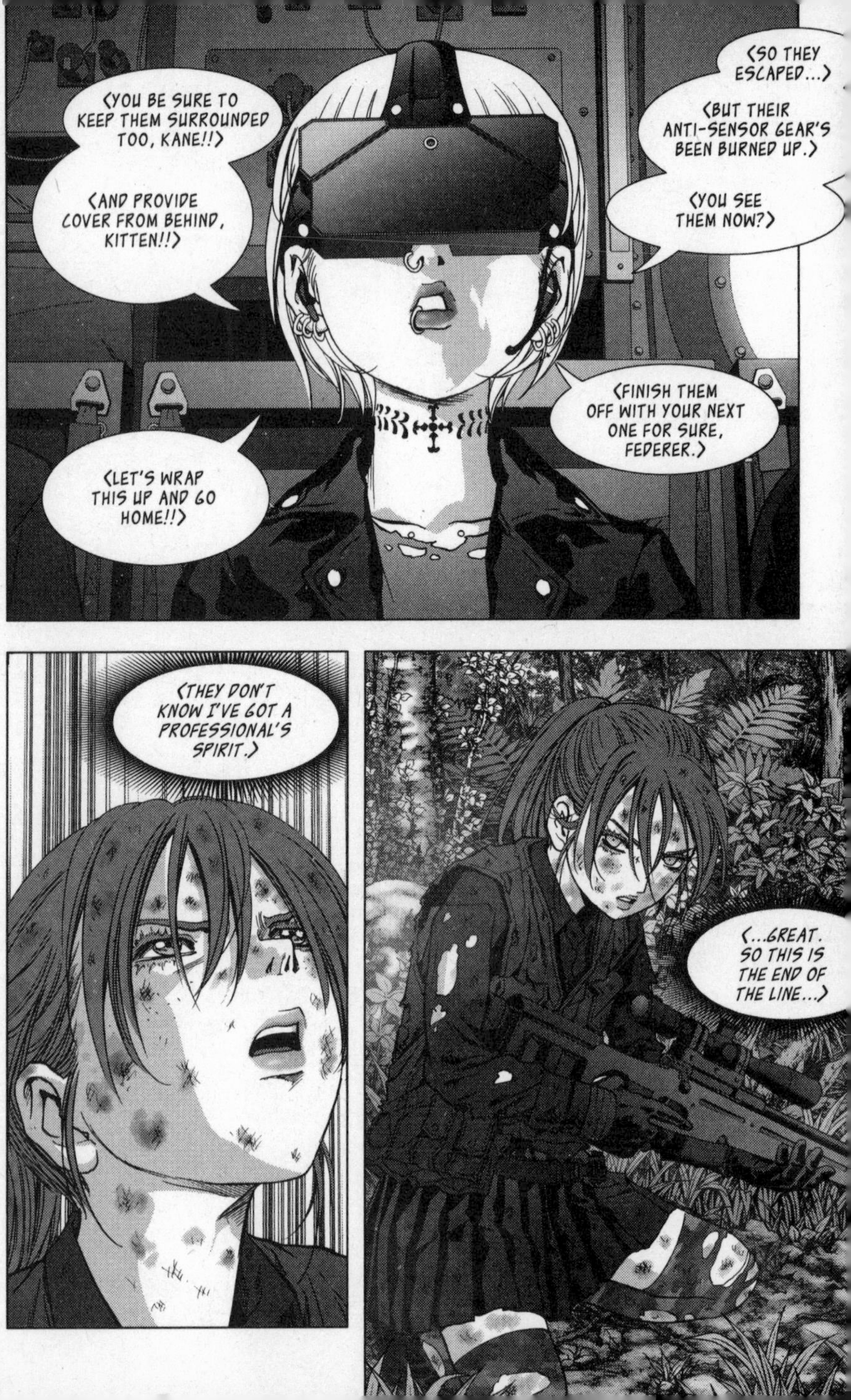
<SO THEY ESCAPED...>
<BUT THEIR ANTI-SENSOR GEAR'S BEEN BURNED UP.>
<YOU SEE THEM NOW?>
<YOU BE SURE TO KEEP THEM SURROUNDED TOO, KANE!!>
<AND PROVIDE COVER FROM BEHIND, KITTEN!!>
<FINISH THEM OFF WITH YOUR NEXT ONE FOR SURE, FEDERER.>
<LET'S WRAP THIS UP AND GO HOME!!>
<...GREAT. SO THIS IS THE END OF THE LINE...>
<THEY DON'T KNOW I'VE GOT A PROFESSIONAL'S SPIRIT.>

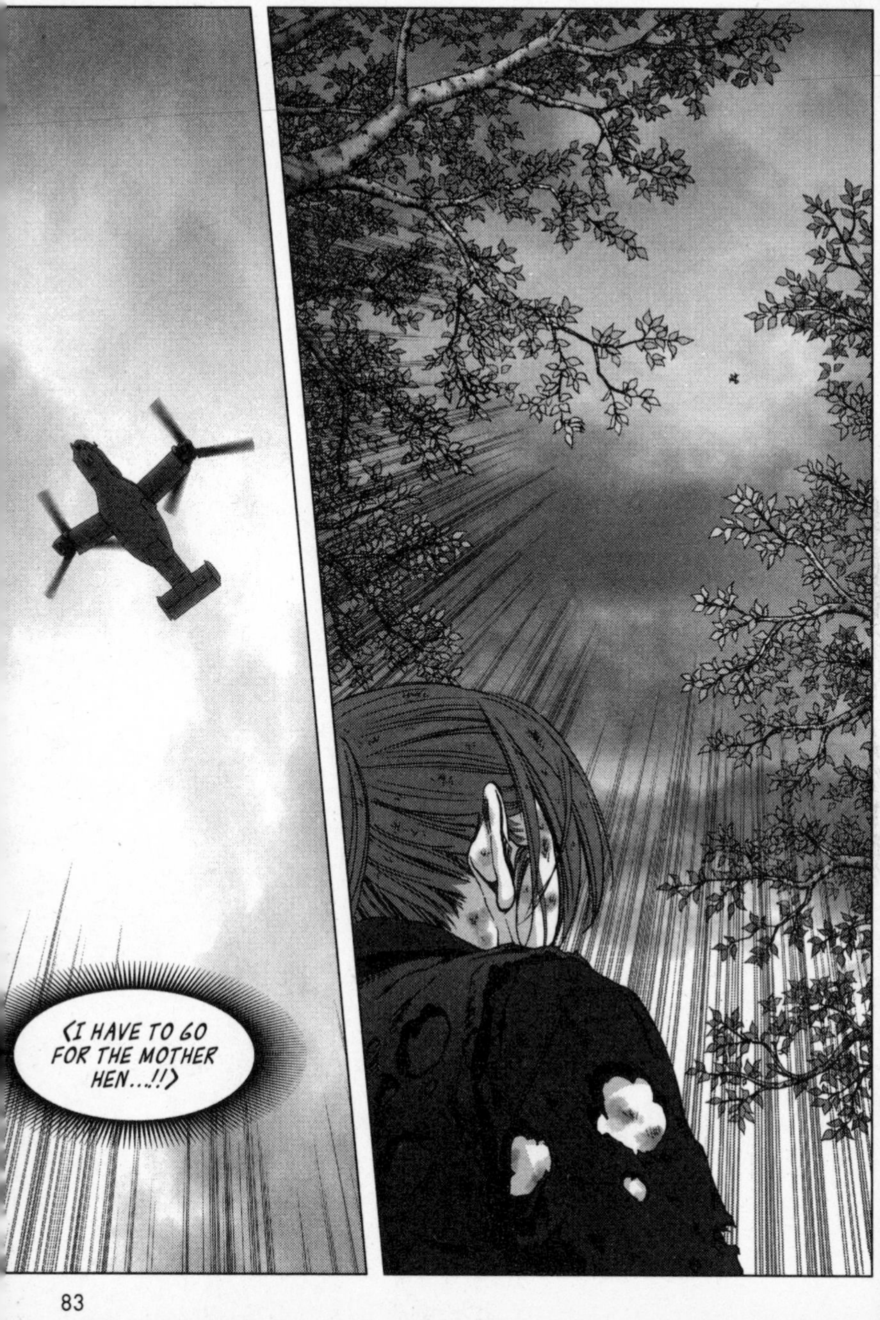

⟨I HAVE TO GO FOR THE MOTHER HEN...!!⟩

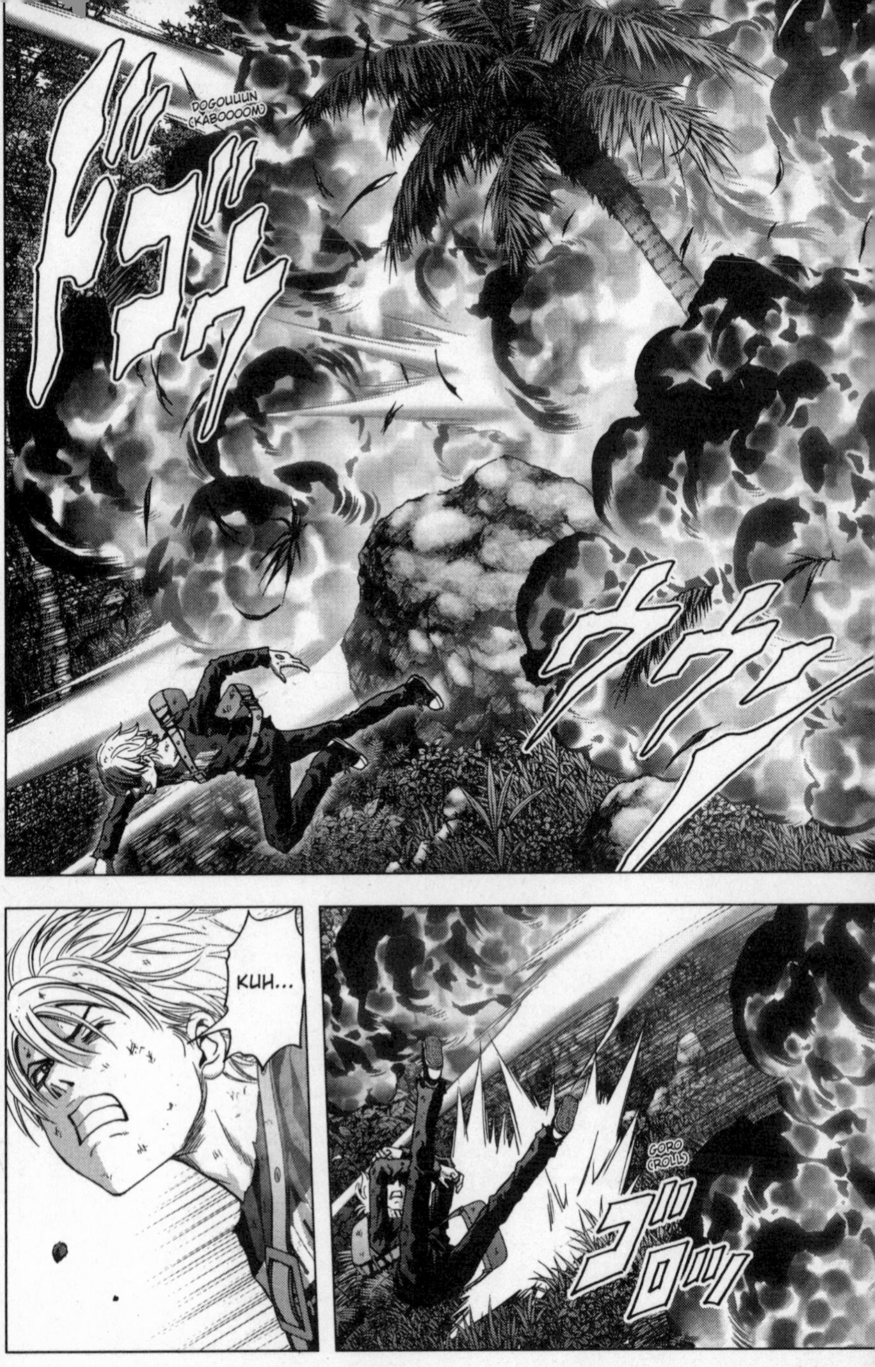
DOGOUUUN
(KABOOOOM)
GORO
(ROLL)
KUH...

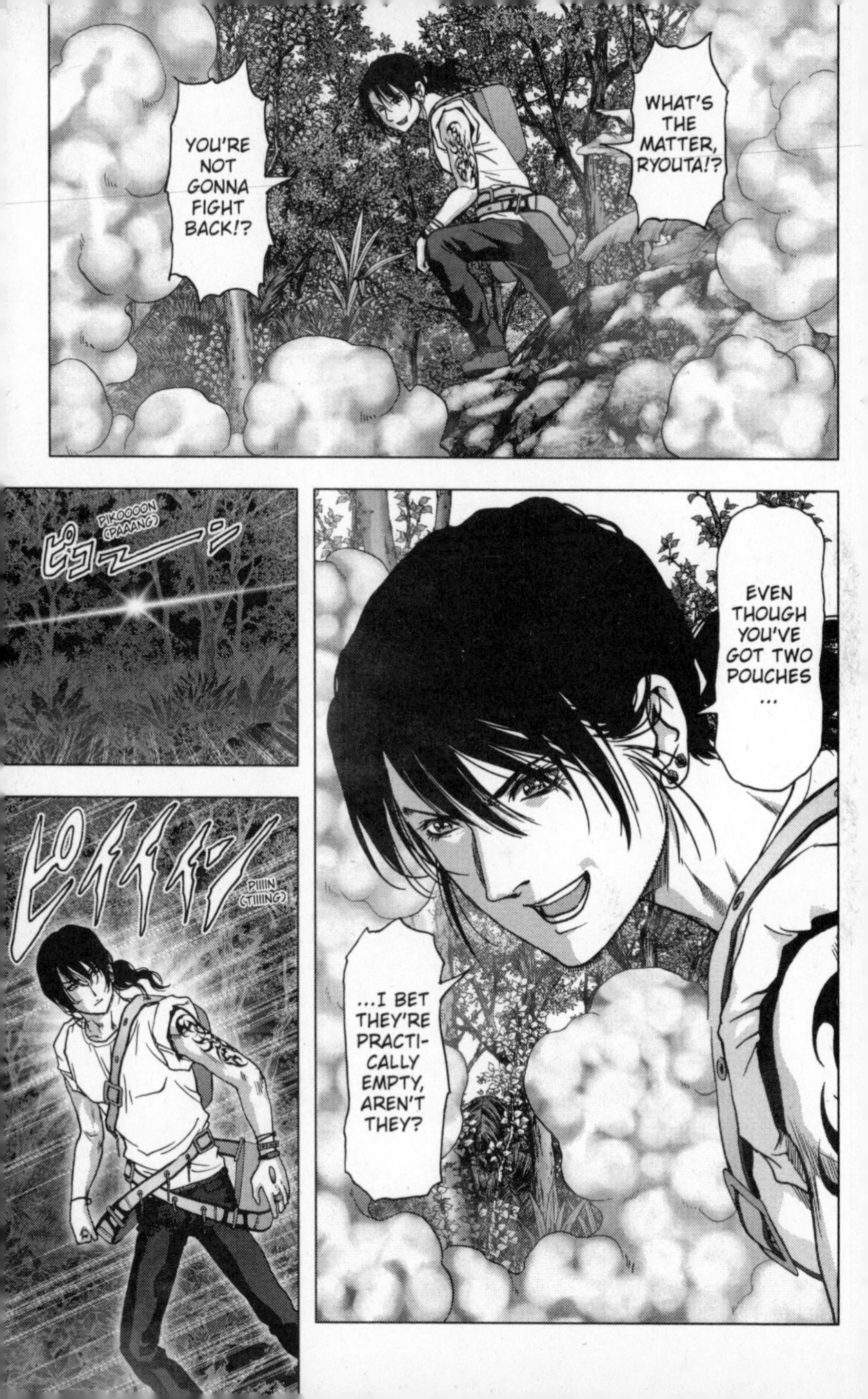
WHAT'S THE MATTER, RYOUTA!?
YOU'RE NOT GONNA FIGHT BACK!?
EVEN THOUGH YOU'VE GOT TWO POUCHES ...
...I BET THEY'RE PRACTI-CALLY EMPTY, AREN'T THEY?
ピコーーン
PIKOOOON (PAAANG)
ピイイイン
PIIIIN (TIIIING)

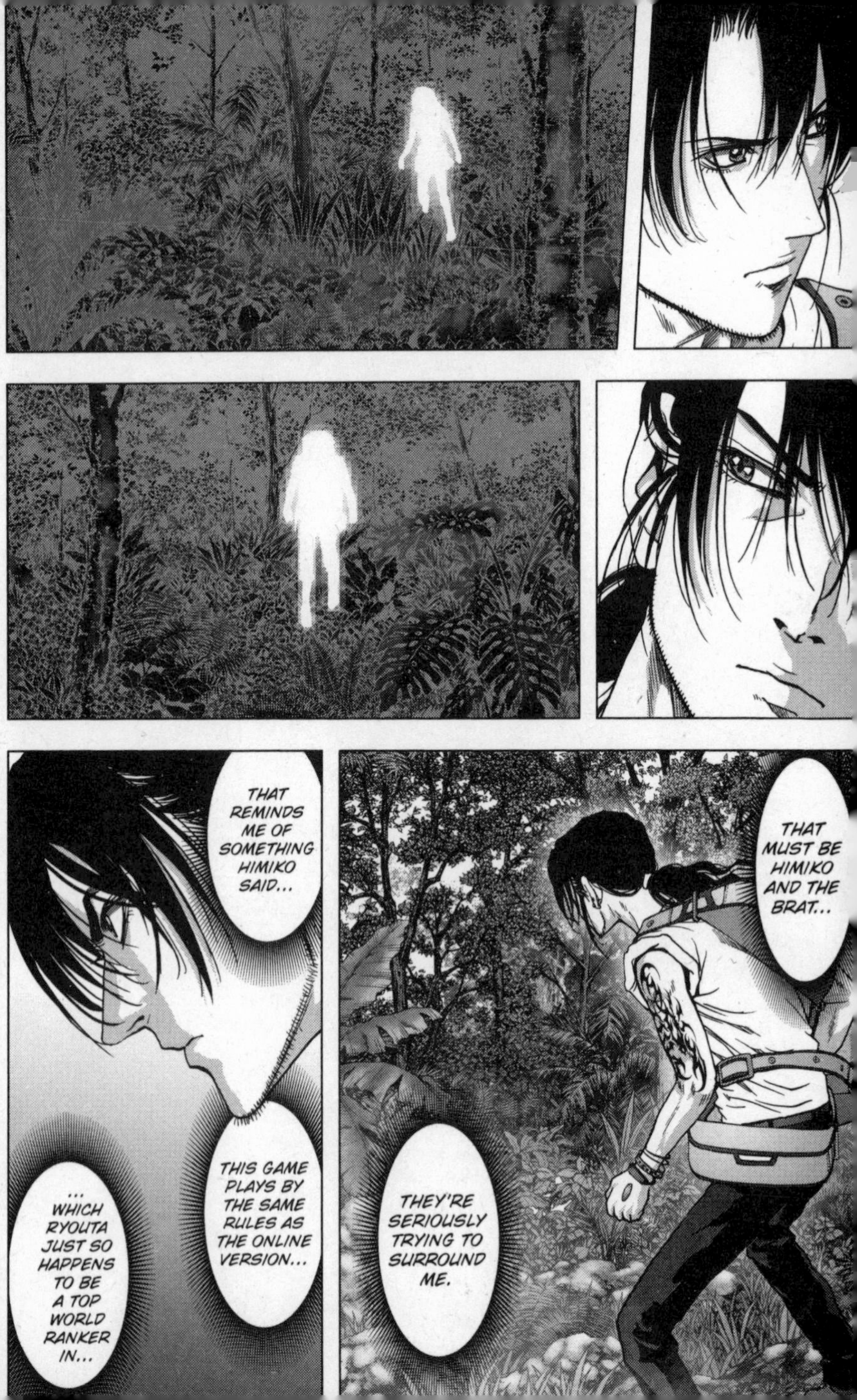
THAT MUST BE HIMIKO AND THE BRAT...
THEY'RE SERIOUSLY TRYING TO SURROUND ME.
THAT REMINDS ME OF SOMETHING HIMIKO SAID...
THIS GAME PLAYS BY THE SAME RULES AS THE ONLINE VERSION...
...WHICH RYOUTA JUST SO HAPPENS TO BE A TOP WORLD RANKER IN...

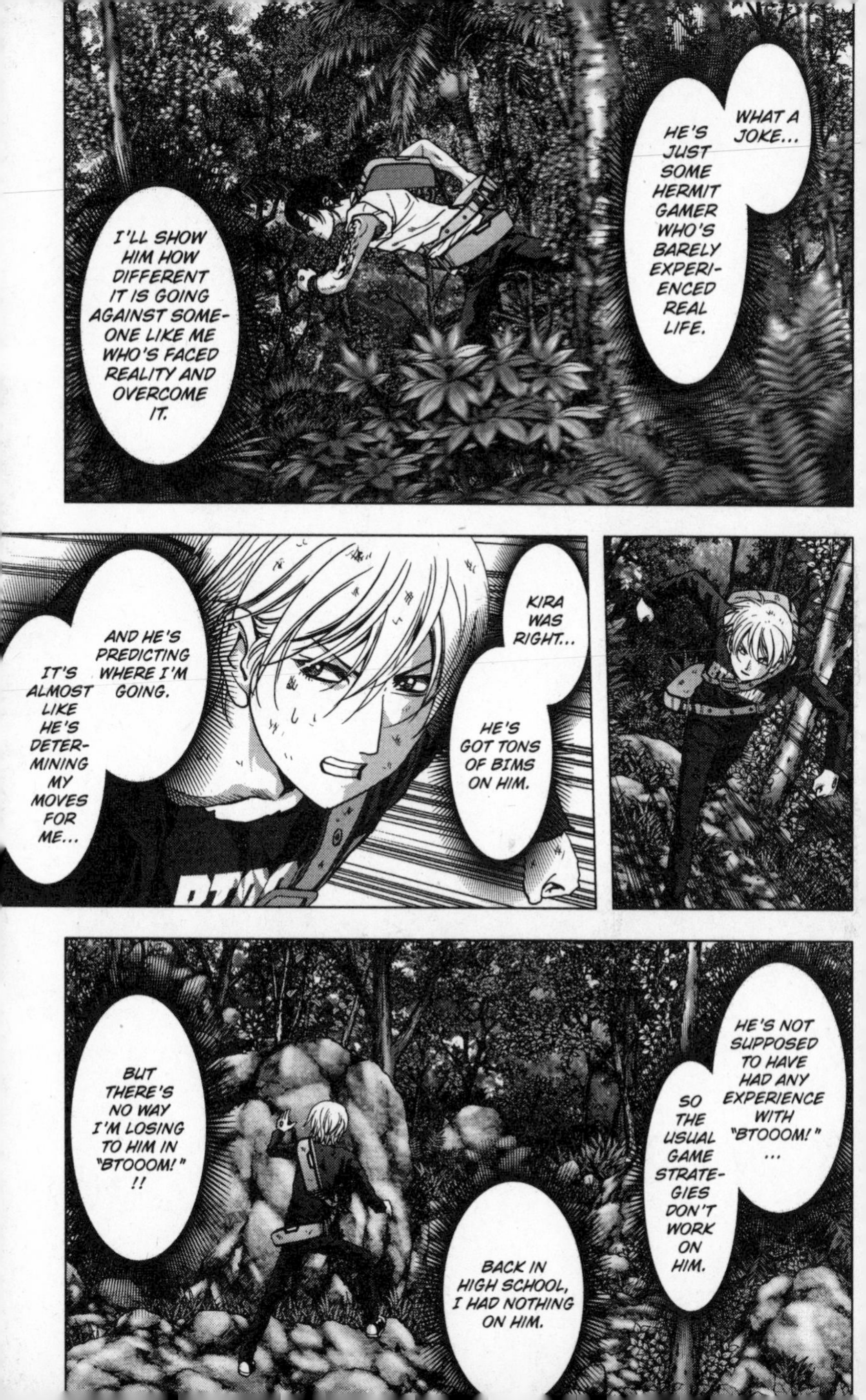
WHAT A JOKE...
HE'S JUST SOME HERMIT GAMER WHO'S BARELY EXPERIENCED REAL LIFE.
I'LL SHOW HIM HOW DIFFERENT IT IS GOING AGAINST SOMEONE LIKE ME WHO'S FACED REALITY AND OVERCOME IT.
KIRA WAS RIGHT...
HE'S GOT TONS OF BIMS ON HIM.
AND HE'S PREDICTING WHERE I'M GOING.
IT'S ALMOST LIKE HE'S DETERMINING MY MOVES FOR ME...
HE'S NOT SUPPOSED TO HAVE HAD ANY EXPERIENCE WITH "BTOOOM!" ...
SO THE USUAL GAME STRATEGIES DON'T WORK ON HIM.
BACK IN HIGH SCHOOL, I HAD NOTHING ON HIM.
BUT THERE'S NO WAY I'M LOSING TO HIM IN "BTOOOM!" !!

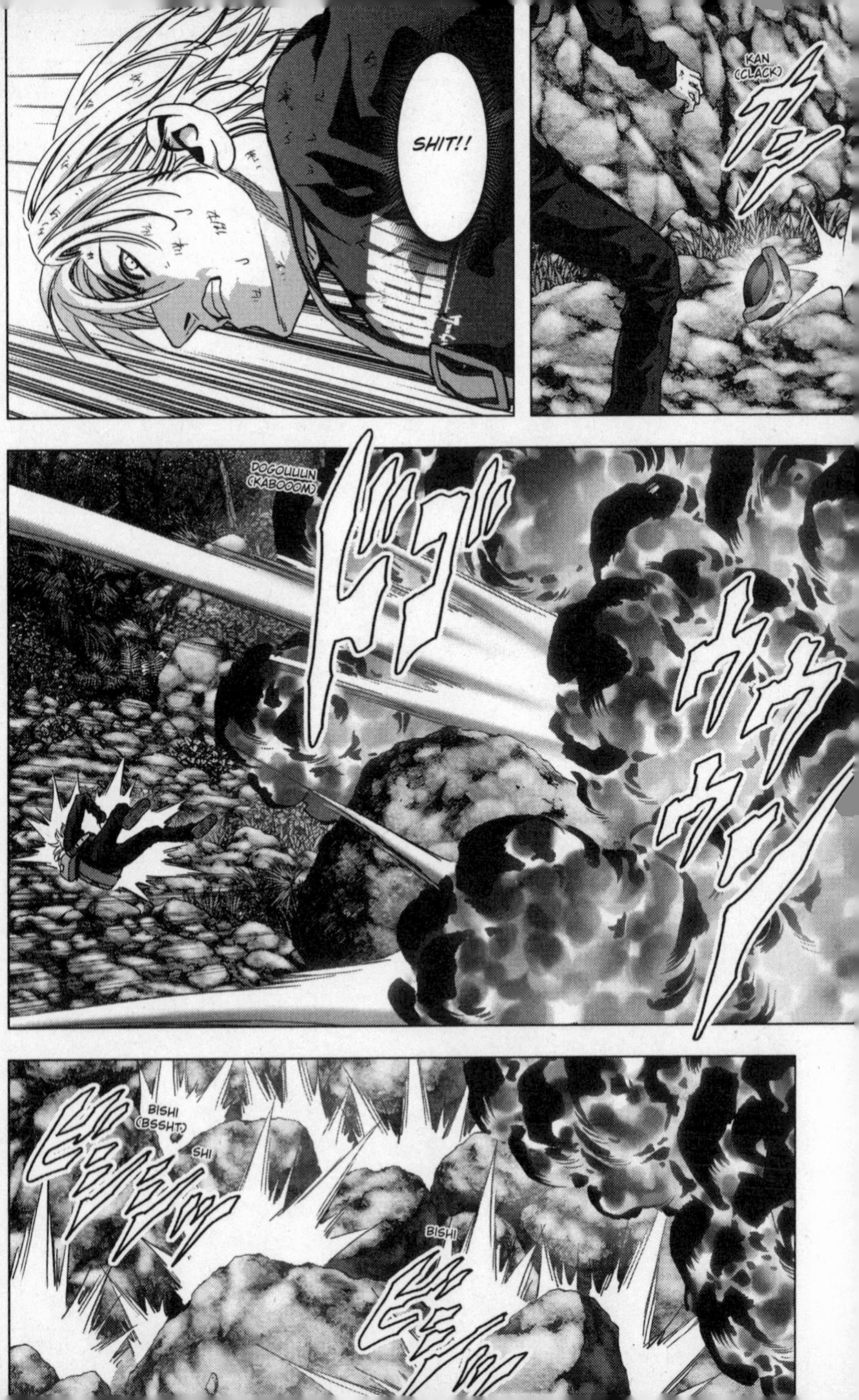
KAN (CLACK)
SHIT!!
DOGOUUUN (KABOOOM)
BISHI (BSSHT)
SHI
BISHI

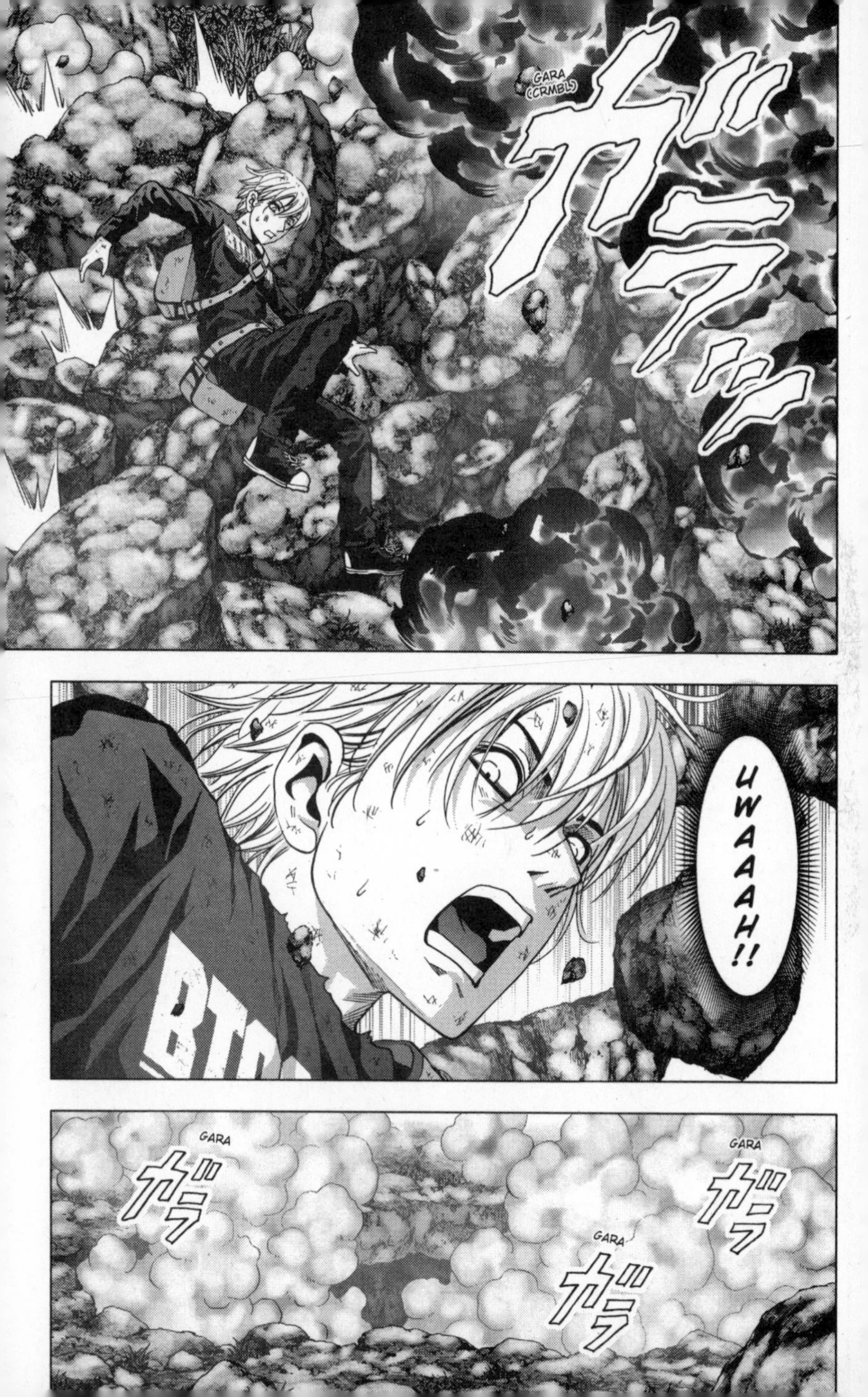
GARA (CRMBL)
ガラッ
UWAAAAH!!
GARA
ガラ
GARA
ガラ
GARA
ガラ

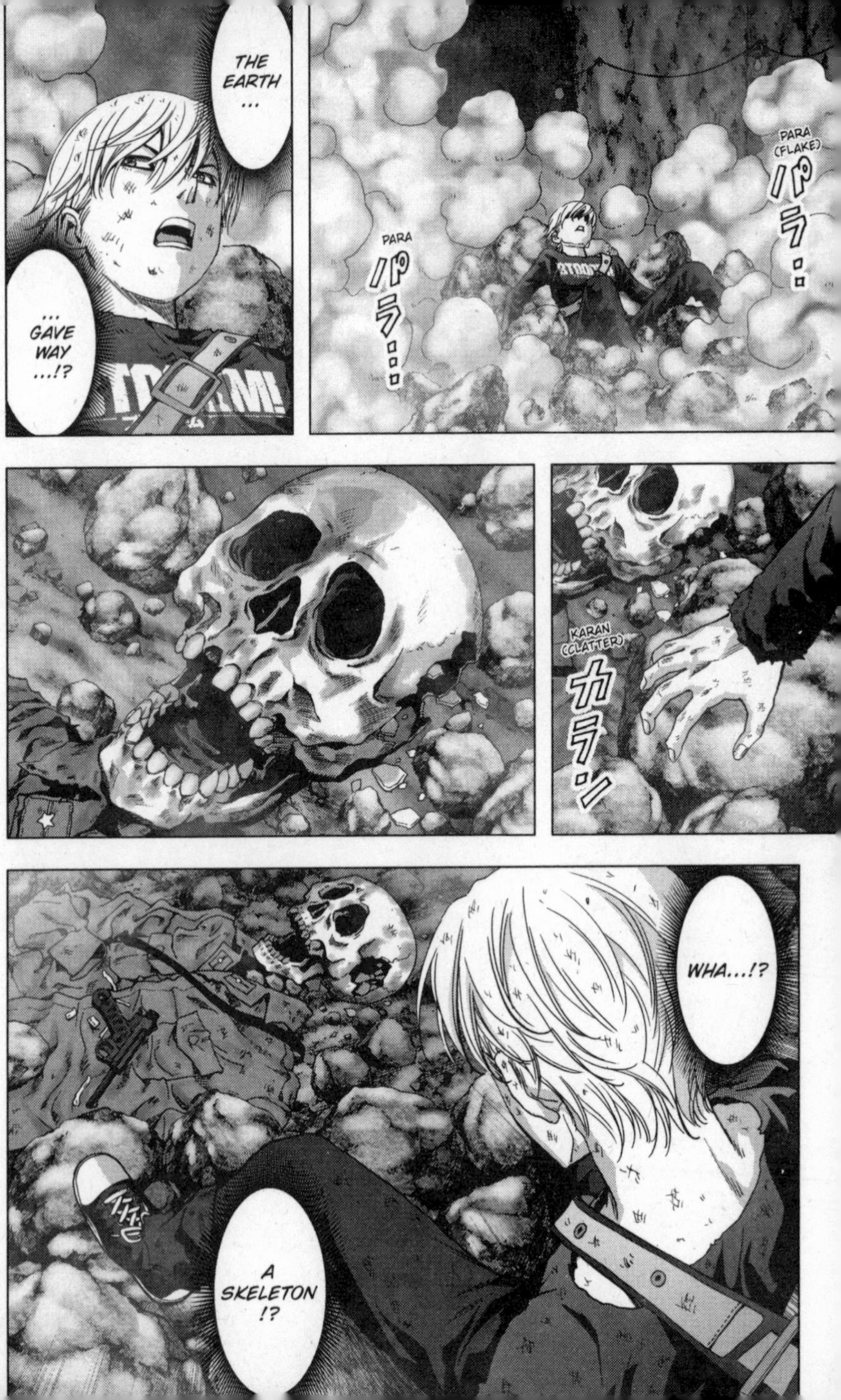
PARA (FLAKE)
パラ..
PARA
パラ...
THE EARTH...
...GAVE WAY...!?
KARAN (CLATTER)
カラン
WHA...!?
A SKELETON !?

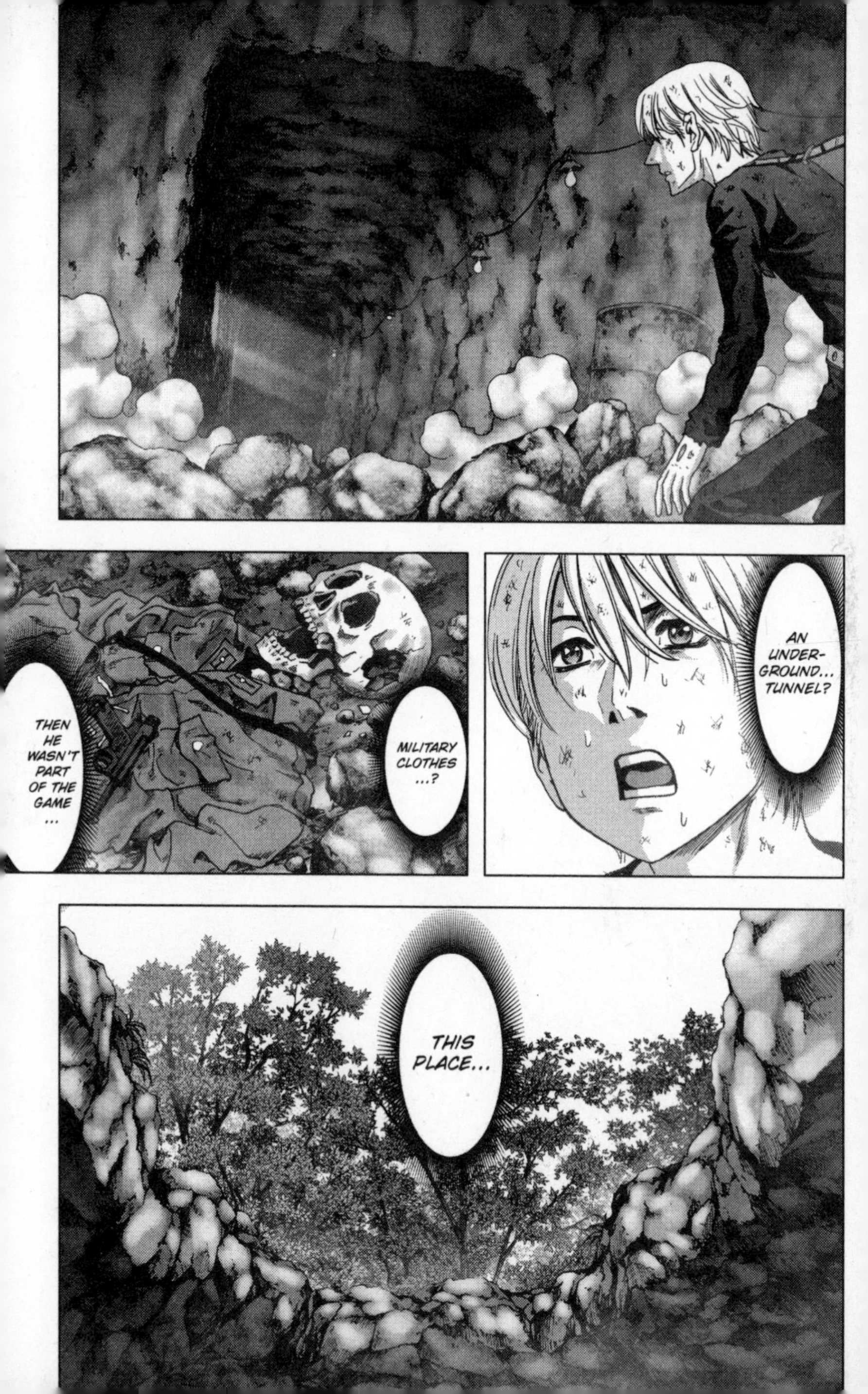
AN UNDER-GROUND... TUNNEL?
MILITARY CLOTHES ...?
THEN HE WASN'T PART OF THE GAME ...
THIS PLACE...

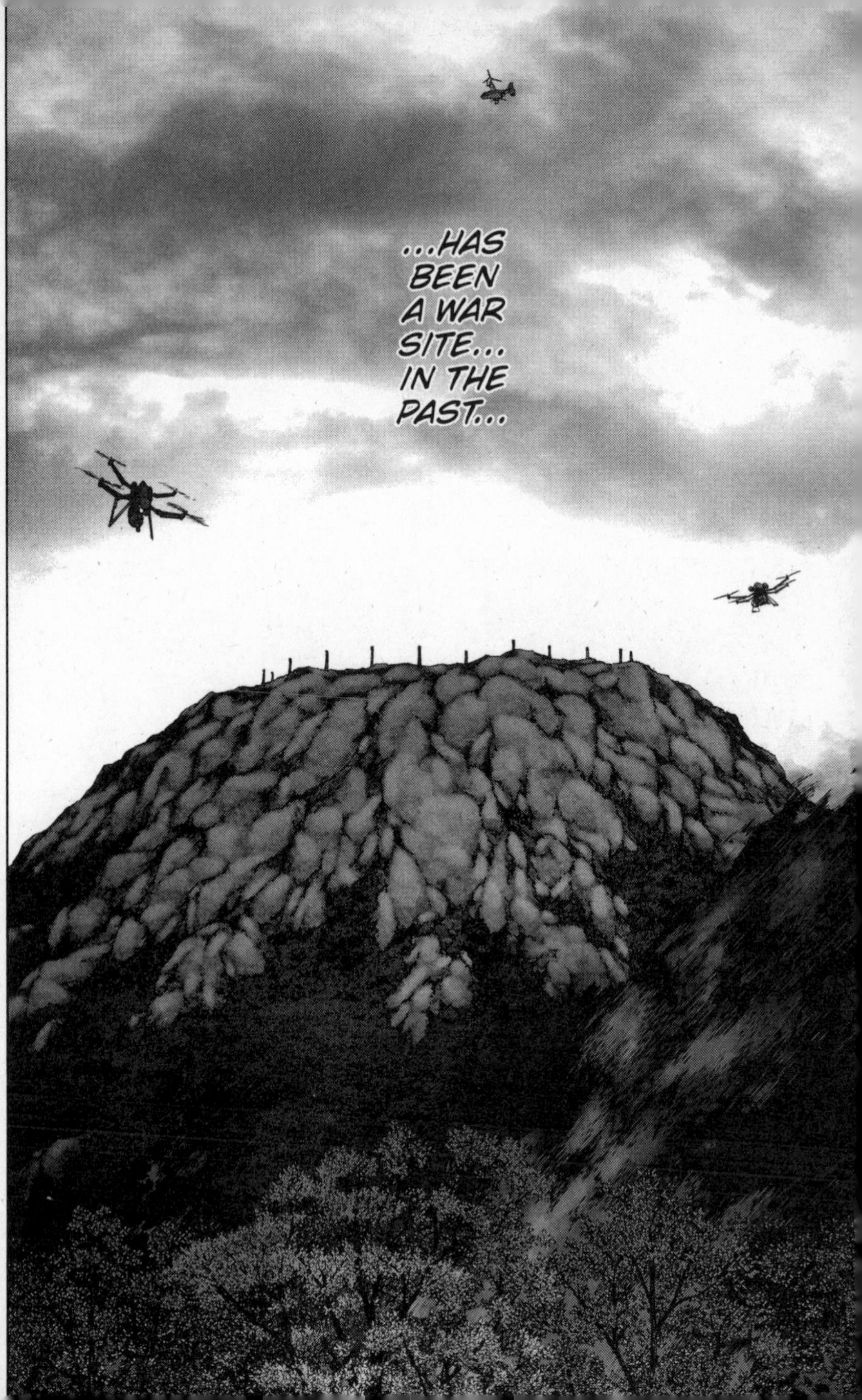
...HAS BEEN A WAR SITE... IN THE PAST...

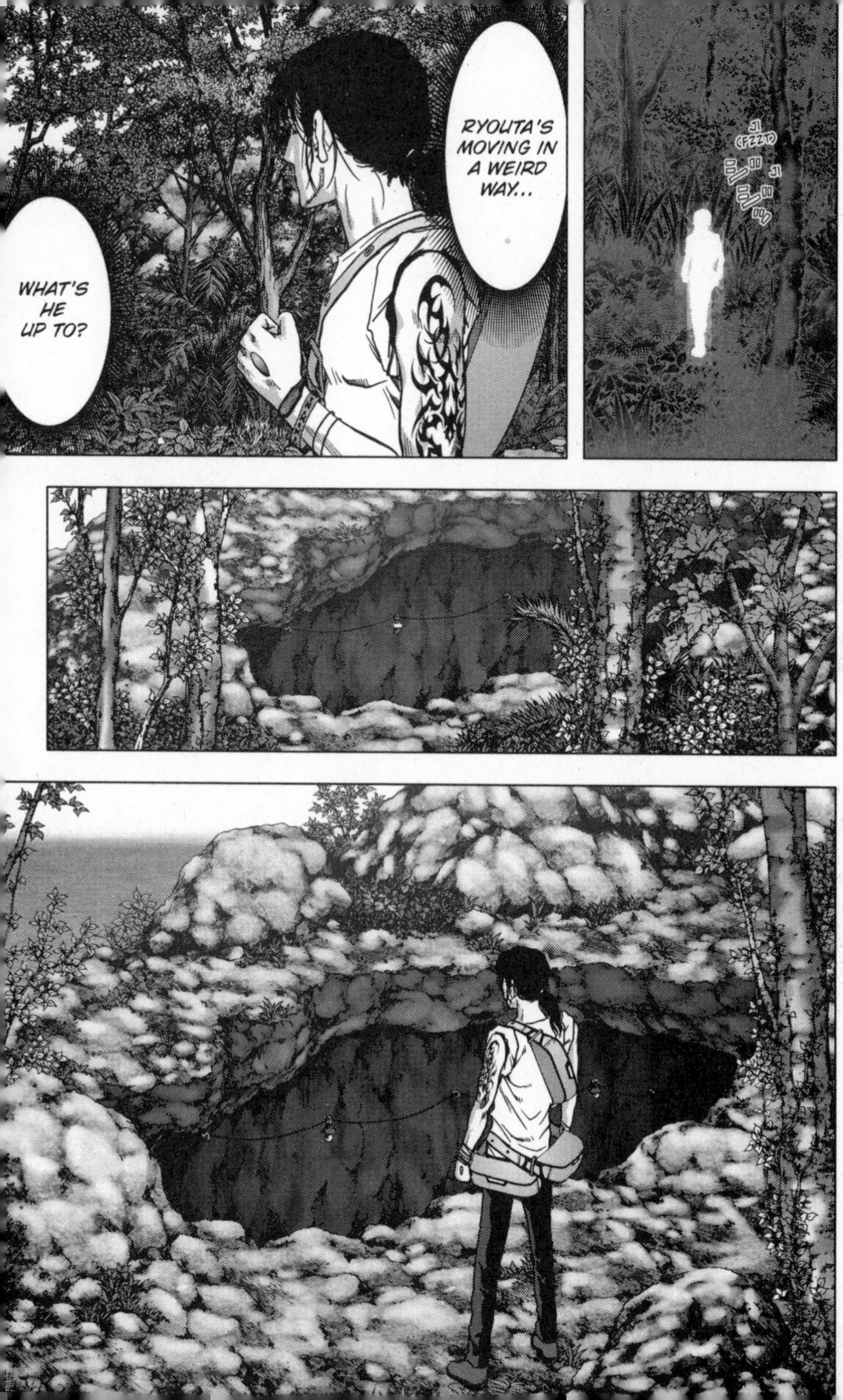
JI (FZZT)
RYOUTA'S MOVING IN A WEIRD WAY...
WHAT'S HE UP TO?

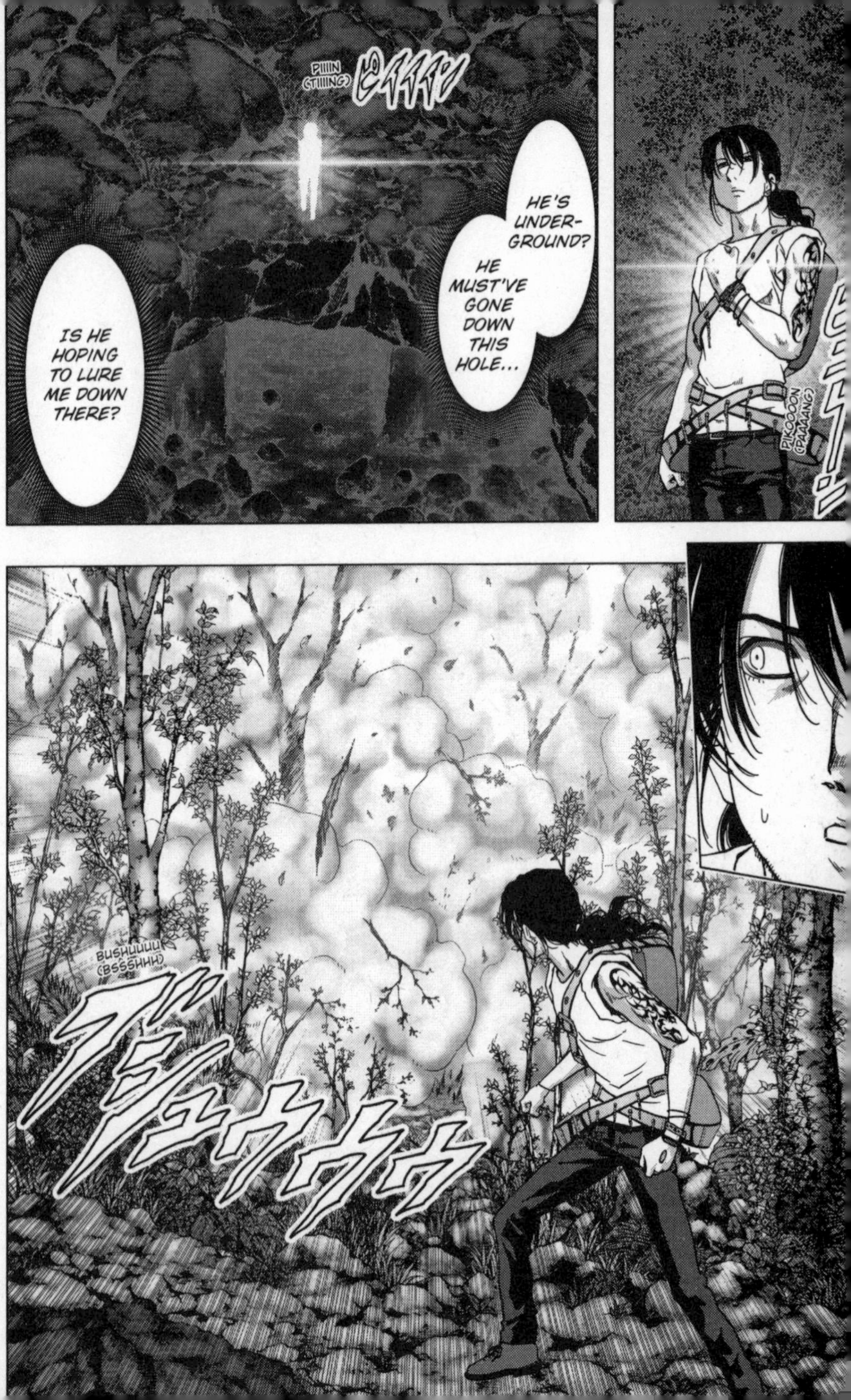
PIKOOOON (PAAAANG)
PIIIIN (TIIIING)
HE'S UNDER-GROUND?
HE MUST'VE GONE DOWN THIS HOLE...
IS HE HOPING TO LURE ME DOWN THERE?
BUSHUUUU (BSSSHHH)

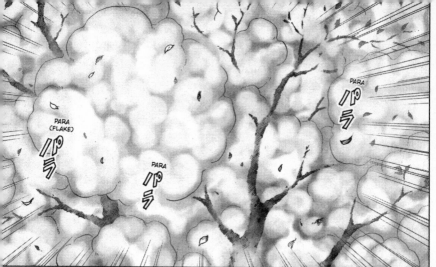

PARA
(FLAKE)
パラ

PARA
パラ

PARA
パラ

GOOO
(WOOO)
ゴオオ

BA
(HOP)
バ

BLAZING GAS!!

WHERE DID THAT COME FROM!?

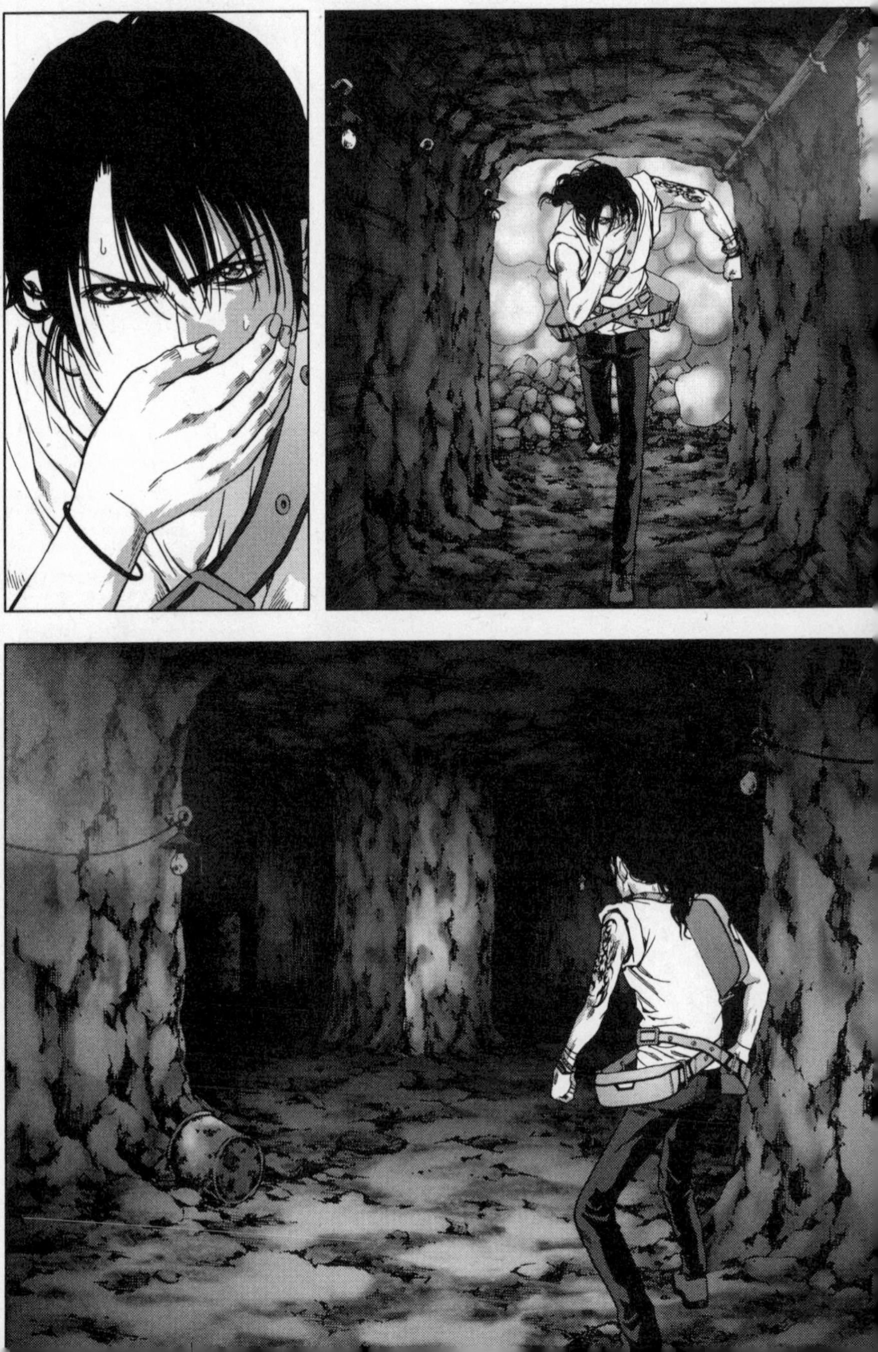

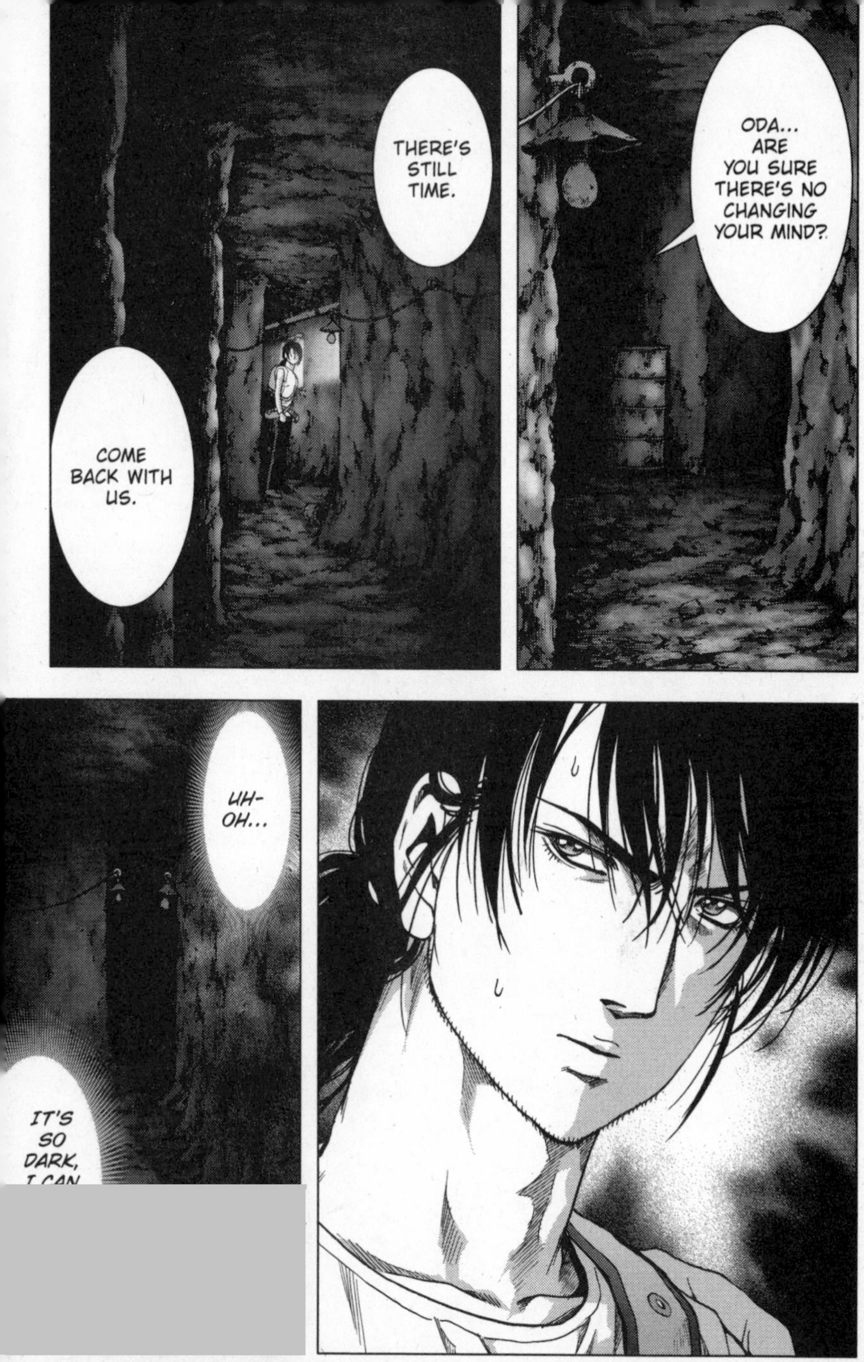
ODA... ARE YOU SURE THERE'S NO CHANGING YOUR MIND?
THERE'S STILL TIME.
COME BACK WITH US.
UH-OH...
IT'S SO DARK,

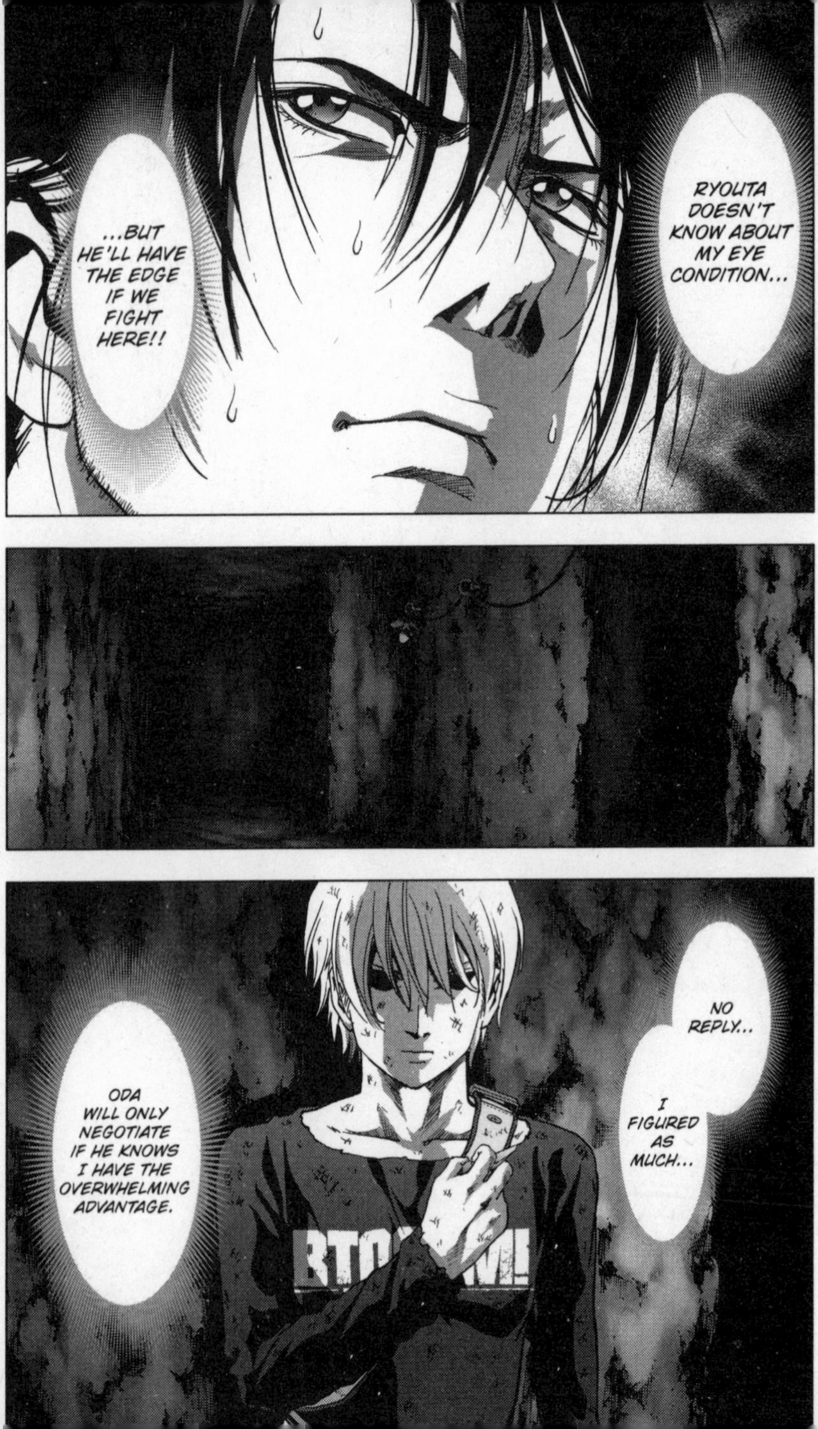
RYOUTA DOESN'T KNOW ABOUT MY EYE CONDITION...
...BUT HE'LL HAVE THE EDGE IF WE FIGHT HERE!!
NO REPLY...
I FIGURED AS MUCH...
ODA WILL ONLY NEGOTIATE IF HE KNOWS I HAVE THE OVERWHELMING ADVANTAGE.

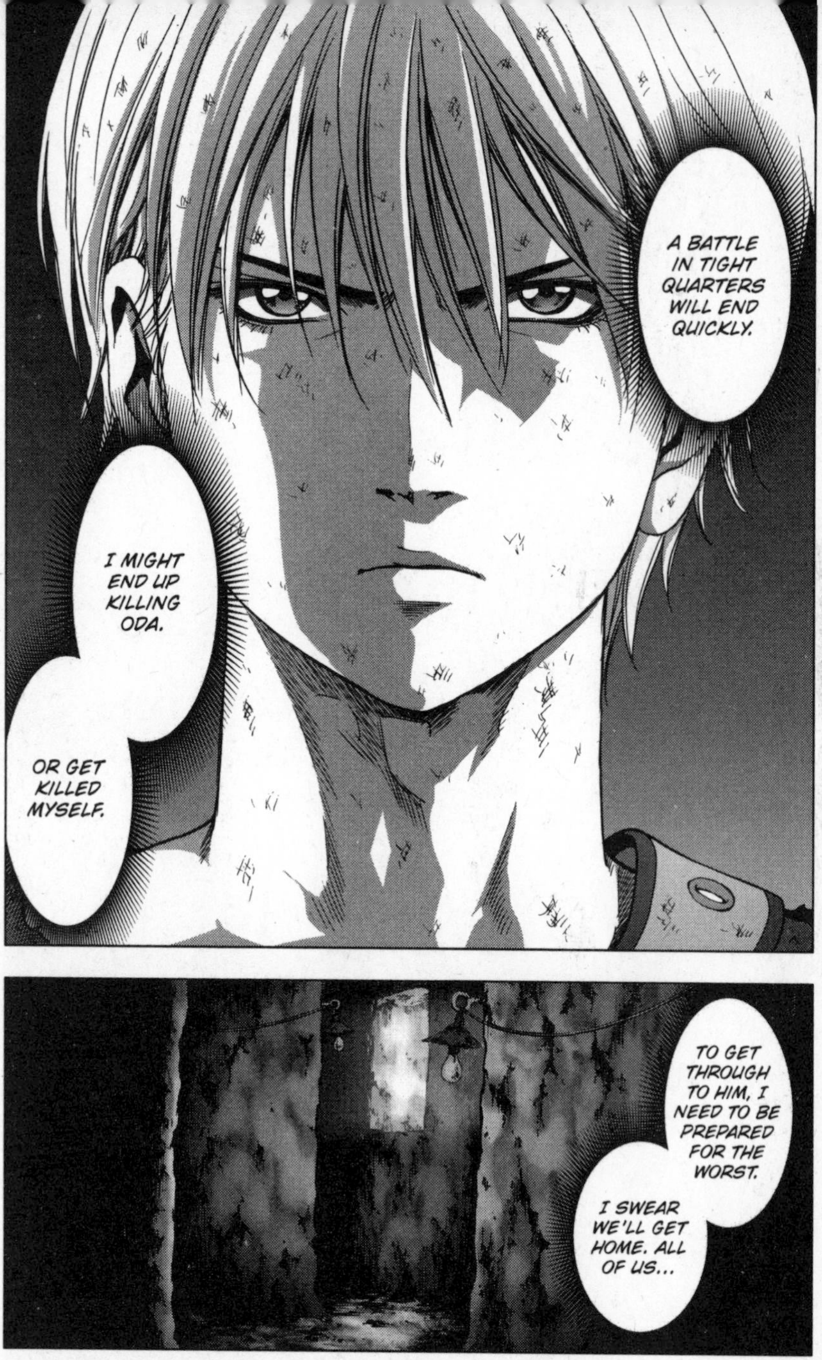
A BATTLE IN TIGHT QUARTERS WILL END QUICKLY.
I MIGHT END UP KILLING ODA.
OR GET KILLED MYSELF.
TO GET THROUGH TO HIM, I NEED TO BE PREPARED FOR THE WORST.
I SWEAR WE'LL GET HOME. ALL OF US...

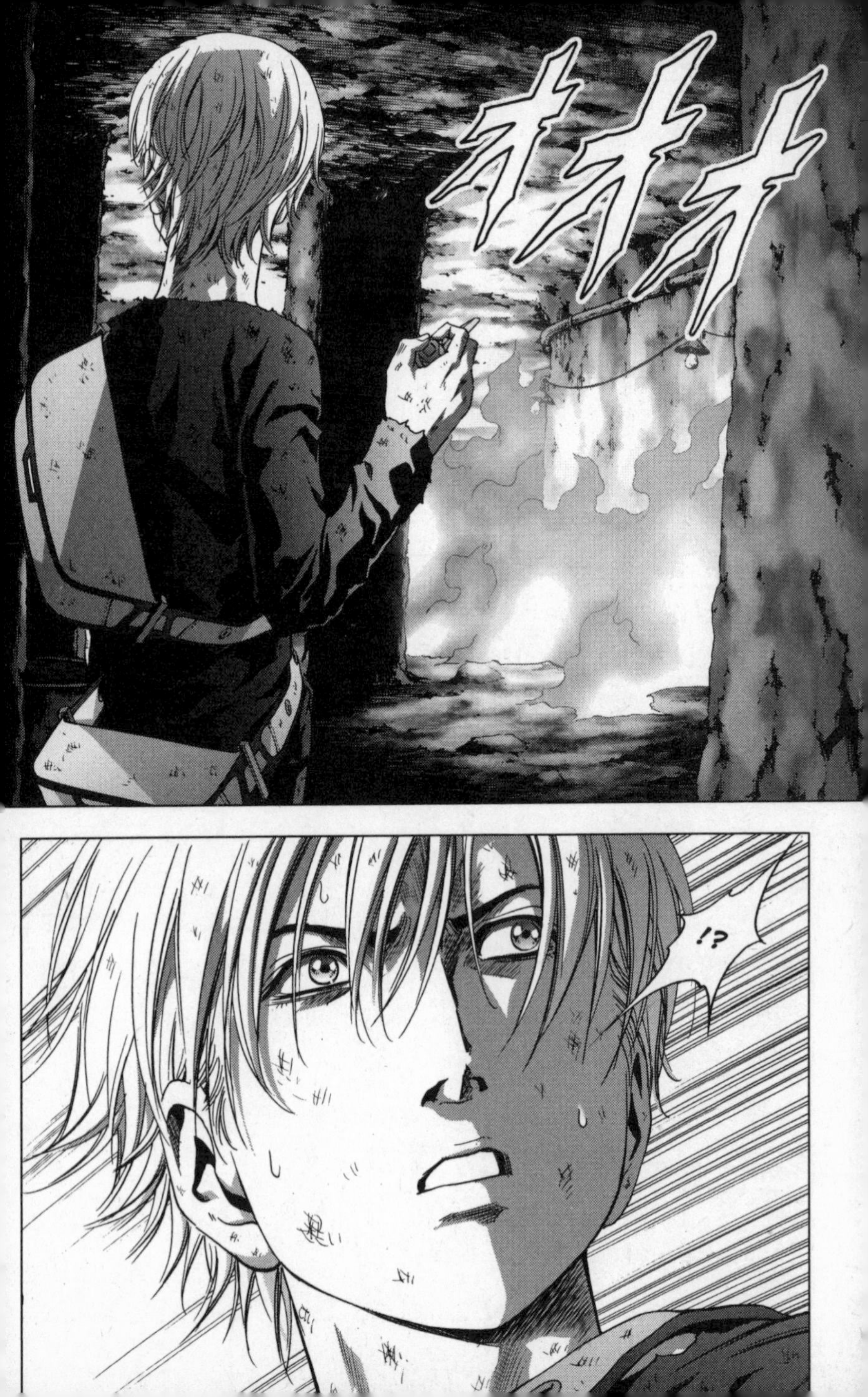
オオオ
!?

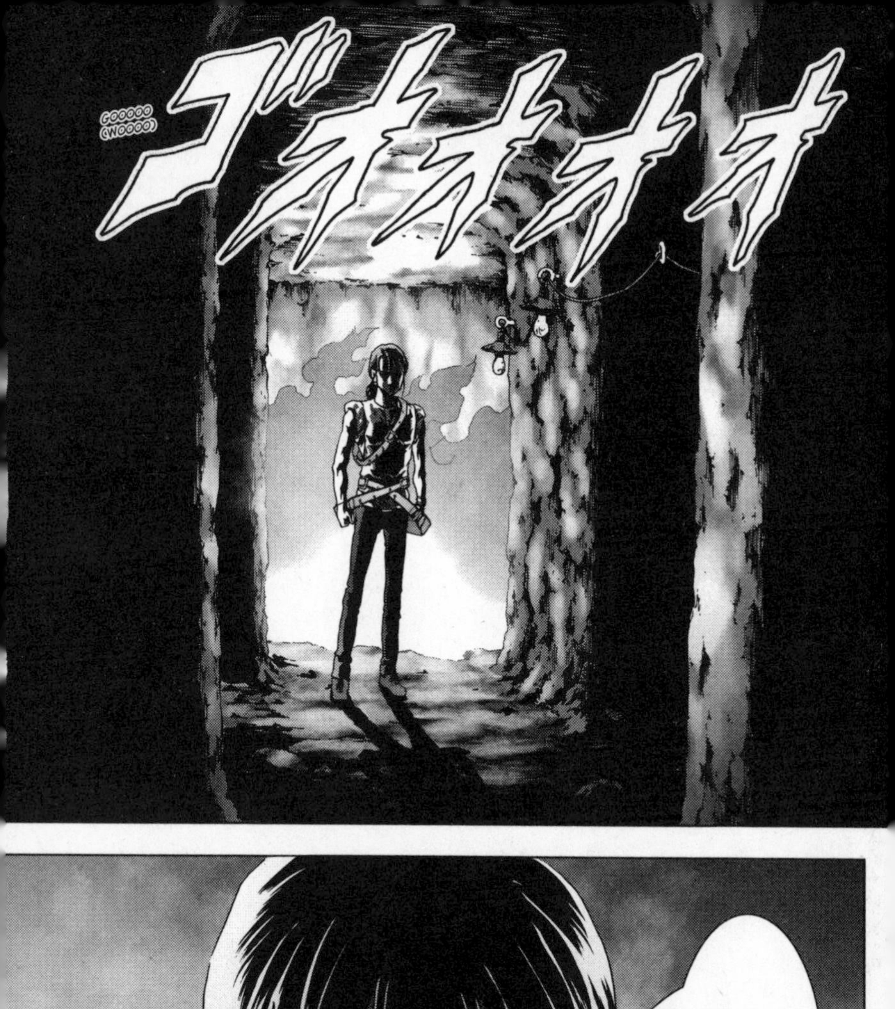
ゴオオオオ
GOOOOO (WOOOO)
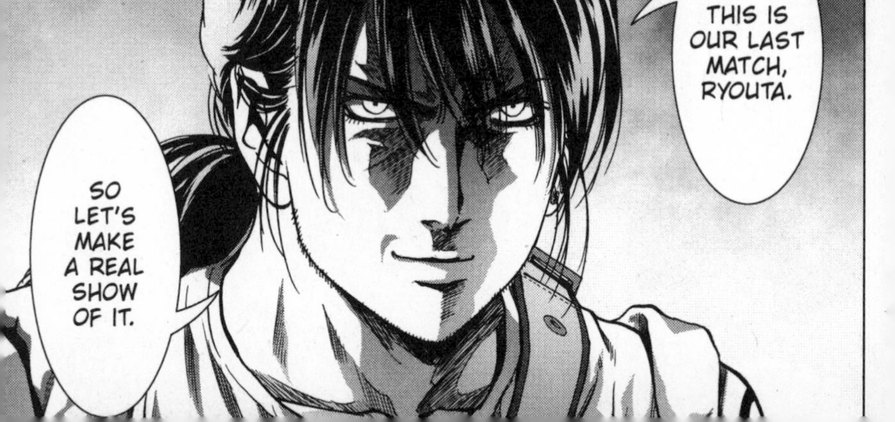
THIS IS OUR LAST MATCH, RYOUTA.
SO LET'S MAKE A REAL SHOW OF IT.

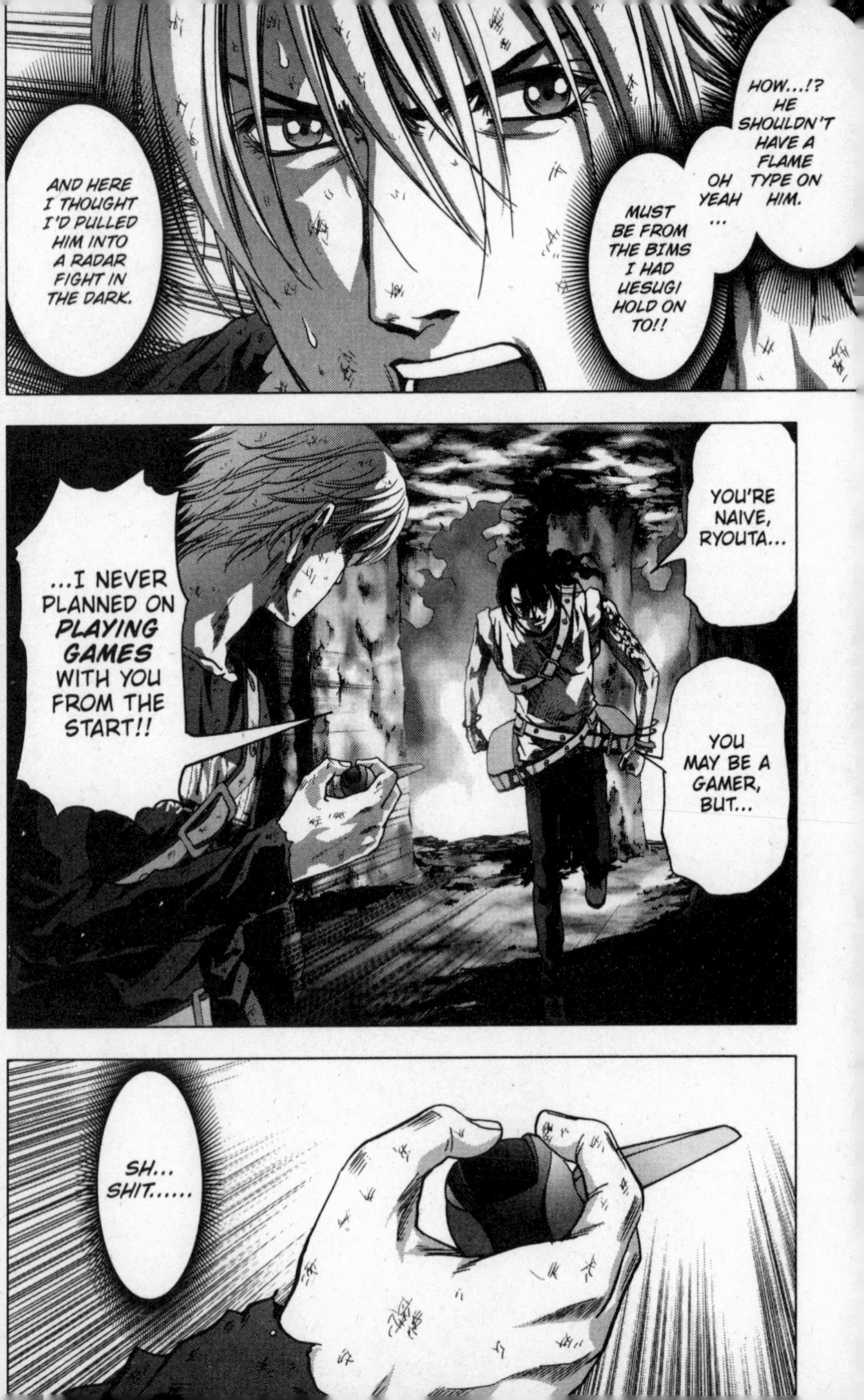
HOW...!? HE SHOULDN'T HAVE A FLAME TYPE ON HIM.
OH YEAH...
MUST BE FROM THE BIMS I HAD UESUGI HOLD ON TO!!
AND HERE I THOUGHT I'D PULLED HIM INTO A RADAR FIGHT IN THE DARK.
YOU'RE NAIVE, RYOUTA...
YOU MAY BE A GAMER, BUT...
...I NEVER PLANNED ON PLAYING GAMES WITH YOU FROM THE START!!
SH... SHIT......

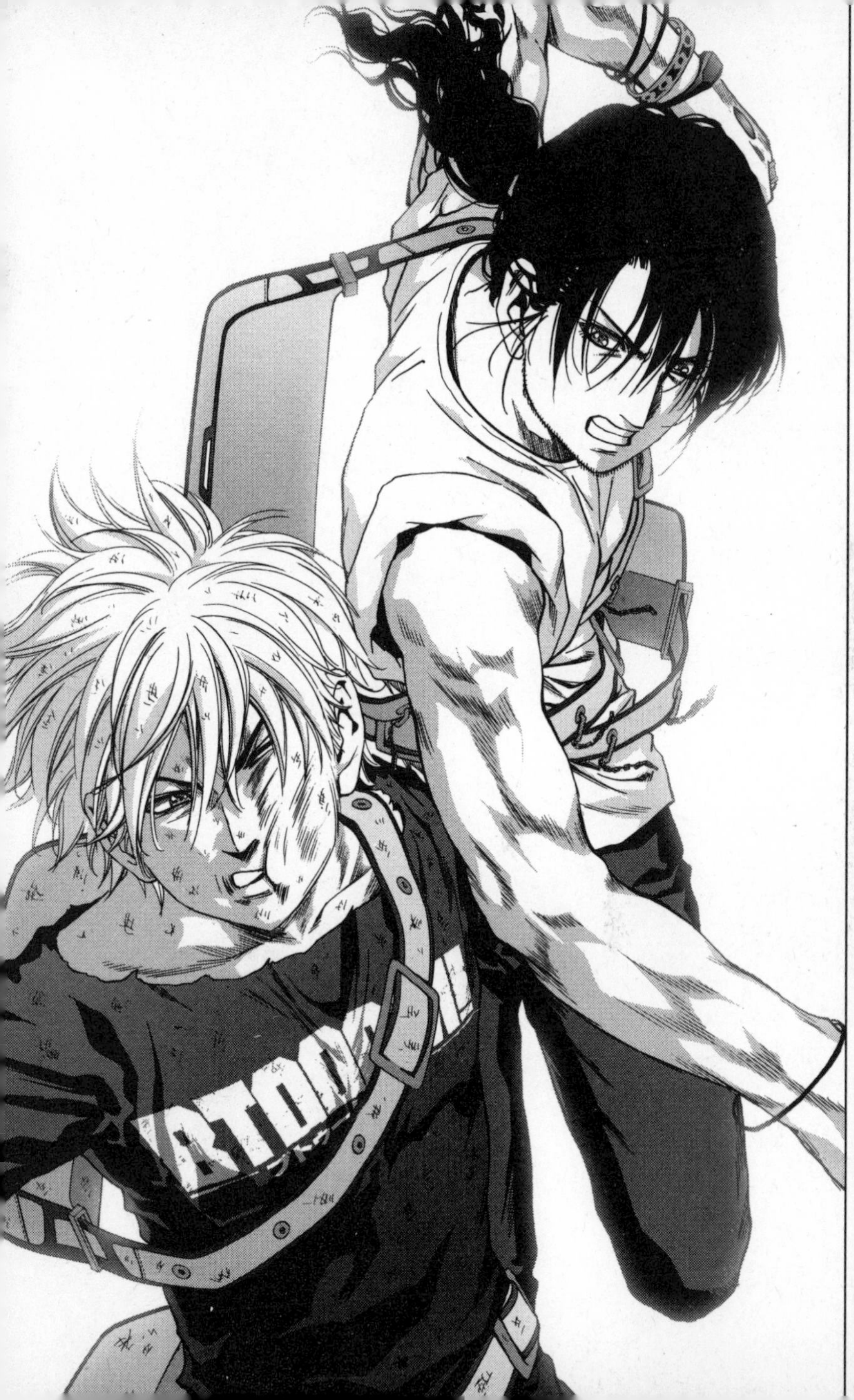

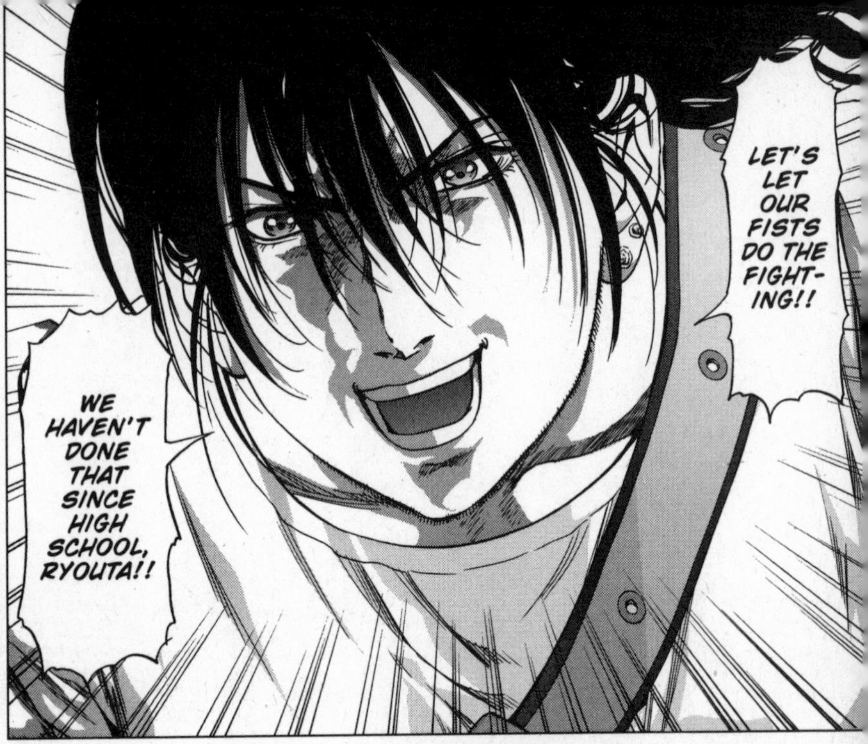
LET'S LET OUR FISTS DO THE FIGHT-ING!!
WE HAVEN'T DONE THAT SINCE HIGH SCHOOL, RYOUTA!!
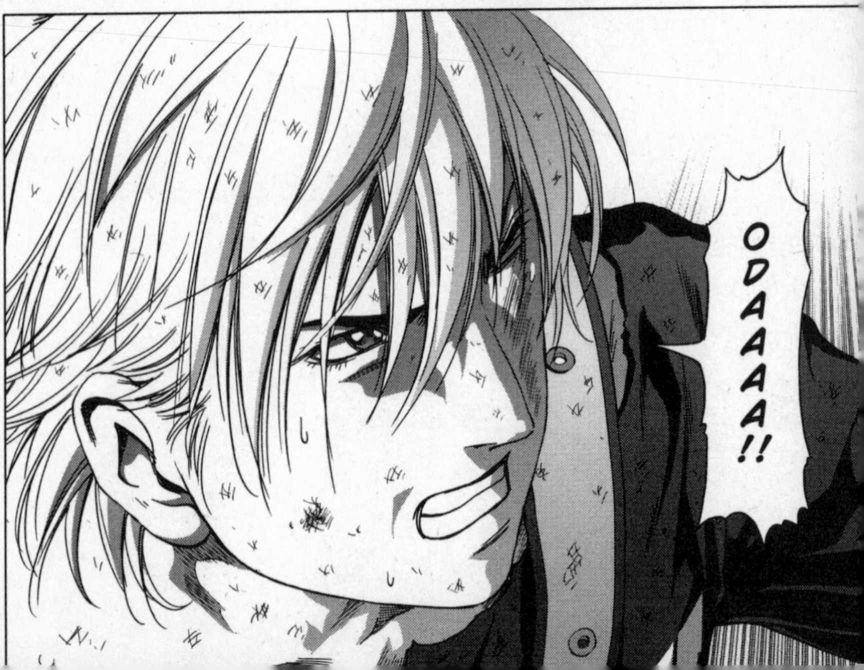
ODAAAAA!!

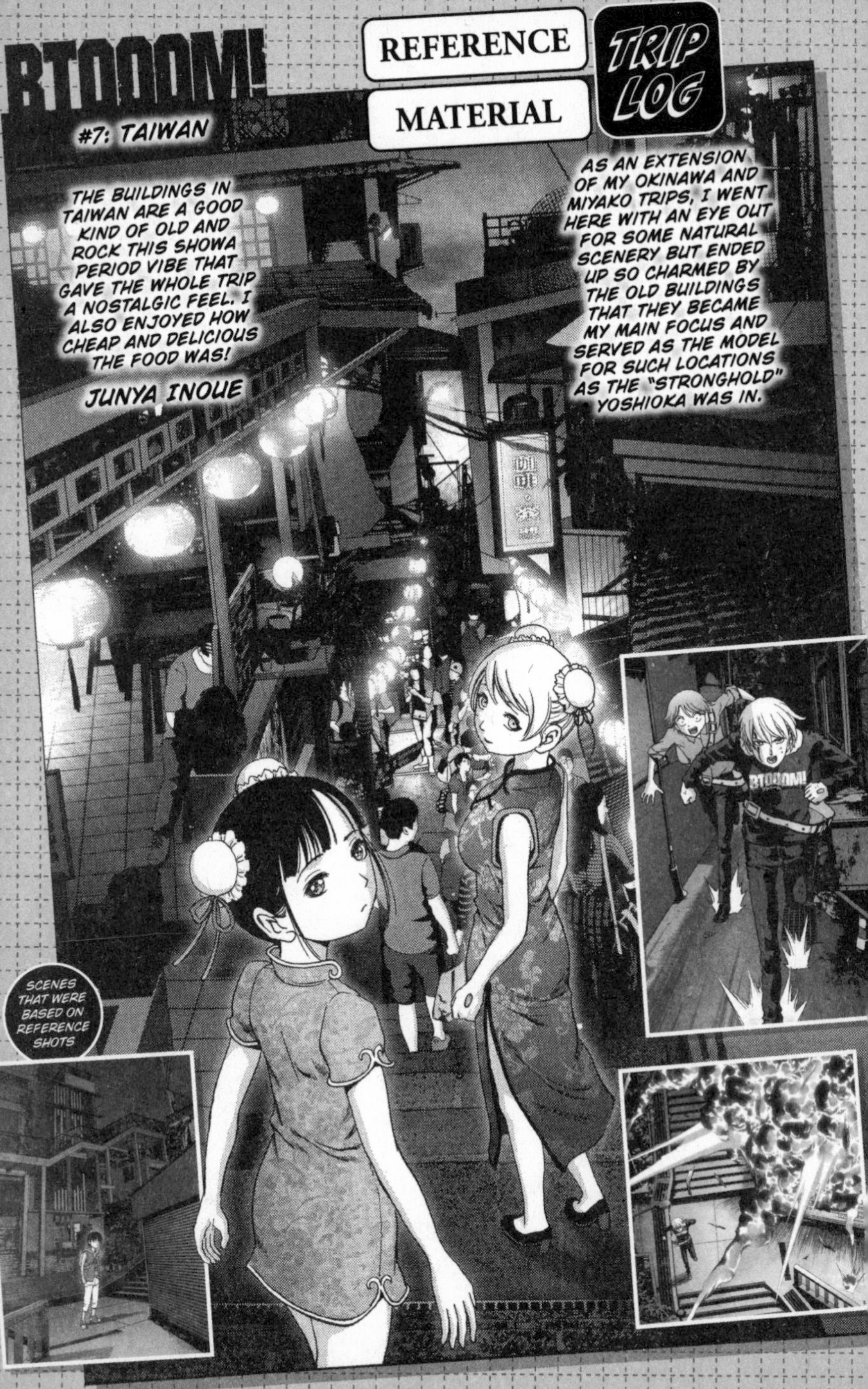
BTOOOM!
REFERENCE
MATERIAL
TRIP LOG
#7: TAIWAN
AS AN EXTENSION OF MY OKINAWA AND MIYAKO TRIPS, I WENT HERE WITH AN EYE OUT FOR SOME NATURAL SCENERY BUT ENDED UP SO CHARMED BY THE OLD BUILDINGS THAT THEY BECAME MY MAIN FOCUS AND SERVED AS THE MODEL FOR SUCH LOCATIONS AS THE "STRONGHOLD" YOSHIOKA WAS IN.
THE BUILDINGS IN TAIWAN ARE A GOOD KIND OF OLD AND ROCK THIS SHOWA PERIOD VIBE THAT GAVE THE WHOLE TRIP A NOSTALGIC FEEL. I ALSO ENJOYED HOW CHEAP AND DELICIOUS THE FOOD WAS!
JUNYA INOUE
BTOOOM!
SCENES THAT WERE BASED ON REFERENCE SHOTS

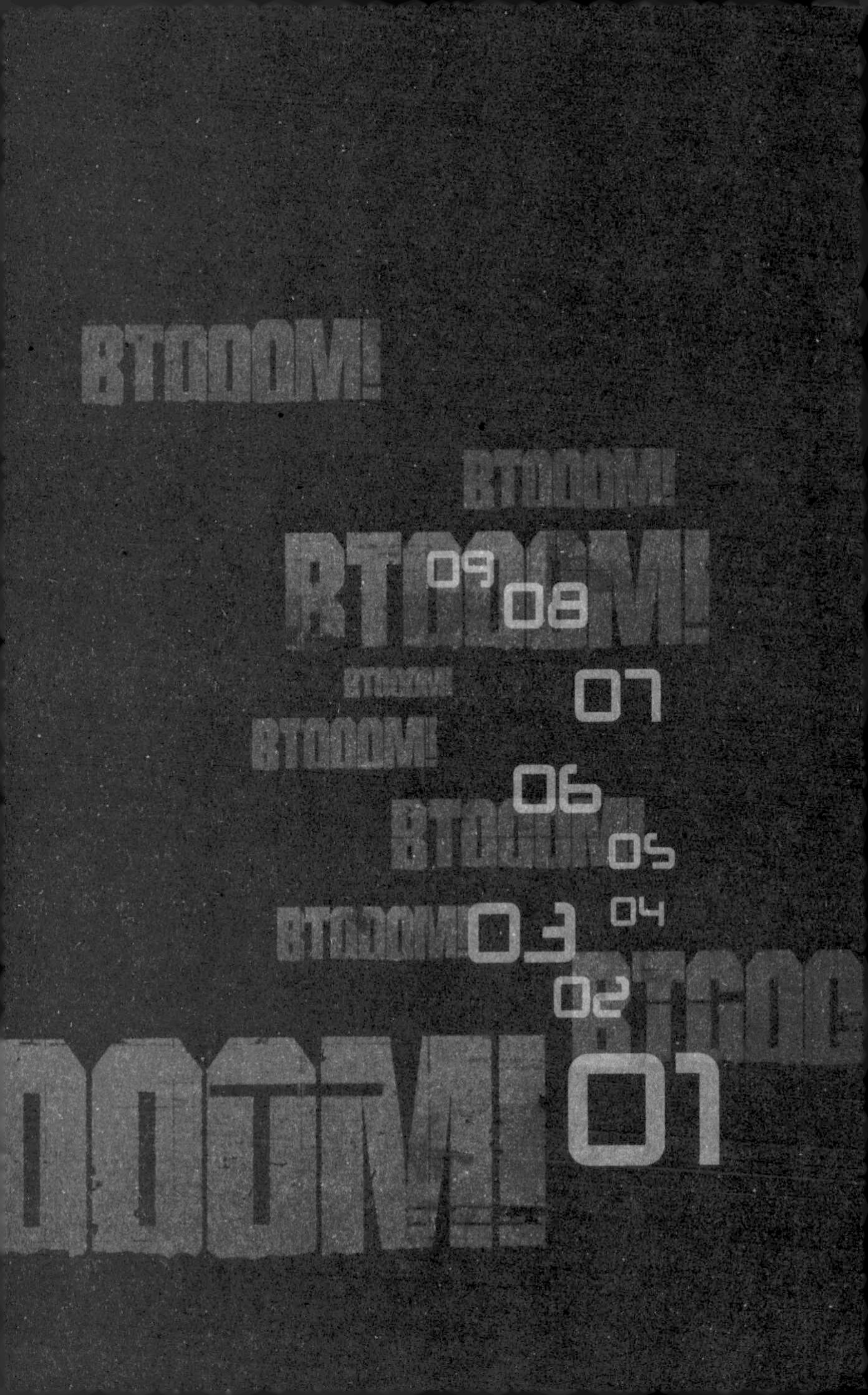
BTOOOM!
09
08
07
06
05
04
03
02
01

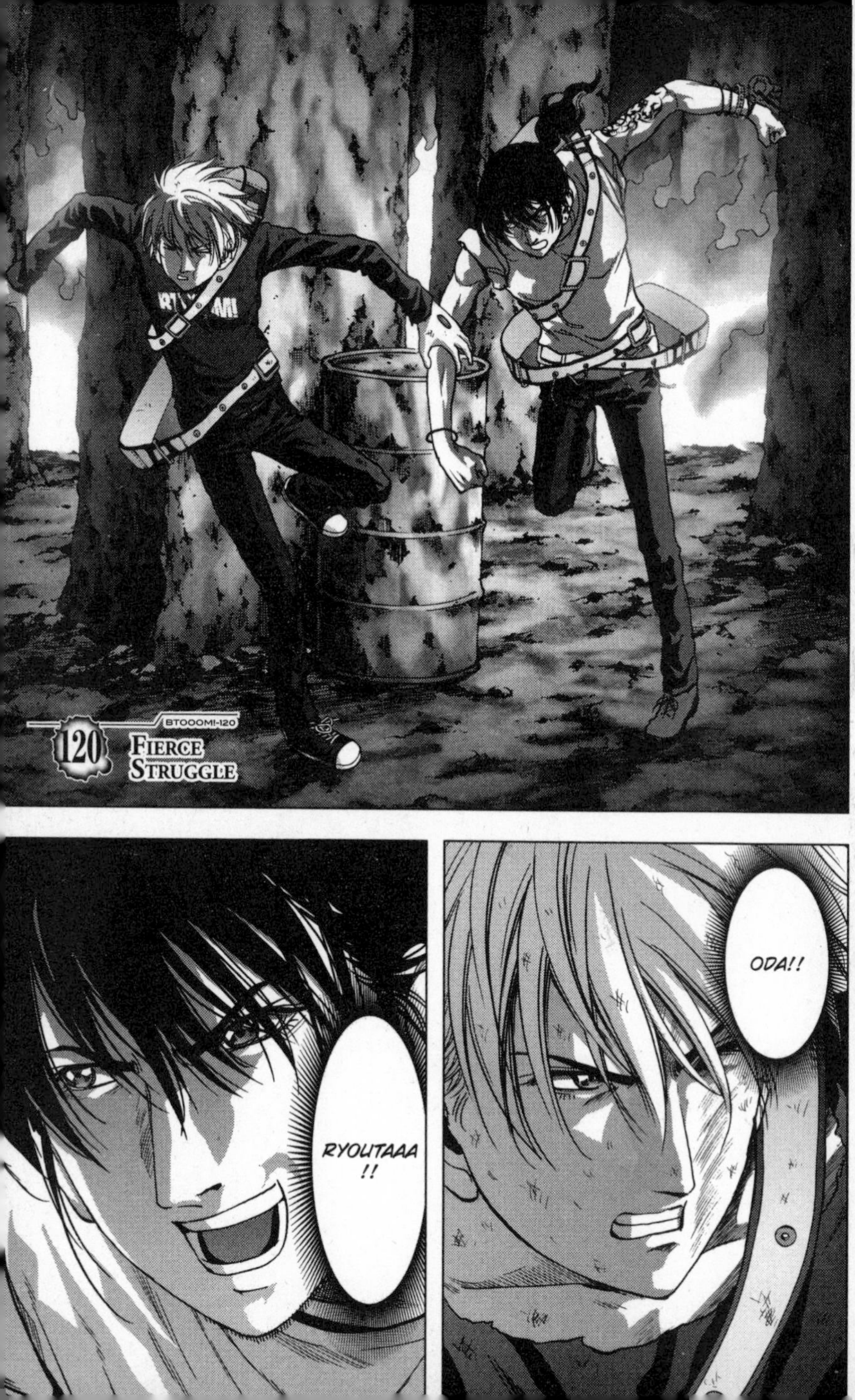
BTOOOM!-120
120
FIERCE STRUGGLE
ODA!!
RYOUTAAA !!

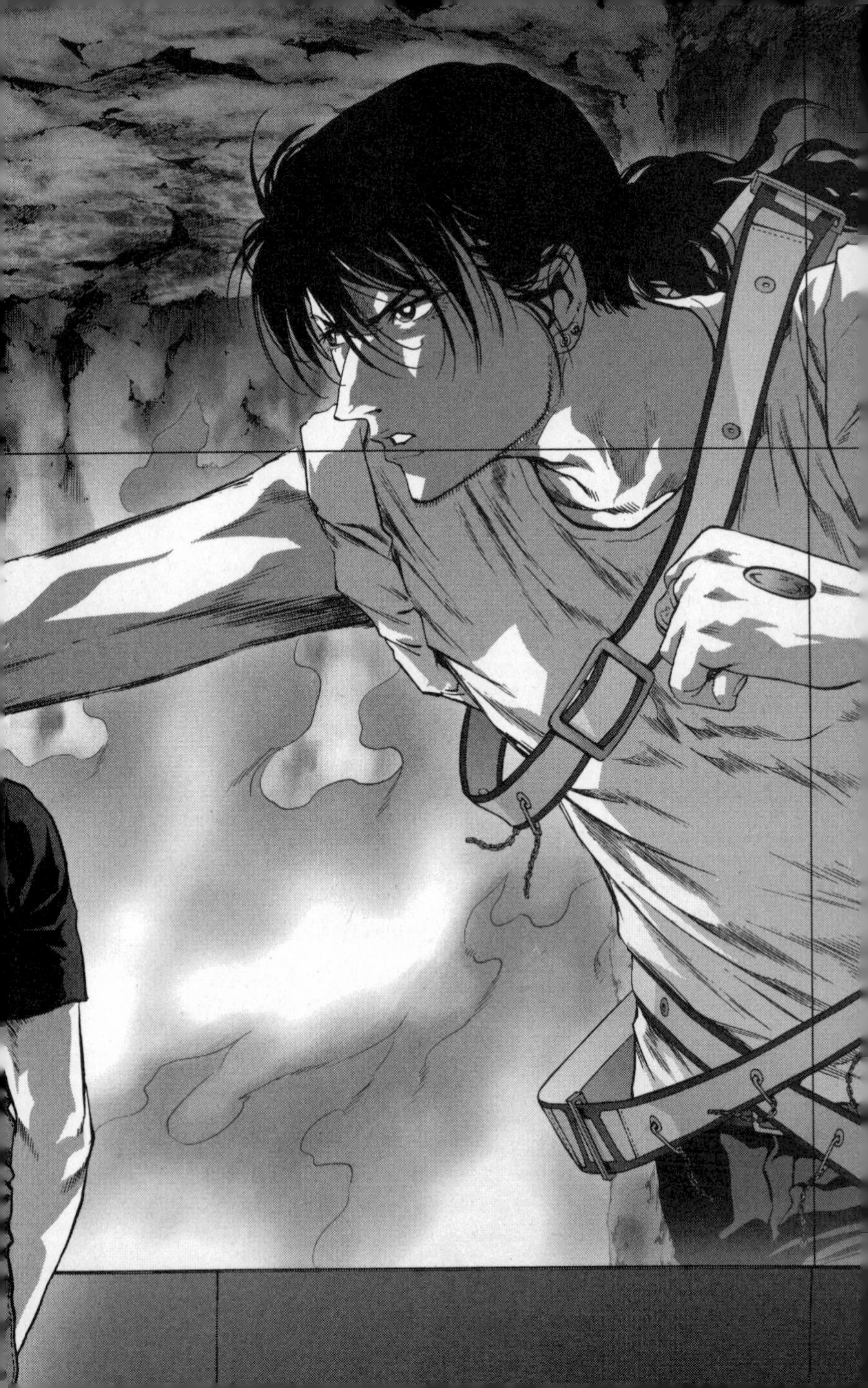

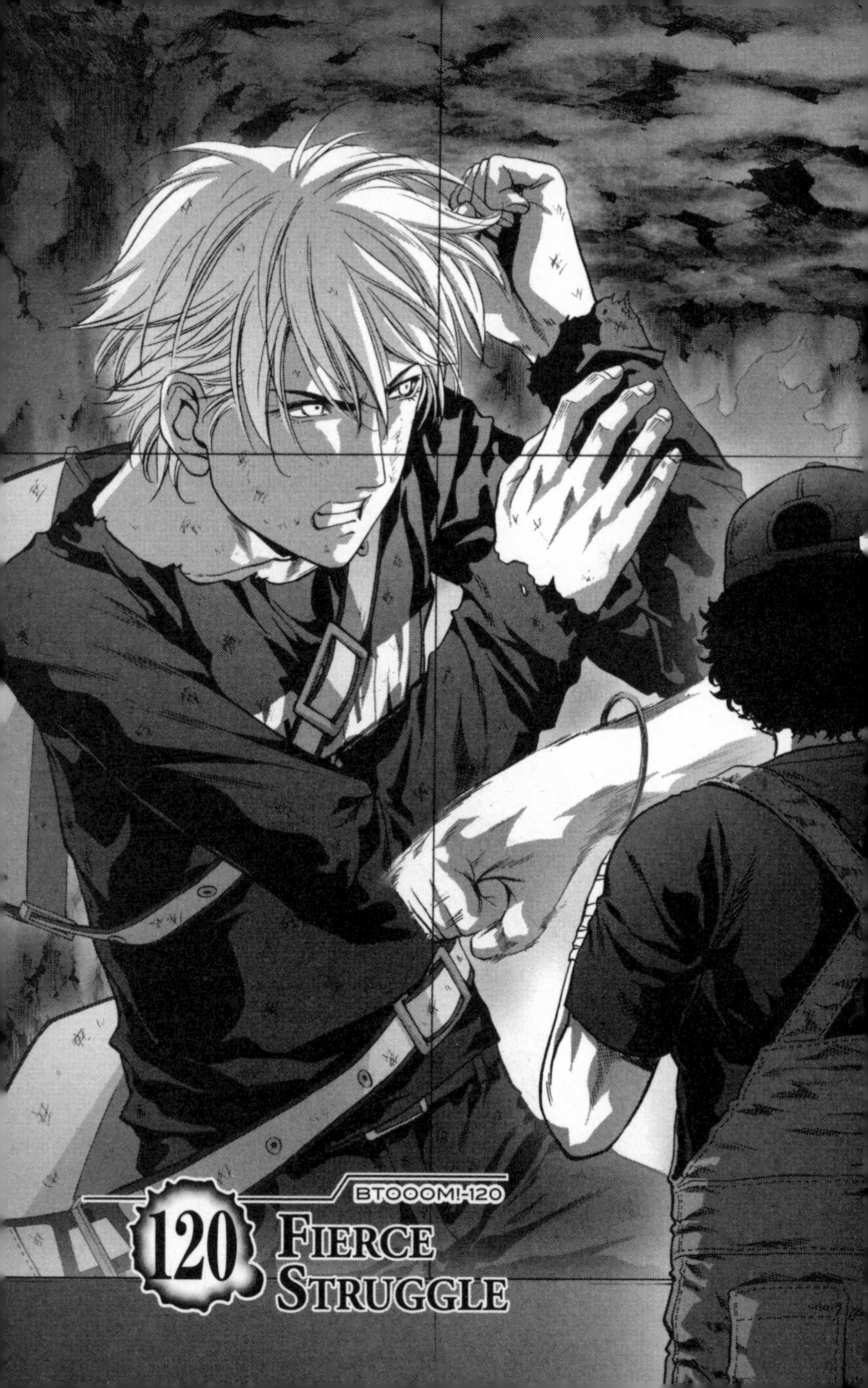
BTOOOM!-120
120
FIERCE
STRUGGLE

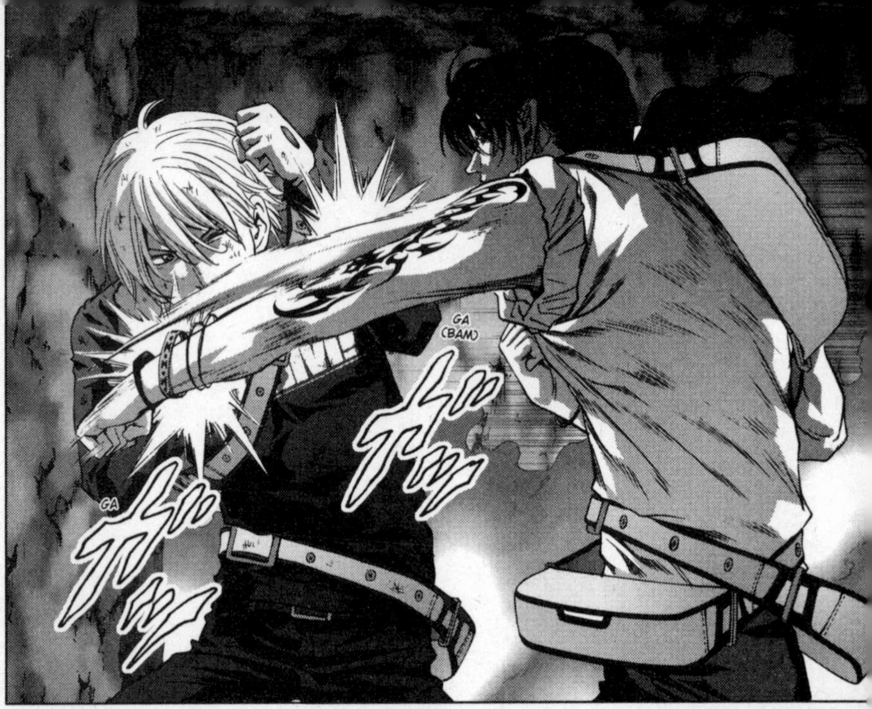
GA (BAM)
ガッ
GA
ガッ
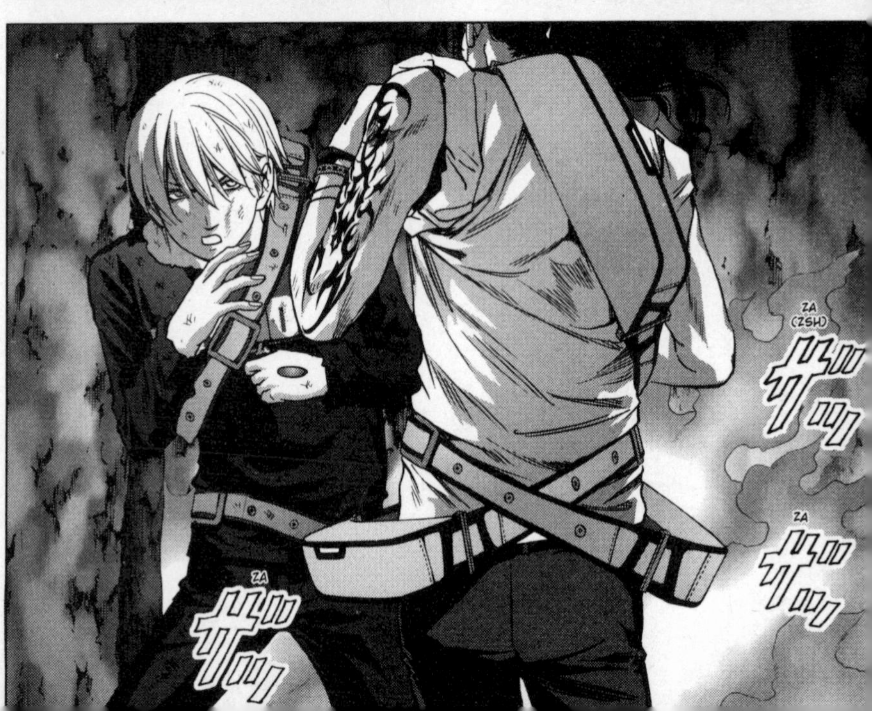
ZA (ZSH)
ザッ
ZA
ザッ
ZA
ザッ

DOGA
(BASH)

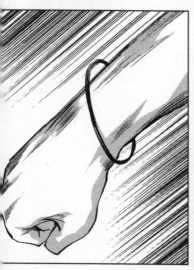

111

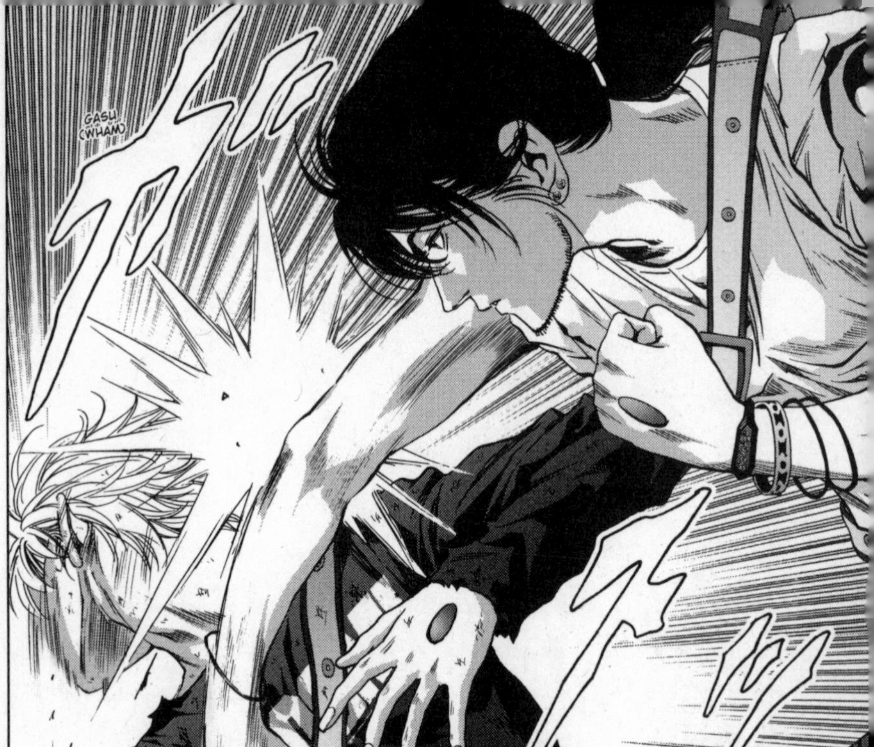
GASU
(WHAM)
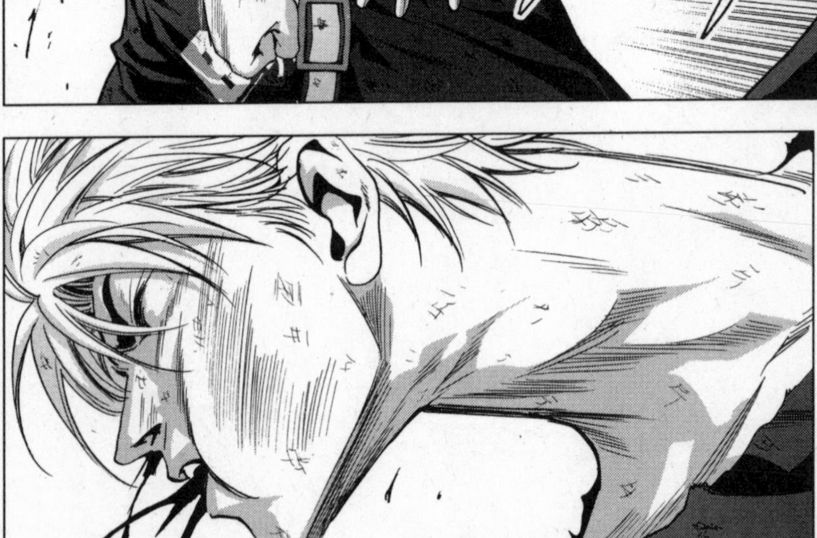

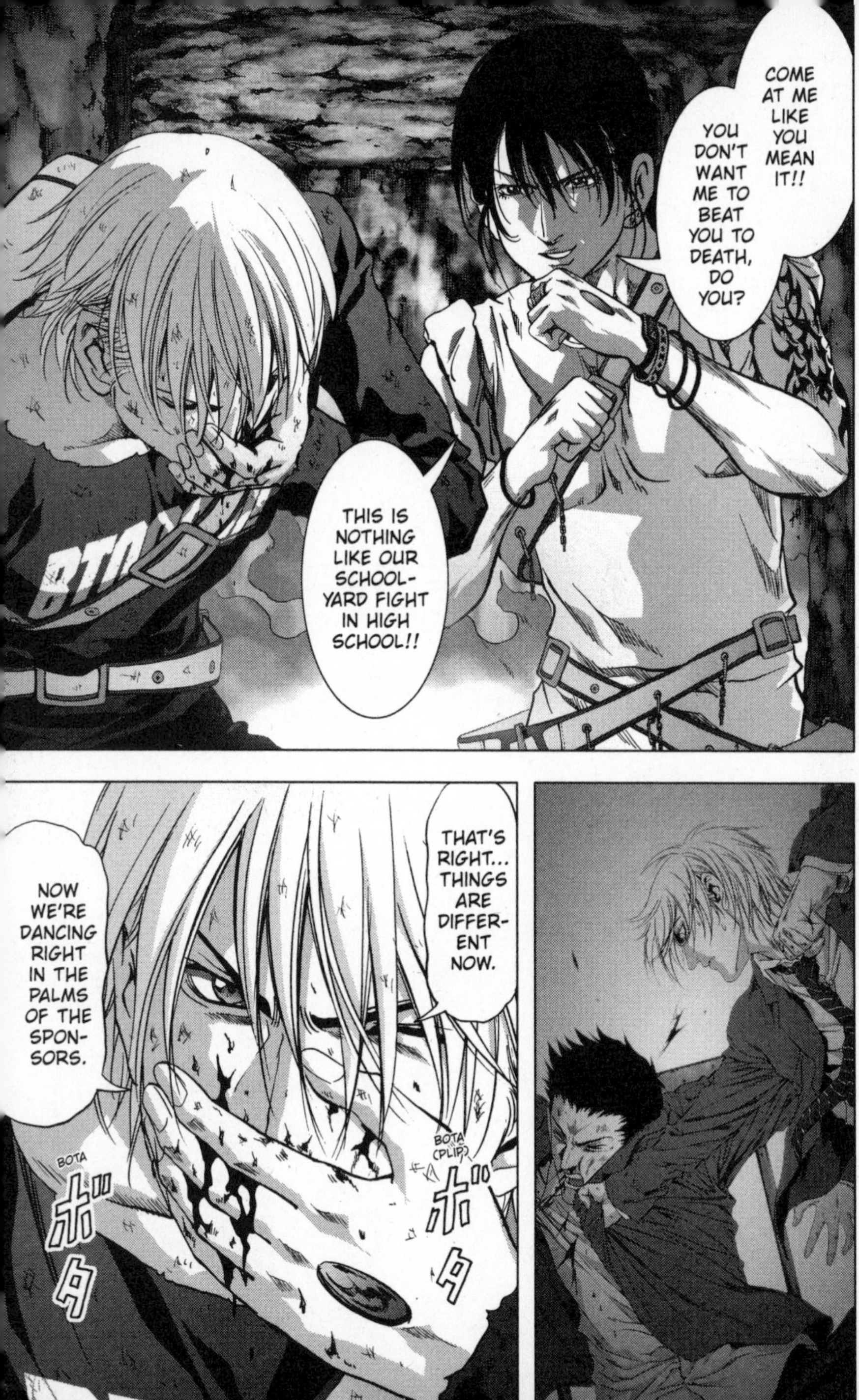
COME AT ME LIKE YOU MEAN IT!!
YOU DON'T WANT ME TO BEAT YOU TO DEATH, DO YOU?
THIS IS NOTHING LIKE OUR SCHOOL-YARD FIGHT IN HIGH SCHOOL!!
THAT'S RIGHT... THINGS ARE DIFFER-ENT NOW.
NOW WE'RE DANCING RIGHT IN THE PALMS OF THE SPON-SORS.
BOTA (PLIP)
ボタ
BOTA
ボタ

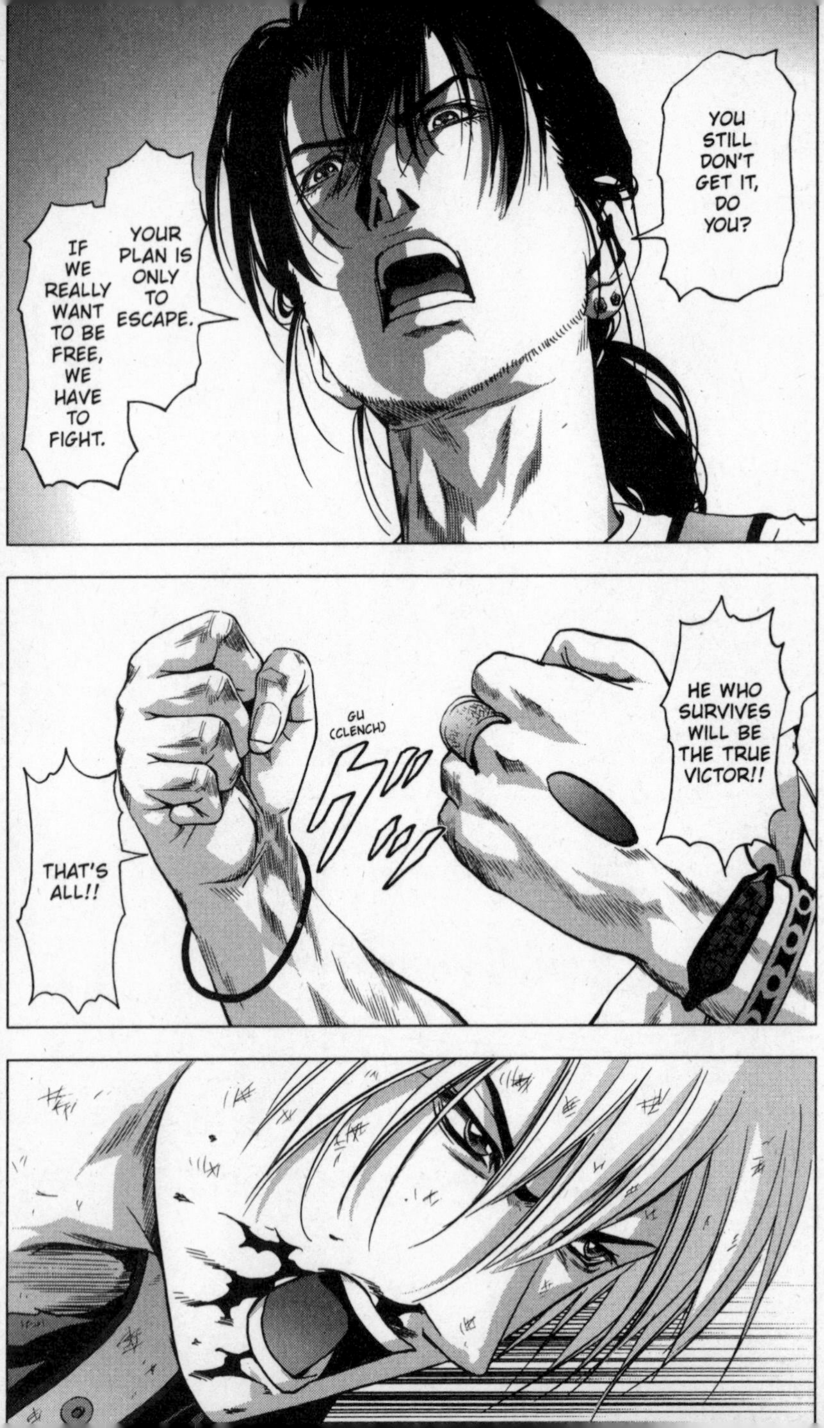
YOU STILL DON'T GET IT, DO YOU?
YOUR PLAN IS ONLY TO ESCAPE.
IF WE REALLY WANT TO BE FREE, WE HAVE TO FIGHT.
HE WHO SURVIVES WILL BE THE TRUE VICTOR!!
GU (CLENCH)
THAT'S ALL!!

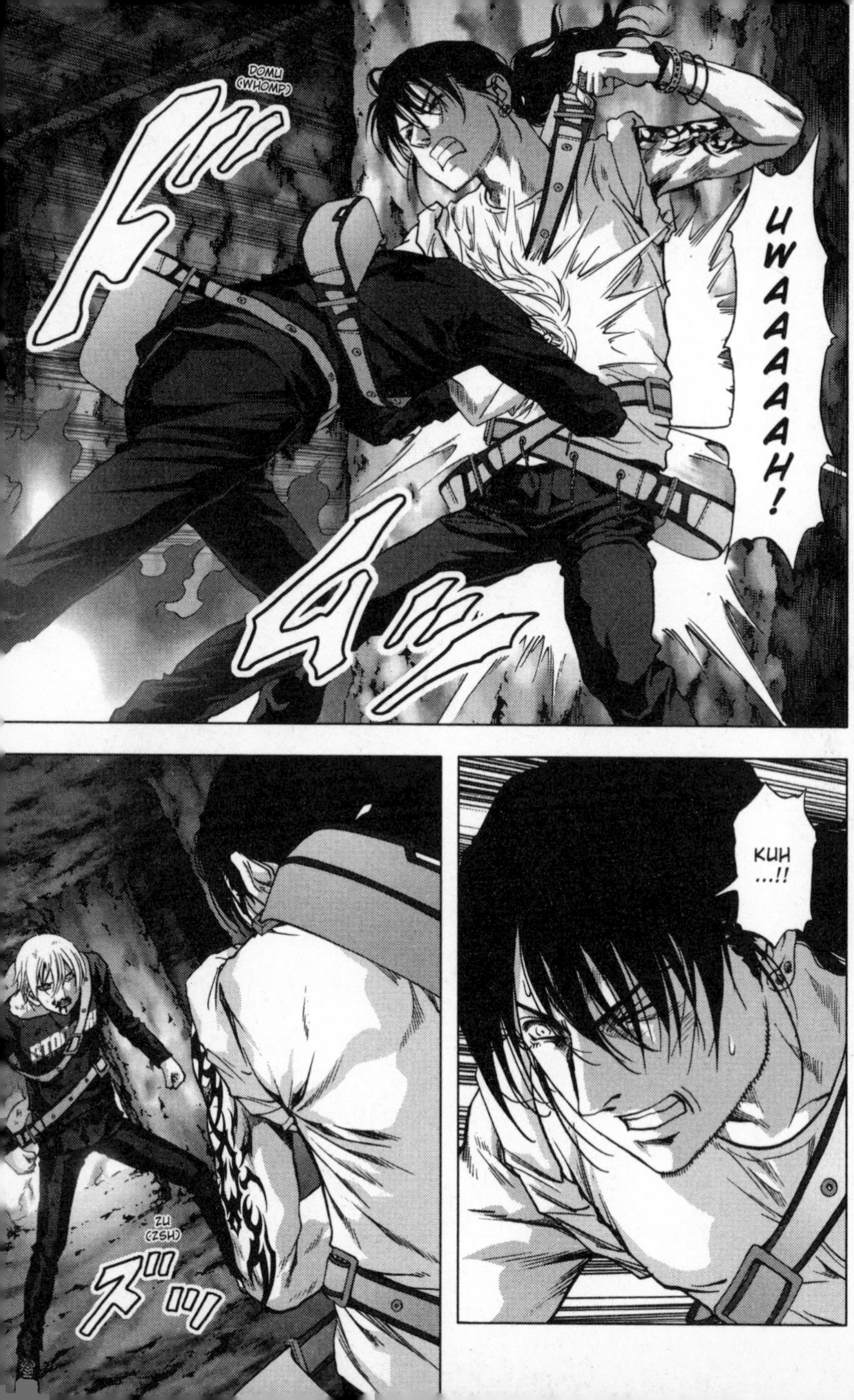
UWAAAAAAH!
DOMU (WHOMP)
KUH ...!!
ZU (ZSH)

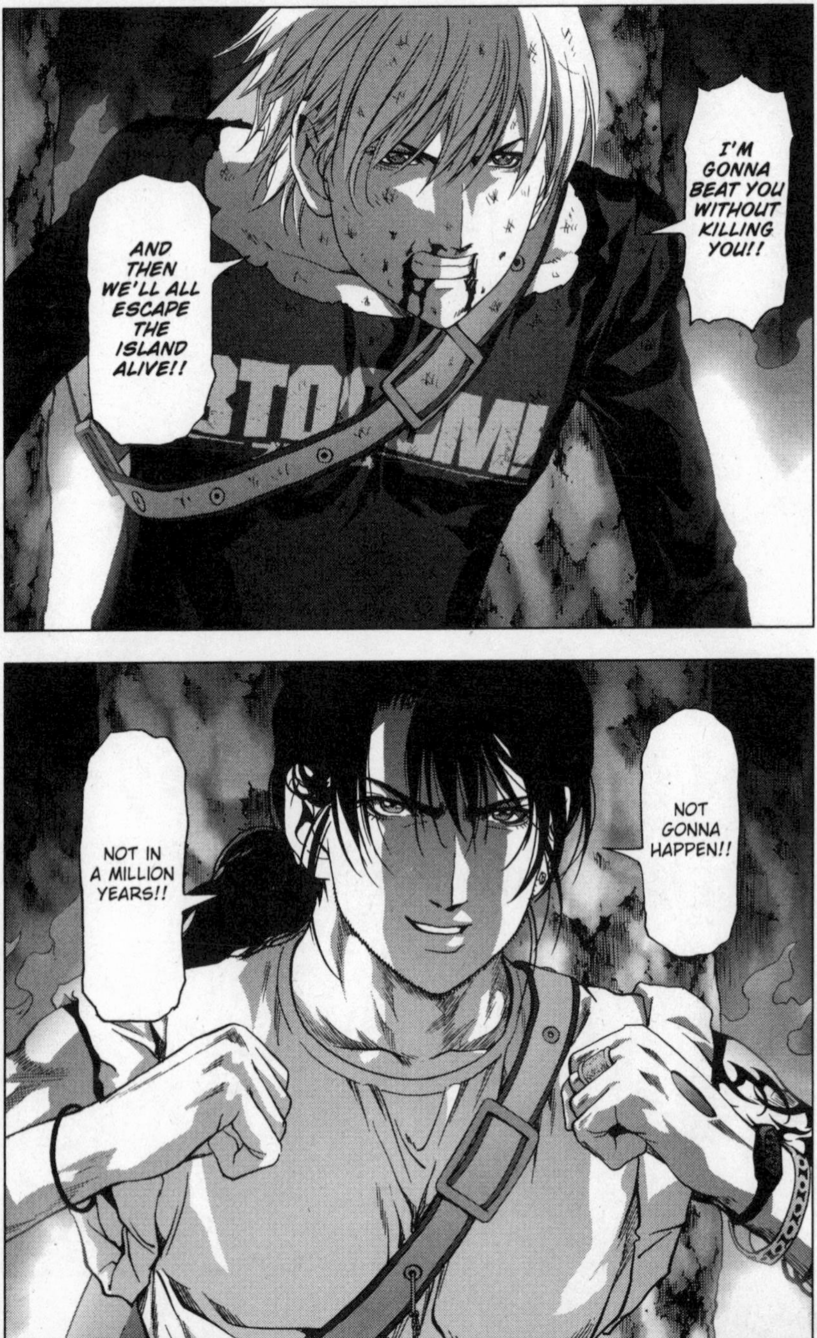
I'M GONNA BEAT YOU WITHOUT KILLING YOU!!
AND THEN WE'LL ALL ESCAPE THE ISLAND ALIVE!!
NOT GONNA HAPPEN!!
NOT IN A MILLION YEARS!!

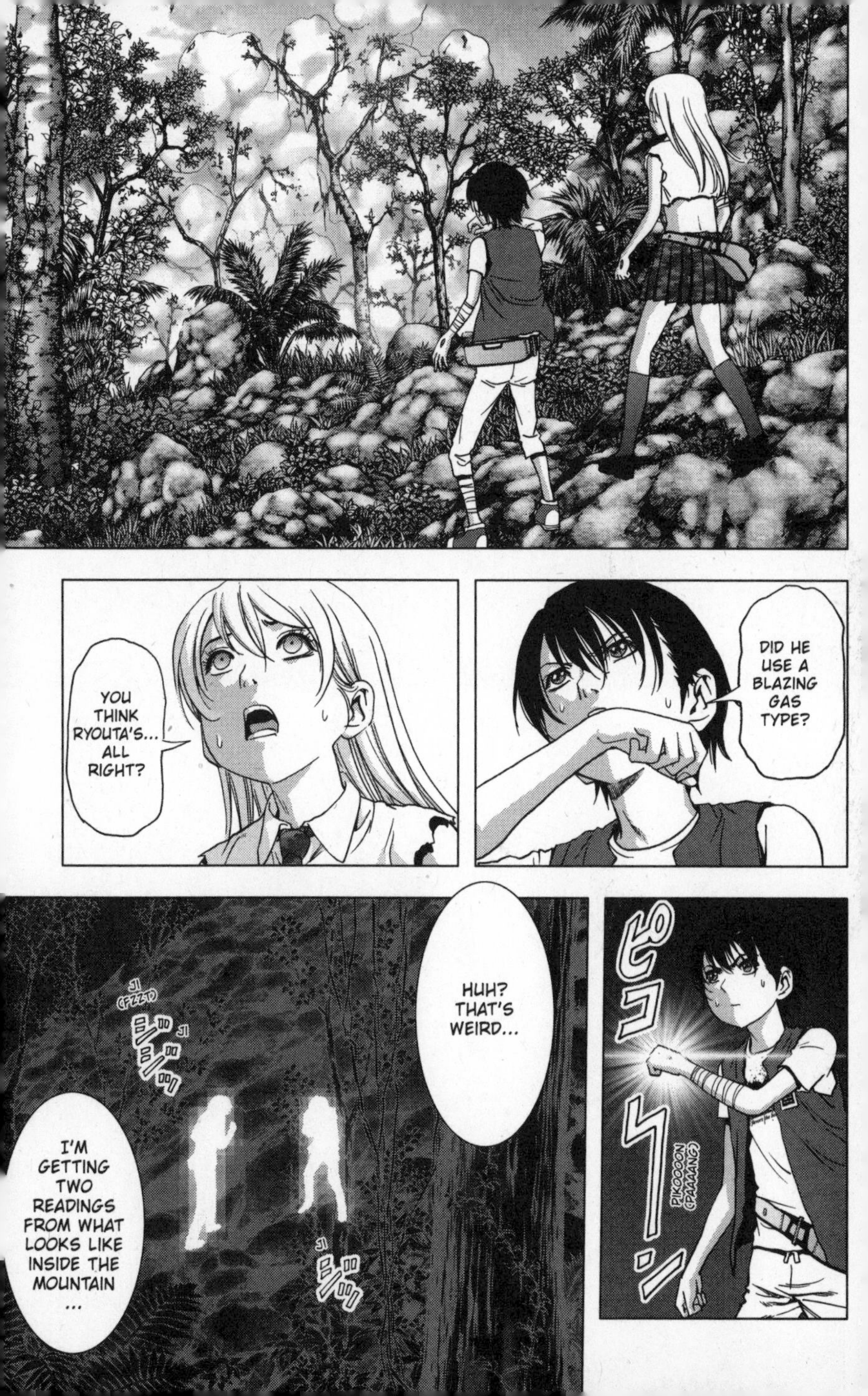

DID HE USE A BLAZING GAS TYPE?
YOU THINK RYOUTA'S... ALL RIGHT?
PIKOOOON (PAAAANG)
HUH? THAT'S WEIRD...
JI (FZZT)
JI
I'M GETTING TWO READINGS FROM WHAT LOOKS LIKE INSIDE THE MOUNTAIN ...
JI

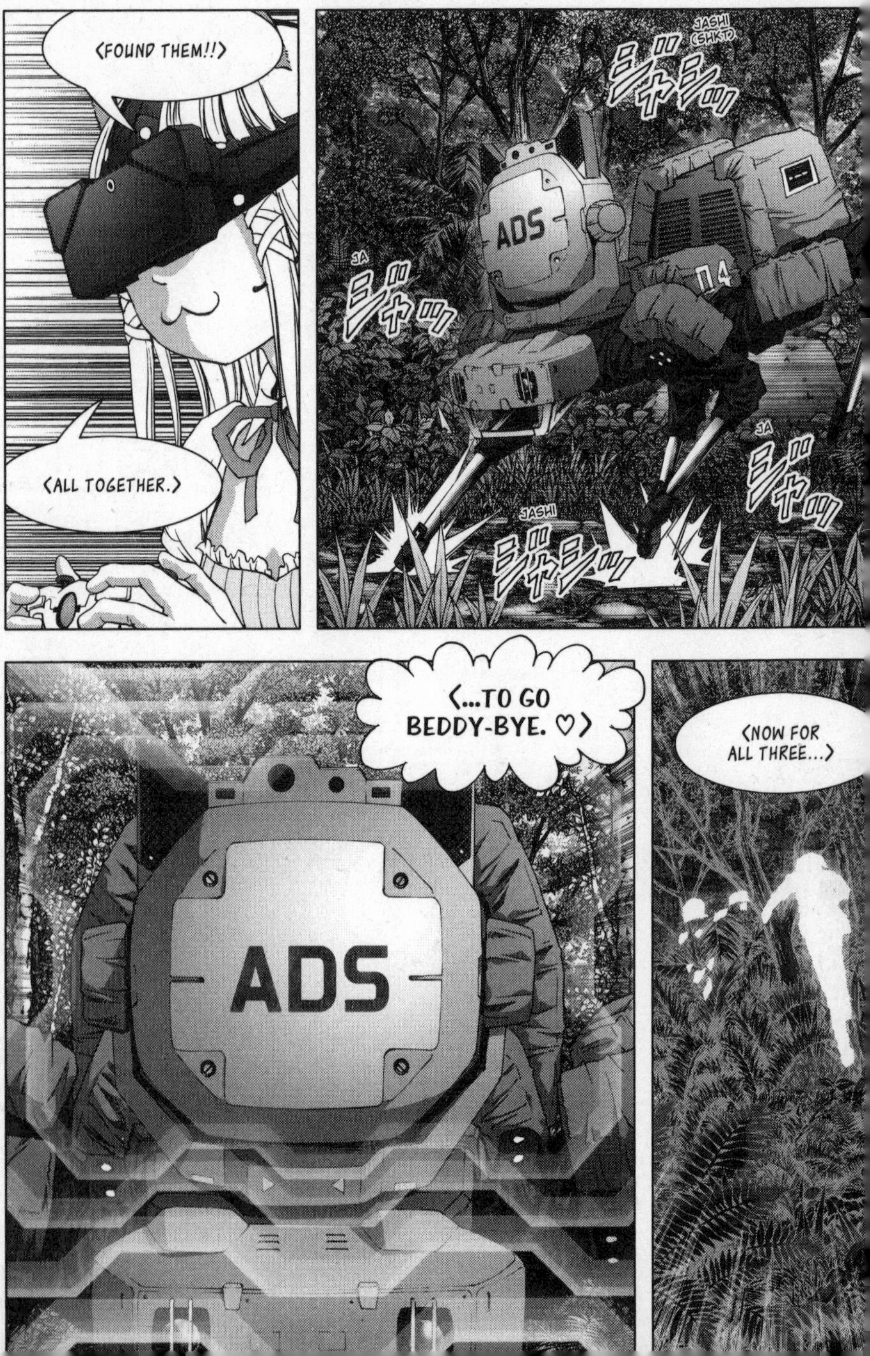
JASHI (SHKT)
JA
JA
JASHI
〈FOUND THEM!!〉
〈ALL TOGETHER.〉
〈NOW FOR ALL THREE...〉
〈...TO GO BEDDY-BYE. ♡〉

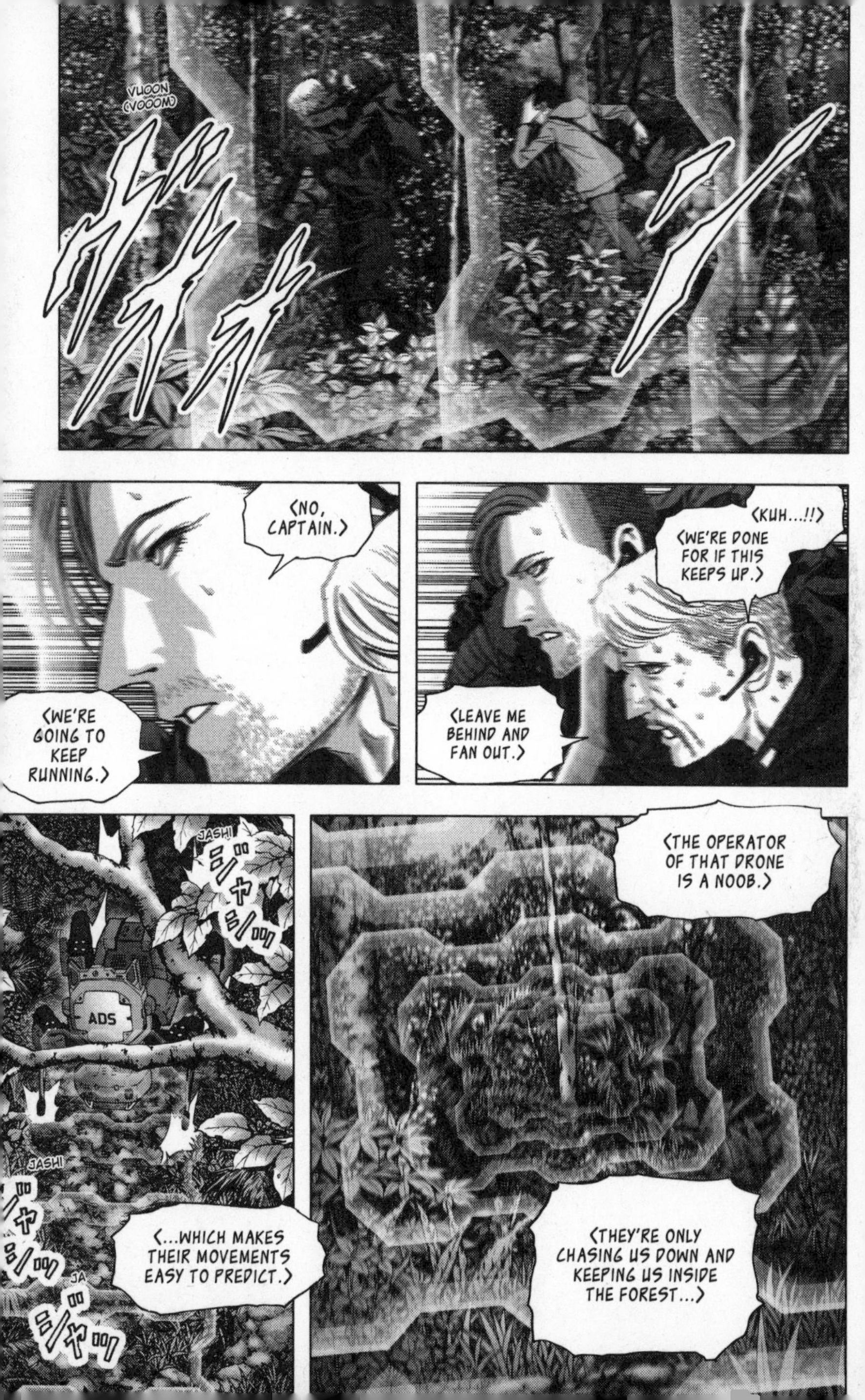

VUOON (VOOOM)
‹KUH...!!›
‹WE'RE DONE FOR IF THIS KEEPS UP.›
‹LEAVE ME BEHIND AND FAN OUT.›
‹NO, CAPTAIN.›
‹WE'RE GOING TO KEEP RUNNING.›
‹THE OPERATOR OF THAT DRONE IS A NOOB.›
‹THEY'RE ONLY CHASING US DOWN AND KEEPING US INSIDE THE FOREST...›
JASH!
ADS
JASH!
JA
‹...WHICH MAKES THEIR MOVEMENTS EASY TO PREDICT.›

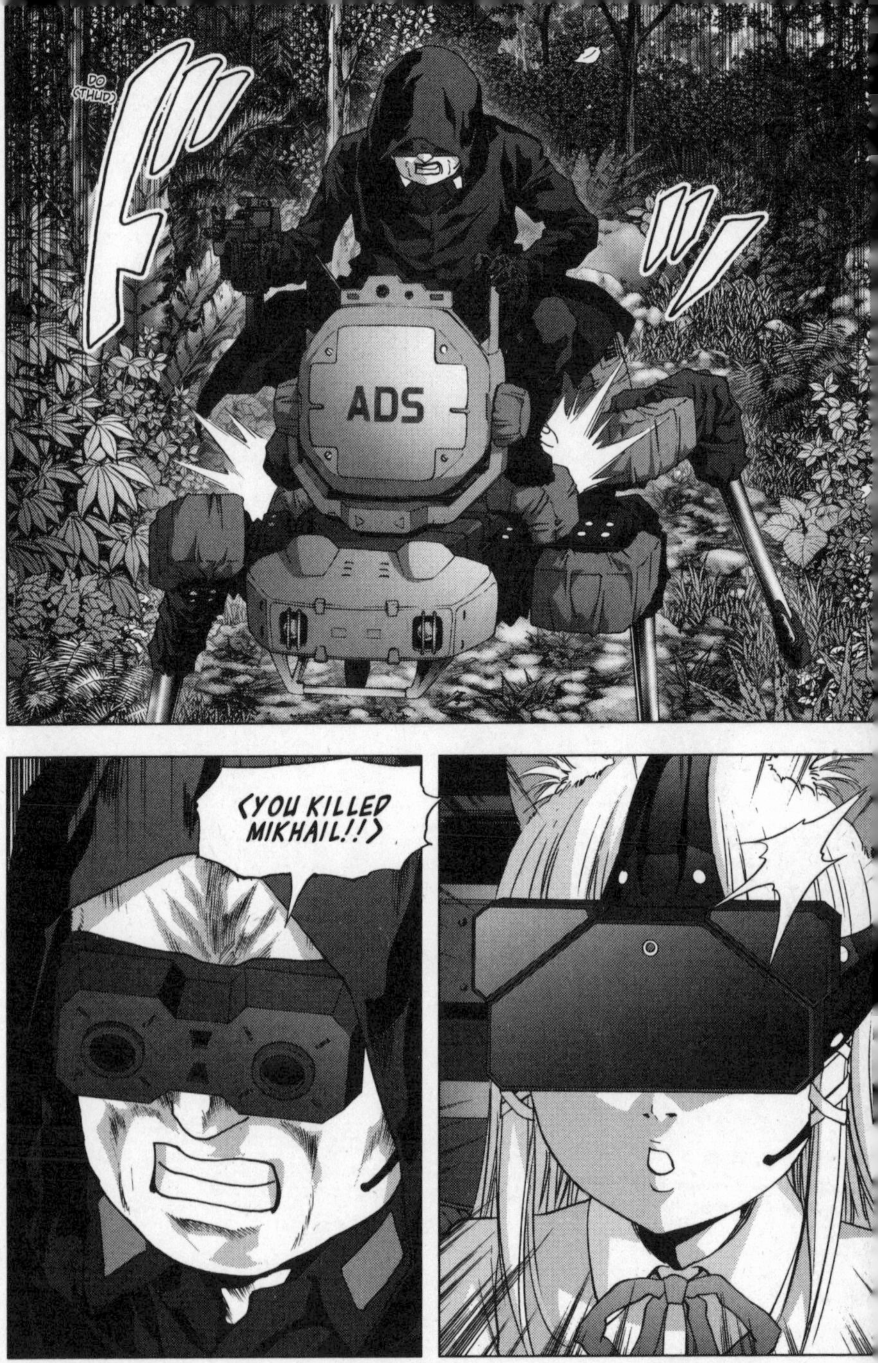
DO (THUD)
〈YOU KILLED MIKHAIL!!〉

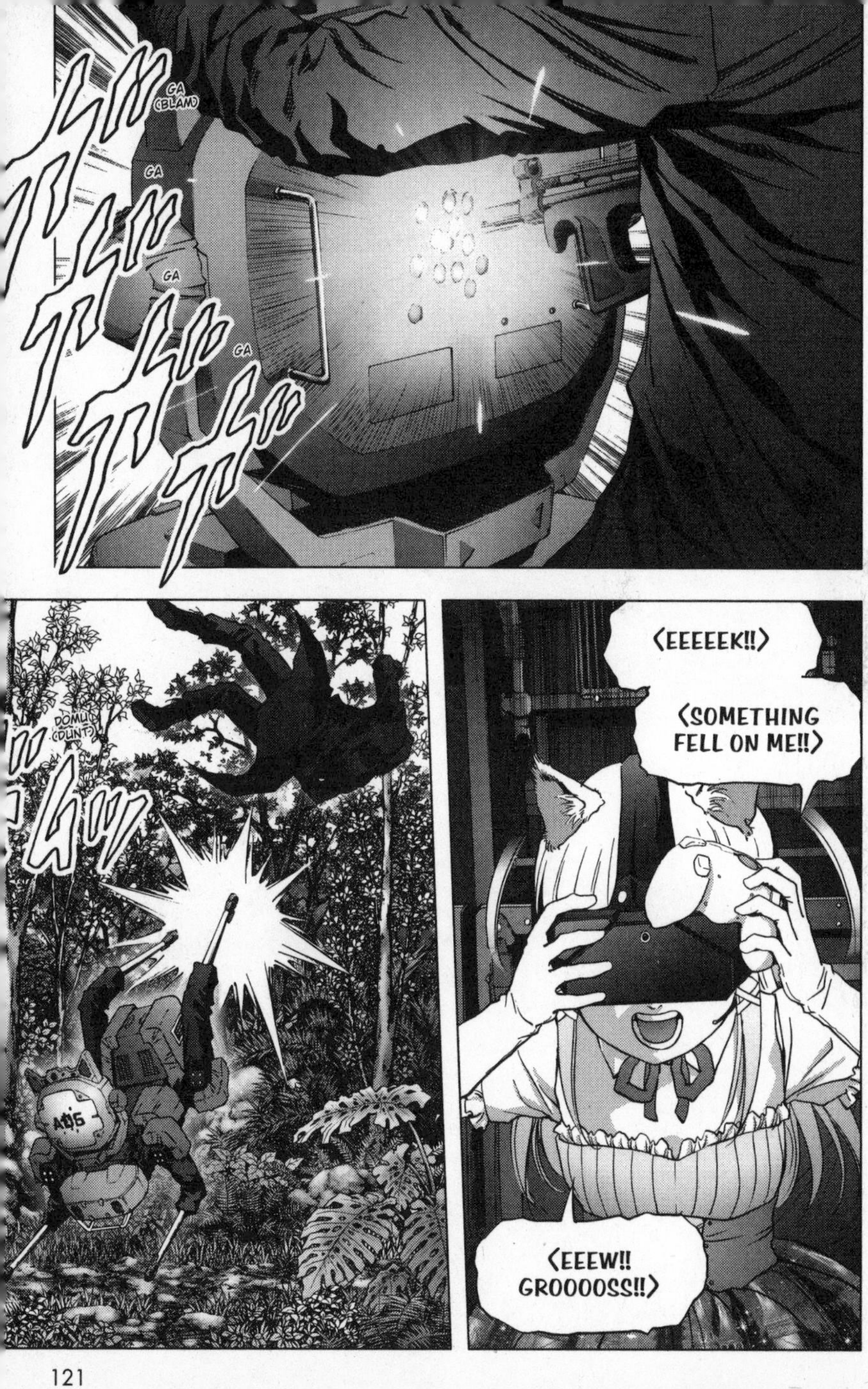
GA (BLAM)
GA
GA
GA
<EEEEEK!!>
<SOMETHING FELL ON ME!!>
<EEEW!! GROOOOSS!!>
DOMU (DUNT)

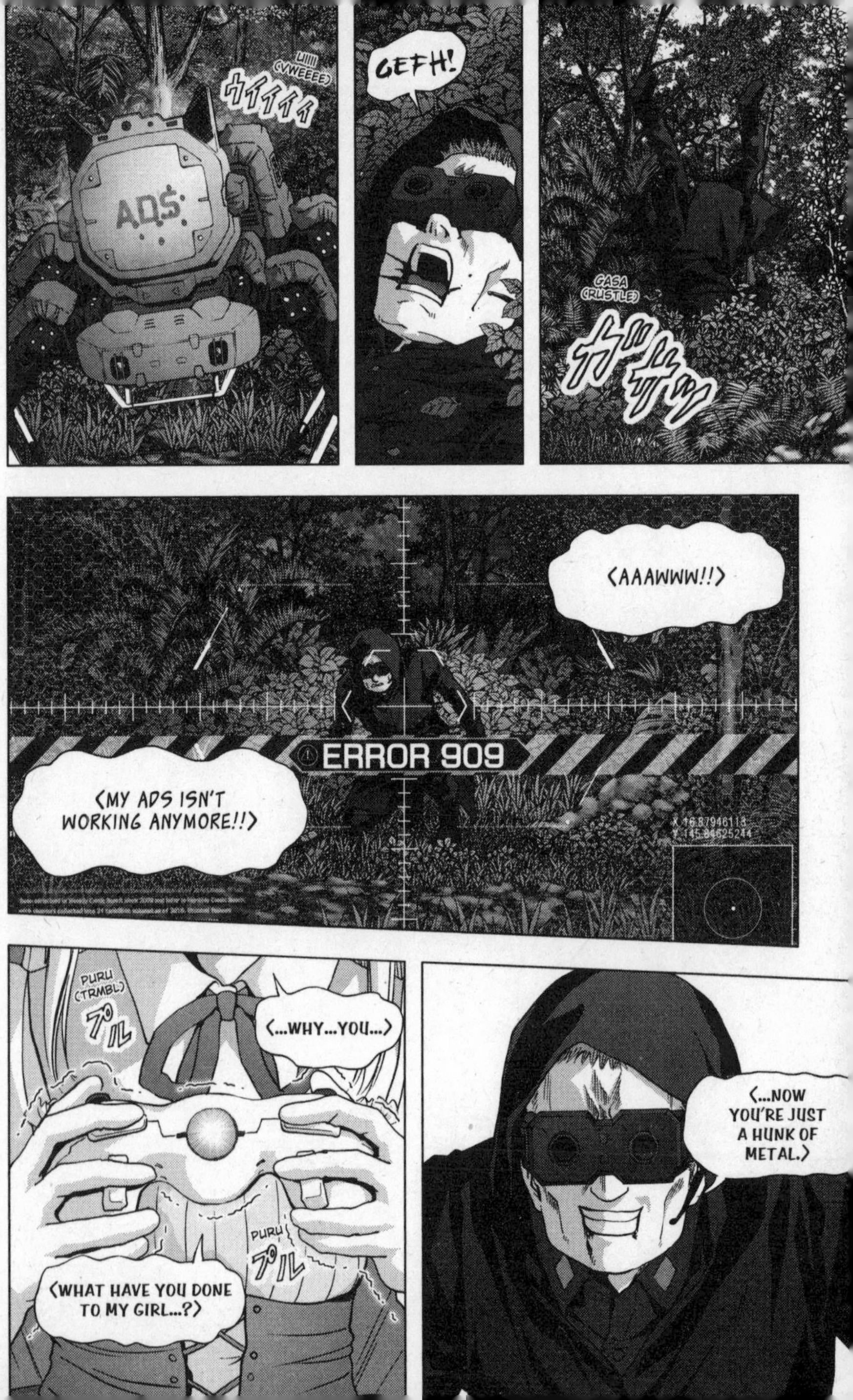
GASA (RUSTLE)
ガサッ
GEFH!
UIIII (VWEEEE)
ウィィィィ
<AAAWWW!!>
ERROR 909
<MY ADS ISN'T WORKING ANYMORE!!>
<...NOW YOU'RE JUST A HUNK OF METAL.>
PURU (TRMBL)
プル
<...WHY...YOU...>
PURU
プル
<WHAT HAVE YOU DONE TO MY GIRL...?>

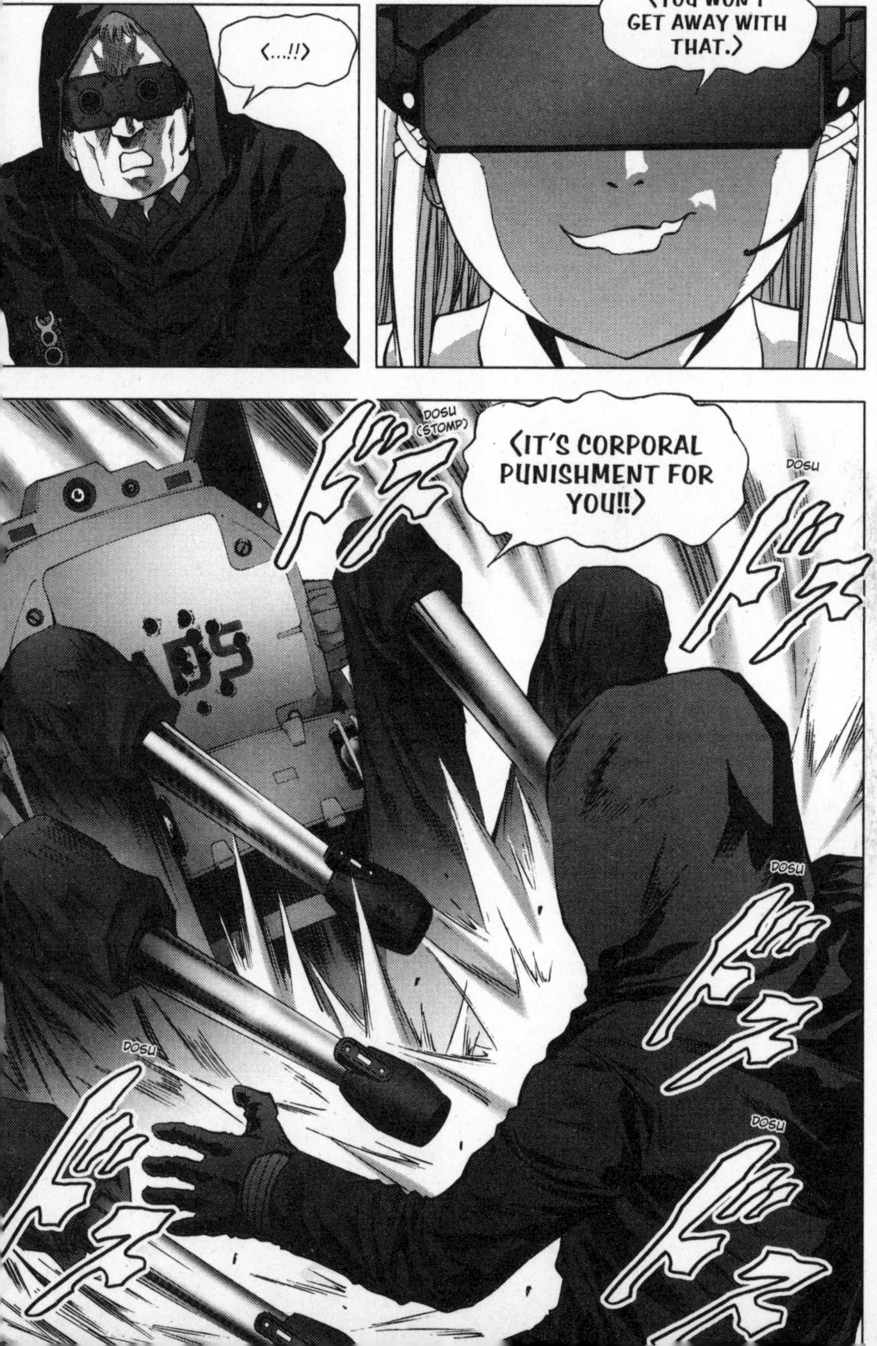
<YOU WON'T GET AWAY WITH THAT.>
<...!!>
<IT'S CORPORAL PUNISHMENT FOR YOU!!>
DOSU
DOSU (STOMP)
DOSU
DOSU
DOSU

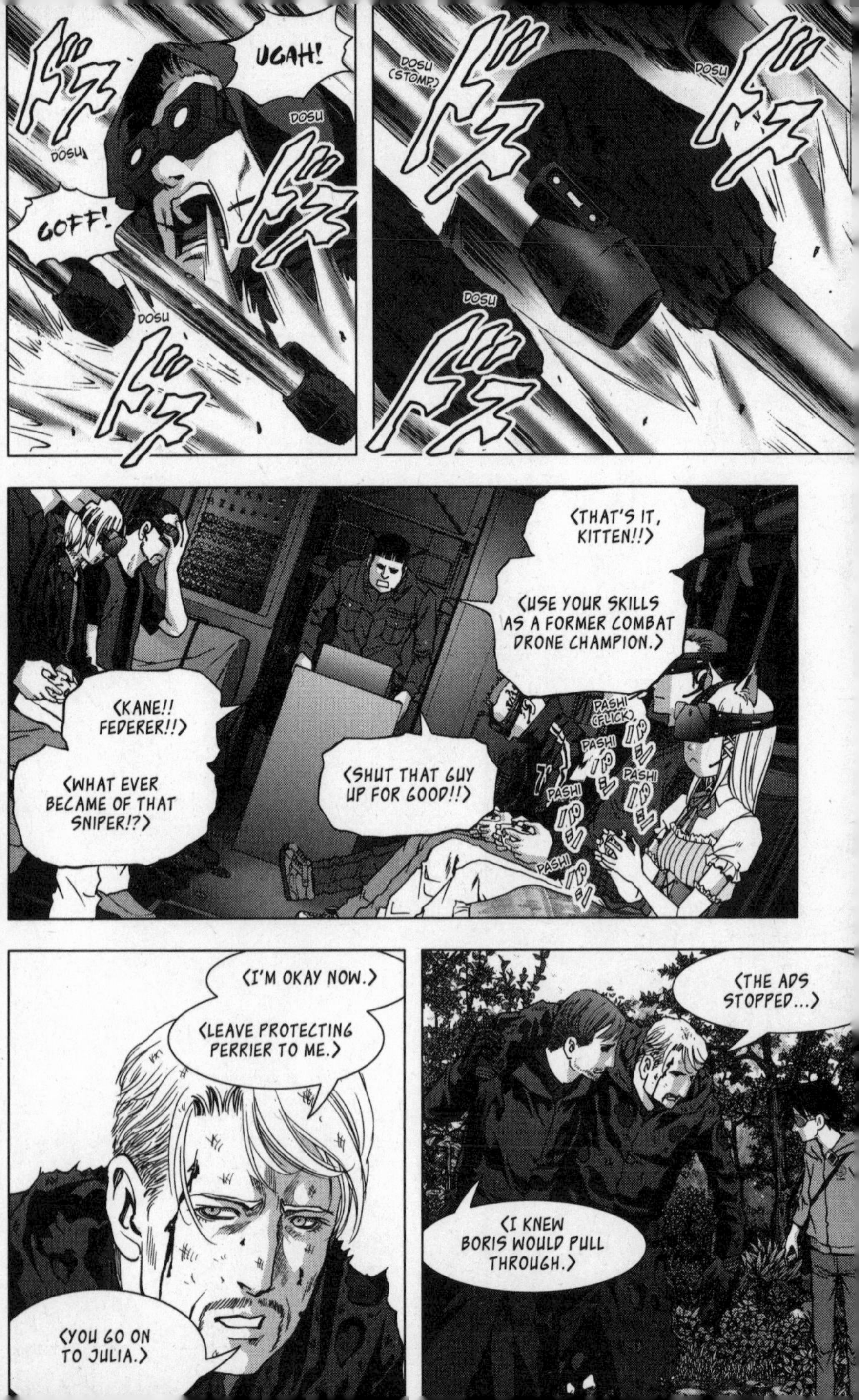
DOSU (STOMP)
DOSU
DOSU
UGAH!
DOSU
DOSU
GOFF!
DOSU
<THAT'S IT, KITTEN!!>
<USE YOUR SKILLS AS A FORMER COMBAT DRONE CHAMPION.>
PASHI (FLICK)
PASHI
PASHI
PASHI
PASHI
<SHUT THAT GUY UP FOR GOOD!!>
<KANE!! FEDERER!!>
<WHAT EVER BECAME OF THAT SNIPER!?>
<THE ADS STOPPED...>
<I KNEW BORIS WOULD PULL THROUGH.>
<I'M OKAY NOW.>
<LEAVE PROTECTING PERRIER TO ME.>
<YOU GO ON TO JULIA.>

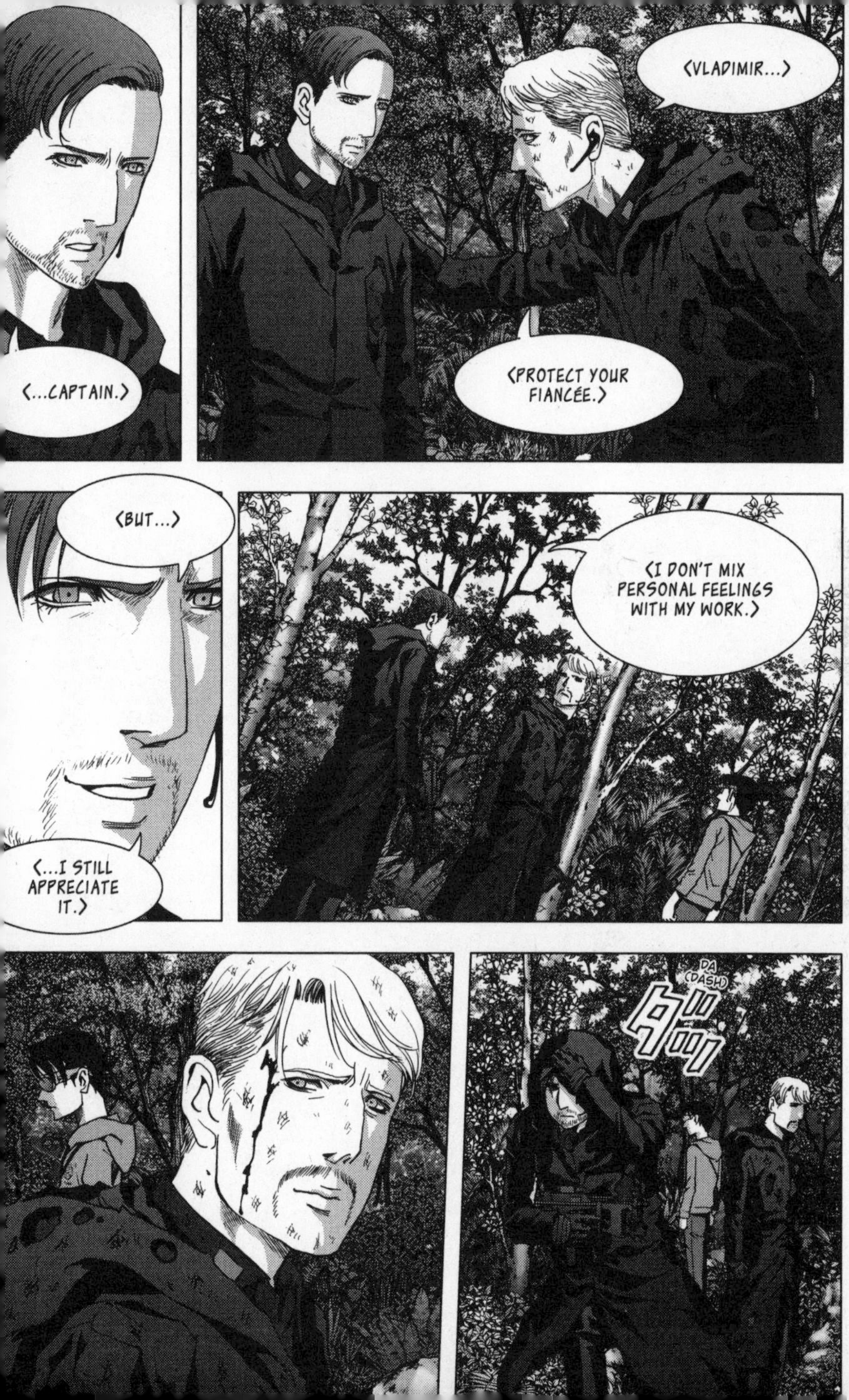
⟨VLADIMIR...⟩
⟨PROTECT YOUR FIANCÉE.⟩
⟨...CAPTAIN.⟩
⟨I DON'T MIX PERSONAL FEELINGS WITH MY WORK.⟩
⟨BUT...⟩
⟨...I STILL APPRECIATE IT.⟩
DA (DASH)

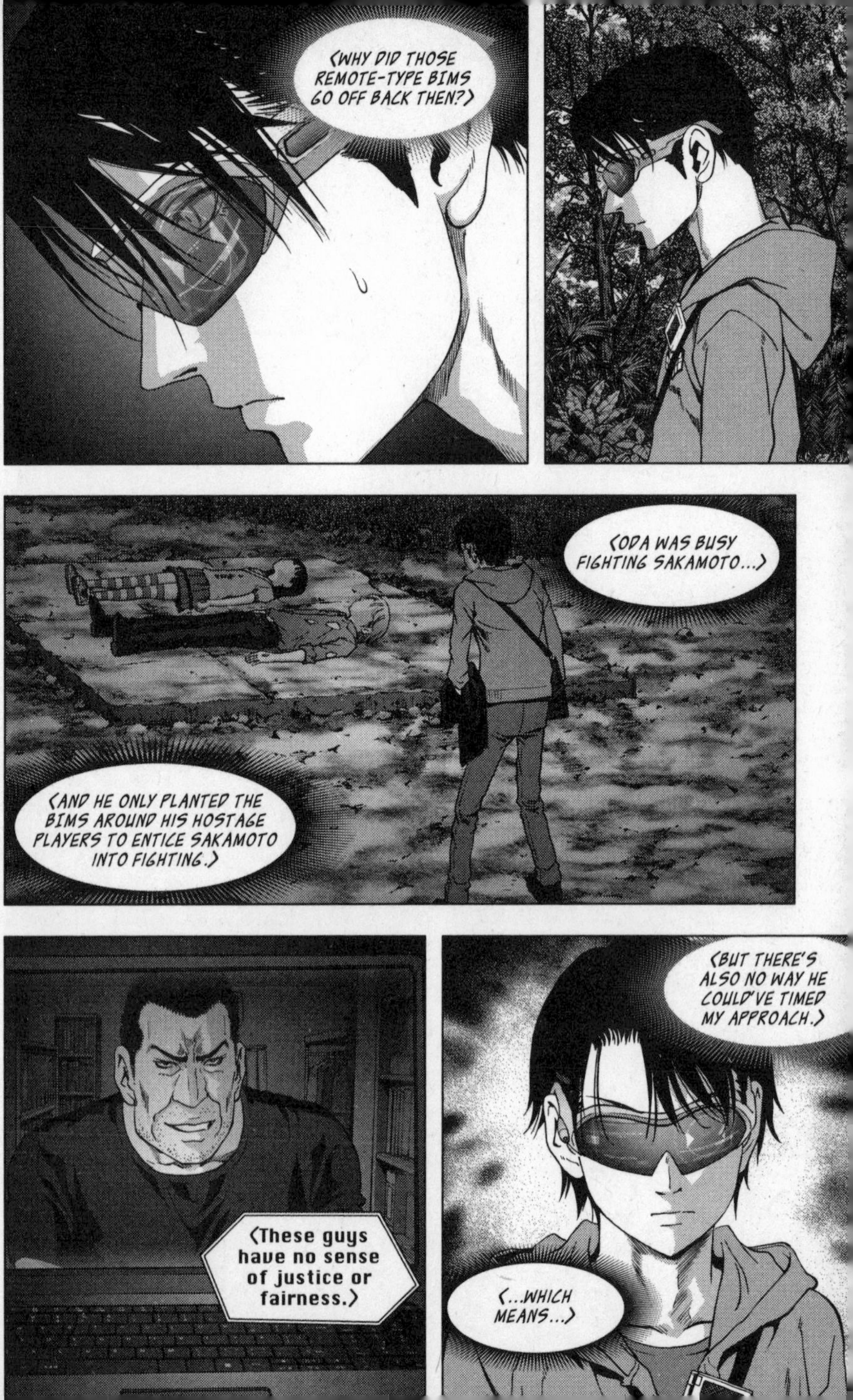

⟨WHY DID THOSE REMOTE-TYPE BIMS GO OFF BACK THEN?⟩
⟨ODA WAS BUSY FIGHTING SAKAMOTO...⟩
⟨AND HE ONLY PLANTED THE BIMS AROUND HIS HOSTAGE PLAYERS TO ENTICE SAKAMOTO INTO FIGHTING.⟩
⟨BUT THERE'S ALSO NO WAY HE COULD'VE TIMED MY APPROACH.⟩
⟨...WHICH MEANS...⟩
⟨These guys have no sense of justice or fairness.⟩

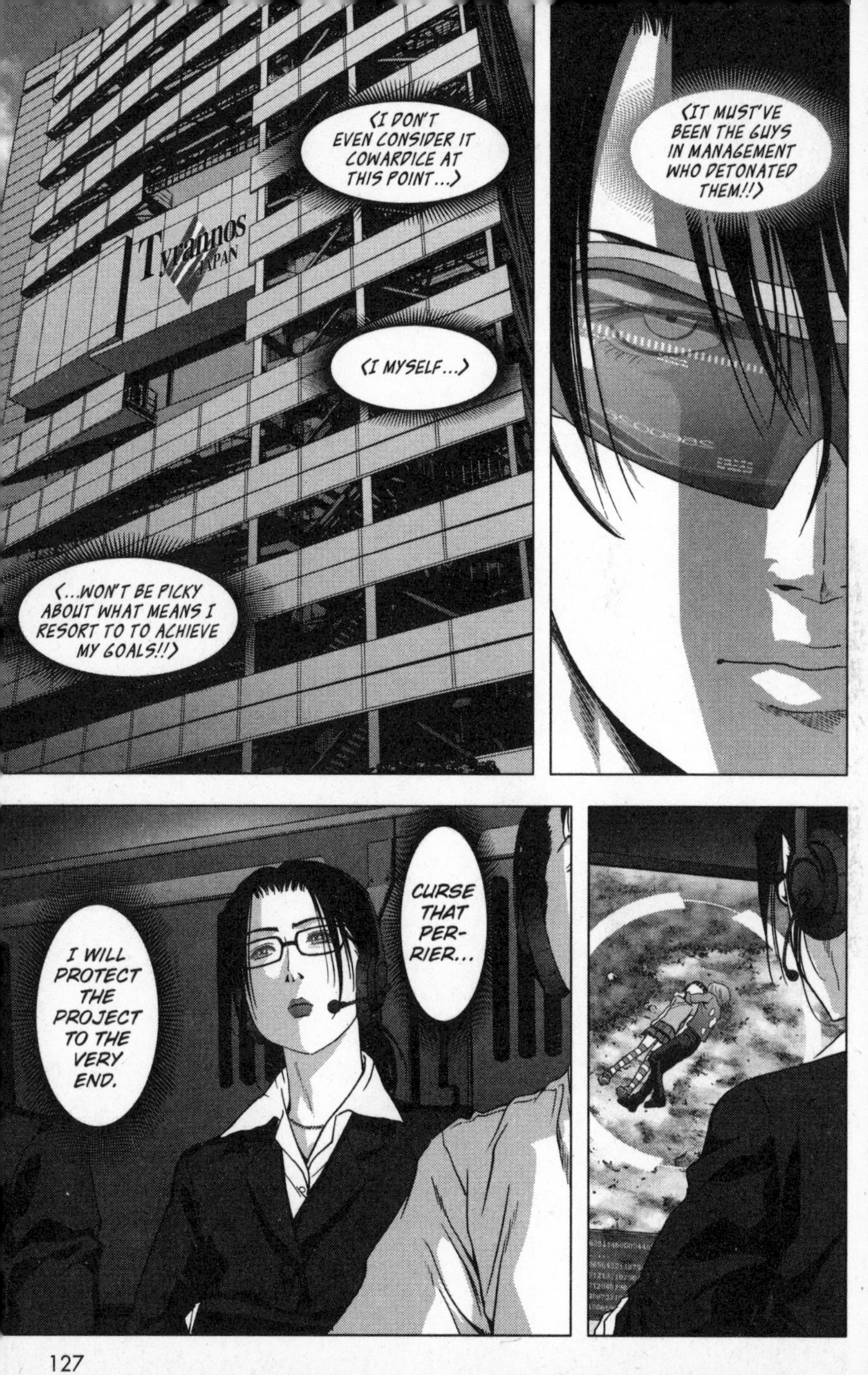
⟨IT MUST'VE BEEN THE GUYS IN MANAGEMENT WHO DETONATED THEM!!⟩
⟨I DON'T EVEN CONSIDER IT COWARDICE AT THIS POINT...⟩
Tyrannos JAPAN
⟨I MYSELF...⟩
⟨...WON'T BE PICKY ABOUT WHAT MEANS I RESORT TO TO ACHIEVE MY GOALS!!⟩
CURSE THAT PER-RIER...
I WILL PROTECT THE PROJECT TO THE VERY END.

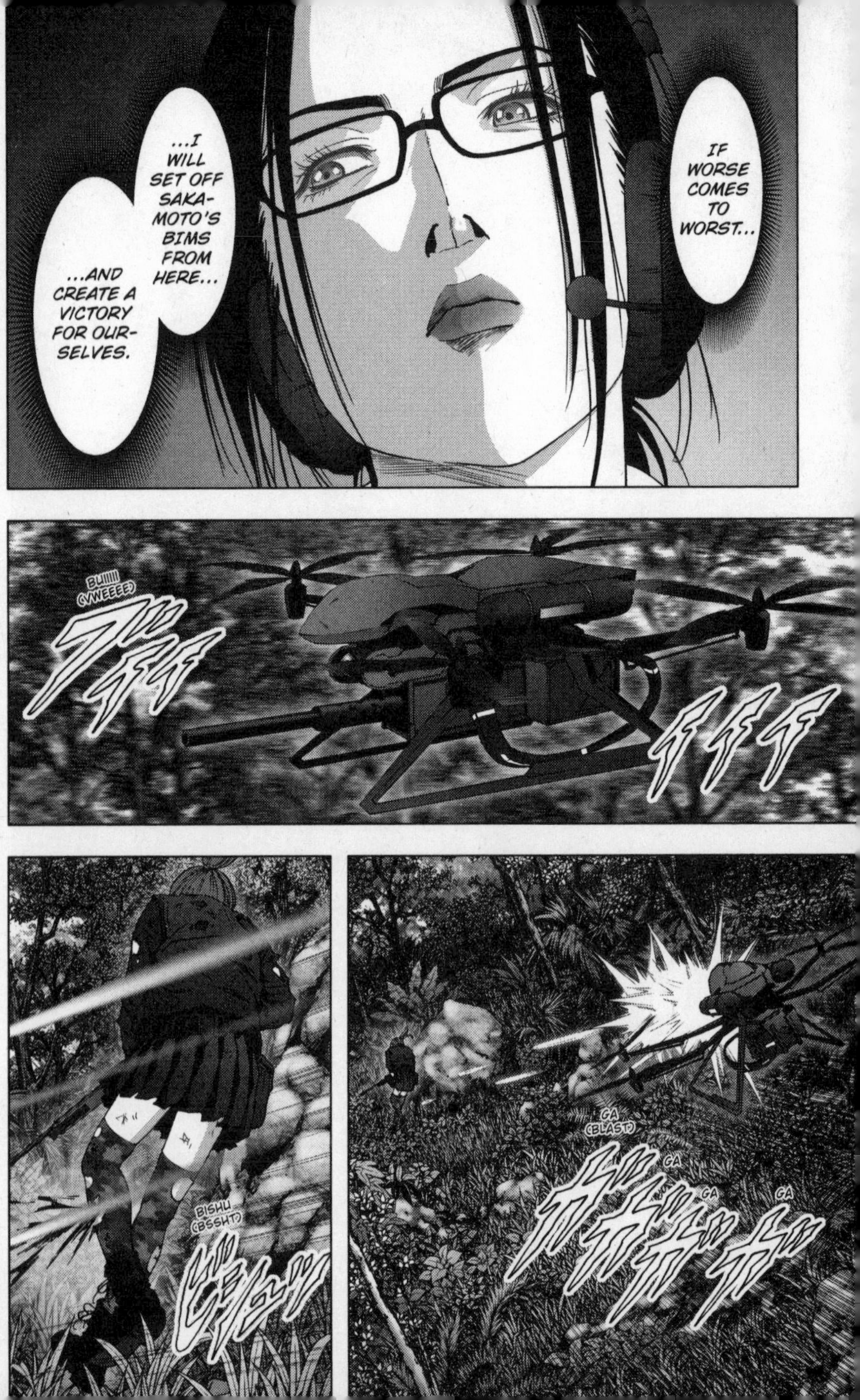
IF WORSE COMES TO WORST...
...I WILL SET OFF SAKAMOTO'S BIMS FROM HERE...
...AND CREATE A VICTORY FOR OURSELVES.
BUIIIII (VWEEEE)
GA (BLAST)
GA
GA
GA
BISHU (BSSHT)

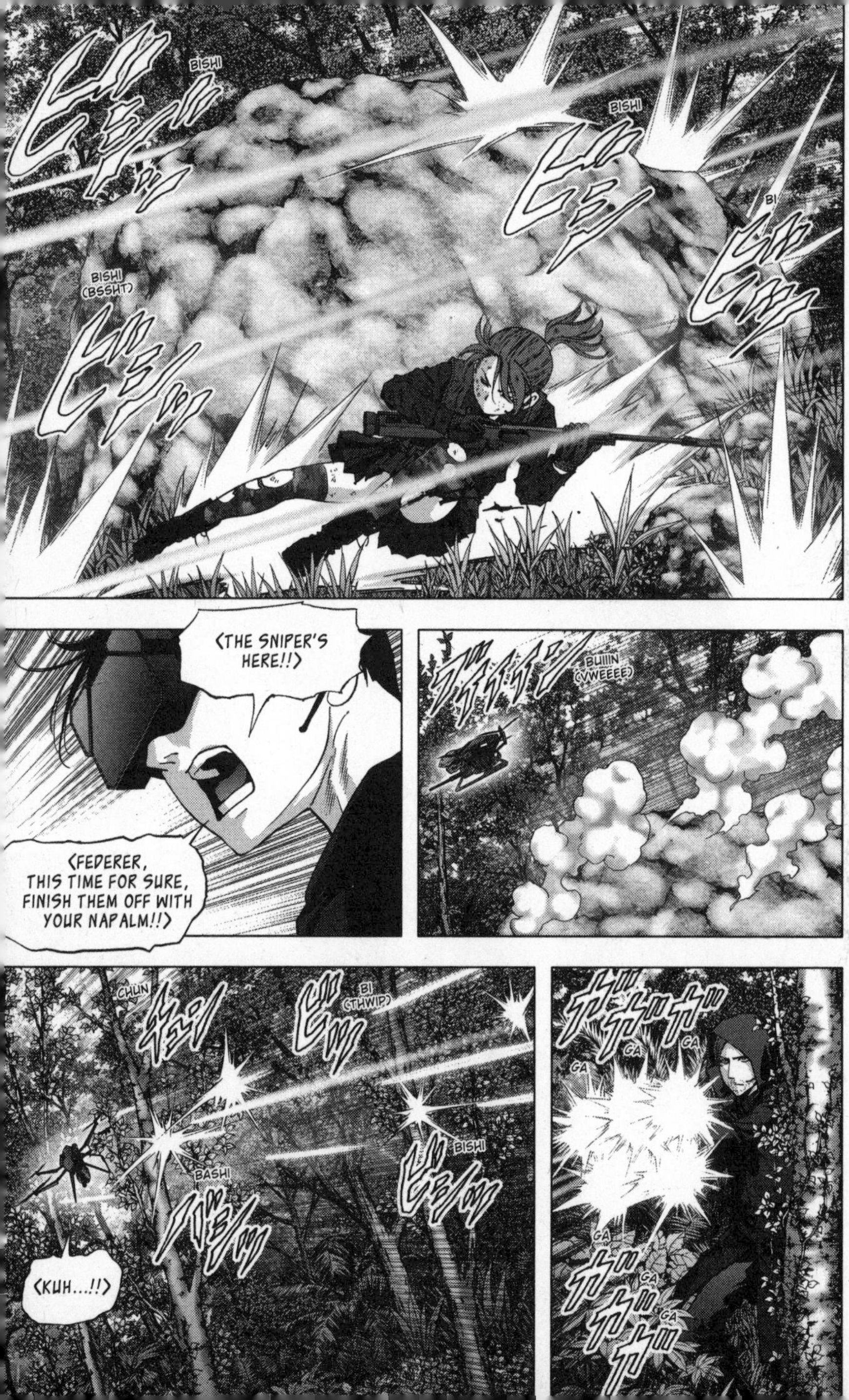
BISHI
BI
BISHI
BISHI (BSSHT)
BUIIIN (VWEEEE)
<THE SNIPER'S HERE!!>
<FEDERER, THIS TIME FOR SURE, FINISH THEM OFF WITH YOUR NAPALM!!>
GA
GA
GA
GA
GA
GA
BI (THWIP)
CHUN
BISHI
BASHI
<KUH...!!>

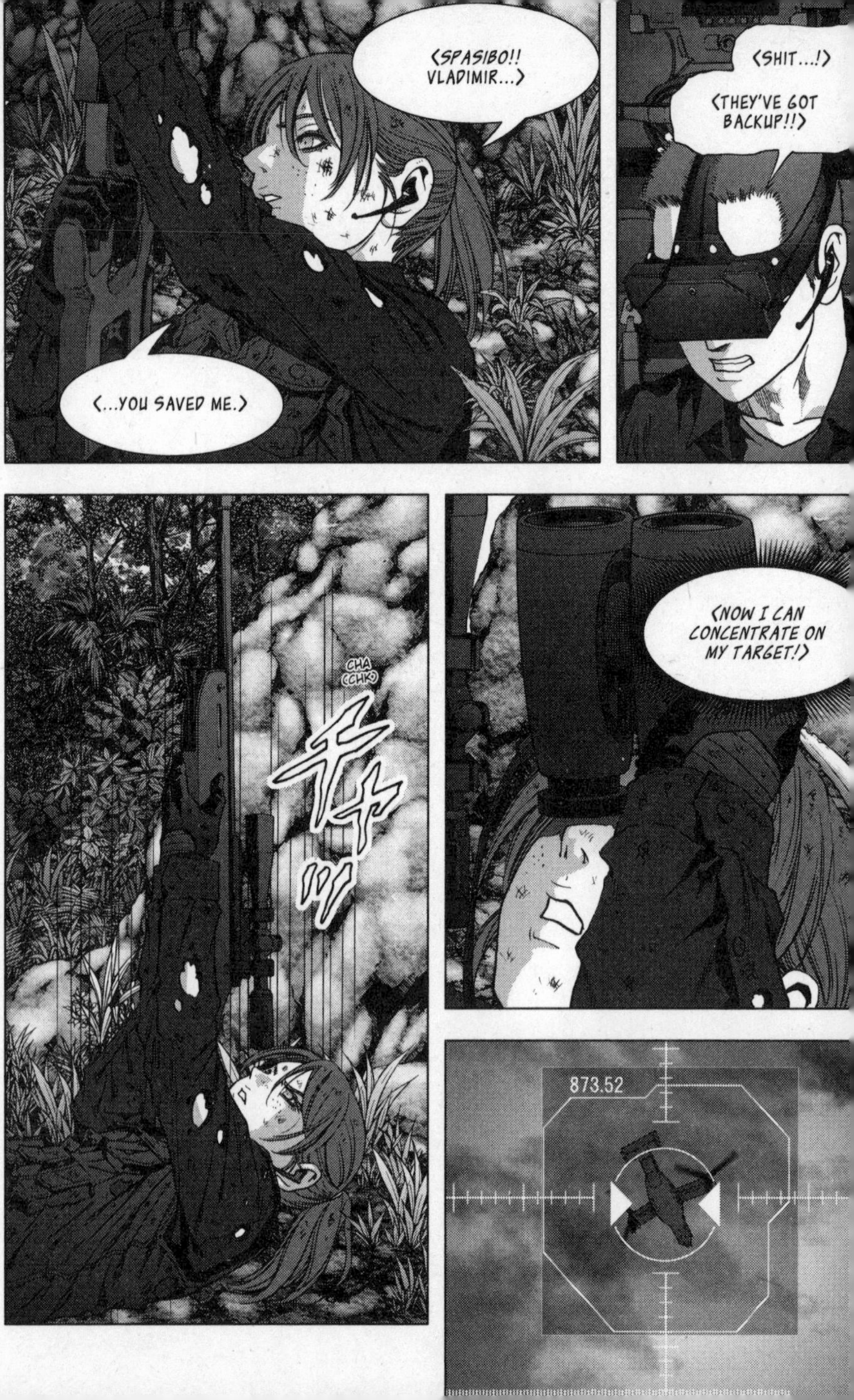

〈SHIT...!〉
〈THEY'VE GOT BACKUP!!〉
〈SPASIBO!! VLADIMIR...〉
〈...YOU SAVED ME.〉
〈NOW I CAN CONCENTRATE ON MY TARGET!〉
873.52
CHA (CHK)

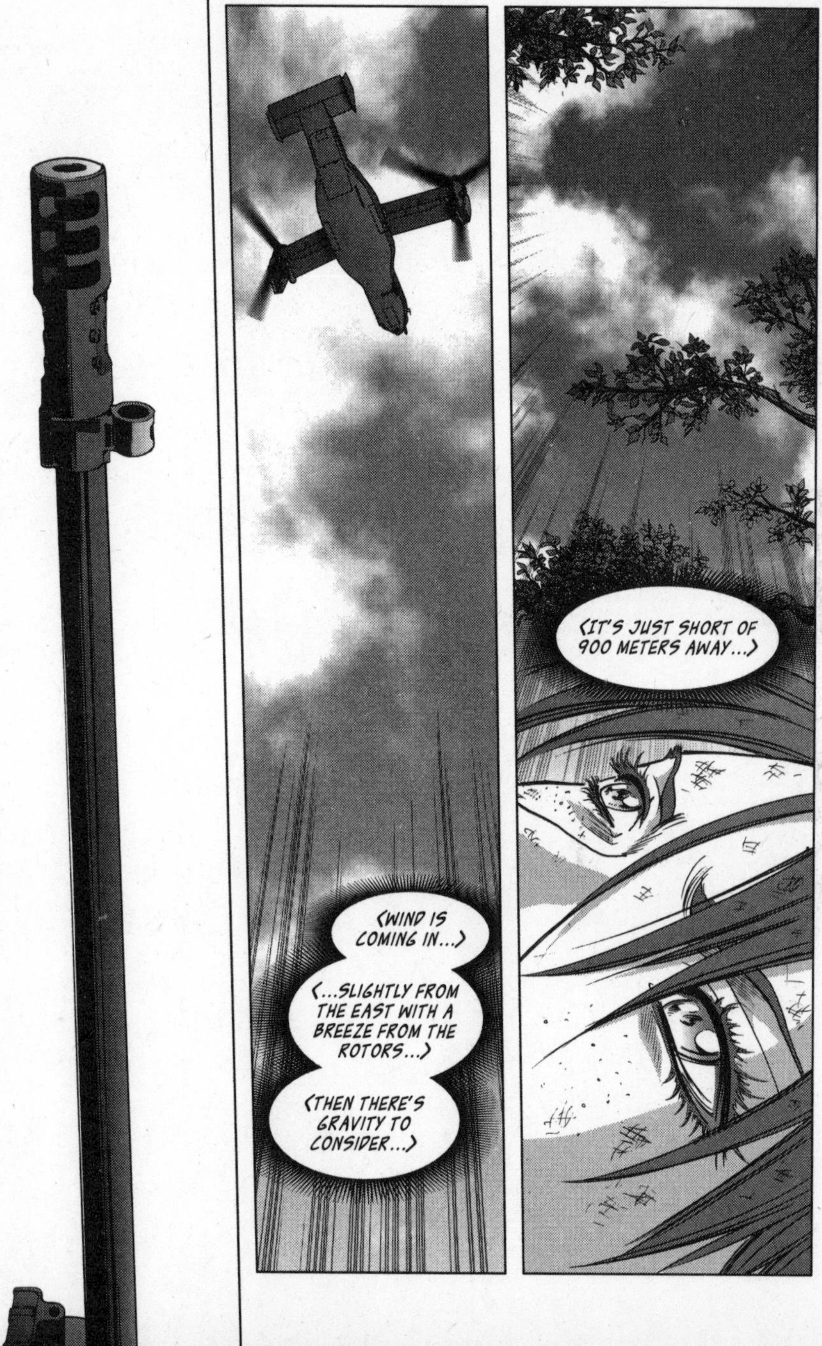

〈IT'S JUST SHORT OF 900 METERS AWAY...〉
〈WIND IS COMING IN...〉
〈...SLIGHTLY FROM THE EAST WITH A BREEZE FROM THE ROTORS...〉
〈THEN THERE'S GRAVITY TO CONSIDER...〉

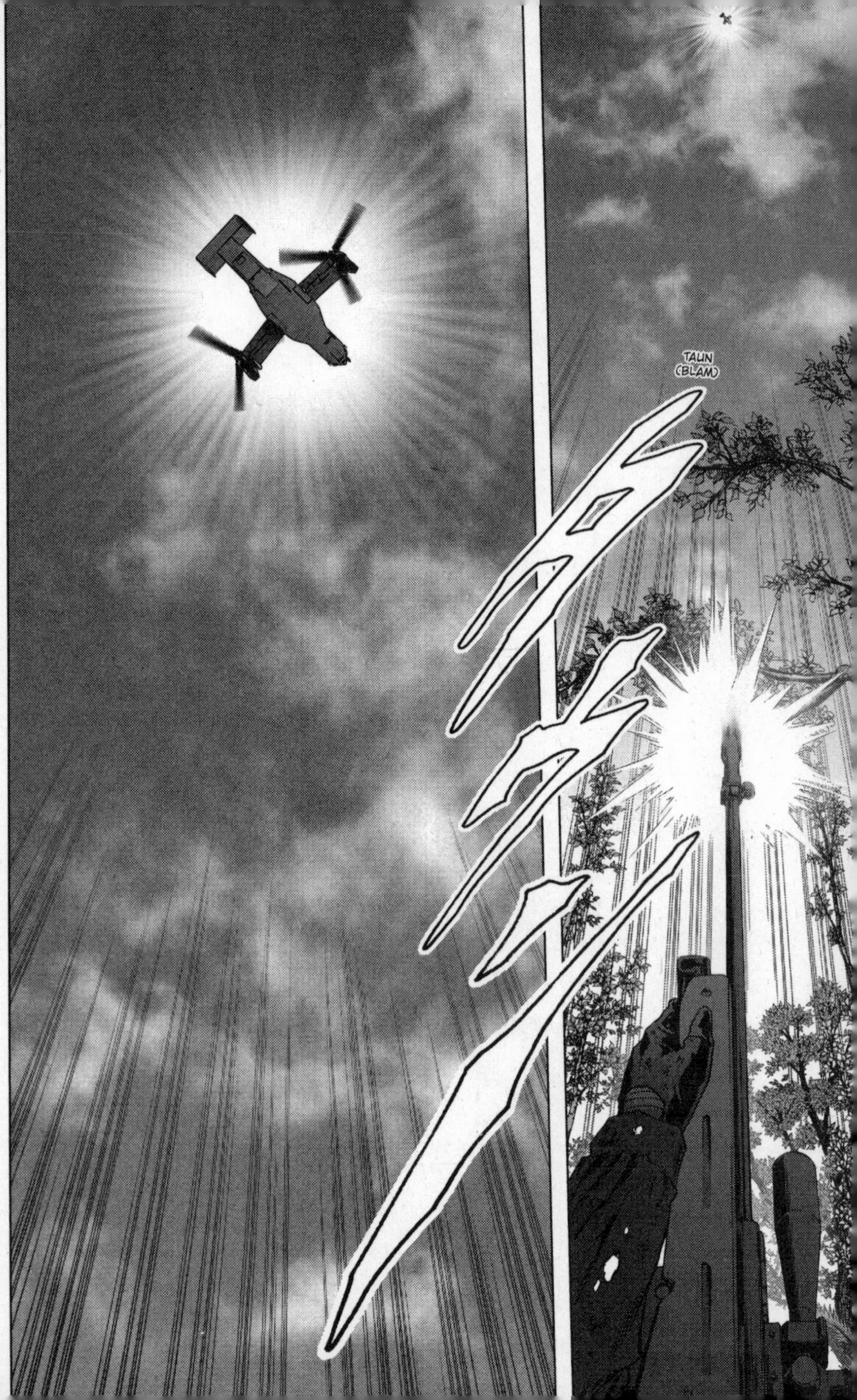
TAUN
(BLAM)

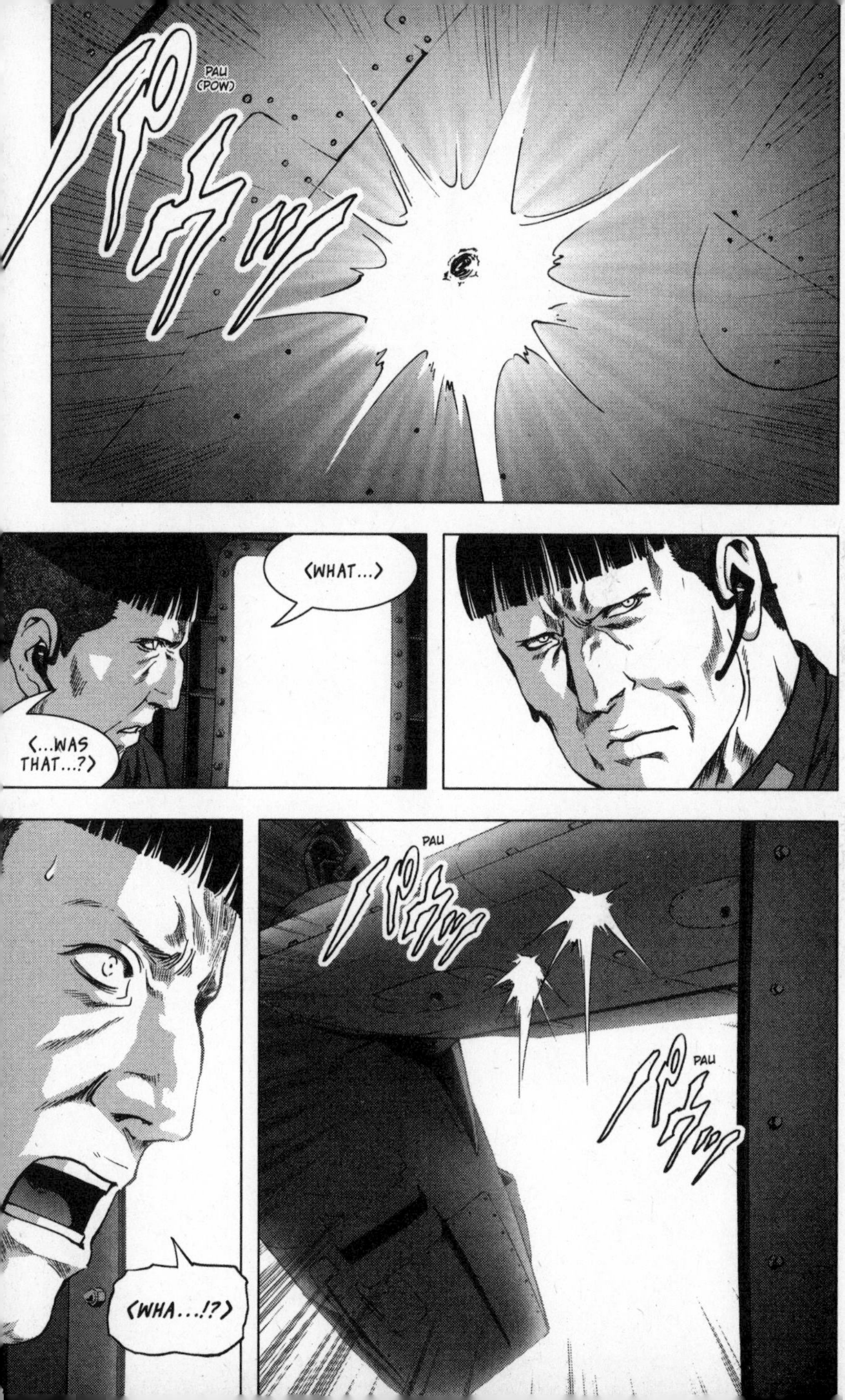
PAU
(POW)
<WHAT...>
<...WAS THAT...?>
PAU
PAU
<WHA...!?>

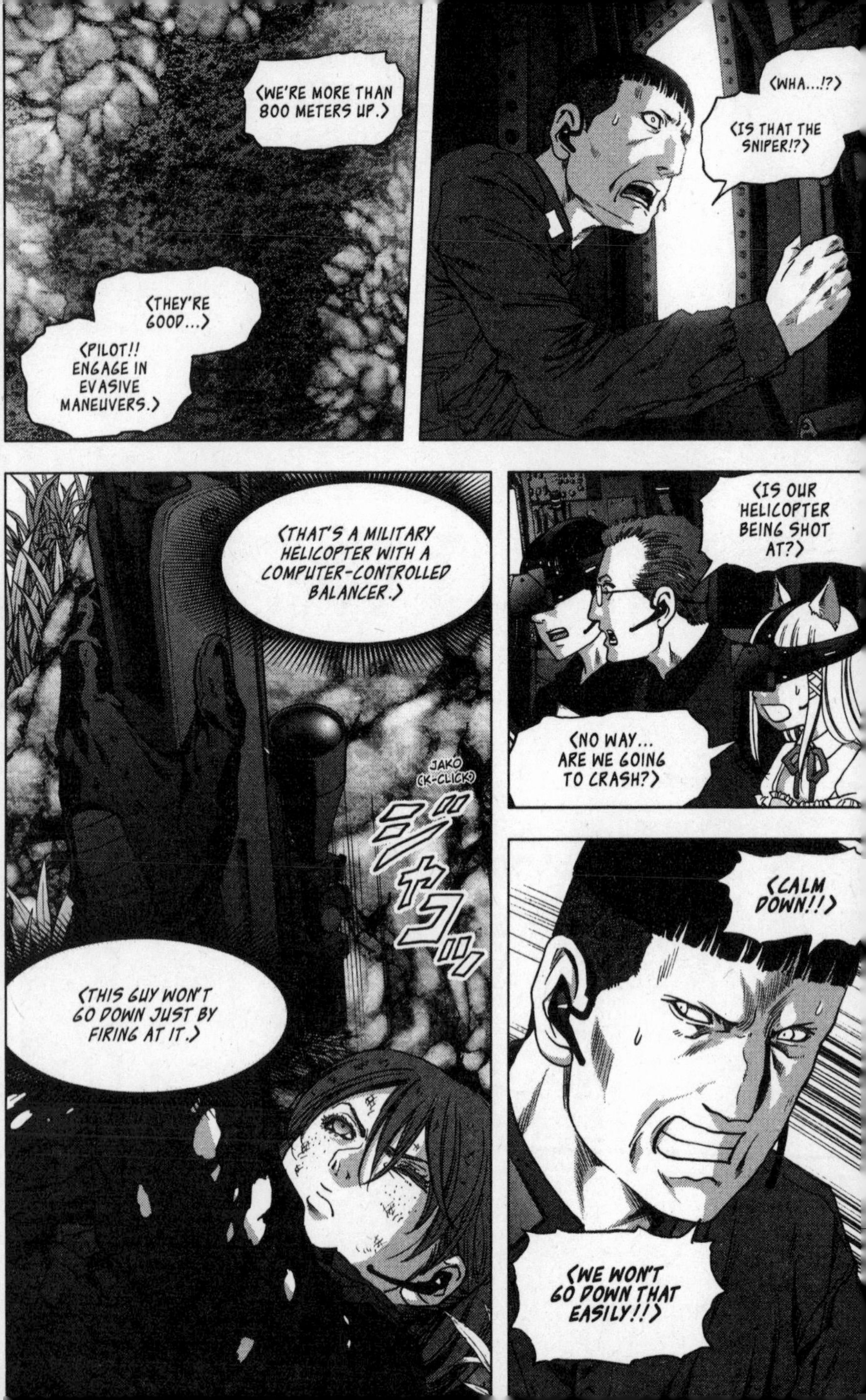
<WHA...!?>
<IS THAT THE SNIPER!?>
<WE'RE MORE THAN 800 METERS UP.>
<THEY'RE GOOD...>
<PILOT!! ENGAGE IN EVASIVE MANEUVERS.>
<IS OUR HELICOPTER BEING SHOT AT?>
<NO WAY... ARE WE GOING TO CRASH?>
<CALM DOWN!!>
<WE WON'T GO DOWN THAT EASILY!!>
<THAT'S A MILITARY HELICOPTER WITH A COMPUTER-CONTROLLED BALANCER.>
JAKO (K-CLICK)
<THIS GUY WON'T GO DOWN JUST BY FIRING AT IT.>

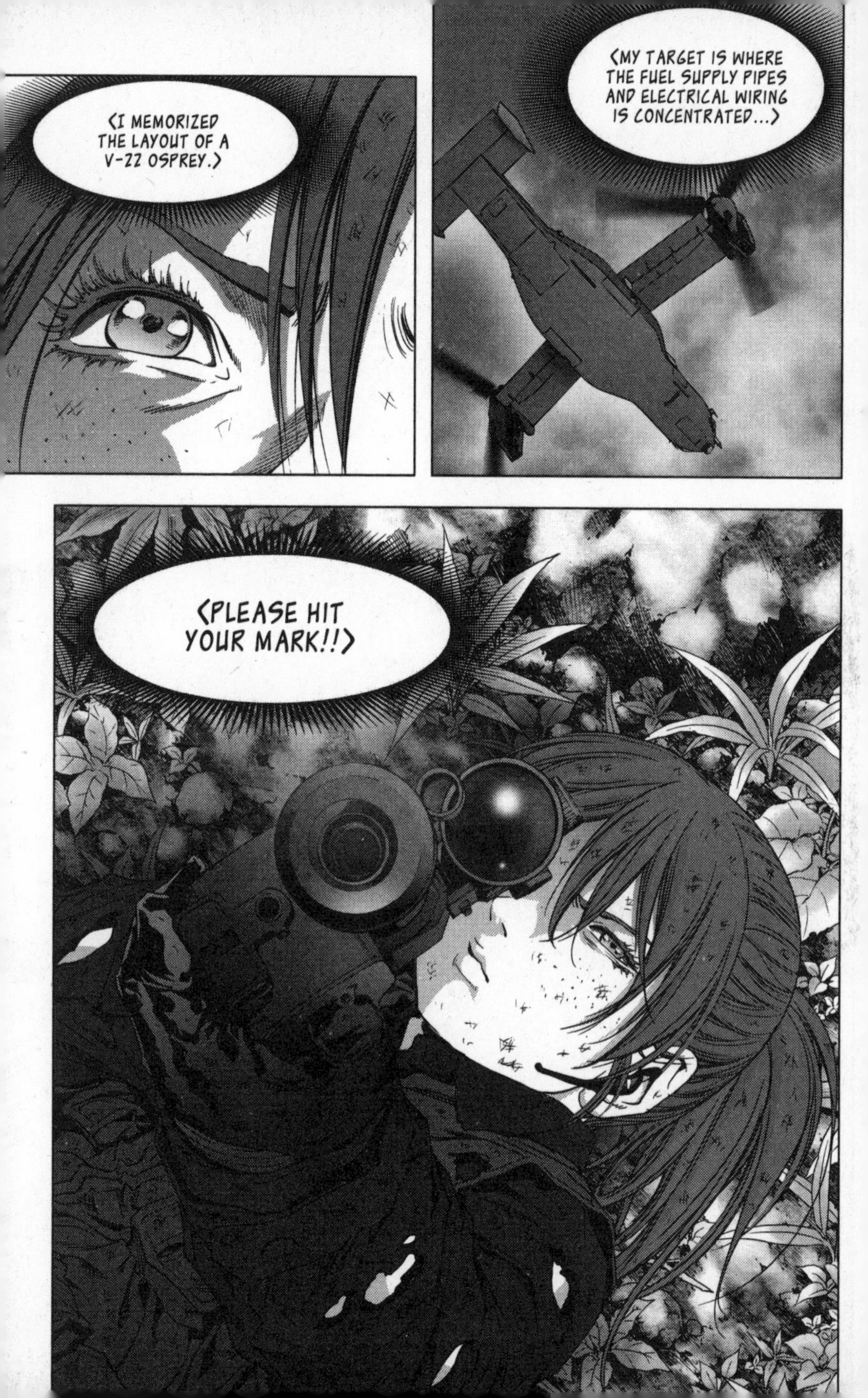
〈MY TARGET IS WHERE THE FUEL SUPPLY PIPES AND ELECTRICAL WIRING IS CONCENTRATED...〉
〈I MEMORIZED THE LAYOUT OF A V-22 OSPREY.〉
〈PLEASE HIT YOUR MARK!!〉

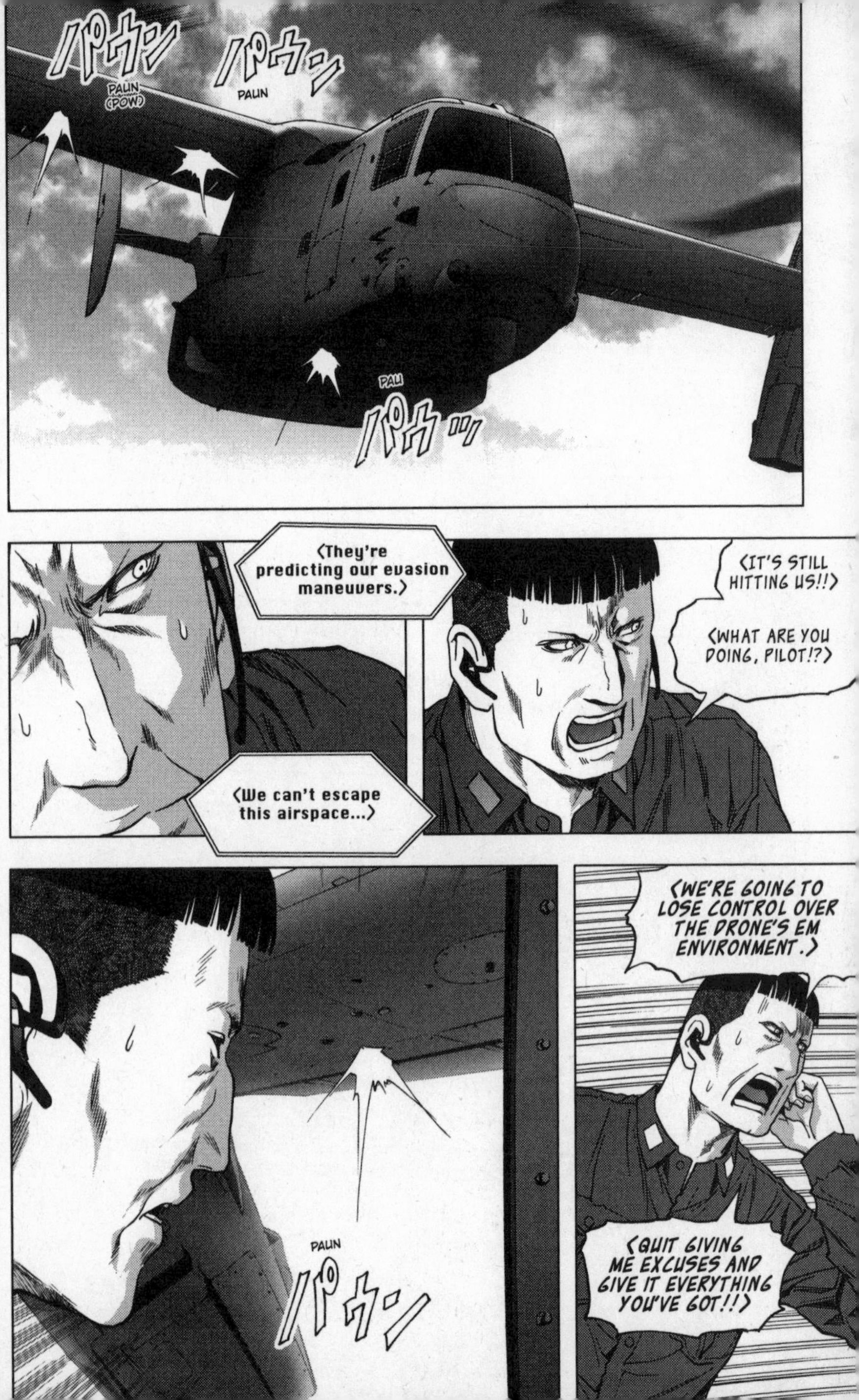
パウン
PAUN
パウン
PAUN
(POW)
PAU
パウッ
〈IT'S STILL HITTING US!!〉
〈WHAT ARE YOU DOING, PILOT!?〉
〈They're predicting our evasion maneuvers.〉
〈We can't escape this airspace...〉
〈WE'RE GOING TO LOSE CONTROL OVER THE DRONE'S EM ENVIRONMENT.〉
〈QUIT GIVING ME EXCUSES AND GIVE IT EVERYTHING YOU'VE GOT!!〉
PAUN
パウン

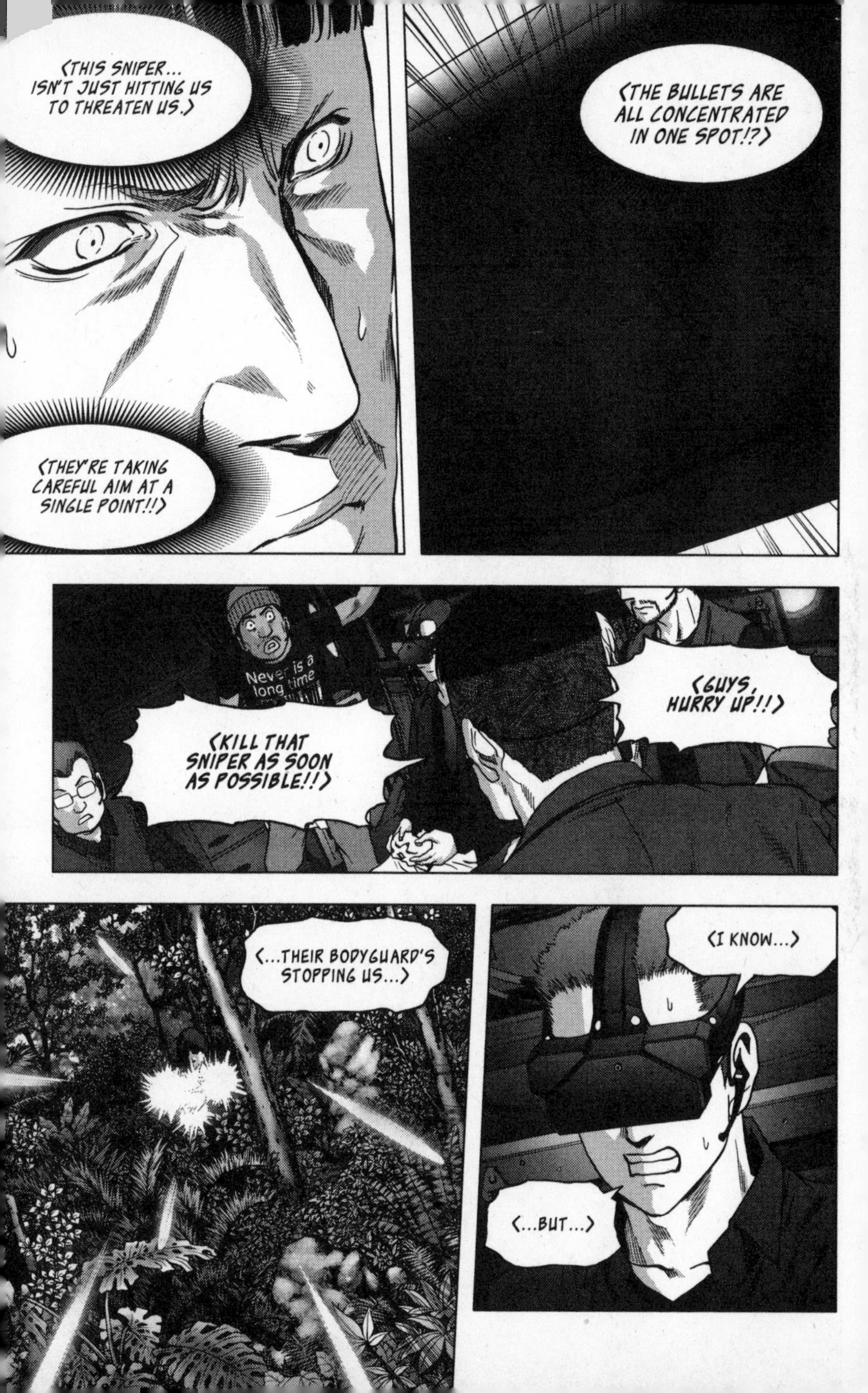
〈THE BULLETS ARE ALL CONCENTRATED IN ONE SPOT!?〉
〈THIS SNIPER... ISN'T JUST HITTING US TO THREATEN US.〉
〈THEY'RE TAKING CAREFUL AIM AT A SINGLE POINT!!〉
〈GUYS, HURRY UP!!〉
Never is a long time
〈KILL THAT SNIPER AS SOON AS POSSIBLE!!〉
〈I KNOW...〉
〈...BUT...〉
〈...THEIR BODYGUARD'S STOPPING US...〉

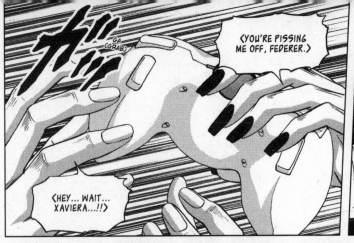

〈YOU'RE PISSING ME OFF, FEDERER.〉

GA (GRAB)

〈HEY... WAIT... XAVIERA...!!〉

〈JEEZUS...〉

BUIIII (BLIZZZZ)

〈I'LL DO IT MYSELF!!〉

GU (CLASP)

BI (BSSHT)

BISHI

BASHI

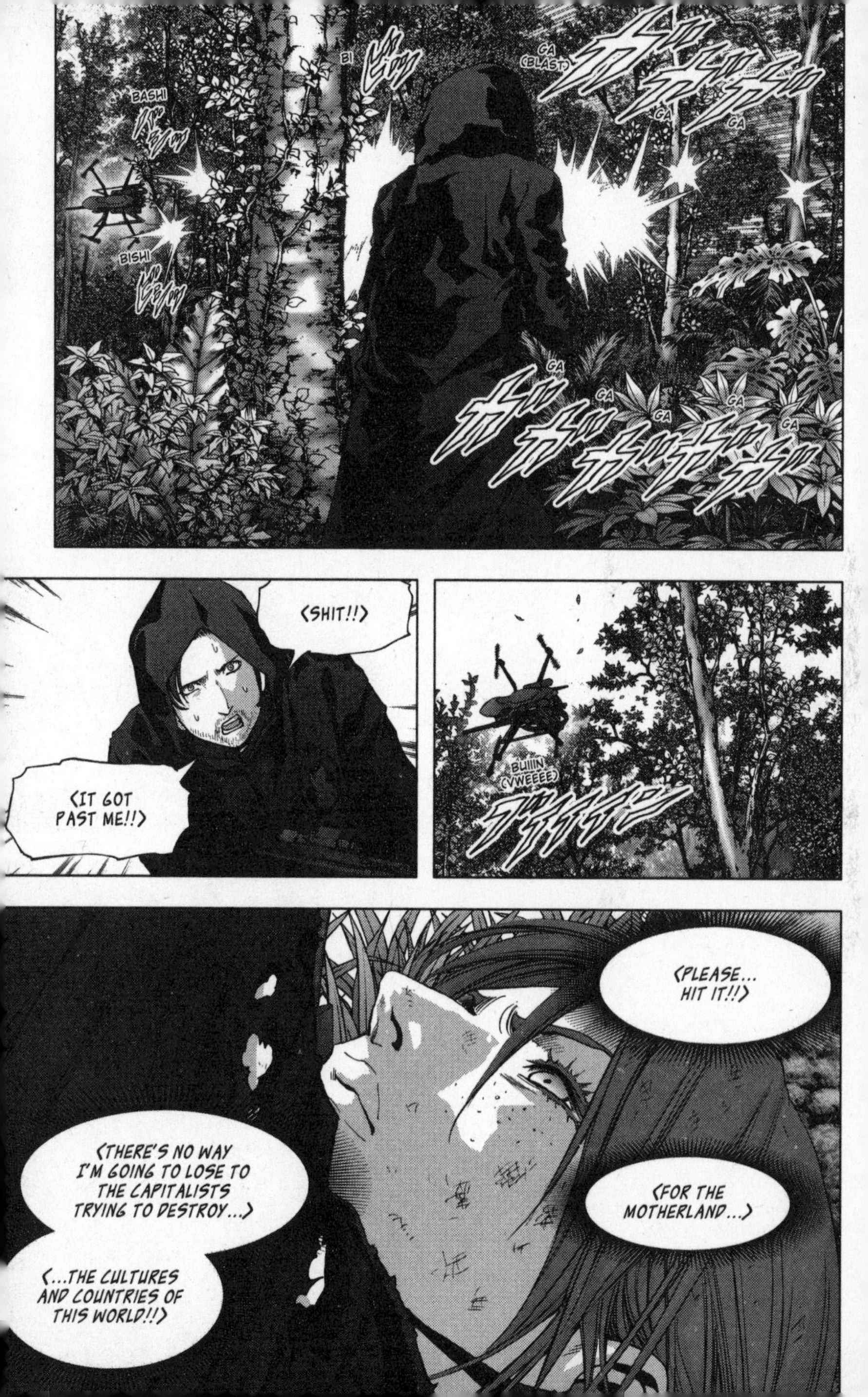
GA (BLAST)
GA
GA
BI
BASHI
BISHI
GA
GA
GA
GA
GA
BUIIIN (VWEEEE)
<SHIT!!>
<IT GOT PAST ME!!>
<PLEASE... HIT IT!!>
<FOR THE MOTHERLAND...>
<THERE'S NO WAY I'M GOING TO LOSE TO THE CAPITALISTS TRYING TO DESTROY...>
<...THE CULTURES AND COUNTRIES OF THIS WORLD!!>

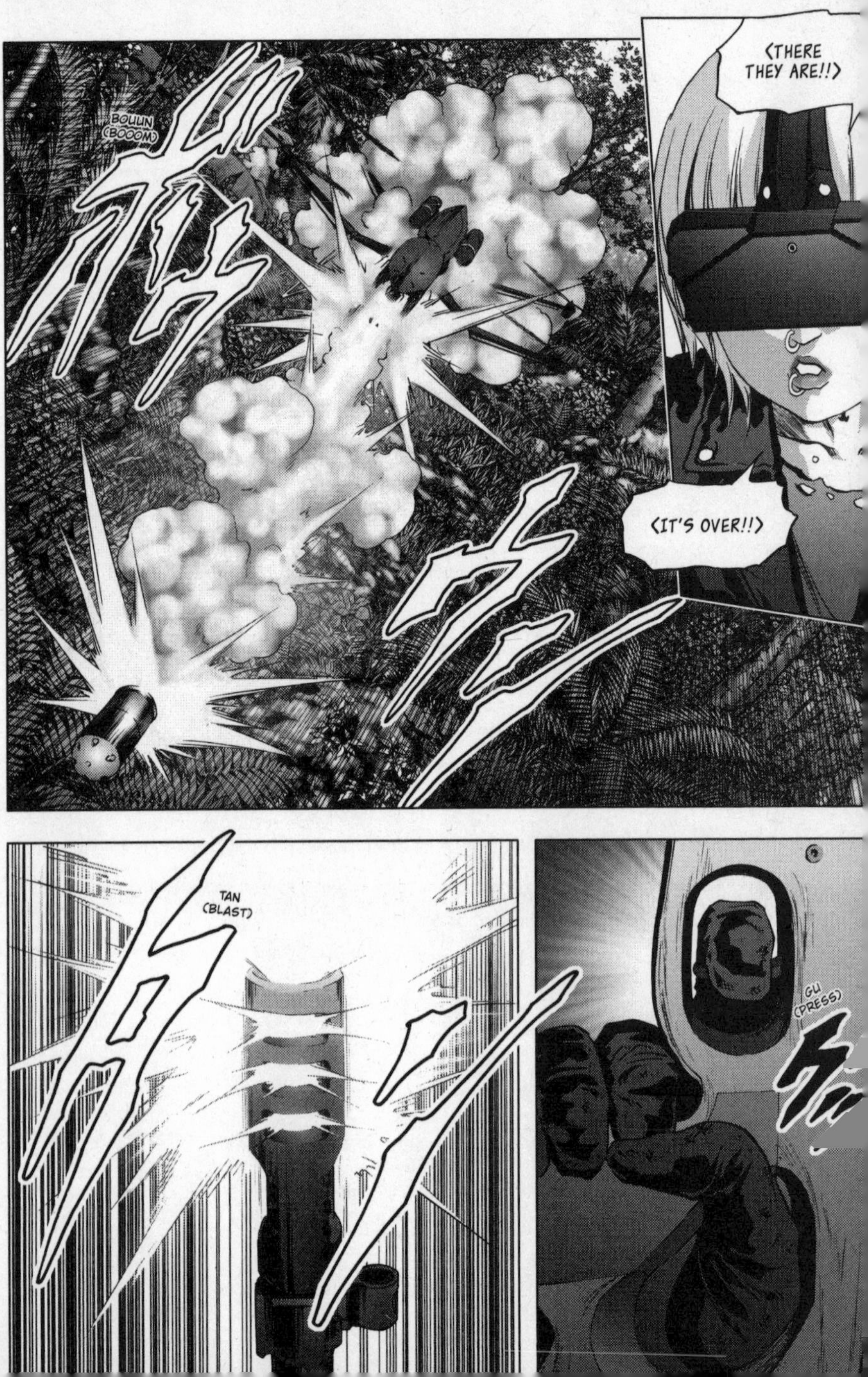
⟨THERE THEY ARE!!⟩
⟨IT'S OVER!!⟩
BOUUN (BOOOM)
GU (PRESS)
TAN (BLAST)

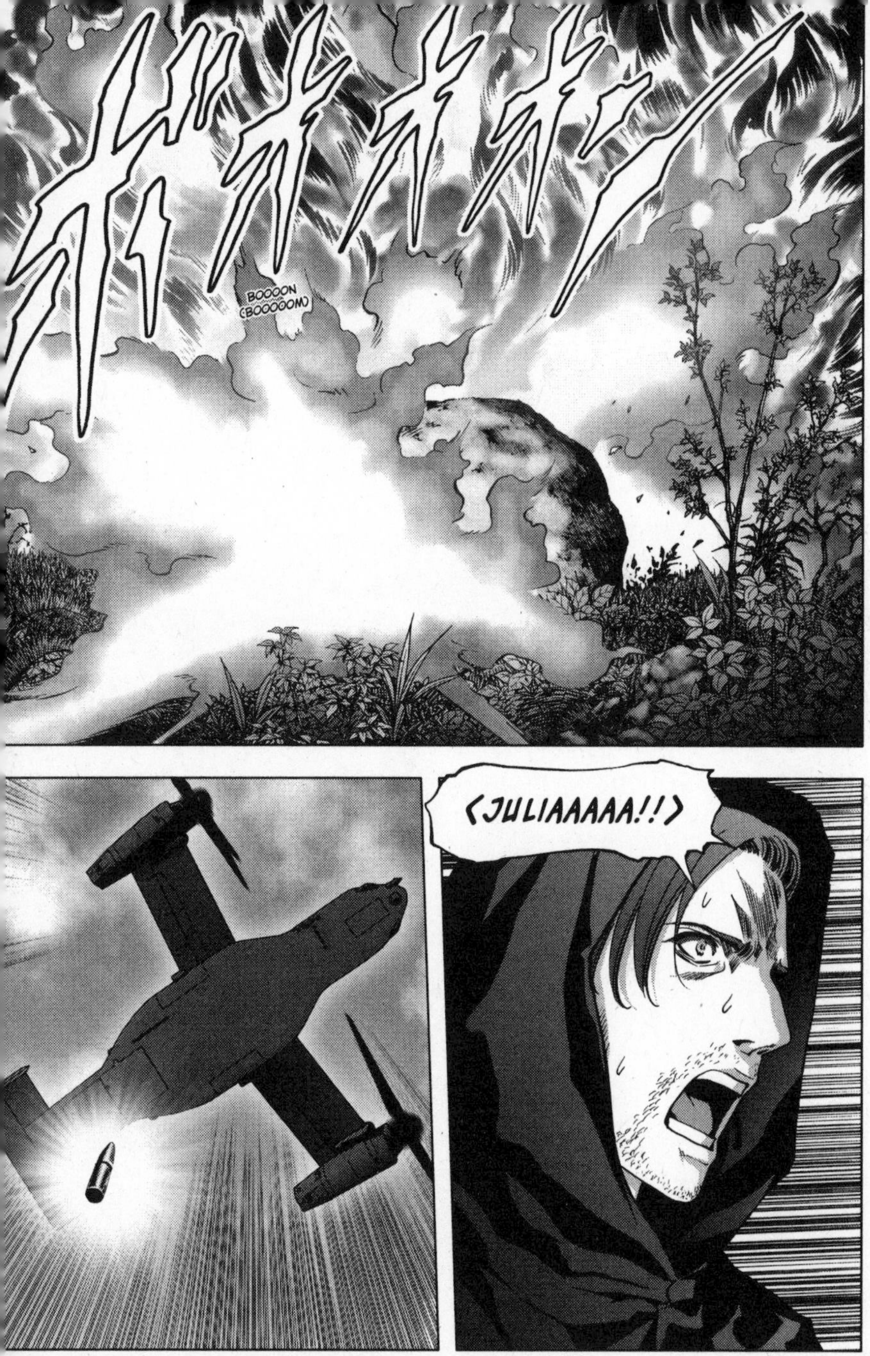
BOOOON
(BOOOOOM)
<JULIAAAAA!!>

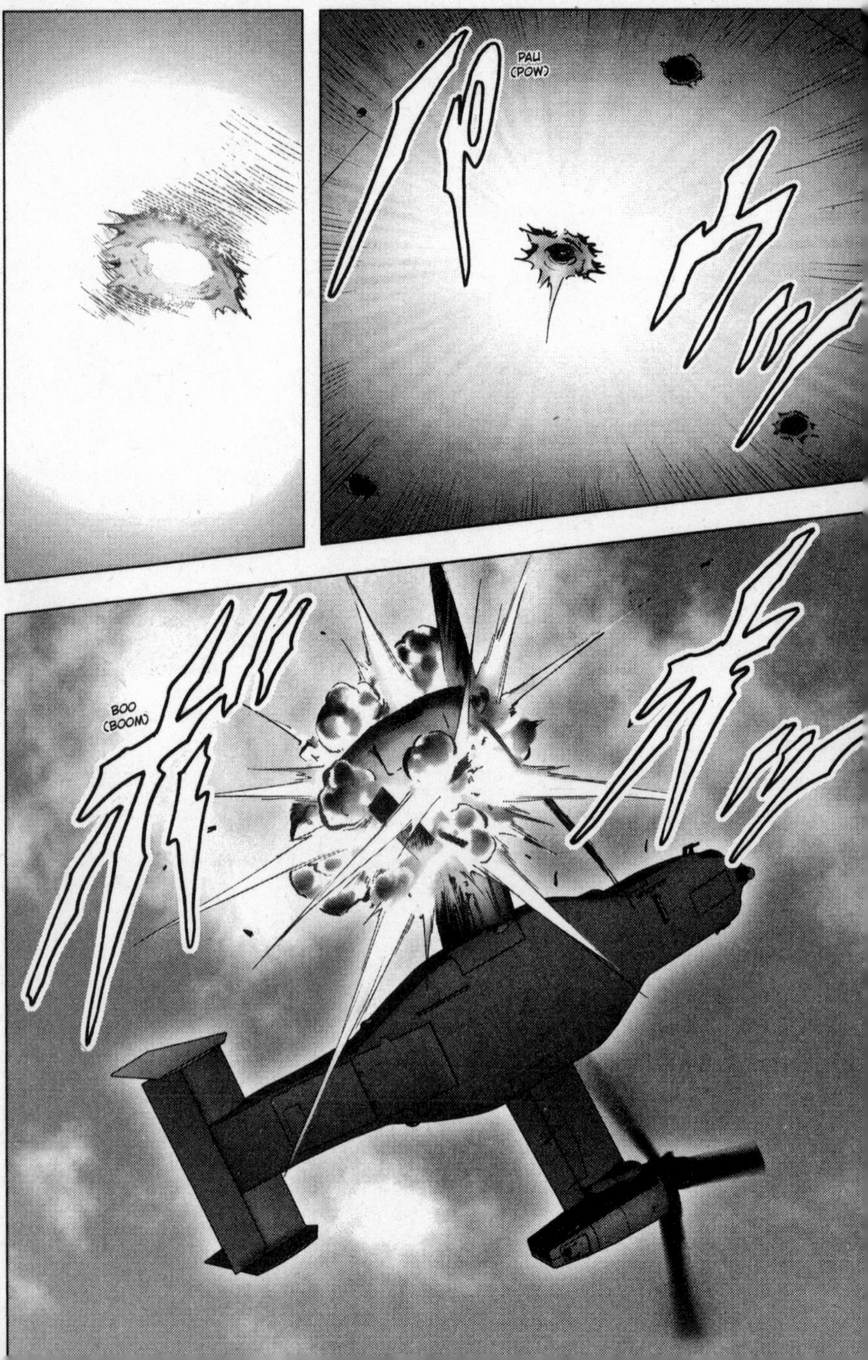
PAU
(POW)
BOO
(BOOM)

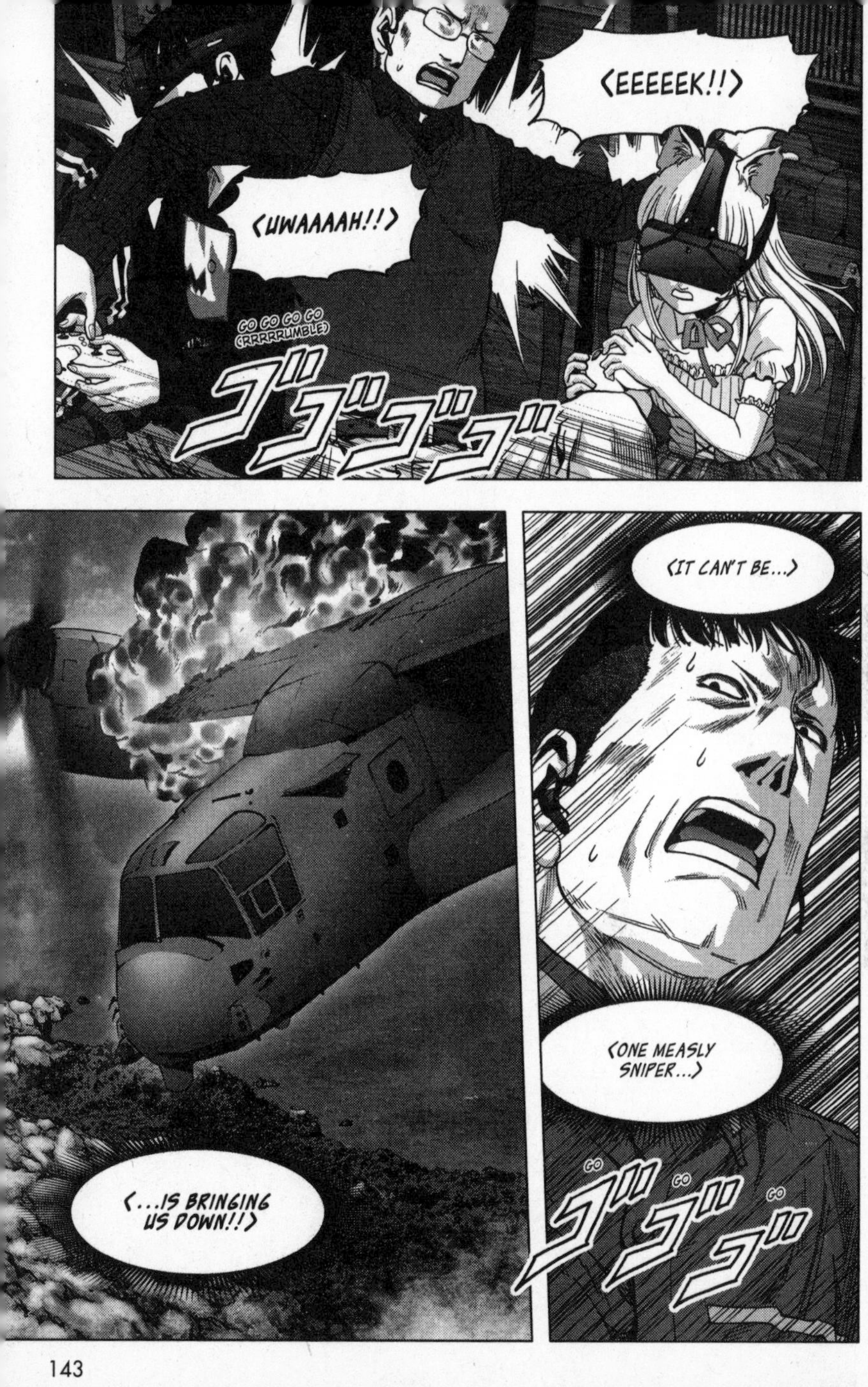

〈EEEEEK!!〉
〈UWAAAAH!!〉
GO GO GO GO
(RRRRRUMBLE)
ゴゴゴゴ
〈IT CAN'T BE...〉
〈ONE MEASLY SNIPER...〉
GO GO GO
ゴゴゴ
〈...IS BRINGING US DOWN!!〉

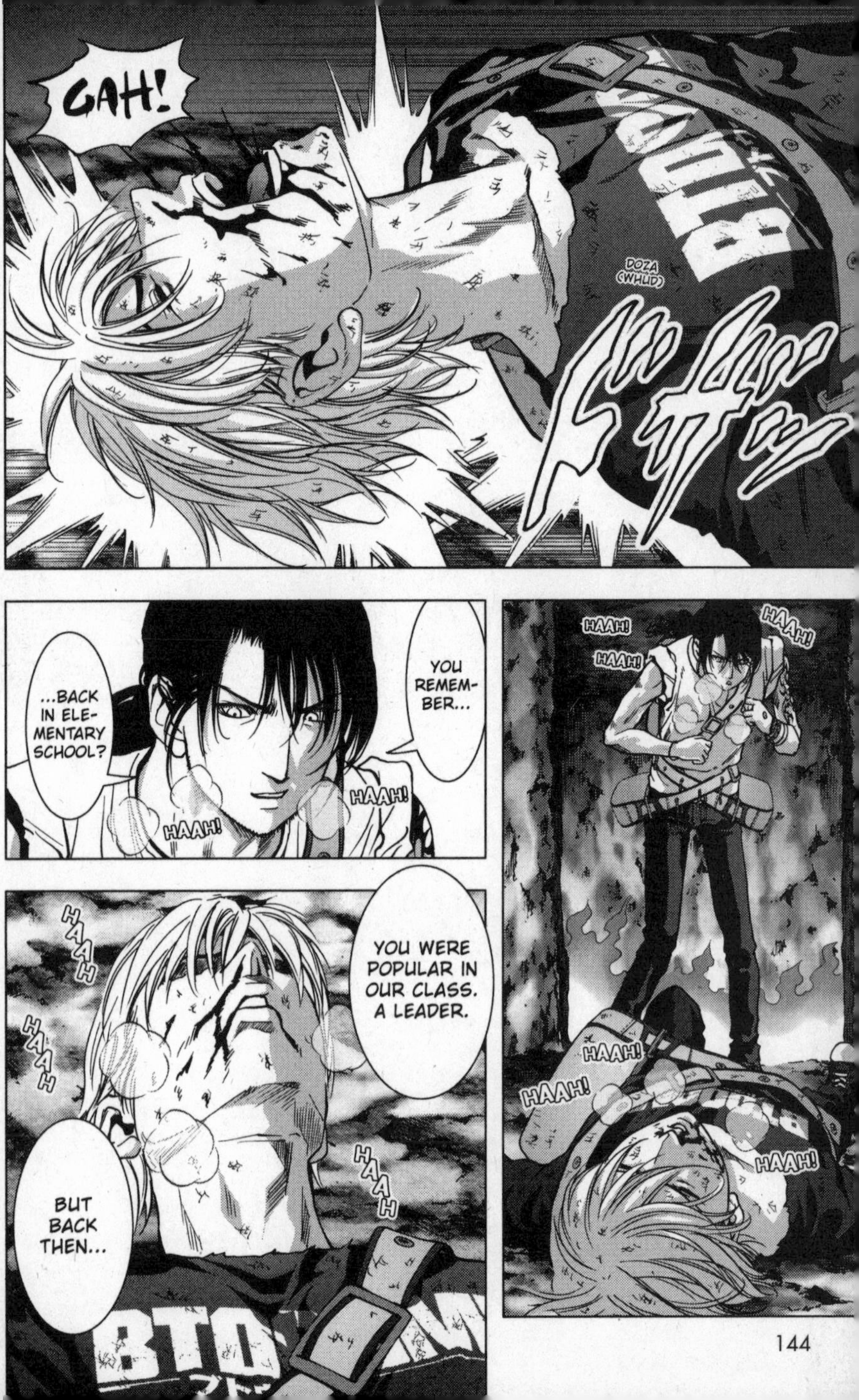
GAH!
DOZA (WHUD)
HAAH!
HAAH!
HAAH!
HAAH!
HAAH!
HAAH!
YOU REMEMBER...
...BACK IN ELEMENTARY SCHOOL?
HAAH!
HAAH!
YOU WERE POPULAR IN OUR CLASS. A LEADER.
HAAAH
HAAAH
HAAAH
BUT BACK THEN...

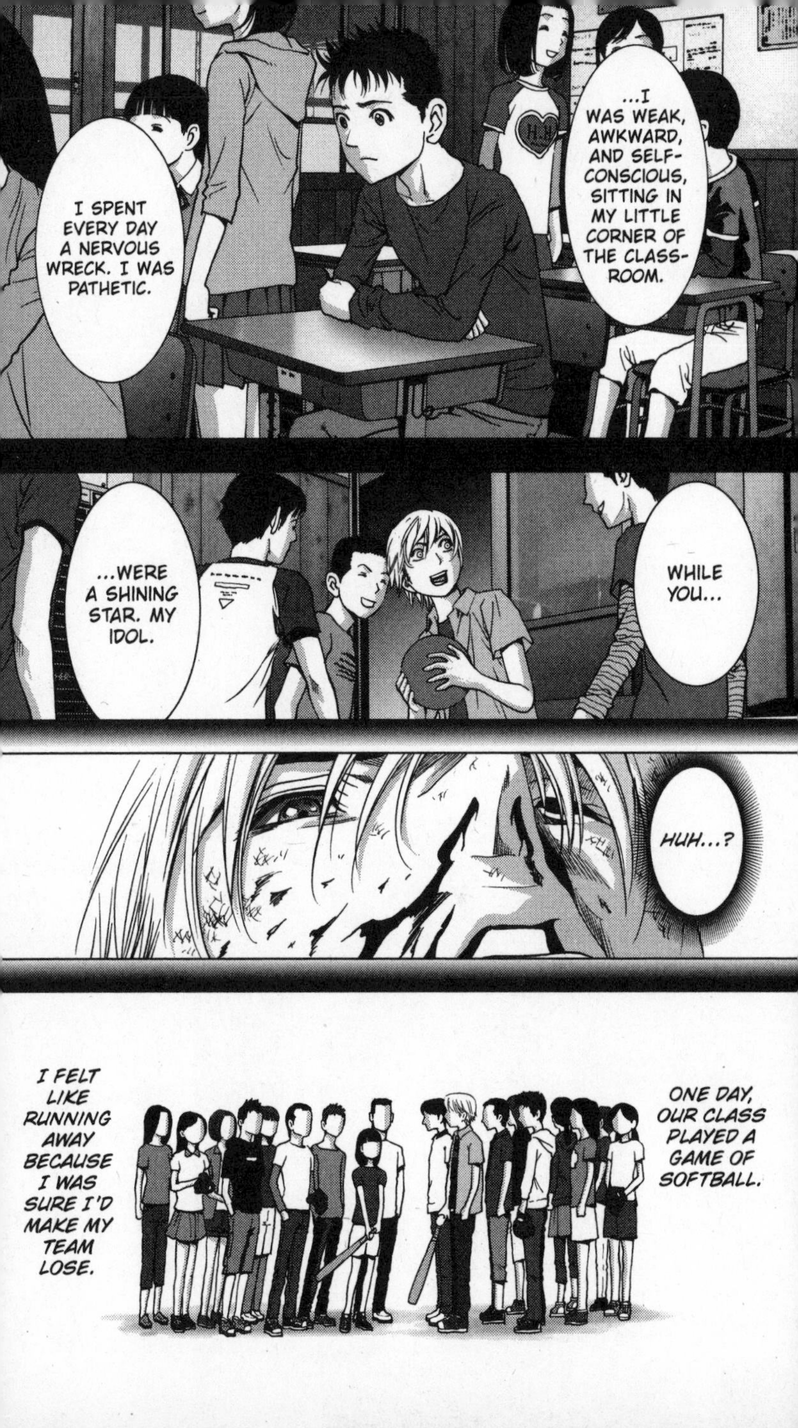
...I WAS WEAK, AWKWARD, AND SELF-CONSCIOUS, SITTING IN MY LITTLE CORNER OF THE CLASS-ROOM.
I SPENT EVERY DAY A NERVOUS WRECK. I WAS PATHETIC.
WHILE YOU...
...WERE A SHINING STAR. MY IDOL.
HUH...?
ONE DAY, OUR CLASS PLAYED A GAME OF SOFTBALL.
I FELT LIKE RUNNING AWAY BECAUSE I WAS SURE I'D MAKE MY TEAM LOSE.

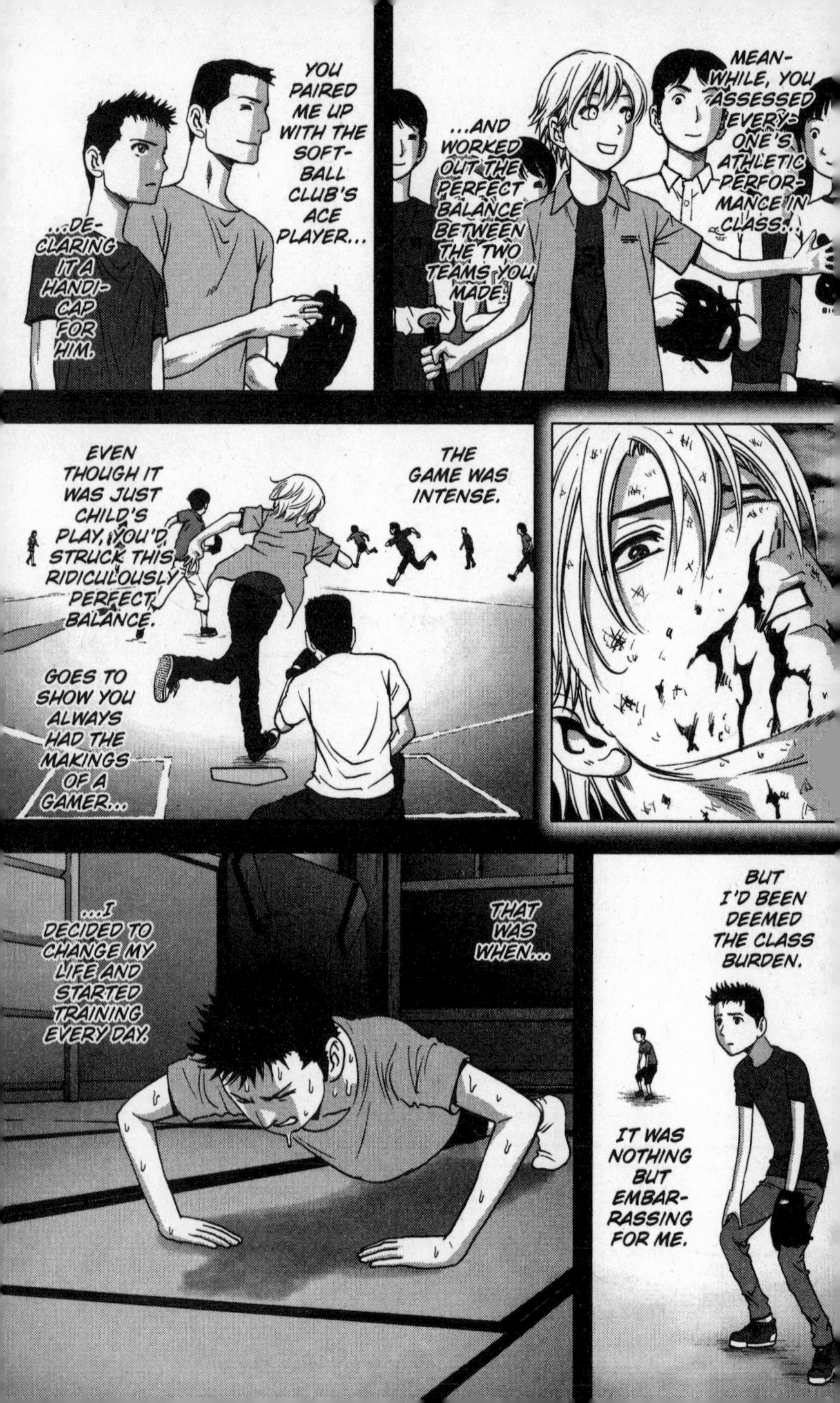
MEAN-WHILE, YOU ASSESSED EVERY-ONE'S ATHLETIC PERFOR-MANCE IN CLASS...
...AND WORKED OUT THE PERFECT BALANCE BETWEEN THE TWO TEAMS YOU MADE!
YOU PAIRED ME UP WITH THE SOFT-BALL CLUB'S ACE PLAYER...
...DE-CLARING IT A HANDI-CAP FOR HIM.
THE GAME WAS INTENSE.
EVEN THOUGH IT WAS JUST CHILD'S PLAY, YOU'D STRUCK THIS RIDICULOUSLY PERFECT BALANCE.
GOES TO SHOW YOU ALWAYS HAD THE MAKINGS OF A GAMER...
BUT I'D BEEN DEEMED THE CLASS BURDEN.
IT WAS NOTHING BUT EMBAR-RASSING FOR ME.
THAT WAS WHEN...
...I DECIDED TO CHANGE MY LIFE AND STARTED TRAINING EVERY DAY.

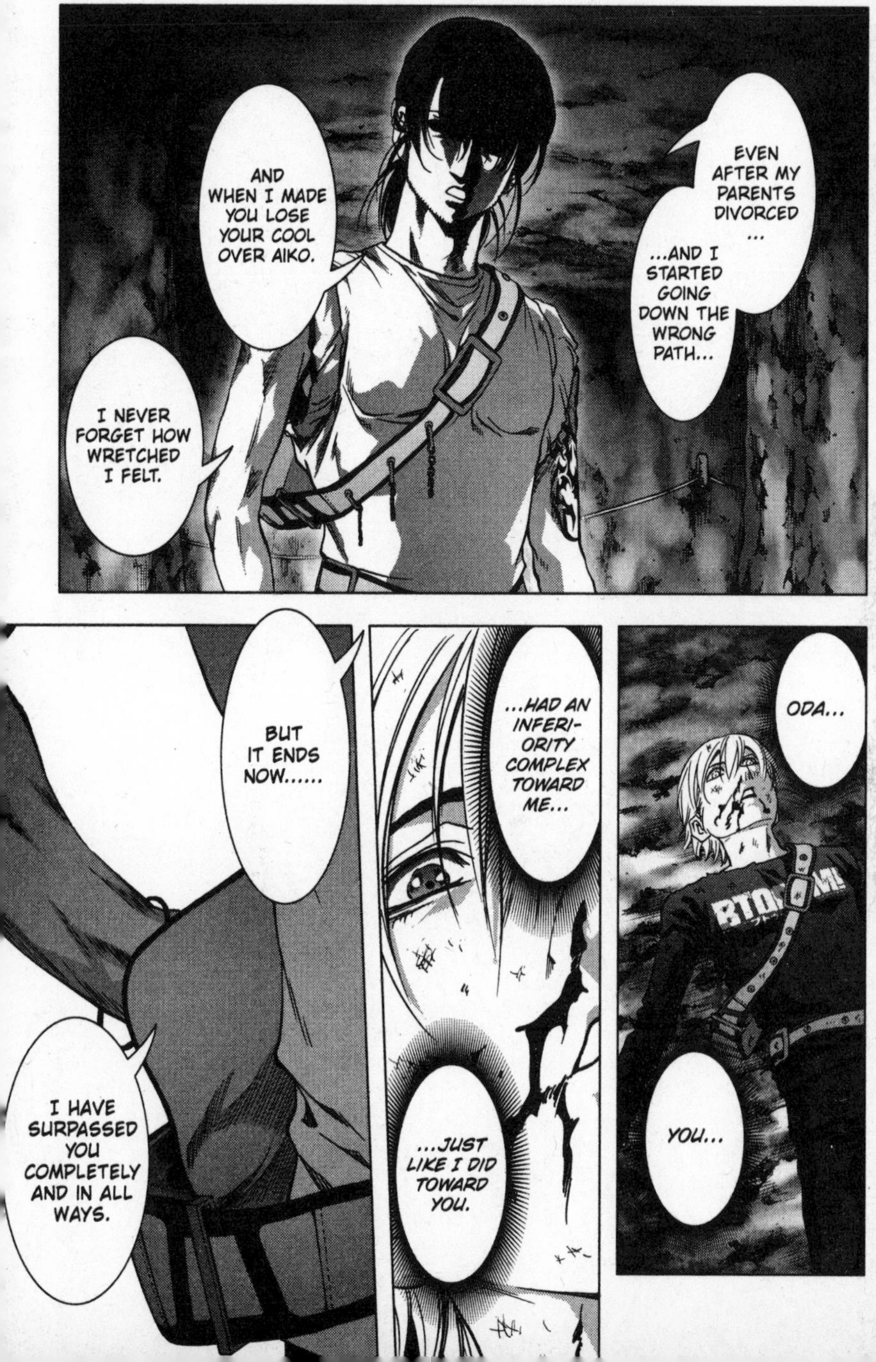
EVEN AFTER MY PARENTS DIVORCED ...
...AND I STARTED GOING DOWN THE WRONG PATH...
AND WHEN I MADE YOU LOSE YOUR COOL OVER AIKO.
I NEVER FORGET HOW WRETCHED I FELT.
ODA...
YOU...
...HAD AN INFERIORITY COMPLEX TOWARD ME...
...JUST LIKE I DID TOWARD YOU.
BUT IT ENDS NOW......
I HAVE SURPASSED YOU COMPLETELY AND IN ALL WAYS.

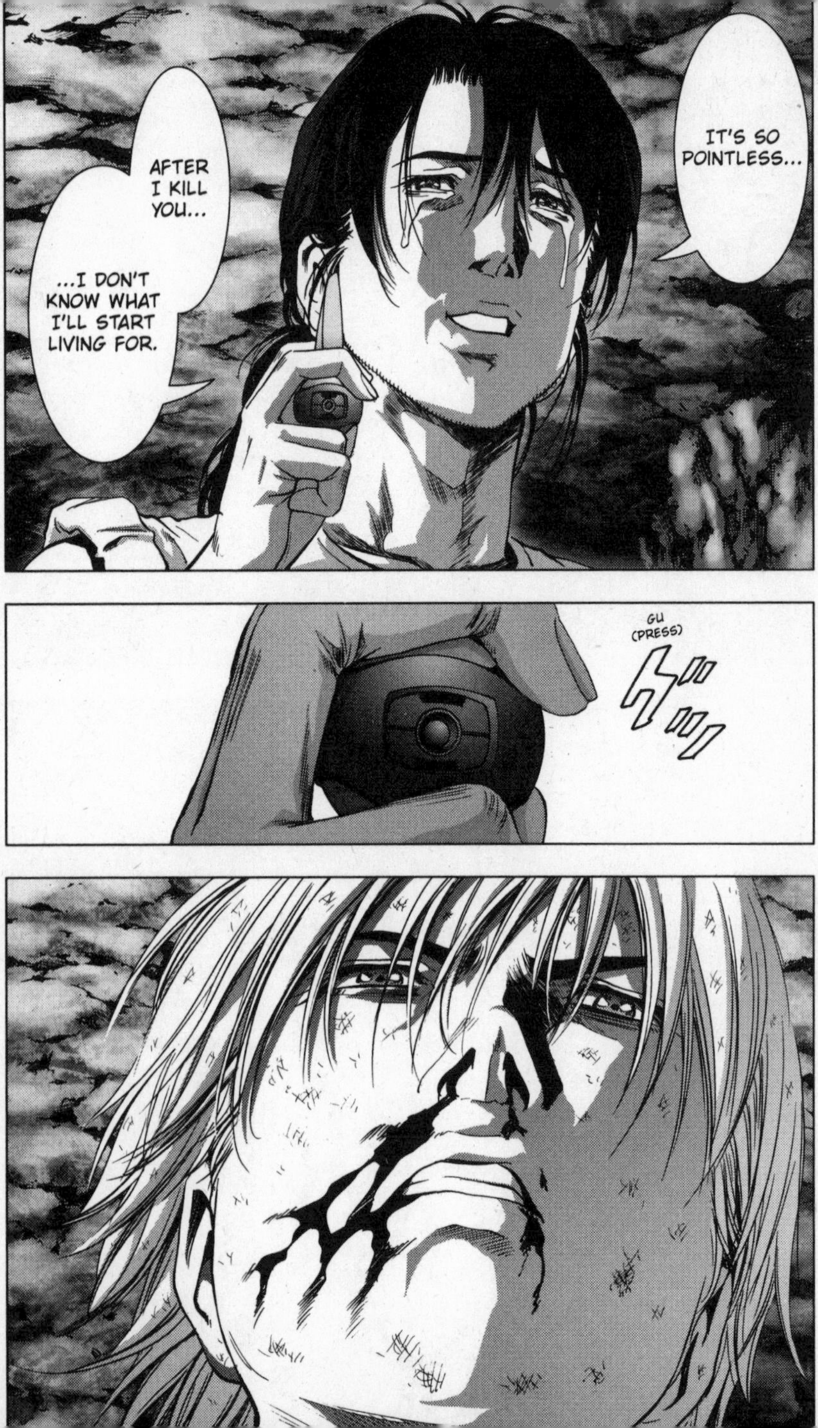
IT'S SO POINTLESS...
AFTER I KILL YOU...
...I DON'T KNOW WHAT I'LL START LIVING FOR.
GU (PRESS)

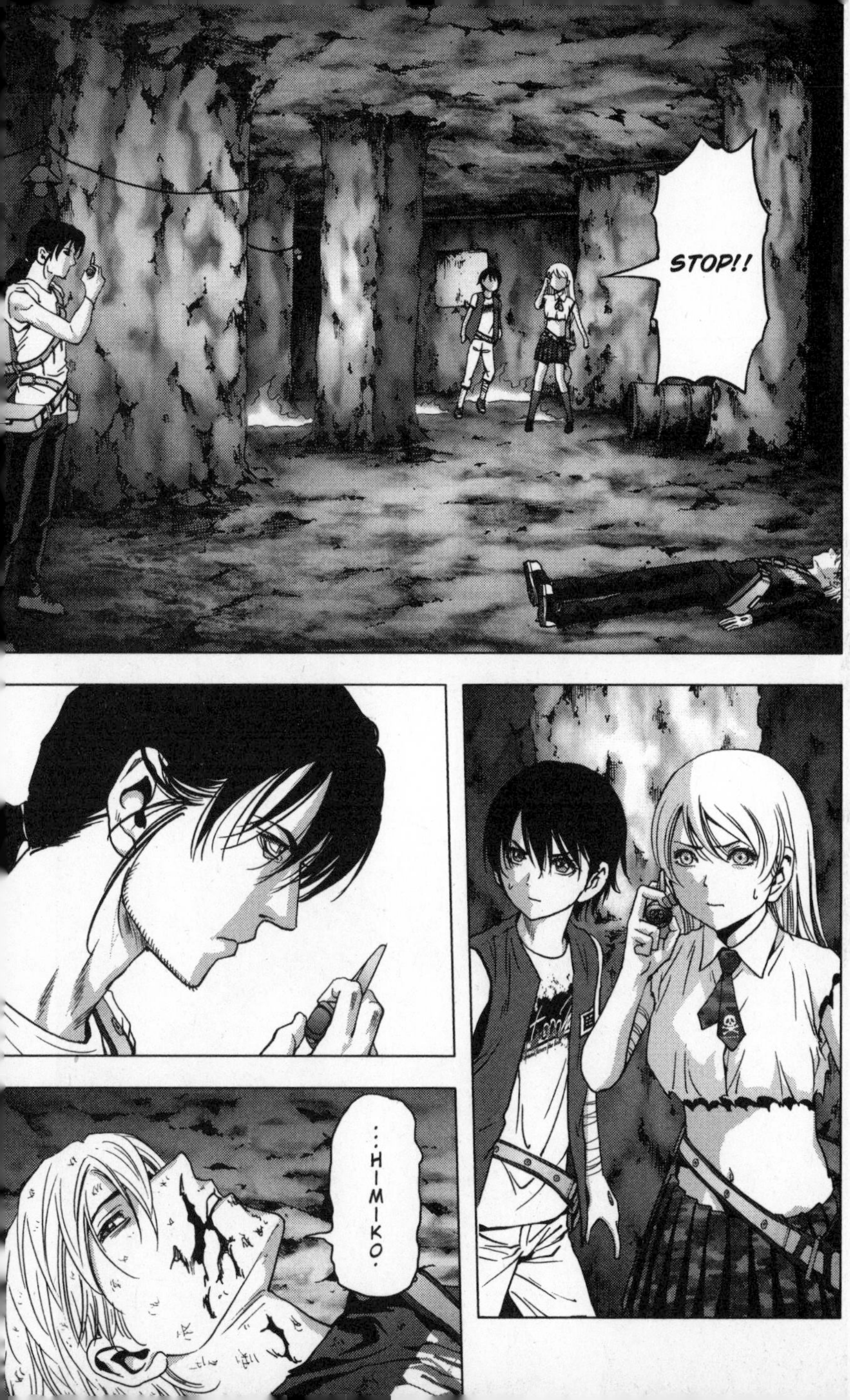
STOP!!
...HIMIKO.

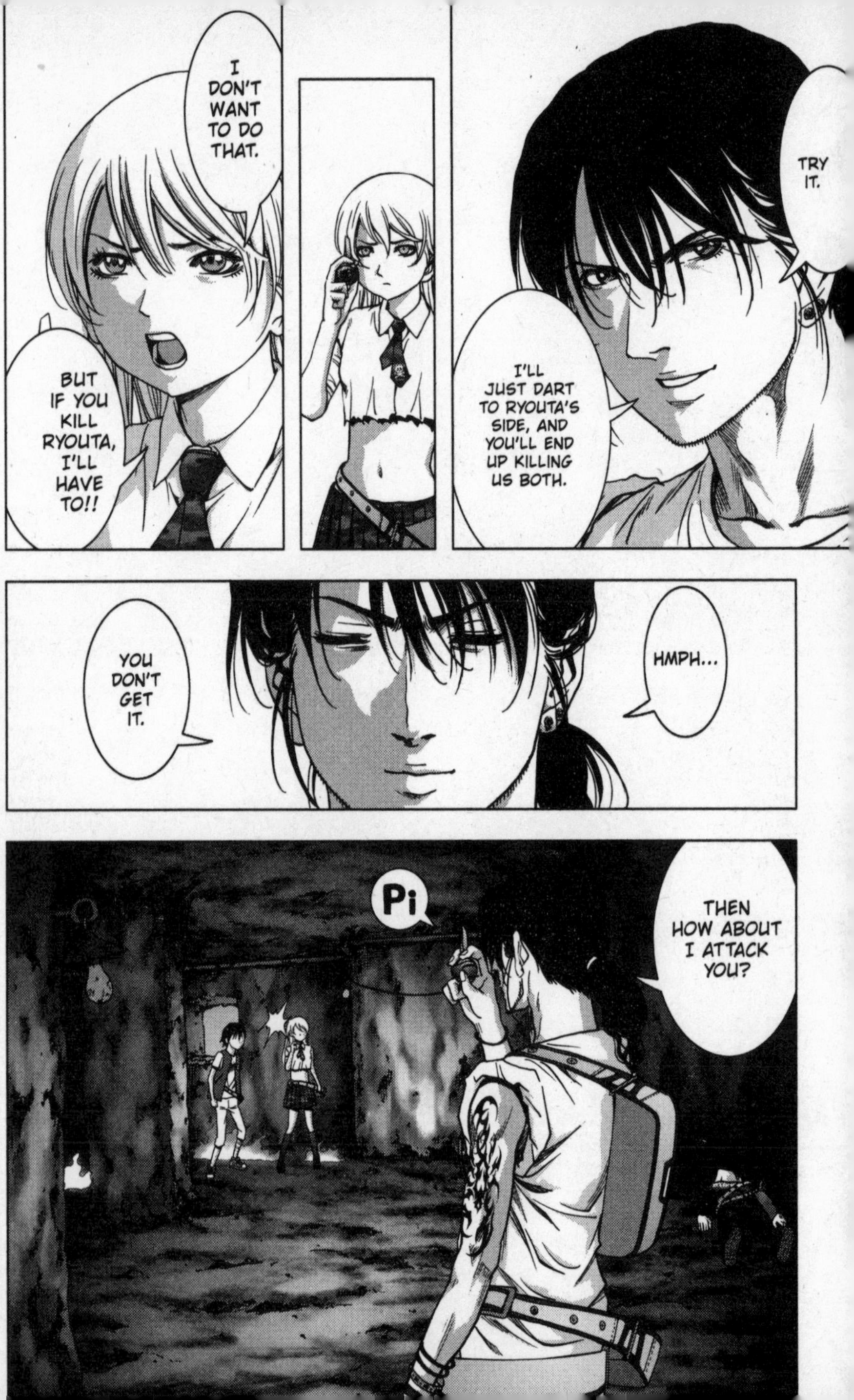
TRY IT.
I'LL JUST DART TO RYOUTA'S SIDE, AND YOU'LL END UP KILLING US BOTH.
I DON'T WANT TO DO THAT.
BUT IF YOU KILL RYOUTA, I'LL HAVE TO!!
HMPH...
YOU DON'T GET IT.
THEN HOW ABOUT I ATTACK YOU?
Pi

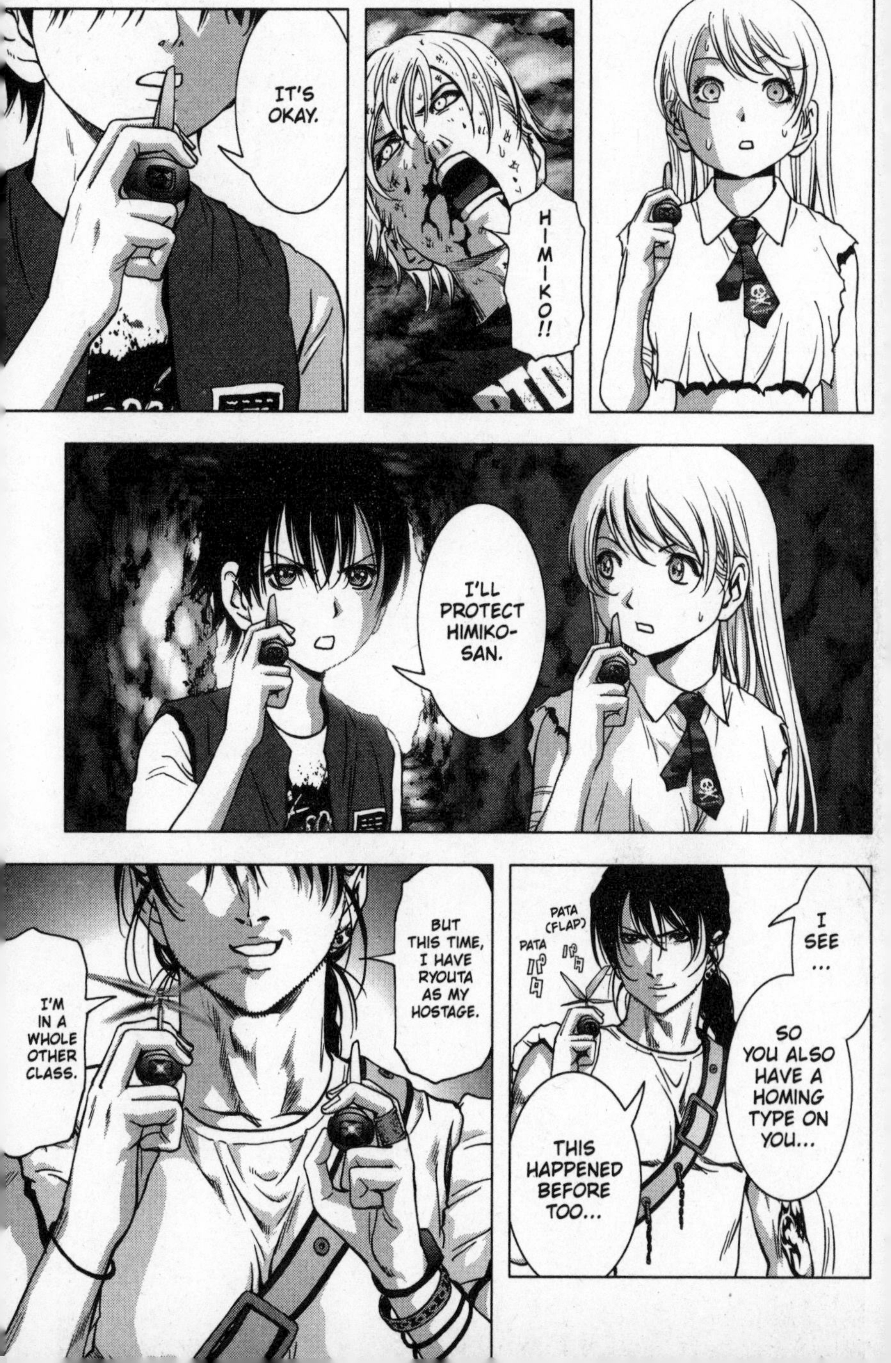
HIMIKO!!
IT'S OKAY.
I'LL PROTECT HIMIKO-SAN.
I SEE...
SO YOU ALSO HAVE A HOMING TYPE ON YOU...
PATA (FLAP)
PATA
THIS HAPPENED BEFORE TOO...
BUT THIS TIME, I HAVE RYOUTA AS MY HOSTAGE.
I'M IN A WHOLE OTHER CLASS.

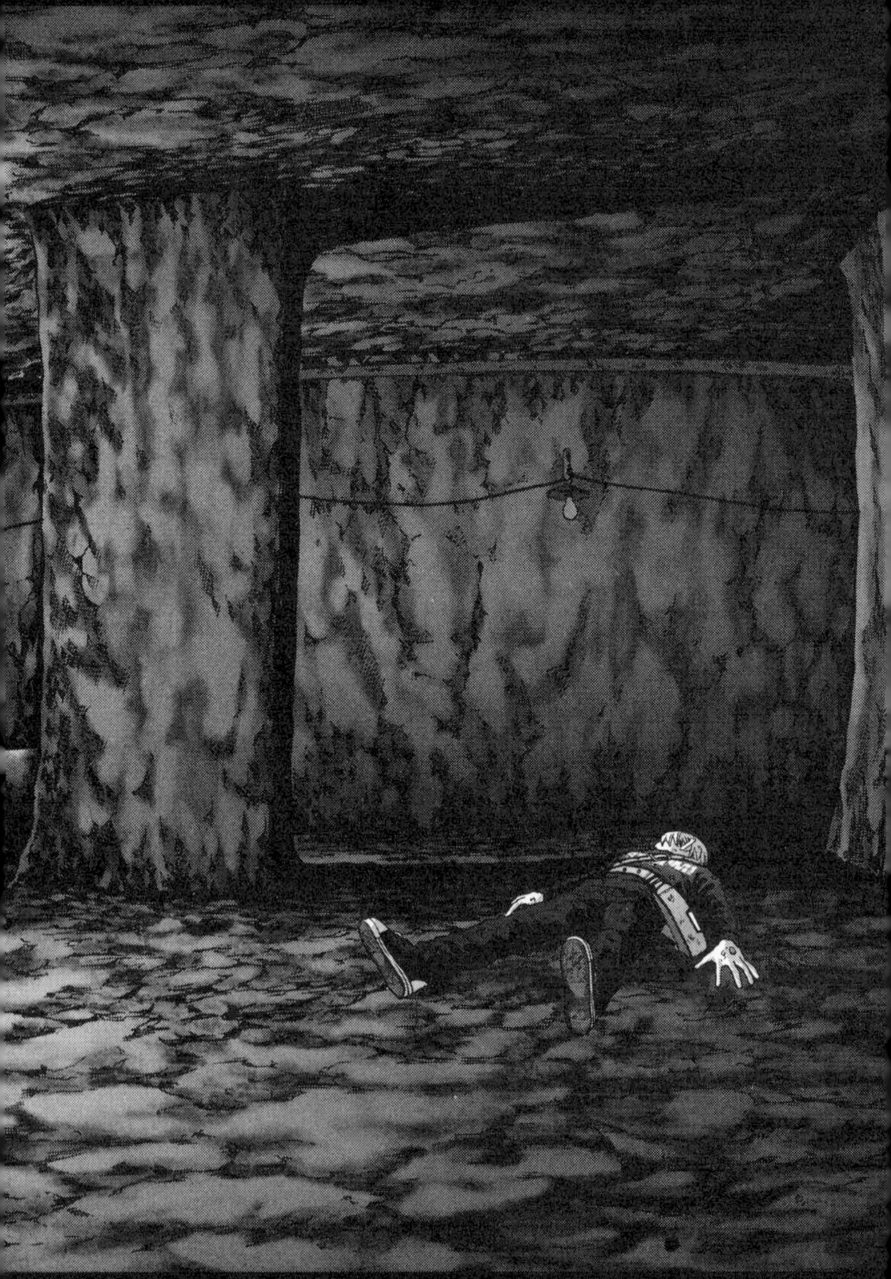

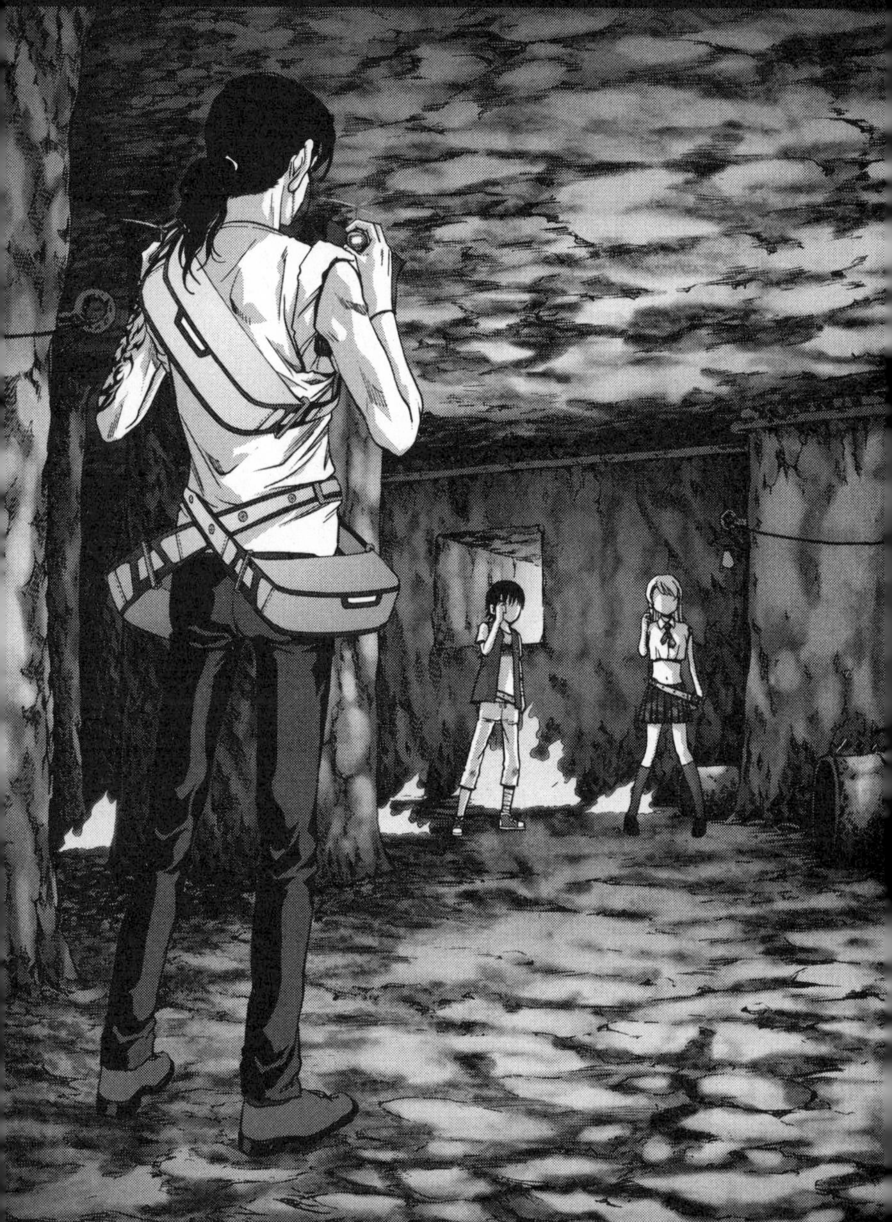

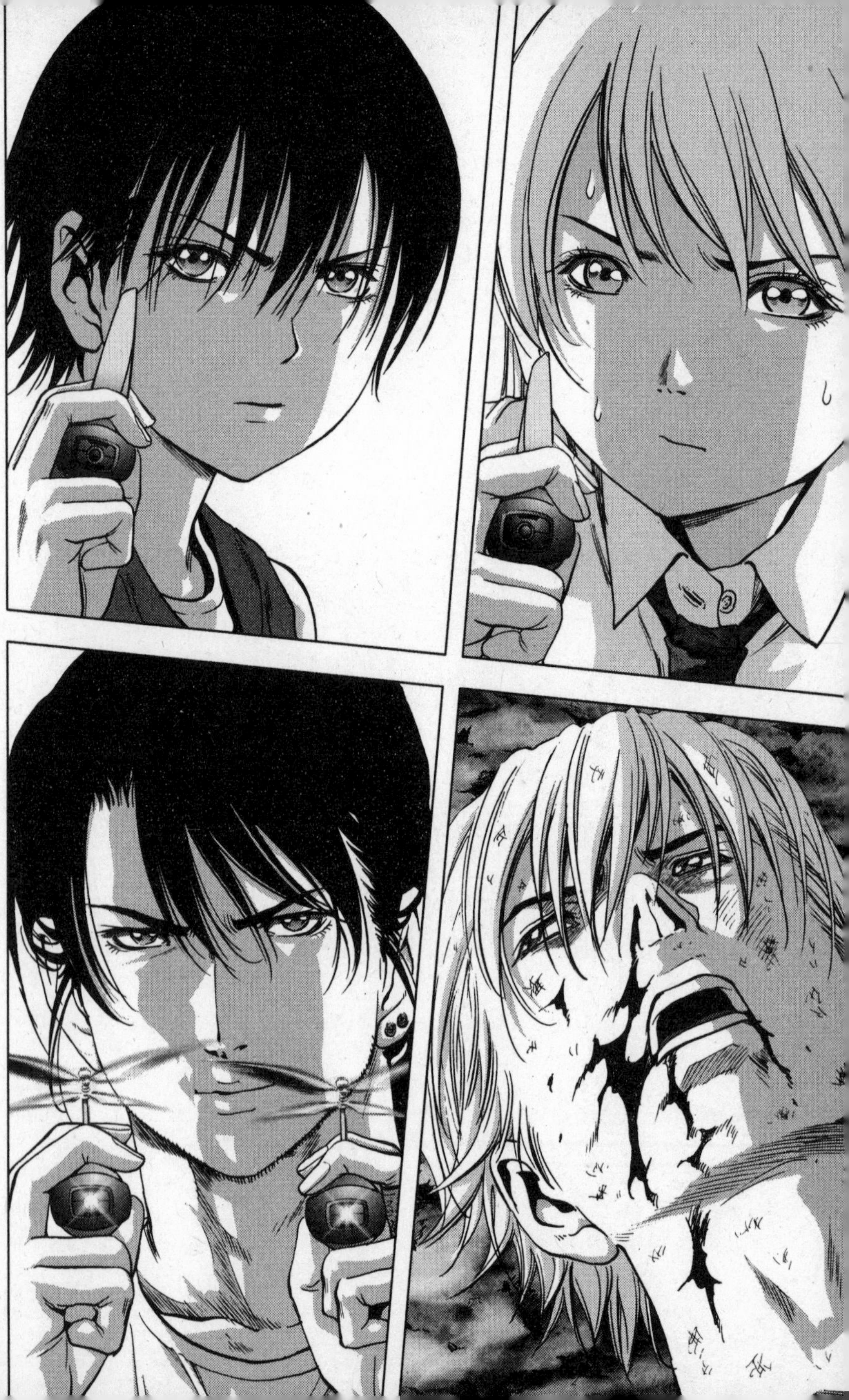

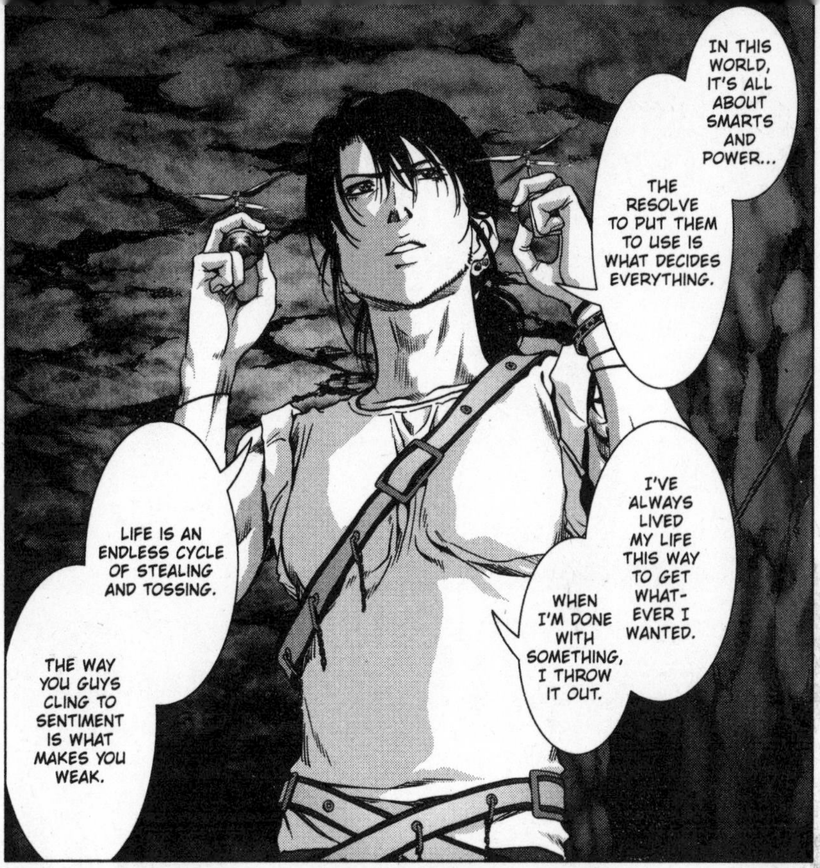
IN THIS WORLD, IT'S ALL ABOUT SMARTS AND POWER...
THE RESOLVE TO PUT THEM TO USE IS WHAT DECIDES EVERYTHING.
I'VE ALWAYS LIVED MY LIFE THIS WAY TO GET WHAT-EVER I WANTED.
WHEN I'M DONE WITH SOMETHING, I THROW IT OUT.
LIFE IS AN ENDLESS CYCLE OF STEALING AND TOSSING.
THE WAY YOU GUYS CLING TO SENTIMENT IS WHAT MAKES YOU WEAK.
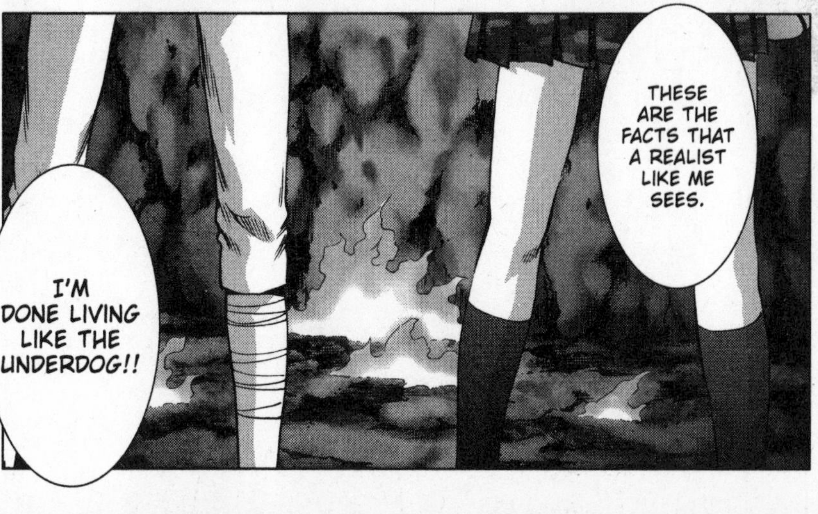
THESE ARE THE FACTS THAT A REALIST LIKE ME SEES.
I'M DONE LIVING LIKE THE UNDERDOG!!

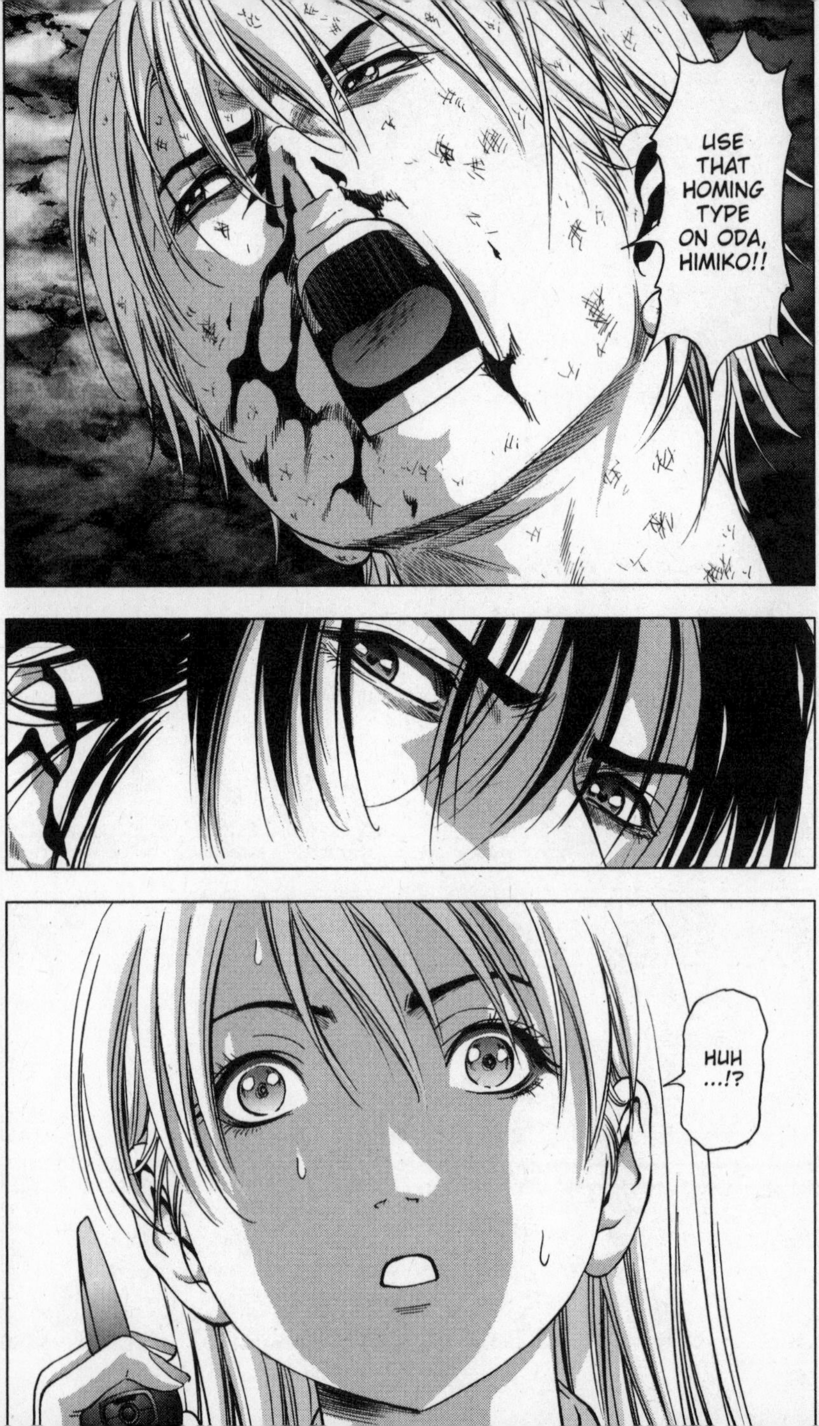
USE THAT HOMING TYPE ON ODA, HIMIKO!!
HUH ...!?

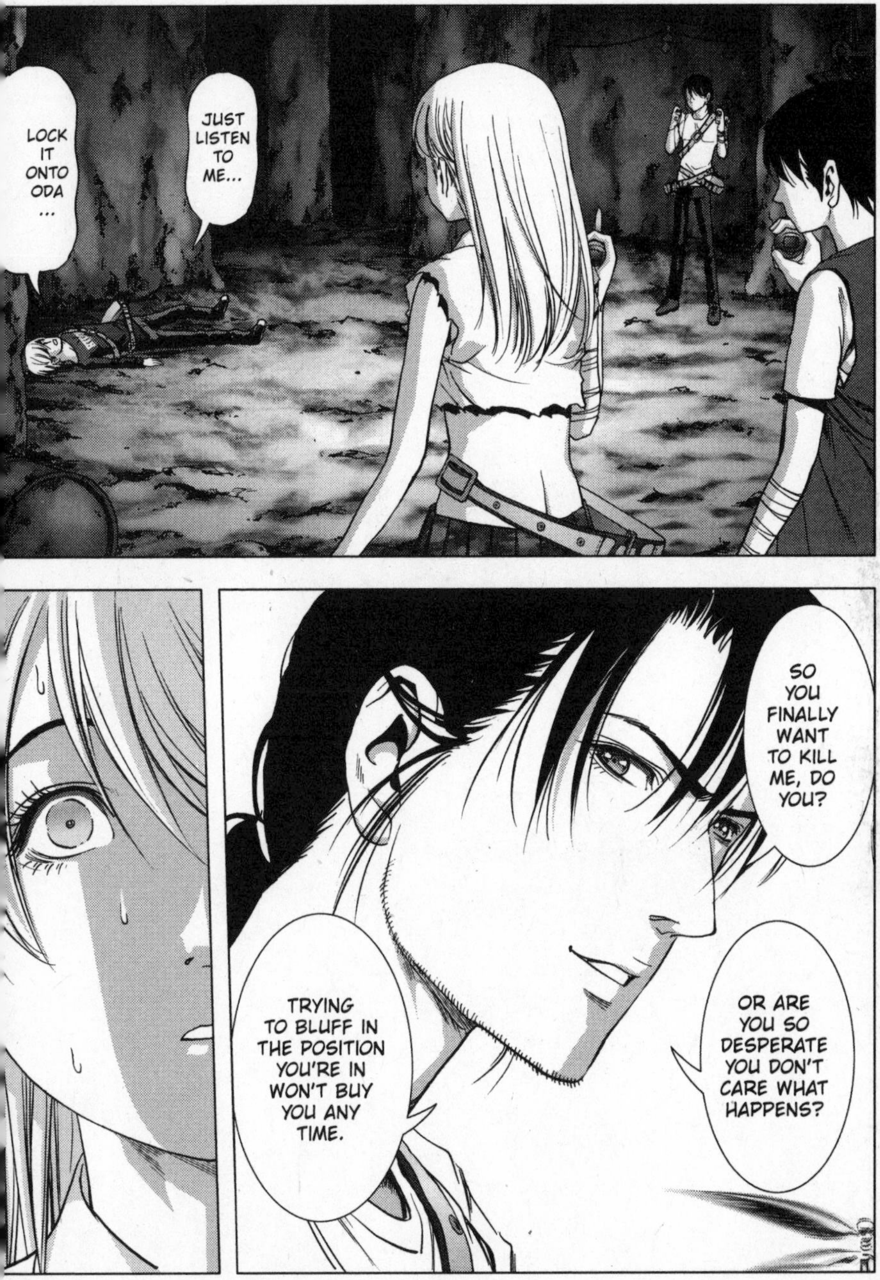
JUST LISTEN TO ME...
LOCK IT ONTO ODA...
SO YOU FINALLY WANT TO KILL ME, DO YOU?
OR ARE YOU SO DESPERATE YOU DON'T CARE WHAT HAPPENS?
TRYING TO BLUFF IN THE POSITION YOU'RE IN WON'T BUY YOU ANY TIME.

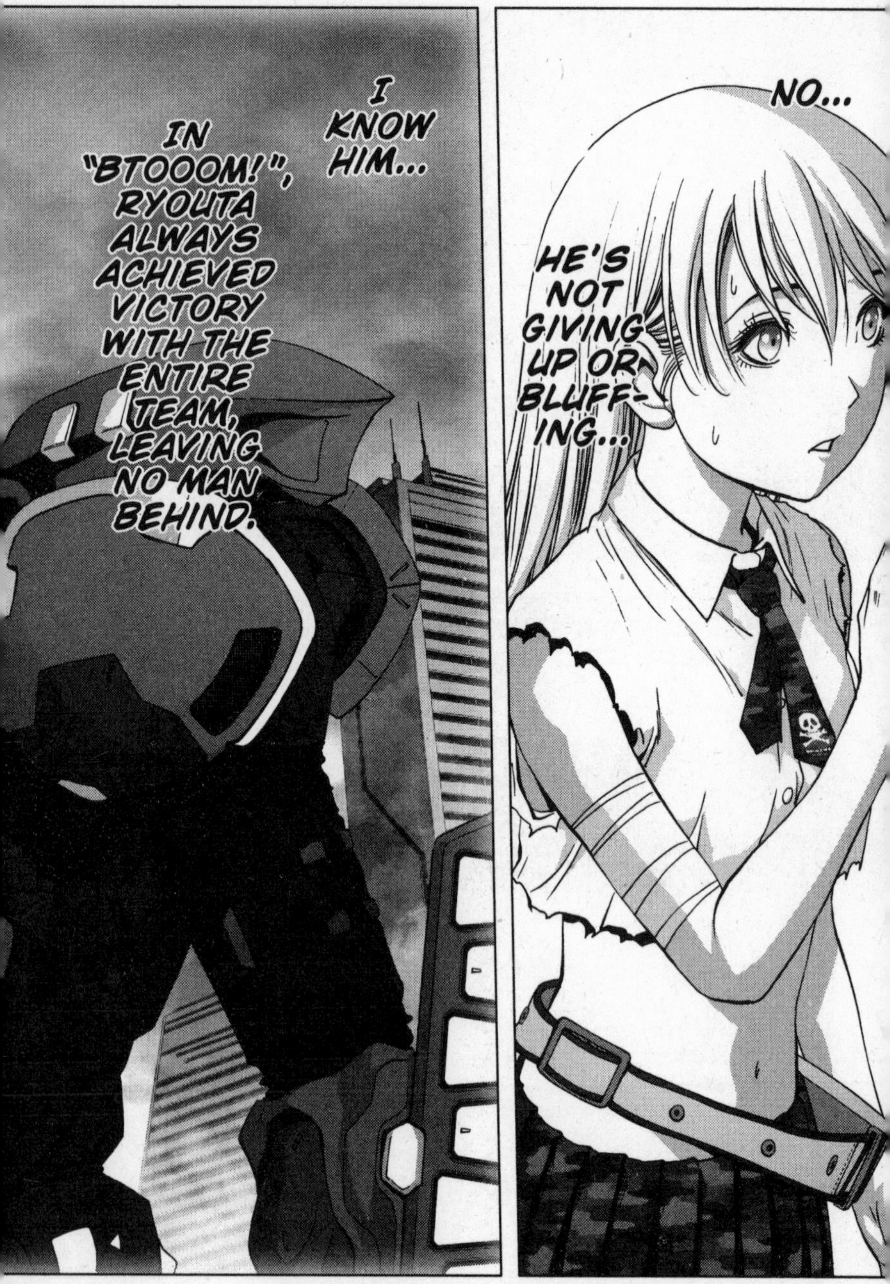
NO...
HE'S NOT GIVING UP OR BLUFF-ING...
I KNOW HIM...
IN "BTOOOM!", RYOUTA ALWAYS ACHIEVED VICTORY WITH THE ENTIRE TEAM, LEAVING NO MAN BEHIND.

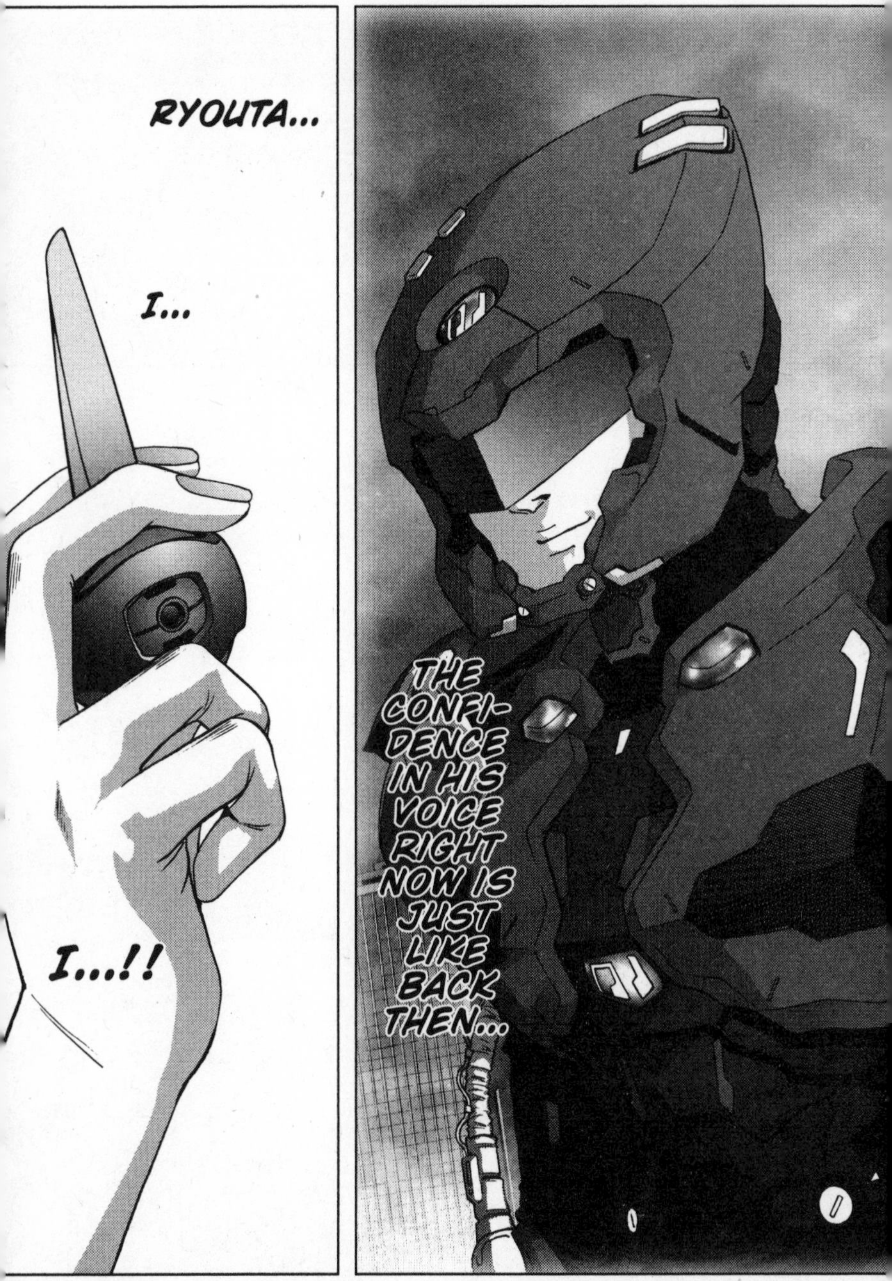
THE CONFIDENCE IN HIS VOICE RIGHT NOW IS JUST LIKE BACK THEN...
RYOUTA...
I...
I...!!

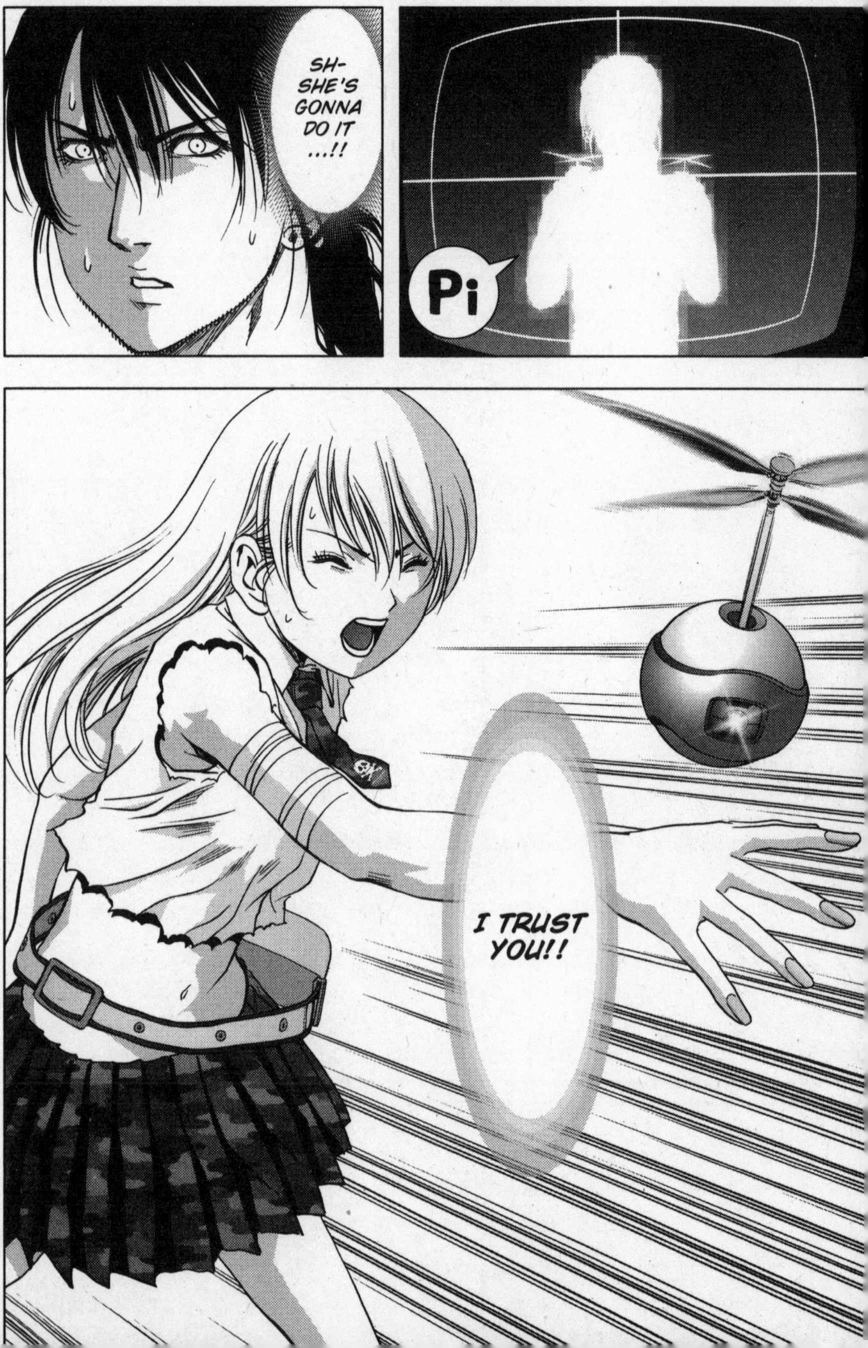
Pi
SH- SHE'S GONNA DO IT ...!!
I TRUST YOU!!

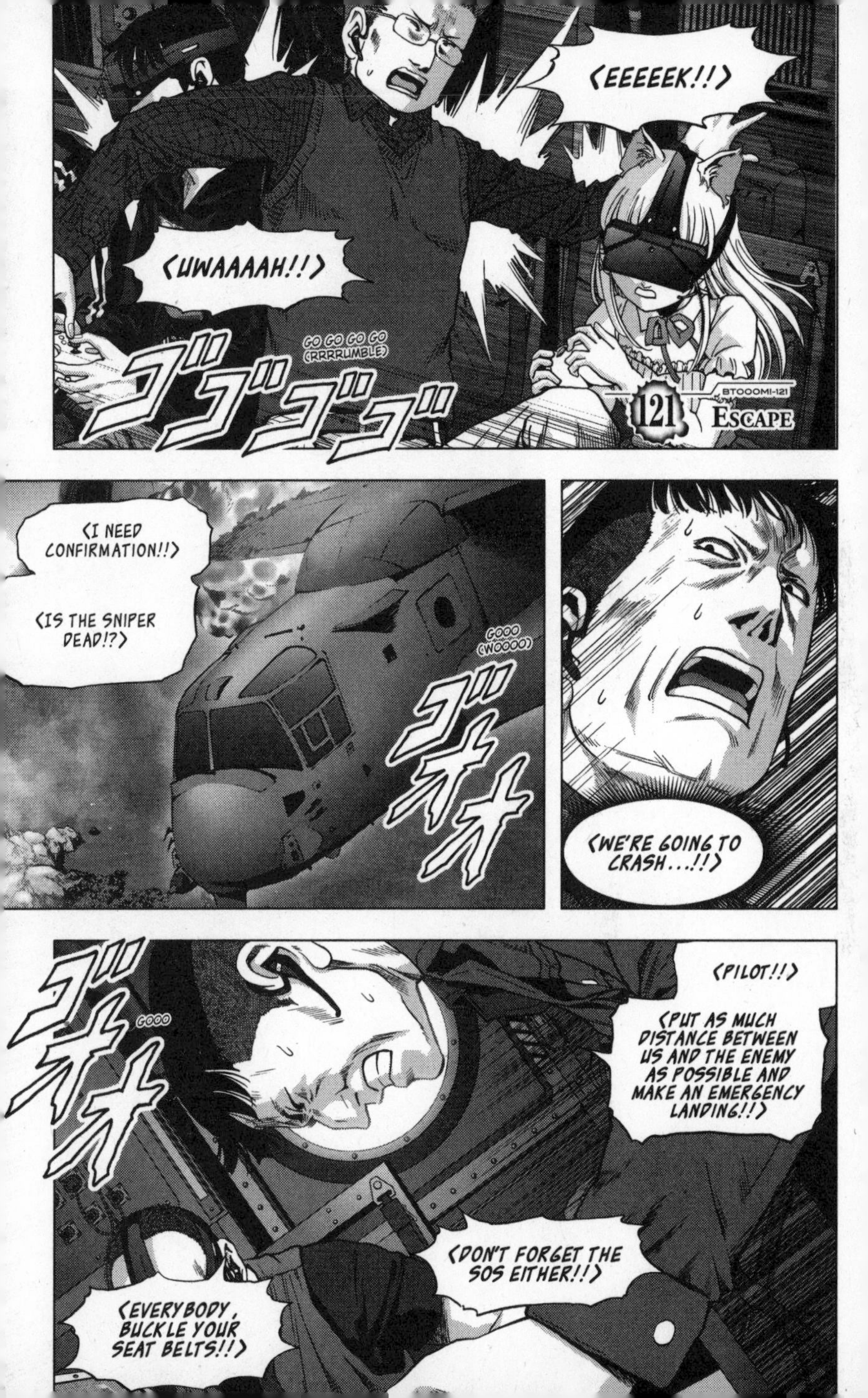
〈EEEEEK!!〉
〈UWAAAAH!!〉
GO GO GO GO (RRRRUMBLE)
BTOOOM!-121
121 ESCAPE
〈WE'RE GOING TO CRASH...!!〉
〈I NEED CONFIRMATION!!〉
〈IS THE SNIPER DEAD!?〉
GOOO (WOOOO)
〈PILOT!!〉
〈PUT AS MUCH DISTANCE BETWEEN US AND THE ENEMY AS POSSIBLE AND MAKE AN EMERGENCY LANDING!!〉
GOOO
〈DON'T FORGET THE SOS EITHER!!〉
〈EVERYBODY, BUCKLE YOUR SEAT BELTS!!〉

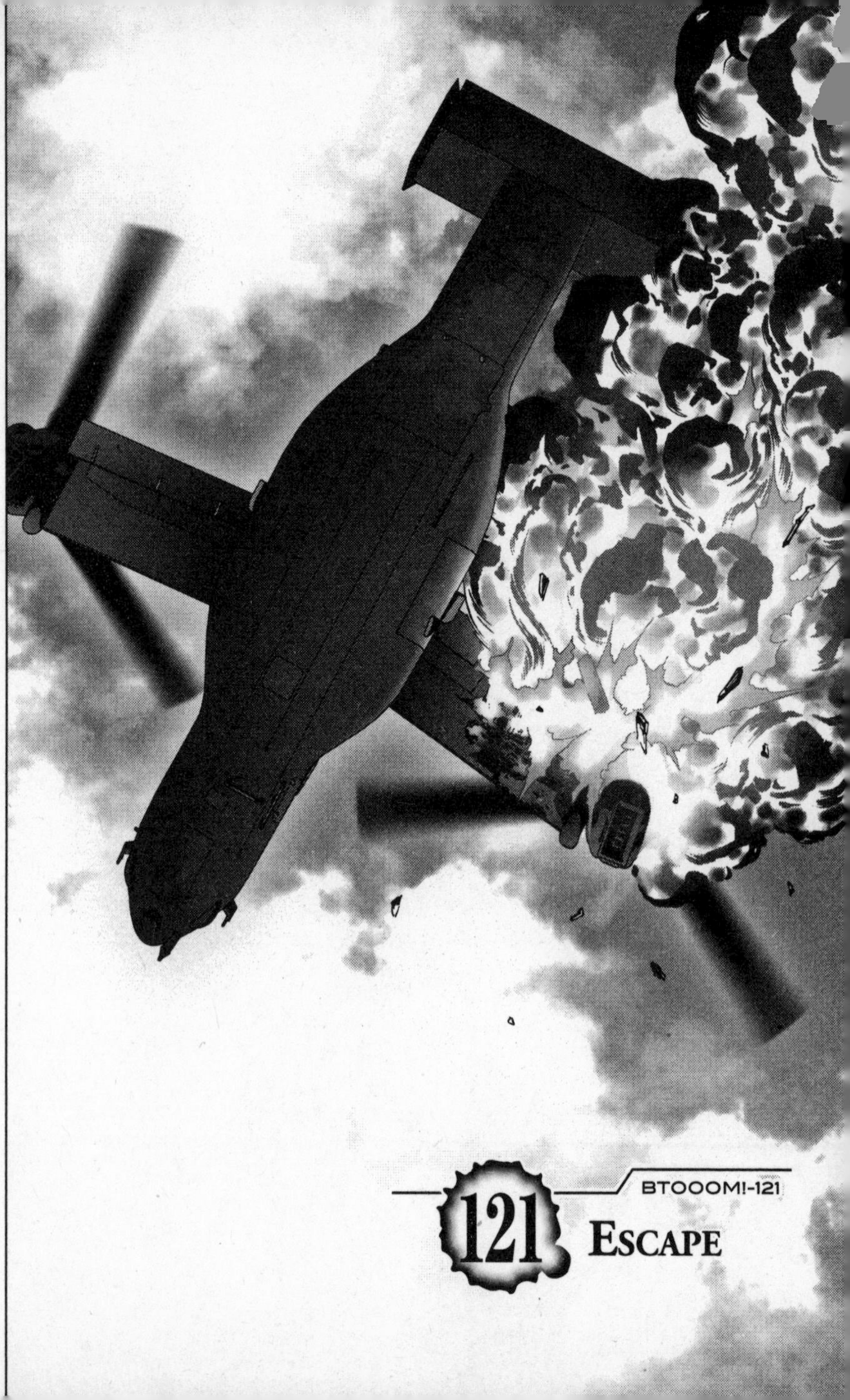
BTOOOM!-121

121 Escape

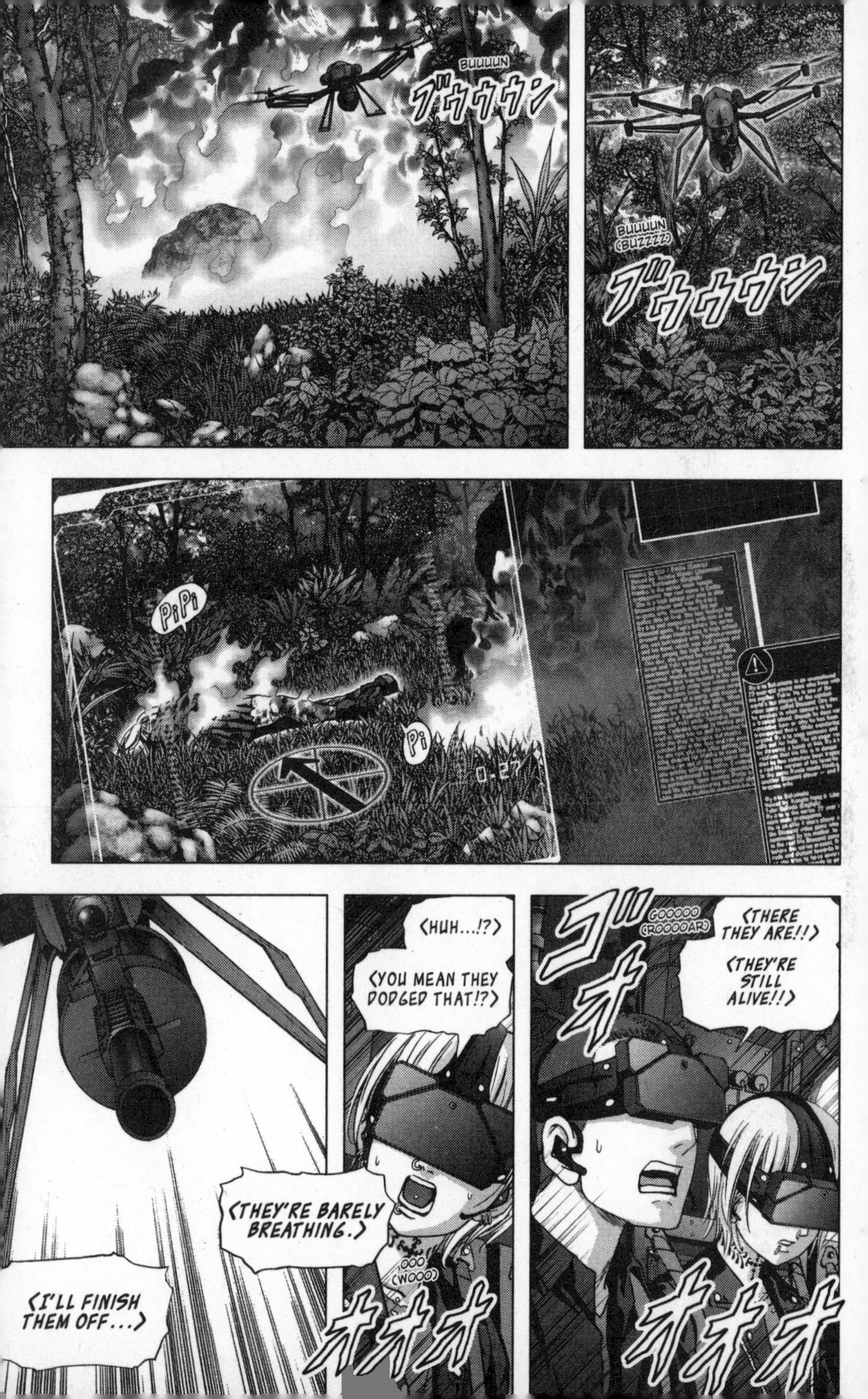
Buuuun
(Buzzzz)
ブウウウン
Buuuun
ブウウウン
PiPi
Pi
Goooo
(Roooar)
ゴオ
〈There they are!!〉
〈They're still alive!!〉
オオオ
〈Huh...!?〉
〈You mean they dodged that!?〉
〈They're barely breathing.〉
ooo
(Wooo)
オオオ
〈I'll finish them off...〉

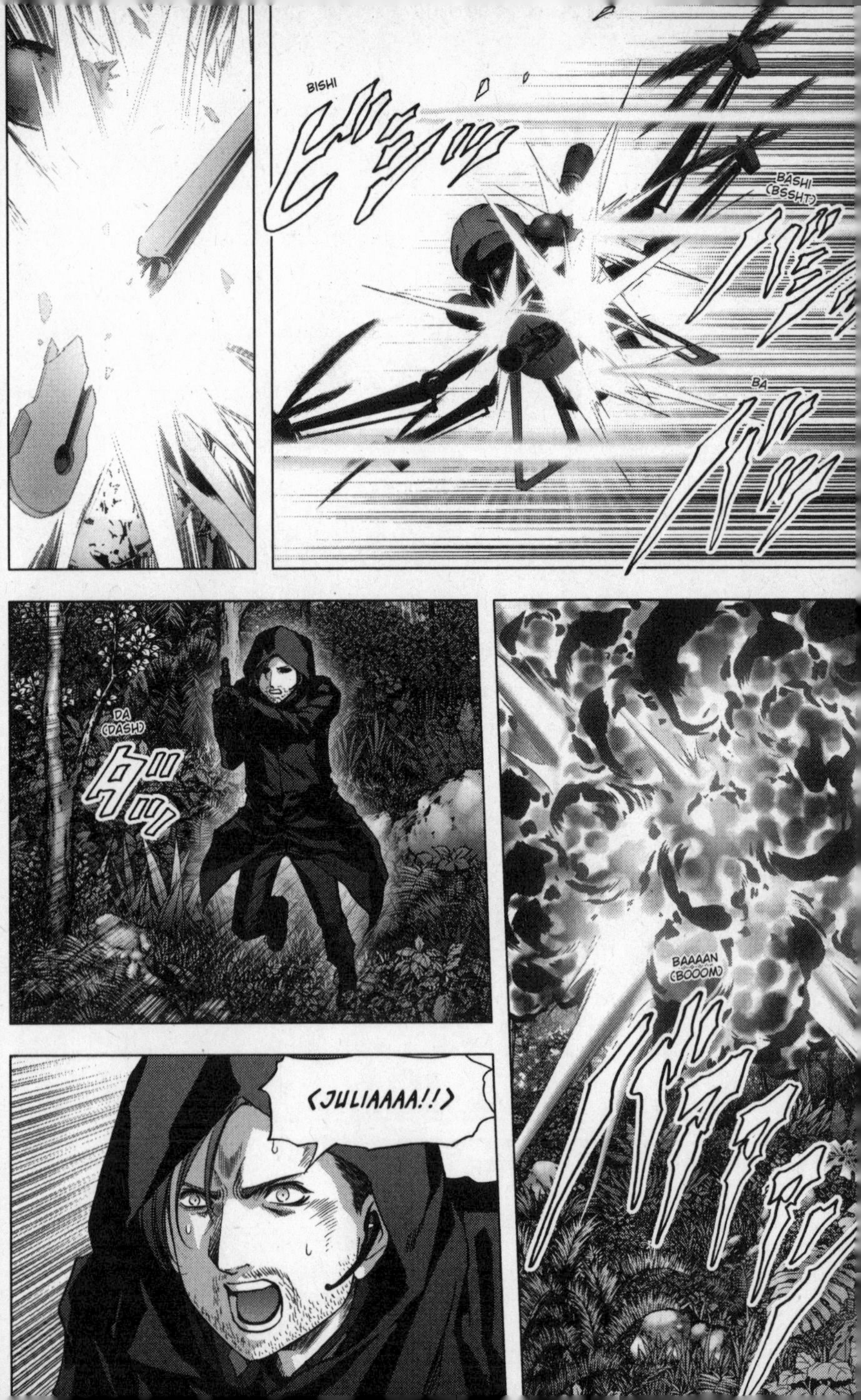
BASHI (BSSHT)
BA
BISHI
BAAAAN (BOOOM)
DA (DASH)
<JULIAAAA!!>

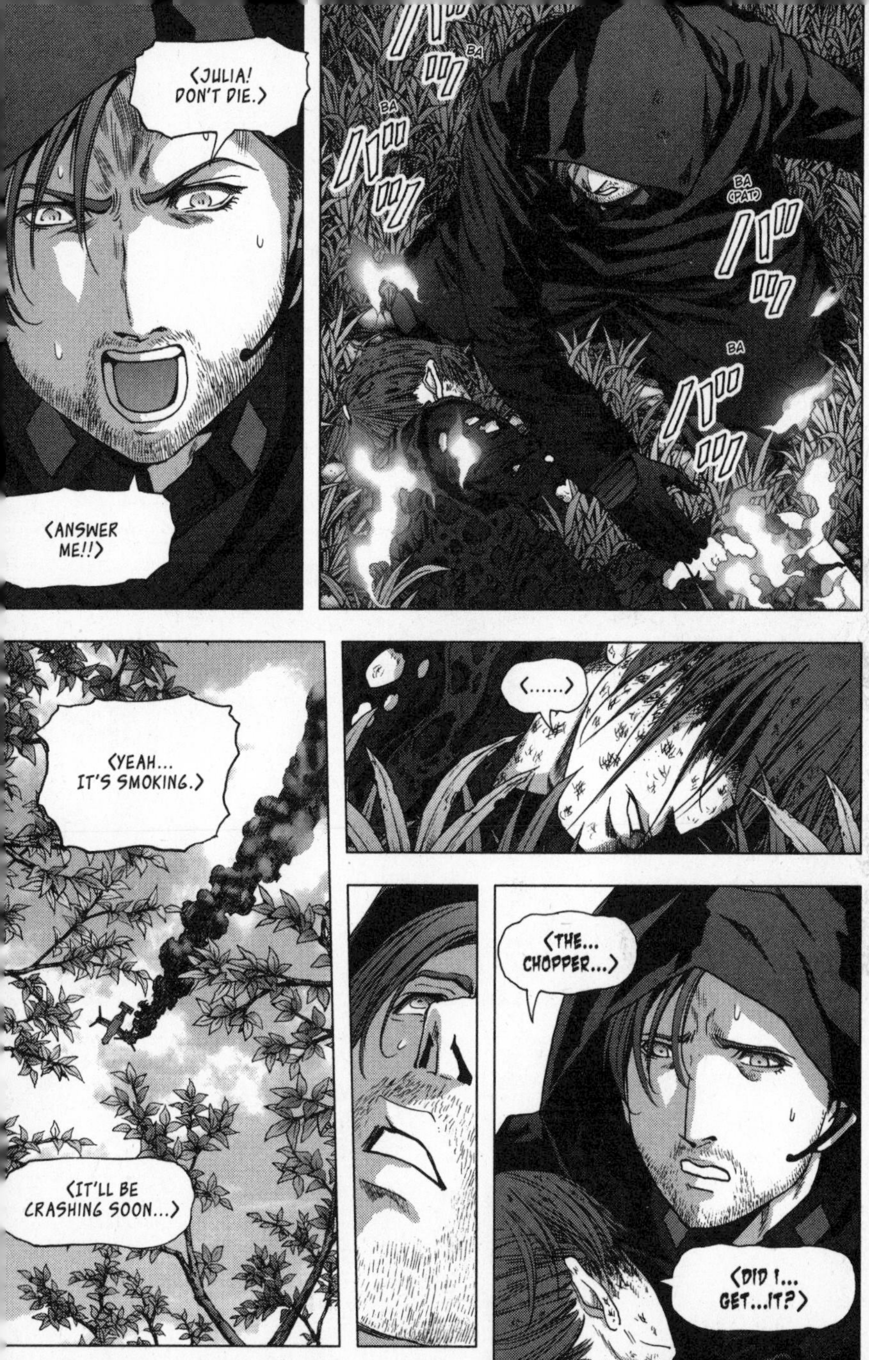
BA
BA (PAT)
BA
BA
〈JULIA! DON'T DIE.〉
〈ANSWER ME!!〉
〈......〉
〈THE... CHOPPER...〉
〈DID I... GET...IT?〉
〈YEAH... IT'S SMOKING.〉
〈IT'LL BE CRASHING SOON...〉

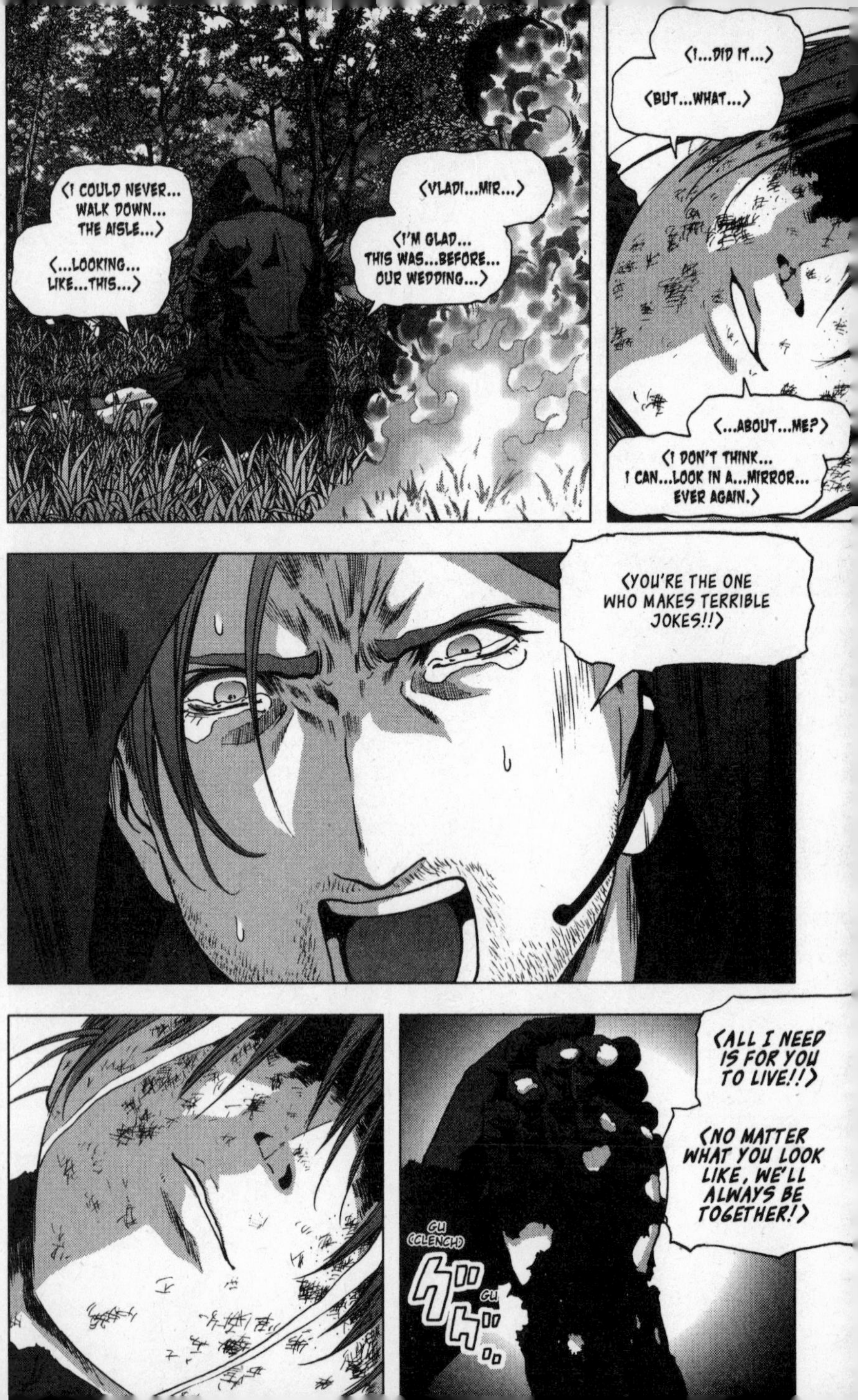

〈I...DID IT...〉
〈BUT...WHAT...〉
〈...ABOUT...ME?〉
〈I DON'T THINK... I CAN...LOOK IN A...MIRROR... EVER AGAIN.〉
〈VLADI...MIR...〉
〈I'M GLAD... THIS WAS...BEFORE... OUR WEDDING...〉
〈I COULD NEVER... WALK DOWN... THE AISLE...〉
〈...LOOKING... LIKE...THIS...〉
〈YOU'RE THE ONE WHO MAKES TERRIBLE JOKES!!〉
〈ALL I NEED IS FOR YOU TO LIVE!!〉
〈NO MATTER WHAT YOU LOOK LIKE, WE'LL ALWAYS BE TOGETHER!〉
GU (CLENCH)
GU

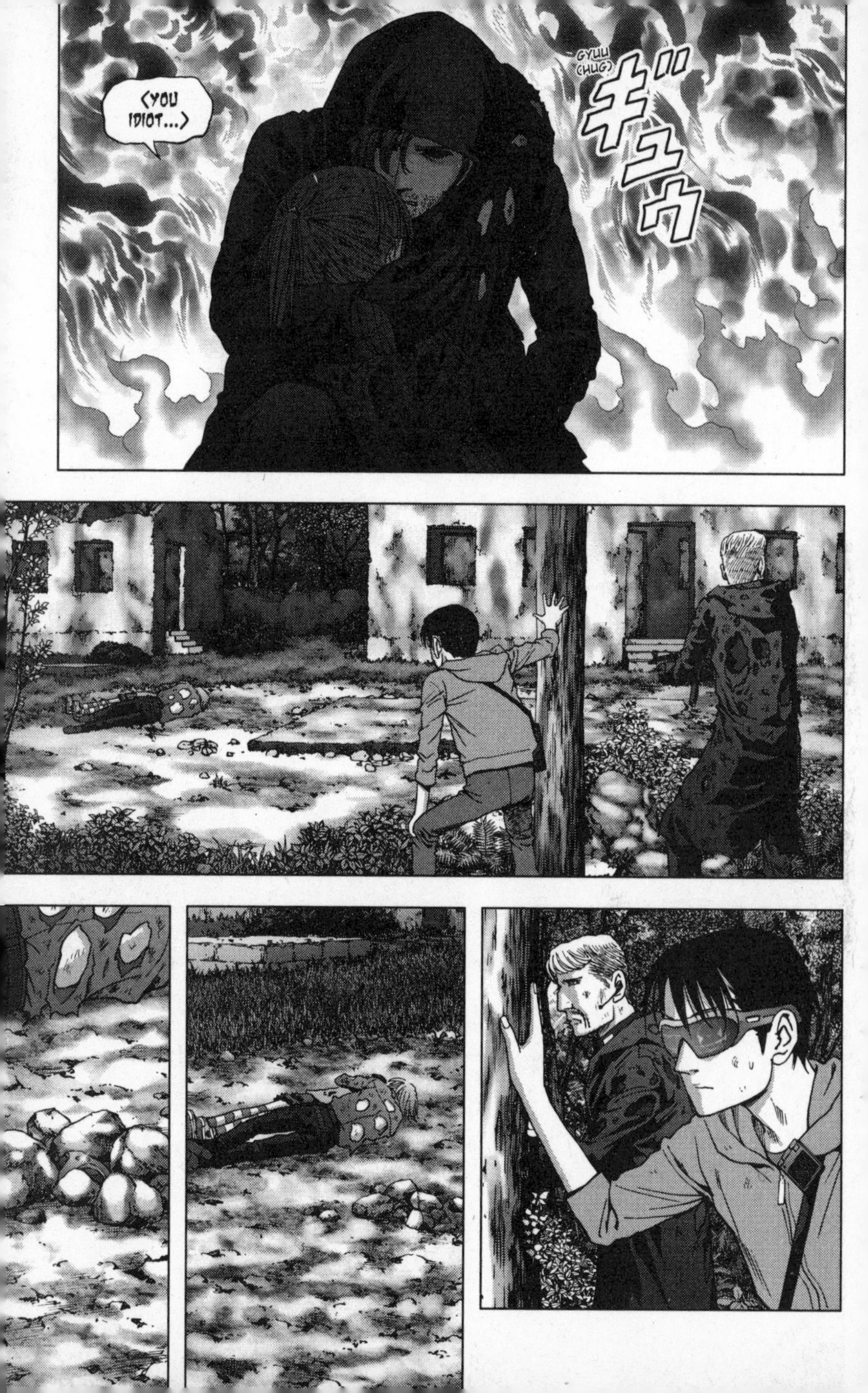
GYUU (HUG)
ギュウ
<YOU IDIOT...>

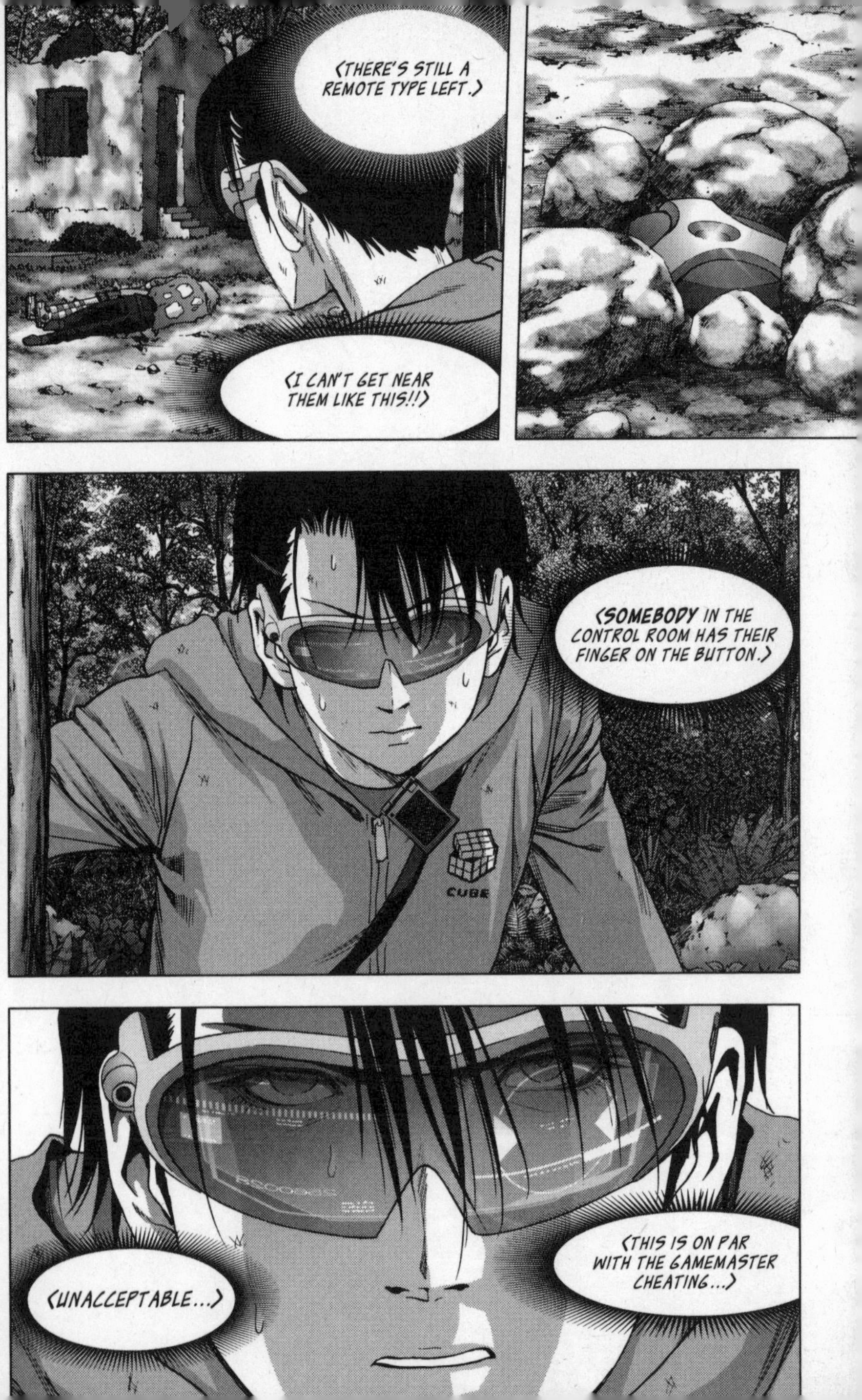
⟨THERE'S STILL A REMOTE TYPE LEFT.⟩
⟨I CAN'T GET NEAR THEM LIKE THIS!!⟩
⟨SOMEBODY IN THE CONTROL ROOM HAS THEIR FINGER ON THE BUTTON.⟩
CUBE
⟨THIS IS ON PAR WITH THE GAMEMASTER CHEATING...⟩
⟨UNACCEPTABLE...⟩

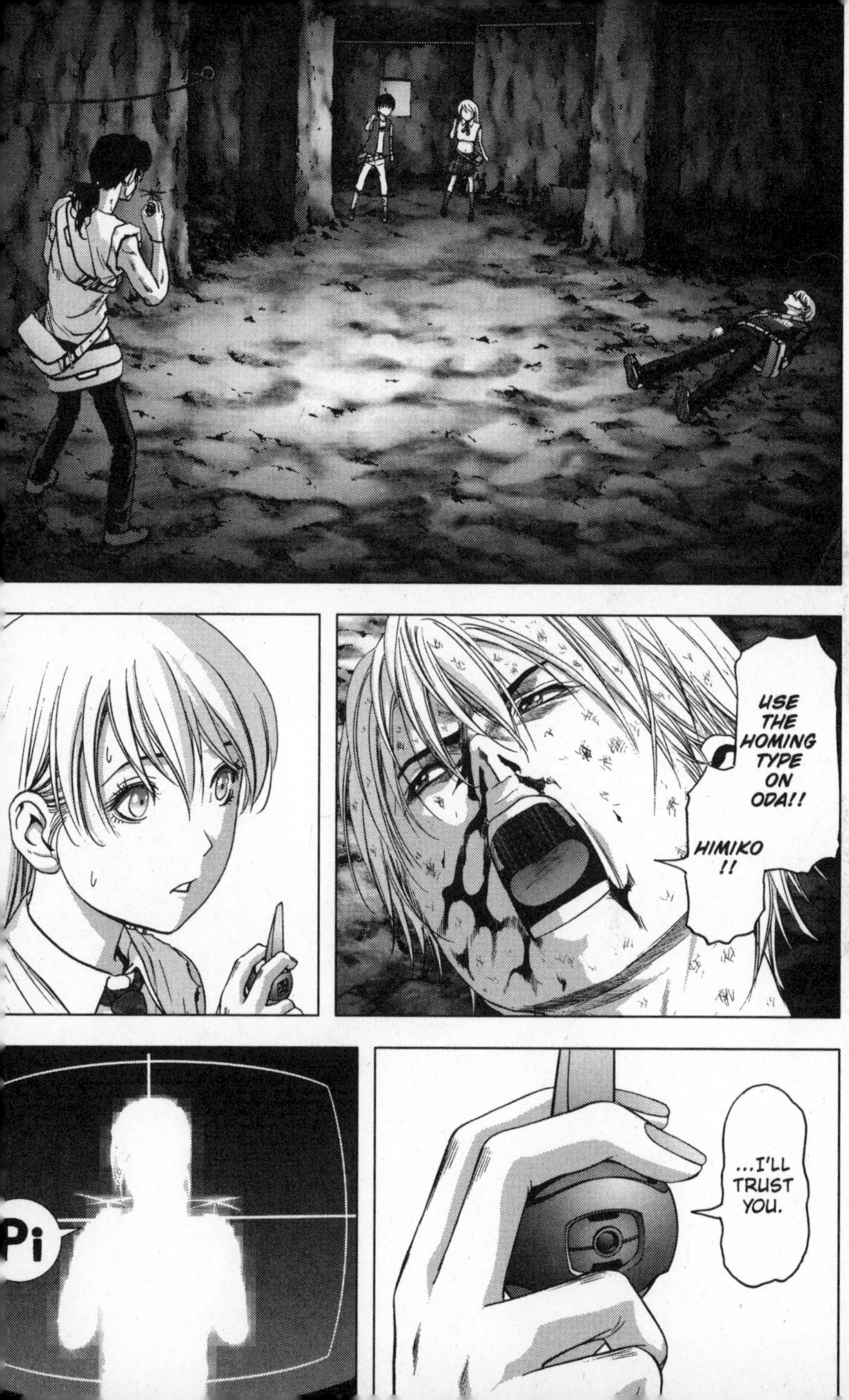
USE THE HOMING TYPE ON ODA!!
HIMIKO !!
...I'LL TRUST YOU.
Pi

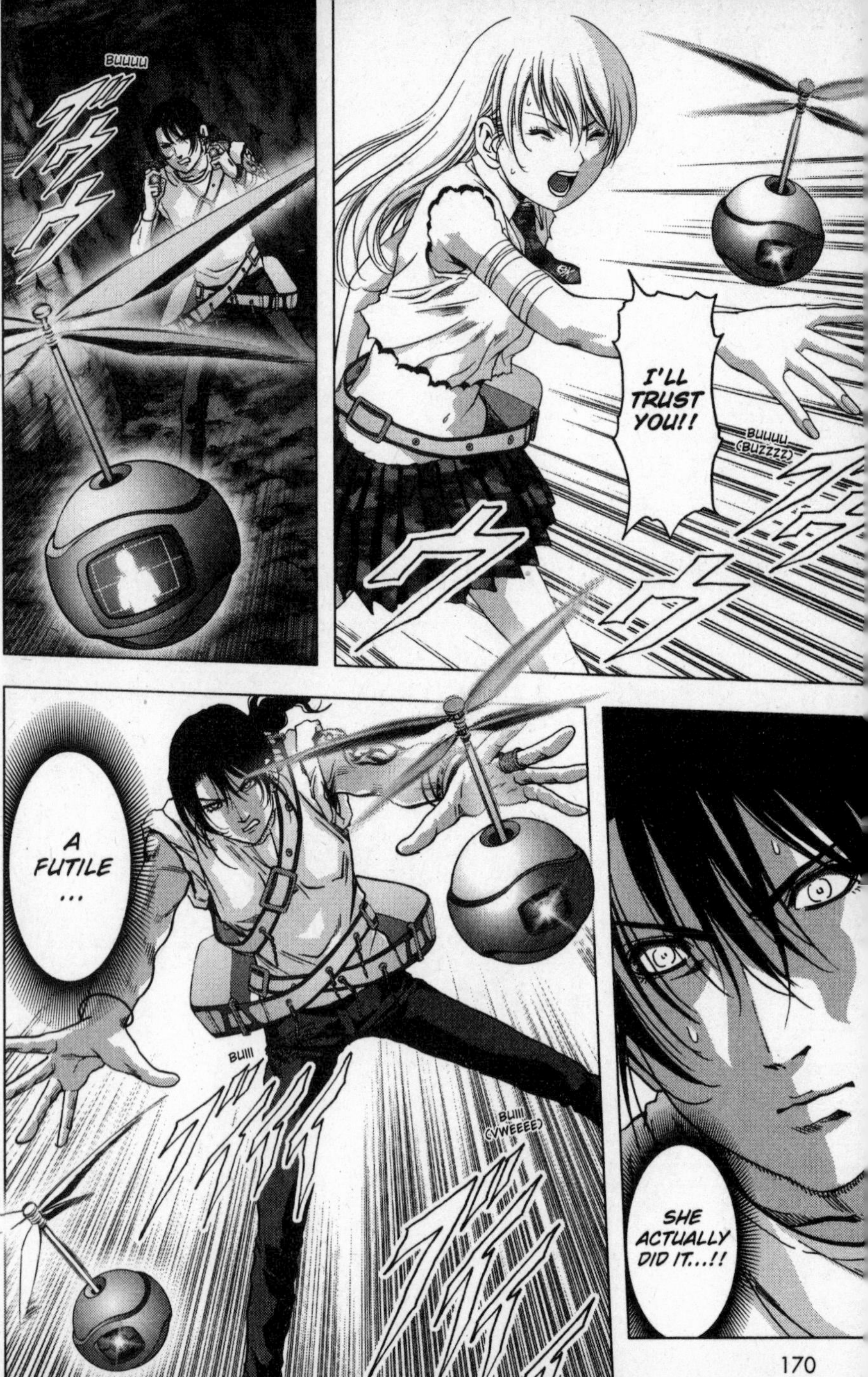
I'LL TRUST YOU!!
BUUUU (BUZZZZ)
BUUUU
SHE ACTUALLY DID IT...!!
A FUTILE ...
BUIII
BUIII (VWEEEE)

...LAST-DITCH EFFORT!!

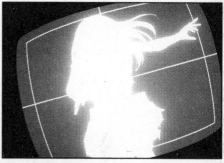

I'VE RELEASED TWO HOMING TYPES LOCKED ONTO THEM.

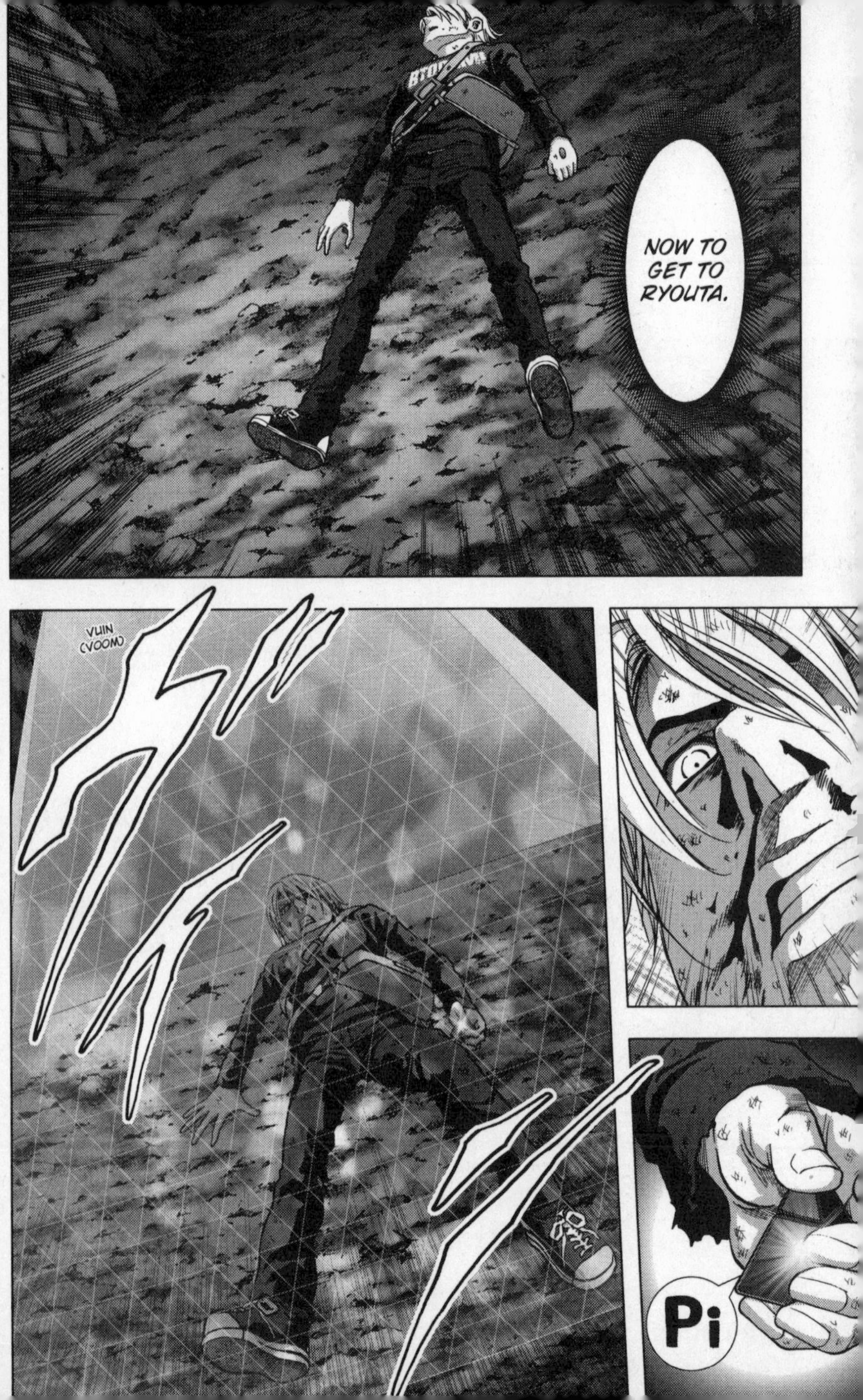
NOW TO GET TO RYOUTA.
Pi
VUIN (VOOM)

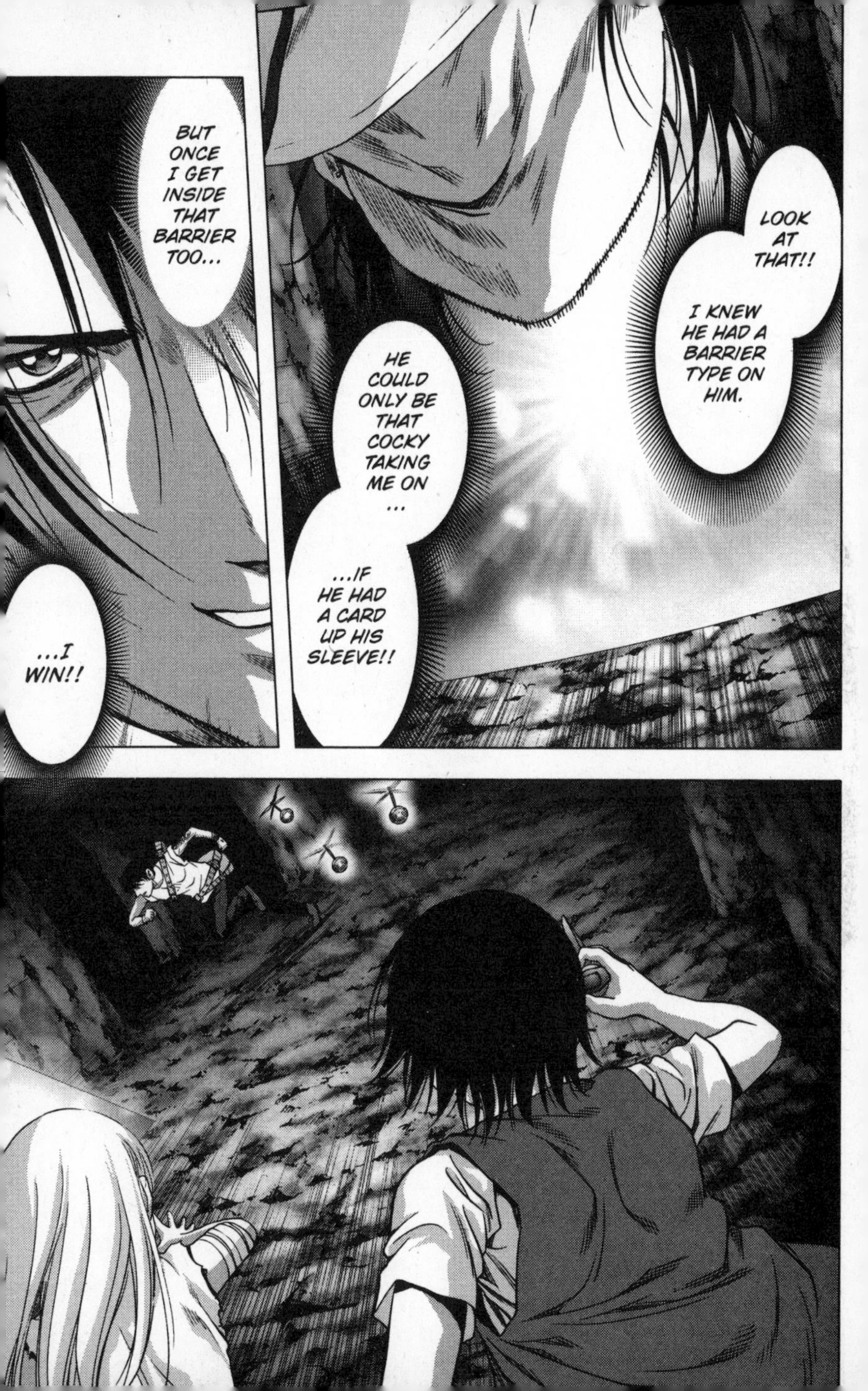

LOOK AT THAT!!
I KNEW HE HAD A BARRIER TYPE ON HIM.
HE COULD ONLY BE THAT COCKY TAKING ME ON ...
...IF HE HAD A CARD UP HIS SLEEVE!!
BUT ONCE I GET INSIDE THAT BARRIER TOO...
...I WIN!!

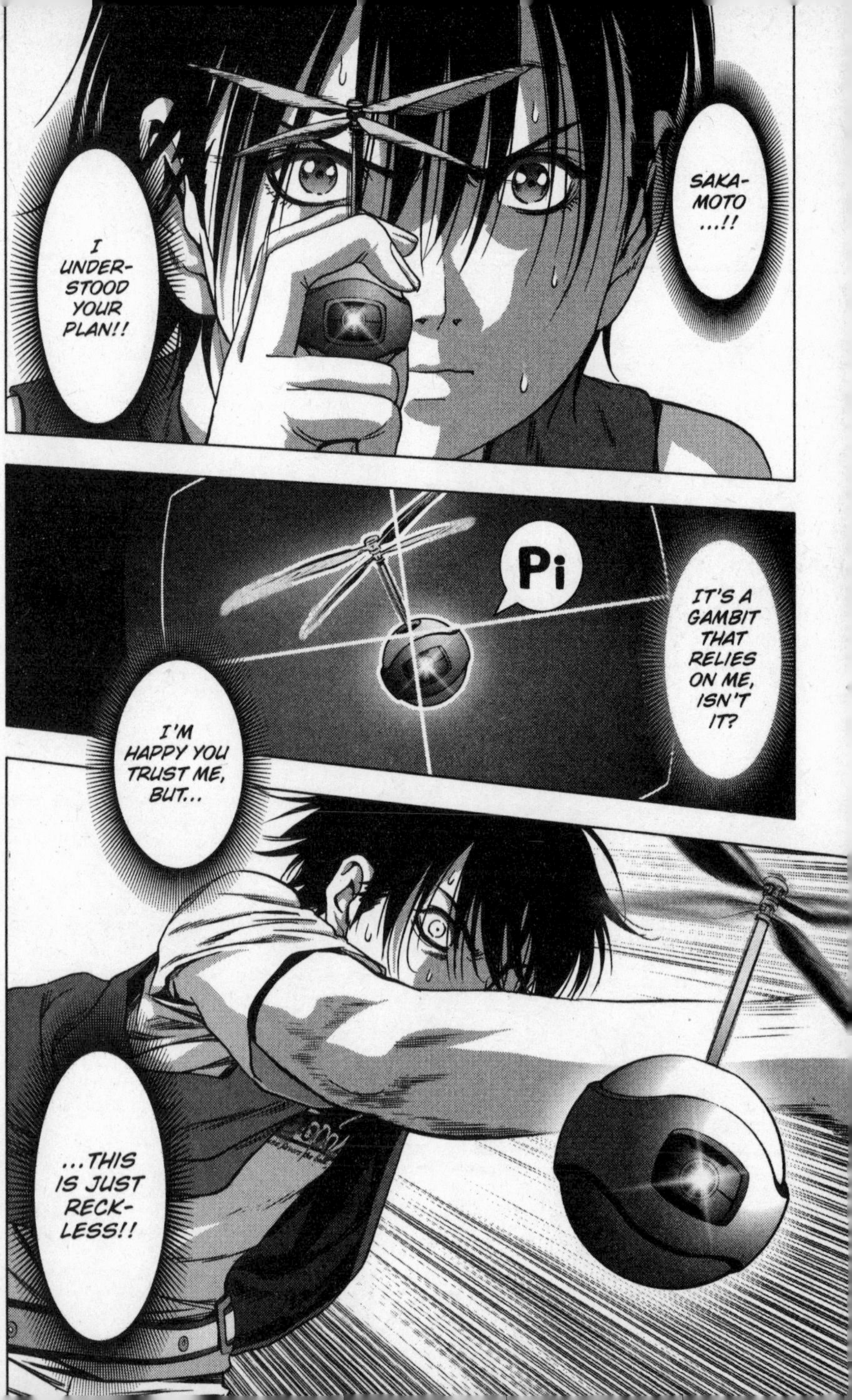
SAKA-MOTO ...!!
I UNDER-STOOD YOUR PLAN!!
Pi
IT'S A GAMBIT THAT RELIES ON ME, ISN'T IT?
I'M HAPPY YOU TRUST ME, BUT...
...THIS IS JUST RECK-LESS!!

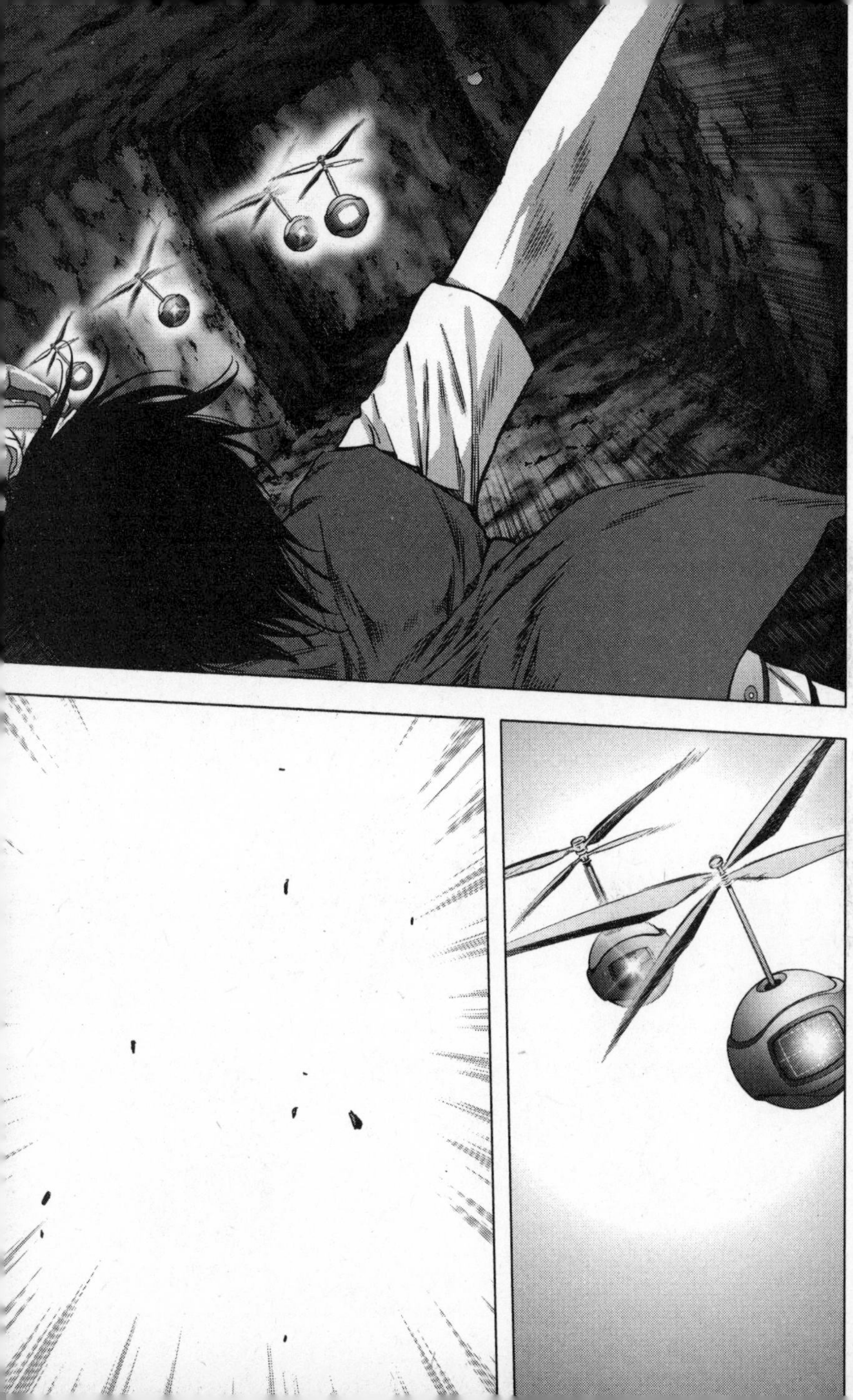

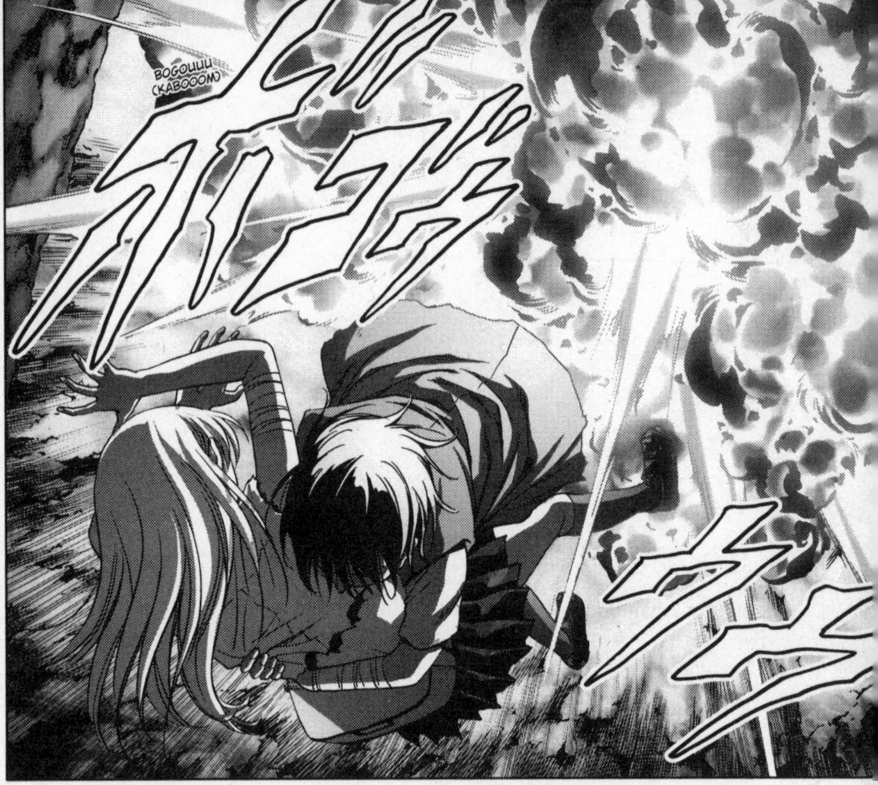
BOGOUUU
(KABOOOM)

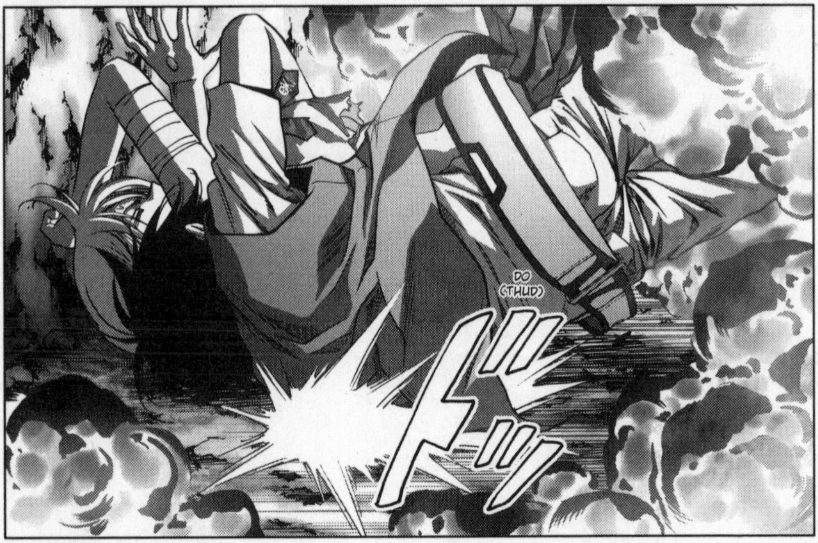
DO
(THUD)

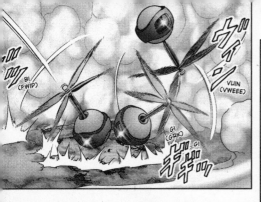

BI
(FWIP)

VUIN
(VWEEE)

GI
(GRK)

GI

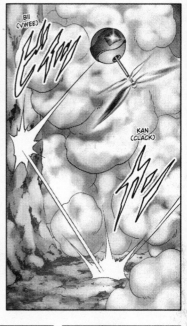

BII
(VWEE)

KAN
(CLACK)

BUIIN
(VWEEE)

BUIIIII

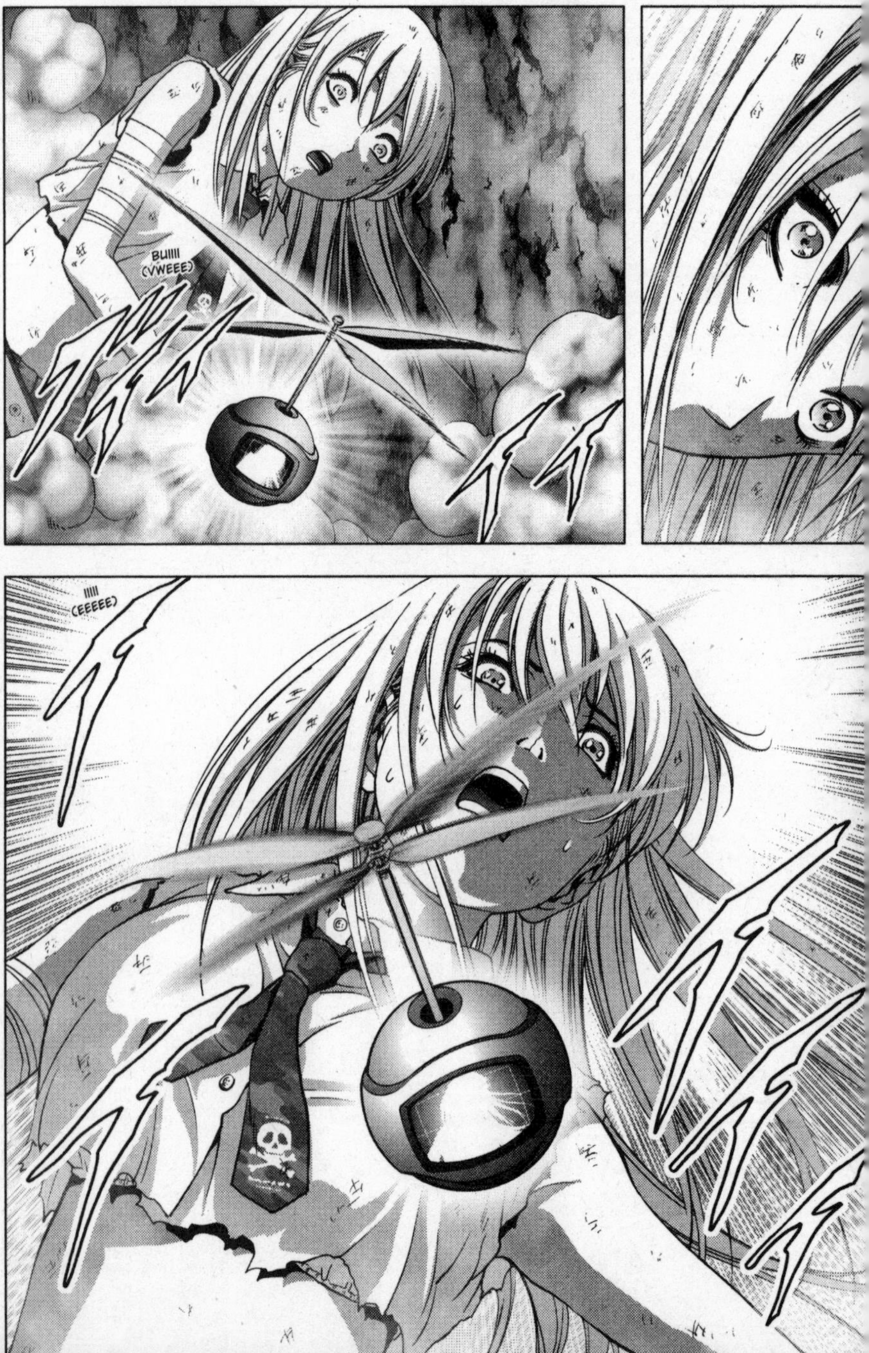
BUIIII
(VWEEE)
IIIII
(EEEEE)

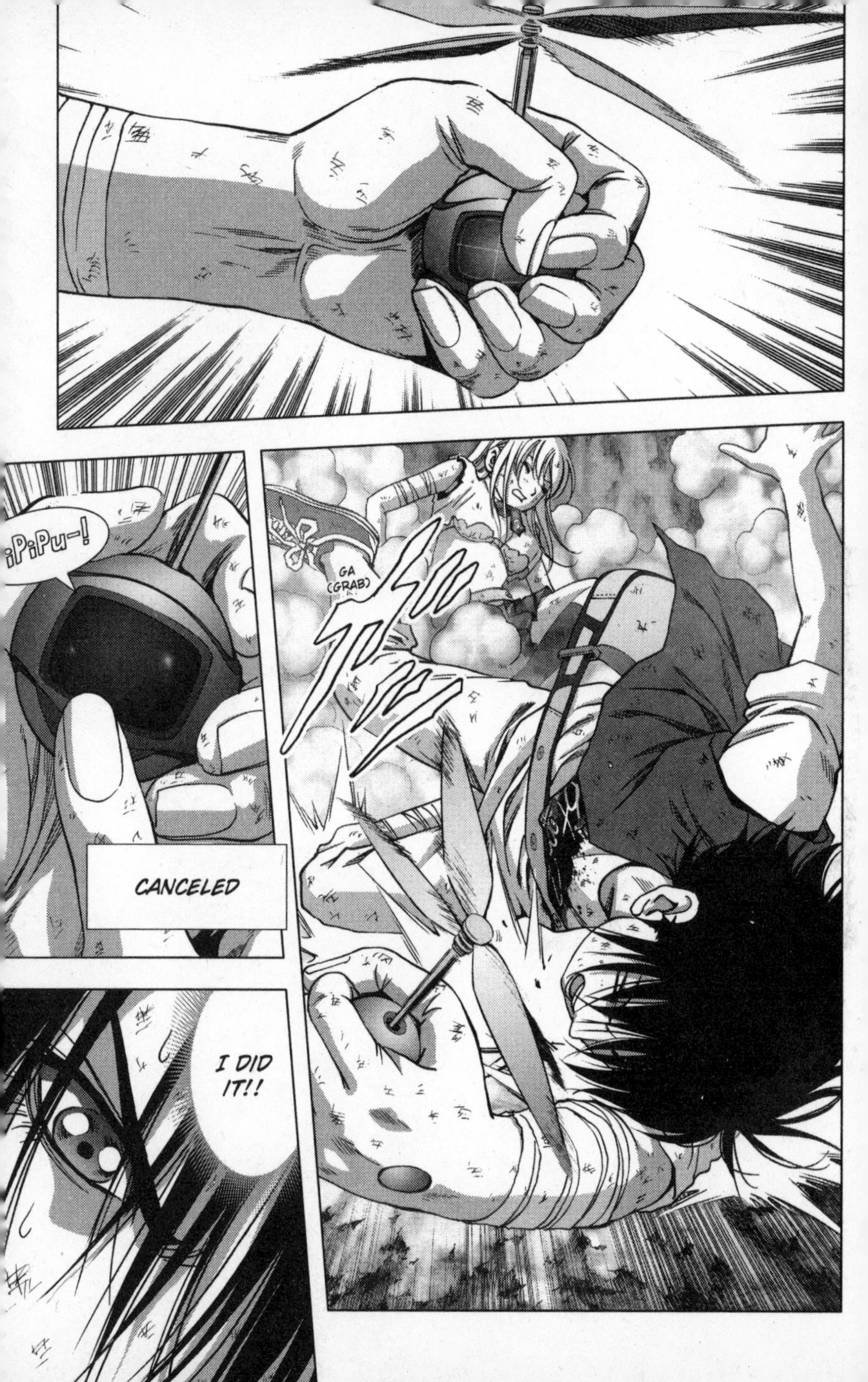
GA (GRAB)
¡PiPu-!
CANCELED
I DID IT!!

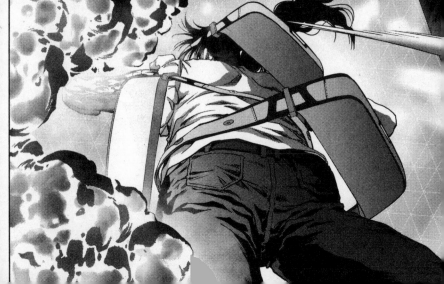

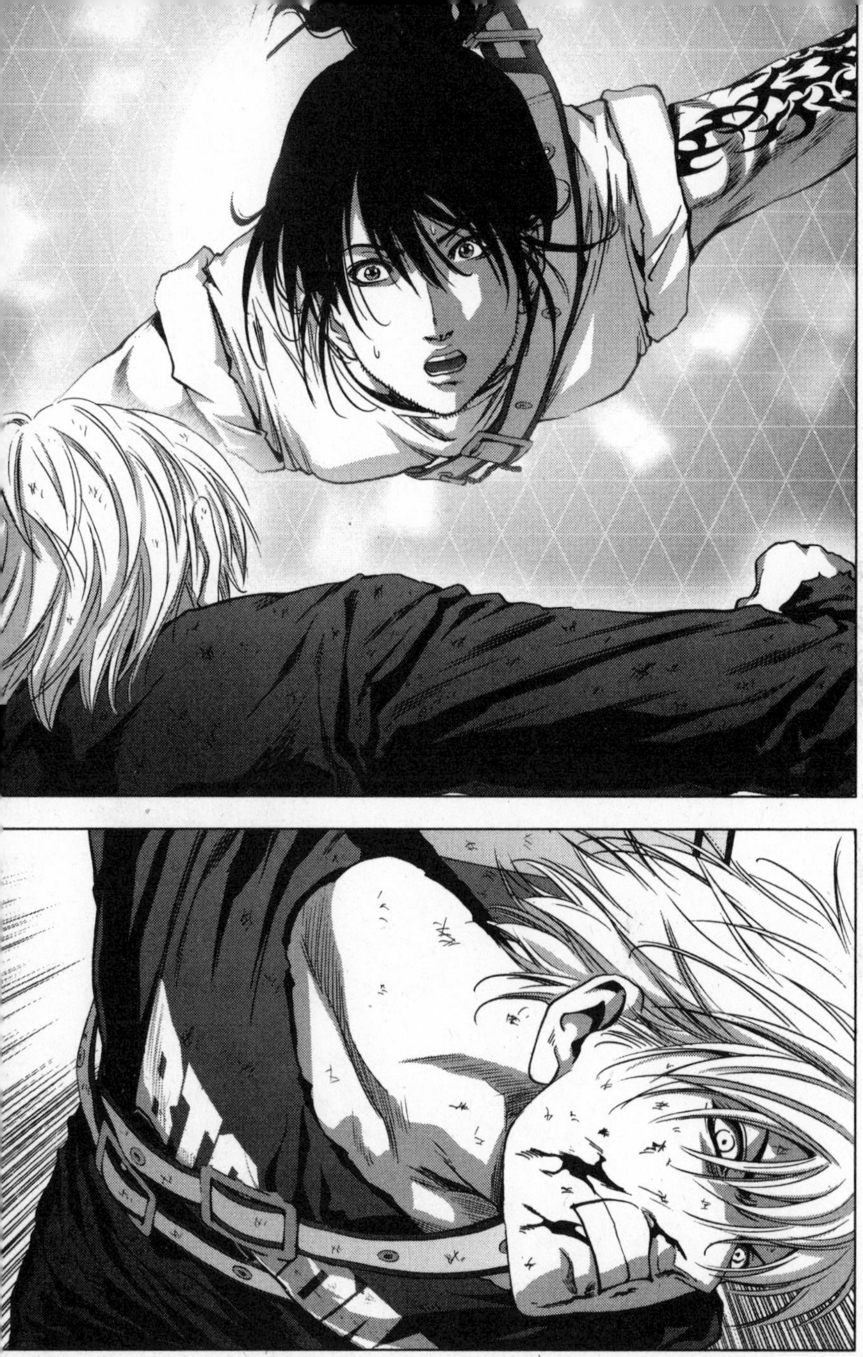

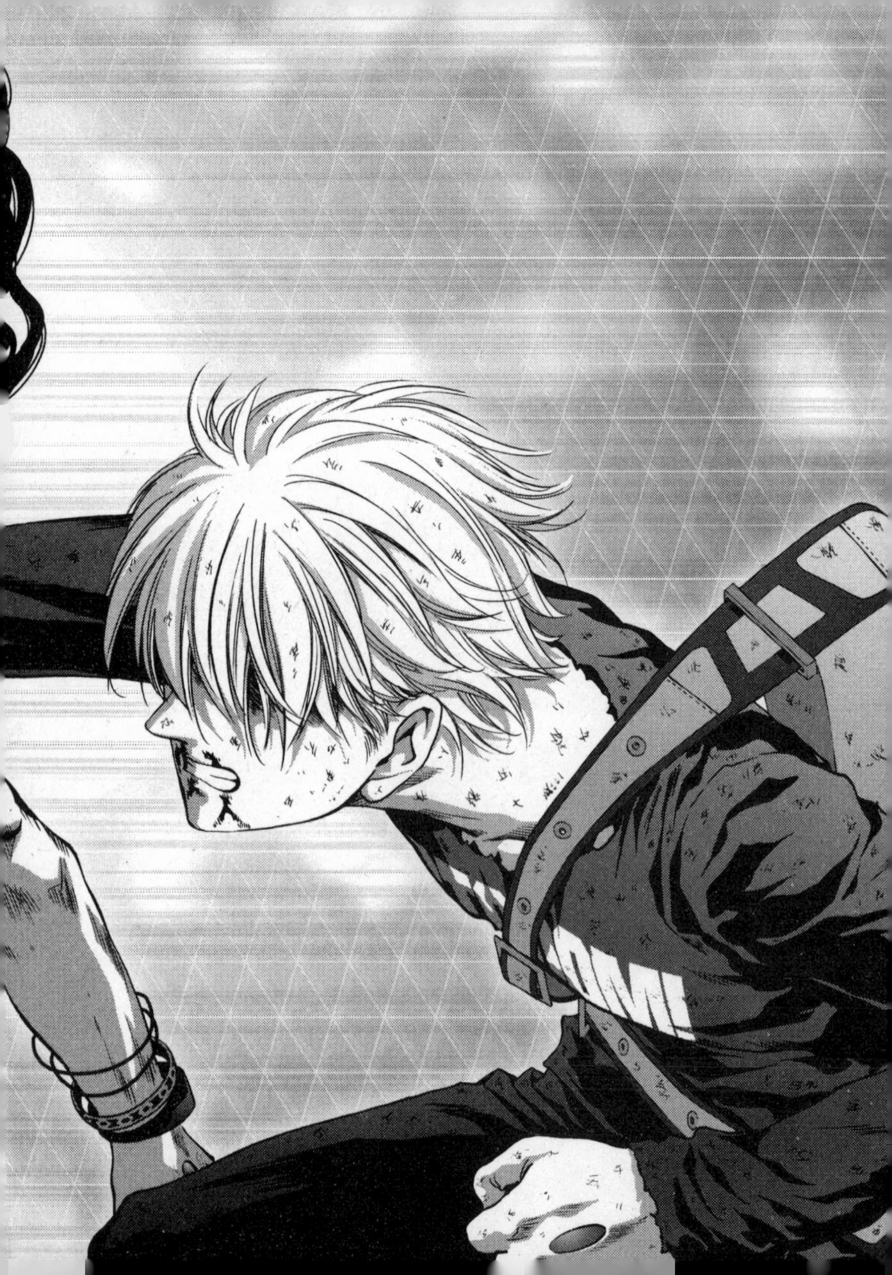

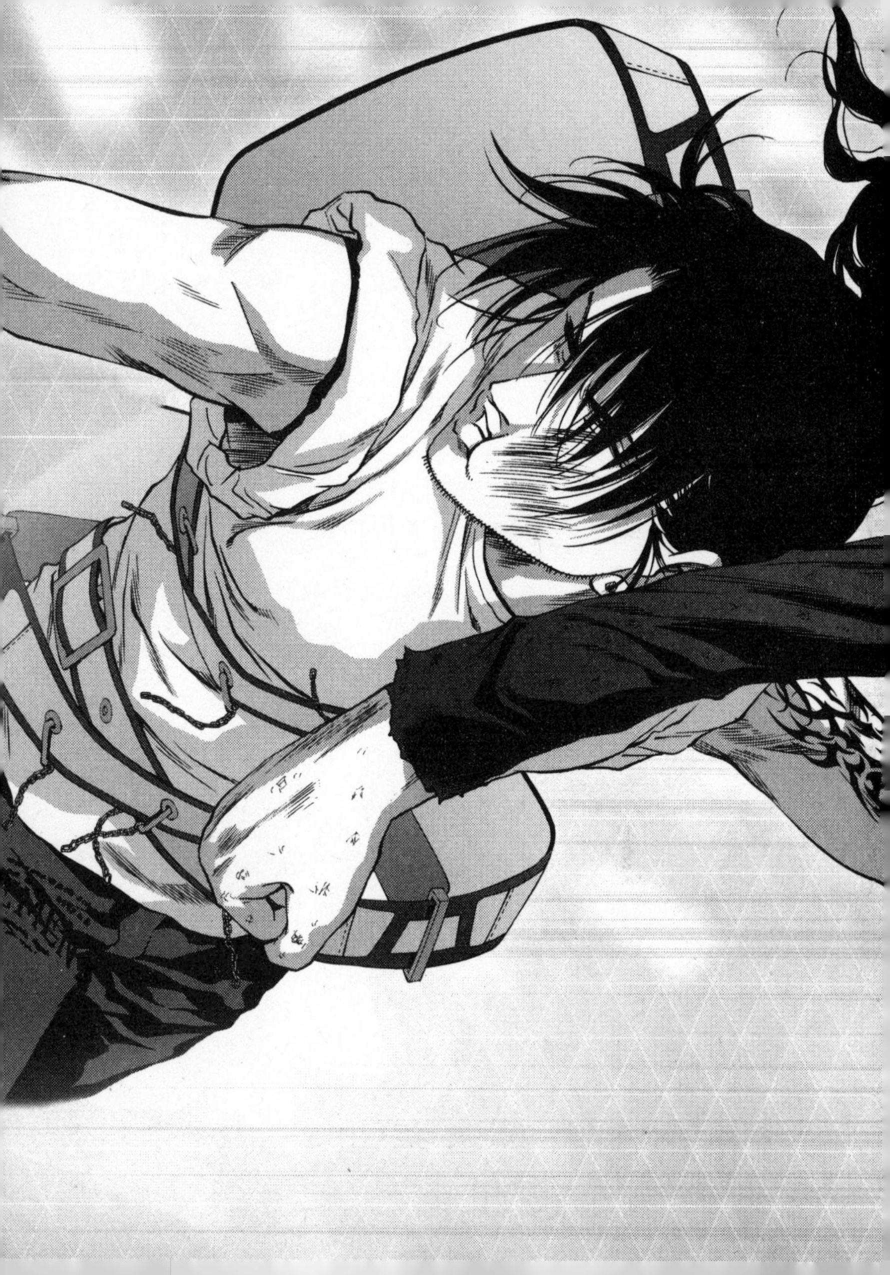

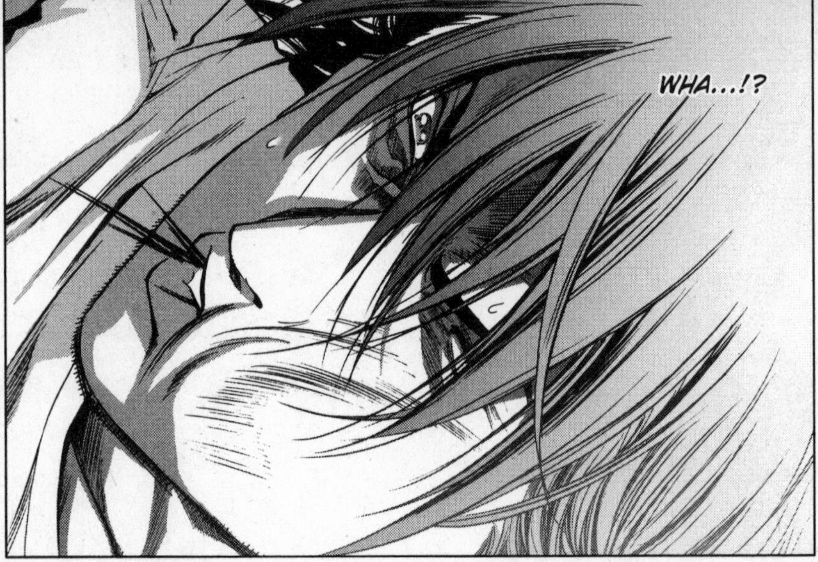
WHA...!?
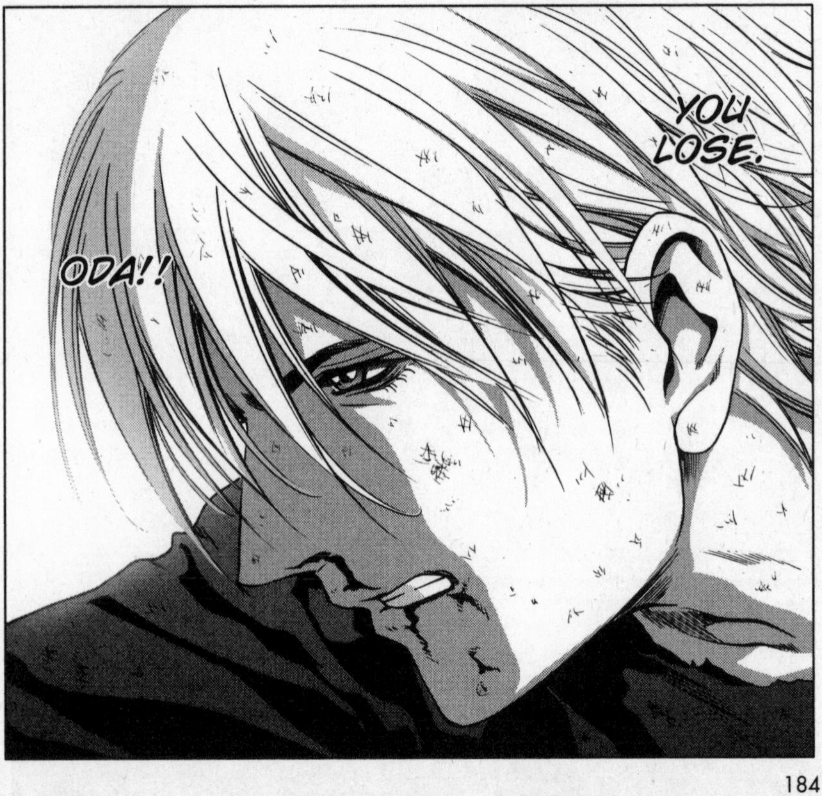
YOU LOSE.
ODA!!

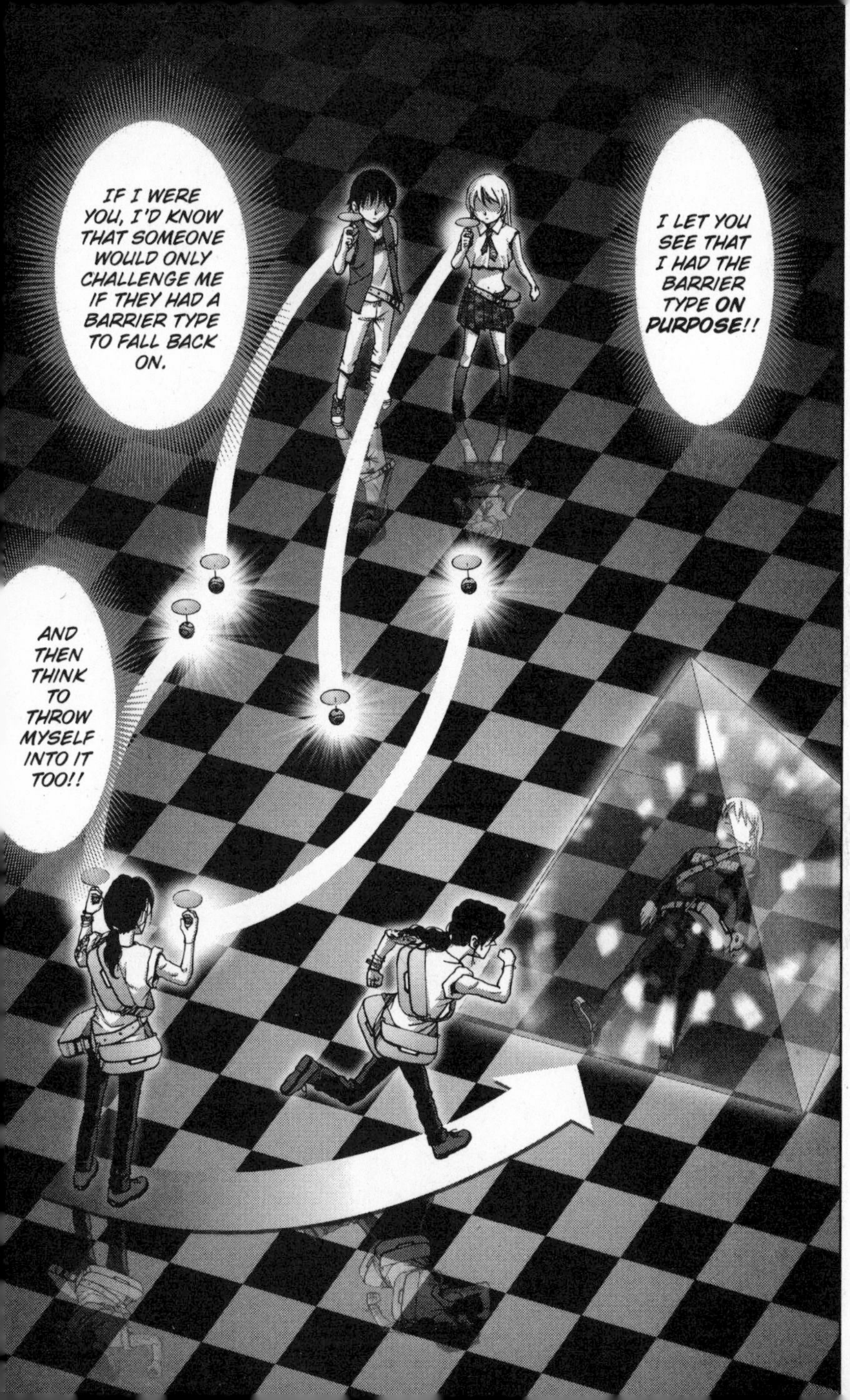
I LET YOU SEE THAT I HAD THE BARRIER TYPE ON PURPOSE!!
IF I WERE YOU, I'D KNOW THAT SOMEONE WOULD ONLY CHALLENGE ME IF THEY HAD A BARRIER TYPE TO FALL BACK ON.
AND THEN THINK TO THROW MYSELF INTO IT TOO!!

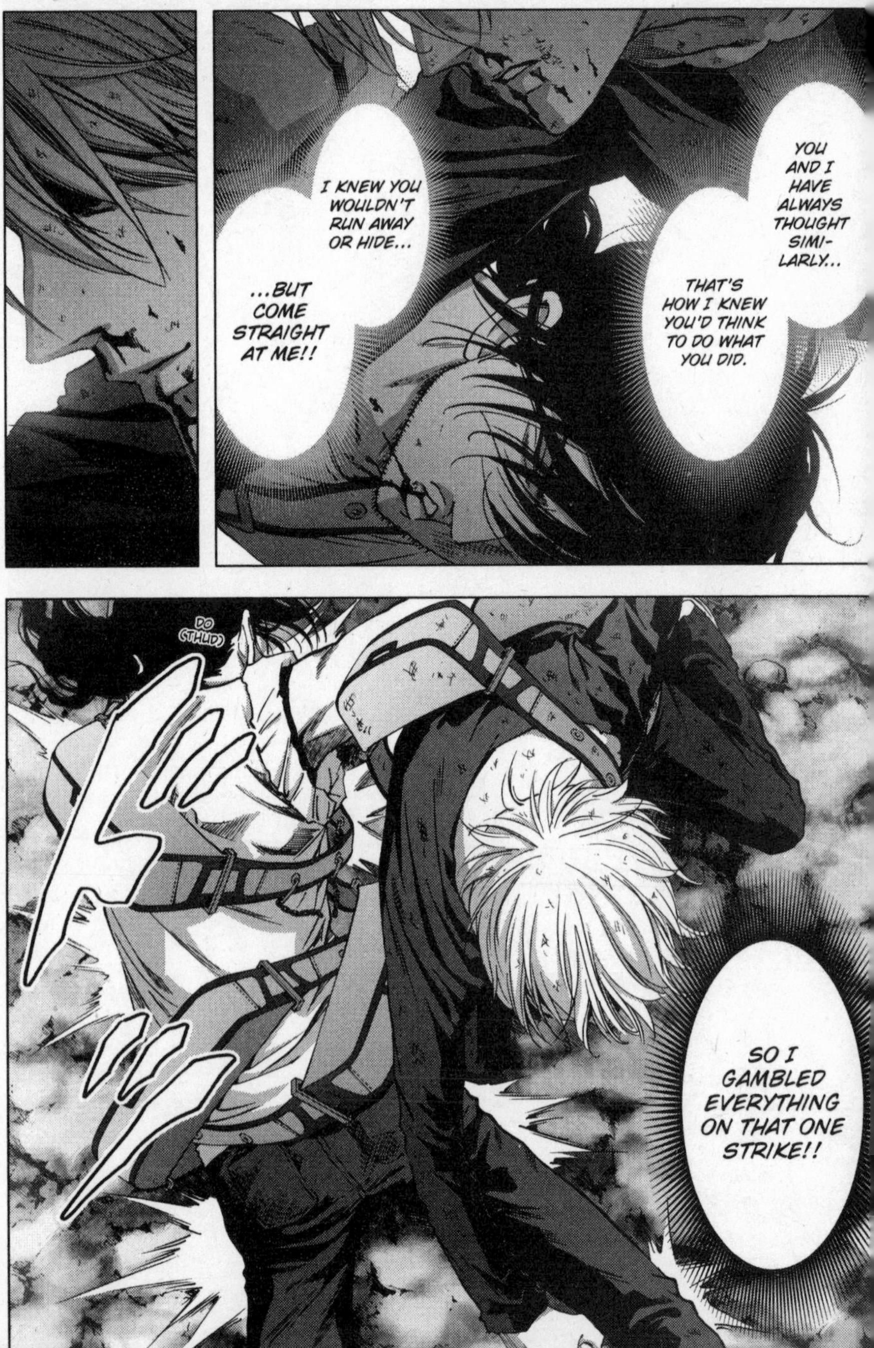
YOU AND I HAVE ALWAYS THOUGHT SIMILARLY...
THAT'S HOW I KNEW YOU'D THINK TO DO WHAT YOU DID.
I KNEW YOU WOULDN'T RUN AWAY OR HIDE...
...BUT COME STRAIGHT AT ME!!
DO (THUD)
SO I GAMBLED EVERYTHING ON THAT ONE STRIKE!!

ザ
(ZSH)

ブウン
(BUZZ)

ビ
(FWP)

ガ
(CLACK)

GA GA GA GA

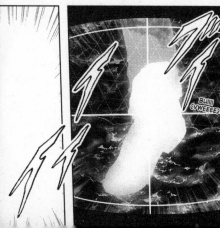

ブ
(VWEEEE)

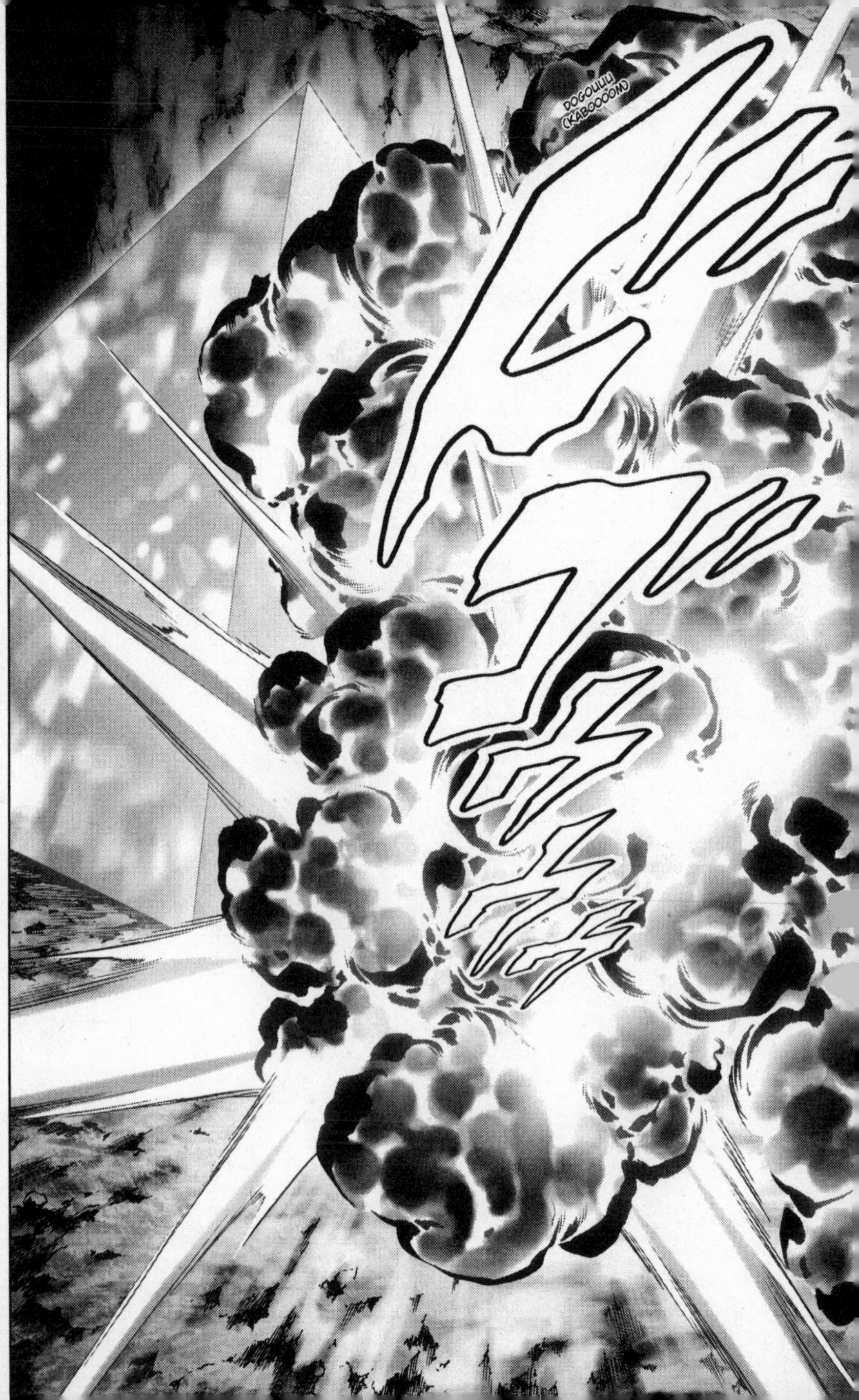
DOGOUUU
(KABOOOOM)

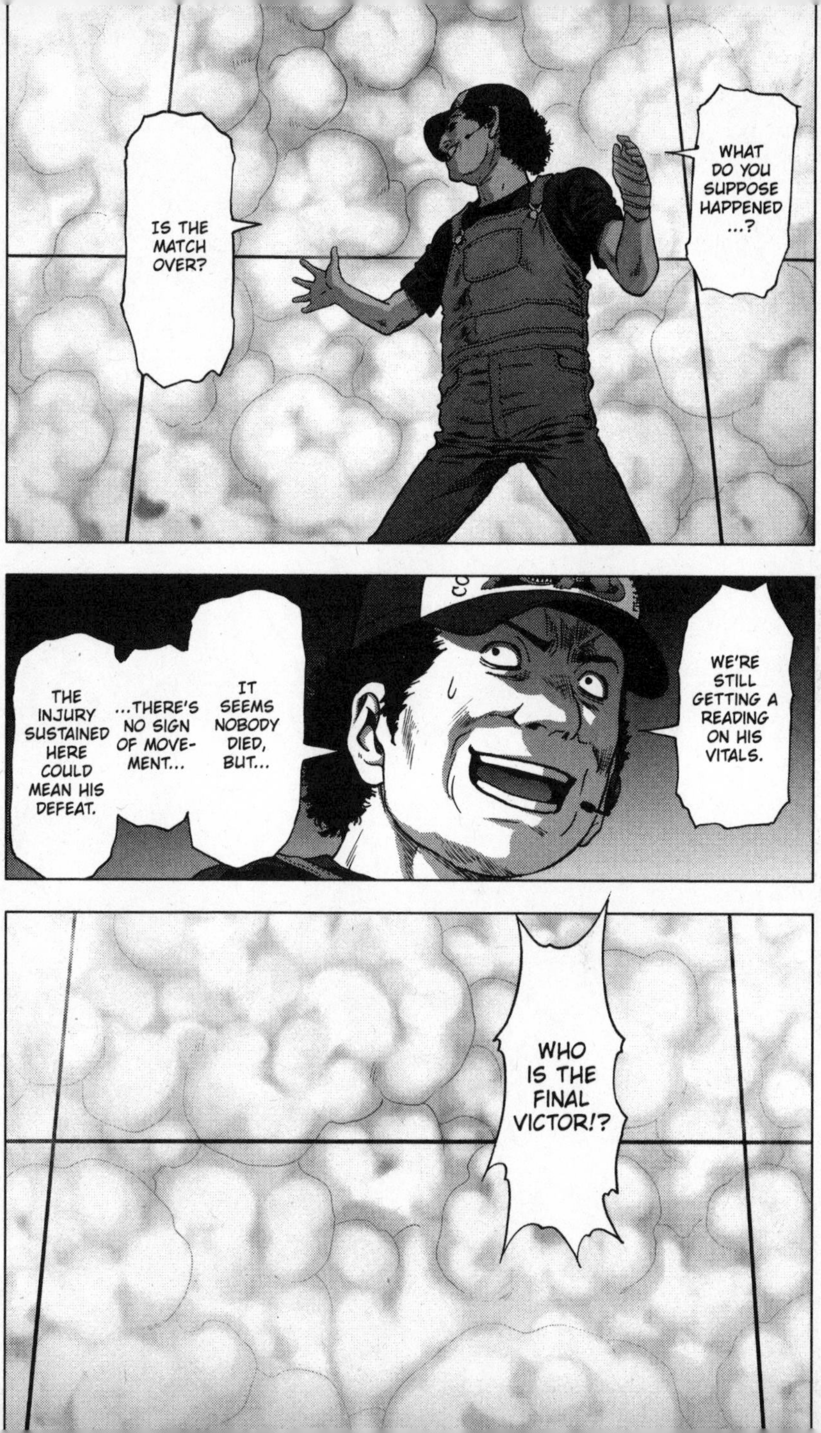
WHAT DO YOU SUPPOSE HAPPENED ...?
IS THE MATCH OVER?
WE'RE STILL GETTING A READING ON HIS VITALS.
IT SEEMS NOBODY DIED, BUT...
...THERE'S NO SIGN OF MOVE-MENT...
THE INJURY SUSTAINED HERE COULD MEAN HIS DEFEAT.
WHO IS THE FINAL VICTOR!?

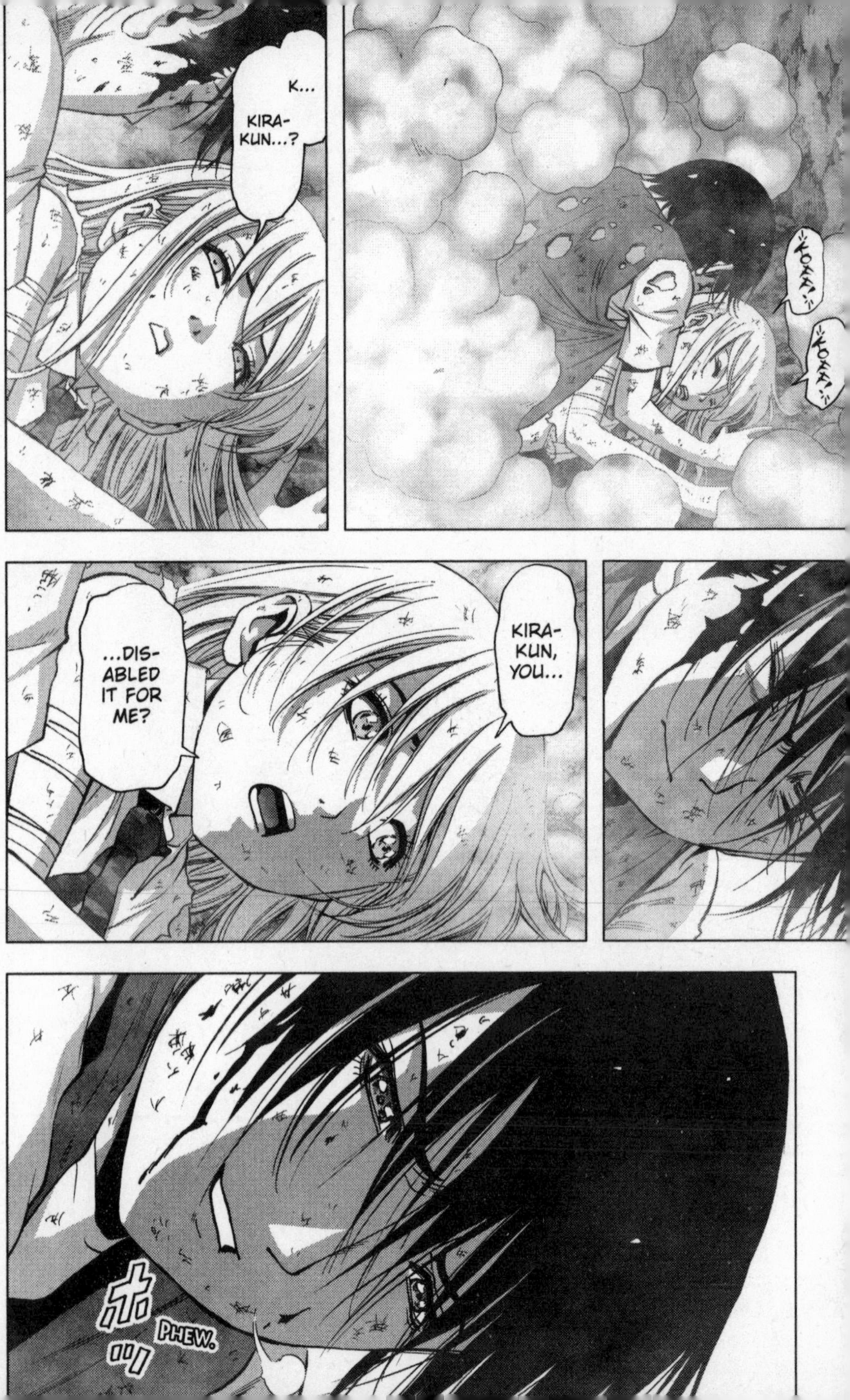
KOFF!
KOFF!
K...
KIRA-KUN...?
KIRA-KUN, YOU...
...DIS-ABLED IT FOR ME?
PHEW.

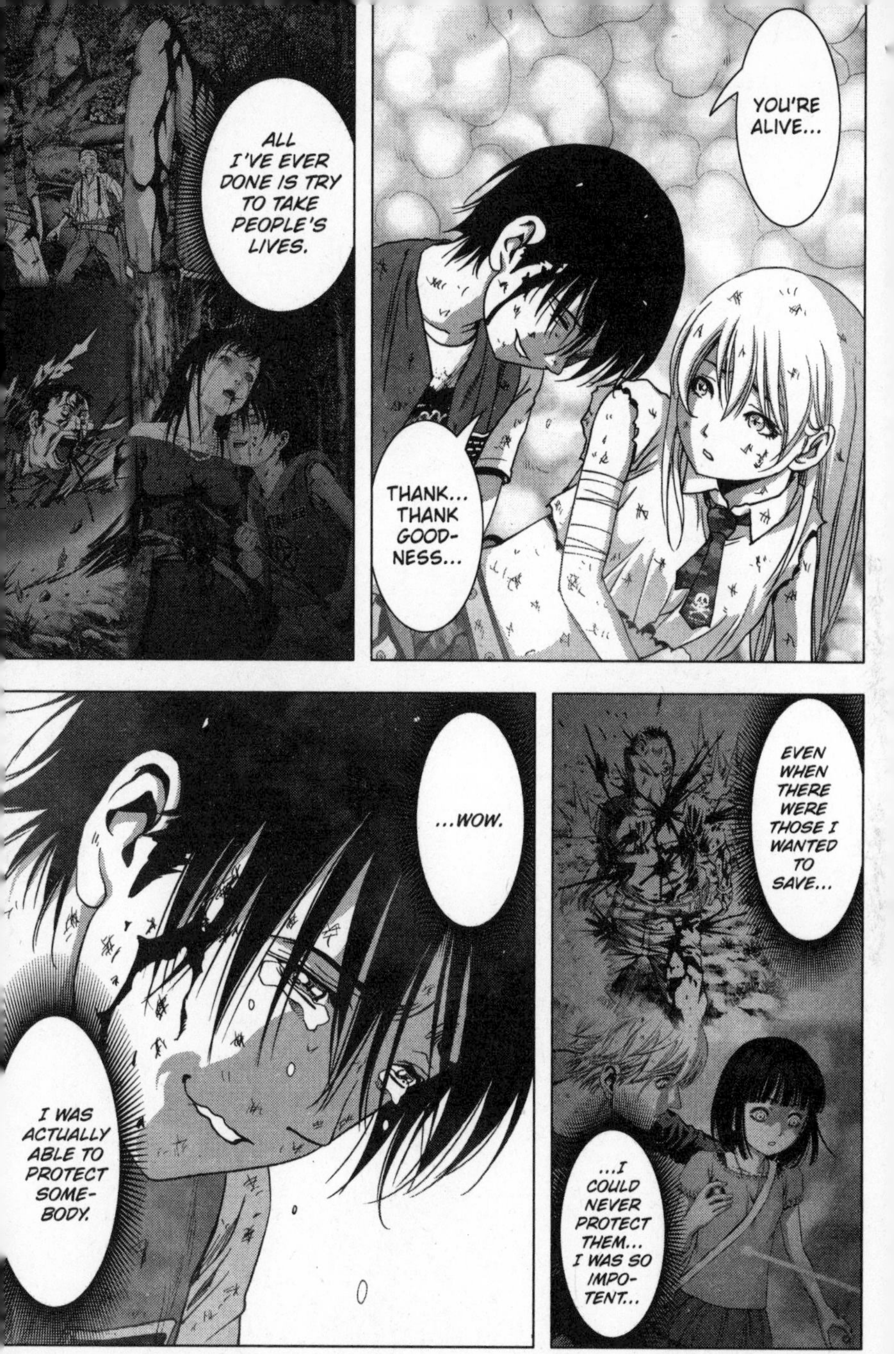
YOU'RE ALIVE...
THANK... THANK GOODNESS...
ALL I'VE EVER DONE IS TRY TO TAKE PEOPLE'S LIVES.
EVEN WHEN THERE WERE THOSE I WANTED TO SAVE...
...I COULD NEVER PROTECT THEM... I WAS SO IMPOTENT...
...WOW.
I WAS ACTUALLY ABLE TO PROTECT SOMEBODY.

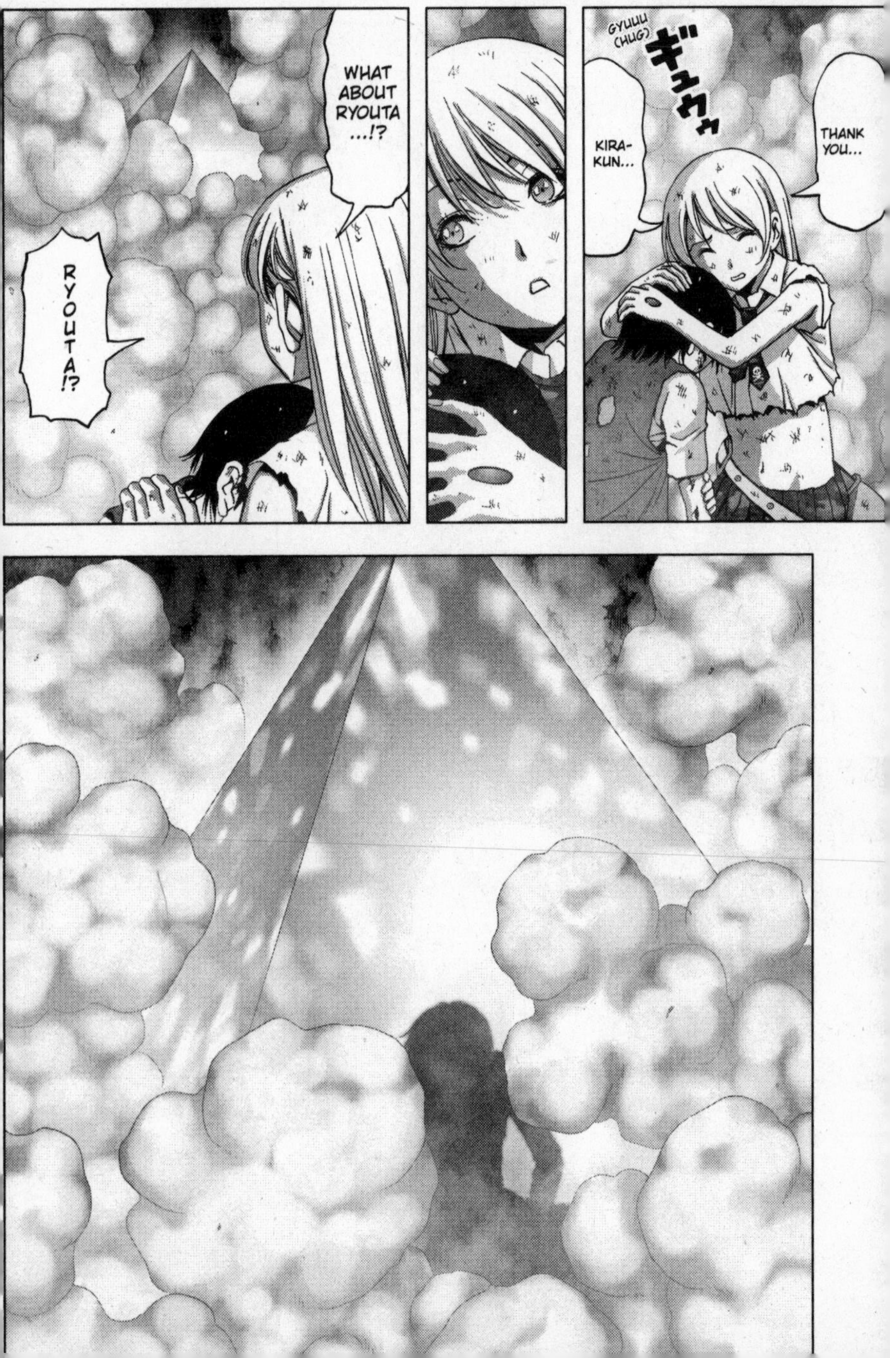
THANK YOU...
GYUUU (HUG)
ギュウゥ
KIRA-KUN...
WHAT ABOUT RYOUTA ...!?
RYOUTA!?

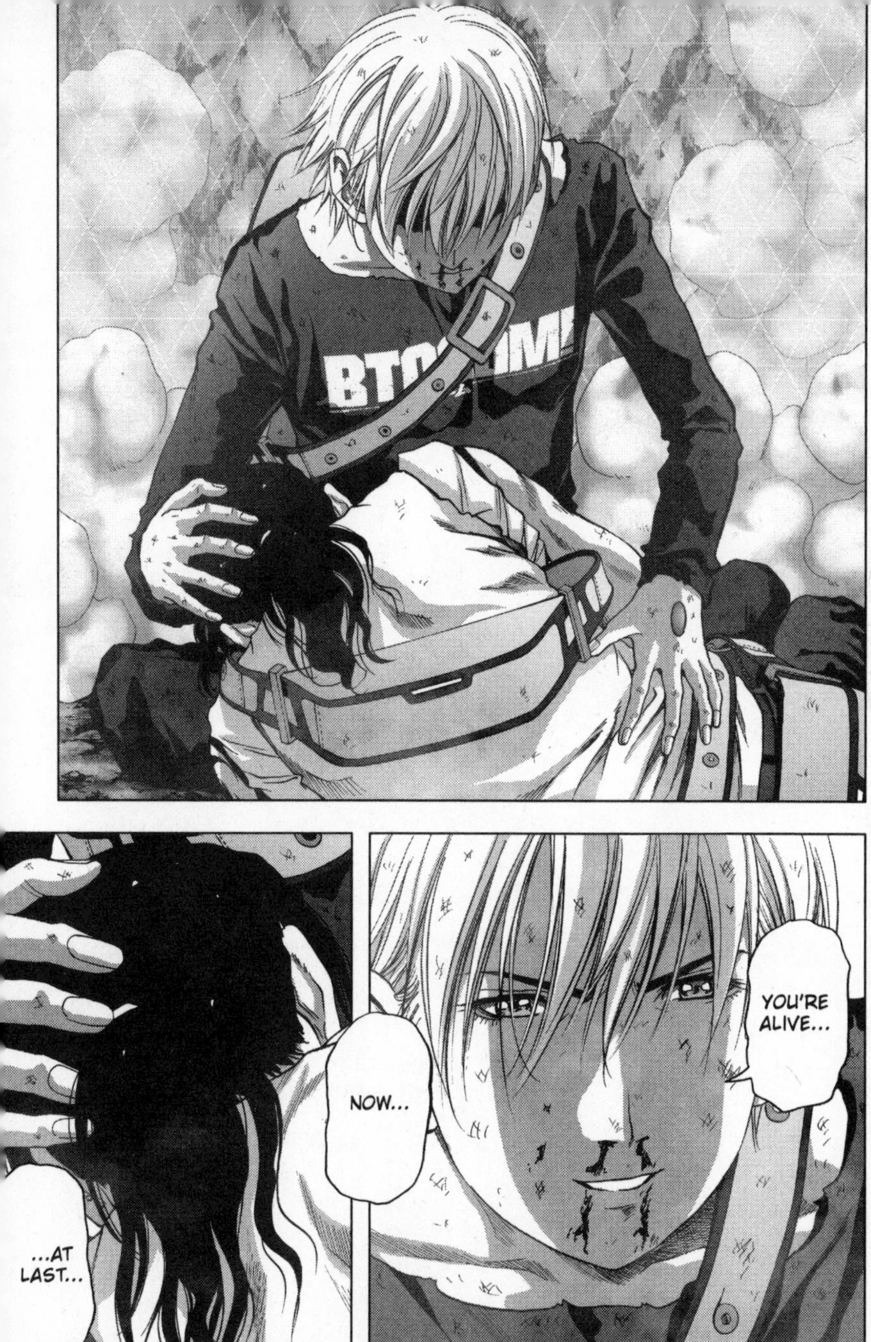
YOU'RE ALIVE...
NOW...
...AT LAST...

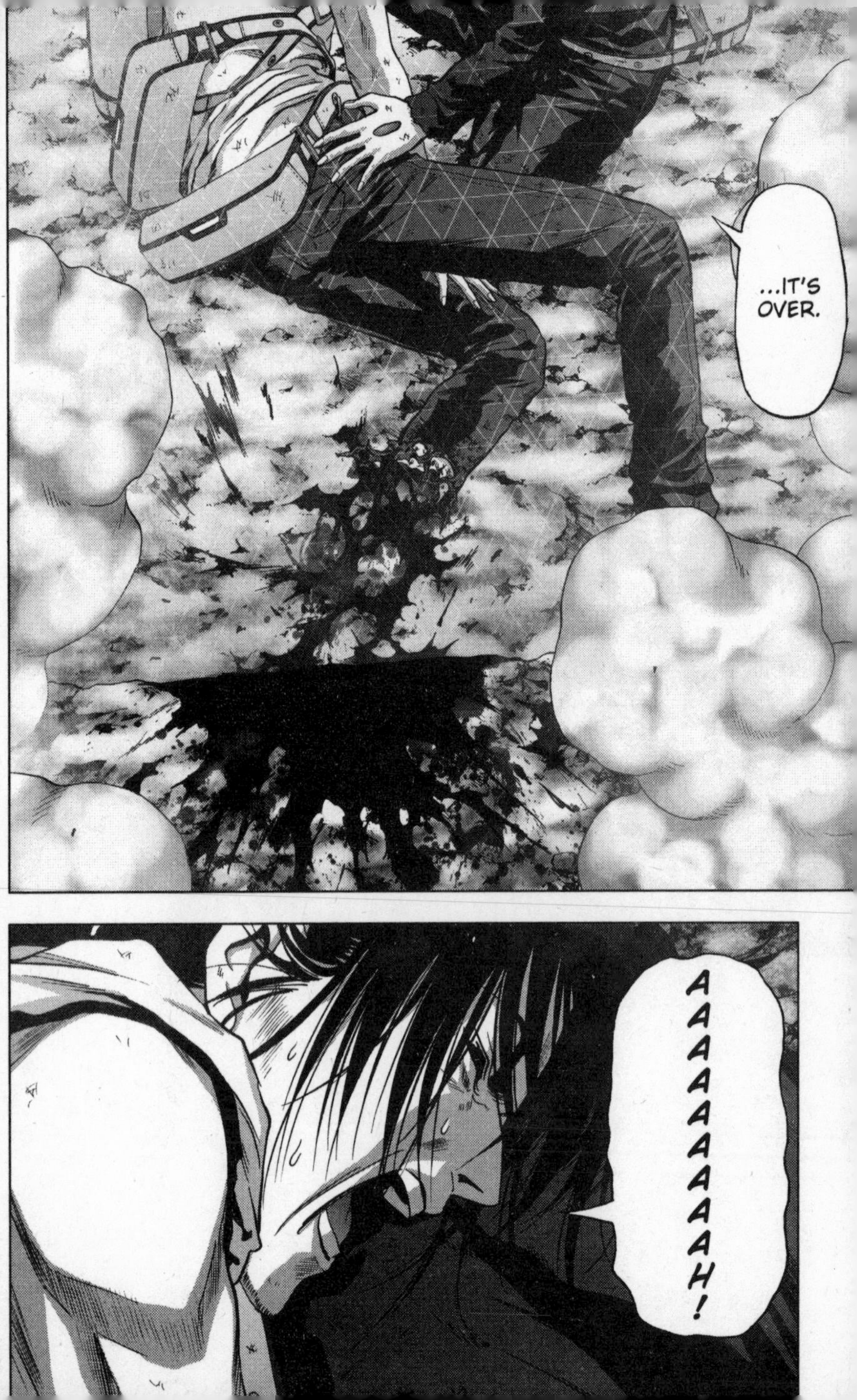
...IT'S OVER.
AAAAAAAAAAAH!

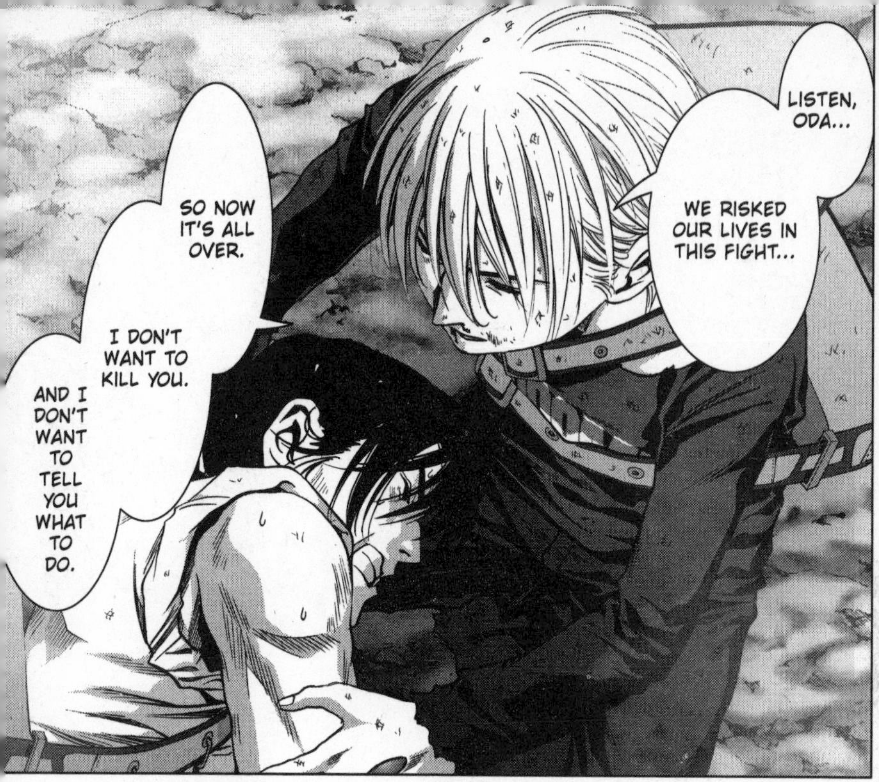
LISTEN, ODA...
WE RISKED OUR LIVES IN THIS FIGHT...
SO NOW IT'S ALL OVER.
I DON'T WANT TO KILL YOU.
AND I DON'T WANT TO TELL YOU WHAT TO DO.
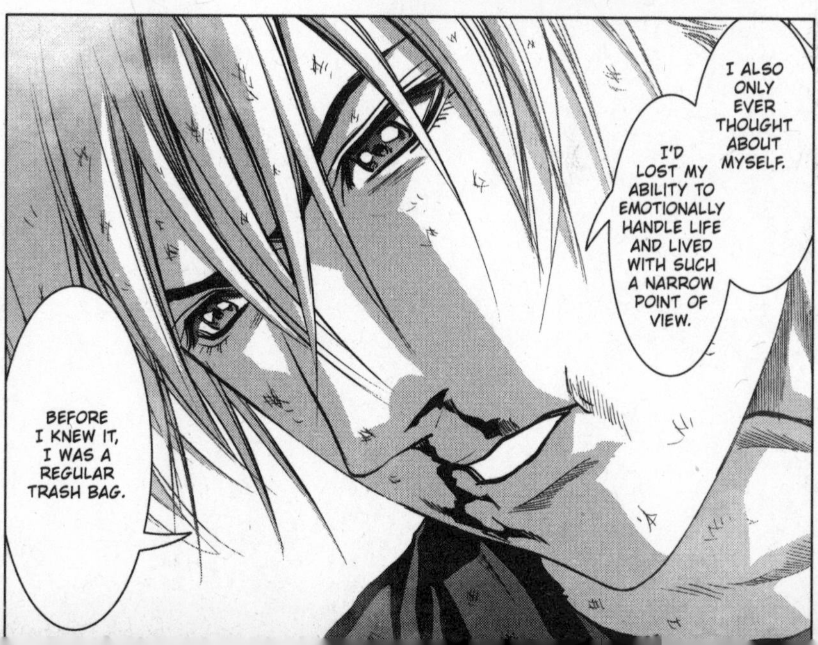
I ALSO ONLY EVER THOUGHT ABOUT MYSELF.
I'D LOST MY ABILITY TO EMOTIONALLY HANDLE LIFE AND LIVED WITH SUCH A NARROW POINT OF VIEW.
BEFORE I KNEW IT, I WAS A REGULAR TRASH BAG.

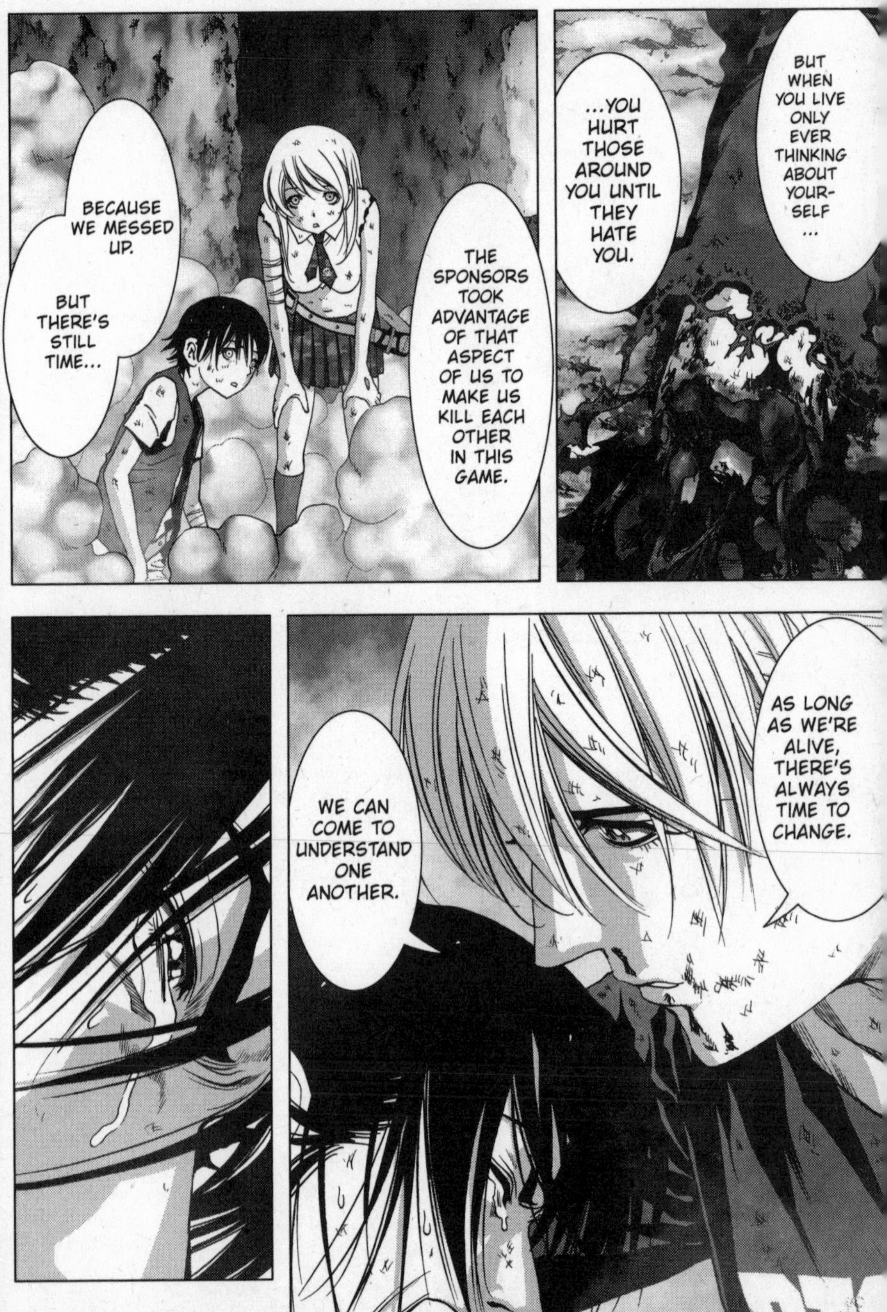
BUT WHEN YOU LIVE ONLY EVER THINKING ABOUT YOUR-SELF ...
...YOU HURT THOSE AROUND YOU UNTIL THEY HATE YOU.
THE SPONSORS TOOK ADVANTAGE OF THAT ASPECT OF US TO MAKE US KILL EACH OTHER IN THIS GAME.
BECAUSE WE MESSED UP.
BUT THERE'S STILL TIME...
AS LONG AS WE'RE ALIVE, THERE'S ALWAYS TIME TO CHANGE.
WE CAN COME TO UNDERSTAND ONE ANOTHER.

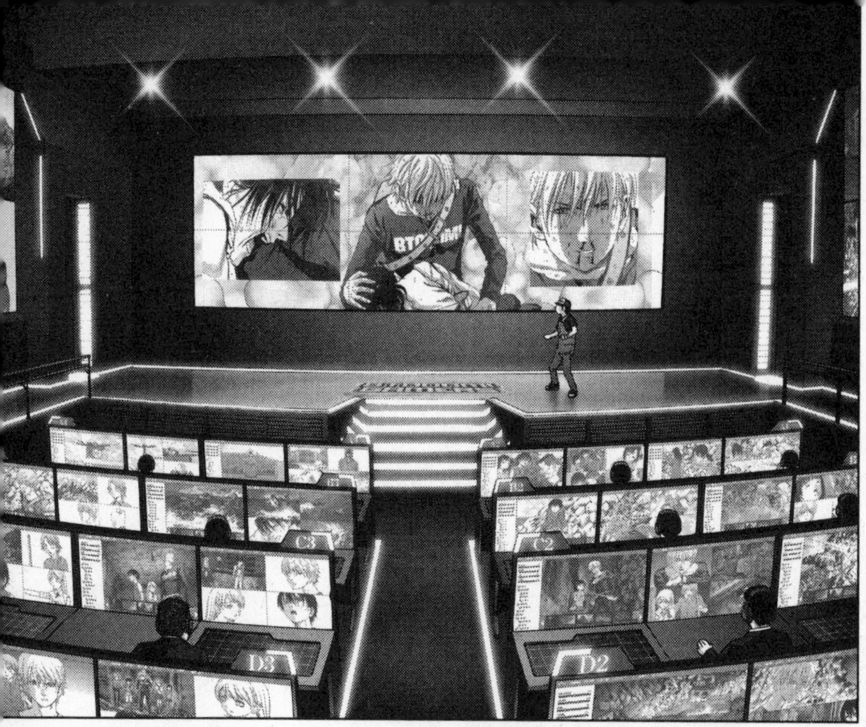
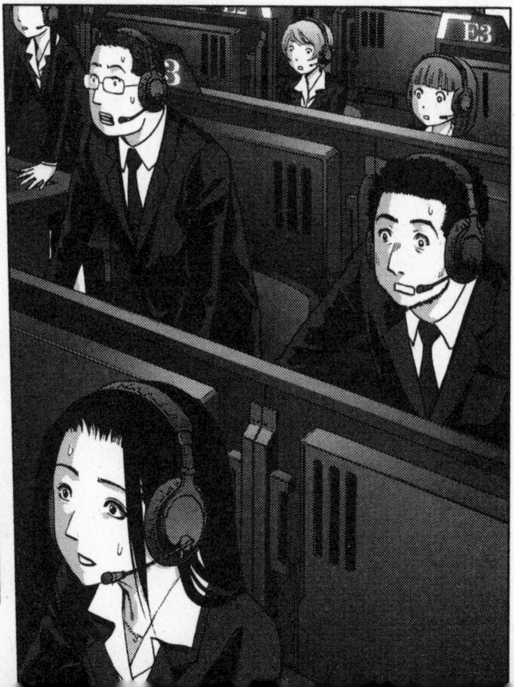
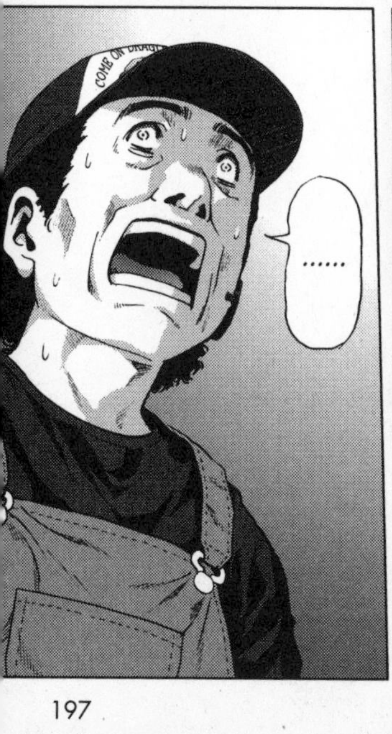
......

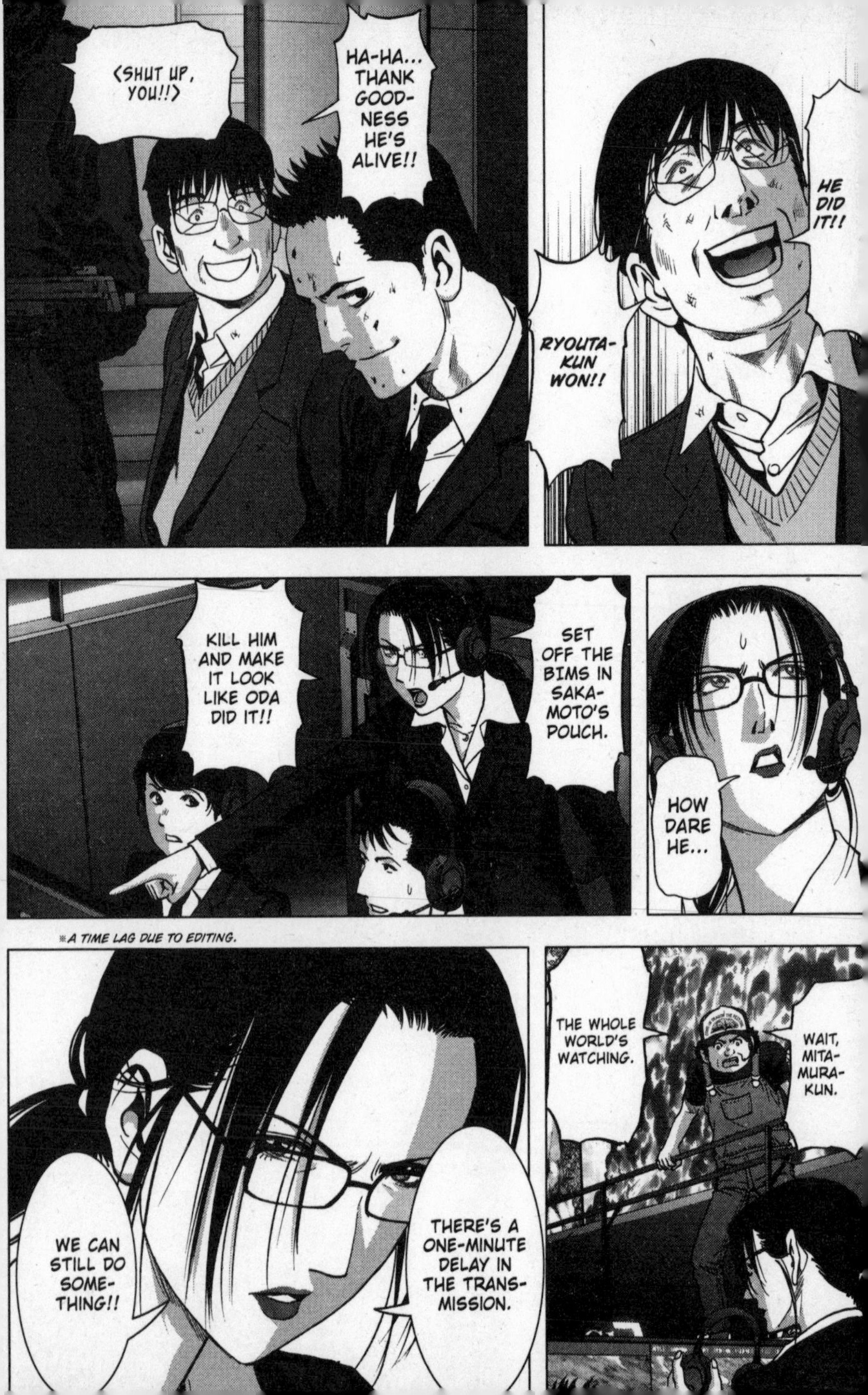
HE DID IT!!
RYOUTA-KUN WON!!
HA-HA... THANK GOODNESS HE'S ALIVE!!
‹SHUT UP, YOU!!›
HOW DARE HE...
SET OFF THE BIMS IN SAKAMOTO'S POUCH.
KILL HIM AND MAKE IT LOOK LIKE ODA DID IT!!
※A TIME LAG DUE TO EDITING.
WAIT, MITAMURA-KUN.
THE WHOLE WORLD'S WATCHING.
THERE'S A ONE-MINUTE DELAY IN THE TRANSMISSION.
WE CAN STILL DO SOMETHING!!

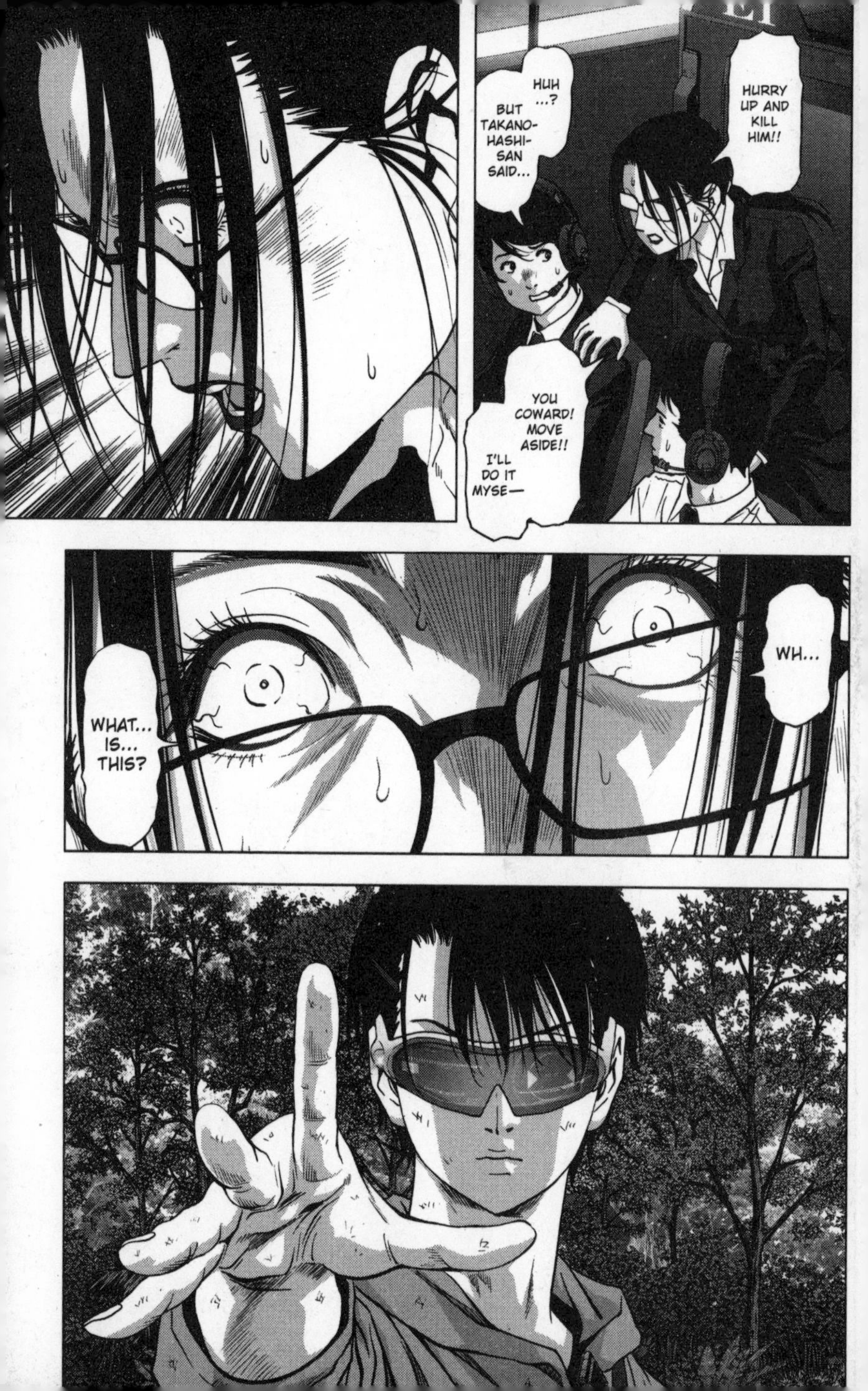
HURRY UP AND KILL HIM!!
HUH ...? BUT TAKANO-HASHI-SAN SAID...
YOU COWARD! MOVE ASIDE!! I'LL DO IT MYSE—
WH...
WHAT... IS... THIS?

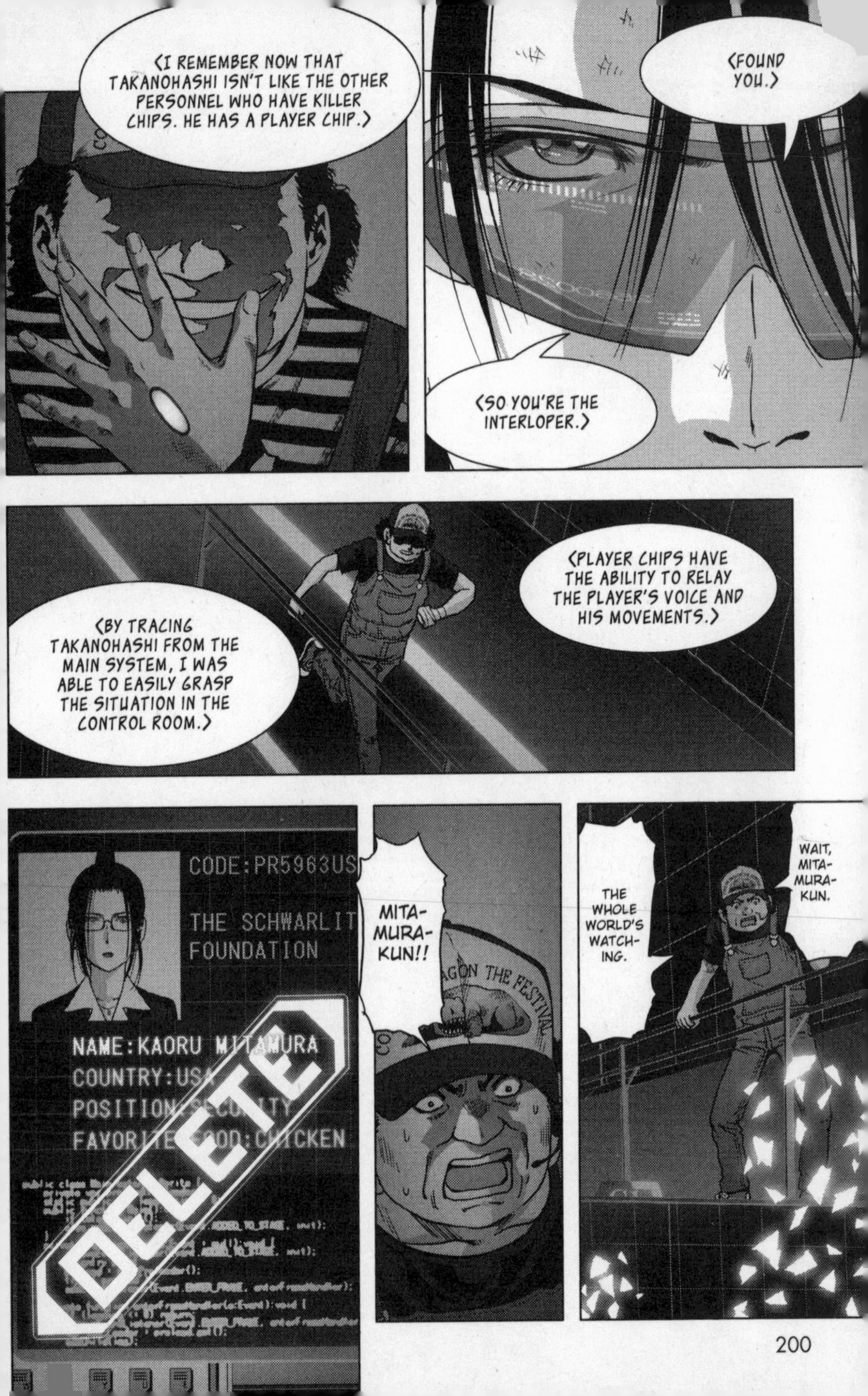
〈FOUND YOU.〉
〈SO YOU'RE THE INTERLOPER.〉
〈I REMEMBER NOW THAT TAKANOHASHI ISN'T LIKE THE OTHER PERSONNEL WHO HAVE KILLER CHIPS. HE HAS A PLAYER CHIP.〉
〈PLAYER CHIPS HAVE THE ABILITY TO RELAY THE PLAYER'S VOICE AND HIS MOVEMENTS.〉
〈BY TRACING TAKANOHASHI FROM THE MAIN SYSTEM, I WAS ABLE TO EASILY GRASP THE SITUATION IN THE CONTROL ROOM.〉
WAIT, MITA-MURA-KUN.
THE WHOLE WORLD'S WATCH-ING.
MITA-MURA-KUN!!
CODE:PR5963US
THE SCHWARLIT
FOUNDATION
NAME:KAORU MITAMURA
COUNTRY:USA
POSITION:SECURITY
FAVORITE FOOD:CHICKEN
DELETE

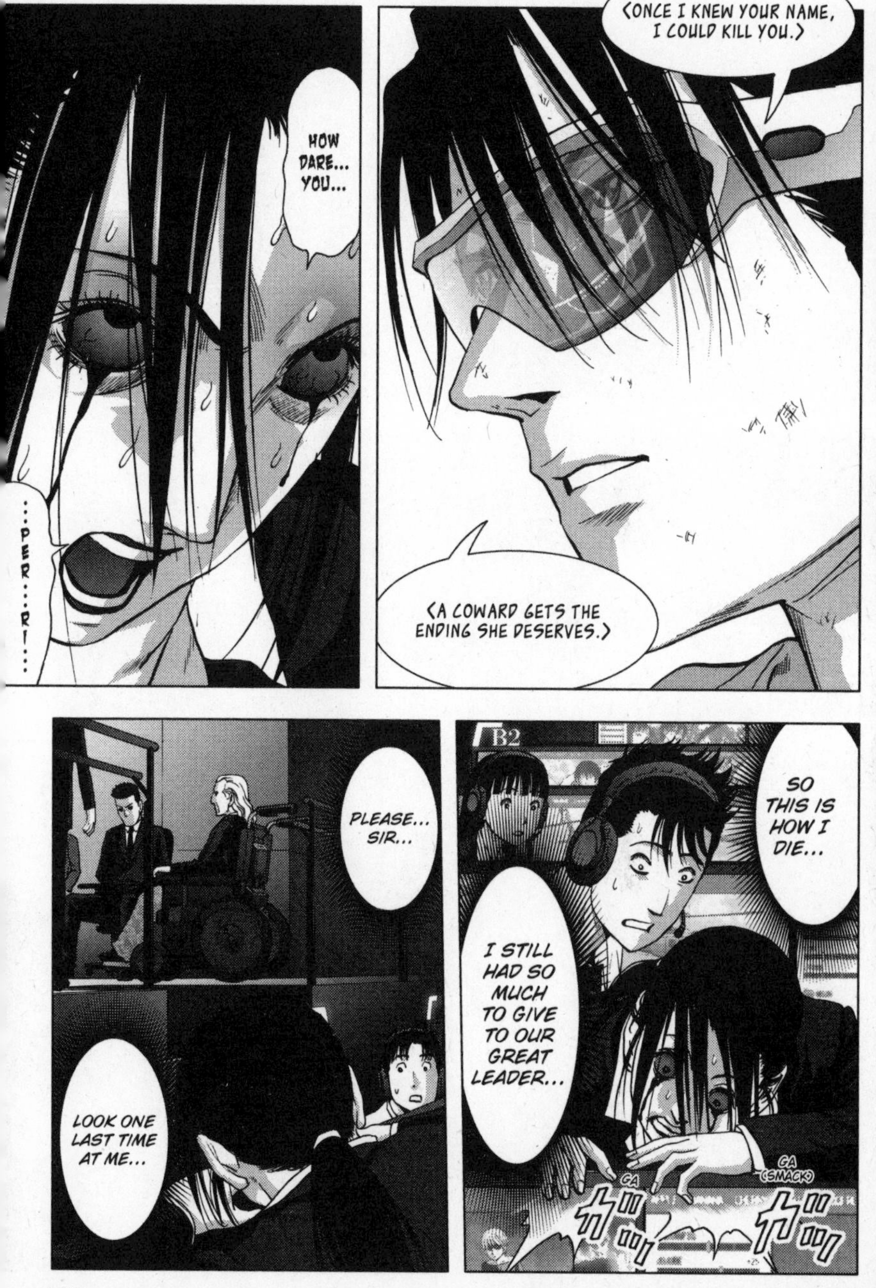
<ONCE I KNEW YOUR NAME, I COULD KILL YOU.>
<A COWARD GETS THE ENDING SHE DESERVES.>
HOW DARE... YOU...
...PER...RI...
SO THIS IS HOW I DIE...
I STILL HAD SO MUCH TO GIVE TO OUR GREAT LEADER...
GA (SMACK)
GA
PLEASE... SIR...
LOOK ONE LAST TIME AT ME...

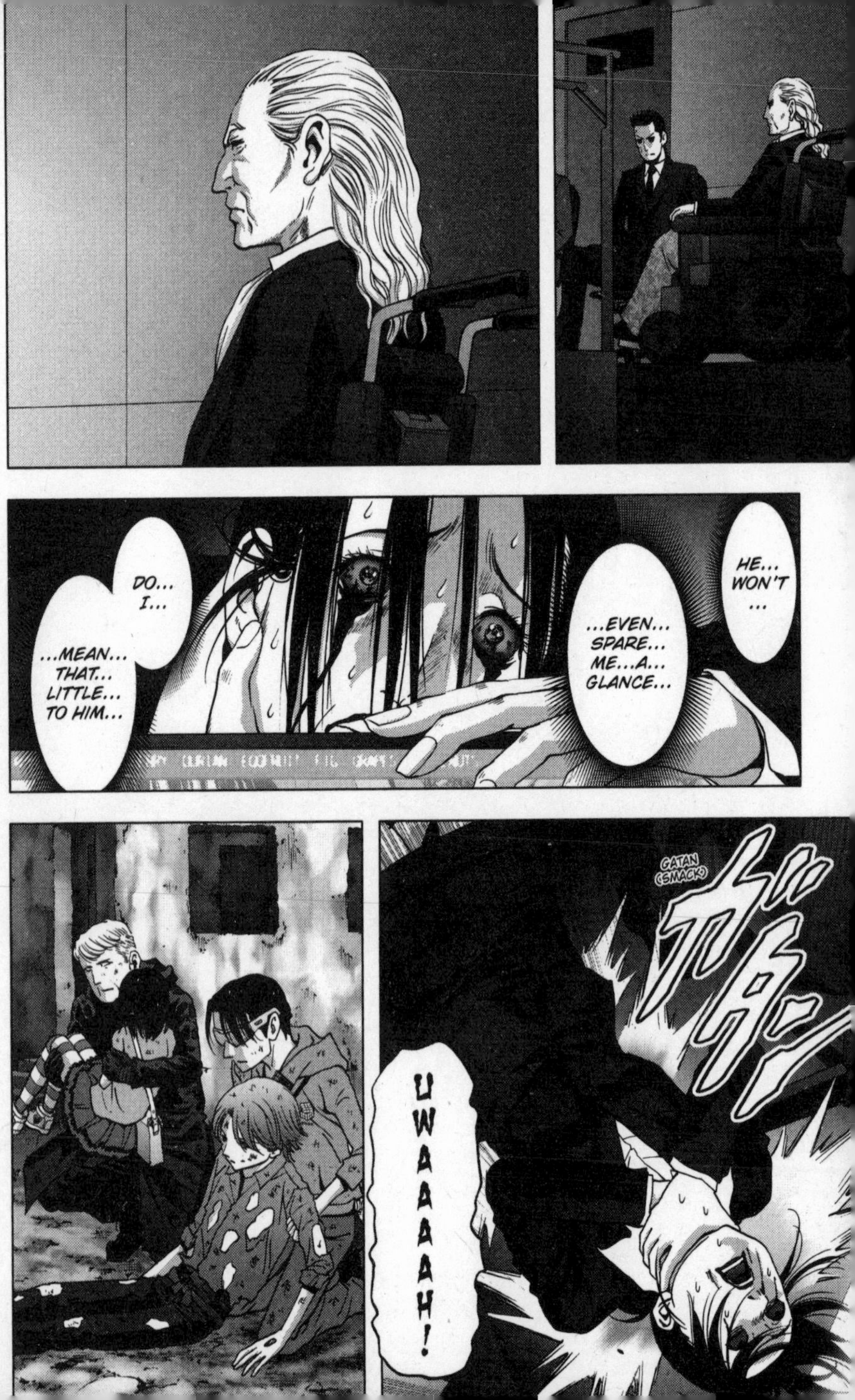
HE... WON'T ...
...EVEN... SPARE... ME...A... GLANCE...
DO... I...
...MEAN... THAT... LITTLE... TO HIM...
GATAN (SMACK)
UWAAAAAAH!

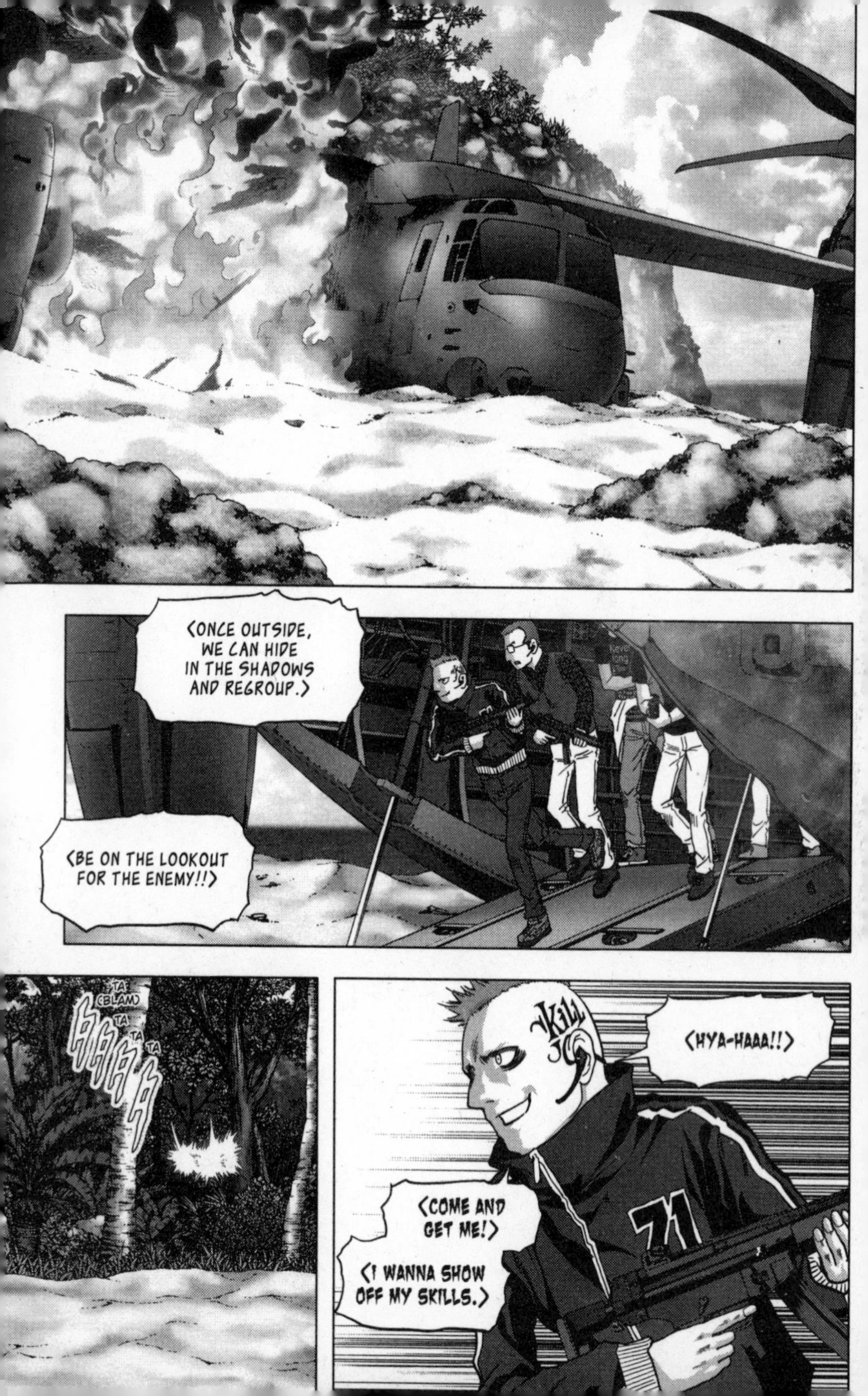
<ONCE OUTSIDE, WE CAN HIDE IN THE SHADOWS AND REGROUP.>
<BE ON THE LOOKOUT FOR THE ENEMY!!>
<HYA-HAAA!!>
<COME AND GET ME!>
<I WANNA SHOW OFF MY SKILLS.>
TA (BLAM) TA TA TA

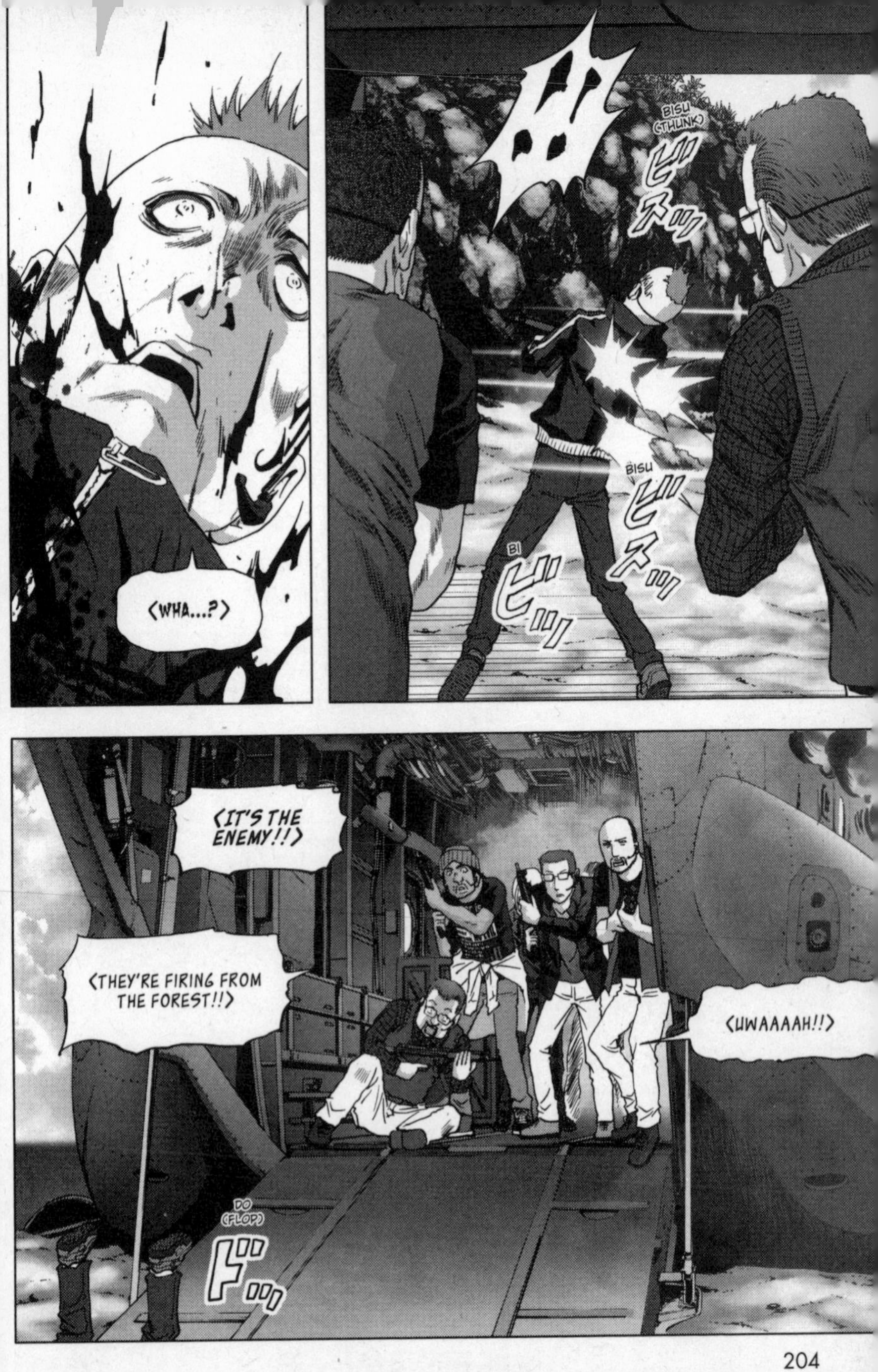
BISU (THUNK)
ビスッ
BISU
ビスッ
BI
ビッ
<WHA...?>
<IT'S THE ENEMY!!>
<THEY'RE FIRING FROM THE FOREST!!>
<UWAAAAH!!>
DO (FLOP)
ドッ

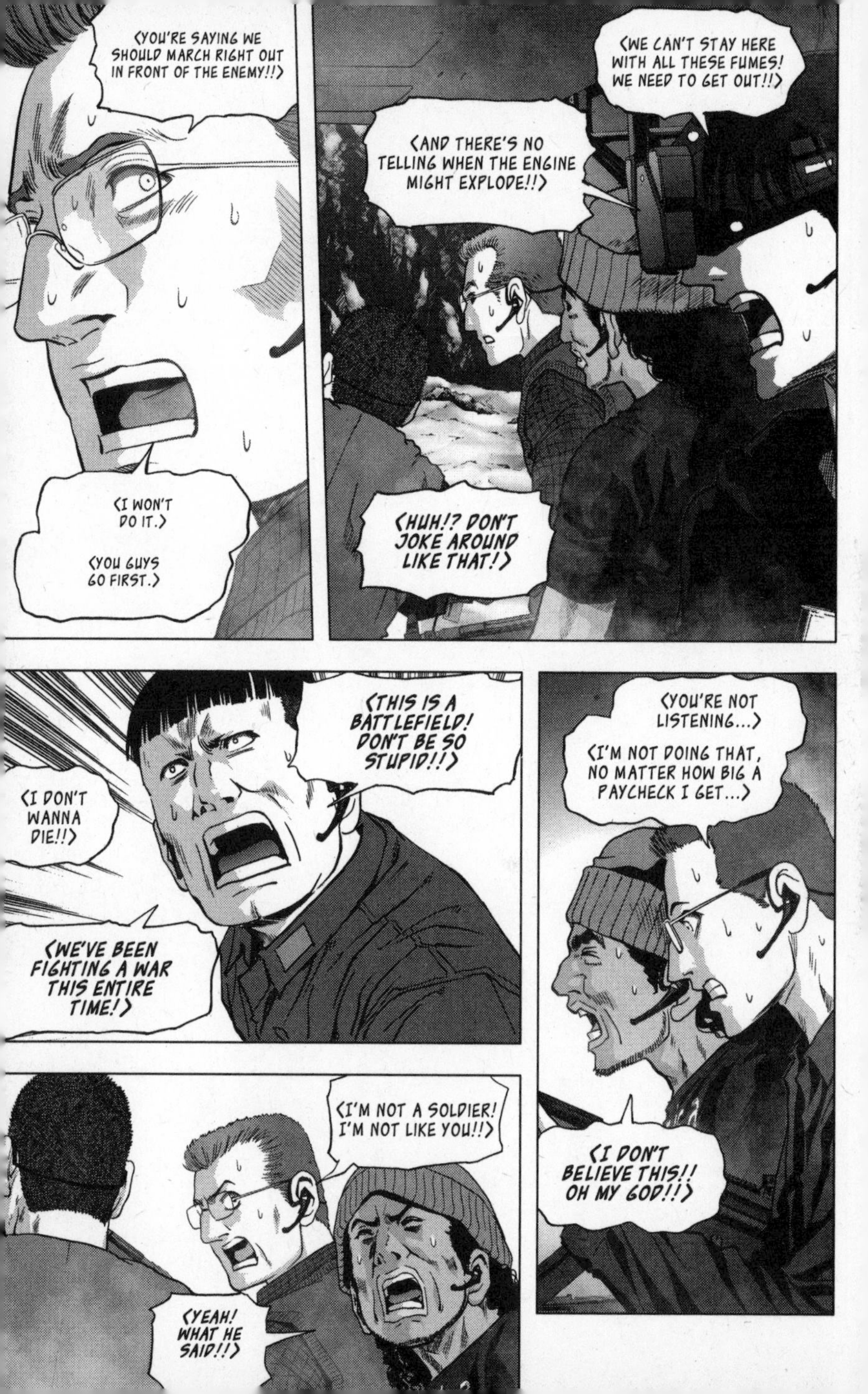
〈WE CAN'T STAY HERE WITH ALL THESE FUMES! WE NEED TO GET OUT!!〉
〈AND THERE'S NO TELLING WHEN THE ENGINE MIGHT EXPLODE!!〉
〈HUH!? DON'T JOKE AROUND LIKE THAT!〉
〈YOU'RE SAYING WE SHOULD MARCH RIGHT OUT IN FRONT OF THE ENEMY!!〉
〈I WON'T DO IT.〉
〈YOU GUYS GO FIRST.〉
〈YOU'RE NOT LISTENING...〉
〈I'M NOT DOING THAT, NO MATTER HOW BIG A PAYCHECK I GET...〉
〈I DON'T BELIEVE THIS!! OH MY GOD!!〉
〈THIS IS A BATTLEFIELD! DON'T BE SO STUPID!!〉
〈I DON'T WANNA DIE!!〉
〈WE'VE BEEN FIGHTING A WAR THIS ENTIRE TIME!〉
〈I'M NOT A SOLDIER! I'M NOT LIKE YOU!!〉
〈YEAH! WHAT HE SAID!!〉

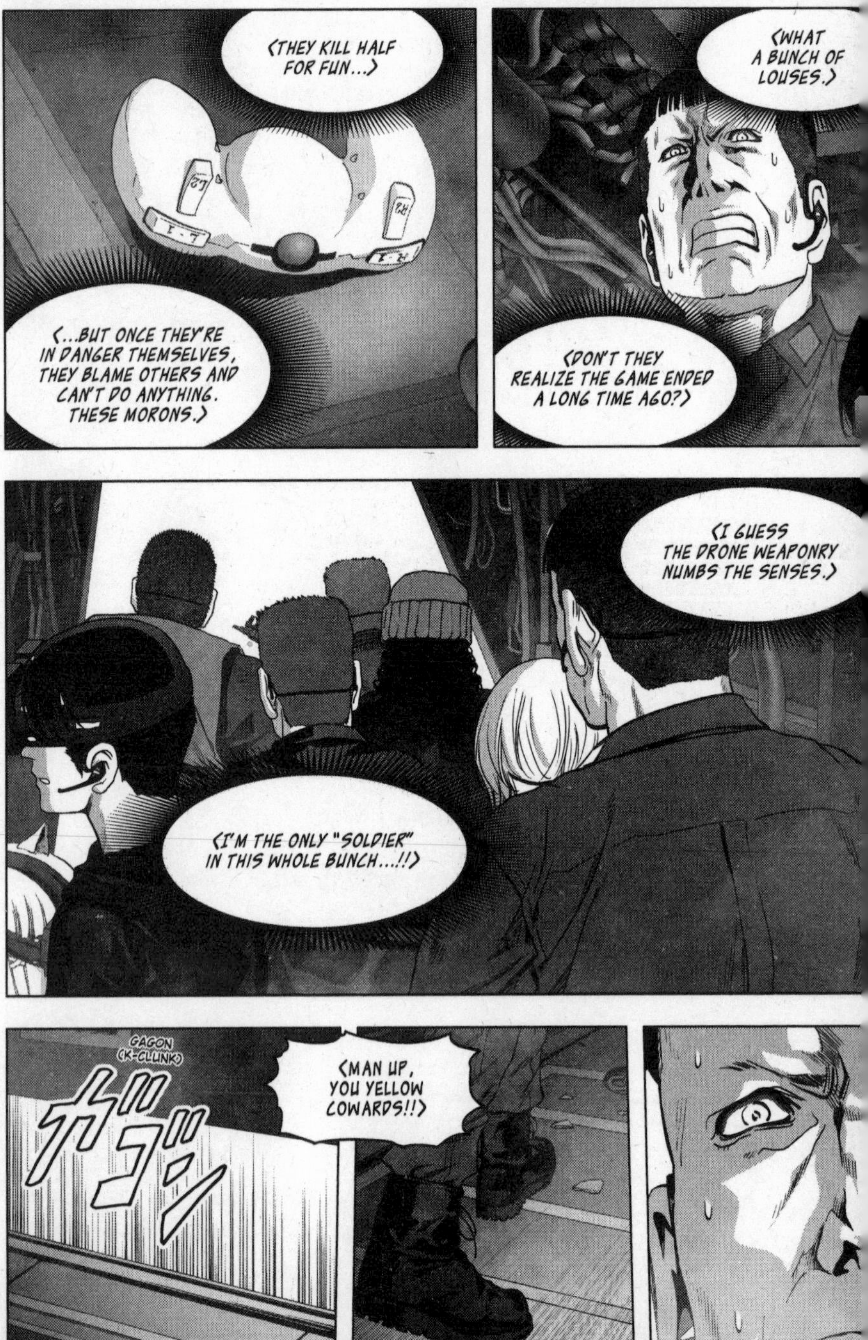
<WHAT A BUNCH OF LOUSES.>
<DON'T THEY REALIZE THE GAME ENDED A LONG TIME AGO?>
<THEY KILL HALF FOR FUN...>
<...BUT ONCE THEY'RE IN DANGER THEMSELVES, THEY BLAME OTHERS AND CAN'T DO ANYTHING. THESE MORONS.>
<I GUESS THE DRONE WEAPONRY NUMBS THE SENSES.>
<I'M THE ONLY "SOLDIER" IN THIS WHOLE BUNCH...!!>
<MAN UP, YOU YELLOW COWARDS!!>
ガゴン
GAGON (K-CLUNK)

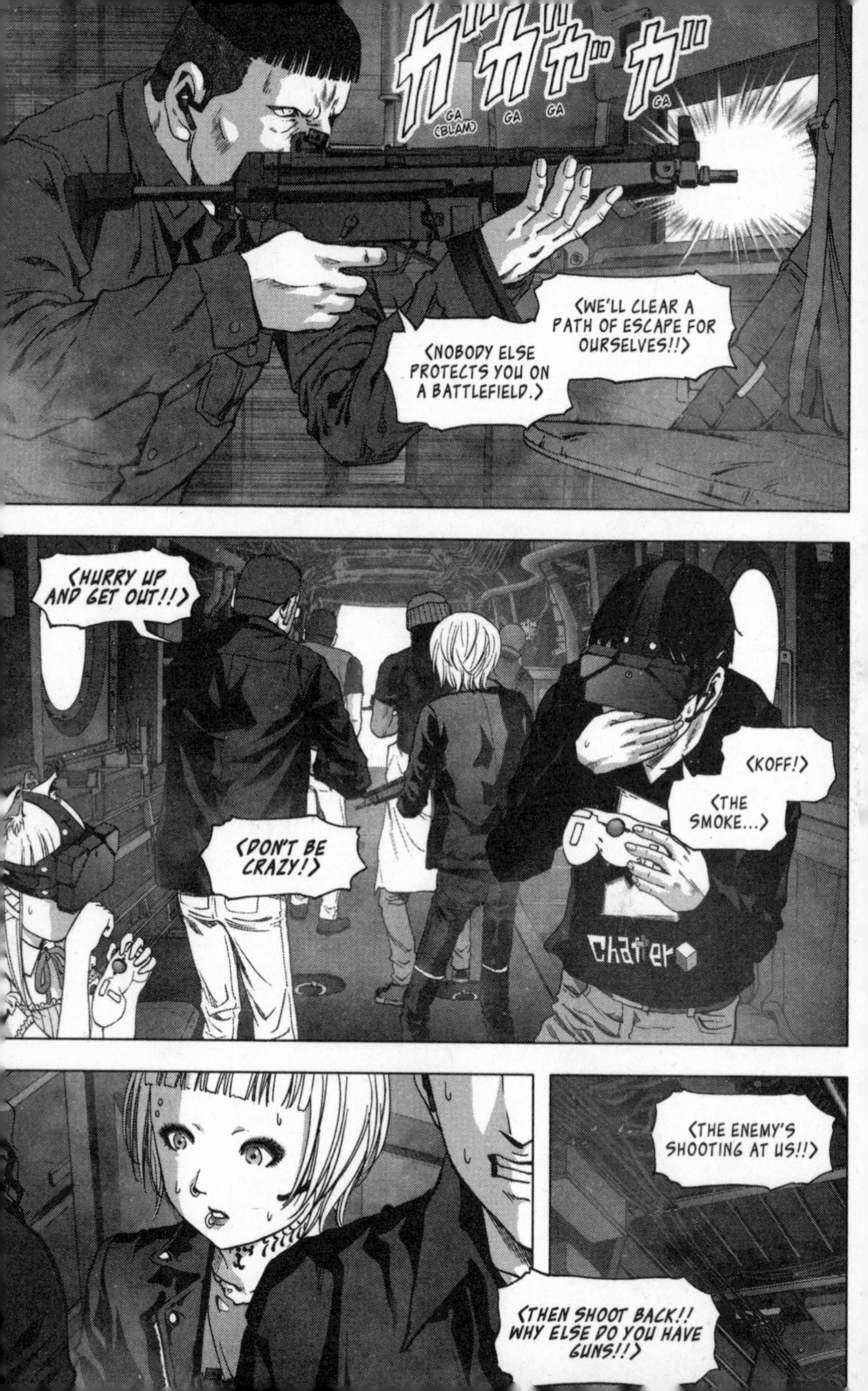
ガガガガ
GA (BLAM) GA GA GA
‹WE'LL CLEAR A PATH OF ESCAPE FOR OURSELVES!!›
‹NOBODY ELSE PROTECTS YOU ON A BATTLEFIELD.›
‹KOFF!›
‹THE SMOKE...›
‹HURRY UP AND GET OUT!!›
‹DON'T BE CRAZY!›
Chatter
‹THE ENEMY'S SHOOTING AT US!!›
‹THEN SHOOT BACK!! WHY ELSE DO YOU HAVE GUNS!!›

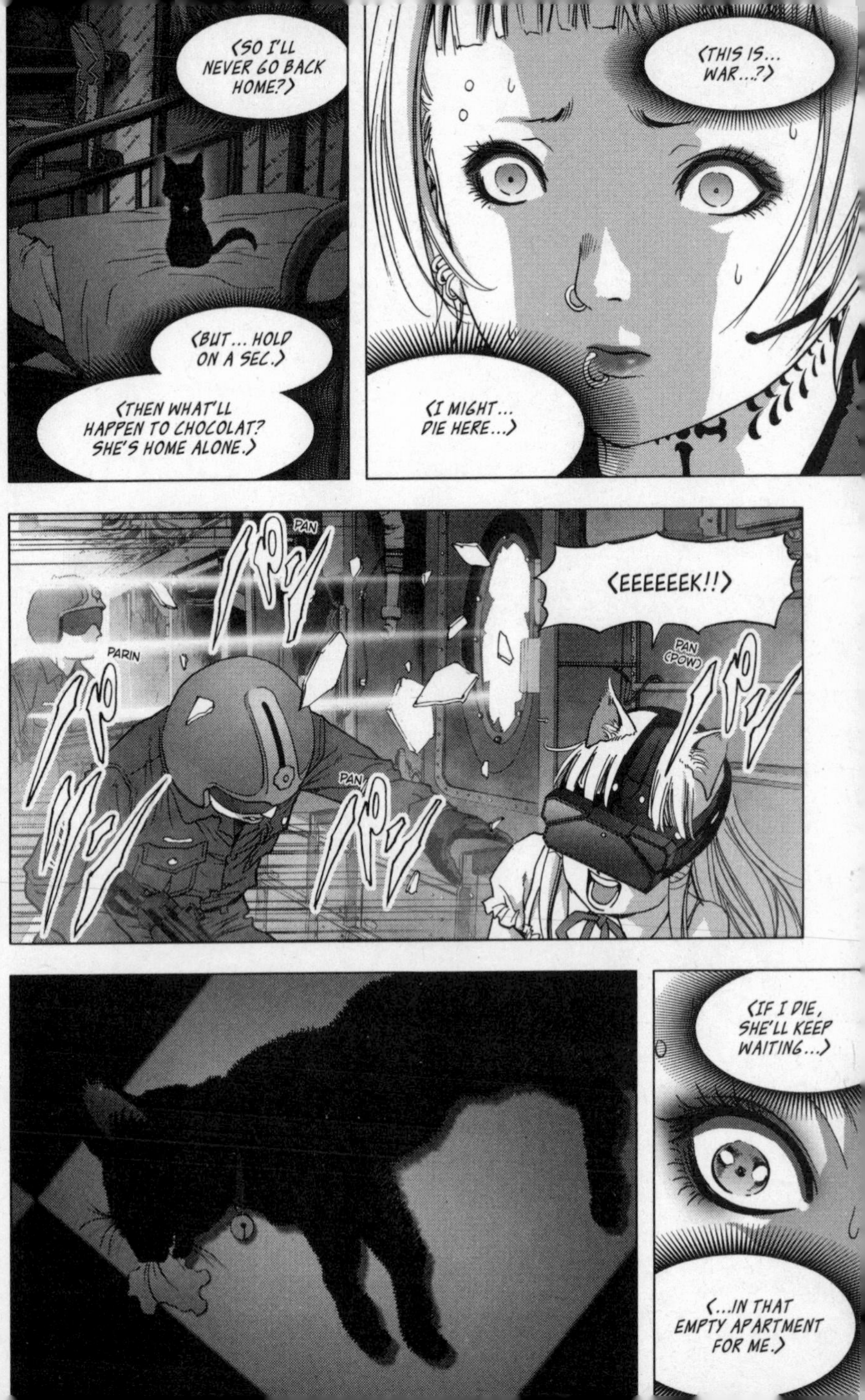
<THIS IS... WAR...?>
<I MIGHT... DIE HERE...>
<SO I'LL NEVER GO BACK HOME?>
<BUT... HOLD ON A SEC.>
<THEN WHAT'LL HAPPEN TO CHOCOLAT? SHE'S HOME ALONE.>
<EEEEEEK!!>
PAN
PAN (POW)
PARIN
PAN
<IF I DIE, SHE'LL KEEP WAITING...>
<...IN THAT EMPTY APARTMENT FOR ME.>

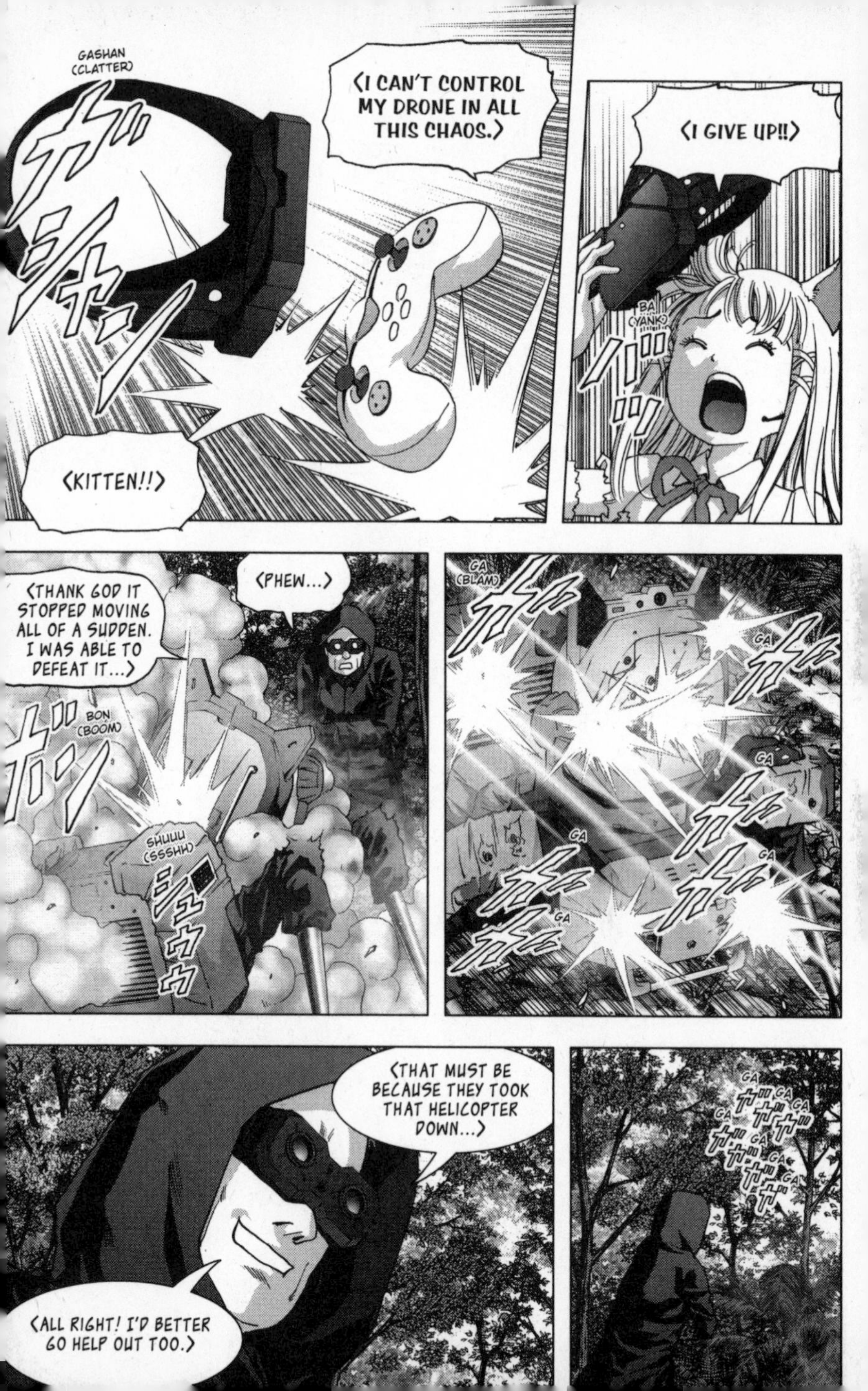
‹I GIVE UP!!›
BA (YANK)
‹I CAN'T CONTROL MY DRONE IN ALL THIS CHAOS.›
GASHAN (CLATTER)
‹KITTEN!!›
GA (BLAM)
GA
GA
GA
GA
GA
‹PHEW...›
‹THANK GOD IT STOPPED MOVING ALL OF A SUDDEN. I WAS ABLE TO DEFEAT IT...›
BON (BOOM)
SHUUU (SSSHH)
GA GA GA GA GA GA GA
‹THAT MUST BE BECAUSE THEY TOOK THAT HELICOPTER DOWN...›
‹ALL RIGHT! I'D BETTER GO HELP OUT TOO.›

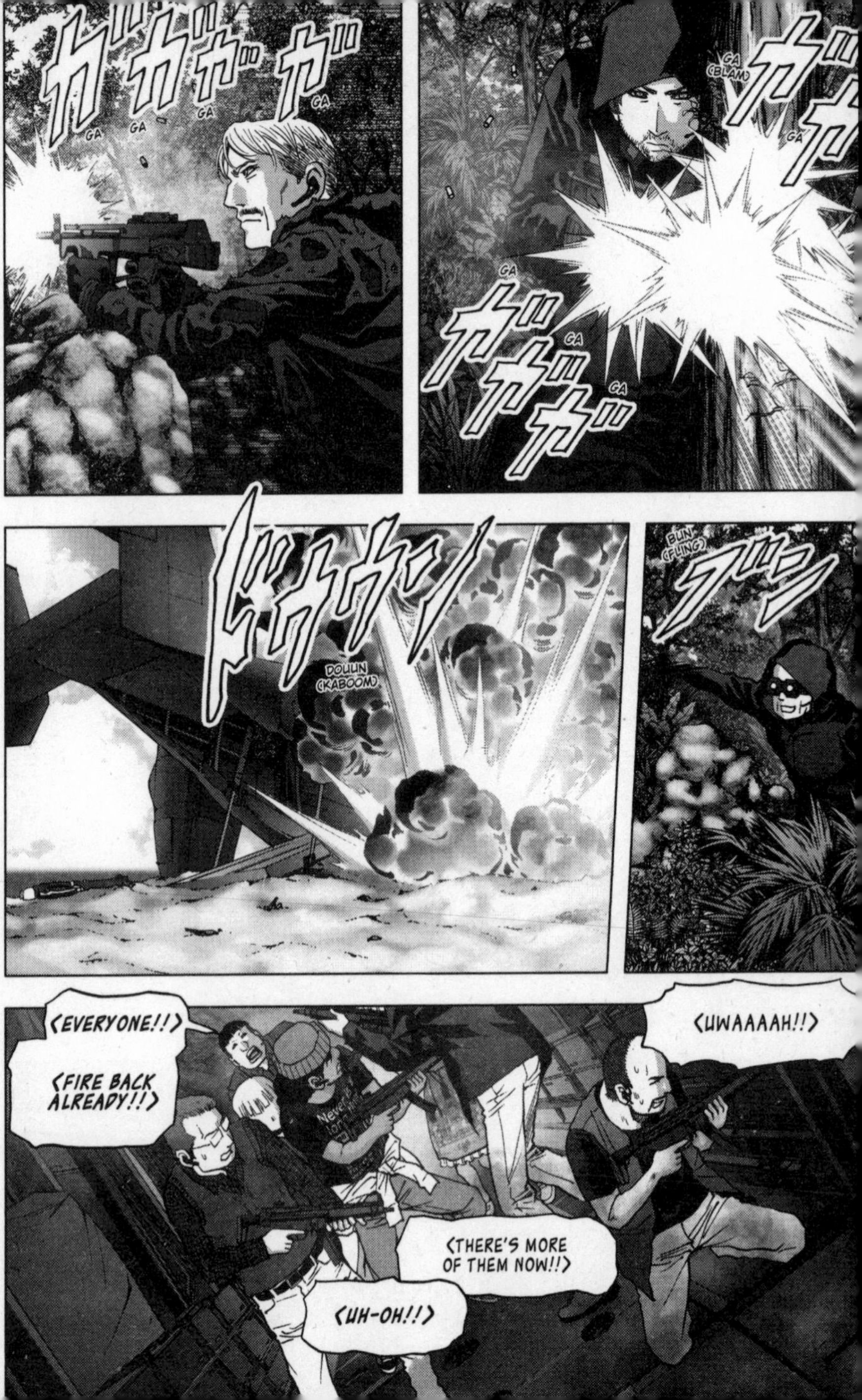
GA
(BLAM)
GA
GA
GA
GA
GA
GA
GA
GA
BUN
(FLING)
DOUUN
(KABOOM)
‹UWAAAAH!!›
‹EVERYONE!!›
‹FIRE BACK ALREADY!!›
‹THERE'S MORE OF THEM NOW!!›
‹UH-OH!!›

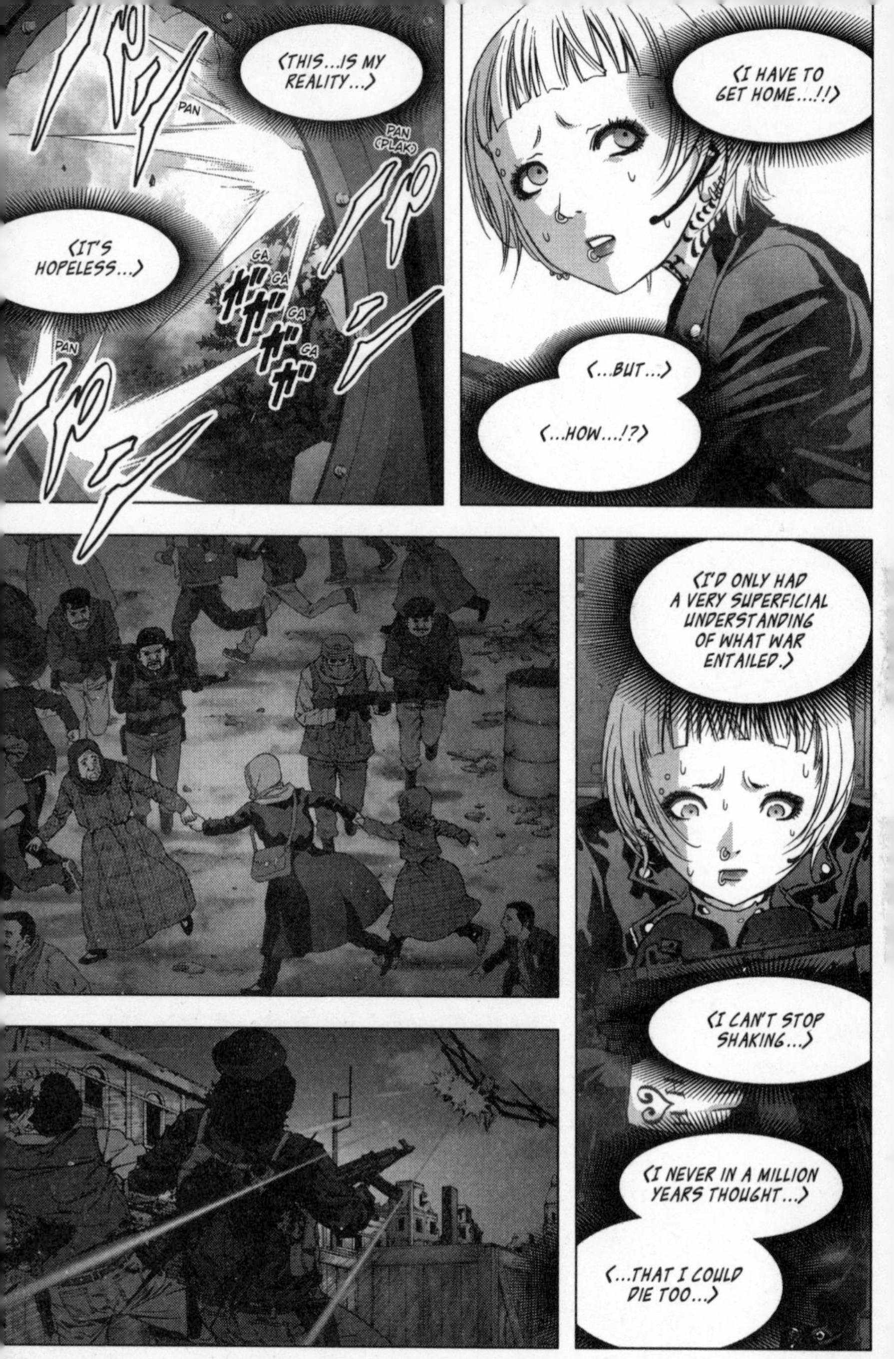
⟨I HAVE TO GET HOME...!!⟩
⟨...BUT...⟩
⟨...HOW...!?⟩
⟨THIS...IS MY REALITY...⟩
PAN
PAN (PLAK)
⟨IT'S HOPELESS...⟩
GA
GA
GA
GA
PAN
⟨I'D ONLY HAD A VERY SUPERFICIAL UNDERSTANDING OF WHAT WAR ENTAILED.⟩
⟨I CAN'T STOP SHAKING...⟩
⟨I NEVER IN A MILLION YEARS THOUGHT...⟩
⟨...THAT I COULD DIE TOO...⟩

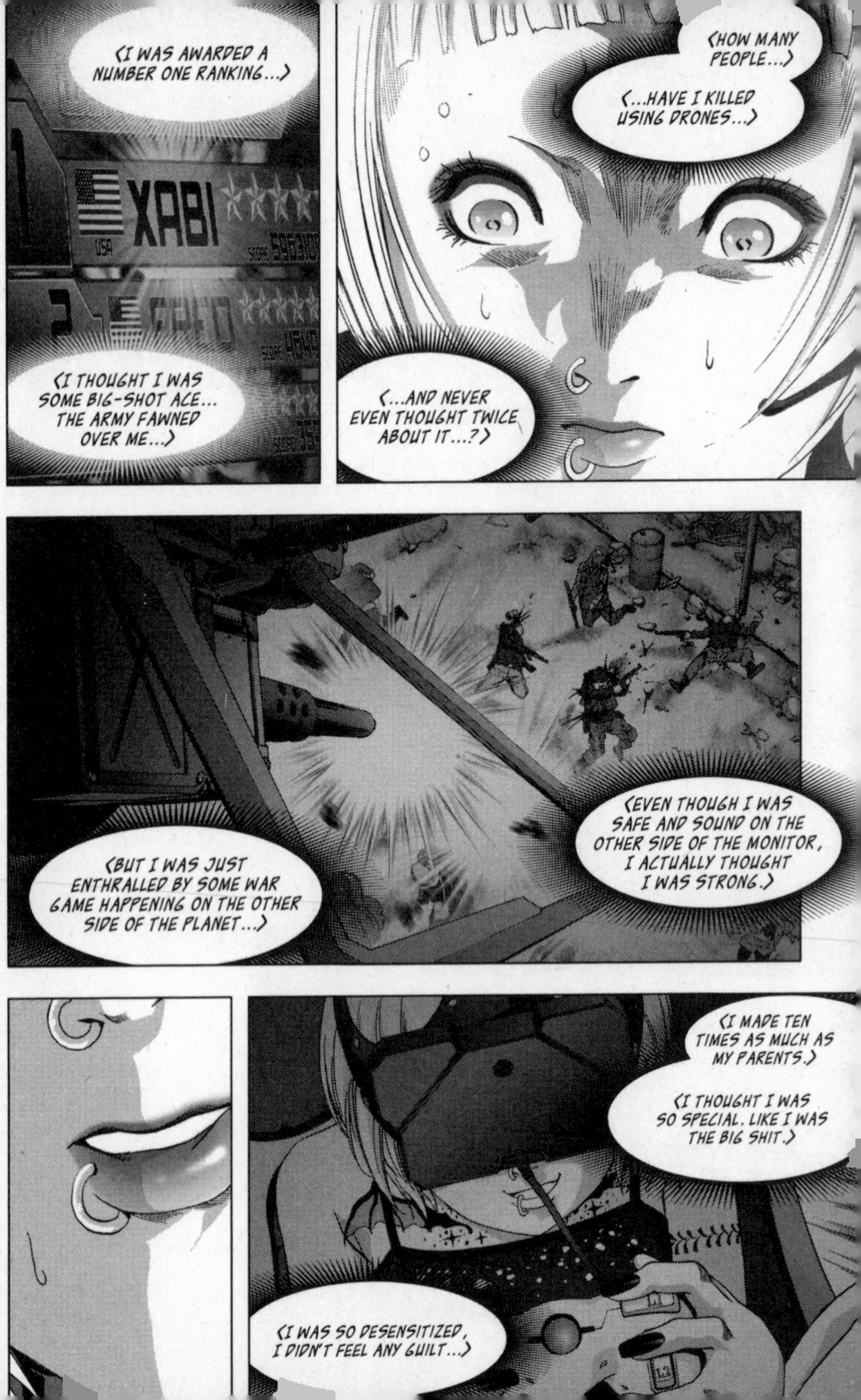
‹HOW MANY PEOPLE...›
‹...HAVE I KILLED USING DRONES...›
‹...AND NEVER EVEN THOUGHT TWICE ABOUT IT...?›
‹I WAS AWARDED A NUMBER ONE RANKING...›
XABI
USA
‹I THOUGHT I WAS SOME BIG-SHOT ACE... THE ARMY FAWNED OVER ME...›
‹EVEN THOUGH I WAS SAFE AND SOUND ON THE OTHER SIDE OF THE MONITOR, I ACTUALLY THOUGHT I WAS STRONG.›
‹BUT I WAS JUST ENTHRALLED BY SOME WAR GAME HAPPENING ON THE OTHER SIDE OF THE PLANET...›
‹I MADE TEN TIMES AS MUCH AS MY PARENTS.›
‹I THOUGHT I WAS SO SPECIAL. LIKE I WAS THE BIG SHIT.›
‹I WAS SO DESENSITIZED, I DIDN'T FEEL ANY GUILT...›

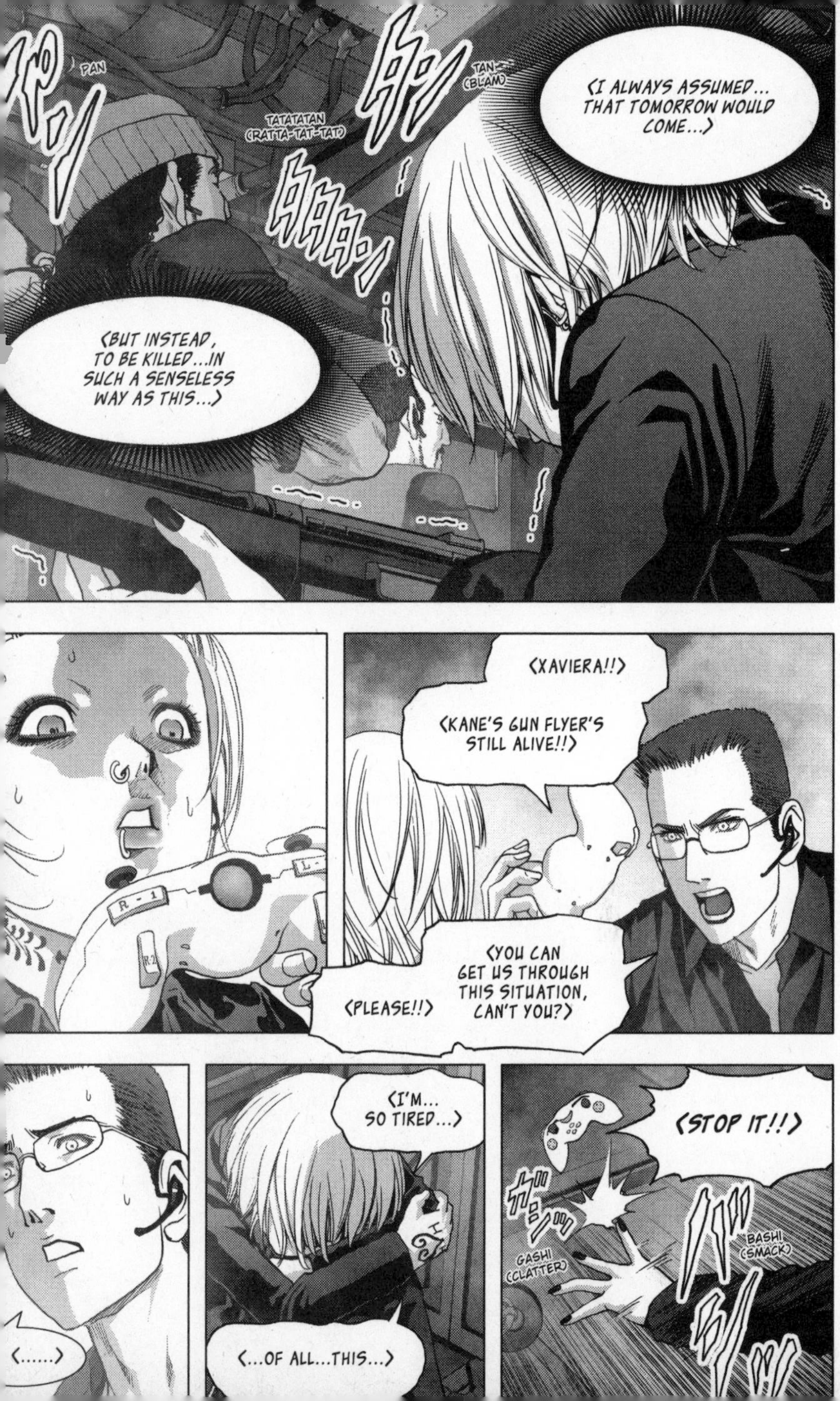
<I ALWAYS ASSUMED... THAT TOMORROW WOULD COME...>
TAN (BLAM)
TATATATAN (RATTA-TAT-TAT)
PAN
<BUT INSTEAD, TO BE KILLED...IN SUCH A SENSELESS WAY AS THIS...>
<XAVIERA!!>
<KANE'S GUN FLYER'S STILL ALIVE!!>
<YOU CAN GET US THROUGH THIS SITUATION, CAN'T YOU?>
<PLEASE!!>
<STOP IT!!>
BASHI (SMACK)
GASHI (CLATTER)
<I'M... SO TIRED...>
<...OF ALL...THIS...>
<......>

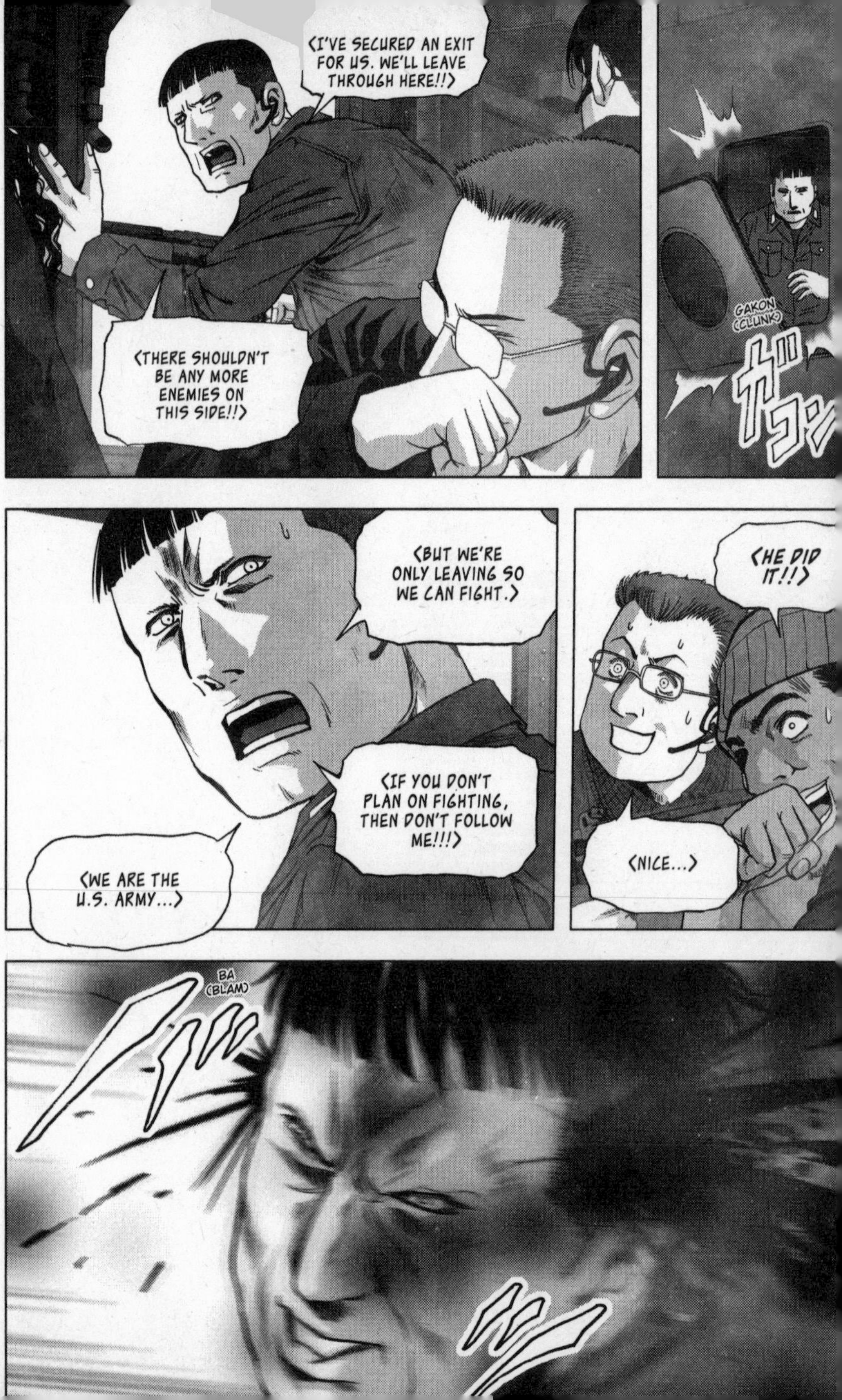
GAKON (CLUNK)
ガコン
<I'VE SECURED AN EXIT FOR US. WE'LL LEAVE THROUGH HERE!!>
<THERE SHOULDN'T BE ANY MORE ENEMIES ON THIS SIDE!!>
<HE DID IT!!>
<NICE...>
<BUT WE'RE ONLY LEAVING SO WE CAN FIGHT.>
<IF YOU DON'T PLAN ON FIGHTING, THEN DON'T FOLLOW ME!!!>
<WE ARE THE U.S. ARMY...>
BA (BLAM)

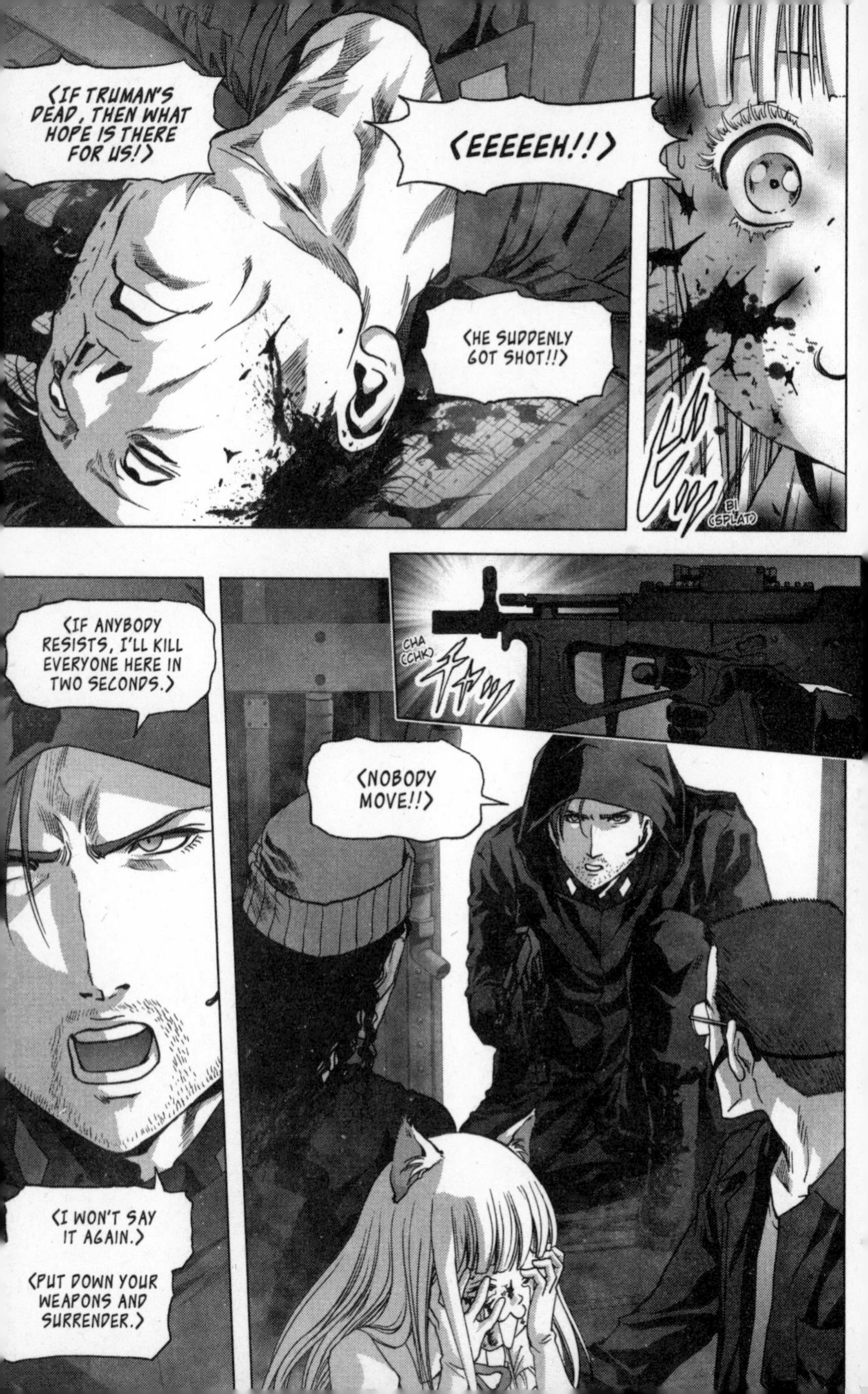
BI
(SPLAT)
〈EEEEEH!!〉
〈IF TRUMAN'S DEAD, THEN WHAT HOPE IS THERE FOR US!〉
〈HE SUDDENLY GOT SHOT!!〉
CHA
(CHK)
〈NOBODY MOVE!!〉
〈IF ANYBODY RESISTS, I'LL KILL EVERYONE HERE IN TWO SECONDS.〉
〈I WON'T SAY IT AGAIN.〉
〈PUT DOWN YOUR WEAPONS AND SURRENDER.〉

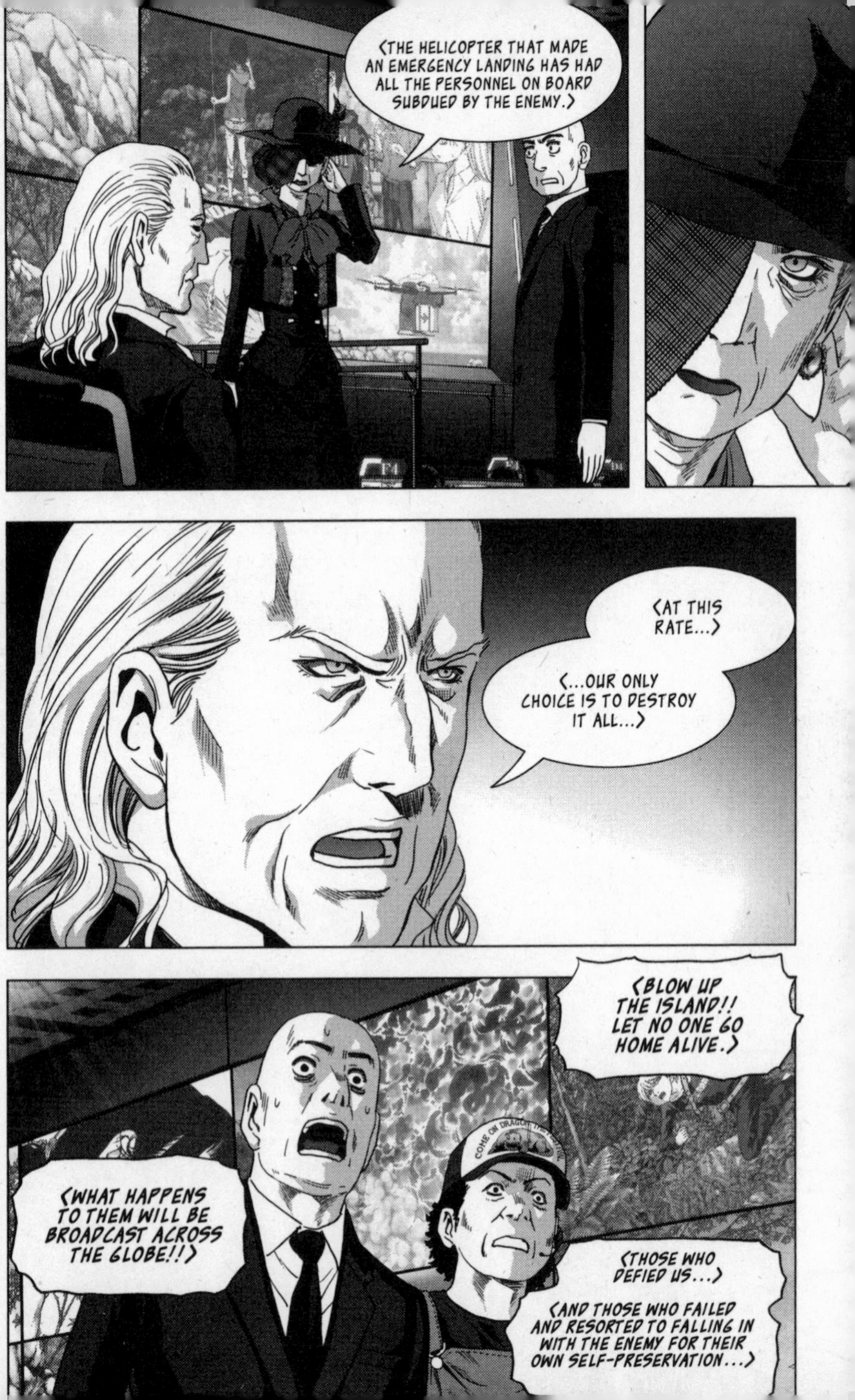
⟨THE HELICOPTER THAT MADE AN EMERGENCY LANDING HAS HAD ALL THE PERSONNEL ON BOARD SUBDUED BY THE ENEMY.⟩
⟨AT THIS RATE...⟩
⟨...OUR ONLY CHOICE IS TO DESTROY IT ALL...⟩
⟨BLOW UP THE ISLAND!! LET NO ONE GO HOME ALIVE.⟩
⟨THOSE WHO DEFIED US...⟩
⟨AND THOSE WHO FAILED AND RESORTED TO FALLING IN WITH THE ENEMY FOR THEIR OWN SELF-PRESERVATION...⟩
⟨WHAT HAPPENS TO THEM WILL BE BROADCAST ACROSS THE GLOBE!!⟩

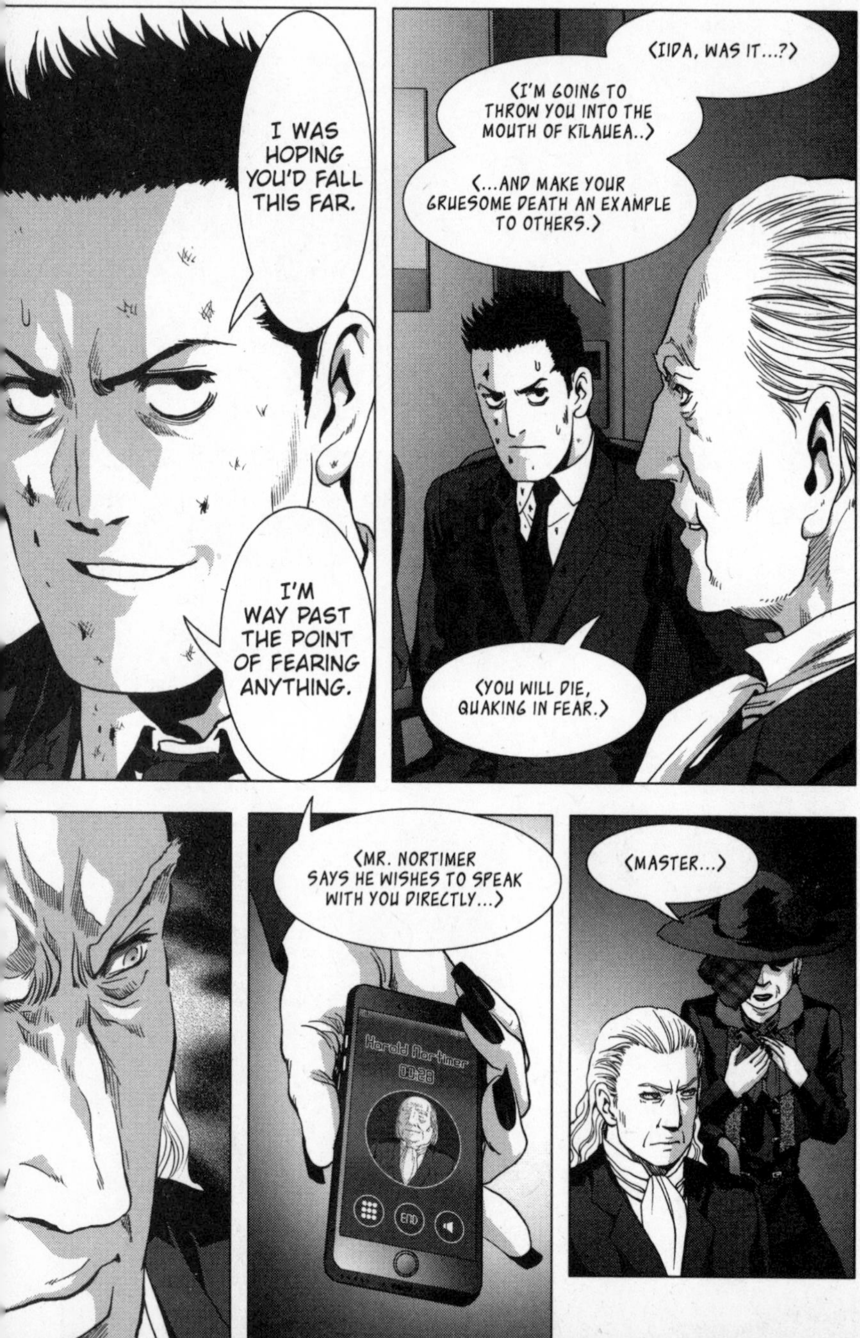
<IIDA, WAS IT...?>
<I'M GOING TO THROW YOU INTO THE MOUTH OF KĪLAUEA..>
<...AND MAKE YOUR GRUESOME DEATH AN EXAMPLE TO OTHERS.>
<YOU WILL DIE, QUAKING IN FEAR.>
I WAS HOPING YOU'D FALL THIS FAR.
I'M WAY PAST THE POINT OF FEARING ANYTHING.
<MASTER...>
<MR. NORTIMER SAYS HE WISHES TO SPEAK WITH YOU DIRECTLY...>
Harold Nortimer
00:28
END

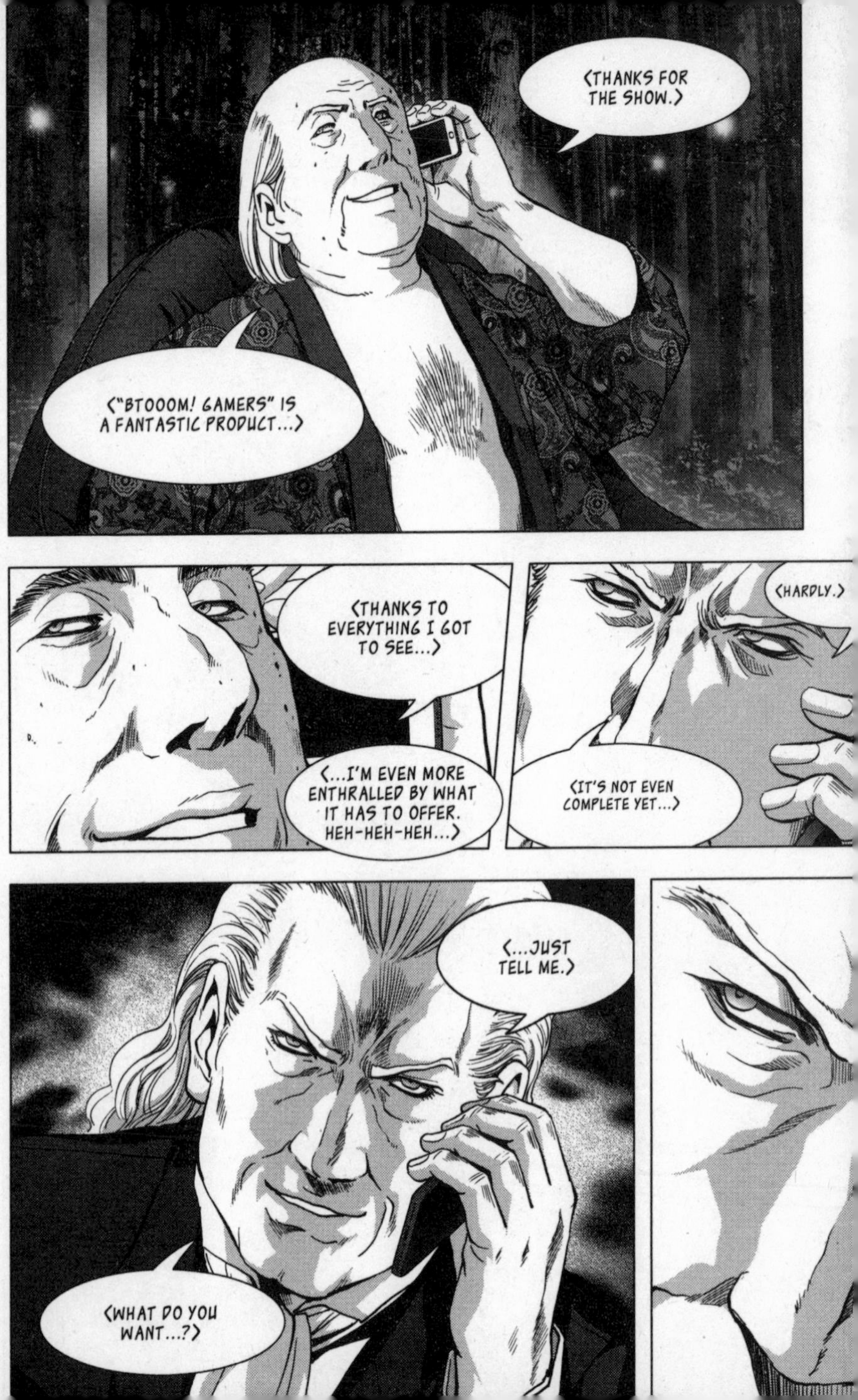
<THANKS FOR THE SHOW.>
<"BTOOOM! GAMERS" IS A FANTASTIC PRODUCT...>
<HARDLY.>
<IT'S NOT EVEN COMPLETE YET...>
<THANKS TO EVERYTHING I GOT TO SEE...>
<...I'M EVEN MORE ENTHRALLED BY WHAT IT HAS TO OFFER. HEH-HEH-HEH...>
<...JUST TELL ME.>
<WHAT DO YOU WANT...?>

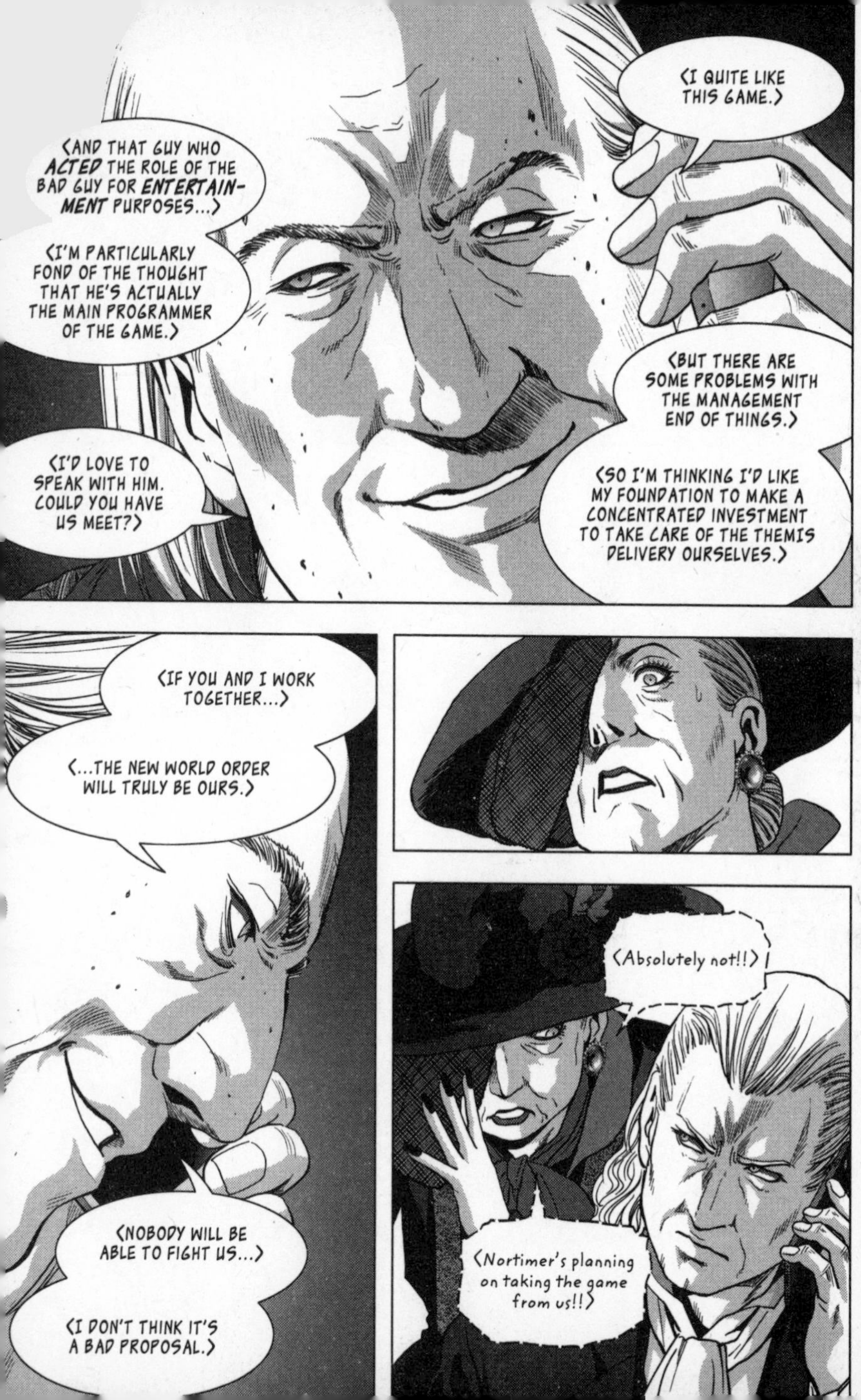

<I QUITE LIKE THIS GAME.>
<AND THAT GUY WHO ACTED THE ROLE OF THE BAD GUY FOR ENTERTAINMENT PURPOSES...>
<I'M PARTICULARLY FOND OF THE THOUGHT THAT HE'S ACTUALLY THE MAIN PROGRAMMER OF THE GAME.>
<I'D LOVE TO SPEAK WITH HIM. COULD YOU HAVE US MEET?>
<BUT THERE ARE SOME PROBLEMS WITH THE MANAGEMENT END OF THINGS.>
<SO I'M THINKING I'D LIKE MY FOUNDATION TO MAKE A CONCENTRATED INVESTMENT TO TAKE CARE OF THE THEMIS DELIVERY OURSELVES.>
<Absolutely not!!>
<Nortimer's planning on taking the game from us!!>
<IF YOU AND I WORK TOGETHER...>
<...THE NEW WORLD ORDER WILL TRULY BE OURS.>
<NOBODY WILL BE ABLE TO FIGHT US...>
<I DON'T THINK IT'S A BAD PROPOSAL.>

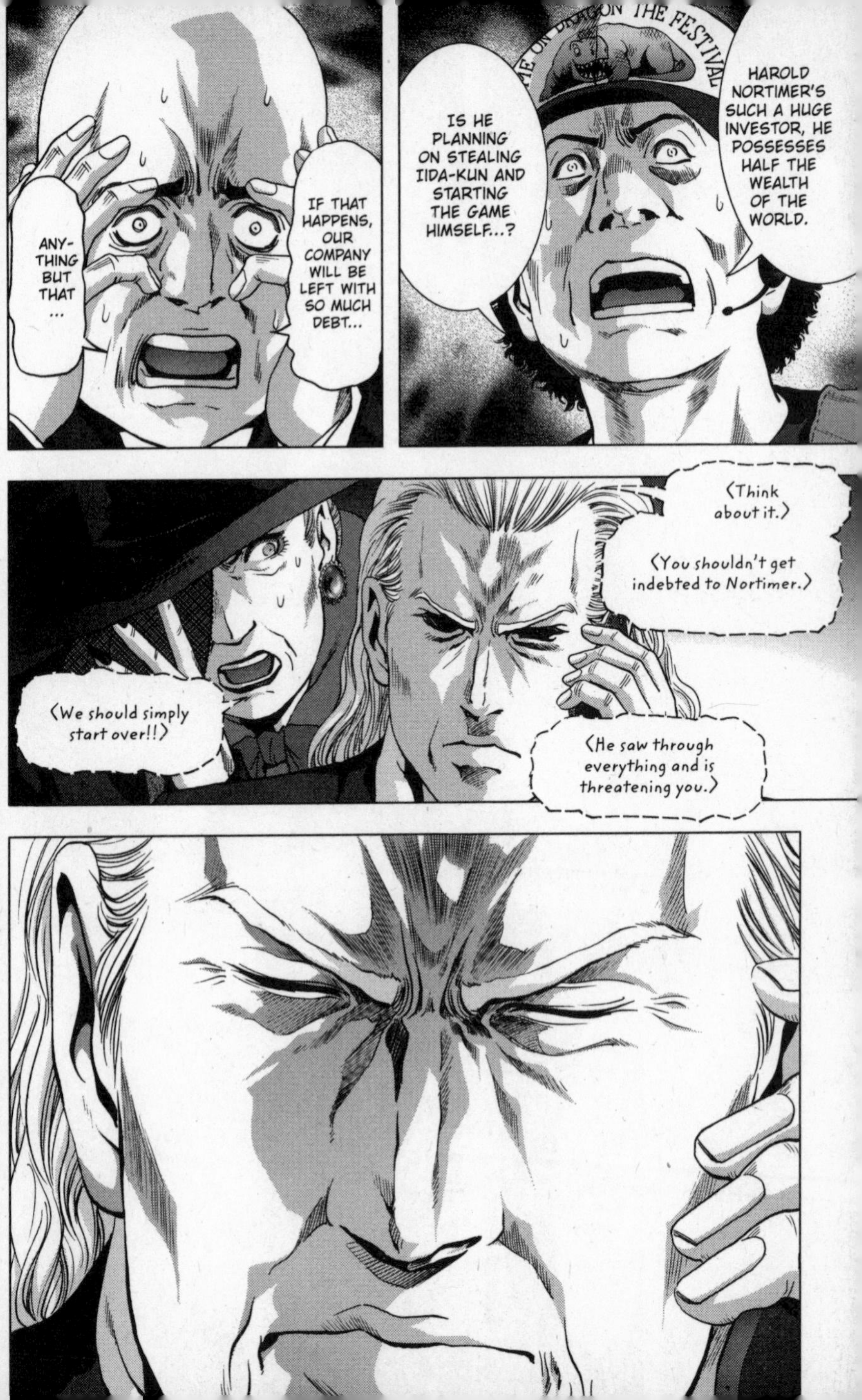
HAROLD NORTIMER'S SUCH A HUGE INVESTOR, HE POSSESSES HALF THE WEALTH OF THE WORLD.
IS HE PLANNING ON STEALING IIDA-KUN AND STARTING THE GAME HIMSELF...?
IF THAT HAPPENS, OUR COMPANY WILL BE LEFT WITH SO MUCH DEBT...
ANYTHING BUT THAT...
〈Think about it.〉
〈You shouldn't get indebted to Nortimer.〉
〈He saw through everything and is threatening you.〉
〈We should simply start over!!〉

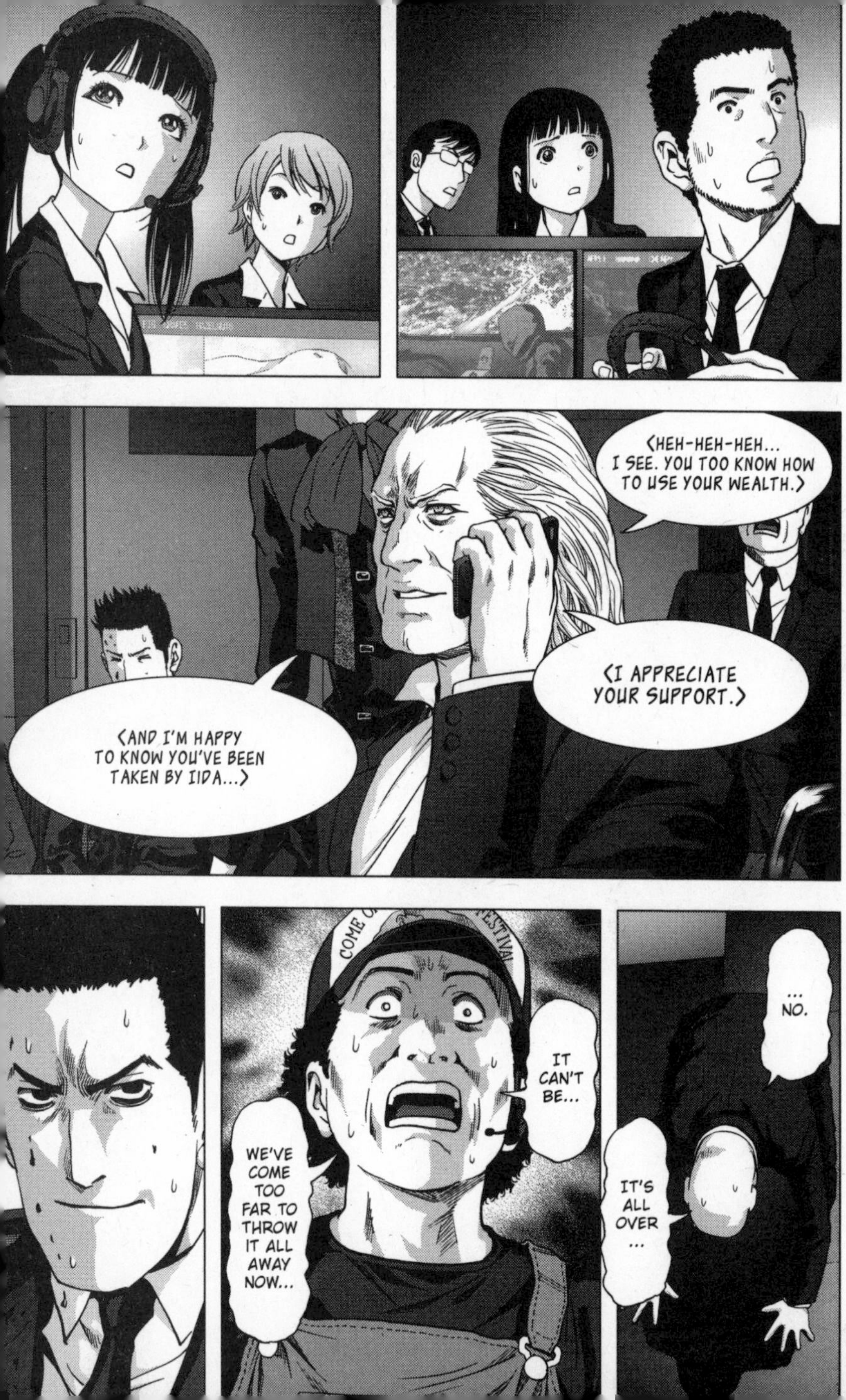
<HEH-HEH-HEH... I SEE. YOU TOO KNOW HOW TO USE YOUR WEALTH.>
<I APPRECIATE YOUR SUPPORT.>
<AND I'M HAPPY TO KNOW YOU'VE BEEN TAKEN BY IIDA...>
...NO.
IT'S ALL OVER ...
IT CAN'T BE...
WE'VE COME TOO FAR TO THROW IT ALL AWAY NOW...

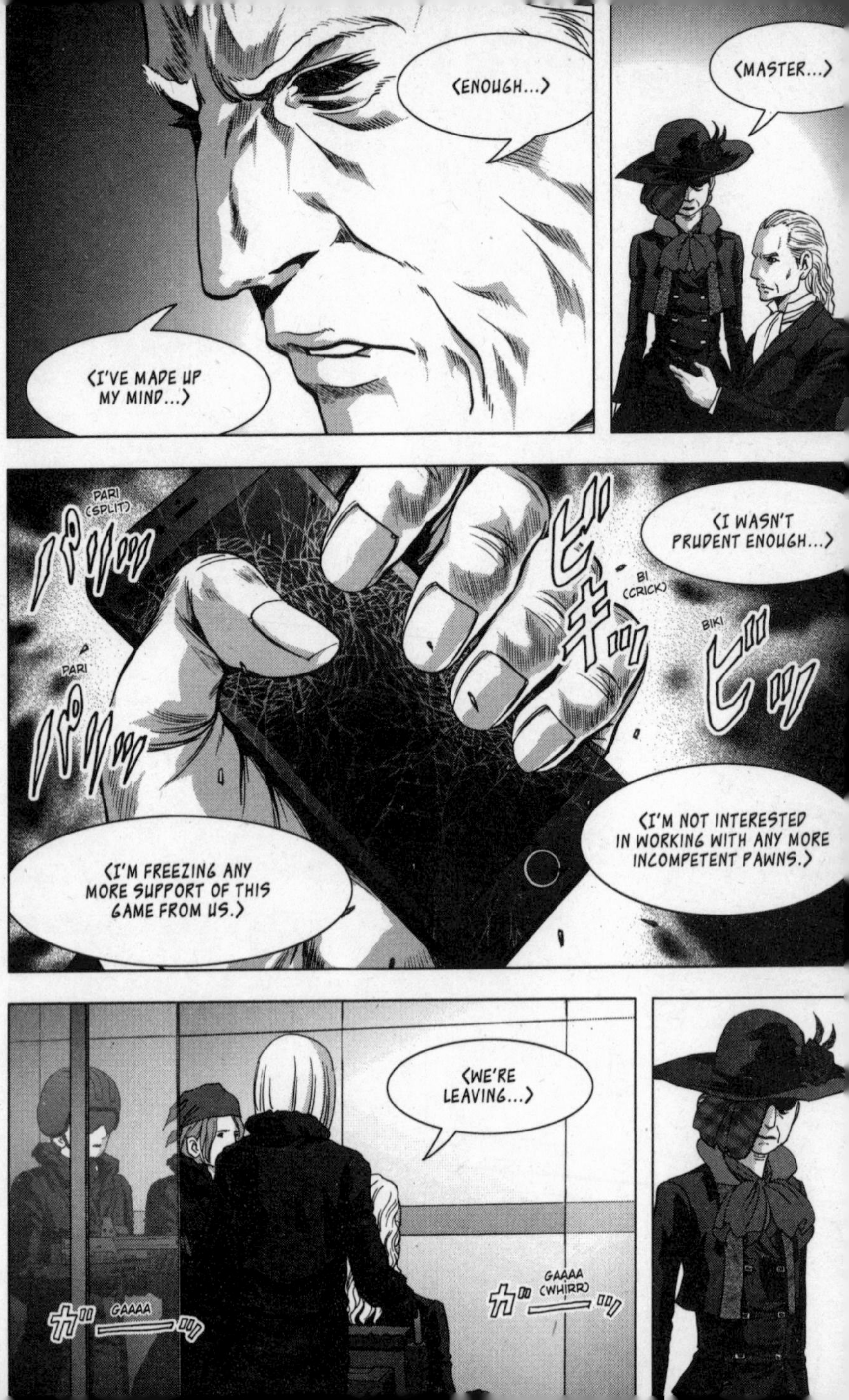

<MASTER...>
<ENOUGH...>
<I'VE MADE UP MY MIND...>
<I WASN'T PRUDENT ENOUGH...>
BI (CRICK)
BIKI
PARI (SPLIT)
PARI
<I'M NOT INTERESTED IN WORKING WITH ANY MORE INCOMPETENT PAWNS.>
<I'M FREEZING ANY MORE SUPPORT OF THIS GAME FROM US.>
<WE'RE LEAVING...>
GAAAA (WHIRR)
GAAAA

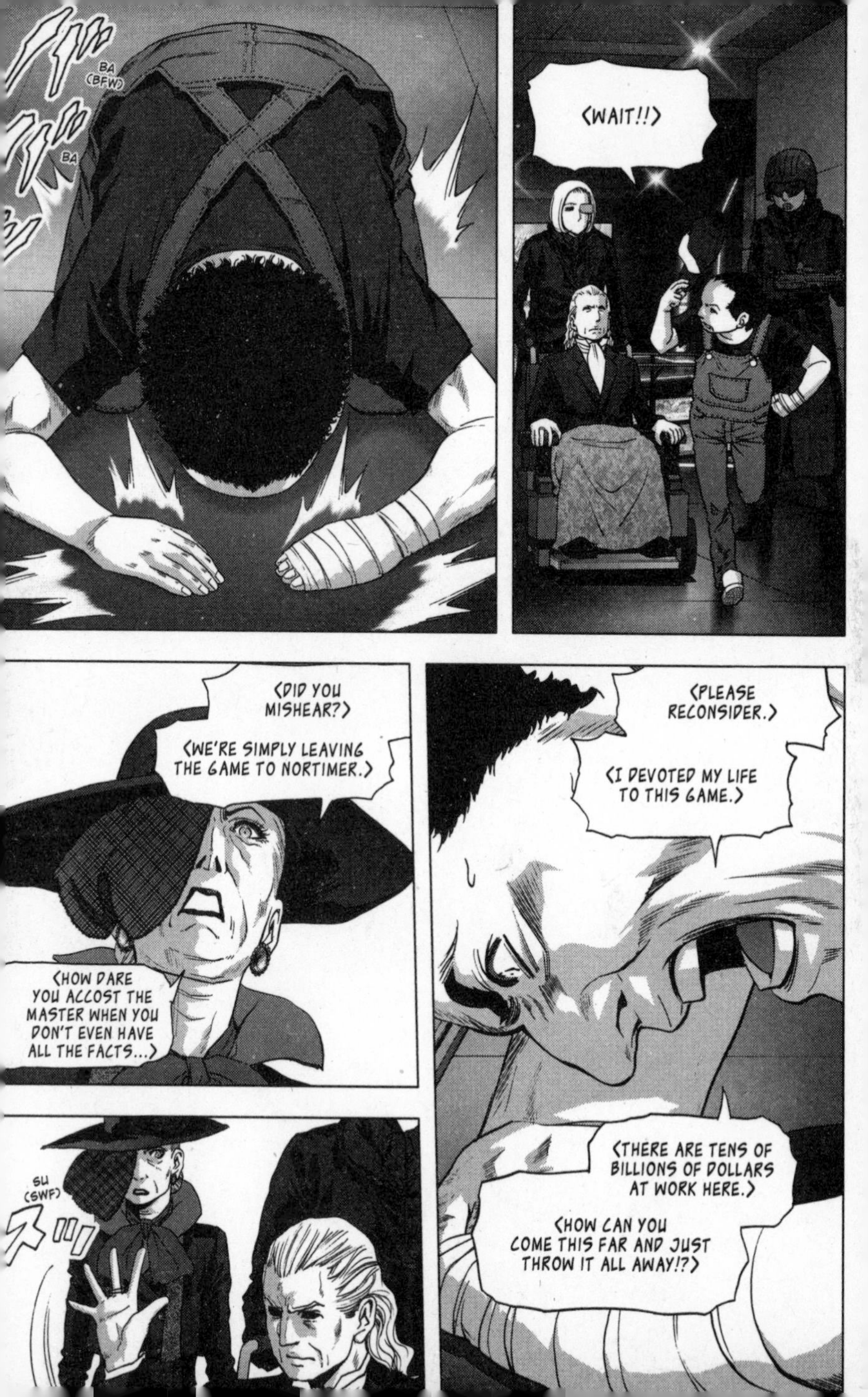
〈WAIT!!〉
BA (BFW)
BA
〈PLEASE RECONSIDER.〉
〈I DEVOTED MY LIFE TO THIS GAME.〉
〈THERE ARE TENS OF BILLIONS OF DOLLARS AT WORK HERE.〉
〈HOW CAN YOU COME THIS FAR AND JUST THROW IT ALL AWAY!?〉
〈DID YOU MISHEAR?〉
〈WE'RE SIMPLY LEAVING THE GAME TO NORTIMER.〉
〈HOW DARE YOU ACCOST THE MASTER WHEN YOU DON'T EVEN HAVE ALL THE FACTS...〉
SU (SWF)

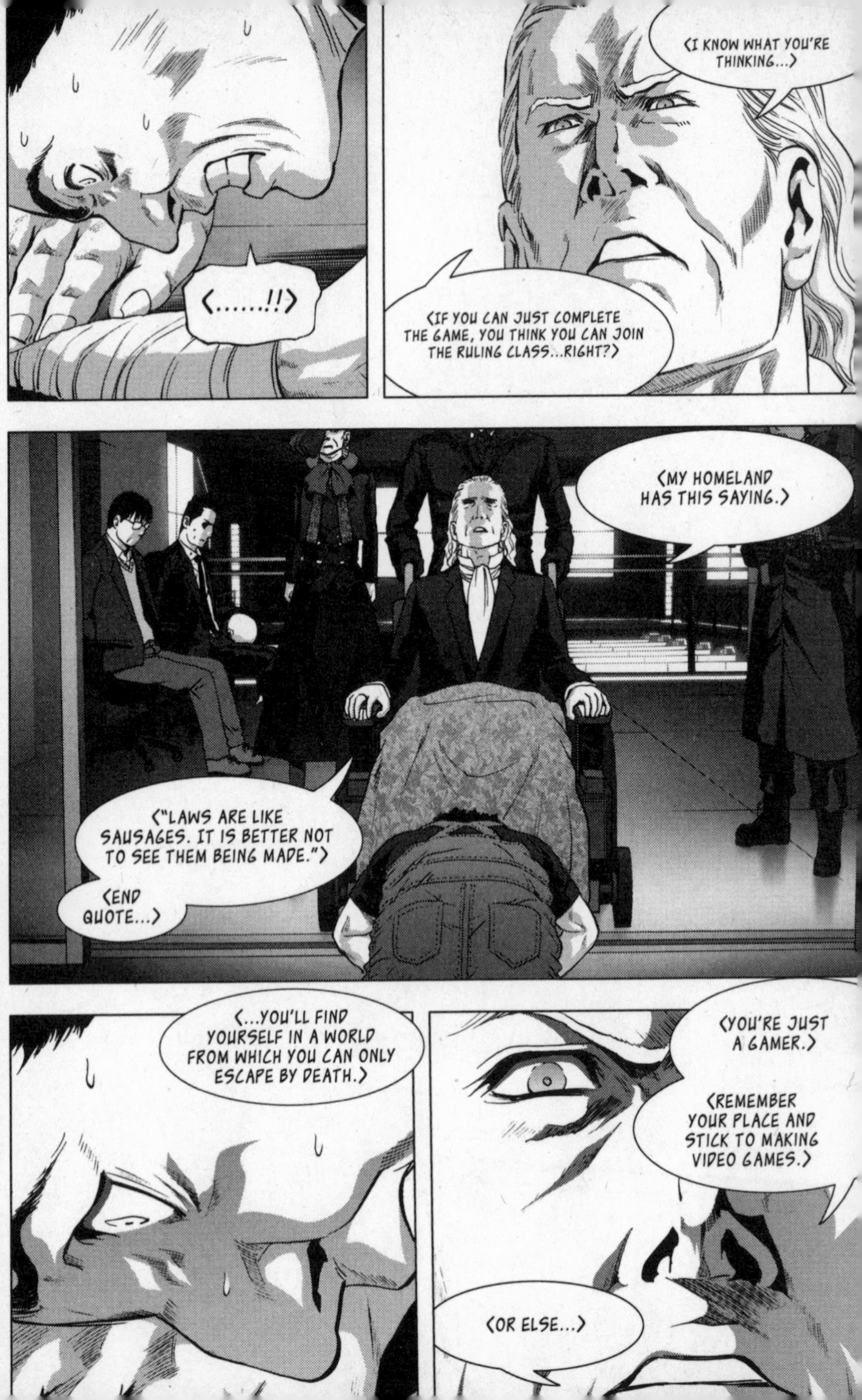
〈I KNOW WHAT YOU'RE THINKING...〉
〈IF YOU CAN JUST COMPLETE THE GAME, YOU THINK YOU CAN JOIN THE RULING CLASS...RIGHT?〉
〈......!!〉
〈MY HOMELAND HAS THIS SAYING.〉
〈"LAWS ARE LIKE SAUSAGES. IT IS BETTER NOT TO SEE THEM BEING MADE."〉
〈END QUOTE...〉
〈YOU'RE JUST A GAMER.〉
〈REMEMBER YOUR PLACE AND STICK TO MAKING VIDEO GAMES.〉
〈OR ELSE...〉
〈...YOU'LL FIND YOURSELF IN A WORLD FROM WHICH YOU CAN ONLY ESCAPE BY DEATH.〉

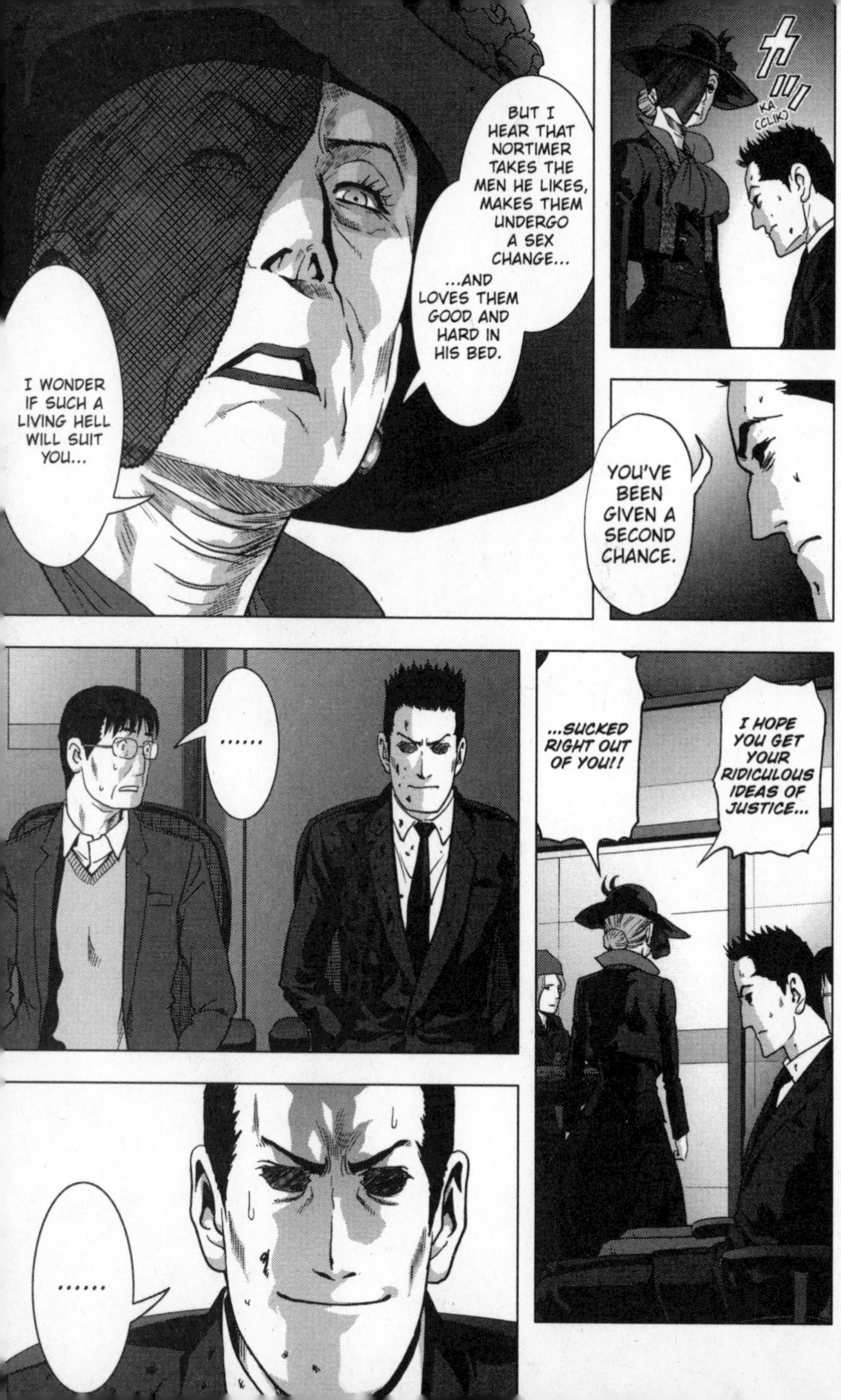
KA (CLIK)
YOU'VE BEEN GIVEN A SECOND CHANCE.
BUT I HEAR THAT NORTIMER TAKES THE MEN HE LIKES, MAKES THEM UNDERGO A SEX CHANGE...
...AND LOVES THEM GOOD AND HARD IN HIS BED.
I WONDER IF SUCH A LIVING HELL WILL SUIT YOU...
I HOPE YOU GET YOUR RIDICULOUS IDEAS OF JUSTICE...
...SUCKED RIGHT OUT OF YOU!!
......
......

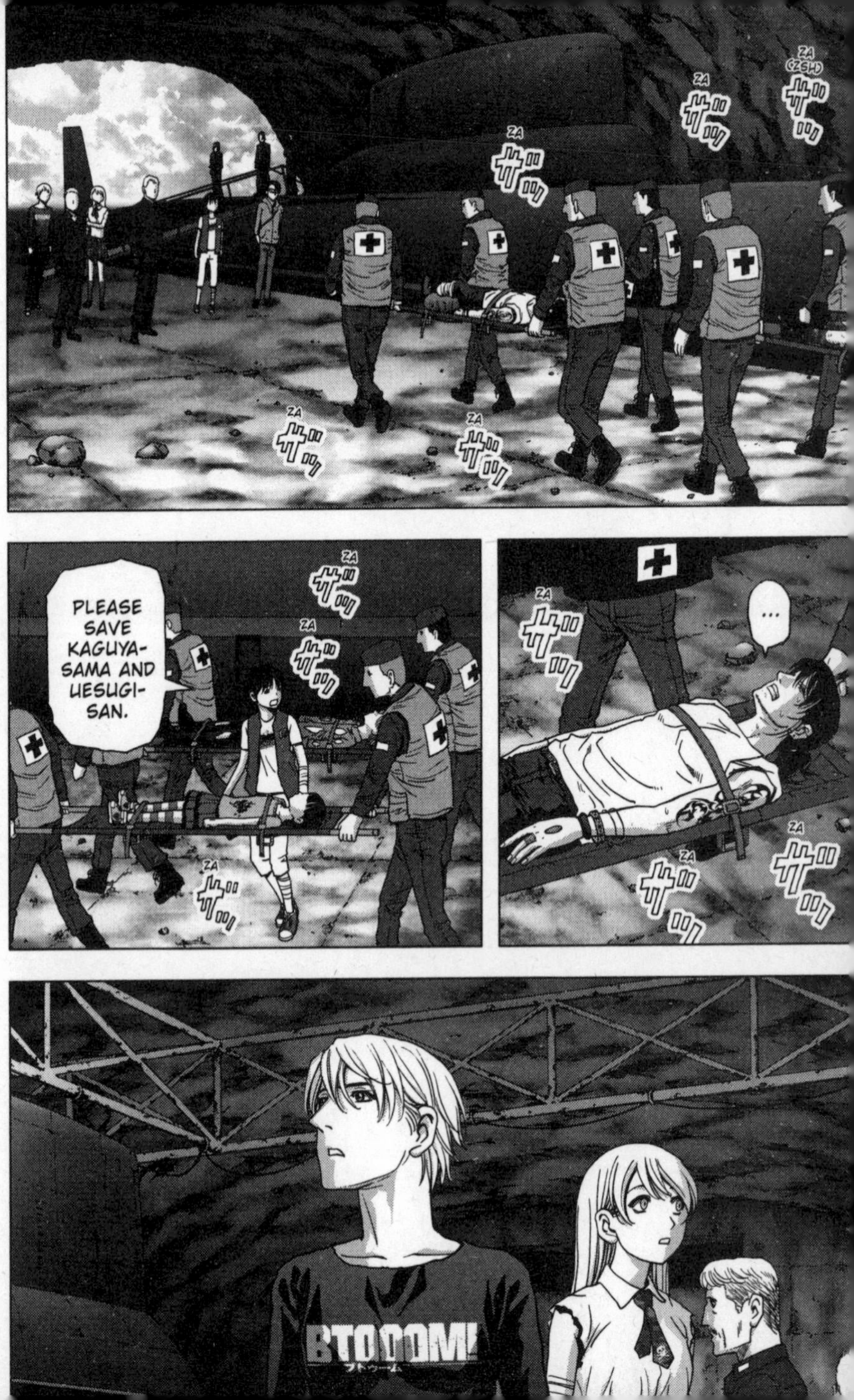
ZA (ZSH)
ZA
ZA
ZA
ZA
ZA
...
ZA
ZA
ZA
ZA
PLEASE SAVE KAGUYA-SAMA AND UESUGI-SAN.
ZA
BTOOOM!

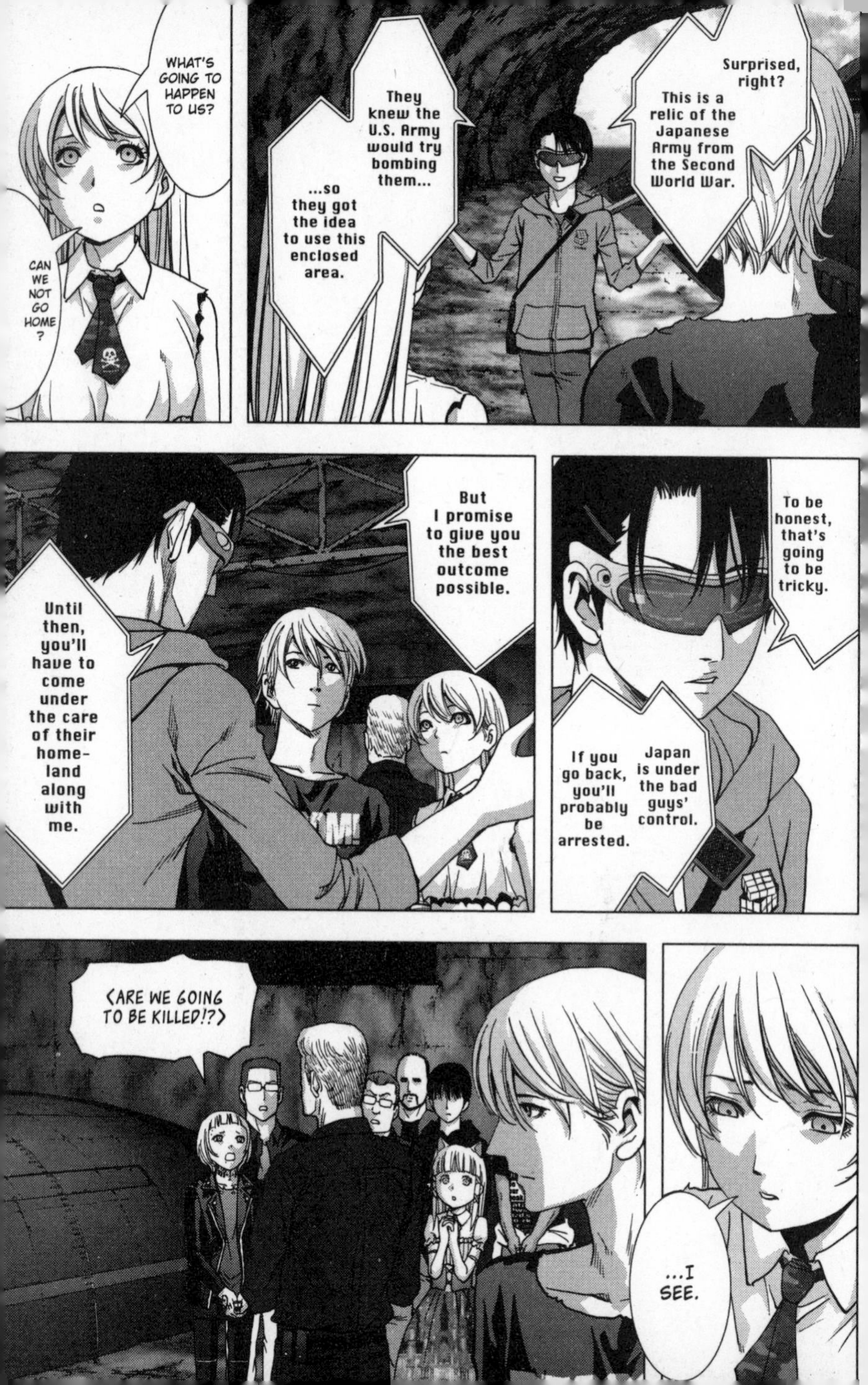
Surprised, right?
This is a relic of the Japanese Army from the Second World War.
They knew the U.S. Army would try bombing them...
...so they got the idea to use this enclosed area.
WHAT'S GOING TO HAPPEN TO US?
CAN WE NOT GO HOME?
To be honest, that's going to be tricky.
Japan is under the bad guys' control.
If you go back, you'll probably be arrested.
But I promise to give you the best outcome possible.
Until then, you'll have to come under the care of their homeland along with me.
...I SEE.
〈ARE WE GOING TO BE KILLED!?〉

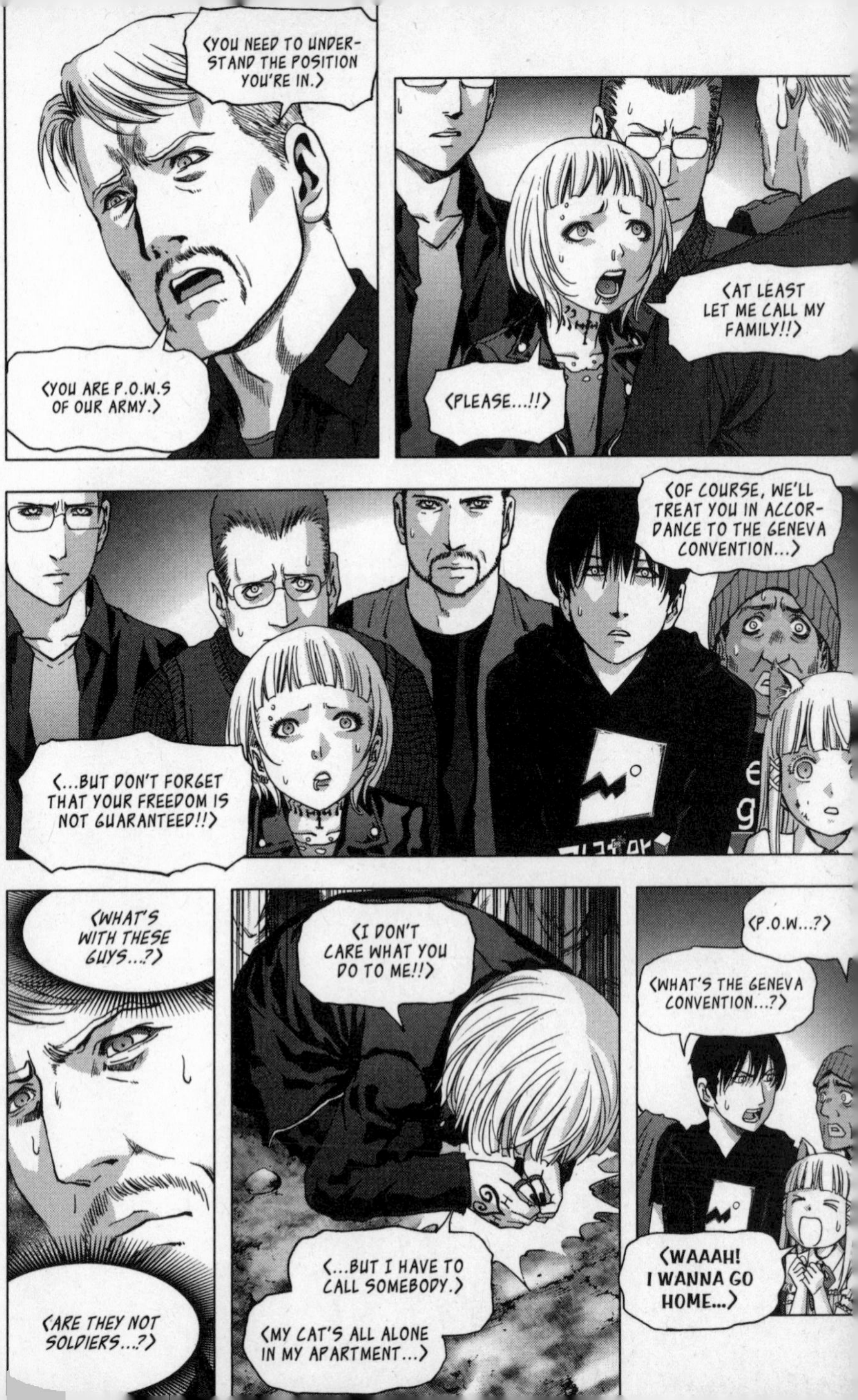
<AT LEAST LET ME CALL MY FAMILY!!>
<PLEASE...!!>
<YOU NEED TO UNDER-STAND THE POSITION YOU'RE IN.>
<YOU ARE P.O.W.S OF OUR ARMY.>
<OF COURSE, WE'LL TREAT YOU IN ACCOR-DANCE TO THE GENEVA CONVENTION...>
<...BUT DON'T FORGET THAT YOUR FREEDOM IS NOT GUARANTEED!!>
<P.O.W...?>
<WHAT'S THE GENEVA CONVENTION...?>
<WAAAH! I WANNA GO HOME...>
<I DON'T CARE WHAT YOU DO TO ME!!>
<...BUT I HAVE TO CALL SOMEBODY.>
<MY CAT'S ALL ALONE IN MY APARTMENT...>
<WHAT'S WITH THESE GUYS...?>
<ARE THEY NOT SOLDIERS...?>

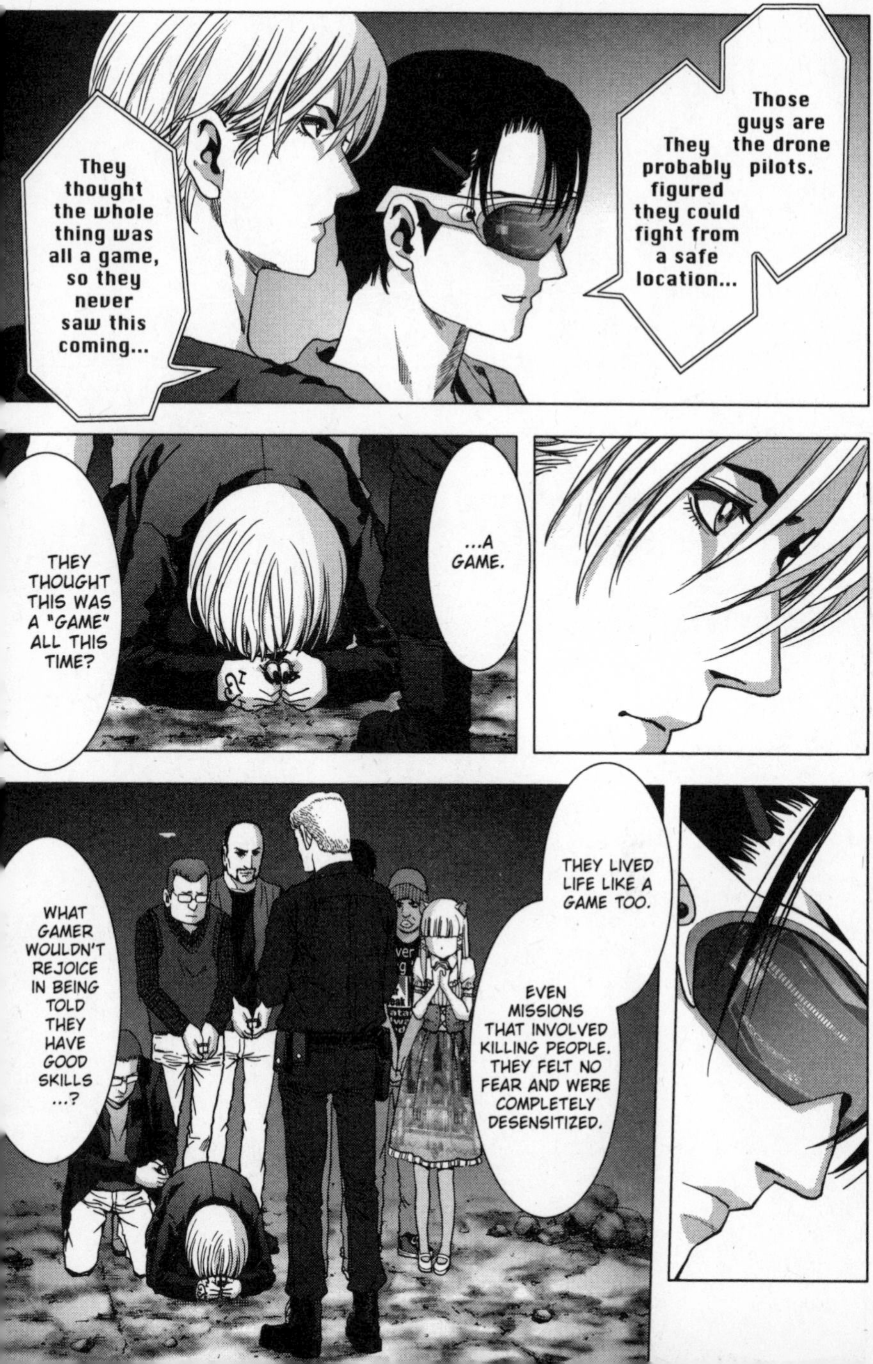
Those guys are the drone pilots.
They probably figured they could fight from a safe location...
They thought the whole thing was all a game, so they never saw this coming...
...A GAME.
THEY THOUGHT THIS WAS A "GAME" ALL THIS TIME?
THEY LIVED LIFE LIKE A GAME TOO.
EVEN MISSIONS THAT INVOLVED KILLING PEOPLE. THEY FELT NO FEAR AND WERE COMPLETELY DESENSITIZED.
WHAT GAMER WOULDN'T REJOICE IN BEING TOLD THEY HAVE GOOD SKILLS ...?

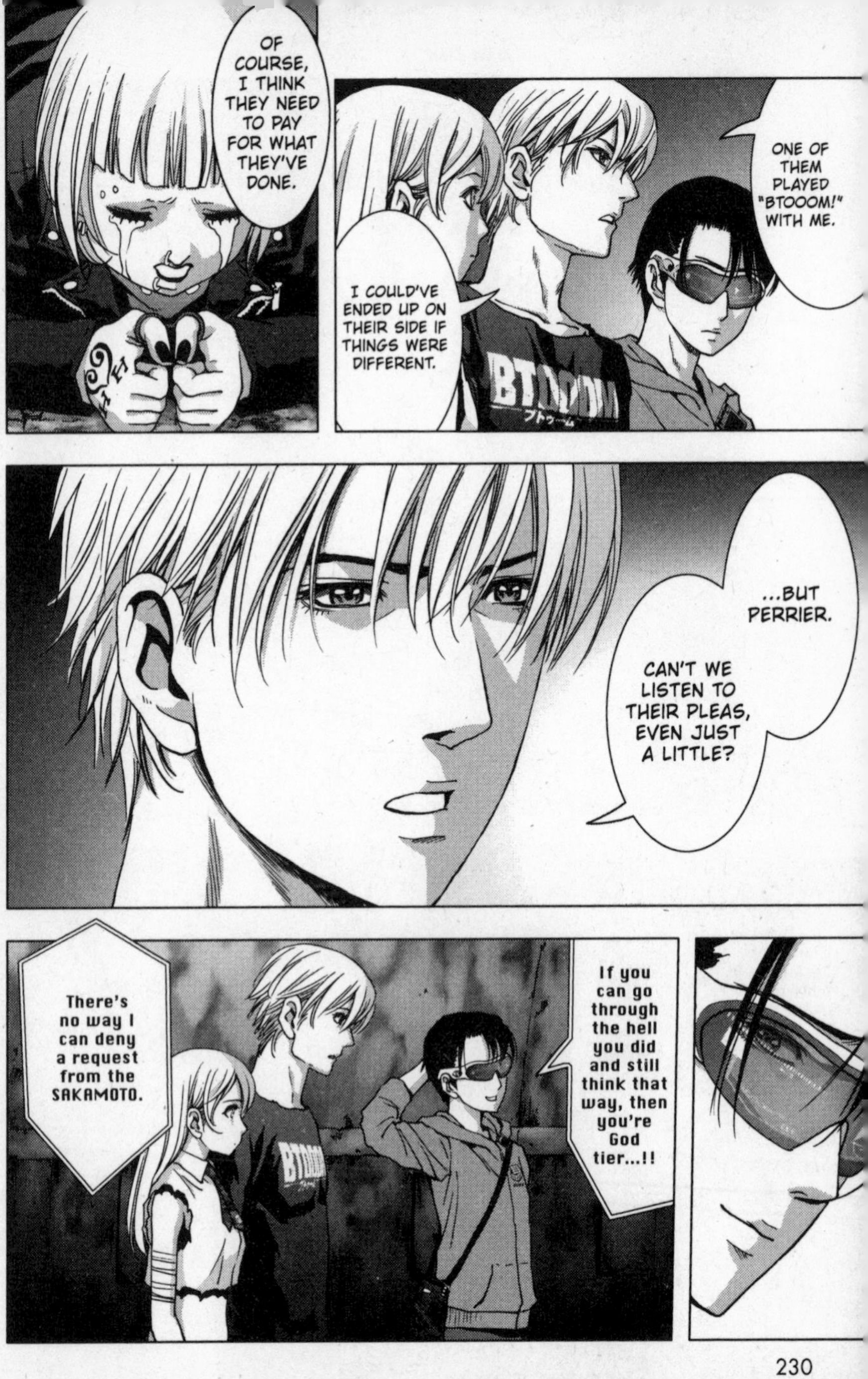
ONE OF THEM PLAYED "BTOOOM!" WITH ME.
I COULD'VE ENDED UP ON THEIR SIDE IF THINGS WERE DIFFERENT.
OF COURSE, I THINK THEY NEED TO PAY FOR WHAT THEY'VE DONE.
...BUT PERRIER.
CAN'T WE LISTEN TO THEIR PLEAS, EVEN JUST A LITTLE?
If you can go through the hell you did and still think that way, then you're God tier...!!
There's no way I can deny a request from the SAKAMOTO.

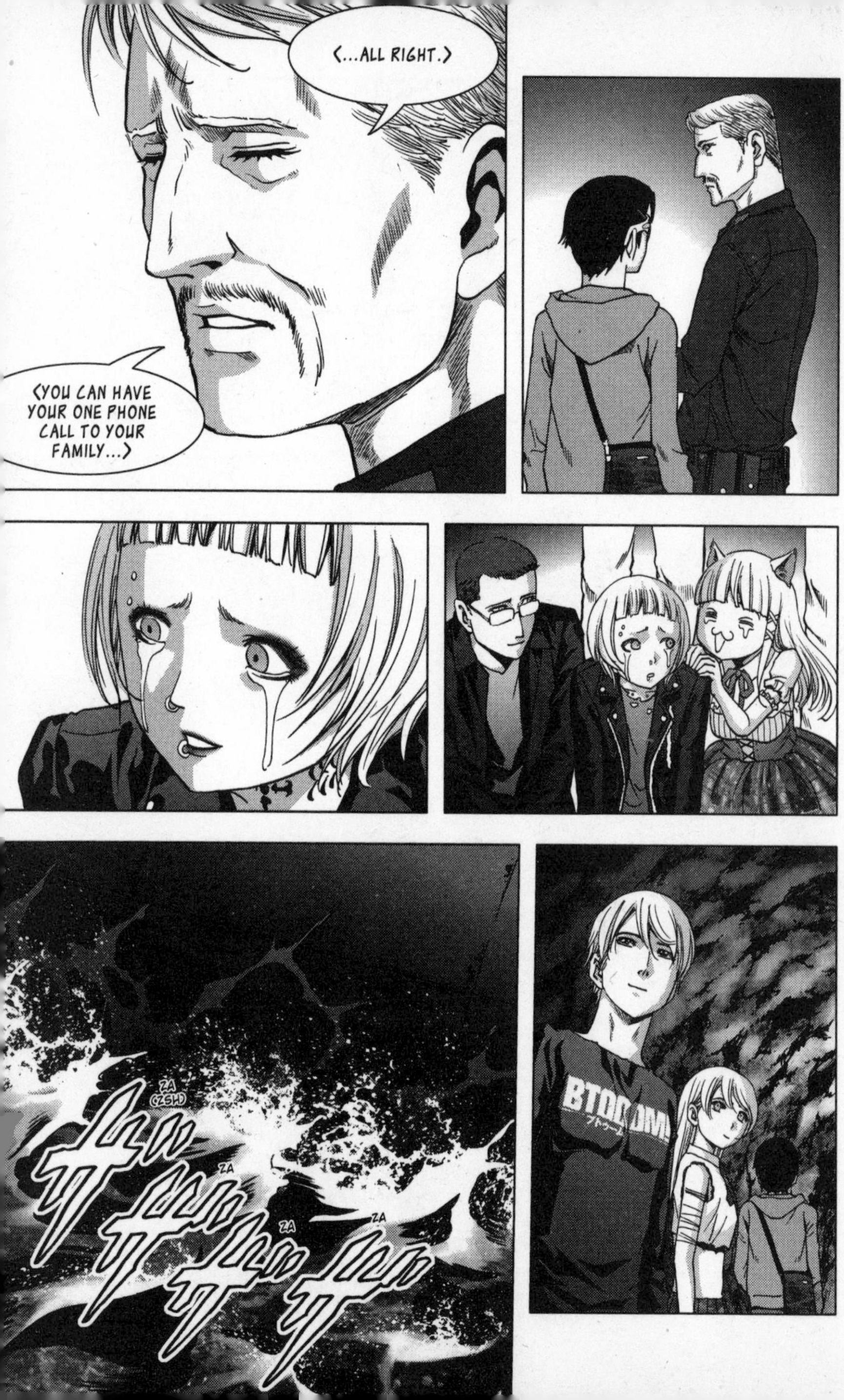
<...ALL RIGHT.>
<YOU CAN HAVE YOUR ONE PHONE CALL TO YOUR FAMILY...>
ZA (ZSHH)
ZA
ZA
ZA
BTOOOM!

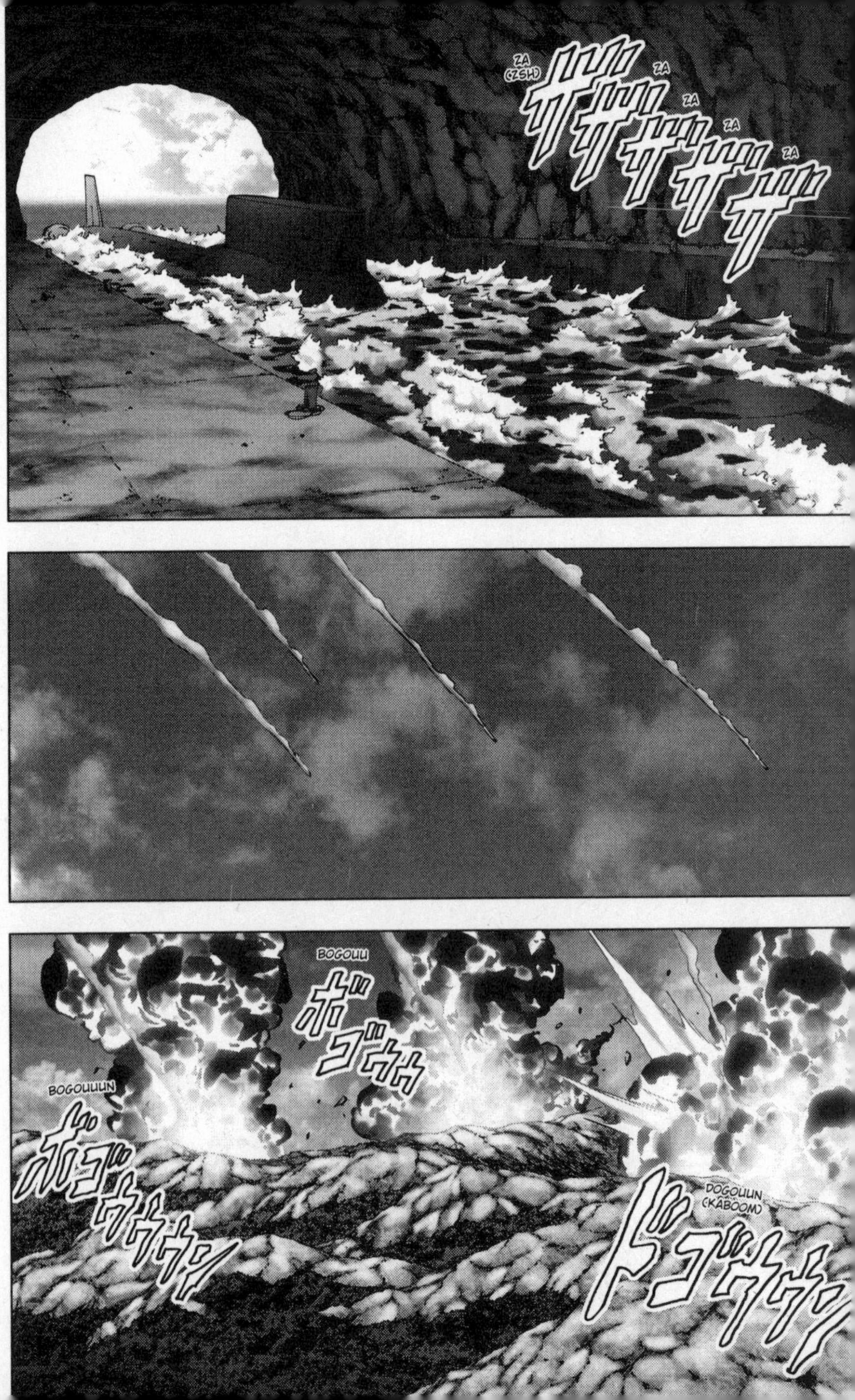
ZA (ZSH)
ZA
ZA
ZA
ZA
ザザザザザ
BOGOUU
ボゴゥゥ
BOGOUUUN
ボゴゥゥゥン
DOGOUUN (KABOOM)
ドゴゥゥン

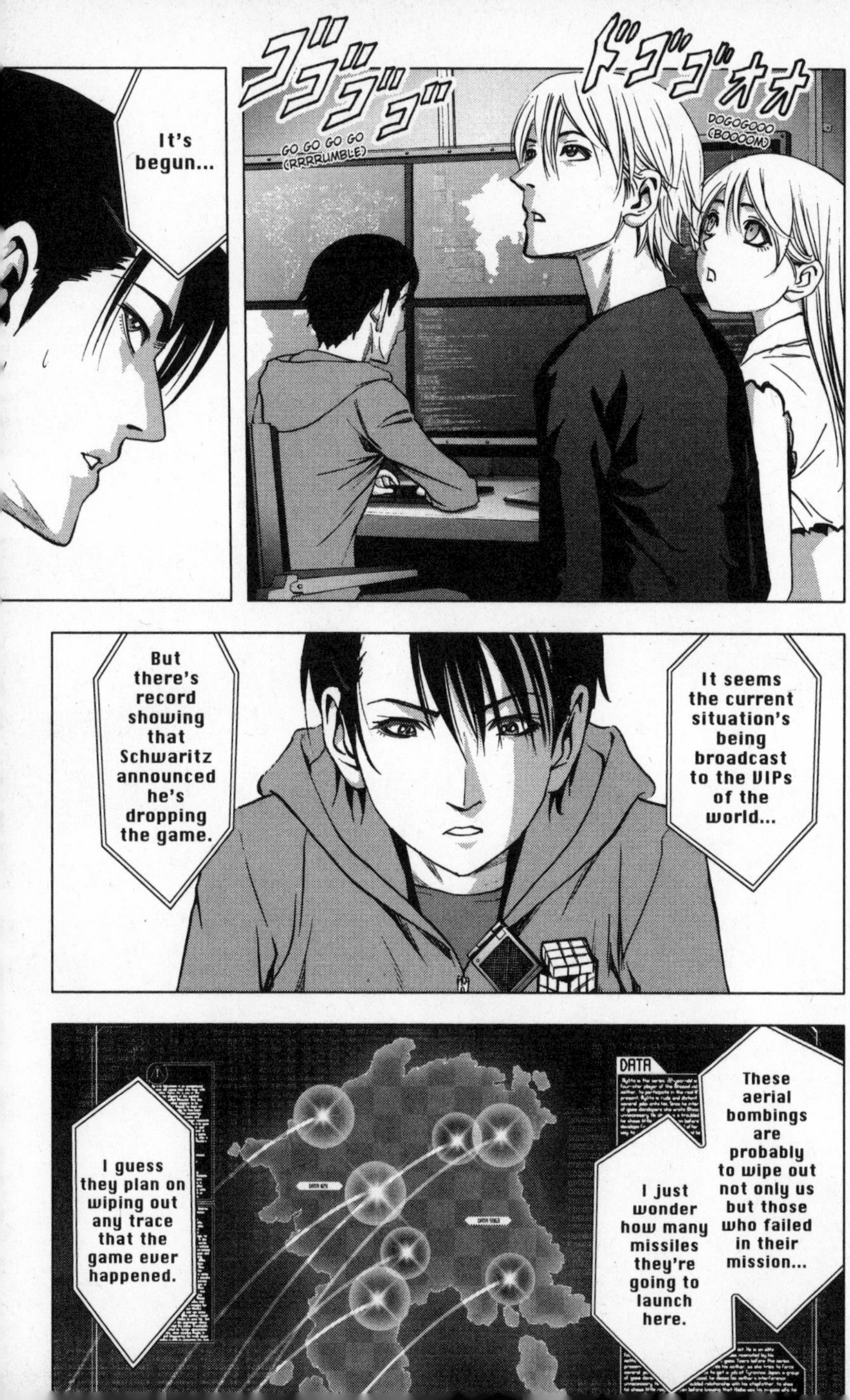
ドゴゴオオ
DOGOGOOO (BOOOOM)
ゴゴゴゴ
GO GO GO GO (RRRRUMBLE)
It's begun...
It seems the current situation's being broadcast to the VIPs of the world...
But there's record showing that Schwaritz announced he's dropping the game.
DATA
These aerial bombings are probably to wipe out not only us but those who failed in their mission...
I just wonder how many missiles they're going to launch here.
I guess they plan on wiping out any trace that the game ever happened.

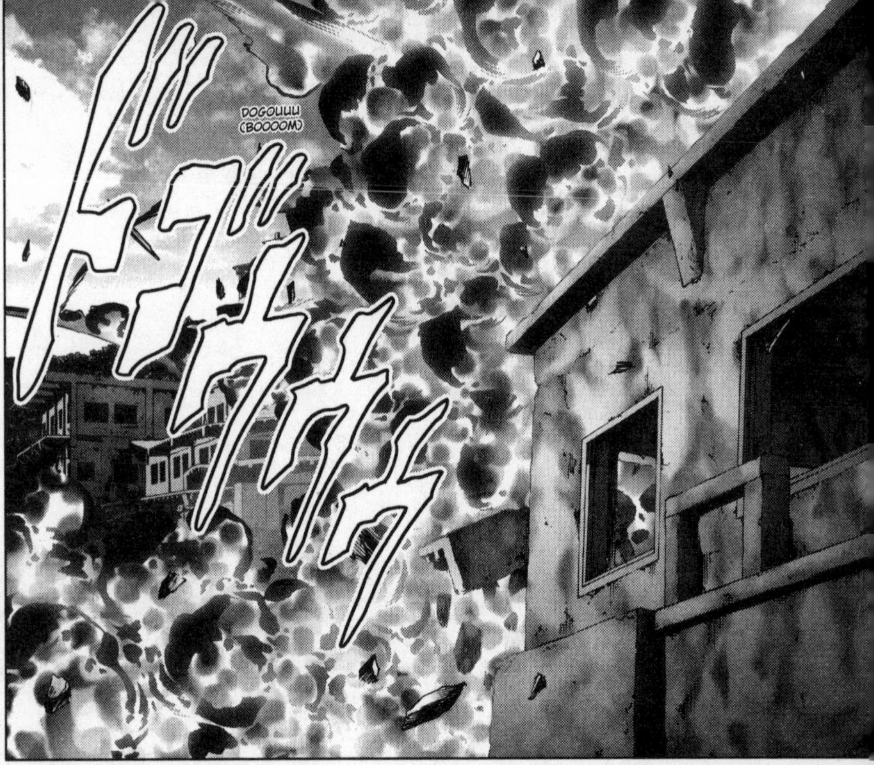
ドゴウウウ
DOGOUUU (BOOOOM)
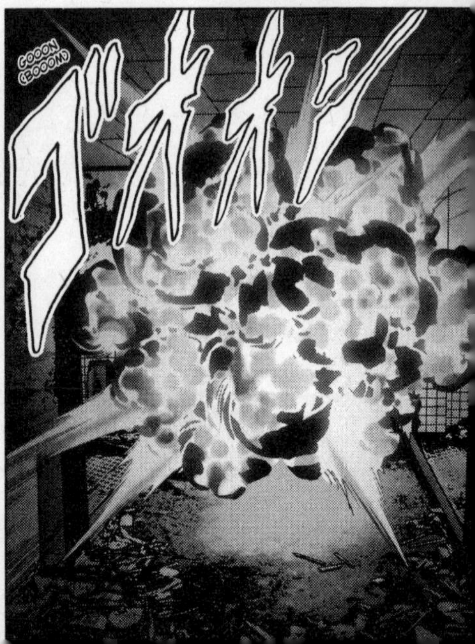
ゴオオン
GOOON (BOOOM)
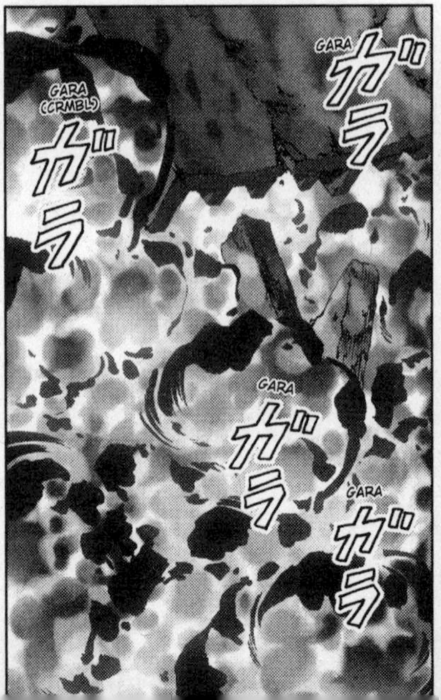
GARA
ガラ
GARA (CRMBL)
ガラ
GARA
ガラ
GARA
ガラ

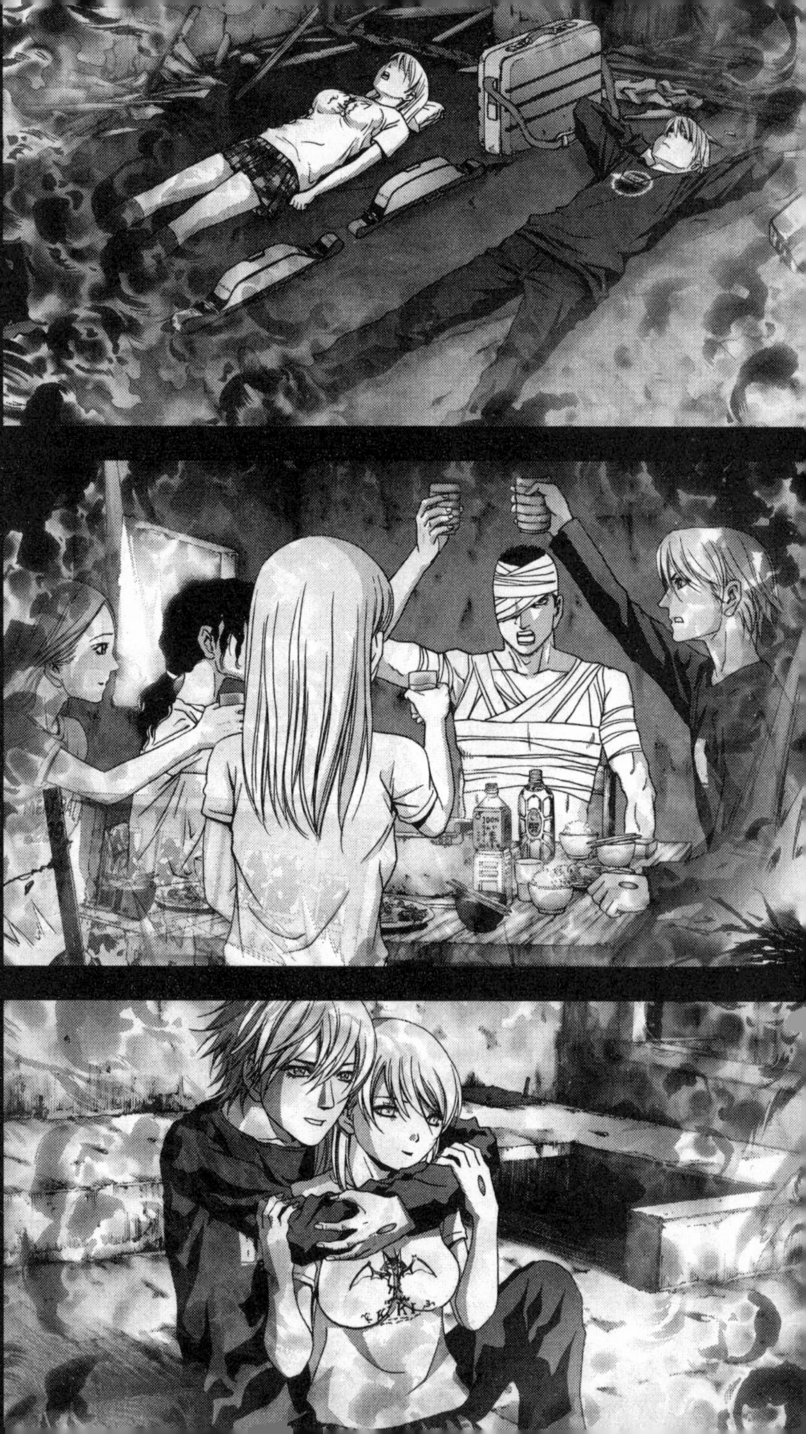

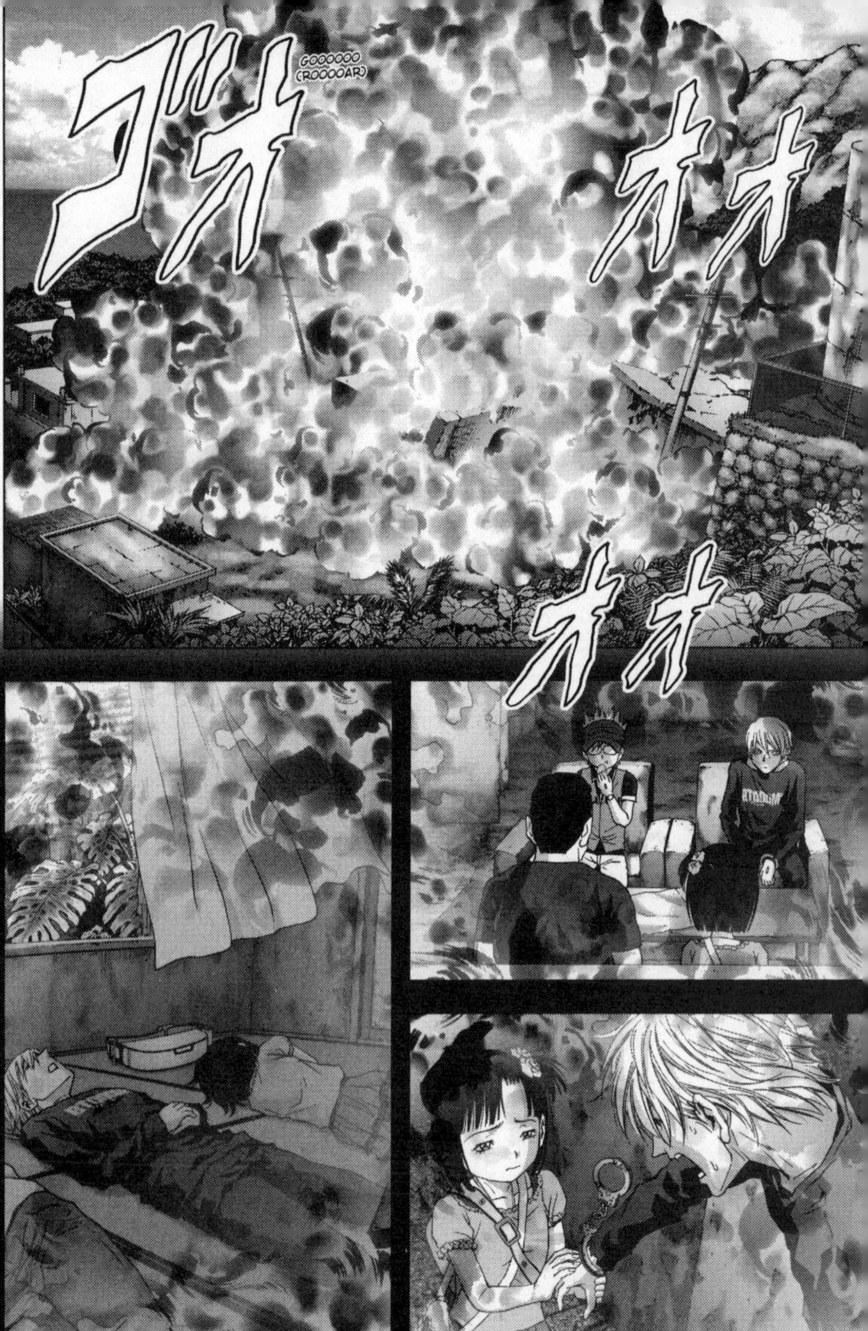
ゴオオオオオ
GOOOOOO
(ROOOOAR)

<WE HAVE TO STOP THE BLEEDING AT ONCE.>
<PREPARE THE BLOOD TRANSFUSION!!>
<CHECK HER BLOOD TYPE...>

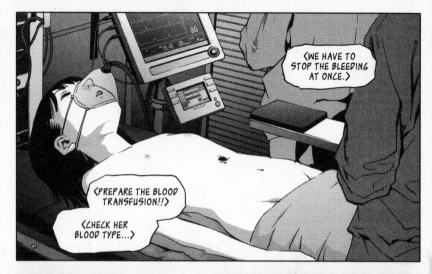

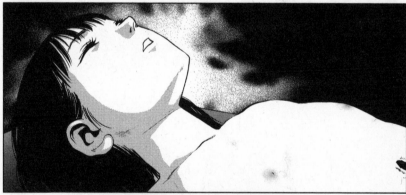

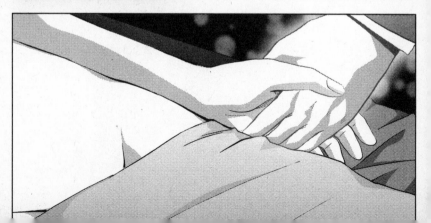

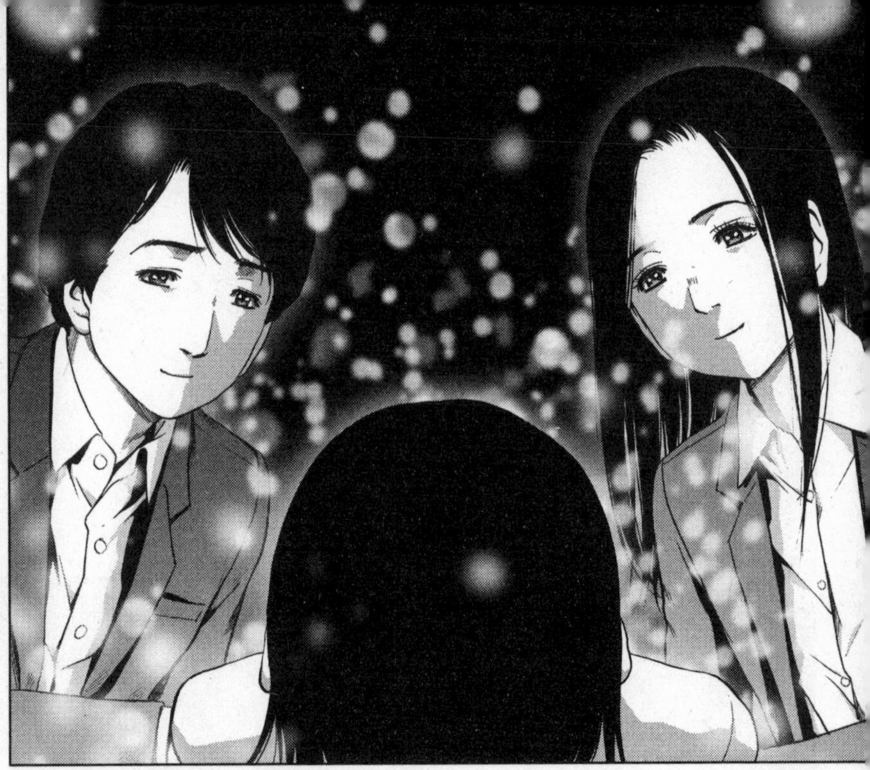

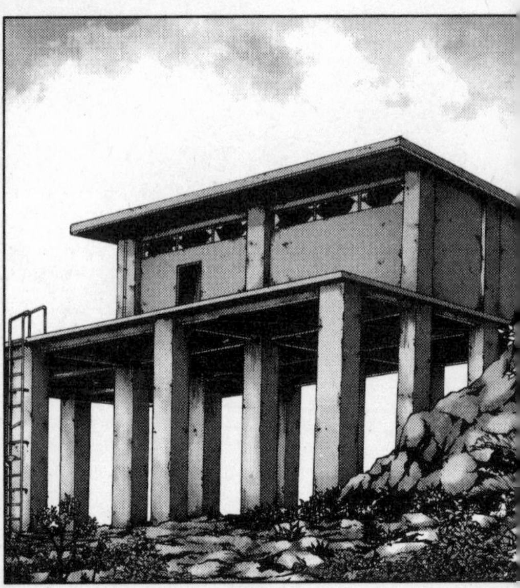

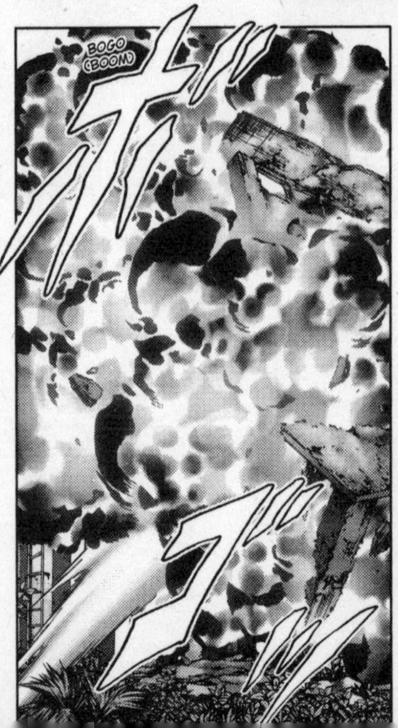
BOGO
(BOOM)

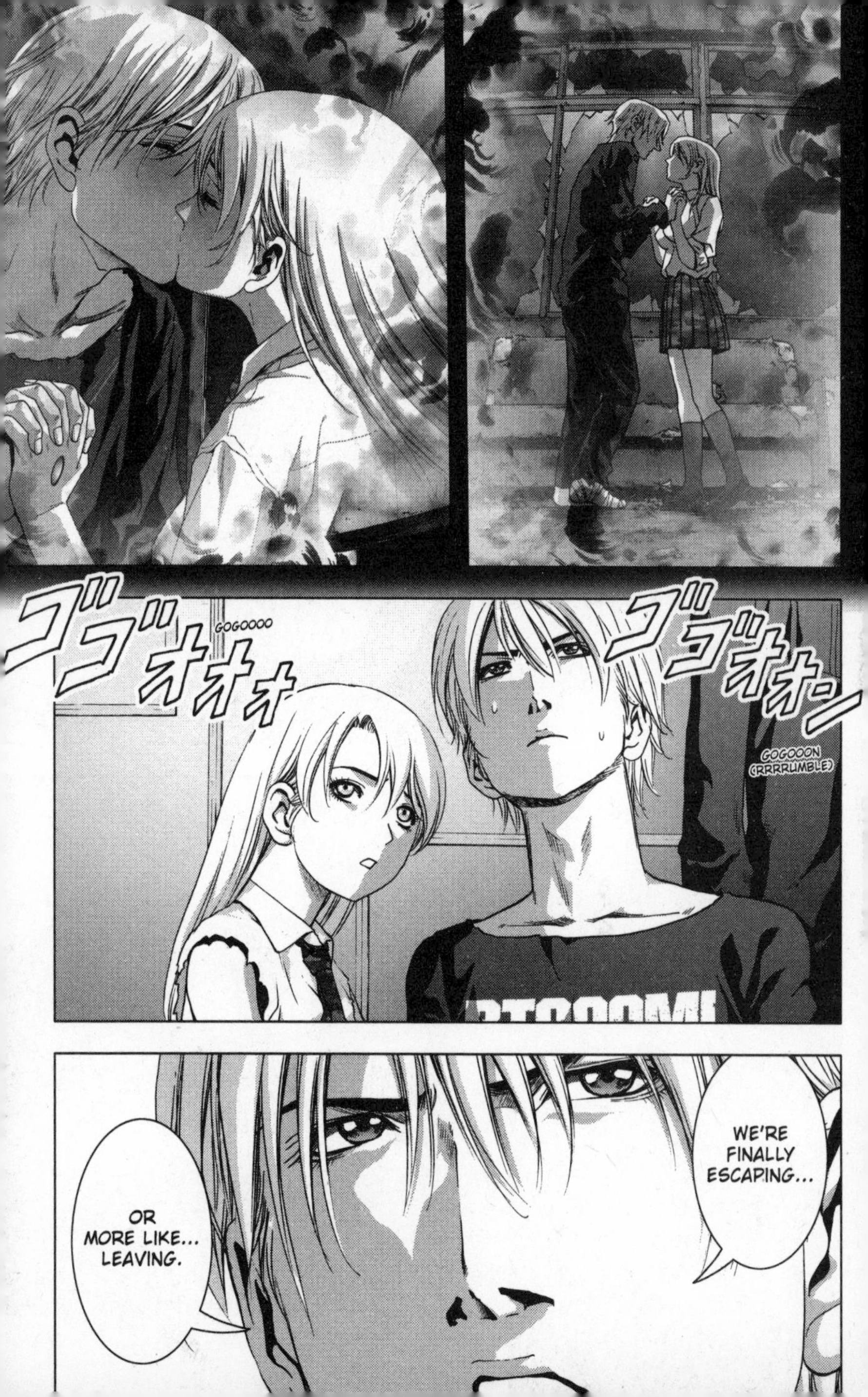
ゴゴオオーン
GOGOOON (RRRRUMBLE)
ゴゴオオォ
GOGOOOO
WE'RE FINALLY ESCAPING...
OR MORE LIKE... LEAVING.

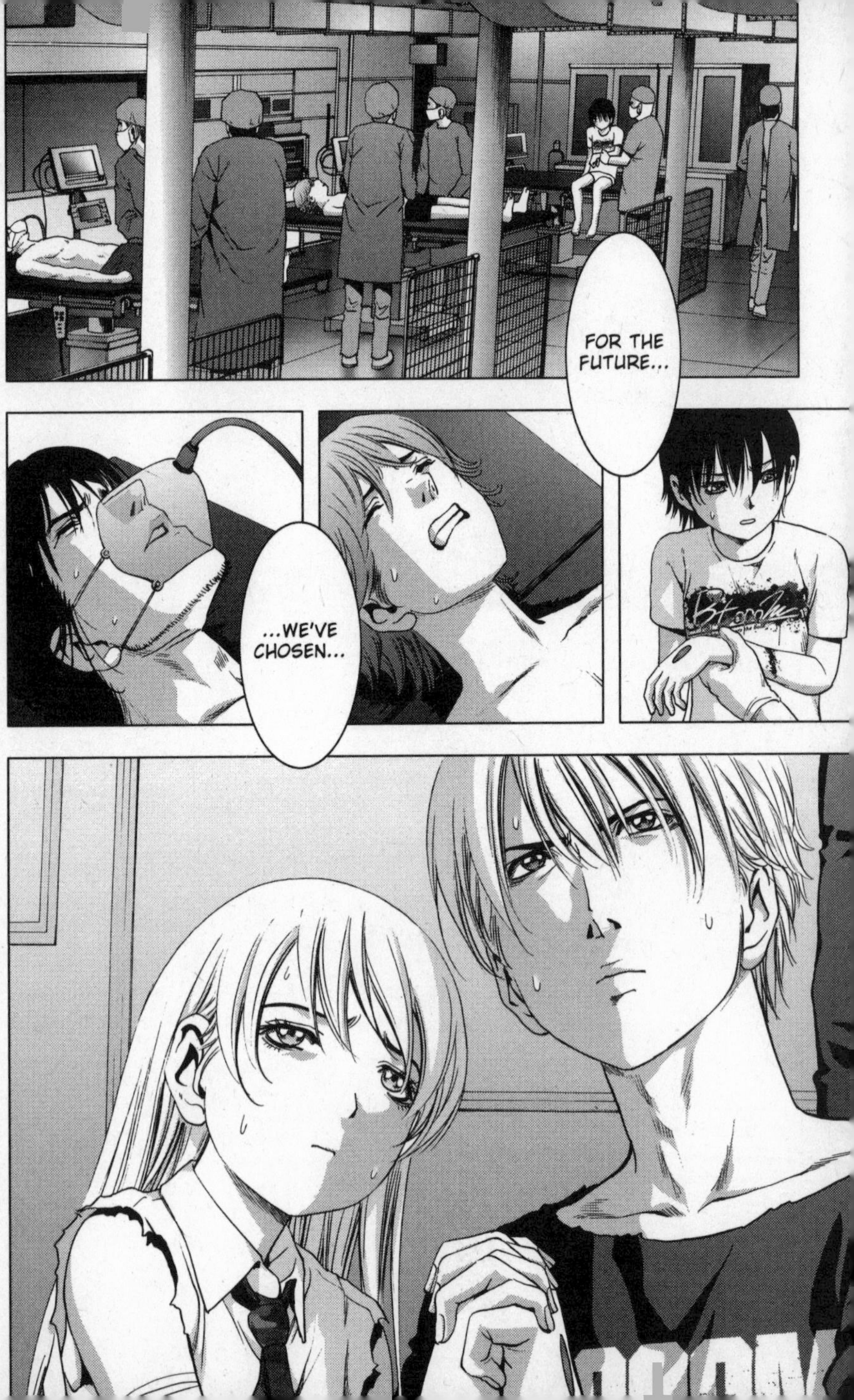
FOR THE FUTURE...
...WE'VE CHOSEN...

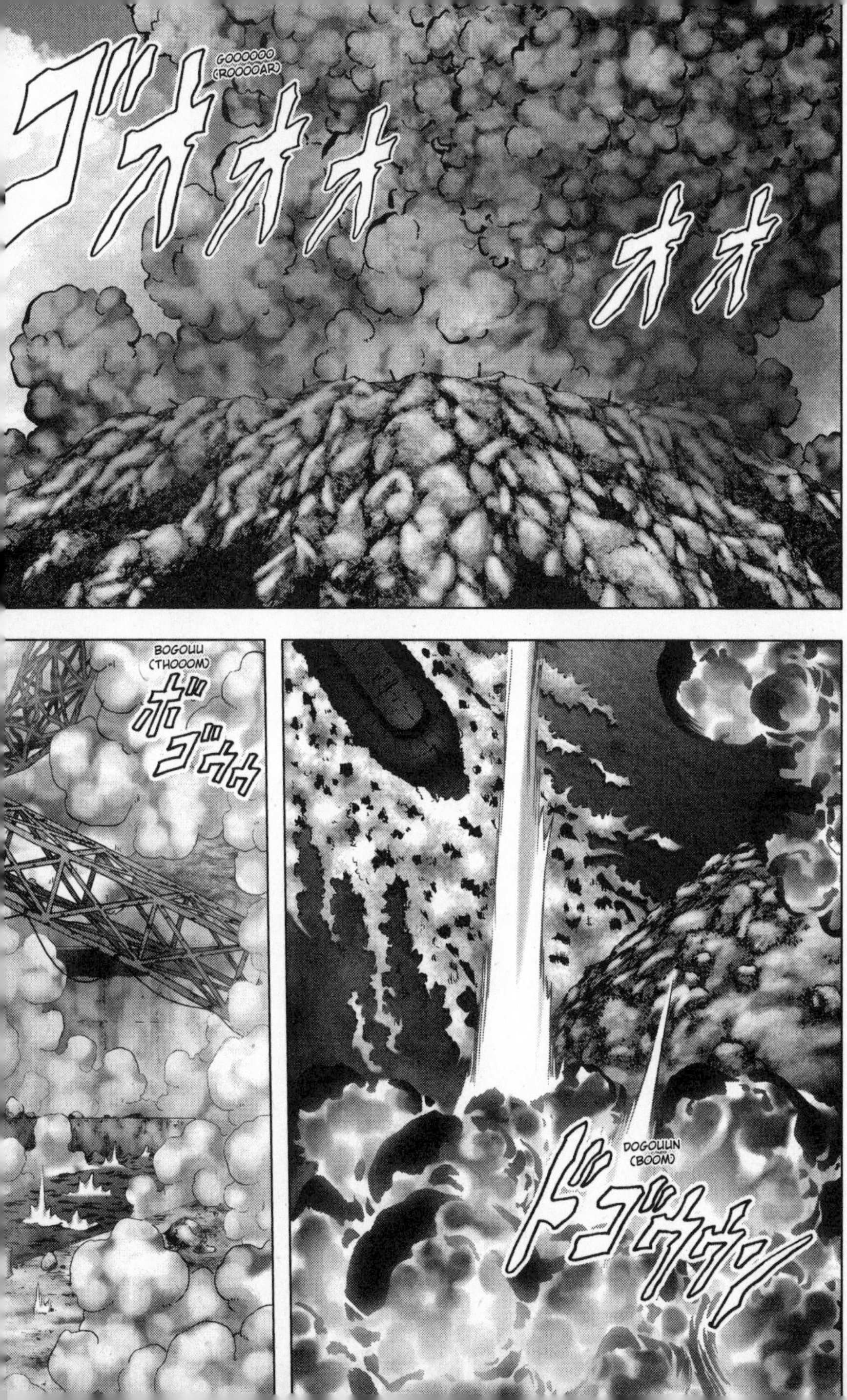
ゴオオオオオ
GOOOOOO
(ROOOOAR)
ドゴウウン
DOGOUUN
(BOOM)
ボゴゥゥ
BOGOUU
(THOOOM)

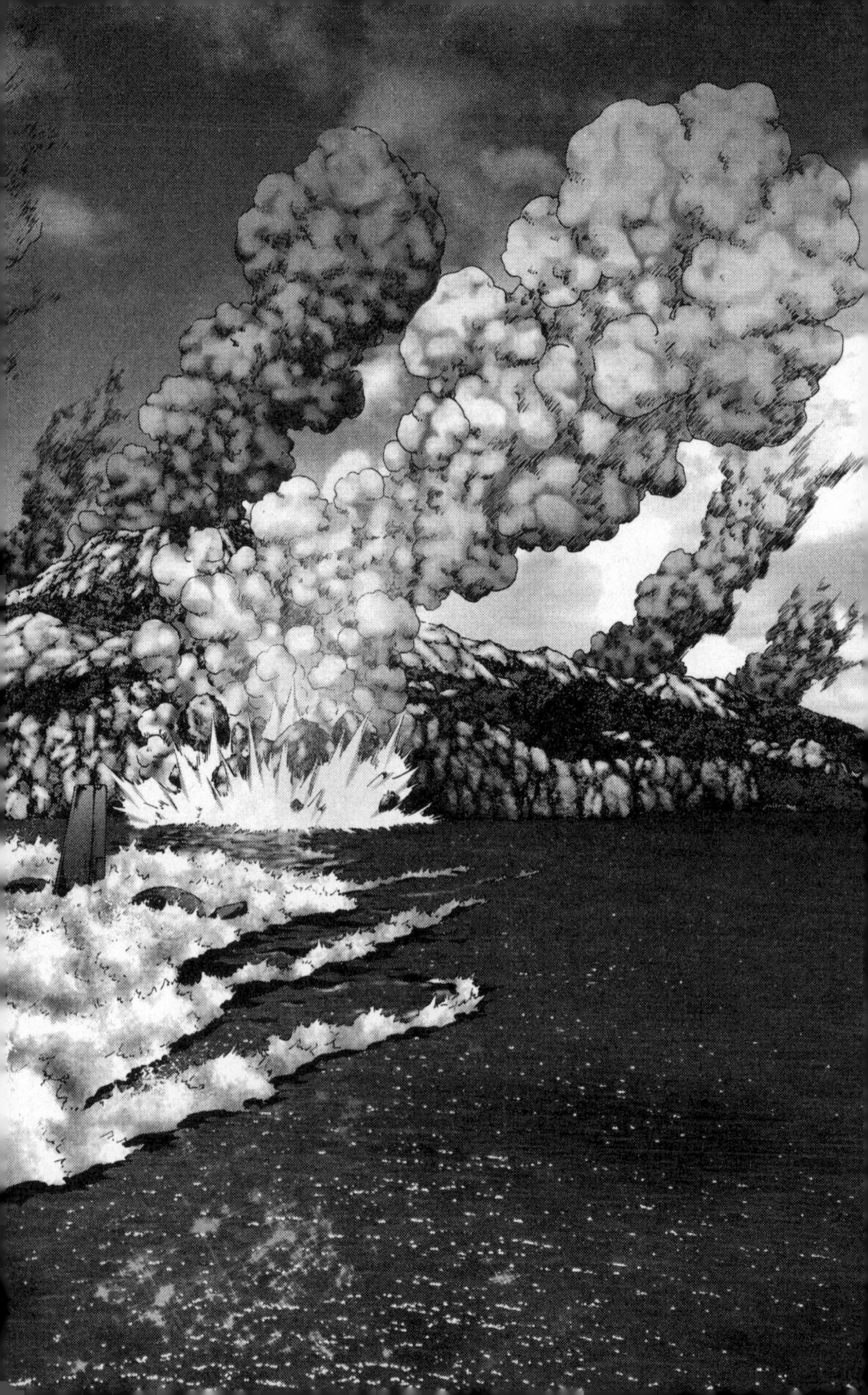

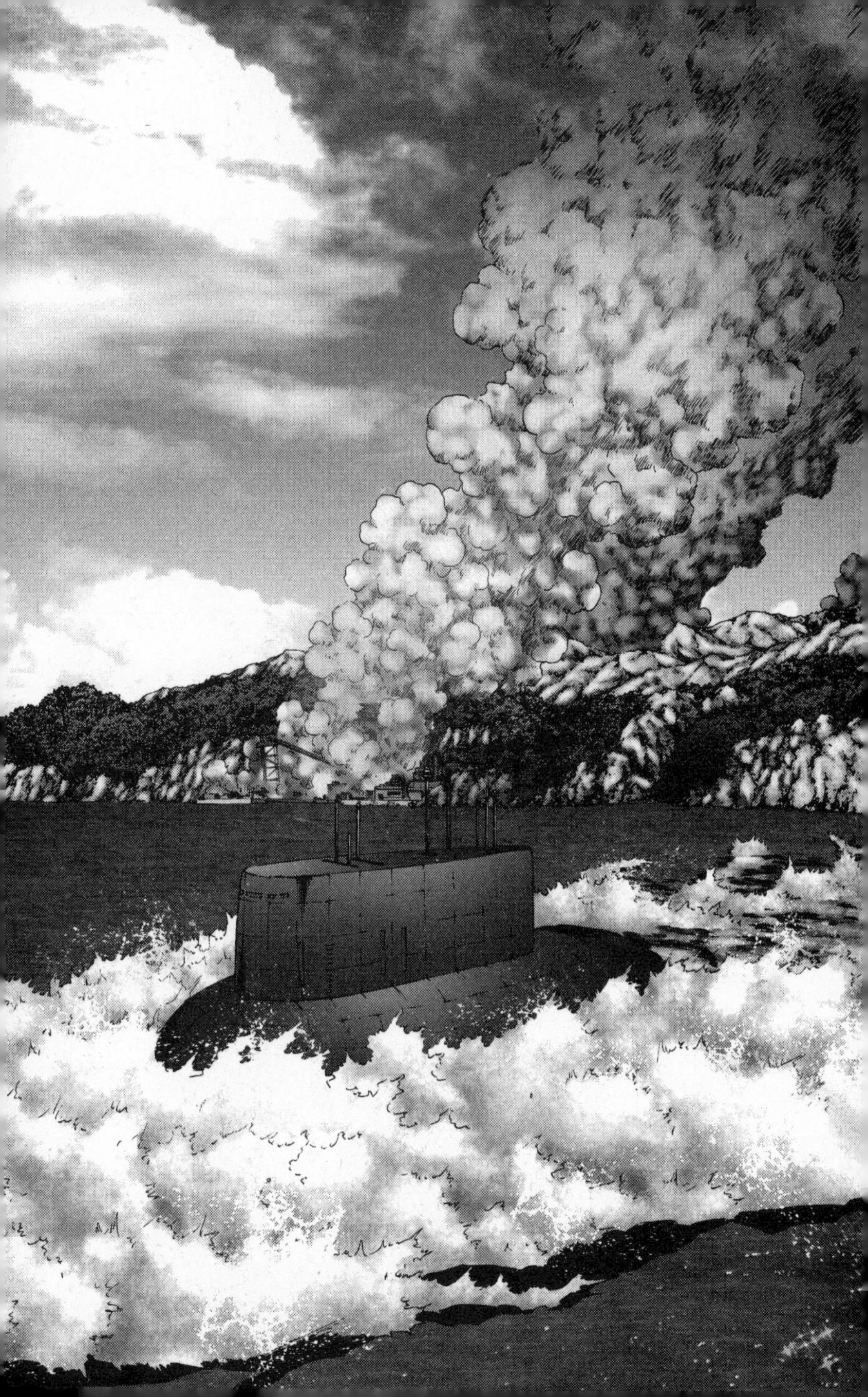

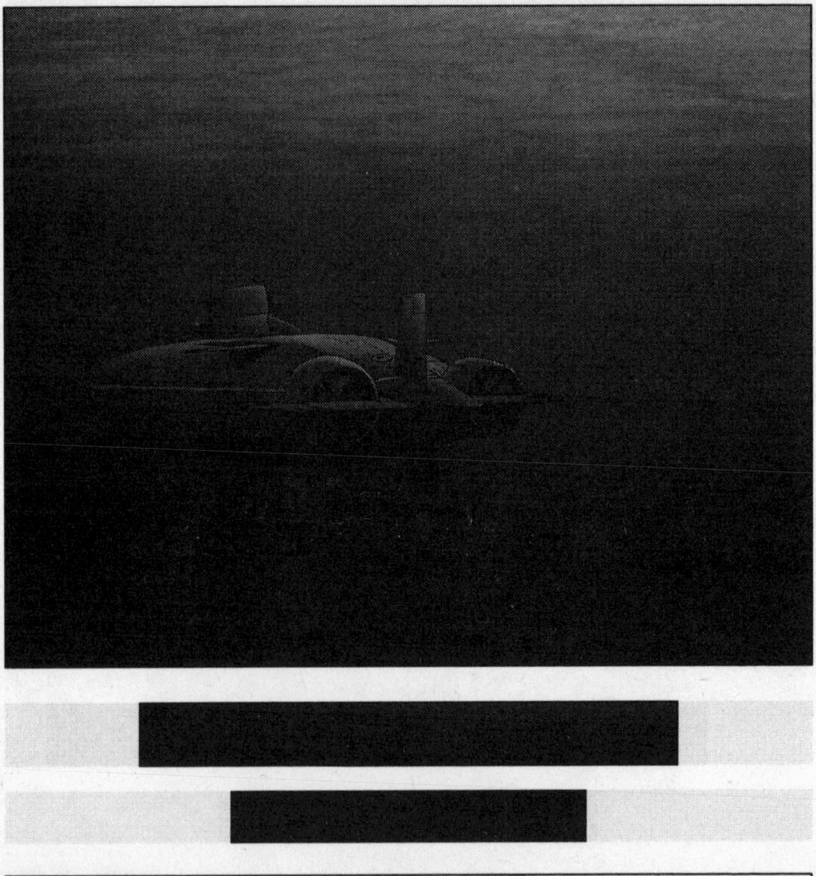

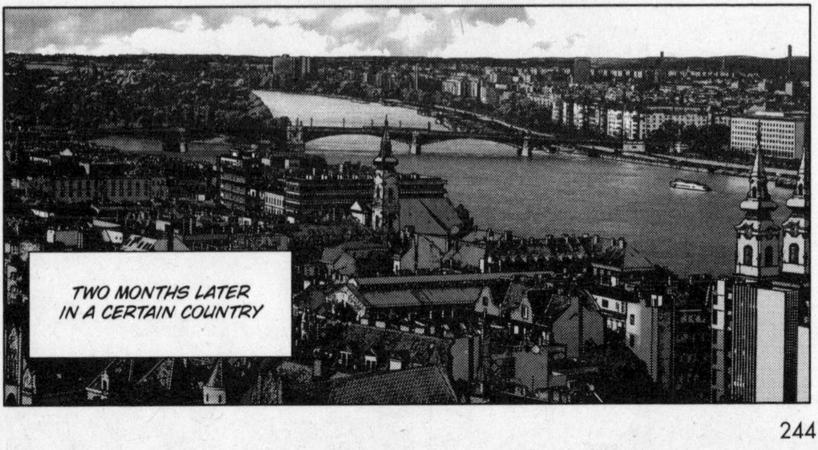
TWO MONTHS LATER IN A CERTAIN COUNTRY

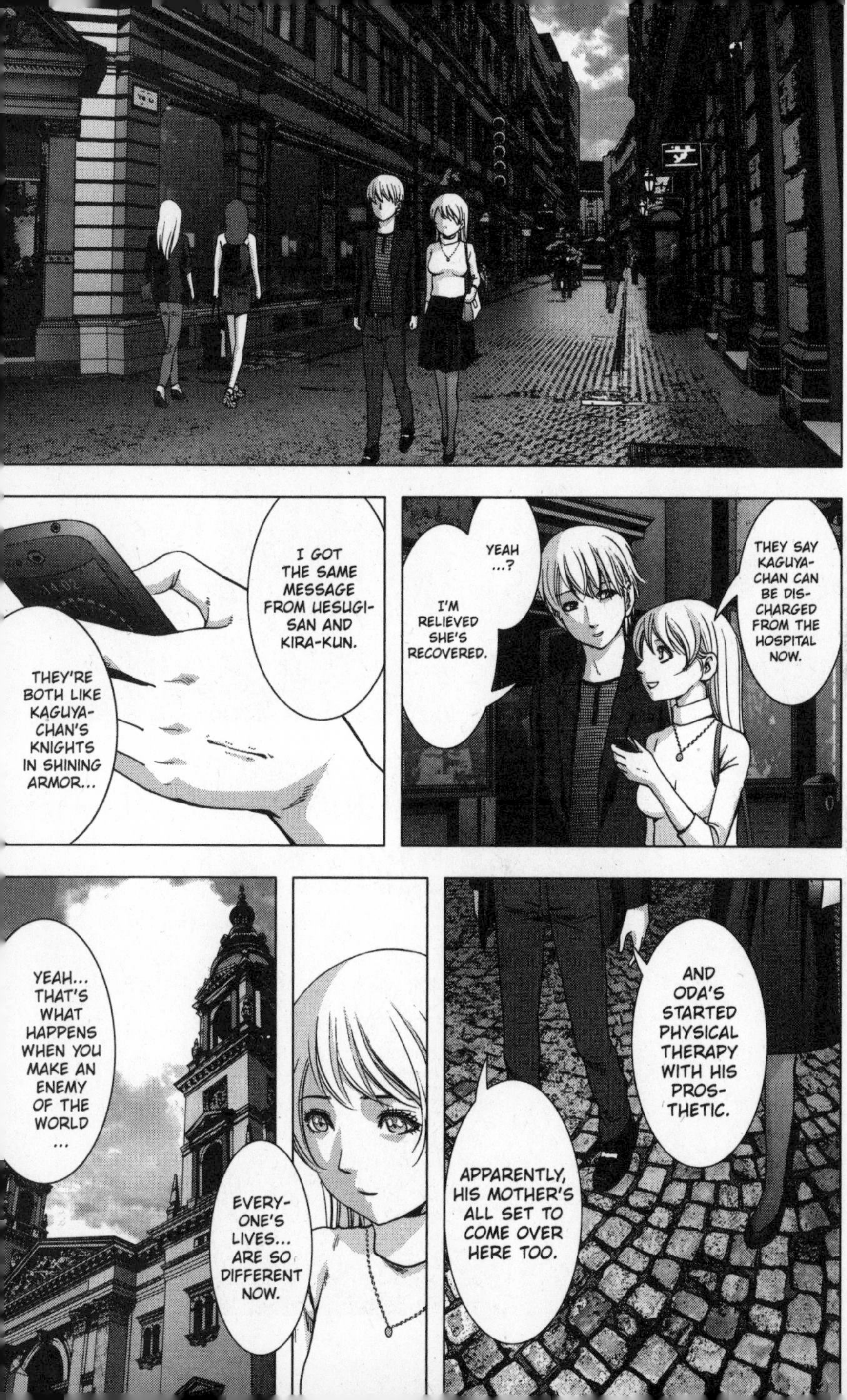
THEY SAY KAGUYA-CHAN CAN BE DISCHARGED FROM THE HOSPITAL NOW.
YEAH...?
I'M RELIEVED SHE'S RECOVERED.
I GOT THE SAME MESSAGE FROM UESUGI-SAN AND KIRA-KUN.
THEY'RE BOTH LIKE KAGUYA-CHAN'S KNIGHTS IN SHINING ARMOR...
AND ODA'S STARTED PHYSICAL THERAPY WITH HIS PROSTHETIC.
APPARENTLY, HIS MOTHER'S ALL SET TO COME OVER HERE TOO.
EVERYONE'S LIVES... ARE SO DIFFERENT NOW.
YEAH... THAT'S WHAT HAPPENS WHEN YOU MAKE AN ENEMY OF THE WORLD...

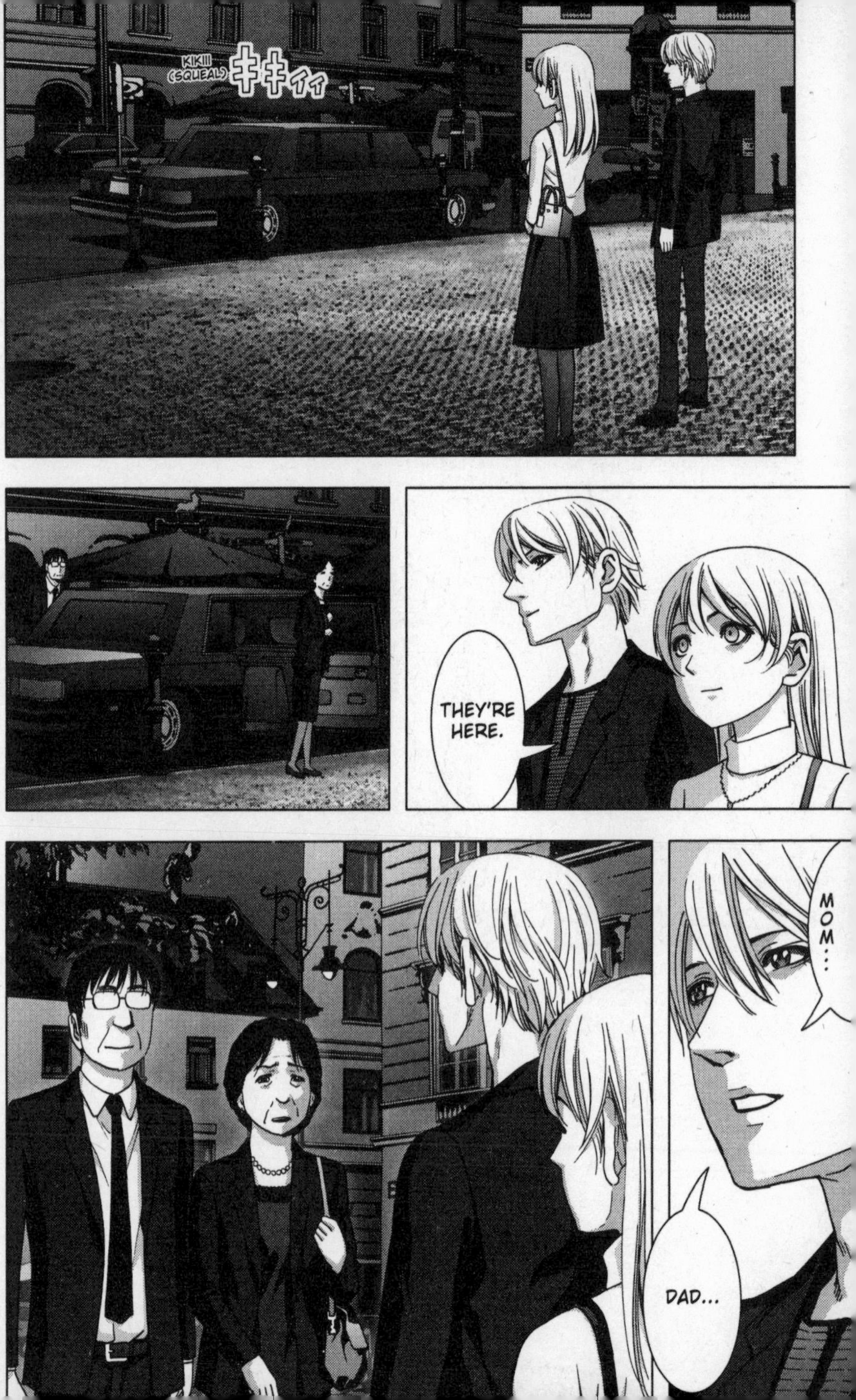
KIKIII (SQUEAL) キキイィ
THEY'RE HERE.
MOM...
DAD...

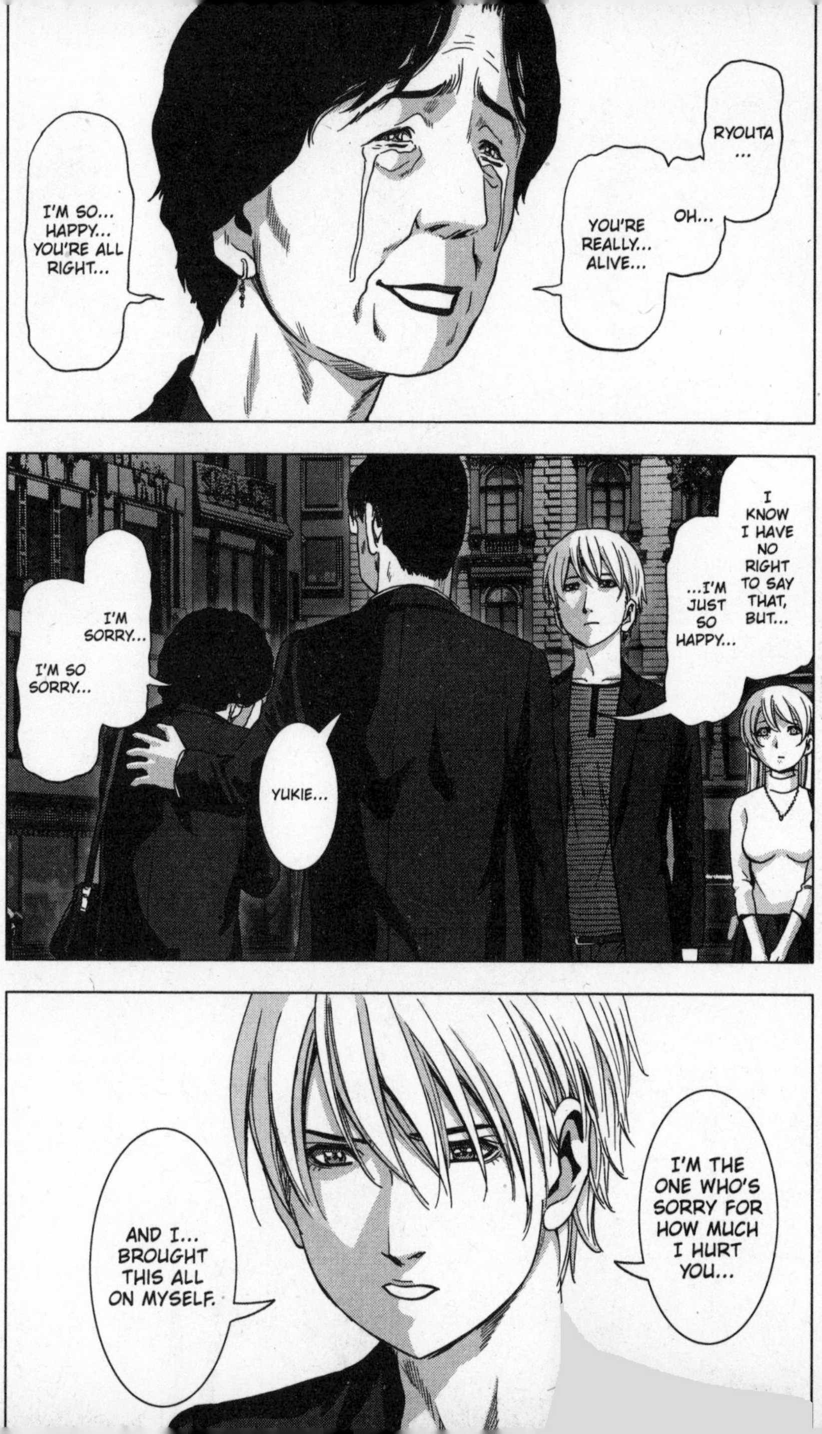
RYOUTA...
OH...
YOU'RE REALLY... ALIVE...
I'M SO... HAPPY... YOU'RE ALL RIGHT...
I KNOW I HAVE NO RIGHT TO SAY THAT, BUT...
...I'M JUST SO HAPPY...
YUKIE...
I'M SORRY...
I'M SO SORRY...
I'M THE ONE WHO'S SORRY FOR HOW MUCH I HURT YOU...
AND I... BROUGHT THIS ALL ON MYSELF.

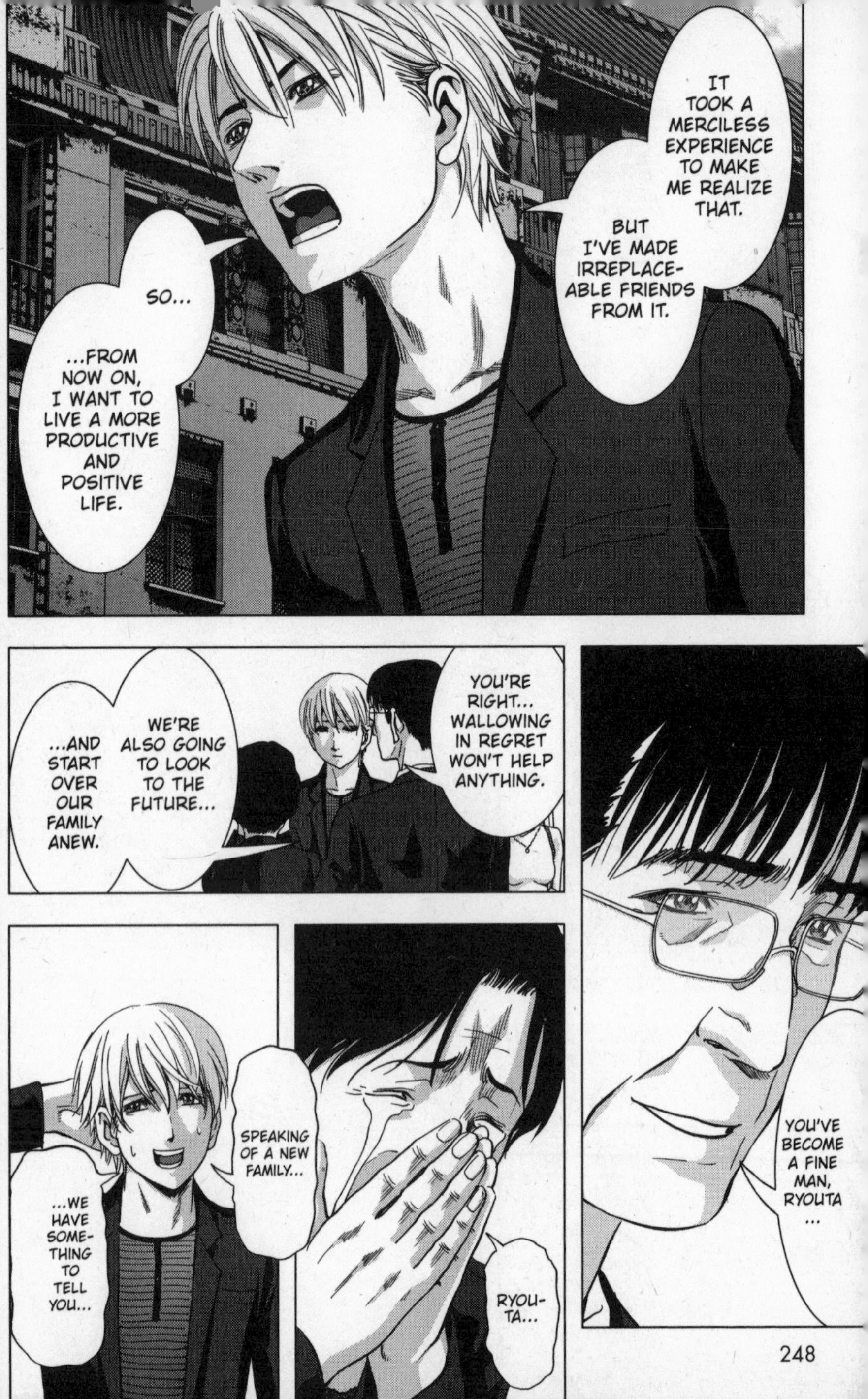
IT TOOK A MERCILESS EXPERIENCE TO MAKE ME REALIZE THAT.
BUT I'VE MADE IRREPLACE-ABLE FRIENDS FROM IT.
SO...
...FROM NOW ON, I WANT TO LIVE A MORE PRODUCTIVE AND POSITIVE LIFE.
YOU'VE BECOME A FINE MAN, RYOUTA...
YOU'RE RIGHT... WALLOWING IN REGRET WON'T HELP ANYTHING.
WE'RE ALSO GOING TO LOOK TO THE FUTURE...
...AND START OVER OUR FAMILY ANEW.
RYOU-TA...
SPEAKING OF A NEW FAMILY...
...WE HAVE SOME-THING TO TELL YOU...

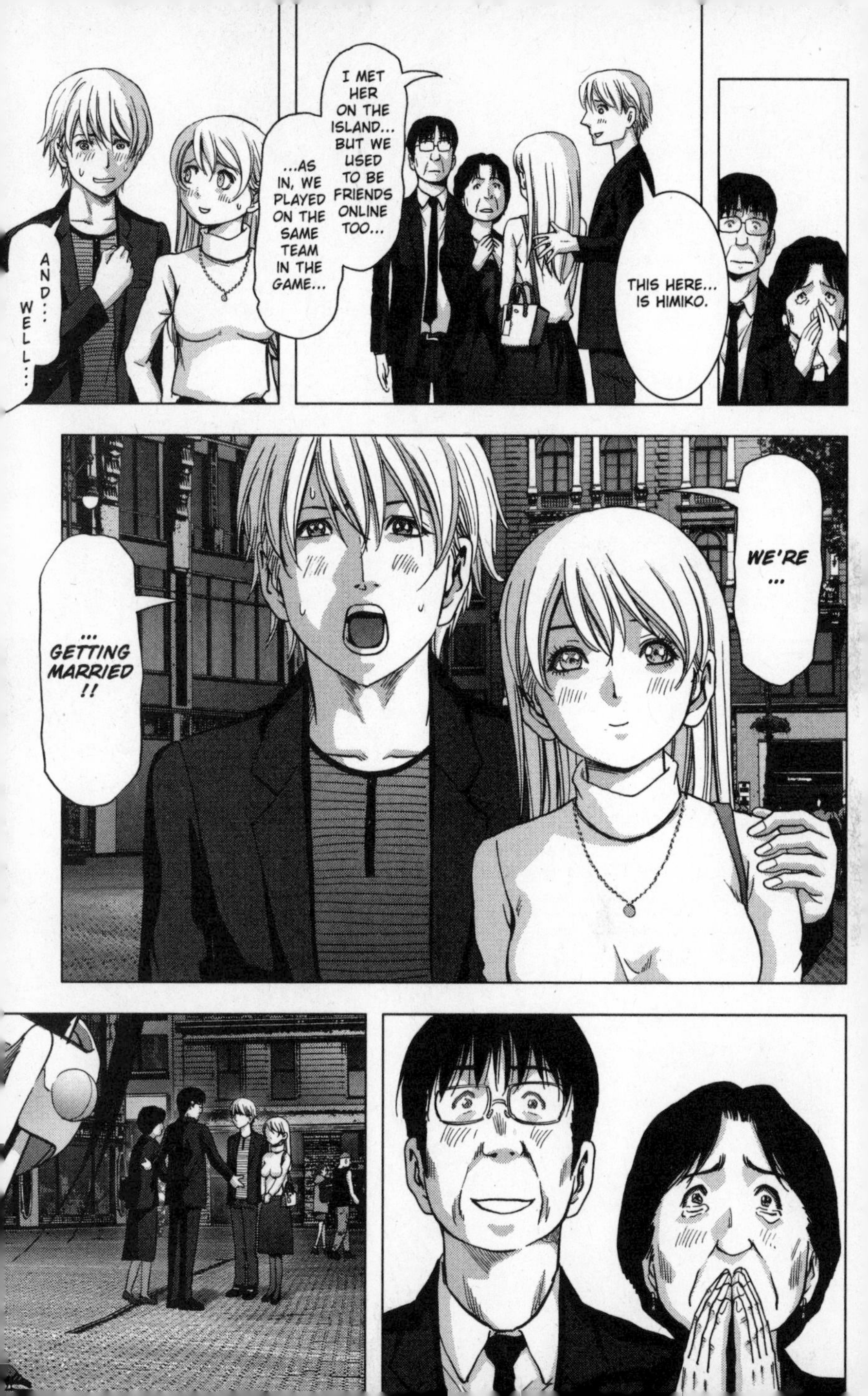
THIS HERE... IS HIMIKO.
I MET HER ON THE ISLAND... BUT WE USED TO BE FRIENDS ONLINE TOO...
...AS IN, WE PLAYED ON THE SAME TEAM IN THE GAME...
AND... WELL...
WE'RE ...
... GETTING MARRIED !!

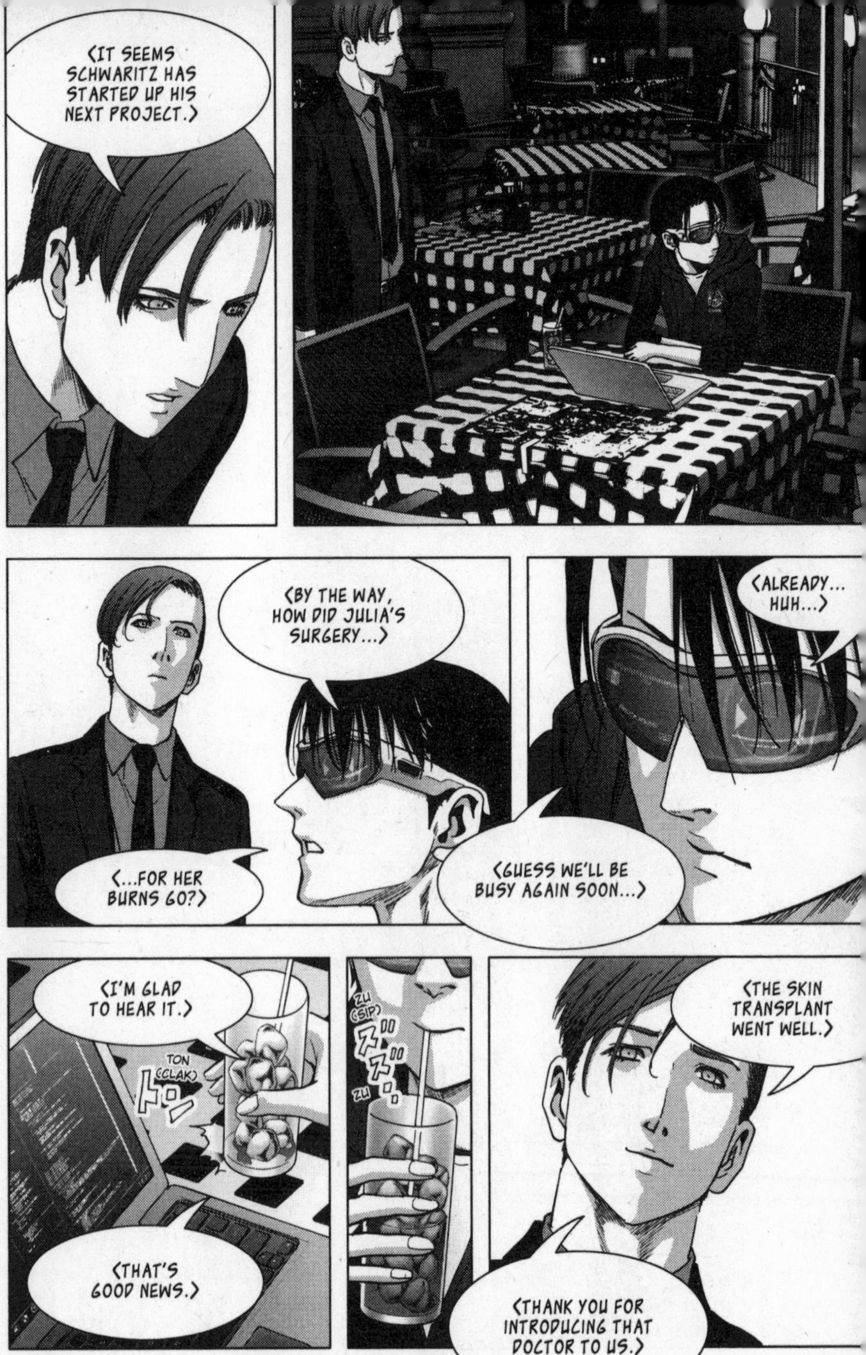
〈IT SEEMS SCHWARITZ HAS STARTED UP HIS NEXT PROJECT.〉
〈ALREADY... HUH...〉
〈GUESS WE'LL BE BUSY AGAIN SOON...〉
〈BY THE WAY, HOW DID JULIA'S SURGERY...〉
〈...FOR HER BURNS GO?〉
〈THE SKIN TRANSPLANT WENT WELL.〉
〈THANK YOU FOR INTRODUCING THAT DOCTOR TO US.〉
ZU (SIP)
ZU
〈I'M GLAD TO HEAR IT.〉
TON (CLAK)
〈THAT'S GOOD NEWS.〉

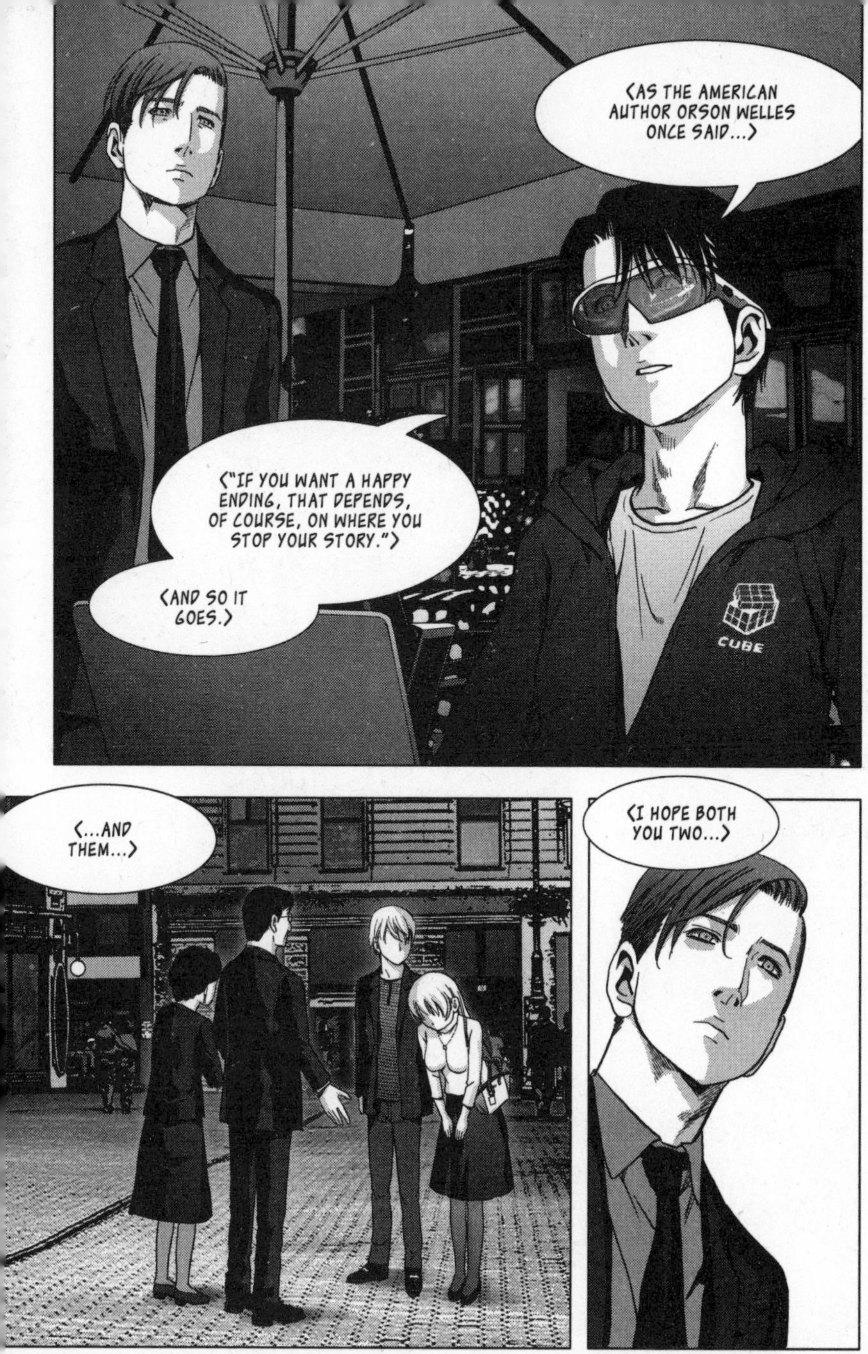
<AS THE AMERICAN AUTHOR ORSON WELLES ONCE SAID...>
<"IF YOU WANT A HAPPY ENDING, THAT DEPENDS, OF COURSE, ON WHERE YOU STOP YOUR STORY.">
<AND SO IT GOES.>
CUBE
<I HOPE BOTH YOU TWO...>
<...AND THEM...>

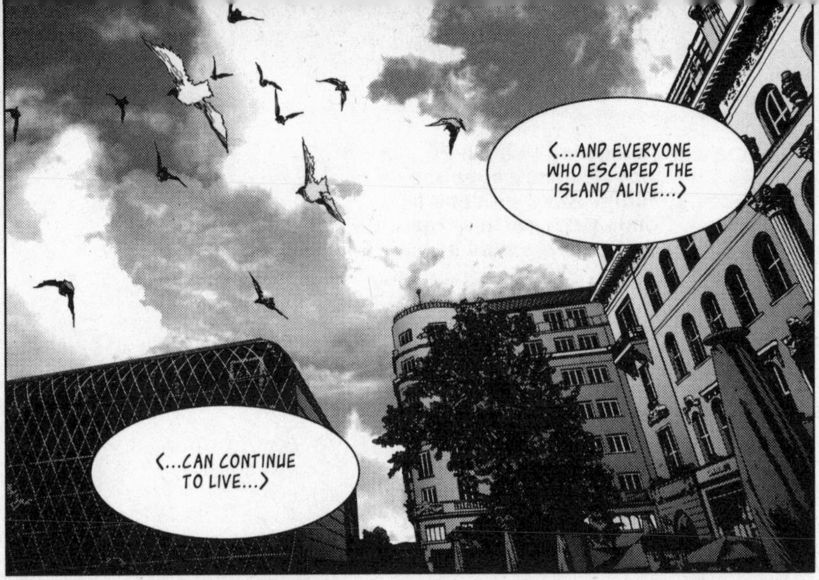
〈...AND EVERYONE WHO ESCAPED THE ISLAND ALIVE...〉
〈...CAN CONTINUE TO LIVE...〉
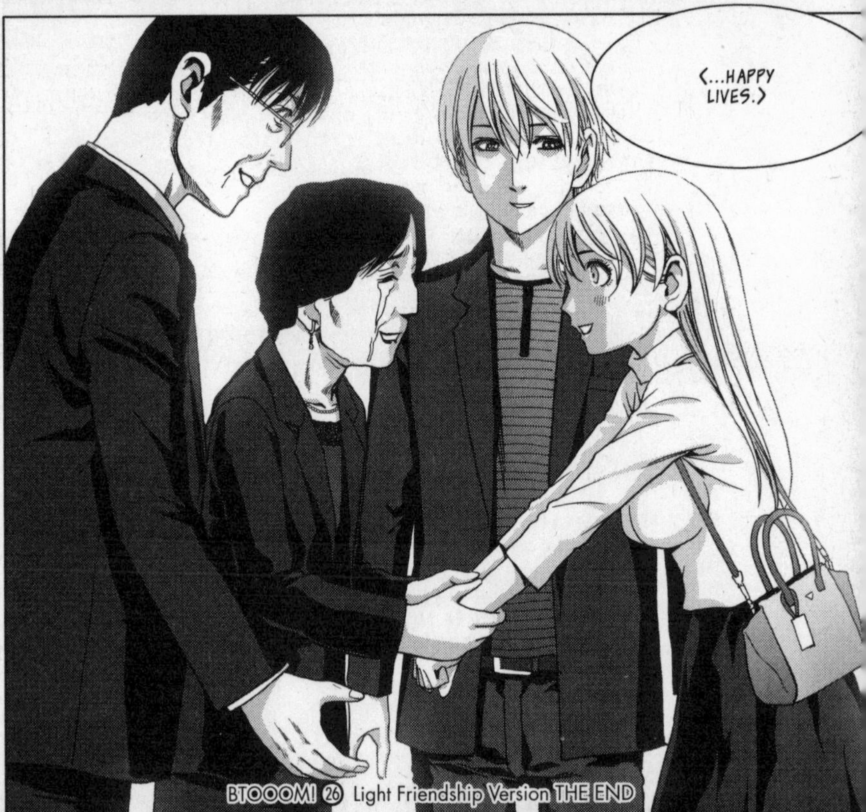
〈...HAPPY LIVES.〉

BTOOOM! 26 Light Friendship Version THE END

Afterword

How did you all enjoy Volume 26, the Light Friendship Version? The manga industry has never seen a manga series that offers two alternate endings like I've done here. Although you can prevail after overcoming difficulties, reality is hard, and it takes a lot of sacrifice... That was the kind of balanced happy ending I wanted to present.

"I don't just want the fight to end. I want to leave some lingering scars." I'm sure this is something that any creator who ponders manga 24-7 has considered, though I'm sure no reader necessarily wants that. I think readers like to be left with a feel-good ending. So should I accommodate the readers' needs? Or pursue my own identity as a writer? After hemming and hawing about it endlessly, I arrived at the unconventional solution of doing both. The idea first came to me while I was writing Volume 13, so I had plenty of chapters to lay the groundwork and got the publisher to agree to make it a reality (heh).

I feel like, in recent years, manga and video games have started to lean toward being about "service." Even though we have all this entertainment available, everyone's too busy to have any time to enjoy it. So consumers only want to see things that amuse them. That's why stories are judged after just one chapter or one volume and dropped lickety-split. I feel that's why the industry is desperate to cater exactly to the audience's tastes so they don't lose them. Subsequently, creators are encouraged to make their stories easy to follow, use expressions that don't bring down morale, and resolve conflicts quickly to keep the readers happy. But then they're also told not to make it feel too cookie-cutter, and the hard work they put in to achieve that very tricky balance has resulted in higher-quality products. I feel that, in such an age, creators are wasting their lives tackling this challenge, but as their sources of inspiration can rapidly run dry, they listen to stories from those around them and use their real-life experiences as the bases for their stories and are very quickly unable to seek new inspiration, all while fighting the fear that their story won't sell... It's so important to put out your antennae and put your social network to work. This plan I made was a challenge to that pressure and stemmed from my realization that I had to try something new.

This Volume 26 Light Friendship Version puts emphasis on "service." This should be thought of as the "official" ending, and a lot of heart was put into it. So on the flip side, the "Dark Reality Version" puts emphasis on my "identity" and conveys exactly whatever I wanted to convey. Of course, my aim is to have you "pick the version you'd more likely enjoy and read that," but I hope you enjoy in partaking in my little experiment as well.

Creator: Junya Inoue

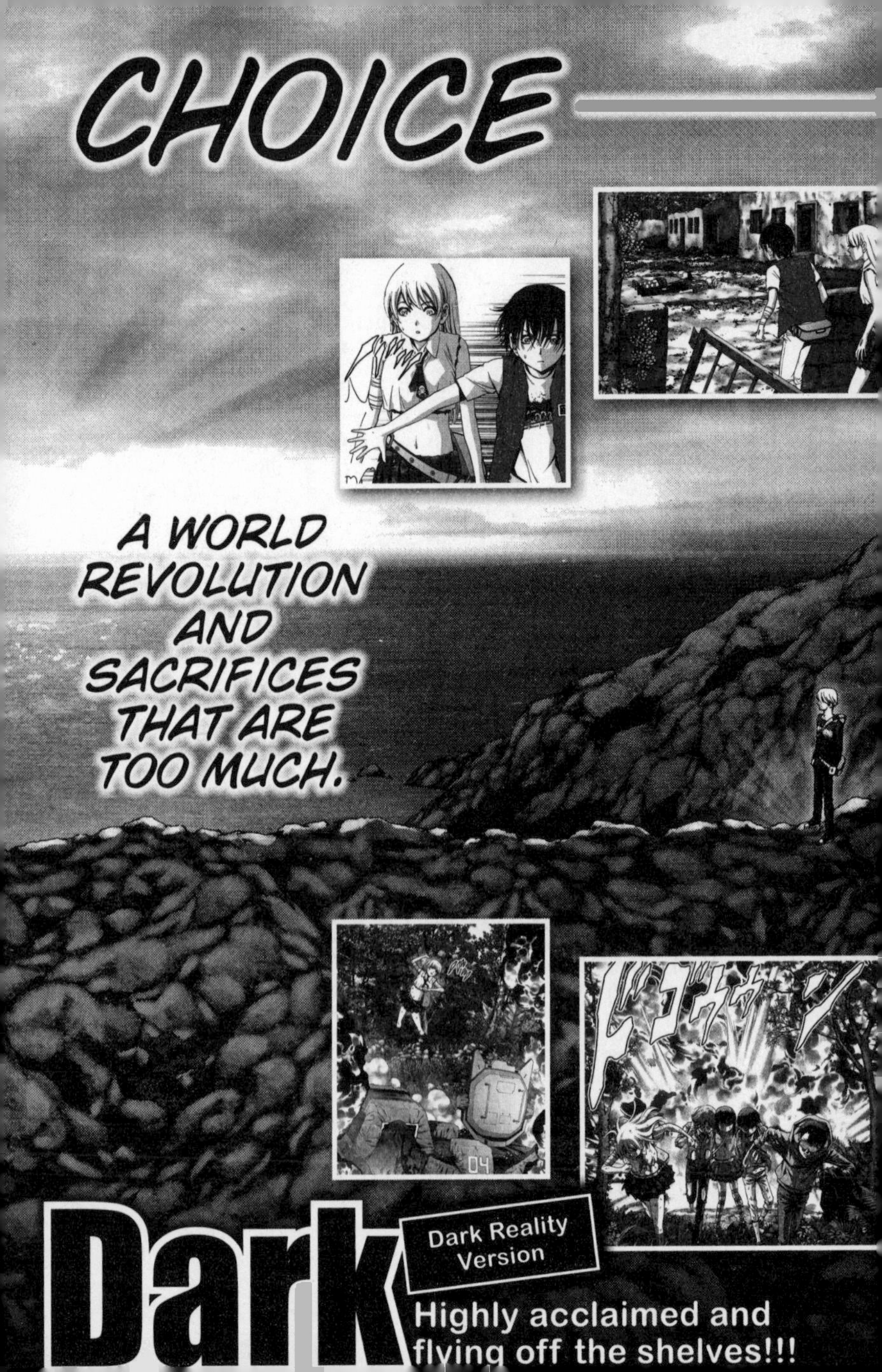
CHOICE
A WORLD REVOLUTION AND SACRIFICES THAT ARE TOO MUCH.
Dark
Dark Reality Version
Highly acclaimed and flying off the shelves!!!

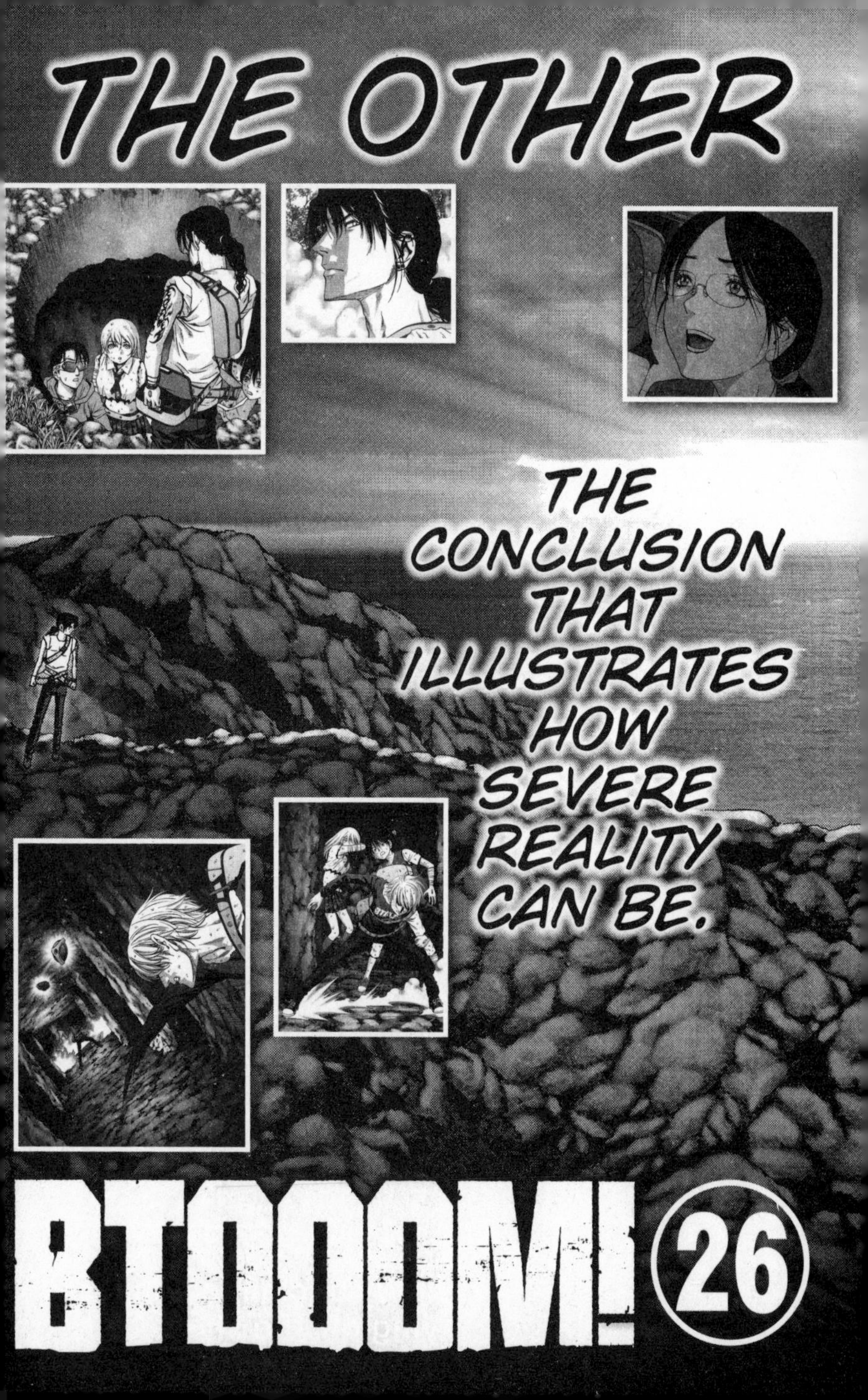
THE OTHER
THE CONCLUSION THAT ILLUSTRATES HOW SEVERE REALITY CAN BE.
BTOOOM! 26

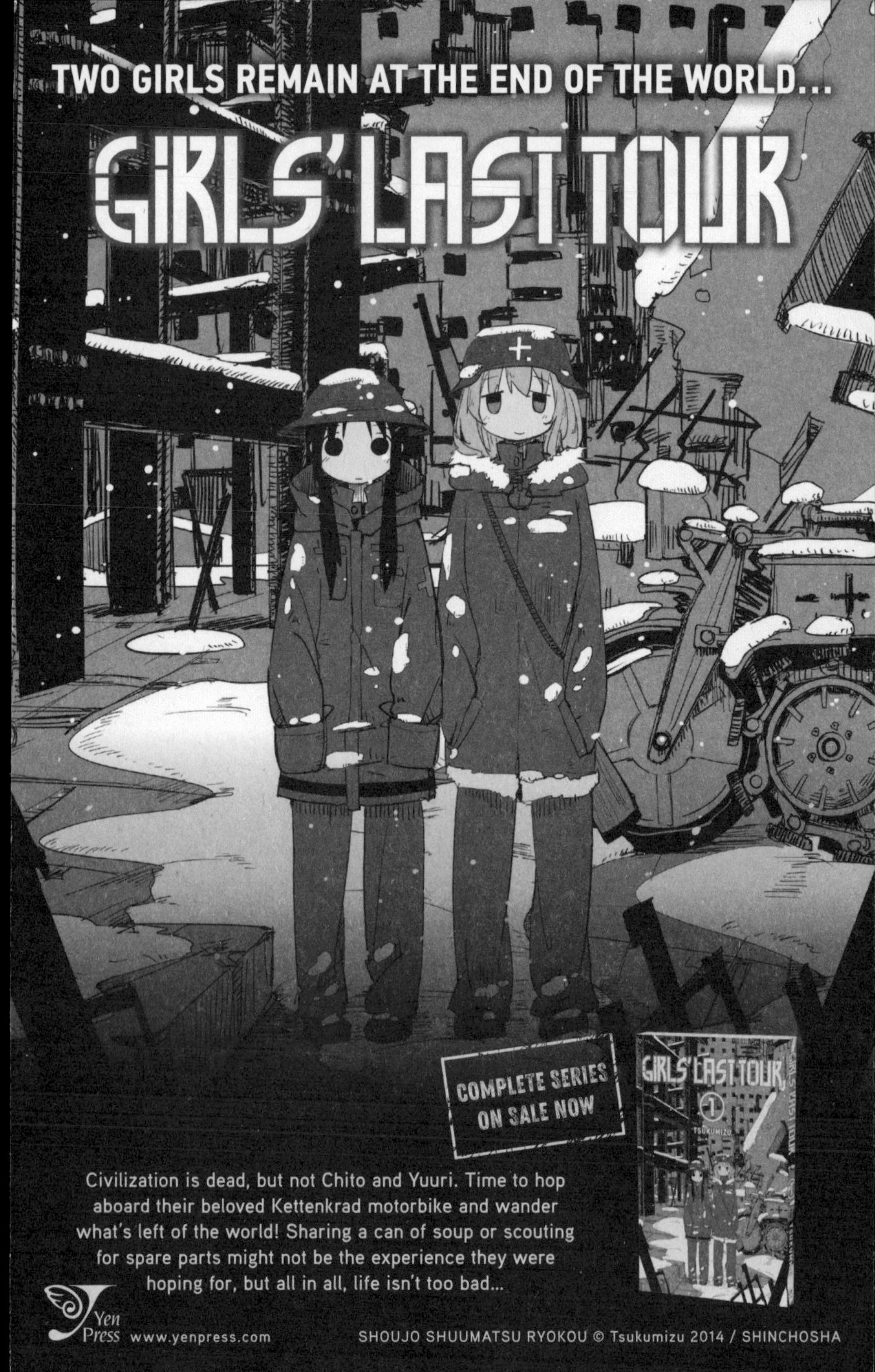
TWO GIRLS REMAIN AT THE END OF THE WORLD...
GIRLS' LAST TOUR
COMPLETE SERIES ON SALE NOW
GIRLS' LAST TOUR 1 TSUKUMIZU
Civilization is dead, but not Chito and Yuuri. Time to hop aboard their beloved Kettenkrad motorbike and wander what's left of the world! Sharing a can of soup or scouting for spare parts might not be the experience they were hoping for, but all in all, life isn't too bad...
Yen Press www.yenpress.com
SHOUJO SHUUMATSU RYOKOU © Tsukumizu 2014 / SHINCHOSHA

BTOOOM! 26 Light Friendship Version

JUNYA INOUE

Translation: Christine Dashiell

Lettering: Phil Christie

This book is a work of fiction. Names, characters, places, and incidents are the product of the author's imagination or are used fictitiously. Any resemblance to actual events, locales, or persons, living or dead, is coincidental.

BTOOOM! © Junya INOUE 2009. All rights reserved. English translation rights arranged with SHINCHOSHA PUBLISHING CO. through Tuttle-Mori Agency, Inc., Tokyo.

English translation © 2020 by Yen Press, LLC

Yen Press
150 West 30th Street, 19th Floor
New York, NY 10001

Visit us at yenpress.com
facebook.com/yenpress
twitter.com/yenpress
yenpress.tumblr.com
instagram.com/yenpress

First Yen Press Edition: March 2020

Yen Press is an imprint of Yen Press, LLC.
The Yen Press name and logo are trademarks of Yen Press, LLC.

The publisher is not responsible for websites (or their content) that are not owned by the publisher.

Library of Congress Control Number: 2013497409

ISBNs: 978-1-9753-0425-6 (paperback)
       978-1-9753-0649-6 (ebook)

10 9 8 7 6 5 4 3 2 1

WOR

Printed in the United States of America